THE YEARS BETWEEN
1909   1969

THE EASTERN NATIONAL STORY

FROM 1930

THE YEARS BETWEEN

1909   1969

Vol. 2

THE EASTERN NATIONAL STORY

FROM 1930

R J C Crawley   D R MacGregor   F D Simpson

Oxford Publishing Company

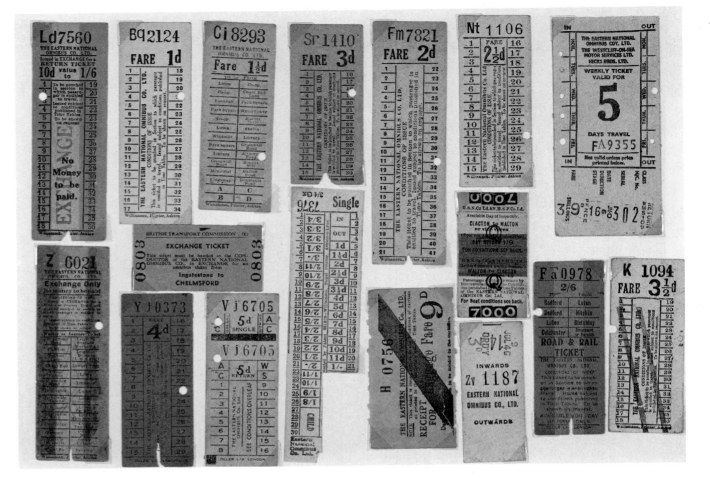

Typesetting by:
Aquarius Typesetting Services, New Milton, Hants.

Printed in Great Britain by:
Netherwood Dalton & Co. Ltd., Huddersfield, Yorks.

Published by:
Oxford Publishing Co.
Link House
West Street
POOLE, Dorset

Acknowledgements

It is again our pleasant duty to offer sincere thanks for help generously given in the course of preparation of the present volume. In addition to those specifically mentioned, there are many others who cannot be named, but to whom we are, nonetheless, equally grateful. We refer to those who have, over the years, perhaps quite unconsciously in the course of reminiscing, looking over old photographs and other transport ephemera, elucidated some fact which, at the time, may have seemed quite trivial but, when blended with many other such seemingly minor matters, produced an invaluable amalgam of information of historical value not obtainable in any other way.

We have again been very happy to have had the services of Eric Axton to supply the majority of the maps and, of course, the benefit of his extensive knowledge of bus happenings in northern Essex. Roger Barton and his co-helpers have contributed much valuable information regarding the Luton/Dunstable area as a result of indefatigable research work. Our information regarding the many small operators in the Grays and Tilbury district owes much to the researches of Mervyn Gibson, and Norman Maxim's recollections of the transport scene in the Southend area of times gone by have been very welcome. Without the benefit of Mr Merton's copious notes on the early omnibus owners in the Dengie Hundred, our story would have been much less complete. A. W. Monk has been of help over many years in a number of ways, and Alan Osborne, founder and chairman of the Eastern National Enthusiasts' Group has again placed his valuable collection of transport material at our disposal.

The senior officers and headquarters staff of Eastern National, both past and present, have been most helpful and generous of their time in providing material and detail information which we must acknowledge with gratitude.

Peter Clark, with whom must be linked the late Norman Bridge, has contributed much of the knowledge of the strange affairs of Canvey Island, but has also made meticulous search of local authority minutes for all South Essex and of the local newspapers, and he also deserves particular mention. When it comes to matters involving vehicle registrations or ownerships, we always turn to John Taylor (with whom we must link the PSV Circle) knowing full well that our enquiries will always receive his fullest attention so willingly given in great detail. Brian Walters, the hard-working curator of the Omnibus Society's timetable collection, has unfailingly provided a great variety of material of whatever nature requested, often involving the packing and despatching of heavy parcels, which has been of the greatest assistance in knowing more of what was happening in the early days. Matters relating to Eastern National in Northampton and Stony Stratford area have been considerably clarified as a result of much help from Roger M. Warwick who has made a special study of this area, and Godfrey Willis's researches, in depth, of the activities of a number of the smaller operators in the Bedfordshire area have been most valuable. Reg Westgate and his co-helpers' work into the happenings along the Eastern National/London Transport border is also acknowledged.

The County Council Library Services of Essex and Bedfordshire and of Southend Borough and their staffs, as do those of the Record Offices in the same areas, have been of the greatest help in locating and making available material and obtaining books. To them a special word of thanks is due.

Wherever possible, the source of the photographs we have used is gladly given, but there are a number of cases where this is not possible, so to those unknown photographers whose cameras have captured scenes from the past, which do much to bring to life matters which no amount of text can achieve effectively, we given thanks.

We pay tribute to Christine Crawley, for producing a very professional typescript from an untidy mass of much corrected and manhandled manuscript.

R. J. Crawley
D. R. MacGregor
F. D. Simpson
1984

Bibliography

A History of Public Transport in the Halstead Area — E. G. Axton
History of British Buses — J. A. B. Hibbs
An Illustrated History of United Counties Omnibus Co. — R. M. Warwick
Kings of the Road — Tilling
London's Buses, Vol. I — Blacker Lunn and Westgate
Motor Transport Year Book — Electrical Press (various years)
PSV/OS Fleet Histories
Numerous periodicals, newspapers, magazines, trade journals, almanacs, timetables, both official and locally published, directories and local guide books far too numerous to mention, have all contributed, in varying degrees, their quota of useful information.

Contents

Introduction

Little need be added to the introduction to the first volume of *The National Story* beyond reiterating, for the benefit of those who may not have read it, that the Eastern National Omnibus Company Ltd. was formed to continue operation of the services in the east of England of its parent, the National Omnibus and Transport Co. Ltd., in association with the London Midland & Scottish Railway and the London & North Eastern Railway companies who, between them, held 50 per cent of its issued capital as a result of the powers granted them by Parliament in 1928.

The National Company's activities in the west of England had, a little earlier, been transferred to its successors, the Southern National and Western National companies, in which the Southern Railway and the Great Western Railway each respectively held a 50 per cent share. The story of these two companies will be related in the third volume.

In Volume One, we adopted a system of chronological survey, followed by detailed appendices dealing with rolling stock, services operated and businesses acquired, an arrangement which is being followed again.

Any information by way of correction or amplification will be welcomed from readers and should be addressed to the Publisher.

Once again the authors wish to place on record their indebtedness to the host of people who have assisted in many ways to make the story more complete or accurate. A list of acknowledgements appears elsewhere, but it is felt that special thanks should be given to the officers and staff of Eastern National, both past and present, who have contributed much during the period of our researches.

R. J. Crawley
D. R. MacGregor
F. D. Simpson
Colchester
1984

Chapter One

The New Partnership 1930-1932

Although the title 'Eastern National Omnibus Company Ltd.' (ENOC) had been registered on 28th February 1929, it was not until the last day of that year that the parent 'National Omnibus and Transport Company Ltd. (NOTC), the London Midland & Scottish Railway Co. (LMS) and the London & North Eastern Railway Co. (LNER), found it possible to sign and seal the agreement, made between them, which set out the general arrangements for the formation and working of the Company and for the bus services being operated.

Even at this late stage, the future of the NOTC's Grays depot and services was still unresolved so, to expedite matters, Grays was excluded from the agreement and left in the hands of NOTC in an agency capacity. The difficulties at Grays arose from the fact that several parties had a varying degree of interest in its destiny. First there was the London General Omnibus Company (LGOC or 'General'), as some of the Grays routes crossed the area agreement boundary which divided NOTC from LGOC territory. Secondly, the LMS was more deeply interested than the LNER as the omnibus services lay almost entirely within its area. Thirdly, of underlying concern, was the fact that Grays garage was the only NOTC depot not operating profitably, largely due to unbridled competition from a host of small operators in the area, many of whom worked on a 'go as it pleased' basis, making it a less attractive proposition for a purchaser. The agreement required the NOTC to forthwith procure an increase in the ENOC's authorized capital from the original £100, of which only seven shares had been issued, to £500,000, by creating 300,000 6 per cent cumulative preference shares and a further 199,900 ordinary shares, all of £1 each. The agreement was to run for five years, during which time the NOTC was to provide management services from its headquarters at 206 Brompton Road, London SW3, as hitherto, for a remuneration of two fifths of a penny per service mile operated. The NOTC was to hand over the whole of that portion of its undertaking situated in the east of England, excluding Grays, together with its engineering and stores departments at Anchor Works, Chelmsford, and the benefit of any agreements subsisting with adjacent undertakings. A half interest in the London—East Coast express coach services passed to ENOC, the other moiety remaining with the NOTC, which intended to retain its depot at Shepherd's Bush, London, from which it would continue to serve the long distance services to both the east and west of England, and where also an existing profitable private hire department flourished by agreement with the LGOC. A clause was inserted, presumably at the insistence of the LNER, lay-ing down that no intermediate traffic could be carried by the ENOC coastal services. This was later to have unfortunate consequences for the Company.

Although 1st January 1930 may be considered the date 'Eastern National' was launched, the public will probably have been quite unaware of any change until the following May, when the first timetables bearing the new company title made their appearance. The purchase price was agreed at £400,000, of which the railway companies contributed £200,000. For operation and organization purposes, the business was divided into two administrative areas known as Eastern and Midland. The former comprised all the Essex operations, some of which strayed over the border into Suffolk here and there, and also into Hertfordshire at Bishop's Stortford. The Midland area covered the Bedfordshire and Huntingdonshire services, some of which extended into adjacent parts of Buckinghamshire, Cambridgeshire, Hertfordshire and Northamptonshire. At the commencement of operations, the ENOC inherited the following premises:

Freehold properties

Bedford	St. John's Road; garage and depot.
Chelmsford	Duke Street; garage, depot and enquiry office.
	Anchor Works, Lower Anchor Street, engineering/stores department.
Clacton-on-Sea	Wash Lane; small garage and extensive coach park.
Colchester	Queen Street; garage and depot.
Huntingdon	Stukeley Road; garage and depot.
Luton	Castle Street; garage and depot (part shared with LGOC).
	Langley Street; garage (formerly Road Motors) now let.
Toddington	Gas Street; small garage with two adjacent cottages.

Leasehold properties

Bedford	The Broadway, St. Peter's; kiosk for enquiries, parcels, etc.
Biggleswade	Church Road; large shed which was replaced in July by larger accommodation, at the Half Moon Inn, together with a cottage leased for twenty one years.
Chelmsford	Baddow Road; enquiry office and shelter.
	Railway Station; waiting-room and section of forecourt with standing for not more than five omnibuses.
Clacton-on-Sea	Pier Avenue; tours and enquiry office.
Colchester	St. John's Street; enquiry and parcels office facing bus park.
Hitchin	3 Bancroft; office and waiting-room.
Luton	14 Park Square; travel bureau and waiting-room, parcels office.
	Manchester Street; small shop used as inspectors office.
St. Ives	North Street; small garage.
Stony Stratford	Wolverton Road; office and waiting-room in public hall.

Sundry rented premises — not tenancies

Brentwood	Yorkshire Grey public house yard; outstation.
Cambridge	Ortona Company's garage; outstation.
Clophill	Flying Horse public house yard; outstation.
Cranfield	Anstee's garage, High Street; outstation.
Danbury	Bell Inn; dormy shed.
Dedham	Marlborough Head public house; garage.
Dunstable	Luton Road; small garage (believed formerly 'Ideal' buses).
Eaton Bray	Chequers public house; dormy shed at rear.
Hitchin	Deamer's garage and Primes garage; two simultaneous outstations.
Leighton Buzzard	North Street; small garage.
Maldon	White Horse public house; outstation for Chelmsford buses.
	Swan public house; outstation for Colchester buses.
Northampton	Bedford Road (United Counties Omnibus Co's. garage); outstation.
Norton (Herts)	Mr Parker's yard opposite Horseshoe Inn; dormy shed.
Rushden	(no information); one bus outstationed here.
St. Neots	Cambridge Street (Ashman's garage); outstation.
Stoke-by-Nayland	Angel Inn; outstation at rear.
Stony Stratford	London Road; depot in yard of Littledale's garage.
Sudbury (Suffolk)	Church Street; outstation at Sayer's jobmasters yard.
Toddington	Bell Yard; any overflow from Gas Street garage.

An interesting clause in the agreement provided for the operation of a service from Colchester to Hadleigh (Suffolk), via Nayland, which in fact never operated. It is thought this may have been connected with the anticipated closure of the Bentley—Hadleigh branch railway which ceased to carry passengers after 29th February 1932. This lay within the Eastern Counties Road Car Company's territory who already worked buses from Hadleigh to Ipswich and to Colchester via Stratford St. Mary, and would, no doubt, have objected to such an intrusion.

Although dealt with fully in Volume One, it should perhaps again be mentioned, for the benefit of new readers, that the NOTC operated a number of bus services on a contract basis for the LGOC in the northern outer London area, from garages at Watford, Ware, Hatfield and Bishop's Stortford. All belonged to the LGOC and their vehicles were used but these carried the 'National' fleetname and the crews wore 'National' uniform, and 'NOTC' adorned timetables and stationery. Bishop's Stortford appeared in the ENOC timetables as one of its depots, but they garaged only two or three buses there by arrangement. Conversely, at Luton, where the LGOC had a few services on the south side of the town, fifteen buses were housed in the ENOC Castle Street garage, an arrangement always officially referred to as 'Luton South', although all were in the same building! These services were transferred to London General Country Services (LGCS) at the end of February 1932.

Chelmsford bus station, shortly after transfer from National to Eastern National in 1929, and viewed from the railway viaduct.

F. Spalding

Four of these Gilford buses with 20 seat Strachan bodies were based at Grays for local services. This one, No. 2925, is about to depart to the Nutberry Estate.

J. F. Higham

According to the agreement, the ENOC was to take over 177 omnibuses, three lorries, one van, five motor cars and two motor cycles. It will be noticed that this figure does not tally with the fleet list, the difference arising from the Grays fleet, which was not included, plus other small discrepancies arising from the allocation of new vehicles ordered by the parent company, and repairs vehicles leaving Anchor Works around the change-over date between the three companies. The agreement contained a second schedule of forty three buses, the oldest in the fleet, some dating back to 1919 which, because of rebodying and fitment of pneumatic tyres, probably stood at inflated values in the Company inventory. It was feared that this value might not be realized when the time came for their disposal, and any deficit so arising was to be borne up to 50 per cent by the old company.

Although they were partners in the ENOC, the two railway companies were still very suspicious of the parent NOTC in which they had no say or control, and insisted upon the following clause being inserted in the ENOC agreement:

'The National Company hereby undertakes and agrees with the railway companies that it will not carry on, or be engaged, concerned or interested, either on its own behalf or on behalf of, or as agent, or manager for, any other person, firm of company in the business of omnibus proprietors and the transport of passengers, goods and merchandise by road . . . and the new company to agree not to put on any new services which will compete directly with the rail services of the railway companies, or either of them without the consent in writing of the railway companies.'

The first Board of Directors was composed of Sir John Jarvis (Chairman), Walter J. Iden (Managing Director), Bert Smith (General Manager) and H. G. Burford who represented the 'National' interest. The railways seem to have regarded the matter of appointments to the Board as being of the utmost importance, the LMS nominees being no less than J. H. Follows (one of its Vice Presidents) and H. L. Thornhill (its Chief Legal Adviser), while the LNER appointed G. F. Thurston (Divisional General Manager, Southern), who was accompanied by C. J. Selway (Southern Passenger Manager). One cannot but feel that these gentlemen would have already been more than fully occupied with their existing duties.

The day to day running of the business followed 'National' practice and was in the hands of a management committee which met monthly at head office, Brompton Road. This comprised Walter Iden, Bert Smith, Frank Bryan (District Manager, based at headquarters), William Morison (Chief Engineer), Richard Hunt (the newly appointed Secretary) and a nominee from each of the two railways.

The first fruits of the partnership would appear to be the inclusion of between thirty and forty pages of train arrival/departure times at the more important stations in the two company timetables. On reflection, this would seem to have been largely a waste of money, for it did not reveal to the reader when the train arrived, or at what time it started back, and there was no information whatsoever concerning intermediate stations. Miniature timetables of the pattern used by the Southern National and Western National companies were infinitely more useful and required but a quarter of the volume of paper!

It is clear that the LMS quickly got down to seeking ways of working more closely with the buses, and a number of changes were soon introduced, as will be noticed in the review of 1930 operational matters. In September, the first links in the 'straight line across Essex' (see map) began to be forged when certain through journeys started over hitherto separate services — viz: 17A, Harwich—Colchester; 5, Colchester—Chelmsford and 42, Chelmsford—Grays, which was now extended to Tilbury Ferry landing stage for Gravesend (Kent) and the south. Through trips were now also running over service 5, and service 21, Colchester—Clacton. Two months later, service 37, Grays—Chadwell St. Mary was also extended to Tilbury town and the landing stage, which not only filled a 'long felt want' but also aimed at the competing 'Tilbury & District' route which it paralleled.

In the Midland area, the first road/rail inter-available return ticket now made its appearance between Bedford and Cambridge, and buses hitherto terminating in town centres at Leighton Buzzard and Dunstable were extended to the railway stations. In October an interesting new facility was service 66, Luton (LMS Station)—Dunstable—Fenny Stratford—Bletchley, as hitherto, rail passengers were required to make inconvenient changes of train. Another was the new 20C route which competed with Mr Vale, connecting Clophill and Ampthill town with the station which was out in the country. The only matter concerning the LNER this year appears to have been the replacing of the Somersham—Ramsey branch train with the new service 39 bus worked from Huntingdon depot.

The Company was still facing much competition and the shadow of the new licensing system, at that time passing through Parliament, prompted a number of old (and new) owners to get new services established before the deadline, in the hope of qualifying for a licence. Thus the ENOC was not only involved in defending its own network against such operators, but was also concerned with its own programme of development. One of the new intruders was 'Rayleigh Motor Services' which, in early summer, started a through service from Southend-on-Sea to Colchester, via Maldon, several times daily, which enjoyed immediate popularity as existing road and rail facilities were poor. The ENOC covered only the Maldon—Colchester section (route 19), but, in July, replied by arranging for one bus to run a connectional service over the Maldon—Southend-on-Sea portion. At the same time it extended service 19 from Maldon to Woodham Ferris, by using layover time, where it connected with route 6, the Chelmsford—Southend service. On 1st August a full six times daily through service commenced using new Leyland Titan double-decks. Other improvements this year were the extension of service 22 from the Hedinghams to Haverhill (despite

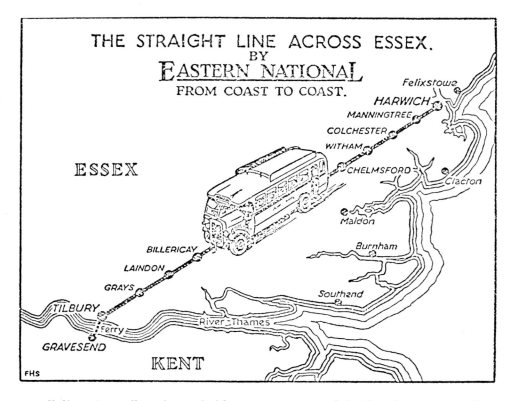

THE STRAIGHT LINE ACROSS ESSEX.
BY
EASTERN NATIONAL
FROM COAST TO COAST.

Felixstowe
HARWICH
MANNINGTREE
COLCHESTER
WITHAM
CHELMSFORD
Clacton
ESSEX
Maldon
Burnham
BILLERICAY
LAINDON
GRAYS
Southend
TILBURY
River Thames
Ferry
GRAVESEND
KENT
FHS

paralleling the railway), probably to prevent exploitation by a competitor, service 32 from Stanford-le-Hope to Corringham and a through booking arrangement for service 17A, the Harwich—Colchester service, with the Eastern Counties Road Car Company's coach service at Colchester for London. This was short-lived, as a few weeks later the ENOC put on its own thrice daily coach service with bookings from all points Harwich—Manningtree—Colchester to all points Romford—London (Victoria). A new service 50 between Chelmsford and Terling came on in July and a new service 45, from Grays to Linford, began in November. In a move against the Lion Associated which invaded the 2 and 2A routes to Writtle/Ongar and Blackmore, with a daily Chelmsford—Epping Town service, route 14 was extended from Chignal Corner to Oxney Green, via Lordship Lane, which gave a quicker journey than the existing services.

The Midland area also had new developments; service 18A was new from Leighton Buzzard to Eddlesborough and Luton, and an express facility was started from Luton to Moggerhanger Sanatorium. Two new routes were started in September; the 7D, Bedford local to Beverley Crescent service and a Henlow—Arlesey service, as yet unnumbered, for Saturday shoppers. In November, there were further changes when services 3A, Dunstable—

Toddington and 25, Biggleswade—Hitchin were upgraded to daily working and 15A was extended from Gamlingay to Waresley. At about the same time, two new routes, 34 and 34A, were started in an attempt to secure a footing along what may be termed the back way between Bedford and St. Neots, going via Thurleigh/Kimbolton or Ravensden/Colmworth. This was occupied by T. F. Allen who continued a daily service started by the somewhat notorious H. H. Clench with his 'Dreadnought' buses (q.v.), and no less than six other small proprietors who sought a rather precarious existence by working variations of the route on market days or at weekends.

It is interesting to note that the Company had, in 1930, provided a substantial network of services over principal routes on Christmas Day, giving one or two out and home trips on the trunk routes with a service on most town routes until 4 p.m., and at Luton, a reduced service was run right up until normal finishing time. Near the end of the year, Cooper's 'Ideal' bus, which worked on the 33 Southend Hotel—Queens Park local route, was absorbed, the ENOC now holding all the timings. On Sundays, Cooper had worked from each terminal to Bedford Cemetery which now became services 33A and 33B.

By October, the position of the Grays garage was settled; the whole network would be handed to the ENOC for operation, except service 40 to Romford, which would continue as a joint operation with the LGOC. However, service 41, Grays—Laindon—Romford market bus was taken off as other operators covered most sections of the route more frequently. A London bus and coach operator, Birch Bros., who started their own service, and had recently acquired other coach services between London—Bedford and Rushden, was making things more difficult for ENOC on its Hitchin—Bedford and Bedford—Rushden routes. Similarly, several small operators were giving some trouble on the west side of Luton and Dunstable of whom more will be heard later. Through coach services by others from London to Chelmsford and beyond caused similar problems on the Brentwood—Chelmsford—Colchester sections where ENOC found itself at a disadvantage by reason of its agreement with the LGOC, which precluded it from running nearer to London.

Premises at Grays, to be added to the ENOC list, comprised a freehold garage at Argent Street and a rented kiosk at Market Hall near the King's Arms bus terminal. It should be noted that after 6 p.m. on Saturdays, all services terminated at the War Memorial by the junction of High Street, London Road and Orsett Road, due to the evening traffic prohibiting use of the King's Arms terminus which was too congested by shoppers, and frequent closing of the level crossing making punctual operation impossible.

The timetables issued in May 1930 were an adaptation of the old 'National' style, but in June a new cover design appeared which was a considerable improvement and new maps were included (see illustration). At the end of the year, there were fifty five services in operation in the Eastern, and eighty eight in the Midland areas.

The Company operated an extensive parcel carrying service on its buses, a

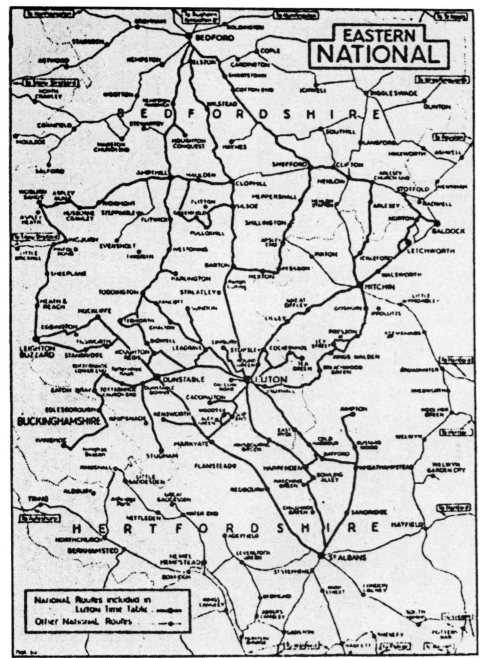

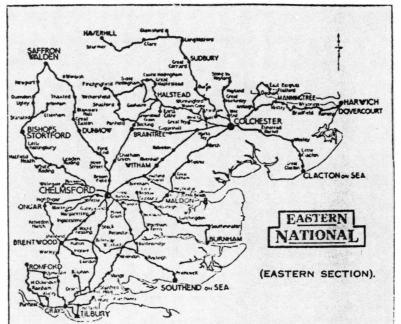

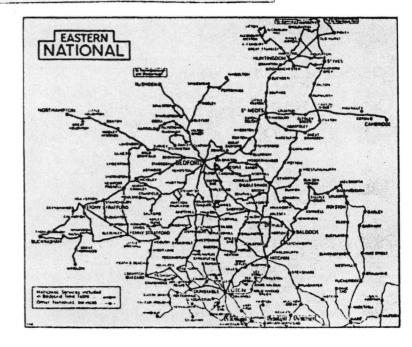

11

facility dating back to the steam car days at Chelmsford. There were agents in almost every town and village throughout the Eastern and Midland areas, with the exception of the Grays district, where the facility was conspicuous by its absence! The buses were used considerably by shopkeepers, wholesalers and factors who would despatch goods by the next out-going bus on receipt of a 'printed matter' order card; postage ½d. Private individuals also found it useful, sometimes in unexpected ways. One enterprising Essex housewife used it to solve a domestic difficulty. She would hail the Wednesday morning market bus to Braintree from Chelmsford, whereupon the driver and conductor would dismount and disappear behind her house, to reappear moments later dragging a heavy mangle which was humped on to the rear platform. A few miles down the road the bus would stop at a cottage occupied by the consignor's daughter, into which the mangle would be dragged. On the afternoon return journey, the whole process would be repeated in reverse, the daughter having meanwhile completed the weekly duty for herself and her neighbours, . . . thanks to the ENOC bus! Unfortunately, the advent of covered tops, enclosed staircases and saloon buses rendered these opportunities rather more difficult, as was another unofficial practice frequently observed on Saturday nights. On late buses for shoppers and cinema patrons, the front portion of the upper deck would often be filled with bicycles, push-chairs and other bulky packages covering several rows of seats, the owners having earlier that day ridden in but they did not, or found it impossible, to cycle home laden with their purchases.

The new legislation mentioned earlier reached the statute book in the shape of the Road Traffic Act, 1930. Herbert Morrison, the Minister of Transport, had been steadily progressing the former Omnibus Bill and Road Traffic Bill through the Commons during the earlier part of the year, and on 1st August it became law. This would have a profound effect on the entire transport industry, more particularly for the small bus owners who now found themselves caught within a new operational framework. They would now have, in common with large undertakings which possessed the necessary resources and expertise anyway, to cope with the making of applications for licences to the newly appointed Traffic Commissioners. By 9th February 1931, every qualifying service would have to be licensed, as would every omnibus driver and conductor, by the licensing authority instead of, as hitherto, the local council. In addition, all public service vehicles would have to undergo a ministry inspection and carry a certificate of fitness. Many small operators who had started with a horse and van had only been able to invest in some rather primitive form of mechanical transport, some of which were rather makeshift affairs adapted from a second-hand van into which seats had been added. An owner with insufficient capital to purchase a suitable vehicle, or

Pausing on layover at Kempston is No. 2996, one of the ten Strachan-bodied Leyland Lion LT2 saloons supplied in 1930.

D. S. Deacon

St. Peter's Church was the terminus for all out of town services from Bedford. Here, No. 3009, one of four Leyland Tiger TS3 saloons, new in 1930, catches the evening sun.

J. F. Higham

one more adept at handling a horse or using a spanner rather than coping with complicated paperwork, now felt it was better to give up the struggle and so sought a buyer for his services. This accounted for quite a few of the many purchases made by the ENOC in the ensuing years which would not have normally been considered for acquisition, but now were taken to ensure that the licences did not fall into the hands of a competitor.

The new Act quickly brought some order out of chaos especially in districts such as Grays, where the local authority had previously issued hackney licences to all-comers. Some owners acted responsibly and did genuinely try to provide a regular and safe service but, it is true to say, others ran only when there was plenty of traffic to be collected, to the disadvantage of the operator who conscientiously provided an all-day service and needed all the passengers he could muster to cover the 'thin' hours.

Full details of individual vehicles purchased new or second-hand appear in *Appendix A*. The fleet numbering system used by 'National' was continued unaltered for a while longer and, although the ENOC, and sister companies Southern and Western National were to be regarded as separate, the fleet nevertheless remained numbered in a common series, as did the Company's

own method of body numbering. The engineering administration for all three companies continued at Chelmsford until satisfactory arrangements were completed in the West Country for its own engineering and stores department.

Thirty three new vehicles joined the ENOC fleet in 1930. The double-decks consisted of eight Leyland Titan TD1 vehicles with the same manufacturer's 48 seat bodies, and eleven AEC Regent 1 chassis, equipped with 50 seat bodies from the Rochester factory of Short Bros. Strachan supplied fourteen 32 seat single-deck bodies, ten on Leyland Lion LT2 and four on Tiger TS3 chassis of the new generation on low slung frames specially designed for saloon passenger bodywork, which superseded the famous PLSC Lion in 1929. The Tiger and Titan enjoyed a similar mechanical specification and were powered by the 6.8 litre six cylinder overhead-cam petrol engine, while the Lion, of not dissimilar build and identical 16ft. 6in. wheelbase, was propelled by the smaller four cylinder unit of 5.1 litres.

Five Dennis vehicles were acquired from Leverett (trading as Ashwell and District) of Ashwell, Herts in 1931. This 32 seat EV model became No. 3058 in the Eastern National fleet and is seen at Cambridge, with an Ortona vehicle in the background.

J. F. Higham

Two Strachan-bodied AEC Regal chassis were delivered in 1931. The driver returns to No. 3062, a 32 seat rear entrance example, standing at Colchester for its journey across Essex to the Tilbury Ferry.

J. F. Higham

During this year, the ENOC embarked on a programme of purchasing businesses large and small, increasing in momentum until a maximum was reached in 1934. Thereafter it continued at a diminishing rate as the number of opportunities for suitable purchases became fewer.

In another way this was a momentous year for the ENOC and its sister businesses, for Thomas Tilling Ltd., which not only had its own omnibus businesses in London and Hove but, for some years had been steadily investing in provincial undertakings, now made a successful bid to the shareholders of the parent National Omnibus & Transport Company, which gave it control of its subsidiaries on 7th February.

George Cardwell, one of Tilling's chief and most experienced executives, was immediately appointed to represent its interest on the board of the ENOC, H. G. Burford resigning to create the vacancy. Cardwell quickly familiarized himself with the business and began to prepare the way for Tilling methods to be introduced. At the Annual General Meeting held at the year's end, two further Tilling nominees took their seats on the Board when Sir John Jarvis vacated the chair and Walter Iden ceased to be Managing Director, although he continued in this office for the parent company a little longer. John F. Heaton now brought Tilling chairmanship to the Board, accompanied by F. P. Arnold, its other nominee, and Bert Smith retained his seat and continued in office as General Manager.

Around May 1931, negotiations for the acquisition of the important bus and coach company trading as 'Silver Queen', and based at Clacton-on-Sea, reached fruition, the deal including the 'Enterprise' services of that town which had latterly come under 'Silver Queen' control. For many years these two concerns had engaged in fierce competition with their buses and charabancs. Between them, they virtually covered the whole of the Tendring Hundred, except the Harwich—Colchester and Brightlingsea—Colchester roads which they avoided by agreement with 'National'/ENOC and Messrs Berry & Sons respectively. The precise date of acquisition is not known, but both concerns were in voluntary liquidation in August 1931. Strange to relate, there was no mention of services of the acquired 'Silver Queen' and 'Enterprise' businesses in the ENOC monthly timetable until the following May.

'Silver Queen' was one of the many creations of W. P. Allen, an earlier London omnibus pioneer who, having disposed of his activities in the capital to the LGOC, moved into the provinces. The Clacton unit was started in 1913 but the outbreak of hostilities in 1914 practically closed it down. After the war, expansion was rapid and several services were also attempted around Colchester from a depot at the rear of the Angel Hotel in the High Street. In the summer, great business was done at Clacton and Walton with excursions and tours from a large stand on the corner of Rosemary Road and Pier Avenue extending back to the Marine Hotel, where the enquiry and booking office was also located. The 'Enterprise' stand was also nearby and Messrs

The interior of Queen Street garage, Colchester. The word EASTERN has prefixed NATIONAL since the change in Company name. The vehicles are (left to right) AEC Regent No. 3021; Gilford No. 3018; AEC Reliance No. 2886; AEC B No. 2329; AEC YC No. 2328 and AEC Regent No. 3087.

F. Spalding

Five Strachan-bodied Thornycroft XC double-decks arrived in 1931 and here No. 3068 stands at Galleywood Common to be specially photographed before entering service.

F. Spalding

Suttons was just around the corner in Pier Avenue, whilst Hicks Bros. of Braintree also had a starting point close by. As the name implies, the 'Silver Queen' fleet was in all-over silver livery, the 'Enterprise' vehicles being in golden yellow and lined out in black, Sutton's coaches were a rich scarlet and Hicks sported blue and yellow.

Between them, 'Silver Queen' and 'Enterprise' operated some twenty eight omnibus services, this total being reduced to twenty two after take-over by combining several routes and allowing two to lapse. The acquired services were numbered in a new series starting at 101, in most instances using the former SQ number with 100 added. The ENOC fleet increased by sixty nine vehicles, fifty three coming from 'Silver Queen' and sixteen from 'Enterprise'. Together, they represented the largest single purchase made by the ENOC until 'Westcliff Motor Services' was acquired in 1952. The services operated by the two concerns at 1931 are as follows:

'Silver Queen'/ 'Enterprise' No.	ENOC No.	Route
1	101	Clacton-on-Sea—St. Osyth
2	102	Clacton-on-Sea—Brightlingsea (joint SQ/E)
3	103	Clacton-on-Sea—Walton, via Thorpe-le-Soken
3A	103A	Clacton-on-Sea—Thorpe Green, via Park Gate corner ('Enterprise' service)
4	Part 121	Colchester—Wivenhoe
5	105	Colchester—Walton-on-Naze
6	104	Clacton-on-Sea—Harwich, via Great Oakley
6A	106	Clacton-on-Sea—Harwich, via Wix
7	107	Clacton-on-Sea—Holland—Walton-on-Naze (joint SQ/E)
8	108	Clacton-on-Sea—Tendring—East Bergholt
† 9	—	Walton-Great Bentley—Brightlingsea
10	110	Harwich—East Bergholt
11	111	Harwich—Thorpe-le-Soken—Walton-on-Naze
† 12	—	Jetty—Town—Cemetery
13	Part 118/9 group	Harwich—Dovercourt (White Horse), via Main Road or Fronks Road
14	114	Rush Green—Town—Jetty (joint SQ/E)
15	115	Magdalen Green—Town—Jetty—Jaywick
16	116	Walton-on-Naze—Lower Kirby
17	117	Clacton-on-Sea—Holland via Station
18	Part 118/9 group	Harwich—Dovercourt (Tollgate), via A135 road
19	do.	Harwich—Parkeston Quay
19A	do.	Harwich—Dovercourt (Memorial), via Main Road
20	104A/B	Harwich—Ramsey—Wix
21	21	Clacton-on-Sea—Weeley—Colchester (joint ENOC/SQ)
21A	121	Clacton-on-Sea—St. Osyth—Colchester
22	122	Parkeston Quay—Dovercourt
+ 23	—	Jetty—Clacton-on-Sea—Holland Cliffs ('Enterprise' service)
+ 24	—	Magdalen Green—Town—Jaywick ('Enterprise service)

Notes: † Services allowed to lapse.
+ Services integrated with others.

With the exception of some town routes, all the services terminated in Rosemary Road on its south side, between Station Road and Pier Avenue, using the street in an east-west directly. The ENOC now closed its Pier Avenue office and transferred its own coaches to the 'Silver Queen' stand.

The writer has one very vivid recollection of an incident concerning 'Silver Queen', in his youth which, but for the grace of God, might well have precluded him from taking any further interest in the buses of this earthly

Short Bros. supplied the bodywork for thirteen AEC Regent double-decks in 1931. Note the small oval window giving light to the space below the rear staircase, a feature of No. 3082 and the rest of its batch.

J. F. Higham

world! He was in a car following a 'Silver Queen' double-deck at Little Clacton, where there are several sharp bends (much sharper than nowadays) and, when negotiating one of them, another 'Silver Queen' bus was met coming in the opposite direction. Neither driver was properly prepared for such an encounter with the result that both front offside hubs met, knocking the steering wheels out of the drivers' hands which caused each vehicle to swerve violently across the road, narrowly missing the front of the car The front wheels of both buses dropped into the ditch on each side but fortunately neither toppled over or suffered damage . . . or provoked passenger complaint! One bus was able to reverse out and immediately managed to pull the other one clear with the aid of a rope which was always carried to cover such contingencies. No police officer witnessed the proceedings and all resumed their journeys little the worse for the mishap.

The very old established business of J. & S. Hinsby at St. Neots was acquired by the ENOC in 1931, removing competition from the Bedford—St. Neots route 4 and 4A, and adding three small market services to the network and five omnibuses to the fleet.

For most of its routes, the ENOC submitted licence applications to the Eastern Traffic Area Commissioners, but some fell within the East Midland Area so a separate application was necessary for them. The ENOC withdrew the original 'Silver Queen/Enterprise' applications and submitted them under its own name.

The Company's endeavours to provide improved facilities throughout its operating area can readily be noticed by examining the number of service modifications during the year. In the Eastern Area, January saw the 40A Grays—Brentwood Hospital service revamped into a daily Tilbury—Grays—Brentwood—Chelmsford through route and the start of a new 1A Chelmsford—Woodham Walter service. Additional trips were put on service 42, Grays—Chelmsford, to discourage the activities of Grays & District. In March, service 14 was extended from Sandon to Danbury Common and a new 52 service to Pleshey replaced one previously run by the former carrier who used a small fourteen seater known as the 'Pleshey Belle'. At Grays, the 31/38 Tilbury—Purfleet service was further strengthened in the fight against the many competing operators. In September, the final metamorphosis of several services across the county from Tilbury to Clacton/Harwich, 'The Straight Line Across Essex', came about when through trips over routes 5, 29 and 42 were combined as service 51, and journeys from Chelmsford (later from Tilbury) to Clacton became service 53.

In the Midland Area, there was also considerable activity. January saw the introduction of eight additional road/rail inter-availability arrangements with the LMS and more services amended to terminate at its stations, notably at Dunstable, Northampton and Rushden. In February, the services worked by H. Leverett, trading as Ashwell & District, appeared in the timetables, although the exact date of acquisition is not known. His main route was the important Hitchin—Royston—Cambridge service which was acquired jointly with the Ortona Motor Co. of Cambridge. His other services became solely

A facsimile of the leaflet announcing the daily coach service between London and Clacton-on-Sea.

A. Driver & Sons

ENOC and were numbered as follows: 35B, Ashwell—Royston market bus; 35E, Ashwell—Letchworth workmen's buses; 41, Hitchin—Cambridge and 41A, Hitchin—Ashwell (short trips). Two buses were now outstationed at Ashwell until the new Hitchin garaged opened.

This year saw the opening of the new Whipsnade Zoological Park for which almost every operator for miles around sought licences. The ENOC secured a daily Luton (LMS) service 53B to the zoo with another, service 67 from Leighton Buzzard, which was unsuccessful and soon withdrawn. The Bedford—Dunstable route 3 was also extended thereto. In June, a new direct service 8D, between Bedford and Biggleswade, was put on and in August, the 36 group of services between Bedford and Cranfield were reorganized, extensions to Moulsoe or Salford becoming 36B, buses going via Marston Church End, 36A, and workmen's buses via Stewartby, 36C.

Further improvements in November included service 7E, Bedford—Bromham/Box End, formerly run by Mr Stevens of Kempston, and a new service 28B to Ampthill, via Stewartby, began. Hinsby's market buses to Huntingdon were added to service 14, to Eltisley Green as 29A (very soon discontinued because the 29 covered the same ground), the service to Staploe became 73, and to Perry, 74. For no apparent reason, the existing

45 service, Huntingdon—Houghton, was renumbered 42A. Another improvement was the complete remodelling of the Park Square premises at Luton into an attractive travel centre with waiting-rooms. On 1st July, a second terminal in Bedford was brought into use at the Fairground in Commercial Road, at which virtually all services entering the town from the south now terminated on weekdays. This was done to reduce the severe congestion caused by buses standing and turning at the St. Peter's terminus. At the same time, the through service to Cambridge was diverted from St. Mary's to terminate at the Midland Road LMS Station.

At Stony Stratford, the frequent local service, 7A, to Wolverton and Stantonbury, was changed to 7B. It ran in competition with no fewer than five local operators who had been a considerable nuisance to the Company and at times among themselves. The ENOC normally ran a half-hourly service but now increased this to every twenty minutes (a.m.) and every ten minutes (p.m.) presumably with a view to qualifying for a larger share of the times to be allocated by the Licensing Authority between the Company and 'The Five'. Perhaps the ENOC hoped that by swamping the road, it would be making its competitors work less profitably, and induce one or more to give up! Vain hope; things did not work out that way, as will be seen later.

One of the sixteen Strachan-bodied Leyland Titan TD1 double-decks, supplied in 1931, is seen in Greys, en route to Purfleet.

J. F. Higham

Sixteen of these Strachan-bodied Leyland TD1 double-decks were supplied in 1931, of which No. 3168 is a typical example.

B. S. Stocker

17

One of the first changes which Tilling introduced was the termination of the joint arrangement between the NOTC and the subsidiary companies for the operation of the coastal express services, which now became the sole property of the area company concerned. Tilling transferred to themselves the 'National' private hire and excursion operations based at Shepherd's Bush, which was now simply a convenient place to garage coaches requiring an overnight stop in London. The business here was valued at £50,000, an amount which included goodwill, vehicles, licences and the NOTC share-holding in London Coastal Coaches. The ENOC portion represented £7,500 of the total value, which included five coaches and a quarter of the shares the NOTC held in London Coastal Coaches, the balance passing to Southern National and Western National.

At the year end, the fleet total had risen from 249 to 361, most of the increase arising from the Clacton acquisitions. New vehicles coming into the fleet consisted of thirty seven double-decks on AEC Regent, Leyland Titan and Thornycroft chassis, with bodywork shared by Strachan and Short Bros. Two Gilford saloons, from a 1930 order, were delivered during the early part of the year together with four Strachan-bodied saloons, two on Leyland PLSC chassis and two on AEC Regal chassis, and Duple of Edgware completed two Leyland Tiger coaches. This was augmented with the large intake of second-hand vehicles bringing the total input to 124 units. The balance of stock comprised the 'Silver Queen' and 'Enterprise' fleets which, with those

Five Beadle-bodied Leyland Tiger TS4 chassis were supplied in 1932 and, in the original form, were 26 seat coaches. Later they were downgraded to 32 seat buses and after such treatment No. 3306 is seen leaving Chelmsford bus station for West Hanningfield.

S. N. White

from Leverett and Hinsby, totalled seventy nine. The variety now finding its way into the ENOC consisted of thirty double-decks, manufactured by Leyland and Thornycroft, and a solitary AEC Regent. One of the acquired Leylands, an 'S' type of 1922 vintage, was not allocated a fleet number and was quickly sold. An even greater assortment of saloons created a substantial non-standard element with such diverse makes as Dennis, Morris, Ford, Daimler, Guy, Leyland, Lancia, Gotfredson, Berliet, Chevrolet and Thornycroft, many of which were soon made redundant.

With the acquisition of 'Silver Queen', the ENOC gained the following premises:

Clacton — Rosemary Road (corner of Pier Avenue); coach stand and
 booking office.
Clacton — Castle Road; principal garage.
Clacton — Jackson Road; secondary garage.
Walton-on-Naze — Naze Park; Foundry garage.
Walton-on-Naze — Kino Stand; bus and coach terminus and booking office.
Dovercourt Bay — Kingsway; garage with coach booking kiosk on forecourt.

Also at:
Bedford — Fairground; new terminal, bus park and enquiry/parcel kiosk.
Clacton — the former ENOC booking office in Pier Avenue closed.

The following additional outstations were now in use, viz:
Ashwell (Herts) — two buses at The Drive (ex-Leverett).
Brightlingsea — one bus in 'Old Tom Marsh's yard'.
East Bergholt — two buses for summer months (location unknown).
Great Oakley — one bus at The Maybush Inn.
St. Osyth — one bus (location unknown).
Tendring — one bus (location unknown) moved to East Bergholt for summer.
Thorington — one bus in the driver's (Joe Carter) front garden.
Thorpe Green — one bus parked on verge outside driver's (Jock Webber)
 house.

The last two named were ex-'Enterprise'; the remainder being ex-'Silver Queen'. In its publicity, the ENOC claimed that in 1931 its 350 omnibuses and coaches had aggregated over eight million miles, covering 175 service routes and had carried twenty six million passengers.

1932

Further changes, as a result of Tilling influence, were apparent at the beginning of the new year when a fresh timetable layout made its appearance. It had a title page which included a summary of contents, and the fare charts were removed to separate fare books, but the through fare between all time-tabled points was placed in the final column after the service times, with a list of available return fares. Timetables were now endorsed 'Until Further

Notice', monthly publication ceasing. The next issue, which appeared in May, contained a completely revised set of company regulations, presumably in line with Tilling practice, which extended to four pages of small print compared to 'National' which had managed to accommodate all its regulations on a single page of larger typeface, with room to spare!

In the Midland Area, there was a general tidying up of service numbers by combining routes over common ground where possible, resulting as follows:

15, Biggleswade—Waresley; now included in 35C Biggleswade—St. Neots
15A, Biggleswade—Henlow; now included in 25 Biggleswade—Hitchin
23, Bedford—Haynes; now included in 8C Bedford—Biggleswade
27, Stony Stratford—Loughton; now included in 31 Stony Stratford—Bletchley
32, Stony Stratford—Deanshanger; now included in 51A Stony Stratford—Fenny Stratford, via Buckingham
51, Stony Stratford—Buckingham; now included in 51A (as above)
41A, Hitchin—Ashwell; now included in 41 Hitchin—Cambridge

Some segregation of services also took place. Service 3A, Dunstable—Toddington was used for journeys via Chalton; those via Tebworth became 3B. The 52 service, Luton—Hitchin—Baldock/Stotfold became 52 and 52B respectively, and service 18, Luton—Leighton Buzzard was for journeys via Hockliffe, those going via Tilsworth becoming 18B. On the same day, the first inter-availability arrangement with the LNER started between Hitchin and Biggleswade. During the spring, extra trips were put on service 5, Bedford—Riseley—Kimbolton, following the demise of A. & F. Wise of Riseley whose licence was revoked. In April, a series of special services for workpeople at the Wolverton factories, operating at special fares not hitherto advertised, now made their appearance in the timetables. These were services 69 from Deanshanger, 70 for Potterspury, 71 from Yardley Gobion and 72 from the Nash/Calverton area. There were also journeys from Old Bradwell and Stony Stratford working as part of the 7B and 31 services.

Finally settled this year, were the operational difficulties of the Stony Stratford—Wolverton-Stantonbury local service. The licensing authority faced a hopeless task in trying to reconcile the conflicting applications lodged by the company and the 'gang of five', who all considered that they each had a better claim than anyone else on 'the times' that would eventually be alloted. The authority neatly avoided any further argument and unseemly wrangling in the traffic courts by determining that the number of buses at present on the service was grossly excessive. By setting a basic frequency of fifteen minutes up to midday, and every seven to eight minutes thereafter, a considerable scaling down from the ENOC's ten minute service, plus whatever else was being worked by 'The Five', was now achieved. All were sent away to work out an amicable operating schedule and return when agreement had been reached. Frank Bryan and his assistants from the Company had an arduous and protracted task seeking a working arrangement acceptable to 'The Five', who could not even themselves agree on how to allocate their own share of 'the times'.

The solution, which came into operation in April 1933, was a masterpiece of ingenuity. The morning schedule was simple, it required only four cars; two from the ENOC and two from 'The Five'. The latter period needed eight cars; three from the ENOC and one each from 'The Five'. The Company worked to a fixed timetable which it could publish in its time book, whereas 'The Five' each worked one of five car schedules numbered 1 to 5, covering seven days, two of which covered long shifts (whole day) and three short shifts from midday to finishing time. Every week each owner moved on to the next numbered shift, thus each performed two long and three short turns every five weeks. The long turns consisted of 15/16 round trips and the short ones varied from 9 to 12 trips departing every 52/53 minutes. None of 'The Five' were to be seen on service before 8.45a.m., between 12.30 and 1.30p.m. or from 5.15 to 6.15p.m. (except Saturdays), as they were all conveying work-people to and from the factories at Wolverton and various parts of the district; so the ENOC put on the extra cars needed to cover these times. Some of 'The Five' operated additional buses at factory times; they were John Bates with up to five buses, J. Brown with three, J. Egglesfield with two, R. Humphrey & Son with four, and Malcolm Jelley with one only, although he was operating services elsewhere (q.v.). All, except the ENOC, worked jointly, honouring each others' return tickets. The timetable, which nobody would dare alter, held good until 24th June 1945 when the United Counties Omnibus Co. acquired the last of 'The Five', the ENOC meanwhile having worked its own fixed set of times without change throughout.

Dennis Lancets were to feature in large numbers and No. 3319 was one of the original batch of five which were bodied by Beadle in 1932.

G. Porter

19

On 13th May 1932, the small service of D. Lodge of Wayside, Wilstead, who ran to Bedford by Cardington and London Road, or by the Elstow Road, was acquired, and his times consolidated with the existing service 30 which now extended to Wilstead crossroads.

In July, a further market bus to St. Neots was put on as service 34B, a variant to 34/34A, and about the same time the 4C Bedford—Goldington Avenue local service became a circular route, returning via Kimbolton Road. This summer saw the inauguration of the first scheduled express service in the Midland Area, to Great Yarmouth. Just prior to the year end, a new Bedford—Old Warden service 8F was started.

By 1932, everybody in the industry was learning to live with licensing and no businesses in the ENOC territory were acquired that year. Somewhat surprisingly, the Company was unfortunate to be refused licences for its London—Colchester—Harwich express route and the Blackmore—Brentwood section of route 2A. The Harwich refusal was a nasty blow for it strengthened the position of Eastern Counties and 'Grey-Green' on the London—Colchester road, with the result that the ENOC was never more than a summer seasonal operator on that route.

Three new services commenced in 1932; service 11A, Chelmsford—West Hanningfield, following revocation of the licence of Davies of Ramsden Bellhouse; service 32B, Grays—Fobbing and 115A, Holland—Jaywick, via the seafront. There was a considerable number of changes at Clacton, no doubt resulting from experience gained, so that services 104B, 113, 116, 117 and 120 were all combined into others which simplified the timetables. The 37A, Grays—Tilbury Ferry service was diverted from Kings Arms to start from Grays (LMS Station, avoiding the level crossing) and in October, service 1A was extended to Maldon.

During 1932, Luton Corporation, which owned a small tramway system, decided it was time to close it down. It had never been extended since opening, so that in addition to being in a rather run-down condition, it left large areas of the borough completely unserved so that others came in to provide local services. Several of these had been started by 'Road Motors' which 'National' inherited in 1925, and others were worked by the 'Blue Bird' services of Hinds & Savage. Negotiations were opened between the Corporation and the ENOC with a view to the Company providing replacement omnibus services in return for a guaranteed annual payment. This proposal, however, was not favourably received by a large number of residents, so the case was submitted to the Minister of Transport who advised the Corporation not to sell its Transport Department. The Corporation now applied for licences to run buses in place of the trams and for all the 'Blue Bird' routes, which had recently come under the control of Mr A. F. England, and for his other services into the country under the fleetnames 'Union Jack' and 'XL Service'.

The ENOC and the LGCS objected to the Corporation's application for services outside the borough and, at the public hearing which took place on 1st December, several of the contentious applications were withdrawn. Clearly there had been some 'behind the scenes' negotiations and agreement reached on most matters prior to the hearing. The Corporation was, however, successful in obtaining licences to run out to Dunstable via the main road and via Houghton Regis, to Bramingham Turn along the Old Bedford Road, and from Round Green to Stopsley along the Hitchin Road. The portions of routes from A. F. England, not granted to the Corporation, were now taken over by the ENOC in exchange for some small transfers to the Corporation, all with effect from 23rd March 1933, details of which can be found in the next chapter.

It is interesting to note that a batch of six Leyland Titans and four AEC Renowns, all double-decks which had been ordered in anticipation, were delivered with destination blinds displaying the points covered by the Luton Tramways! The year saw the intake of forty one new vehicles. As a matter of policy the Board had discussed, some two years earlier, the possibility of discontinuing the purchase of AEC chassis since it discovered that this manufacturer had been supplying competitors on more favourable terms than those it had, itself, enjoyed! Even so, it took another fourteen chassis to be built and delivered for 1932 before the long allegiance with AEC was finally severed. Nine of these arrived as Strachan-bodied Regent double-decks; four came from Short Bros. as 66 seaters on the six-wheeled Renown chassis, and Duple provided a solitary Regal coach. Leyland were favoured with an order for nine new TD2s with 56 seat Strachan double-deck bodies.

To enable 66 passengers to be carried on a double-deck bus, the six-wheeled AEC Renown provided the answer. Short Bros. provided the bodies and four worked from Luton on heavily-trafficked services. Later all were switched to Chelmsford depot where No. 3334 is seen about to leave for Maldon.

and five TS4 Tigers with 26 seat Beadle coach bodies. The intake was completed by eight 32 seat Beadle saloons on Tilling Stevens B39A7 chassis and five Dennis Lancets, carrying identical bodies. The use of Tilling Stevens Motors (TSM) vehicles had been an inherent feature of all Tilling Group businesses which was, however, soon to be abandoned. It is worth recording that 1932 was the last year in which new vehicles received territorial registrations, dependent upon the operating district to which they were first allocated. From now on, only Essex County Council marks would be used, reflecting the location of the Company's head office. The territorial registration marks used were EV, HK, NO, PU, TW, VW and VX from Essex; BM, MJ, NM and TM from Bedfordshire; UU and XA from London County Council and EW from Huntingdonshire.

The years from 1929 to 1932 may perhaps be summarized as a period of adjustment to the very changed conditions invoked by the joint railway ownership, the new licensing arrangements, and the top control having passed from 206 Brompton Road to 20 Victoria Street SW1 (Tilling Headquarters). This preoccupation, however, did not interfere with the accession of a large new piece of operating territory in East Essex, or implementing sundry improvements to the facilities offered to the travelling public. So far as the railways were concerned, some co-operation with the LMS was evident, but virtually nothing was to be witnessed in the ENOC's assocation with the LNER.

Chapter Two
Effects of New Legislation 1933-1935

The period covered by this chapter saw the Company pass through considerable change, at the end of which it had assumed the shape it was to retain for the next twenty years. During these three years, nearly forty omnibus and coach undertakings, of all sizes, were absorbed. There were also transfers of some services from the ENOC to neighbouring concerns with some loss of territory, which was more than made up elsewhere.

It has been said that the heavy programme of buying out businesses reflected the difference between the policies of the former 'National' management and that of Tilling. Examination of the factors behind this phenomenon show that matters largely outside both the Company and Tilling control were the true cause. One was the new licensing system and another was the new legislation which received Royal Assent on 13th April 1933, creating the London Passenger Transport Board (hereafter referred to as the LPTB or the Board), which was given an absolute monopoly of all road/rail passenger transport within its 'special area'. Soon it was seen that in certain parts its boundary had not been drawn up with full regard to the possible effects it might have on the travelling public. Thirdly, a once only peculiarity, was side effects arising from Luton Corporation's decision to play a major role in pursuit of which it purchased several private omnibus services. Lastly, the normal commercial market, in which business could change hands for all sorts of reasons, was now more active than hitherto, because of the monopoly value attached to a road service licence.

One of the requirements of the new licensing system was the necessity for all applications for services, or even the smallest alterations thereto, to be published in an official periodical known as Notices and Proceedings. Through this media, everyone engaged in the industry could learn exactly who was doing what. Licensing had fairly quickly eliminated many of the fringe operators who would today be called 'cowboys' but in those days were generally referred to as 'pirates'. A small number had obtained licences but those who failed to adhere to the conditions attached quickly found that they paid the penalty of suspension or revocation of the licence if they did not mend their ways. Traffic officials of the larger concerns were alerted to watch for any infringements by competitors, and information so gleaned was passed back to the licensing authority who would arrange for its enforcement officer to check the workings of a suspected operator. Furthermore, objection could be lodged by any aggrieved party when the time arrived for the annual renewal of licences.

Some small proprietors who were used to 'free enterprise' and working with the minimum of paperwork, found the new conditions alien to their nature, so were not sorry to find a purchaser, if only for the value of the licence. By 1933, there was considerable activity in the 'transfer market' with more businesses on offer which could be purchased without fear of any unauthorized newcomer appearing on the scene. Thus we find the ENOC continuing its programme of taking over competing or complementary businesses. The considerable amount of money required did not pose any problems, as the parent NOTC possessed ample capital reserves as a result of the railway companies who, having bought a 50 per cent stake in the business, would now also subscribe for 50 per cent of any new capital raised, in order to maintain their holding on an equality with the NOTC.

The Grays area, which had always been the Company's most difficult spot prior to licensing, clearly exemplifies how quickly the new system brought order out of chaos. Of forty seven or forty eight separate proprietors identified as working some kind of stage/express service, four or five made no attempt to apply for licences, preferring to throw their lot in with another applicant more likely to be successful. Fourteen of the forty-two firm applicants were rejected in their entirety, twenty five operators received the

A fine view of Chelmsford bus station after extension and redevelopment of the corner site and demolition of the old Counting House building. This view should be compared with the first illustration. Note the generous use of publicity material fixed to all available wall space.

F. Spalding

licences sought, although subject to modification in certain cases, and three were granted a part only. By the end of 1932, one owner had had his licence revoked for misconduct and another failed at the first attempt at renewal. Two more did not bother to renew. In 1933 some were selling out to the ENOC and a little later several were compulsorily acquired by the LPTB, so before three years had elapsed, only six licensed operators remained working in the town.

Early in 1933, the ENOC began to eliminate some of the competition. During February and April two lady proprietors, Mrs Mummery of Little Thurrock and Mrs Paxman of Grays, who both worked on the very busy Tilbury—Grays—Purfleet route, were acquired, but no vehicles were taken over from either. At about the same time, negotiations were put in hand with E. Adams and F. W. Keeling, also of Grays, who traded separately but worked together jointly as 'The Local Bus' on the short Grays—Nutberry Estate route, who were taken over in February and March. Their times were combined with the ENOC 32A service which now held four of the six trips per hour authorized, the other two remaining with the Benjamin family which continued to trade as 'Our Bus' until 1951, when it was finally acquired.

Competition in the Chadwell St. Mary sector was eliminated in June with the purchase of another pair of operators; J. J. Naish of the village, who ran direct into Grays, and A. R. Greenslade's 'Tilbury & District Motor Services'. The latter held licences for two services from Chadwell St. Mary to Tilbury (Civic Square) where they bifurcated to (a) the Dock Station LMS or (b) over the hairpin bridge to the ferry. The ex-Naish service and the one to the ferry were now combined with the ENOC service 37A, and the Dock Station route became a new 37B service. No buses were taken from either operator.

The LPTB legally commenced business on 1st July 1933. The ENOC was scarcely affected as most of its services lay outside the 'special area', except at Grays where the 'powers that be', in its wisdom in planning the Board's boundary, took the line clean through the centre of the town! This effectively bisected all the east-west cross town services compelling thousands of daily passengers, who had hitherto enjoyed a through service, to leave one bus, walk to another terminal and queue again! A perfect example, and there were others, of the, at times, complete indifference of the Board or legislature to the needs and convenience of the travelling public.

Conversely, the ENOC acquired from the LPTB the severed eastern section of some through services whose owner had required the Board to purchase in order to secure severance compensation. The following services on the west side of the town passed from the ENOC to the LPTB on 31st August 1933:

Another interesting view, but this time taken inside the bus station to catch a glimpse of the rear of vehicles. The double-deck on the extreme right is Thornycroft XC No. 3067. Moving left, the identifiable vehicles are Leyland TD1 No. 3017, AEC Regent No. 3063, Thornycroft XC No. 3068, AEC YC No. 2226 and Leyland PLSC3 No. 2823.

F. Spalding

Five 32 seat dual-purpose saloons were supplied by Eastern Counties in 1932 on the popular Dennis Lancet chassis. Here No. 3423 has arrived at the London terminal in readiness for its express return trip to Jaywick Sands.

31, Grays—Purfleet—Rainham (Sundays only)
36, Grays—Aveley—Rainham—Romford (daily)
G/N 40, Grays—the Ockendons—Upminster—Romford
(daily joint with the LGOC)

The 38 Grays—Purfleet (daily) route lingered on with the ENOC until 17th April 1934 while the Board was negotiating the purchase of the following who were still working on this route: R. Clark, Mrs Coe, F. R. Harris, J. Harvey, Smith & Godden, Day & Bedingfield and the 'Tilbury Safety Coaches' of Cecil Rudkins.

The following services on the east side of the town came to the ENOC via the LPTB on 24th March 1934; the Tilbury—Grays—Ipswich—Great Yarmouth summer express service, formerly owned by Tilbury Coaching Services Ltd., with some excursions and tours from the two towns. This Yarmouth service became the nucleus of the extensive group of coastal services gradually developed by the ENOC in this area. During July, two further transfers were completed, viz: (a) P. W. Day and C. R. Bedingfield, who ran from Balmoral Avenue to Stanford-le-Hope and Grays or Shell Haven, which became ENOC services 58 and 59, and (b) the 'Tilbury Safety Coaches' of Cecil Rudkins, also known as 'Swallow Coaches', who had been one of the main contenders on the Tilbury—Grays—Purfleet road with six vehicles allowed on his licence. Rudkins operated several other services as follows:-

Route	ENOC No.
Purfleet—Tilbury Hospital (for visitors)	abandoned
Tilbury, Dock Road—Nutberry (peak hours)	57
Tilbury, Civic Square—Orsett Infirmary (visitors service)	54
Tilbury, Civic Square—Stifford Hospital (visitors service)	55
Tilbury, Civic Square—West Tilbury, Wilsons Farm (seasonal for pea-pickers)	56 †
Excursions and tours from Dock Road (Rudkins garage) and Calcutta Road (Labour Club)	continued

† *Not advertised in the public timetables*

In certain areas the combined effect of licensing, and the creation of the LPTB, completely altered the established pattern of bus/coach operations. This was particularly the case in West Hertfordshire/Buckinghamshire where several services which were outside the Board area went into the melting pot, to re-emerge in a completely new pattern which bore little resemblance to the old, so it became necessary for the demarcation lines between several 'area agreement companies' to be redrawn. Certain well-known names in the omnibus world were to now disappear for all time. The major changes may be summarized as follows:

(a) The LPTB took over the whole of the former LGCS on 1st July 1933 and the Amersham & District Company's services on 24th November 1933, except for one or two very minor sections, plus many smaller concerns from within those areas.

(b) The Aylesbury Omnibus Company's (AOC) network was completely dismembered as detailed later.

(c) The ENOC lost its Stony Stratford garage and group of services to 'United Counties Omnibus Company' (UCOC) which was another component of the Tilling empire based on Northampton.

(d) The UCOC also received a further substantial wedge of territory in which it had not previously worked.

(e) The City of Oxford Company received several services to the west of Aylesbury.

The reasons for these changes may be more readily understood by taking a backward look at some earlier events. The AOC started life in 1920 as the Aylesbury Motor Bus Company, owned by E. W. Young who was proprietor of The County Garage and Motor Works. He steadily built up a network of over twenty routes which, by 1931, extended as far as Thame, Bicester, Buckingham, Fenny Stratford, Leighton Buzzard, Dunstable, Berkhamsted, Amersham and High Wycombe. On 17th August 1931, the 'Premier Line', which worked some Green Line type coach services from this area and elsewhere into London, took over the working of the Aylesbury Motor Bus Company's routes, using its own coaches under a hiring arrangement with Young. A little later it secured the entire business and transferred operations to its newly built garage in Bicester Road, whereupon the business became the Aylesbury Omnibus Company Ltd. on 26th October 1931, using the fleetname 'Aylesbury Line'. 'Premier Line' was the ill-starred associate of the well-known Premier Omnibus Company of London. Both companies had great difficulties in obtaining licences for their bus/coach services, some of which they had been compelled to withdraw after prosecution and fines for operating unlicensed, in anticipation that one would be forthcoming. This resulted in a large surplus of almost new Leyland Tiger/Titan coaches, many of which were being bought on hire-purchase, the instalments for which were falling into arrears, so the Aylesbury operation was arranged in an effort to find remunerative work for some of them.

'Premier Line' still urgently needed additional services and many attempts were made to obtain further licences with little success. The AOC expanded on 12th October 1931 by taking over the 'Viking' coach service. This ran from Oxford, via Thame, to London, via Princes Risborough, Wendover and Tring, but was topped and tailed on 20th May 1932 to re-emerge as a stage service from Thame to Aldbury. Connections for London passengers were arranged at Wendover with the 'West London' coaches, with through bookings, and at Tring LMS Station with London trains. It became service 10 in the AOC series, vacant since the previous user, a Tring—Buckland Common service, having been transferred to 'Amersham & District' about two years earlier. The AOC made a further effort to expand on 3rd March 1933 when application was lodged to extend the 18 Aylesbury—Winslow—Buckingham service to Northampton, via Towcester which, had it been successful, would have had some interesting consequences. It passed through an area hitherto neglected by the major companies except for a service by 'Midland Red' from Banbury to Northampton. This ran only three days a week and had been put on a few years earlier as a threat to the former Northampton Motor Omnibus Company which was developing to the west and south of Northampton. This apparently innocuous application, however, turned out to be the catalyst which started a whole chain reaction.

Tilling were well aware of the financial and licensing problems of 'Premier Line' and the AOC, and saw to it that its actions were well monitored by the ENOC and UCOC, the latter being most concerned about the proposed extension to Northampton. This passed through the one district still open to the UCOC for further development, for UCOC was tightly contained on north and west by Midland Red and on the east, and a good deal of the south, by the ENOC. There were a number of small bus operators working on this road whose services ran mainly to Banbury, Northampton, Towcester or Stony Stratford and Bletchley. If many of these got into the wrong hands, it would be a decided inconvenience. At a conference quickly summoned at 20 Victoria Street, London, an immediate decision was made to buy off the AOC, so eliminating any further problems in this area, and overtures were addressed to the AOC Board. Well aware that it would soon compulsorily lose the whole of its London bus business and all its coach interests to the LPTB, as well as part of the AOC for which compensation would be received, the Directors felt there was no point in attempting to expand what little there would be left, due to the difficulty in obtaining licences. Mutually acceptable terms were soon agreed and arrangements concluded for the ENOC to take over the entire AOC business on 11th May 1933 as a wholly-owned subsidiary in an agency capacity, so far as the omnibus services and licences were concerned, but with the rolling stock passing to the ENOC at once. The ENOC now withdrew the AOC application to run to Northampton and commenced negotiations with two of 'The Five' working on the 'Wolverton Local', as detailed in the previous chapter, and the UCOC opened negotiations with some of the Buckingham operators.

About the end of May, Tilling made known to the ENOC and UCOC its ideas for the 'carving of the Aylesbury duck'. From the east side there was a slice each for the LPTB and the Amersham & District Company, and one from the south (the High Wycombe service) for Thames Valley, who had shared the route for a long time; arrangements no one would quarrel about. There would be three or four slices on the west side which would be handed to the City of Oxford Company in whose territory they clearly lay. Of the

Bert Smith, former Traffic Manager with the old National Company, and Eastern National's General Manager from 1929 until his retirement in November 1937. He was, for many years, a Director of London Coastal Coaches, and also a Director of 'Borough' and 'Rayleigh Motor Services' and Aylesbury Omnibus Company.

A. L. Smith

25

rest of the bird, the Winslow and Buckingham slices should go to the UCOC, as they entered the area that the company wished to develop, and the ENOC would receive the rest of the carcase. These proposals brought forth a very sharp reaction from the UCOC management which strongly felt that the remaining slices should be divided fifty-fifty between itself and the ENOC. A series of meetings was held at Victoria Street in which Stanley Kennedy and J. H. Mills of the UCOC were engaged in a tug of war with George Cardwell and Bert Smith of ENOC, with J. F. Heaton, who was Chairman of both sides, sitting in as umpire! It was not by any means an easy matter to resolve, for there were several rather awkward obstacles to be cleared. The presence of 'Midland Red' on the Northampton road was an inconvenience, as was the ENOC services based on Stony Stratford which reached out to Buckingham and Winslow, coupled with the problem 'Wolverton Local' worked by the ENOC and 'The Five'. In correspondence, Bert Smith declared the ENOC's strong preference that the UCOC should not come on to that road at all, in view of the extreme difficulties endured in securing the co-ordinated time-table. It would upset the status quo which should not be disturbed on any account. George Cardwell wanted to see some joint services by both companies, which would have been beneficial from the public point of view, but this was found impractical because the UCOC paid its road staff on a lower scale of wage than that enjoyed by ENOC's employees. While these discussions continued, the negotiations with the small operators were set aside, until a solution would be found rather late that summer. Eventually a compromise was made in which the AOC services lying north of the Aylesbury to Leighton Buzzard road were to be handed to the UCOC with effect from 1st December, together with the ENOC services at and around Stony Stratford, but not its two services to Bedford, or its share in the 'Wolverton Local'.

Meanwhile, the carving of the non-controversial parts of the AOC began on 1st July when the Tring Station—Aldbury section passed to the LPTB, continuing at intervals, as detailed in the following tabulation, until 20th December when the LPTB received the final slice, by which date the 'Aylesbury' had become a very dead duck!

On the day prior to taking over the 'Aylesbury', the ENOC acquired a service from Tring to Leighton Buzzard through Long Marston and Cheddington. This had been part of the 'Chiltern Service' of E. Prentice & Son Ltd., whose main line between Aylesbury and Watford had been taken over by the LGCS just before the LPTB assumed control. The Leighton Buzzard route lay outside the 'special area' so was resold to the ENOC, who numbered it 16A.

The ENOC now resumed and completed negotiations with John Bates to take over his 'Blue Bus Service', and applied for his licences on 25th August, which were granted on 27th October. Because the ENOC did not wish to operate a five weekly rota, as Bates had, but wanted a fixed timetable to go into its timebooks, it took over the number four car working rota for the Stony Stratford—Stantonbury service, and the remaining four operators now

Break-Up of the Aylesbury Omnibus Co. Ltd. 1933

AOC No.	Route	Notes	Destiny and No.		Date
1	Aylesbury—Tring—Berkhamsted		LPTB	301	20.12.33
2	Aylesbury—Tring—Dunstable		ENOC	101	1.12.33
3	Berkhamsted—Tring—Dunstable	+	—	—	—
4	Aylesbury—Weston Turville (circular)		ENOC	102	1.12.33
5	Tring—Long Marston		ENOC	103	1.12.33
6	Aylesbury—Marsworth—Long Marston		ENOC	104	1.12.33
7	Aylesbury—Rowsham—Wing—Leighton Buzzard		ENOC	105	1.12.33
8	Aylesbury—Bierton	†	UCOC	47	1.12.33
9	Leighton Buzzard—Great Brickhill		UCOC	51	1.12.33
10	Thame—Princes Risborough—Wendover—Tring (Rly. Stn.)	*	abandoned		1.12.33
11	Leighton Buzzard—Stewkley—Fenny Stratford		UCOC	48	1.12.33
12	Leighton Buzzard—Winslow—Aylesbury		UCOC	46/49	1.12.33
13	Leighton Buzzard—Winslow		UCOC	49	1.12.33
14	Leighton Buzzard—Wing		part EN and UC	18 49	
15	Aylesbury—Princes Risborough—High Wycombe		TVT	30	30.9.33
16	Aylesbury—Wendover—Halton Camp		ENOC	106	1.12.33
17	Aylesbury—Great Missenden (section of 17)		ENOC	107	1.12.33
17	Great Missenden—Amersham—Chesham (section of 17)		'A & D'		21.7.33
18	Aylesbury—Hoggeston Turn or North Marston—Winslow—Buckingham	††	UCOC	46	1.12.33
19	Aylesbury—Haddenham—Thame		C of O	82	3.8.33
20	Aylesbury—Chearsley—Thame		C of O	81	3.8.33
21	Aylesbury—Bishopstone—Marsh		C of O	83	3.8.33
22	was not in use		—	—	—
23	Aylesbury—Waddesdon—Marsh Gibbon—Bicester		C of O	98	3.8.33
24	Aylesbury—Stoke Mandeville		ENOC	108	1.12.33
25	Aylesbury Town Service—Bicester Road—Southcourt		ENOC	109	1.12.33

Notes: + Denotes route 3 was a connecting service, buses on services 1 and 2 were timed to meet at Tring, going either way, where passengers could interchange.
† Denotes the UCOC withdrew its route 47 during 1935, whereupon the ENOC became sole operator on the direct Aylesbury—Leighton Buzzard section.
* Denotes that the Tring Station—Aldbury section passed to the LTPB on 1st July 1933.
†† Denotes the AOC applied to extend the Buckingham route to Northampton, via Towcester and Blisworth, on 3rd March. The ENOC withdrew the application on 2nd June in view of the uncertain future of the AOC.

Code A&D = Amersham & District Motor Bus and Haulage Co. Ltd. — taken over by the LPTB on 24th November 1933.
C of O = City of Oxford Motor Services Ltd.
TVT = Thames Valley Traction Company Ltd.

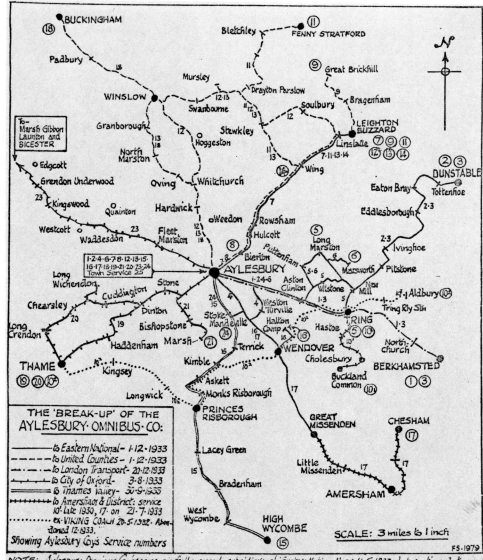

THE 'BREAK-UP' OF THE
AYLESBURY OMNIBUS CO.

– – – – – to Eastern National - 1·12·1933
– – – – – to United Counties - 1·12·1933
–·–·–·– to London Transport - 20·12·1933
–··–··– to City of Oxford - 3·8·1933
–···–··· to Thames Valley - 30·9·1933
+++++++ to Amersham & District: service
10 late 1930, 17. on 21·7·1933
·········· ex VIKING COACH 20·5·1932. Abandoned 12·1933.
Showing Aylesbury Co.'s Service numbers

NOTE: Aylesbury Omnibus Co. became a wholly owned subsidiary of 'Eastern National' on 11·5·1933, but continued to work its services as 'Aylesbury Line' up to the disposal dates shown: its last day being 19.12.1933.

rotated on schedules 1, 2, 3 and 5 every four weeks. As the number four working was one of the short shifts, it favoured the four remaining owners who would now be working two long turns every four weeks, instead of every five weeks as hithero. Bates' other two licences were for a workmen's service to the Morris Works at Cowley, a Stony Stratford—Old Bradwell route consisting of two trips on Saturday evenings and three on Sundays, some excursions and tours from Wolverton, and a school contract. It is believed that the ENOC assumed operation on 1st December 1933.

The services transferred from the ENOC to the UCOC at Stony Stratford were as follows:

ENOC No.	Route	UCOC No.
13	Stony Stratford-Winslow	part 40
24	Stony Stratford—Woburn Sands—Woburn	38
24A	Stony Stratford—Little Brickhill—Woburn	39
31	Stony Stratford—Bletchley—Stoke Hammond	part 37
51A	Stony Stratford—Deanshanger—Buckingham—Nash—Bletchley—Fenny Stratford	part 36
69	Potterspury—Stony Stratford—Wolverton	42
70	Deanshanger—Stony Stratford—Wolverton	44
71	Yardley Gobion —Stony Stratford—Wolverton	43
72	Wolverton—Nash—Galverton—Wolverton (circular)	45

(Services 69, 70, 71, 72 are marked "works services".)

When the services changed over on 1st December, the ENOC opened a new outstation at the 'Bull Hotel' yard in Stony Stratford with one double-deck and two saloons, where the UCOC had garaged two out-stationed buses for its Northampton service. The latter now travelled round the corner to Wolverton Road where they joined four saloons and three double-decks left by the ENOC (ADCs Nos. 2383 and 2386, Lions Nos. 2402 and 2403 and Titans Nos. 2850, 2909 and 3073) for transfer to the UCOC, which also took over the garage, office and waiting-room. The ENOC road staff at Stony Stratford were not very happy with the changed arrangements, for those being transferred to the UCOC had to take a cut in their wages, or seek employment elsewhere. On the same day, four ex-'Aylesbury Line' 26 seat Leyland Tigers, registered GK441, GK444, GN5142 and GN5143, were transferred from the AOC to the UCOC with the Leighton Buzzard routes. An old Dennis open-top double-deck was also intended for transfer but was deleted from the agreement following a check by a vehicle examiner, who put a stop notice on it.

On 15th December, the UCOC applied for the ex-Bates licences which were granted on 26th February, on which day his vehicles passed from the ENOC to the UCOC. On the same day, the UCOC also took over the services and vehicles of M. E. Jelley of Cosgrove who was the second member of 'The Five' on the 'Wolverton Local'. Negotiations had been started by the ENOC during the summer, but had been held over. Jelley operated several services (detailed below), two of which the ENOC took over but were worked by the UCOC for one week, the ENOC taking up the running on 6th March 1934.

Route	Became
Leighton Buzzard—Ivinghoe	ENOC 16B
Leighton Buzzard—Northall	part ENOC 18A
Cosgrove—Leighton Buzzard (by two routes)	part UCOC 56
Cosgrove—Stony Stratford—Wolverton	part UCOC 43
Mursley—Leighton Buzzard	part UCOC 56

The service from Cosgrove to London, via Stony Stratford, Stewkley, Leighton Buzzard, Dagnall and Hemel Hempstead, passed to the UCOC, who withdrew it entirely after only a few weeks of operation. The ex-Bates and Jelley workings between Stony Stratford and Stantonbury now became UCOC service 41.

UCOC now concluded matters regarding the Northampton—Buckingham routes where three owners were acquired on 19th February and a few small services were passed over to 'Midland Red'.

This completes the metamorphosis of omnibus services in this area which concern the ENOC, although there were some less complex transfers along the South Bedfordshire, Hertfordshire and Essex borders, and with Luton Corporation, which will be dealt with in geographical sequence.

An interesting departure was the supply of one Park Royal-bodied Leyland TD2 in 1933. Five sister vehicles received almost identical bodies, but built by Eastern Counties. Vehicle No. 3431 awaits collection from the Willesden factory in London.

C. K. Bowers

The next to be considered was the 'country end' from Dunstable to Leighton Buzzard, of Beaumont and Priest's coach route from London trading as 'Beaumont—Safeway', the name being a combination of two amalgamated concerns. This was incorporated into the existing ENOC 18 Luton—Dunstable—Leighton Buzzard route, the other portion being incorporated into the Green Line service to Dunstable, leaving Leighton Buzzard without a London coach service.

The combined effect of the formation of LPTB and Luton Corporation's entry into the transport scene was the cause of some reshuffling of services, both within and without the borough, in 1933. The ENOC was concerned with the following changes which occurred on 23rd March. It took over the ex-'Bluebird' service, between Luton, Hexton and Pegsdon, from Luton Corporation and numbered it 12A. Service 16 was extended from Eddlesborough to Tring to include some former AOC timings and some from 'XL' via Luton Corporation. Service 18/18B was increased in frequency and extended to Wing and Burcott, to include former 'Union Jack' and 'XL' times received via Luton Corporation, and the aforementioned 'Beaumont—Safeway' transfer. The Company's service 19, Luton—Houghton Regis—Dunstable and 58, Luton—Leagrave—Houghton Regis, were transferred to Luton Corporation for inclusion in services which it had acquired from 'Union Jack' and 'XL'. The ENOC also gained some additional timings on its own 53 direct service to Dunstable and the extension of its service 56, Limbury—Luton (Vauxhall factory main gate), as an all day service.

The 'Bluebird', 'Union Jack' and 'XL' businesses had all been purchased by Luton Corporation from A. F. England's Union Jack (Luton) Omnibus Company Ltd. which he retained, using it for the purchase of further businesses. Over the years, he was a source of considerable irritation to both the ENOC and the LPTB, of which more will be seen later.

A smaller batch of changes occurred in the following August when the last remaining outside operator in this sector was purchased. This was Bright Brothers of Dunstable who traded as 'Brights Luxury Coaches' from a depot at the rear of Scott's garage. Their main activity was a Dunstable—Eddlesborough daily service which was now merged into service 16 and a Friday market bus to Leighton Buzzard which became service 18C. A new service, numbered 52D, was started by the ENOC from Luton to Stopsley and Lilley, via Hart Lane, running every hour, for which H. E. Hill, owner of the appropriately named 'Strawhatter' coaches at Luton, had earlier sought to obtain a licence. The LPTB had taken his London express coach route with his garage and fleet, but could not use his express summer coastal services which were resold to the ENOC during February, together with eight Gilford coaches. The coastal routes went to Bournemouth, Southsea, Margate and Great Yarmouth with valuable pick-up points at Harpenden, St. Albans and Watford. The Margate service had not been in Hill's possession very long and it was formerly in the hands of B. E. Barrett of the Langley Garage, Luton.

Moving eastward to Royston, the ENOC took over the working of the two outer ends of the former LGCS service 31 (316 on Sundays and bank holidays) from Hertford and Ware to Puckeridge where it divided, half continuing via Buntingford and the other via Braughing and Barkway. The first now went no further than Buntingford and the other stopped at Puckeridge, the boundary points. The Royston—Buntingford section became ENOC service 64 and Royston—Puckeridge became 65, both being worked by a bus outstationed at the Green Man Inn, Royston. The loss of the through Royston—Ware facility led to a rapid decline in patronage.

Also working over the Buntingford route was the 'People's Motor Service' developed by Thurgood of Ware, probably better known for his coach-building activities, which diverted, as necessary, to serve villages off the main route. This was not acquired by the Board until December, whereupon services 64 and 65 were reorganized, the former continuing from Buntingford, via Hay Street and Great Hormead, to Braughing and Puckeridge, where it extended to Standon. Service 65 now worked from Royston to Barkway only, except on Sundays when one trip went through to Puckeridge.

On 17th March 1933, the ENOC was able to remodel route 13 from Bishop's Stortford to Saffron Walden, following a somewhat unusual sequence of events on that road. The 'Acme Pullman' service had not long been acquired by the LGCS, but had been kept in being as a separate concern because of the enormous goodwill it enjoyed with the travelling public. Its main business was a half-hourly service between London and Bishop's Stortford, but a few journeys were projected north to Stansted, Saffron Walden or Newmarket over which the minimum fare was only 3d. Anticipating its inability to run beyond Bishop's Stortford, the Board had reached agreement with 'Varsity Express' of Cambridge to continue operation of this section which followed the 'Varsity' route for much of the way. The ENOC, however, considered it had a good claim to some extra journeys over its Bishop's Stortford—Saffron Walden route, as noted above, and 'Eastern Counties' (ECOC), who were at that moment in the throes of taking over Bush and Twiddy's of Norwich ('East Anglian Highways'), who also used this road, did not look very favourably on the 'Acme' times going to a competitor while it still lacked a Cambridge—London service. The Traffic Commissioners were anxious to use this opportunity to secure standardization of fares on this road, which caused some delay in the issuing of licences. Matters had still to be completed as 1st July drew near, when the ECOC put in an application for the transfer of 'Varsity' services. On 30th June, some one appreciated that the ex-'Acme' service could not legally go beyond Bishop's Stortford after that day, but neither the ECOC or 'Varsity' had taken any steps in the matter as no licences had come through. It is understood that the ENOC depot inspector at the small Bishop's Stortford garage received a telephone call 'out of the blue' to inform him that . . . 'You will be doing the Newmarkets from tomorrow . . . and the last one down to Newmarket tonight to be ready to work the morning one up! The ENOC somehow managed to overcome the legal problems involved, sorted out a

Typical 1930s' publicity, mounted on the wall inside Chelmsford bus station. Note the West Country destinations, and the cost of a return trip to Penzance at 50/- (£2.50).
Eastern National

29

Above: An advertisement indicating the extent of the Company's services.

Above left: A former 'Premier Line' Leyland TS3 26 seat coach, acquired from the Aylesbury Omnibus Company in May 1933. It is seen here at Kingsbury Square, Aylesbury, shortly before departure to Halton RAF camp.

J. F. Higham

Left: Three Dennis 4 ton double-decks were taken over from the Aylesbury Omnibus Company in 1933, this particular vehicle having originally been with Premier Omnibus Company Ltd. This rather dated vehicle remained with Eastern National for barely twelve months, during which time it carried the 'Aylesbury Line' fleetname.

J. F. Higham

hiring arrangement between the parties, and maintained the service until 4th August, on which day 'Varsity' took up the Newmarket workings, which ultimately passed to the ENOC on the 15th of the same month.

One important result of fare revisions was the considerable protection which the ENOC enjoyed between Bishop's Stortford and Saffron Walden, as Newport was now the only intermediate fare point. Also, on 4th August, there was a reverse transfer when the Board took over from the ENOC the Ongar—Epping Town section of service 2, Chelmsford—Epping. This had only been in the ENOC's possession since 29th May, following the revocation of the licences of Associated Coaches (Ongar) Ltd. with effect from midnight of the 31st instant, the ENOC taking over two days prior to the revocation coming into effect. This concern had an express route to London which had been taken over a few weeks earlier by the LGCS for similar reasons. The ENOC also acquired a daily Chelmsford—Blackmore service from the same operator which was embodied in its existing 2A service.

On 10th November, the highly important coach service, hitherto provided by Edward Hillman's Saloon Coaches Ltd., between London (Bow) and Chelmsford, via Brentwood, passed to the ENOC, the LPTB having earlier acquired the very frequent timings up to Brentwood. The service was combined with the existing service 10, Chelmsford—Brentwood, between which points there was now a fifteen minute headway, with a half-hourly extension to Bow, where the former Hillman coach station was used for terminal purposes. This was not only situated opposite Bow Road Underground Station and the Bow Road LNER Station, but also next door to Bow LMS Station, the forecourt of which would soon become the terminus for this service. Hillman's coaches had continued approximately every hour beyond Chelmsford to Colchester, with three departures daily going through to Clacton-on-Sea, and others to Norwich, Yarmouth or Southwold. The Company was very anxious to acquire the Colchester and Clacton workings, which would have gone some way to putting it on level terms with the ECOC and 'Grey-Green' for a share of the express route traffic on that road. Hillman's Clacton service gave patrons seven hours by the sea for 6/6d return, which was raised to 8/6d at summer weekends; i.e. 130 miles for 42½p in high season! It enjoyed immense popularity and on fine Sunday mornings, it was not uncommon to see a convoy of eighteen to twenty Hillman Gilford coaches heading for Clacton.

The ENOC's aspirations to have a place on this road were unfortunately thwarted for the ECOC and 'Grey-Green' now put their heads together, a case of strange bedfellows in adversity, and with the railway standing counsel, and other objectors too, were able to mount a formidable opposition. The situation was aggravated further by the unfeigned hostility of the licensing authority to anything associated with 'Hillman', and the obsession which existed to ensure the ENOC did not obtain a London—Chelmsford fare point for its own express services, a facility enjoyed by all those in opposition. Not surprisingly, the Company lost its application on both counts. It was now ordered that all Hillman's long distance services, which the commissioners

Rebodying was a relatively economic way to update the appearance of vehicles, and here is a Leyland Lion PLSC3, new in 1928, but carrying a 1933 Eastern Counties body.

J. F. Higham

Eastern Counties supplied twenty of these 32 seat dual-purpose bodied Dennis Lancets. Vehicle No. 3483 is seen at Aylesbury Market Place en route to Bierton. Note the wheel nut guard and the half-drop window that has become loose in its frame; a common fault with movement in timber-framed bodies.

declared to be 'entirely redundant', (in spite of the heavy carryings) were to be purchased by the ECOC and 'Grey-Green' by agreement with Hillman, bringing immediate suppression to an enterprise which had done more to popularize road travel than anyone else in the area at that time.

This brings to a close the effects on the Company wrought by the creation of the LPTB, so attention can now be focused on a number of other acquisitions of the more usual character.

In May 1933, the ENOC secured control of The Borough Services Ltd., a transaction of rather more than ordinary interest as it had some far reaching effects. 'Borough' was a go-ahead Southend-on-Sea operator who had recently obtained a controlling interest in 'Rayleigh Motor Services' of that town, from which it ran into Southend by two routes, but had also inaugurated the first Southend—Colchester through services as mentioned in the previous chapter. As a result of being the first to put on a through Southend—Grays route, 'Borough' had successfully put its nose into two ENOC operating centres. The purchase of 'Borough' was an astute move, probably engineered by George Cardwell of Tilling, from whom, no doubt, 'Borough' was able to extract very favourable terms. It was followed up by converting 'Rayleigh' into a subsidiary of 'Westcliff' (still independent at this date) which nominated three Directors, the ENOC nominating two, an arrangement which secured for Tilling a toe-hold within the 'Westcliff' enclave, albeit via the back door. Within two years, Tilling had been able to persuade a sufficient number of 'Westcliff's' four hundred shareholders to part with the requisite shares to give it effective control.

The ENOC now transferred the 'Borough' Colchester services to itself which were integrated with its existing 19 service Southend—Colchester, via Danbury, and the few 'Borough' trips via Latchingdon became service 19A. The other 'Borough' routes remained as 'Borough' because the ENOC could not itself work within the 'Westcliff' area. The Southend—Grays service was now numbered 70 and the 'Borough' service between Leigh and Eastwood became 71. The express service to Enfield also continued with 'Borough'.

At Southend-on-Sea, the 'Borough' services started from the LNER Station forecourt, conveniently adjacent to the ENOC's own standings there, which soon became sufficiently busy to justify opening an enquiry-cum-travel bureau at 3 Bradley Street, immediately facing its bus terminals. The Company also took over the 'Borough' garage at 49 London Road, just a short distance away, and very close to the 'Westcliff' garage. The ENOC could now feel it was at last firmly established in the premier resort of Essex, right at the centre of the 'Westcliff' domain.

Early in 1933 there was an increase in the price of petroleum spirit, only a penny or twopence (pre-decimal), which, at that time, would have been considered fairly onerous, but today would seem scarcely noticeable. The Company felt it should recoup the extra cost by making a small increase in fares, and duly submitted proposals to the Traffic Commissioners for the Eastern Area. At that date a fare increase was almost unheard of, so there would be little precedent to assist in the preparation of such an application.

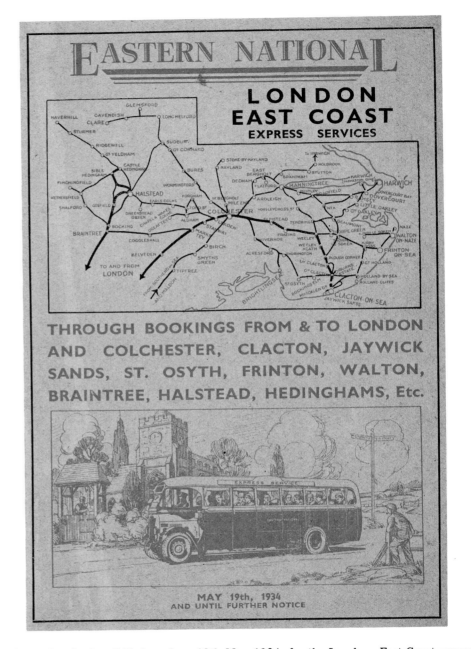

A facsimile of a handbill, issued on 19th May 1934, for the London—East Coast express services.

The Traffic Commissioners considered that the Company was seeking too large an increase, pointing out that this would raise ordinary return fares above 1d per mile which it had fixed as the standard in its area. A fresh application was submitted in which the Company raised as many of its sub-standard fares to agree with this level as was practicable, and at the same time removed several anomalies from its fare tables and altered some concessionary fares (scholars and workmen), which appeared to be on a low basis. Now accepted, the Company had to be content.

A facsimile of a notice issued in October 1934 to announce the revision to service 13 between Bishop's Stortford and Saffron Walden from the beginning of November.

A. Driver & Sons

1934

On 1st January 1934, the joint working with the ECOC on the Bedford—Cambridge, Hitchin—Cambridge and Clacton—Ipswich routes terminated for some undisclosed reason. The ENOC now continued operation of them by itself which required two buses to be outstationed at Cambridge in the ECOC garage in Hills Road, and one at Ipswich in a rather dilapidated building in Silent Street, the property of the ECOC. No longer would ECOC buses be seen working into Bedford, Hitchin or Clacton.

At about the same time as 'Borough' was acquired, arrangements were completed with T. W. H. Griffiths of Halstead for the purchase of his 'Pullman' service to Colchester, which competed with the ENOC service 18. Here there was a third operator, S. Blackwell & Sons of Earls Colne, with whom there was an agreement with the parent 'National' company dating back to the early 1920s. After taking over Griffiths' service, the ENOC started to rationalize and with studied disregard for the spirit of that agreement, neatly deleted any timing which followed a Blackwell departure, but continued to work those leaving just prior. Needless to say, Blackwells never forgave that action and relationships were never the same again. When Blackwells decided to dispose of their business, it went to Hedingham Omnibuses in whose hands the service still flourishes. 'Harry' Griffiths obtained employment with the Company until his retirement, at which time he had charge of its Halstead depot.

Two small acquisitions were now effected in the Midland Area. Towards the end of May, agreement had been reached for the purchase of Jack Dawson's service from Bedford, via Kempston and Wootton to the Cranfield district, which was distinguished for its unusual title, 'Malebird Bus Service'; very puzzling until one discovers that its proprietor, a man with a dry sense of humour, was landlord of the Cock Inn at Wootton! His times were accommodated into the existing 36 group of services, with suitable diversions on certain journeys, the Lidlington service becoming a new 36D. A. M. Bonham's 'Milton Service', based on Milton Ernest, was taken over on 1st September 1933. His three routes were:

(a) Bedford—Clapham—Milton Ernest—Odell—Sharnbrook
(b) Bedford—Clapham—Milton Ernest—Riseley—The Deans—Kimbolton
(c) Bedford—Thurleigh via Ravensden or Clapham.

Of these (a) was combined with service 6, which now became a daily operation as far as Odell, the Sharnbrook portion being abandoned; (b) which was a Sunday only working, became a new 5A; and (c) was slotted into the existing 34 group of services.

The 1933 accessions were rounded off on 18th December when Akers' 'Bird Motor Services' was acquired. He had a well-established daily stage between Halstead and Braintree which descended from a horse-bus service of great antiquity. One of his drivers, Eli Bacon, who died not so very long ago, probably had the unique distinction of being the ENOC's only driver who could claim to have driven a horse-bus and motor omnibus over the

Twenty four more Eastern Counties-bodied Dennis Lancets were supplied in 1935, of which No. 3532 is a typical example.

Eastern National

Six Eastern Counties-bodied Leyland TD3 double-decks joined the fleet in 1935, and here No. 3557 pauses for its official photograph near the Lowestoft factory.

A. Boughton

EASTERN NATIONAL

Associated with the L.M.S. and L.N.E. Railways.

NEW "SUNSHINE SALOON" SUPER LUXURY COACHES

FOR THE

LONDON-CLACTON-JAYWICK SANDS EXPRESS SERVICE

New Coaches of the very latest type now operate on the above Service, and their striking appearance and comfortable appointments will greatly enhance the comfort of passengers by this Route.

The wide windows allow extensive views of the Countryside traversed, and the sliding roofs permit of the maximum amount of sunshine and fresh air.

FOR FULL DETAILS OF TIMES & FARES—SEE OVERLEAF.

A facsimile of a leaflet describing the new Dennis Lancet super luxury coaches to be found on the London—Jaywick Sands service. Only two vehicles were supplied exactly to this pattern; Nos. 3584 and 3585 which had Dennis 32 seat central entrance bodies.

A. Driver & Sons

same route! Akers had also been an 'early bird' with an express service to London, via Braintree, starting from the Hedinghams, running four times daily, which drew the cream of the traffic on this route. There was also a market service to Sudbury, but he does not appear to have catered for excursions and tours. His depot in Rosemary Lane, Halstead became the company's first real garage in the town and eleven saloon vehicles were taken into the fleet. One was a nearly new AEC with Duple bodywork of an extremely luxurious character, which adorned ENOC's express coach leaflets for the next few years. It enjoyed a very long stay with the Company, lasting until 1958. The former 'Bird' routes were now numbered 23 and 24.

In January, John Kemp & Son of Tillingham sold their Friday market bus service from Bradwell-on-Sea to Chelmsford. It was combined with the existing 9 Burnham-on-Crouch—Chelmsford route, which now required a bus to run out twenty four miles to take up service, and another twenty four miles to return home. Such was the determination to gain the service, to preclude it passing to 'Quest Motors' of Maldon who already enjoyed a virtual monopoly of the district.

There were few changes to the Company's other services, but although the extension of service 49 across Chelmsford town from Springfield Park to Brownings Avenue for interworking with service 14A, now became 14B, the section from Woodham Walter to Maldon of service 1A was abandoned in favour of the local operator (Rolf) who was taken over many years later. In the Midland Area there was considerable revision to the Bedford– Hitchin and Rushden routes, a bus being outstationed at the latter, due probably to competition from Birch Brothers coaches.

Another spell of acquisitions started in June with a further ten operators disposing of their services before the year was out, four passing to the LPTB as already noticed. The first was R. H. K. Johnson of Colne Engaine who had recently assumed the refused licence for the Halstead—Hedinghams service of a Mr Pudney. This was combined with the existing route 22 to Haverhill. Johnson also worked Halstead—Pebmarsh, Great Maplestead—Braintree, via Greenstead Green, and a workers service to Rippers Factory at Sible Hedingham which the ENOC numbered 30, 29 and 33 respectively.

In August, the 'East Bergholt & District Service' of Mrs E. S. Furber came into the fold. It operated a daily service to Colchester, via Manningtree and Mistley, becoming 17A, together with excursions and tours from seven points. It was descended from a carriers service of the Peck family, carried through more than one generation.

Pattens Coaches Ltd. of Runwell Road, Wickford was acquired during September. Formerly it had traded as 'Wickford Omnibus Services Ltd.' which was a very short-lived business, and before that it was the Wickford Carriage Company of a Mr Spurling. Six Dennis saloons, which belonged to J. Patten junior and not the company, were taken over together with the garage in Runwell Road which the ENOC retained until 1939. Patten's route was of considerable importance to the Company as it was a frequent daily service passing through Billericay, Wickford and Nevendon to Pitsea,

which established the ENOC into the area now covered by Basildon New Town. In may have had serious consequences had it been allowed to pass into other hands. It was combined with the existing 4 service, Chelmsford— Billericay, now entering the town via Wood Street instead of via Beehive Lane as hitherto.

In July, E. Scott & Sons disposed of their 'Golden Arrow' service jointly with the ECOC, who acquired the major portion, the ENOC receiving a new market route from Ramsey to St. Ives which became service 38A, and a few other timings which were integrated in services 39 and 44. One Dennis Lancet was included in the purchase.

The ENOC attained a third service to Cambridge in August when J. Goates of Arrington Bridge sold his 'Cambridge Blue Motors' to the Company. He operated a daily through service from Bedford, via Biggleswade, Wrestlingworth, Arrington and Orwell, which became 29A. Two ENOC buses were outstationed at Arrington until the advent of a Company garage at Biggleswade. The last take-over of the year was A. T. Rickards' service which worked three days a week from Wingrave to Aylesbury, via Cublington, which the ENOC numbered 110.

Photographed at Bishop's Stortford garage is the former Underwood AEC Regal; new in 1932, acquired in 1935, rebodied by Beadle in 1942 and sold in 1957, making it one of the longest serving PSVs in the fleet. During the 1940/41 period, No. 3577 also saw service whilst on loan to London Transport.

Surfleet

35

The Company was now paying greater attention to the provision of town services, where better utilization of vehicles could be achieved, than on country routes which often had to work with wide headways. Four were started this year — viz: the 30A, on the London Road at Bedford; the 51 town circular from Letchworth Station; and Hitchin to High Dane (51C) or Redhill (51B). There was some reorganization at Aylesbury where service 102 was combined with 108 to run circular via Stoke Mandeville and Weston Turville. Service 103 to Tring, via Marsworth was combined with the 104 to Puttenham and Long Marston, retaining that number, and service 105 lost its identity as it was covered by extending service 17 from Bedford to Leighton Buzzard through to Aylesbury.

1935

New Year's Day, 1935, was celebrated by the ENOC operating the former 'Quest' network of services of J. W. Gozzett of Maldon, who had a monopoly of the Dengie Hundred, that large tract of Essex which lies between the Blackwater and Crouch tidal estuaries. Gozzett had been successful in putting together a fair network of services, including a daily London coach route, in this thinly-populated area given over almost entirely to agricultural pursuits. Several others had succumbed when trying to open up services in the district. Twelve licences for stage routes and six for excursions and tours with a fleet of fourteen (mostly Gilfords) passed to the ENOC. The ten services acquired from 'Quest' were as follows:

Route	ENOC No.
Maldon—Great Totham—Witham	60
Maldon—Southminster—Burnham-on-Crouch	61
Maldon—Southminster—Steeple—Bradwell-on-Sea	62
Maldon—Purleigh—Stow Maries—Wickford	63
Maldon—Heybridge Basin—Goldhanger	64
Maldon—Mill Beach	65
Maldon—Cock Clarks—North Fambridge	66
Maldon—Town Service	67
Maldon—Braintree (Crittall's Works)	68
Maldon—Danbury—London (King's Cross) coach service	—

There were also excursions and tours from Maldon and a number of the towns and villages in the area. Gozzett's business incorporated elements from the following defunct operators: 'Pride of the Marshes'; 'Pride Associated'; A. A. Ford; 'Burnham & District'; Essex Public Company; and a Mr Gridley. Details of these can be found in the acquired operator appendix.

J. W. Gozzett was owner of a flourishing motor garage and car agency at The Causeway, Heybridge, an activity in which the family is still today engaged, and also have interests as travel agents.

A facsimile of a special announcement that Eastern National are about to commence the London—Great Bardfield service, previously run by The Horn Motor Coach Company. The AEC Regal coach featured at the bottom was used on many leaflets during the 1930s and was acquired with the Bird Motor Services, Halstead, in December 1933, becoming No. 3510.

A. Driver & Sons

With the purchase of 'P. H. Underwood's (Blue and Cream) Saloon Omnibuses', also in January, the ENOC secured an entry to Mersea Island, although the parent 'National' Company had, in 1920, made a short-lived attempt to establish a presence on a very competitive road where never less than four proprietors, and often more, were seeking a living. However, Underwood was the sole operator running to East Mersea, which was his base, in continuation of an old family carrier service. Three stage licences and four buses were acquired. His services were Colchester—Abberton—West Mersea; West Mersea—East Mersea; and Colchester—Blackheath—Fingringhoe, which last had been taken over from a Mr Day, the ENOC respectively numbering them 75, 76 and 77. Licences for all the Mersea operators carried two peculiar conditions — viz: (a) any bus must, on request by a passenger at the West Mersea terminal by the church, continue to The Hard at the fare of one penny, and (b) any passengers, on arrival at the Bus Park, Colchester, could demand conveyance to the North Railway Station for a fare of 4d, so long as they had boarded prior to reaching the municipal boundary. Both were in continuance of a long-established local custom.

Buses on the Mersea service had to cross The Strood, a causeway which linked the mainland with the island, generally covered with water at high tide. It did not affect horse-drawn traffic, although there were many stranded vehicles in the early motor bus days, a situation enjoyed to the full by any passing rival. A former Mersea resident writing in an Essex magazine a few years ago mentioned the keen competition between 'Berry's Buses' and the rival 'Primrose' (plus others — Ed) . . . 'Many an exciting ride did we have, each bus being timed to run close to its rival with the resultant neck-and-neck race for the whole ten miles to get to each bus stop before the other so as to snatch up passengers waiting there.' These practices ceased after the new licensing arrangements of 1931, when a co-ordinated timetable on a regular twenty minute headway came into force. Journeys were allocated to the operators as follows:

Berry and Sons	9 to 10	Weekdays
Brown's (Blue Bird)	6 to 7	Weekdays
Mersea Co. (Primrose)	10 to 12	Weekdays
Thorpe's (Reliance)	9 to 10	Weekdays
Underwood	9	Weekdays

On Sundays each performed about two fewer journeys

In summer some operators extended to Seaview Avenue for the beach

During June, one more competitor in the Grays area was removed with the purchase of Stanford Motors Ltd. off Albert Haxell and George Suckling who also included the workings of Huggin's 'Victory' bus. Three services were being operated to (a) Thames Haven/Shell Haven which became ENOC service 35; (b) to Grays direct, or via Horndon-on-Hill; and (c) to Corringham and Fobbing as service 36. Three buses were included in the transaction and for a few years the ENOC occupied its garage in Corringham Road.

Christmas in Huntingdonshire would not be complete without a little Company publicity. St. Neots Market Place provides a convenient spot for the driver to park the Dennis Ace and, if he is flooded with enquiries, a quick telephone call to the depot will soon provide further assistance.

Two small businesses with services in the Wickford area were taken over in July. One was S. A. Amos of Ramsden Heath who traded as S. A. A. Motors, and the other was E. Davies of Ramsden Bellhouse, one of whose services was already being worked by the ENOC following revocation of the licence; service 11A, Chelmsford—West Hanningfield. The earlier operations of this pair were many and various and generally very ephemeral. Davies' routes also embraced part of a Mr Kershaw's activities after he had been in difficulty with the licensing authority. At the time of takeover, Amos had been working daily from Ramsden Heath to Billericay which the ENOC embodied into service 4, Chelmsford—Billericay—Wickford—Pitsea. His Monday market bus to Wickford, via Brock Hill, was now joined to a Davies service working to Rettendon, via Chalk Street, which became a new 12B service. A new 12A service was now made up from the following odds and ends:

(a) ex-Amos	Friday market bus to Chelmsford (direct via Stock 'Ship')	
(b) ex-Davies	Saturday cinema bus to Chelmsford (direct via Stock 'Ship')	
(c) ex-Davies	Weekday commuter service to Wickford Railway Station via Jackson's Corner (peak hours only)	
(d) ex-Davies	Wickford—Runwell Hospital (for workers)	
(e) ex-Quest	Wickford—Runwell Hospital (for workers)	
(f) ex-Davies ex-Kershaw	Wickford—Rettendon Turnpike (to connect with services 19/19A to Maldon in place of service 63 Maldon—Wickford, now withdrawn)	

Services by Davies and Kershaw between Wickford and Basildon, and Wickford and Shotgate, were abandoned as they were well covered by other operators. It should be mentioned that the businesses of both Amos and Davies had been seriously affected by Patten (mentioned earlier) and 'Westcliff Motor Services' when they put on regular through services to more distant destinations such as Chelmsford, Pitsea, Southend-on-Sea, Romford and London.

A number of inter-related changes to other services were also introduced on 11th July. Services 60, Maldon—Witham and 67, Maldon Town route were combined as 60; services 61 and 62 to Burnham/Bradwell were revised, providing improved facilities, the outstation bus at Bradwell being moved to Southminster Station yard where it joined others owing to lack of accommodation at Maldon. Of service 63, Maldon—Wickford, the section Maldon—Purleigh formed part of a new 66 service to North Fambridge, the old section, via Cock Clarks and Hazeleigh, being abandoned. The ex-Kemp extension of service 9 to Bradwell was taken off, now going no further than Burnham as before, and through passengers used connecting facilities, although the return 'connection', which required a wait of forty five minutes at Southminster, could hardly be described as such.

C. M. Taylor's 'Horn Coaches' of Braintree became part of the ENOC on 24th August, bringing a further London express service and three stage routes. The express duplicated the recently-acquired 'Bird' service to London from Braintree, so there was room for some rationalization of timings. This service also possessed fare points from London and Romford to Chelmsford, which was probably one of the main reasons for taking it over. The stage routes were Braintree—Greenstead Green, recently acquired from C. S. Cummings' 'Royal Blue'; Braintree—Felstead Beet Sugar Factory, and Braintree—Great Bardfield daily, which was extended to Great Sampford on Wednesdays. The latter route also embraced T. Sullens & Son, and Ben Adams' former services. When the applications for transfer to the ENOC were heard, all were granted with the exception that the two fare points so desired has been deleted from the fare chart by the licensing authority, causing much frustration for the Company. The same opposition as before had done its work again. The ex-'Horn' services were numbered 21, 21A and 21B; service 21 having just become vacant as its previous user, Colchester—Clacton, via Weeley, had been joined to services 19/19A Southend—Colchester, to give an hourly through service to Clacton-on-Sea. Taylor's garage in Rayne Road was also taken over with four Gilford and two AEC coaches.

Fourteen of these 20 seat Dennis Aces completed the intake of new vehicles in 1935. Familiarly known as 'flying pigs', because of the snout-like appearance, they were well suited to narrow country lanes where the short wheelbase made them highly manoeuvreable. Here, No. 3603 stands at Clacton bus station prior to departure to Point Clear Bay.

At the same time as the applications for the 'Horn' business were heard, the ENOC put in an application for the licences of Rose Brothers of Chelmsford, trading as 'Primrose Coaches' who, inter-alia, operated an approximately hourly coach service daily to London, but once again the Company met a re-buff when it was told . . . 'the commissioners are not prepared to authorize the transference of this licence so as to enable the service to be continued without modification by new operators' . . . No objection was made to transfer Rose's other licences, but the ENOC, at this time, was only really interested in this business if it could obtain the London service, so it became a case of 'No Sale'. Rose Brothers continued to operate until 1958 when the ENOC bought their other licences, the London service having, by then, become almost unsaleable due to the electrification of the railway taking most of the traffic from the coaches working on the Colchester road. The Company would have been wiser arranging for 'Horn' and 'Primrose' to be converted into limited companies, which could have continued operation of the service without transfer of licences.

On 30th December, the ENOC had more success with the transfer of another 'Primrose' service; this being the fleetname of the 'Mersea, Colchester & District Transport & Bus Co. Ltd.,' which had been working on the Mersea road since 1909 and now decided to dispose of the omnibus section, which included three Guy single-decks which had earlier seen service with a North London independent.

During 1935, there was scarcely any service changes in the Eastern Area beyond those already mentioned. In the Midland Area some new services had been introduced. These were as follows:

7E Bedford—Stevington via Bromham (August)
10 Baldock—Bygrave (November)
34B Bedford—Renhold via Salph End, (part of a general overhaul of the
    34 group of services to the St. Neots district)
53B Luton—Dunstable (Hambling Place), providing new local facilities in
    that town (31st October)
20D Luton—Clophill, via Ampthill, (a Sundays only diversion of service
    20B — November)
One service, 28A, Bedford—Stewartby direct, was withdrawn, the 36 group of services now covering

In 1934 the Company celebrated its 'Silver Jubilee Year', although to be more correct, it was twenty five years since the birth of the fleetname 'National' on a Clarkson steam bus, which featured in its publicity material. The ENOC claimed it was operating 250 routes, and carried 40,000,000 passengers annually. This represented an increase of 75 omnibus services and an extra 14,000,000 passengers compared with the figures published in 1931.

At the close of 1935, the Company had reached the territorial position in which it was to remain with little change for some years. The 'big spend' was

1934 'National' Silver Anniversary leaflet.

now over, for there were few outside operators of any significance now willing to dispose of their businesses. Stage services became stabilized, so increased earnings had to be sought elsewhere, hence a new emphasis was made to develop the seasonal express services and the excursions and tours aspect of the business, coupled with greater efficiency of operation.

The engineering department contributed to this efficiency by purchasing 106 new vehicles over the period 1933–1935. The Guildford manufacturer, Dennis, was favoured to supply no fewer than ninety of the new machines, seventy six of them on Lancet chassis and fourteen on the small normal control Ace chassis. The Dennis Company supplied the twenty seat bodies for the Ace and locally-built Eastern Counties bodies were provided for the Lancets. All had petrol engines. The balance of new vehicles was made up of fifteen double-decks and one coach on Leyland Titan and Tiger chassis. A further six Leylands of older vintage were rebodied, five PLSC Lions in 1933 and a Tiger in 1935, and these helped to update the appearance of the fleet.

Ironically, the acquisition of many operators invariably brought with it an assortment of vehicles, many of which could not be considered standard. Some of these were disposed of as soon as a new replacement was ready. Others, which were generally sound and reliable, were given a longer period of service with the Company. It is interesting to note that fifteen different makes of vehicles were obtained from the twenty operators acquired, and by far the most popular model was the Gilford (46 units), with Leyland in second place (18), Dennis (16) and AEC (11). There were seven REOs, five Chevrolets, and three each of GMC, Bedford and Guy. Morris and TSM were represented twice each and there were solitary examples of Albion, AJS, Star and Commer. Altogether 120 vehicles were bought this way, fifty in 1933, forty in 1934 and thirty in 1935.

Chapter Three

Peace and War 1936-1940

The period of five years covered in this chapter is one of contrast. It opens with the Company comfortably enjoying a hitherto unknown period of tranquility, but concludes with the country enmeshed in total war; one not only fought on the battlefields in foreign lands or on the seas, but also in the air, both over enemy and homeland territory.

The battles on the bus routes and in the traffic courts were now over, and all licensed operators could go about their business peaceably. Timetables were all agreed by the licensing authority and accepted by the operators concerned. Fare cutting was a thing of the past, and no one lived in fear of unexpected competition popping up. The 'cowboys', who had not come into line, were now eliminated.

The necessary reorganization following the creation of the London Passenger Transport Board, which required integration or transfer of services as seen in the last chapter, was now completed and the Company was able to settle down to a quiet period in which more attention could be devoted to the finer and less pressing aspects of omnibus and coach operation.

The take-over of other businesses now became less frequent, or urgent, and were generally of lesser importance than hitherto. In many cases, it can be said the acquisitions were made not so much for the value of the service, but to ensure that the licence did not pass to another operator seeking to expand, now that there was little prospect for the introduction of new services.

There was now a higher level of activity in the excursions and tours section, with many new picking-up points arranged over the smaller towns and villages instead of operating solely from the Company's depots and offices.

Another important improvement in facilities for its customers was the opening of new omnibus stations providing off-street loading etc. The Company was justifiably proud of these purpose-built premises as exemplified in leaflets it issued to mark their opening. The Clacton-on-Sea opening leaflet reads . . . 'covers over 26,000 sq. ft., is conveniently situated close to the shopping centre of the town and within easy reach of the sea. Passengers will now be enabled to wait in comfort . . . There is a large sized Waiting Room and Enquiry Office approached from a covered platform, affording every comfort and convenience . . . The Parcels Office will deal with the acceptance of parcels for conveyance, or to be left until called for, under the 'Left Luggage' arrangement.'

'The new building also comprises a Cashier's and General Office, Conductor's Paying-in Room etc. together with the Local Superintendent's Office, each of which is situated on the first floor, whilst for the use of the Staff, a comfortable Mess Room is also provided.'

'Heating for the whole building is supplied by 'Iron Fireman' Mechanical Stokers, located in the Boiler Room below the building.'

'The new Omnibus Station will improve the operation of the Company's Services and represents a further facility for the convenience of the travelling public.'

'Always at your Service'

All the new garages and bus stations in the Tilling Group of Companies, however, varied by reason of differing requirements and shape of site. Each bore a certain affinity, and although devoid of any unnecessary decorations, were extremely functional, bright and clean-looking, and possessed a certain dignity and appearance of fitness for purpose. The man responsible for these works was H. J. Starkey who had charge of the Tilling architectural and surveying section at its London headquarters. Many of his designs can still be seen all over the country, from Cornwall to Northumberland.

During the period now under review, Eastern National built new omnibus stations at Jackson Road, Clacton-on-Sea; at High Street, Maldon; and at St. Peters, Bedford. There had been considerable difficulty in handling traffic at all of these places and no comfort for passengers who had to wait on the street. Furthermore, the 1929 omnibus station at Chelmsford, which had now become totally inadequate for the traffic being handled, was demolished, and a completely new structure incorporating a greatly enlarged

The small capacity coach was also in demand for village private hire, and the forward control Dennis Ace, affectionately known as the Pug, provided the answer. Six of these 20 seat vehicles were supplied, and here No. 3612 poses for the camera outside the Guildford factory.

Dennis Bros.

garage was built over the old site. The area which had been extended north to Fairfield Road permitted all buses to enter and leave without reversing. In the earlier years, garage facilities had been a low priority but now received much attention. The Bedford, Colchester and Luton garages were all enlarged to house the ever increasing vehicle allocations, and entirely new garages were built at Aylesbury, Halstead, Hitchin and Huntingdon, where the buses had, hitherto, stood out in a variety of premises with minimum facilities for servicing. Some additional small depots came into use at Stanford-le-Hope, West Mersea, Wickford and Brightlingsea as a result of businesses taken over. A new enquiry-cum-booking office was opened in Bradley Street, Southend-on-Sea opposite the LNER (now Victoria) Railway Station.

Life in the countryside was beginning to change rapidly with country folk now commuting to the nearest town for the daily work, and greatly increased numbers of children needed transportation as more village schools only provided education for infants and juniors. This required the gradual introduction of daily omnibus services to many villages which had only previously enjoyed market and weekend facilities, although this tended to increase the 'peak hour' problem for the Company.

The country was now generally climbing out of the long depression, and increased spending power enabled many families to enjoy a summer holiday for the first time, or more frequently enjoy a trip by bus or excursion coach at the weekend. Greatly increased summer services had to be introduced at the Company's resort areas, sparked off by the appearance of the very popular holiday camps which provided all inclusive 'organized' leisure.

One business was taken over in the Eastern Area in 1936, but no vehicles changed hands. A long standing local service, provided by Coppin & Son between Orsett and Grays, it had descended from a horse-drawn service dating back to the 1890s. In the Midland Area the Company was very glad to finally buy out Mr A. F. England's 'Union Jack' undertaking for the second time. It will be recalled that he had earlier been active in the Luton/ Dunstable district where his services were now in the hands of Eastern National and Luton Corporation. Immediately afterwards, he bought the Lamb Brothers 'Renown' service from Luton to Flamstead and then transferred his attentions to Bedford, buying up R. A. Carding's 'Wonder Bus' service, which operated two local routes, and also T. F. Allen who ran to

The well-proportioned lines of the 1936 batch of Bristol JO5G dual-purpose vehicles is clearly appreciated in this view of No. 3629 waiting at St. Peter's, Bedford. The kiosk in the background was the Company's office until the bus station was developed nearby.
Bedfordshire Times

The beautiful lines of the Eastern Coach Works styling is clearly visible in this view of No. 3667, just as it leaves the Lowestoft factory.
A. Boughton

St. Neots, previously trading as 'Dreadnought' of H. H. Clench. Another acquisition here was Taylor's 'Reliance' service from Meppershall who had recently taken over some timings from S. Groom in the Henlow to Hitchin area, which was almost certainly done to prevent Birch Brothers from buying them. This former London operator owned a coach route from London through Welwyn to Hitchin, Bedford and Rushden which carried local traffic north of Welwyn. It had been assiduously developed by Birchs who used fast semi-luxury coaches, causing considerable concern to the Company and the railways too, all of whom used every opportunity and excuse to object to any application put forward by Birchs which, nevertheless, continued to flourish.

Because the 'Renown' service was almost entirely within the LPTB area, it was transferred to that body after only a few months of operations as route 83. The Bedford services were numbered from 80 to 82 and the Grays—Orsett service of Coppin was combined with the existing 32 Grays—Stanford-le-Hope service. This opened the way for a general revision and tidying up of services at Grays, where there were a number of overlapping routes after taking over Stanford Motors and Messrs Day & Bedingfield, all of which was accomplished as follows:

(a) Service 32B Grays—Stanford—Fobbing was withdrawn. The latter section was joined to the Stanford—Red Hut section of service 58 to form a new 36 service. The Grays—Stanford section was, of course, well-covered by services 32, 35 and 70 etc.

(b) The Stanford—Shell Haven portion of service 58 was combined with the existing 35 service, Grays—Stanford—Shell Haven or Coryton.

(c) Service 32B was now allotted to a new Grays—Blackshotts Lane local route and co-ordinated with Benjamin's 'Our Bus' service on a combined ten minute interval.

(d) Service 37, Grays—Chadwell St. Mary, via Little Thurrock was now combined with service 45, Grays—Linford, using the same roads.

(e) The terminal for routes 32, 37A, 37B, 44 and 45 was moved from the War Memorial to Grays LMS Railway Station.

(f) On the same day, four special new services for workers at the new Bata Shoe Factory at East Tilbury started from Pitsea, Tilbury Town, Grays and Laindon, numbered 80 to 83 respectively.

(g) Service 31, Grays—Tilbury was now increased from six to eight buses hourly.

(h) The Grays—West Hanningfield section of route 11A was withdrawn, all of which was served by certain parts of services 4, 11, 12A/B, 32, 35, 51/3, or 70.

(i) Service 57, Nutberry—Tilbury now terminated at Tilbury Dock Station, instead of Feenan Highway, except for one scholars' bus.

(j) A new service 59, for work-people from the Red Hut through Stanford and Corringham to Thames Haven, was also started.

(k) A new evening service 83, on Wednesdays and Saturdays from East Tilbury to Stanford-le-Hope was started, but soon withdrawn due to insufficient patronage.

The excursions and tours operated by Taylor of Meppershall were later secured by Birch Bros., but the bus services taken over by the Company were as follows:

(i) Shillington—Pegsdon—Hitchin (Tuesday only) became service 27A
(ii) Henlow Camp/Cinema/Village—Hitchin became service 27
(iii) Henlow Camp—Hitchin Station, for RAF personnel included in existing service 25
(iv) Meppershall—Hitchin, via A600 (Tuesday only) became service 27B
(v) Henlow Village/Camp—Hitchin; two routes became 28 and 28A

In 1937 the ex-Taylor operations were reorganized when services 27B, 28 and 28A were all incorporated into existing 9A and 9B routes and lost their identity. The Southern end of service 9, the original Bedford—Ampthill—Shefford—Baldock—Hitchin route, was merged into service 8A, Biggleswade—Hitchin and the rest, now redundant, was abandoned. At Aylesbury, the 108 Weston Turville circular route was also taken off as it was largely covered by services 106/7 and other local operators.

In the Eastern Area, a new town service in Chelmsford appeared near the year end. Formed from a part of service 4, Chignal Corner—Bus Station, it continued to Wood Street via New Writtle Street, but service 4B ceased when Galleywood Racecourse was closed. Service 21B, Braintree—Greenstead Green was merged into service 33, which was rerouted to embrace it. Trips via Convent Hill, Bocking on service 23 were now numbered 23A and the Sunday only 27 service, Colchester—Braintree, ceased.

A couple of years after securing a foothold on the Colchester—West Mersea road in 1935, Eastern National was glad to buy out the two remaining operators. The first was Berry of Colchester who had been on that road since the 1880s and who had the first PSV licence in the area in 1898. They also worked to Rowhedge, Fingringhoe and Brightlingsea, and twelve buses of seven different makes were acquired. On 11th October the last Thorpe Bros. 'Reliance' came in but excluded vehicles. They had a route to Great Wigborough, formerly the 'Xmas Bus Service' of P. W. Christmas, who also kept the Kings Head at that village. These purchases now gave the Company full control of all routes south of Colchester, except on the short run to Rowhedge where Mr Fale and Mr Warner still plied for hire. During June, the excursions and tours operated by Leggett Dyer & Co. of Dovercourt were acquired and, in December, Ashdown's 'Rodney' bus service between Chelmsford and Little Baddow was bought but, for many years, he continued with excursions, private hire and contract operations.

'Eastern National' was now in a position to introduce certain changes in the timetables of the Mersea Road services which, hitherto, had been impossible with between four and six operators sharing the times. When Underwood was taken over, his services became 75 for West Mersea, 76 for East Mersea and 77 for Fingringhoe, via Blackheath. When 'Primrose' was taken over in the December following (1935), its identical route to West Mersea became 75A and its trips via Peldon Village, 75B, which was done so that Eastern National buses could be identified as to whether they were working an ex-Underwood or ex-'Primrose' timing! Similarly, after acquiring Berry, their identical route became 75C and the trips via Fingringhoe became service 75D, but after Thorpes came into the net, the need for this separate identification no longer existed, so services 75A and 75C could now become 75, and 75A was reissued for the ex-Thorpe Great Wigborough route. A new branch service to Abberton Reservoir was given the number 75E, the

Berry routes to Fingringhoe, via Old Heath 77A, to Rowhedge (Albion) became 77B and to Brightlingsea, 78. Eastern National retained the former 'Primrose' garage at West Mersea and Berry's premises at Victoria Place, Brightlingsea.

In the Clacton area, there were several minor changes including diversion of some journeys from Clacton to Walton, via Elm Tree Avenue, Frinton. A new service for scholars from the railway station to St. Monica's School was numbered 107A and three new town services, incorporating portions of other services, were started, i.e. 115, Magdalen Green—Jaywick Sands; 115A, Holland-on-Sea—Jaywick Sands, via Sea Front; and 116 as the last, but via the station and town centre. There was also a new service 120 from Harwich to the new holiday camp at Dovercourt Bay. The Midland Area routes, 64/5 had worked from an outstation at Royston to Standon, but were now all combined to run via Buntingford as service 64, at the same time being transferred to the Eastern Area for operation from Bishop's Stortford garage. Here it had to be renumbered completely out of sequence to 164, as 64 was already in use at Maldon. There were a few other small changes in the Midland Area to note. The ex-'Union Jack' local services 80 and 80A were now merged into service 1; service 7E was merged into 7C, and the 36 com-

Clacton omnibus station with Bristol double-decks on view. No. 3653 is destined for Southend, and shows the roof-mounted route indicator, while No. 3736 is loading for Walton. The position of the registration numberplate in the centre of the radiator had now become standard Company practice.

Eastern National

The attractive lines of the Eastern Coach Works body is seen again in this view of No. 3721 on one of the Grays local services. This design of single-deck was very typical of the immediate pre-war period.

D. S. Giles

44

plex of routes to the Cranfield district became even more complicated, as new journeys from Cranfield to Newport Pagnell became 36E, trips to North Crawley became 36F and the existing trips to Moulsoe, 36G. The 35C service from Biggleswade to Hitchin was integrated into service 52C, Hitchin—Stotfold Green.

On 4th April 1938, Eastern National commenced operation of the services of Mr Wilson, trading as 'Clavering & District', who had built up a fantail of routes north of Bishop's Stortford, mainly of the market day/weekend variety, which extended as far as Saffron Walden, Royston and Debden. Each served a goodly number of villages hitherto neglected by Eastern National or its predecessor 'National', although parts of the area had some facilities from other small owners passing through to Bishop's Stortford, notably Drayton Bros. from Barley, Weedon from Chrishall and Hicks from Dunmow. Wilson's routes into Bishop's Stortford were numbered 13A, 13B, 13C, 13D and 13E, those to Saffron Walden became 39A, 39B and 39C and that to Royston, 40, although the existing service 40A was from Chelmsford to Tilbury Ferry, via Brentwood! One Bedford bus came with the business. During this year, the two remaining excursion and tour operators at Harwich and Dovercourt, namely Starling & Sons and H. A. Wells, were purchased, which brought additional picking-up points at Parkeston Quay and Upper Dovercourt with one coach from Starlings.

A view of one of the first Bristol K5G double-decks to be supplied with Eastern Coach Works bodies in 1937. Here, No. 3735 displays one of the very short-lived suffixed route numbers which occupied considerable lengths of linen and necessitated much turning of the handle.

There were three acquisitions in the Midland Area in 1938. Firstly the 'Westoning & District' stage routes of Seamarks Bros. (but not their tours) became Eastern National services 21, 23 and 24 on 2nd June. Next was Lewis Slade of Offord D'arcy, trading as 'Offordian', to Huntingdon or St. Neots, including his excursions and tours formerly run by Rowlatt & Miles of St. Neots. These services became 4B and 4D on 28th March and, on the same day, Donne's 'Huntingdon Coaches' daily service between that town and St. Ives, via Houghton, became 43, while some short trips to Wyton were added to the 44 route between Huntingdon and Ramsey.

Two new minor routes started in Bedford, the 30B to Shortstown for work-people, and the 30C from Ampthill Road to London Road for scholars. In Essex, a short spur off route 22, Halstead—Haverhill, served Little Yeldham and route 43 from Brentwood to Billericay, which now, after almost total annihilation by competition, operated on Saturdays only with an extension to Stock. This proved of little benefit so was again cut back to Billericay.

The dark shadow of possible conflict in Europe became more threatening in 1938 and preparations for our defence were activated. Shadow factories for aircraft and other munitions were being established, and new aerodromes being built in the Company's territory for the defence of London called for increased transport facilities for the construction gangs. In full co-operation with the authorities, detailed plans were worked out by the Company for the provision of vehicles for the transport of large numbers of service personnel of Northern Command to the coast in the event of an emergency. Plans were also made for the evacuation of the civilian population from coastal districts, and of children from London to 'safe' reception areas, and for the equipping of a considerable number of single-decks for use as ambulances, should it become necessary to move casualties or complete the evacuation of hospitals.

During the spring of 1939, the 'Sally Bus Service' of the Knight family at Yardley Hastings, which ran from Olney/Lavendon to Northampton, was bought and numbered 50A and two buses continued to be outstationed there in a small garage which Knights had acquired with Alfred Minney's 'Comfy Bus', with whom they were in competition for some years. A double-deck was also lodged in the yard in Chase Park Road. Mrs Goggins' 'Transit Bus', which worked from Wiston or Nayland to Colchester, was also acquired and combined with service 15. She also had a service to Layer Road Football Ground which became service 28, some excursions and tours from Great Horkesley and Mile End and three vehicles came with the purchase. Mr Warner decided to give up running his Rowhedge service this year and his licence was combined with that of the Company, but no extra times appear to have been operated.

There was an interesting transfer from 'United Counties of Northampton' to 'Eastern National' of some services, and five omnibuses previously operated by Meadows & Son of Barton Seagrave, near Kettering, which the former had acquired on 4th December 1938. Some of these routes penetrated into the territory of both companies. Agreement for the division of this business could not be reached until April 1939 and did not become effective until 31st July, which resulted as follows: services 75, 77 and 78 became 'Eastern National', but service 76, Kettering—Thrapston—Huntingdon, became joint with 'Eastern National' which worked it solely on Mondays to Fridays, with 'United Counties' sharing it on Saturdays and Sundays. The routes concerned were:

75 Huntingdon—Spaldwick—Kimbolton—Catworth (Saturdays only)
76 Huntingdon—Spaldwick—Catworth—Thrapston—Kettering (daily)
77 Thrapston—Catworth—Old Weston—Leighton Bromeswold—
    Alconbury—Huntingdon (Saturdays only)
78 Thrapston—Catworth—Old Weston—Leighton Bromeswold—
    Catworth—Keyston—Thrapston, circular, (Tuesdays only)

With the declaration of war in 1939, some of the emergency plans came into operation almost immediately, especially those concerned with the evacuation arrangements. During this period no fewer than 320 buses were concentrated on certain railheads for the distribution of over 40,000 mothers and children to their temporary new homes in the country, which was not accomplished without some inconvenience to the regular travellers; but it had to be done. Several hospitals were also transported in their entirety to safer areas, and eighty buses were continuously earmarked for military use at short notice.

The first intimation to the public of the impending introduction of wartime timetables appeared in the buses on 18th September. It took the form of the notice here reproduced, and was to take effect as from 23rd September, which coincided with the date for the start of winter services.

EASTERN NATIONAL

IMPORTANT NOTICE

WAR-TIME SERVICES WILL COME INTO OPERATION ON SATURDAY, 23rd SEPTEMBER, 1939.

DURING DAY-TIME THE MAJORITY OF ROUTES WILL BE SERVED BY PRACTICALLY A NORMAL SERVICE, AND AFTER DARK BY A REDUCED SERVICE ON MOST ROUTES.

FULL PARTICULARS OF THESE WAR-TIME SERVICES CAN BE OBTAINED FROM THE LOCAL OFFICES OF THE COMPANY.

THE COMPANY REGRETS ANY INCONVENIENCE TO WHICH THE PUBLIC MAY BE PUT AS A RESULT OF THE UNAVOIDABLE ALTERATIONS.

HEAD OFFICES : NEW WRITTLE STREET, CHELMSFORD   Phone 3431 (3 lines)   EN 40 4P 1939

Early casualties of the war were the two Company timetable books which had for some years been produced by Waterlows of Dunstable, who found they could not continue production because of heavy Government commitments. Alternative arrangements had to be made at short notice with Index Publishers, also of Dunstable, who were able to produce a somewhat condensed timetable book in time for a further batch of service reductions during October in both the Eastern and Midland areas. These continued to be issued in this form until 1943.

The majority of service reductions were effected by thinning out evening journeys after the 'peak hours' and some careful pruning of lightly-used trips during the daytime. A few services or sections of route of lesser importance were withdrawn completely, although in most instances there were alternative facilities available by other services of the Company or other operators. In the Eastern Area the following were the principal withdrawals:

  2B Bus Station—Wood Street section; withdrawn
   3 Howe Street—Dunmow section; withdrawn
   7 Chelmsford—Halstead; withdrawn entirely
  12 Chelmsford—Billericay—Southend; withdrawn entirely
  20 Sudbury—Long Melford—Clare; withdrawn entirely
  36 Red Hut—Stanford—Fobbing; withdrawn entirely
  38 Grays—Horndon—Stanford-le-Hope; withdrawn entirely
  39 Saffron Walden—Chelmsford; withdrawn entirely
  43 Brentwood—Billericay; withdrawn entirely
  44 Grays—Bulphan; cut from daily to Friday/Saturday only
54/55 Tilbury—Orsett/Stifford Hospitals; withdrawn entirely
 101 Clacton-on-Sea—St. Osyth; withdrawn entirely
 103 Clacton-Thorpe—Walton; split to run Clacton—Thorpe/Walton Kirby only
 108 Clacton—East Bergholt; withdrawn entirely
 111 Harwich—Walton; withdrawn entirely
114, 115, 115A, 116, 117 Clacton locals; all withdrawn
 120 Harwich—Dovercourt camp; all withdrawn

The Midland Area did not offer the scope for so many withdrawals as it was a reception area and there were no seasonal services, but the following were suspended for the duration of the war:

 10 — Baldock—Bygrave
18C — Edlesborough—Leighton Buzzard
 22 — Newport Pagnell—Bletchley—Stoke Hammond
30C — Bedford School Service
33C — Bedford—Bromham (local)
 35 — Biggleswade—Luton
35D — Biggleswade—Hitchin, via Southill
 45 — Huntingdon—Houghton

The London Essex express services B and C were reduced by one third, and all the coastal summer services withdrawn for the duration. It should be mentioned that in 1936 letter designations began to be allotted to these services which, at 1939, were as follows:

A	London—Colchester—Clacton	ex-'National' 1929
B	London—Braintree—Halstead	ex-'Bird' 1933/'Horn' 1935
C	London—Danbury—Maldon	ex-'Quest' 1934
D	Bedford—Colchester—Clacton	New ENOC 1933
E	Bedford—St. Neots—Great Yarmouth	New ENOC 1932
F	Luton—St. Albans—Watford—Bournemouth	ex-'Strawhatter' 1934
G	Luton—St. Albans—Margate	ex-'Strawhatter' 1934
H	Luton—St. Albans—Portsmouth—Southsea	ex-'Strawhatter' 1934
J	Luton—Round Green—Stopsley—Great Yarmouth	ex-'Strawhatter' 1934
K	Enfield—Edmonton—Westcliff—Southend-on-Sea	Operated by 'Borough Services'
L	Tilbury—Grays etc.—Ipswich—Lowestoft—Great Yarmouth	ex-'Tilbury Coaching' 1934
M	Luton—Hitchin—Baldock—	New ENOC 1936
N	Tilbury—Grays—Laindon—Clacton—	New ENOC 1937
P	Bedford—Shefford—Baldock—Dovercourt Bay	New ENOC 1937
Q	Luton—Hitchin—Baldock—Dovercourt Bay	New ENOC 1937

The first big problem for both drivers and conductors, with wartime operation, was coping with the 'black-out'. The driver had to manage with a single masked headlamp, constructed to throw a very short narrow beam towards the kerb. At first, the only interior lighting permitted was by the entrance to assist passengers to see the steps, and the conductor had to do his work by using a small torch attached to the belt of his ticket machine. However W. J. Morison, the Company Engineer, quickly devised a very ingenious yet simple contrivance to assist the conductor, which consisted of a neat hooded lamp suspended from an electrified batten fixed to the ceiling down the centre length of the saloon, which could be drawn along as the conductor progressed up the car. Later, a system of modified lighting was permitted, so that passengers were not sitting in total darkness.

Early in 1940 the old established business of C. Simpson & Sons was acquired. It was based at Leaden Roding, the centre of that very rural area known as The Rodings from the large number of villages taking their name from the river which flowed through that district. They operated two trunk

The 1938 Eastern Coach Works body on No. 3751 had been extensively rebuilt by the time this photograph was taken in the late 1950s. Becoming No. 1271 in the 1954 renumbering, the vehicle is seen descending North Hill, Colchester.

This Bristol L5G was new in 1938 and numbered 3780. By the time it was photographed standing at the former 'City' stop in Brentwood, the Eastern Coach Works body had been repainted and the post 1954 number, 275, had been allocated.

routes which crossed at Leaden Roding, one from Chelmsford to Bishop's Stortford and the other from Dunmow to Brentwood, with several other market services, all of which had been developed from a carriers cart service. At about the same time the very small service run by a Mr Tween in the same area from Good Easter to Chelmsford was taken over. Hitherto, the only activities of Eastern National within this area was its own route to Bishop's Stortford, which consisted of but a single journey each way on Thursdays and Fridays, with four on Saturdays and Sundays (Service 8) and service 46 to Willingale on Fridays and Saturdays only. The above services were integrated as follows:

2B   (existing) Some trips deleted, duplicated by Simpson's times.

3A   Former Simpson's Dunmow—Brentwood route daily.

8   Former 'Eastern National' and Simpson's services between Chelmsford and Bishop's Stortford combined, now all run via Hatfield Broad Oak and formerly served only by Simpson.

8A   Ex-Simpson's Bishop's Stortford to Matching Green service on Thursdays, Fridays and Saturdays, but formerly run through to Leaden Roding.

8B   Ex-Simpson's Bishop's Stortford to Hatfield Broad Oak, via Woodside Green service on Thursdays and Saturdays only, and formerly run through to Leaden Roding, via Great Canfield.

8C   The ex-Tween route Chelmsford—The Chignals—Good Easter on Tuesdays, Fridays and Saturdays.

46   Chelmsford—Roxwell—Willingale now extended to Matching Green (ex-Simpson's) on Fridays with extras to Willingale.

Simpson not only had excursions and tours from five of The Rodings, Dunmow, Bishop's Stortford and Hallingbury, but also from Chelmsford, which had earlier been taken over from Browne Bros.

Tilling decided this year that no useful purpose was being served in maintaining the 'Borough Services' separate identity just for the necessity of respecting an early operating agreement vis-a-vis 'National' and 'Westcliff' now that the latter was also in Tilling ownership. They accordingly arranged for 'Borough' omnibuses to cease operating their three services on 29th October. Service 70, Southend-on-Sea—Grays became Eastern National, simply by changing the fleet name transfers and legal lettering on the buses which, for some years, had been switched from the parent company in accordance with operating requirements. Operating from Leigh-on-Sea were services 71 and 72 and these were transferred to 'Westcliff' with whom they had hitherto been worked jointly. This was also a simple matter; the service was reduced by one half by deleting the 'Borough' timings from the timetable, and 'Westcliff' continued its share exactly as before. One more well-known fleetname in South Essex passed into oblivion but several years elapsed, however, before the company was finally wound up.

Eighteen vehicles formed the original 'Borough' stock when taken over, but only five of these, Nos. 3432, 3435, 3440, 3442 and 3443, lasted until at least 1940. It is considered that vehicles Nos. 3433, 3436, 3439 and 3441 were not replaced when disposed of in 1934, 1937, 1939 and 1938 respectively, but that the following replacements were arranged on the rest so that the 'Borough' fleet was maintained at fourteen vehicles throughout:

No. 3409 for 3444 in 1934	No. 3639 for 3438 in 1936	No. 3543 for 3434 in 1938
No. 3547 for 3446 in 1935	No. 3644 for 3445 in 1936	No. 3555 for 3437 in 1938
No. 3561 for 3448 in 1935	No. 3645 for 3447 in 1937	No. 2805 for 3449 in 1938

The introduction of the diesel engine, and the enormous savings it made in the cost of operating, brought about one of the most significant changes in the fleet during the late 1930s. Some of the petrol-engined vehicles, particularly the heavier double-decks, could barely manage five miles per gallon but, once an oil engine had been fitted, the fuel consumption not only improved to about 10 m.p.g., but the price per gallon of Derv was also considerably less. Together, this attracted a saving which had to be grasped.

As early as 1931, the Company had taken delivery of one AEC Regent, No. 3063, which was fitted with an oil engine, and this was watched comparatively with its petrol-engined sisters. Six months later something mysterious happened which caused No. 3063 to exchange its engine with the petrol unit in another Regent, No. 3020. Perhaps there had been an accident. Both vehicles were identical, so the experiment continued on No. 3020. Apart from this, no other oil engines appeared in the fleet until late 1934 when, like many other Tilling companies, they generally began to adopt diesel engines as more and more conversions got underway. The Company converted 71 vehicles between then and 1939, 63 of them being double-decks and, of the total converted, 59 were of Gardner manufacture. In addition to this, the intake of new vehicles between 1935 and 1940 brought in 183 fitted with oil engines so that, collectively, by this date, 225, or virtually half the fleet, were operating on the cheaper fuel and travelling almost twice the distance per gallon. It is worth mentioning that three Leyland Tiger coaches, Nos. 3663, 3664 and 3665, which had been delivered new in 1937 with Leyland 8.6 litre oil engines, each lost them in 1939 for the petrol units swopped with TD3 double-decks Nos. 3556, 3559 and 3561. This change further illustrated the common-sense approach in not only providing the heavy double-deck with an oil engine at the expense of the light Tiger coach, but also utilizing three otherwise 'wasted' petrol engines in a chassis which now benefited from its celebrated quick acceleration!

Altogether 188 new vehicles were supplied during the five years ending 1940. When analysed, this represents 153 Bristol, 24 Leyland and 11 Dennis,

and bodywork was shared between ECW (155), Brush (27) and Dennis (6). Divided into types, they sub-totalled 9 coaches, 22 dual-purpose saloons, 64 single-decks and 93 double-decks. A total of 36 older vehicles were rebodied during the period 1938—40 and this continued the programme to update earlier vehicles to the latest pattern and design. Eastern Coach Works supplied new saloon bodies for one 1934 Dennis Lancet, six 1928 Lions and four 1929 Lions, while Beadle completed eleven saloon bodies on 1928 Lions and a further nine on 1929 Lions plus five double-decks on 1930/1 Leyland Titan chassis.

Forty eight vehicles were acquired from other operators during the period comprising thirteen TSM saloons from North Western Road Car Co., Stockport, ten Bedford, seven Dennis, five Leyland, four Albion, three Gilford and one each of AEC, Chevrolet, Commer, Maudslay, Morris and Thornycroft.

In late 1939, the Government conferred powers upon the military authorities which enabled them to take over civilian vehicles in cases of emergency. Bus companies were immediately vulnerable to this action in that their rolling stock was readily suitable for use as troop transporters or for conversion to ambulances, etc. There were sometimes heated exchanges when, on occasions, the Captain of the local platoon would enter one of the

One of the Luton-based Bristol K5G double-decks is seen here on a local service in its younger days.

Company's garages and, with a recently acquired air of authority, would hand the foreman a piece of paper and demand the release of several buses which had appealed to him in the yard outside. Very little time was allowed to 'get them ready' before a group of soldiers arrived to take them away. The Company could resist the seizure of any vehicle on the grounds that it was required to provide an essential service for the community, but very rarely were they able to reverse the decision of the War Office, and the vehicles had to go for an unspecified length of time. Many buses were requisitioned in this way and, although precise figures are unknown and much overlapping occurred, it would not be unreasonable to estimate that at least ninety were involved in this exercise alone. When they had finished with them, the Ministry of Supply would offer the vehicles back to their owners but, by that time, many had been so ill-treated that several could only be regarded as insurance write-offs, and the necessary war damage claims had therefore to be submitted. Those that were less damaged were sent to Dartford for Messrs Beadle to refurbish or rebody, as the case might be, but three vehicles, Nos. 3313, 3314 and 3316 respectively escaped this and ended up as temporary waiting-rooms at Hitchin, Colchester and Bishop's Stortford.

In October 1940, London Transport's cry for help was answered by many provincial operators providing the vehicles which they could spare. Eastern National managed to release five, Nos. 2357, 2534, 3002, 3320 and 3577, and all were safely returned to the Company by August 1941.

This Bristol K5G has just arrived in Aylesbury on service 110 from Cublington. Of the 1940 batch, all twenty K5Gs were allocated to the Midland Area where they were to remain for the rest of their lives.

V. C. Jones

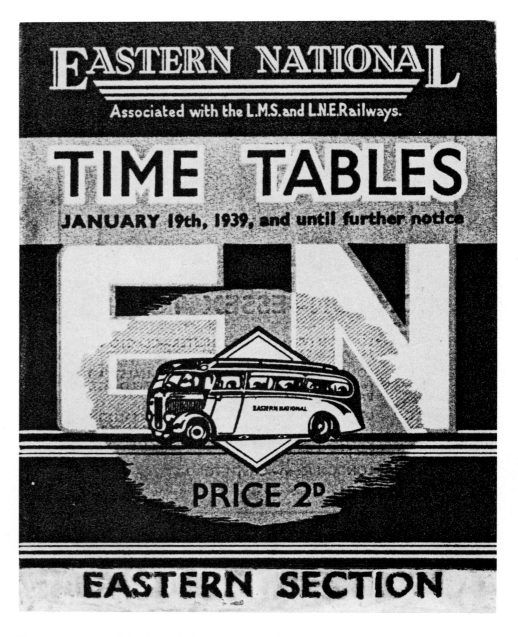

Timetable cover of the late 1930s, in green, yellow and white. It was printed by Waterlows of Dunstable, and replaced in October 1939 by an economy wartime issue. Actual size was five and a half inches by four and three eighths inches.

Chapter Four

Battling On   1941-1946

As the war progressed, the process of 'call-up' of men pursued its inexorable course, so that ultimately more than 600 of the Company's workforce of about 2,000 had joined the forces. By way of replacement, women were employed in as many categories as possible, including the workshops and garages as well as for platform duties. This not only required a heavy and continuous programme of training but also entailed the provision of suitable accommodation, rest room facilities, etc., which did not exist at certain premises. It is believed that the garage at Bishop's Stortford was the only one that remained an all-male establishment right through the war. The men here were determined they would keep it that way, a resolve in which they were successful by dint of heavy overtime and rest day working, postponement of retirement by older staff, and recall of former staff already in retirement.

Coping with the 'peak hour' travel needs and the huge influx of additional workers, the demand for transport facilities had first doubled then trebled at certain industrial centres straining the Company's resources in vehicles and manpower to the limit. There were many vital engineering works within the area served by the Company, in spite of the generally rural nature of the district. At Chelmsford, there were Crompton Parkinson, Hoffman and Marconi; at Luton there were the Vauxhall/Bedford and Commer Motor Works, with AC—Delco at nearby Dunstable, to mention just a few, and each was making very important contributions to the war effort.

The collapse of France was followed by the threat of invasion so that some of the 'safe' areas, to which thousands of evacuees had been sent, had now a reverse role to play as they became coastal defence zones. People had to be moved to safer areas further inland, and most of the normal residents of Clacton and Walton, for example, who were not required for essential work locally, were also required to leave, as military and coastal defence units were strengthened. Most of the hotels, boarding houses, holiday camps and many private houses were requisitioned for use as army billets and offices. Those civilians remaining were issued with permits and no one could enter the area without one. All buses and trains were stopped at check points where permits and passengers were examined. Gun emplacements, defence batteries, searchlight units and observer posts were set up, on which camouflage experts found ample scope for employing their artistic ingenuity in transforming these concrete erections into innocuous looking objects such as refreshment stalls, ornamental shelters, public conveniences or ice-cream kiosks, among the former public lawns and gardens! In this area the bus services were drastically cut; all the town services were withdrawn and only a skeleton network covered the rest of the district. The vehicles so released were a relief to other hard-pressed places.

When the German submarine campaign was at its height, early in 1942, the Ministry of War Transport ordered the withdrawal of all express coach services to assist the deteriorating situation regarding stocks of fuel and rubber for tyres. This caused the London—Halstead/Maldon coach service to end and a few weeks later the Chelmsford—Bow (East London) route was cut at Brentwood. Further reductions were effected on 16th November when all journeys departing after 9p.m. were cancelled, and all Sunday services before 1p.m. also ceased.

In spite of all the difficulties, two businesses were acquired during the year. One was the small service of Mr Wilkinson which worked three days a week from Flacks Green, near Terling, to Chelmsford, which required but one vehicle. The other was the rather more important 'Blue Coach' service of Mr Gammond, which ran daily from Bedford to Oxford by way of Newport Pagnell, Stony Stratford, Buckingham and Bicester. It had long been an irritation to Eastern National, United Counties and the City of Oxford companies over whose territories it crossed. Overtures, with a view to purchase it, had been made from time to time, but all were steadfastly turned down, Gammond having made it quite openly known that he would never sell his service to the Company. It was a lucrative service, especially at weekends, when Gammond's entire fleet of five vehicles, plus other hirings, were sometimes required for a single timing. This was due to the very poor railway facilities which often entailed a wait of an hour or more at Bletchley.

Vehicle No. 3874 was fitted with an interior gas producer plant, access to which was through large doors at the rear. Seen here in 'as delivered' condition, the bus is set up for 'black-out' service with masked headlights and white profile lines.

C. F. Klapper

Junction. The service was a good example of the small proprietor noting what the public wanted . . . and providing it. The arrangements of inter-company territorial agreements seem to have often inhibited the parties from considering the possibilities of cross boundary joint operation, until another party had provided it.

Thus, when Gammond felt it was time to take retirement, he turned his eyes westward, and offered his service to J. H. Watts who headed the Red & White Group, and with whom he had some rapport. His service connected with the latter's London–South Wales express services at Oxford. In June 1941, Watts secured an option on Gammond's business and formed a new company, 'Blue Coach Service (Bedford) Ltd.' of which he and his chief executive, T. J. Jones, were the Directors, and applications were made for the transfer of the licences.

Discovery of who was behind the new company set alarm bells ringing at Tilling and BET headquarters, and formal objections to the application were immediately lodged by all three companies who feared a link might be established with Birch Bros. at Bedford, or other independent operators en route. Watts was called to a meeting with George Cardwell of Tillings and J. S. Wills of BET, following which an agreement was made on 25th November, whereupon Watts would withdraw from proceeding with the purchase that would instead be jointly made by the three companies with effect from 1st January 1942, each to contribute in accordance with the mileage of route within their respective territories. This worked out as Eastern National 17/55ths, United Counties 14/55ths and City of Oxford 24/55ths. The latter was to operate the service and sent two AEC saloons to Gammond's garage at Bedford, retaining three of his drivers. It turned out there were some operational difficulties here and, in the following August, operation was assumed by Eastern National. After the war, City of Oxford joined in operation when the service was doubled in frequency, while United Counties provided extra workings over the middle section or relief vehicles as required.

On 29th September 1942, service 107, Aylesbury–Wendover–Great Missenden was extended to Amersham jointly with the LPTB Country Services in lieu of the Green Line coach route withdrawn that day by Ministerial Order. This was now numbered 369 by the Board, and restored

A view of Maldon depot in 1941. This was the centre of the gas producer operation. Vehicle No. 3306 tows trailer No. 6 out of the depot, enabling the camera to record the nine year Beadle-bodied Leyland Tiger for posterity. The doorway at the back of the garage led to a sizeable yard, which served as a storage place for all Company vehicles withdrawn from service.

Bus & Coach

No. 3887 was one of three Leyland Titan TD2 double-decks acquired from Plymouth Corporation in 1945. Upon acquisition, the Weymann body was rebuilt and a Gardner 5LW engine was fitted. The vehicle is seen standing at Jaywick Sands kiosk.

the former bus route jointly worked by the Aylesbury Omnibus and Amersham & District companies until they had been divided on 21st July 1933.

During the period of heavy bombing raids, Eastern National had its share of damage and the dislocation that followed. Chelmsford suffered on 23rd May 1943 when a heavy raid was concentrated on the town, which almost completely destroyed the garage in which twenty four omnibuses were wrecked beyond recovery. Next morning, the workers were still brought into the town using buses that were still operational, but many were entirely without glass, had destination blinds in ribbons, gashed panels and roofs, and the interiors still littered with debris. The prompt response to calls for help from other depots, and from its neightbour, 'Westcliff', was of enormous assistance during the period of cleaning and patching up that followed. The very prompt and almost heroic action of the garage staff at the Colchester premises averted what might have been a major disaster when they tackled a large incendiary bomb which had penetrated the building close to the fuel pumps. There was another rather similar happening at the Clacton depot.

In 1943, there was another call from the Ministry of War Transport for a further reduction in mileage to help prolong the diminishing stocks of fuel and rubber. This was mainly accomplished by widening the headway of the more frequent local services, as most country routes had already been trimmed to an almost irreducible level. A number of other measures were also introduced about the same time, including a programme of fixed stopping places which was steadily organised over the year in co-operation with the police, local authorities, licensing authority and, where applicable, other operators. This required white markings laid down on the highway in areas where there were no 'stop' signs and was of considerable help to a driver during the hours of black-out, as he now knew where to look for passengers. Likewise the conductor/conductress found it easier to know the name of an approaching stopping place to be called out (see reduced facsimile of one of the notices advising the public of the arrangements).

Because of the intense pressure on the Chelmsford district services at peak times, the Company felt compelled to introduce a priority system over other passengers for workers and scholars travelling on weekly or season tickets. This operated on the basis set·out on the facsimile of the notice reproduced here, and received the approbation of the Minister. As it worked so well, it was soon extended to other districts of the Company. Compulsory queueing when six or more passengers were assembled at a bus stop was also made official at this time by Ministerial Order.

Many single-deck buses now had the seating altered. Instead of the usual two and two placed transversely, the seats were rearranged around the perimeter, which produced a much wider gangway to accommodate up to thirty standing passengers. Authorized under the Standing Passenger Order 1941, they came to be known as 'standee buses' and their use was confined as much as possible to short journeys. Some passengers, lucky enough to be seated, found their toes were very vulnerable to being trodden upon if the

EASTERN NATIONAL

THE WESTCLIFF-ON-SEA MOTOR SERVICES LIMITED.

THE CITY COACH COMPANY, LIMITED.

FIXED 'BUS STOPS BETWEEN

SOUTHEND/RAYLEIGH and RAWRETH

The attention of the public is drawn to the fact that
As from MONDAY, 9th AUGUST, 1943,
VEHICLES OPERATED BY THE ABOVE COMPANIES WILL STOP TO TAKE UP AND SET DOWN PASSENGERS ONLY AT THE UNDERMENTIONED POINTS.

OUTWARD FROM SOUTHEND.

Tyler's Avenue *	— — — —	T
Victoria Avenue, Trolley Pole P.4, South of Dowsett Avenue §	— —	C
L.N.E.R. Station, Forecourt †	— — — —	T
Great Eastern Avenue, Trolley Pole P.13	— — —	R
Harcourt Avenue, Trolley Pole P.21	— — —	R
Spread Eagle Hotel, Trolley Pole P.32	— — —	C
Priory Park, Trolley Pole P.40 —	— — —	R
Outside 497, Victoria Avenue, Lamp Post —	— —	C
Prince Avenue, outside "Nelldene," Bus Post	— —	R
Hobleythick Lane, Bus Post, 30 yards East,	— —	C
Coleman's Avenue	...st of Entrance	C
Opposite Waterworks —	Roundabout	C
Southbourne Grove	, South of Roundabout	C
Entrance to Hydro Dividers L	—	C
Brendon Way, Lamp Post	...29 — —	R
Kent Elms Corner, Bus Po	...0 — —	R
South of Brooklands	Pole P.12 —	R
Rochford Corner,	— —	R
Memorial Hall	...y Pole P.5 § — —	T
Jones Corn	— —	T
Boswor	— —	
East	Route via Down Hall Road	
...Corner	— — — —	C
...Hall Chase	— — — —	R
...klayer's Arms Signpost	— — — —	C
...ooley Drive	— — — —	C
Rawreth Lane Corner	— — — —	C
Hillcrest	— — — —	R
Junction Brooklyn Drive	— — — —	R
Cheapside	— — — —	R
Marina Avenue	— — — —	C

C—Compulsory Stop.   R—Request.
T—Terminus.   *—Operative to City Coach Co., Ltd., only.
†—Operative to "Eastern National" only.
§—Operative to "Westcliff and City."

THE REASON WHY---Fixed 'Bus Stops are being instituted as indicated above in order to meet the need to conserve precious Fuel and Rubber. This means that your 'Bus may no longer be able to pick you up or set you down just where it has done for years, but please be tolerant and help the Conductors who are doing their best to assist you.

Passengers are conveyed subject to the advertised conditions published by the operating Companies concerned. Services liable to alteration without the customary notice in view of the National emergency.

Issued by
THE EASTERN NATIONAL OMNIBUS CO., LTD.
Head Offices : New Writtle Street, Chelmsford. 'Phone 3431 (3 lines).
THE WESTCLIFF-ON-SEA MOTOR SERVICES, LTD.
Head Offices : 17,21 London Road, Southend-on-Sea. 'Phone 49411.
THE CITY COACH CO., LTD.
Head Offices : Ongar Road, Brentwood.   'Phone 1204/5.

bus made an unexpected lurch, or when passengers were struggling to board and alight in the semi-gloom.

One surprising event of 1943 was the appearance, in spite of the paper and printing shortages, of a completely restyled Company timetable for its two areas. It was now in the true Tilling style, double size pages, Gill Sans typeface throughout, printed in blue ink and all tables bordered. Brightly coloured covers bearing a semi-pictorial map adorned the outside. Most of the Company publicity at this time was aimed at securing the utmost co-operation from the travelling public, for which purpose that popular artist and cartoonist Fougasse was commissioned by Tilling, some of whose work is shown here, with a few other exhortations taken from the timetables of the period. In 1944, a Tilling corporate emblem appeared on timetables and handbills. It was based around a representation of Crewe House, its London headquarters, but for some reason it was never used on its vehicles or stationery.

The following year brought a happy turning point in the war. The fear of invasion was now past and everyone was waiting for the allied invasion of Europe. The defence troops at the coast were now largely moved elsewhere for the new role they would be playing. This released a number of the requisitioned properties, and a steady trickle of residents started to return to the area. This called for an improved omnibus service, and the first glimmer of restored facilities came on 23rd October. Although not in itself of very great significance, it was nevertheless a welcome reversal after four years of continued cut backs. The improvements included a few extra short journeys from Clacton to Thorpe Green, and from Harwich to Oakley or Wix. Jaywick was served once again with two daily journeys, as was Coppin's Green, and three additional runs went to Walton-on-Naze. In the Midland Area, service 39, Ramsey—Somersham, was projected into Eastern Counties territory via Colne, and Earith to Bluntisham for scholars. A further modest instalment of improved facilities was made on 4th March 1945 when there were generally increased services all round the Clacton area.

By one of those strange quirks of misfortune, when all thought of danger from enemy bombs had been dismissed, there occurred an awful tragedy on the Luton—Hitchin road. A US army lorry was carrying a load of bombs when it caught fire. The driver had run to warn the occupants of some nearby houses of the impending danger, at which precise moment one of the Company's double-decks drew up behind the lorry completely unaware of the situation. Almost immediately the load exploded killing three passengers and injuring many and causing the bus, No. 3660, to become a write off.

The General Election of 1945 returned a Labour Government to office on a manifesto containing sweeping measures for the nationalization of all sources of energy and power, transportation of both goods and passengers, whether by road, rail or canal, and the docks and waterways. There was little detailed information as to the extent, or by what means these aims were to be accomplished. It was, however, realized within the industry that in taking over the railways, the Government would automatically become a substantial shareholder (in some cases up to 50 per cent) in many of the major omnibus companies, which left it in a state of considerable doubt as to its future position.

It would seem that the new Government had itself not yet formulated any very definite plans for carrying out its intentions. From the time it assumed office, the Transport Bill was gradually developed but did not appear until 1947. The effects thereof will be examined in the next chapter.

Although the slight relaxation in the release of fuel for civilian use was most welcome, the Company was still desperately short of rolling stock which still included many units which, in the normal way, would have been replaced many years before. Many items of equipment were still unobtainable, compelling the engineering department to resort to cannibalization of vehicles unfit for service in order to keep others rolling, and much ingenuity was called for in adapting components for further service that would normally have been thrown out.

However, 3rd March 1946 was a day for rejoicing, for Sunday morning services were restored after a lapse of three years. Five weeks later came restoration of the through Chelmsford—Bow service, which had not run west of Brentwood for four years. In the Midland Area there was a programme of increased frequency and later journeys given on many routes, as well as the Sunday morning resumption. The first coastal express since 1939 appeared at Easter between London and Clacton, and those to Halstead/Maldon resumed on 16th April. The Midland Area ran its coastal summer routes to Yarmouth and Southend once again, and the Tilbury to Yarmouth and Clacton services were also restored. At Bedford, a long awaited cross-town

After the return from loan to London Transport, the ten Guy Arab double-decks spent most of the time at Braintree and Clacton depots. The utility Brush bodies can be recognized on No. 3882 and her sister vehicle, seen here at Clacton.

Vehicle No. 3015 was one of the last to be rebodied by Eastern Coach Works in 1943 to the pre-war design. This vehicle was based at Halstead depot for over a decade, but is seen here at Clacton shortly before its withdrawal in 1952.

service, the new 48A from Mile Road to Clapham, was started as was a new service 67 Tuesday/Saturday market bus between Bletchley and Leighton Buzzard. An extension of service 77 from Huntingdon now gave a service to Old Weston and Brington. A most important new facility was the upgrading, on 28th July 1946, of the infrequent 66 service, Maldon—Stow Maries to operate six times weekdays from Maldon (East Station) through to Woodham Ferris Station, offering rail connections at each end in lieu of the branch line closed in 1939. From this it may be inferred that it was not intended to reopen the line.

Some of the Clacton area local services reappeared during the summer to serve the visitors, many of whom would not have had a seaside holiday for several years, and many youngsters would be seeing the sea for the first time.

The bus industry at this time was enjoying record breaking passenger carryings, and would have been able to do much more in the way of coastal express services and excursions and tours but for the shortage of vehicles. Although the war was over, there was still strict rationing of many commodities, clothing, petrol, coal etc. Consumer goods had still not returned to the shops and neither had television. The public could only spend its money on travel and entertainment.

Meanwhile, the Company could only do its best to cope with this boom by restoring services and getting back to normal as rapidly as new rolling stock was delivered, and when the staff situation had improved in step with the return of men from the forces.

The circumstances of wartime operation was greatly apparent in the scale of new rolling stock supplied, the considerable amount of vehicle rebuilding and, to assist in the effort to conserve resources, the adaptation of vehicles to operate on alternative fuels.

During the period 1941—46, only twenty eight double-decks entered the fleet, three of which were second-hand Leyland Titans from Plymouth Corporation. The new vehicles were supplied by Bristol (15) and Guy (10), and all carried 'utility' constructed bodywork by ECW (13), Brush (10) and Duple (2). All were fitted with oil engines except the three second-hand TD2s, which were converted by the Company from petrol to Gardner 5LW before going into service.

In order to acquire the Plymouth vehicles, the Company had to seek requisition from Tilling headquarters. Several other companies in the Tilling Group were also in a similar position and badly needed replacements but, during the war, even if the vehicles could be found, the authority of the Regional Transport Commissioner had first to be obtained before any could

Sixteen vehicles were rebodied by Beadle during the period 1941-1946, one of the last being No. 3428. Still very much in pre-war styling, Beadle managed to incorporate much salvaged material from the old body during this rather difficult time. The 1933 Leyland TD2 is pictured at the entrance to Colchester Castle.

W. J. Haynes

Seen at Colchester bus park is a former Enterprise Omnibus Company (Clacton) Leyland Tiger TS2 which the Company acquired in 1931. Taking the fleet number 3217, the original Metcalfe body was replaced in 1945 by this East Lancs 31 seat saloon.

J. C. Gillham

be transferred from one area to another. Plymouth was in a position to release fifty one double-decks in 1945, and Tilling negotiated for thirty seven of them (all low height) but had to use Western National's help, as agent, in order to secure the best, and liaise with the RTC for the release of them. Most of the vehicles were checked over at Western National's Plymouth depot before collection took place and it was suggested that a skilled fitter should travel down in a van with spare batteries, magnetos, carburetors and timing chain! Some idea of their general condition can be interpreted from this instruction. Plymouth's Titans, Nos. 49 and 50 (Weymann-bodied) and No. 75 (Leyland-bodied), took the Company's number 3886—3888 respectively.

Single-deck deliveries were even less plentiful with sixteen new vehicles arriving, almost all of them in 1946! The exception was a most interesting Bristol L6GG/ECW 31 seat saloon, new in 1942, with an integral gas producer unit stowed neatly in the rear luggage locker. More will be explained about the gas producer system later but the integral unit had certain disadvantages, not least the danger of setting the vehicle on fire, so it was later removed and the vehicle changed to a conventional 5LW oil engine, and the seating capacity increased to 33. As will be described a little later, the Dartford-based company, John C. Beadle, was responsible for much of the Company's vehicle rebuilding programme and essential repairs. Despite the enormous volume of work entrusted to them during the difficult wartime period, Beadle was also commissioned by the Government to manufacture aircraft components, and the production of lightweight pre-stressed aluminium structures gave them the necessary knowledge and ideas which became the embryo of the revolutionary type vehicle — the chassisless bus. When the production of aircraft components finally ceased, Beadle was left in possession of a considerable stock of aluminium extrusions, and immediately set about turning these into the framework of a lightweight bus body, under which mechanical components of selected manufacture could be used. Beadle had close associations with the Rootes Group, so the Commer Company was an obvious choice for the supply of running units for the prototype chassisless vehicle bearing the production number, JCB 1. The vehicle joined the Company's fleet in 1945 as No. 3923 and later the Commer petrol engine was changed to a Gardner 4LK oil unit. The balance of new single-decks was completed in 1946 with the delivery of another Beadle chassisless bus, this time having Bedford running units. It is interesting to note that the Bedford components in this vehicle had originally been in a Southern National Company coach, No. 499, which had been severely damaged near Yeovil in 1940 and since then had been laid up pending repairs. The parts were instead sent to Beadle for fitment to JCB 2 (Southern National No. 2000), which in the end received Leyland units from another Southern National vehicle, so the Company's new saloon, No. 3924 (JCB 3) was the first of many to be supplied with Bedford units, and proved to be a very successful and economical vehicle to operate.

Two second-hand vehicles were acquired with Simpson's business in 1941;

one, a Bedford WTL coach and the other an Albion Victor Saloon, both with 26 seats. These had been disposed of twelve months later.

As early as 1939, during the period leading up to the outbreak of war, transport undertakings were seeking alternative fuels for propulsion, not only to reduce costs (tax on Derv was already beginning to increase), but to save on the prime supply of petrol and diesel. A lot of work had already been done during World War I and the Government, now realizing its importance, encouraged the larger operators to research into and perfect the possibilities of fuel alternatives, and develop machinery that could easily convert existing vehicles to operate on a chosen form.

The Company's engineer, William Morison, who had himself many years previously, designed and manufactured his own motor car, the WJM, was now engaged in designing suitable equipment to replace pure petrol/oil propulsion. First the fuel to be used had to be selected and experiments were carried out using such combustibles as charcoal, butane, anthracite, lignite, naptha, methane, calor gas, coke, paraffin, tar, town gas, peat, propane, coal and wood. Anthracite and coal seemed best suited, and various grades of these were tried as its quality and reaction differed according to the area of the country where it was mined. The preferred choice was singled out as

RUNNING WITHOUT PETROL

A considerable number of 'Buses have been adapted by the Company to run on PRODUCER GAS

★ALREADY THE " EASTERN NATIONAL " AND THE COMPANIES ASSOCIATED WITH IT, HAVE RUN 2,500,000 MILES BY THIS MEANS, SAVING 415,000 GALLONS OF IMPORTED FUEL

A facsimile of a Company notice indicating the savings that had been made by the introduction of gas-propelled vehicles.

Eastern National

Welsh anthracite, and Morison and other engineers up and down the country, next set about designing the best burners, filters, separators and fittings on which this fuel would work when applied to both petrol and oil engines. While this work was progressing, the cost of anthracite gradually increased as demand for it began to outstrip supply! In September 1939, for example, the price had been less than 50 shillings per ton (£2.50) but within twelve months had more than doubled to prices ranging from 115 shillings (£5.75) to 122 shillings per ton (£6.10). The first trials in buses used the producer plant housed in the rear locker, but the better arrangement was to mount it on a small trailer behind the vehicle. Before this could be approved, a small piece of legislation had to be hastily rushed through Parliament and, in October 1939, the position was cleared by the Public Service Vehicles (Drawing of Gas Producer Trailers) Order 1939, which enabled a bus or coach to draw a trailer solely for the carrying of gas supplying equipment to the drawing vehicle.

In February 1940, John F. Heaton, Chairman of Thomas Tilling Ltd., announced that enough materials were at hand at Bristol to manufacture six hundred gas producer plants and, from this supplier, Eastern National obtained thirty six trailers to convert the entire fleet at Maldon depot. Special equipment was installed with bunkers and cleaning facilities, so that the trailers could be detached and serviced while the bus was working with another trailer coupled. Modifications had also to be made to the induction system on engines using special injectors or carburettors. For best performance the compression ratio on petrol engines had to be increased to about 7:1, while on oil engines it was decreased to between 8 and 11:1.

Drivers had to be selected and given special instructions as to the attitudes in driving with gas, in order to obtain the best results. Some of the drivers were women and they too were expected to have some basic ideas of mechanical contrivances and be able to attend to minor adjustments in the system should it become temperamental. Eight trailers were supplied to the neighbouring 'Westcliff' Company and the following Eastern National vehicles are known to have been among those which were used on gas at Maldon.

No. 3304 Leyland TS4 coach	No. 3532 Dennis Lancet single-deck
No. 3305 Leyland TS4 coach	No. 3542 Dennis Lancet single-deck
No. 3306 Leyland TS4 coach	No. 3607 Dennis Ace single-deck
No. 3307 Leyland TS4 coach	No. 3663 Leyland TS7 coach
No. 3308 Leyland TS4 coach	No. 3664 Leyland TS7 coach
No. 3510 AEC Regal coach	No. 3665 Leyland TS7 coach
No. 3520 AEC Regal coach	No. 3874 Bristol L6GG single-deck

The rebodying programme which had been proceeding steadily up until 1940 was another to suffer disruption over the next five years. Some vehicles now received body swops or rebodies because of the destruction to the original body. All rebodies supplied at this time were built to 'utility' standards, so it was not expected that many years service would be had from them before returning for improvements later on. Forty five vehicles were rebodied during the period 1941—46, sixteen by Beadle, fourteen by ECW, ten by East Lancs., three by Duple, one, and probably the last, by Willowbrook as well. On top of this, the most noticeable cause of vehicle absence was the constant stream of repairs and alterations that had to be undertaken, much as a result of hostilities. One vehicle was sent to the East Lancs. Works for repair and twelve to Eastern Coachworks, now removed from Lowestoft to Irthlingborough, Northamptonshire, but Beadle was relatively close at Dartford to undertake a considerable volume of jobs, some large, some small, but all beyond the scope of the Company during this critical time. Several vehicles returned to Beadle a second time, and some a third, in tune with repeated calls for attention. The 1941 Standing Passenger Order had entailed the removal of seats and the rearrangement of interior layouts which, of course, had to be reverted to standard later on. Beadle undertook much of this work on behalf of the Company, which accounts for some 140 jobs passing through the Dartford factory.

The Company was not spared total losses in enemy raids. Resulting from a fire at Grays garage in 1942, Bristol double-decks, Nos. 3636, 3637 and 3638 were gutted beyond repair. Then came the worst single incident during hostilities when, in May 1943, the following twenty five vehicles based at Chelmsford were severely wrecked; but one, No. 3584, eventually returned to service in 1949 after extensive repair.

No. 3021 AEC Regent double-deck	No. 3533 Dennis Lancet single-deck
No. 3065 Thornycroft double-deck	No. 3539 Dennis Lancet single-deck
No. 3066 Thornycroft double-deck	No. 3542 Dennis Lancet single-deck
No. 3319 Dennis Lancet single-deck	No. 3552 Dennis Lancet single-deck
No. 3323 AEC Regent double-deck	No. 3560 Leyland TD3 double-deck
No. 3325 AEC Regent double-deck	No. 3584 Dennis Lancet coach
No. 3404 Dennis Lancet single-deck	No. 3600 Dennis Ace single-deck
No. 3406 Dennis Lancet single-deck	No. 3683 Bristol J05G single-deck
No. 3411 Dennis Lancet single-deck	No. 3757 Dennis Lancet single-deck
No. 3414 Dennis Lancet single-deck	No. 3759 Bristol L5G single-deck
No. 3417 Dennis Lancet single-deck	No. 3776 Bristol L5G single-deck
No. 3440 AEC Regent double-deck	No. 3873 Bristol K5G double-deck
No. 3477 Dennis Lancet single-deck	

Following this, the Company tightened up on its vulnerable locations as best it could and introduced a system of night vehicle dispersal as a precaution against such a great number of buses being attacked in one raid. At Chelmsford, for example, several vehicles were moved to the waste ground at Bell Meadow at the rear of Bell Hotel in Tindal Square. The further loss of vehicle No. 3396 and the chassis of No. 3758 at Chelmsford, in February 1944, might have been much worse had it not been for these preventive measures being taken.

The disposal of fifty seven other vehicles which had left the fleet by the end of 1945, has not been traced and the fate of these can only be left to conjecture. Some would have justifiably been sold, due to age or being non-standard, but the destiny of the remainder to the military authorities and the subsequent loss or destruction cannot altogether be ruled out.

It would be appropriate here to mention the colour schemes used on the vehicles. The fleet was, at formation in 1929, in the process of changing from red to green, and this policy was continued through to completion by 1931. The shades of green varied, and much experimenting was carried out with darker bands of green to break up the large area of bodywork. By the time Tilling acquired its interest, most double-decks had mid-green panels, three dark green bands, white roofs and window surrounds, black wings and dark green wheels. Another version had light green roofs, excepting the rear dome which was also finished in white. The contemporary coach or dual-purpose livery was virtually the opposite with dark green lower panels, white waist band, dark green roof and window surrounds, black wings and light green wheels.

Tilling influence brought about the substitution of cream in place of white and, by the mid-1930s, a most elaborate colour scheme incorporating thin lining out beneath the waist bands, and the beading between contrasting colours picked out in black, produced a most attractive combination.

The differences between double-deck, single-deck and coach gradually gave way to a common theme, but repainting was done according to a scheduled maintenance programme and it was never true to say that the whole fleet had reached one uniformity before fresh ideas had been introduced along different lines. From about 1938, coaches were painted preominantly green with cream relief, black wings, light brown window surrounds, green roofs, while buses lost the lining out to become mid-green with cream bands separated by black beading. The light brown areas on coaches later gave way to green.

Wartime finish was usually dark grey, often hastily applied, and sometimes revealing the Company's name in original style after the masking had been removed around it. After the war, the 1938 style was reintroduced and more or less remained unchanged through to the late 1960s.

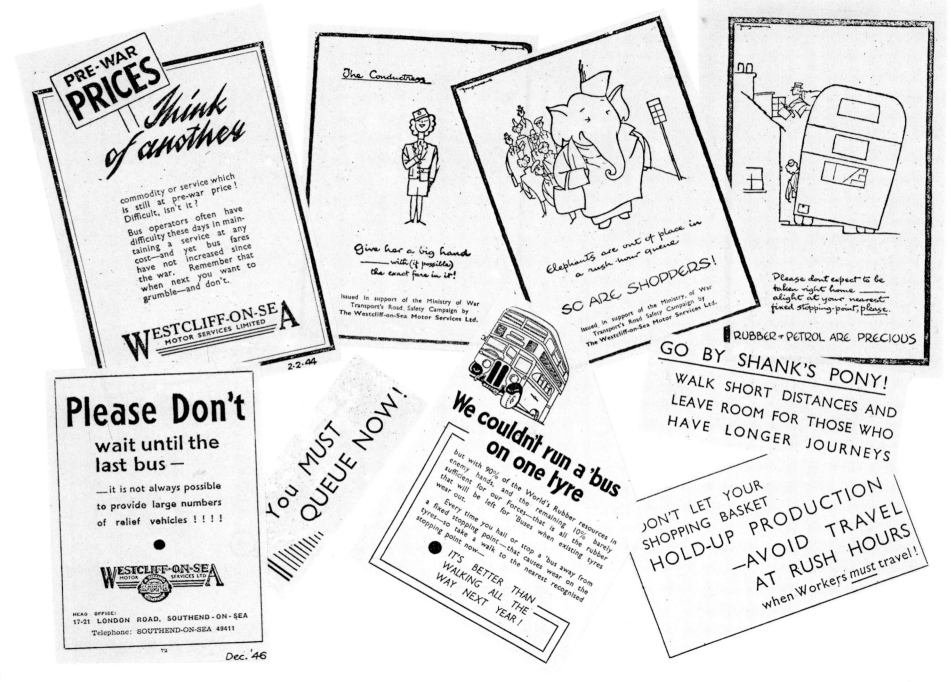

PRE-WAR PRICES

Think of another

commodity or service which is still at pre-war price! Difficult, isn't it?

Bus operators often have difficulty these days in maintaining a service at any cost—and yet bus fares have not increased since the war. Remember that when next you want to grumble—and don't.

WESTCLIFF-ON-SEA MOTOR SERVICES LIMITED

2.2.44

The Conductress

Give her a big hand — with (if possible) the exact fare in it!

Issued in support of the Ministry of War Transport's Road Safety Campaign by The Westcliff-on-Sea Motor Services Ltd.

Elephants are out of place in a rush-hour queue

SO ARE SHOPPERS!

Issued in support of the Ministry of War Transport's Road Safety Campaign by The Westcliff-on-Sea Motor Services Ltd.

Please don't expect to be taken right home — alight at your nearest fixed stopping-point, please.

RUBBER & PETROL ARE PRECIOUS

GO BY SHANK'S PONY!

WALK SHORT DISTANCES AND LEAVE ROOM FOR THOSE WHO HAVE LONGER JOURNEYS

DON'T LET YOUR SHOPPING BASKET HOLD-UP PRODUCTION

—AVOID TRAVEL AT RUSH HOURS when Workers *must* travel!

Please Don't

wait until the last bus —

—it is not always possible to provide large numbers of relief vehicles ! ! ! !

WESTCLIFF-ON-SEA MOTOR SERVICES LTD

HEAD OFFICE: 17-21 LONDON ROAD, SOUTHEND-ON-SEA Telephone: SOUTHEND-ON-SEA 49411

72

Dec. '46

You MUST QUEUE NOW!

We couldn't run a 'bus on one tyre

but with 90% of the World's Rubber resources in enemy hands, and the remaining 10% barely sufficient for our Forces—that is all the rubber that will be left for 'Buses when existing tyres wear out.

Every time you hail or stop a 'bus away from a fixed stopping point—that causes wear on the tyres—so take a walk to the nearest recognised stopping point now.

IT'S BETTER THAN WALKING ALL THE WAY NEXT YEAR !

Chapter Five

Nationalization and What Followed 1947-1954

The dreaded Transport Act became law this year, but still did very little to clarify the future role of the bus and coach industry. The British Transport Commission, which was set up to implement the Government's intentions, established several Executives to control particular sectors of the industry on behalf of the Commission, to which the undertakings acquired would be transferred. The railways were so vested on 1st January 1947 except those controlled by the London Passenger Transport Board which continued unchanged but reconstituted as the London Transport Executive. As a result of taking over the railways, the BTC had already become possessed of several large road haulage companies such as Pickfords, Carter Paterson, etc., with a large shareholding in all the railway associated bus companies, together with a few others acquired with the electricity supply companies, which had hitherto been unable to hive them off.

The Road Transport Executive was soon split into a Road Passenger Executive for the omnibus and railway interests and the Road Haulage Executive, which created British Road Services to continue operation of the acquired haulage firms.

Early in 1948 it became known that Sir Frederick Heaton, Chairman of the Tilling Group, was engaged in exploratory talks with the BTC who had so far made no move or pronouncements regarding its policy for the future organization of the industry. Heaton was endeavouring to discover whether it might be more beneficial for the shareholders if a negotiated sale at a reasonable figure could be arranged, rather than wait only to be compulsorily taken over on, what might be, less favourable terms.

In September, the whole uncertain situation suddenly changed overnight after Heaton 'dropped a bombshell', by letting it be known that he had reached an agreement with the BTC to acquire the entire Tilling Group of omnibus companies and its substantial road haulage interests. The terms were not disclosed until November, which showed that it would permit a distribution of £5 of BTC 3 per cent stock for every £1 of Tilling stock held. The settlement also included transfer of the Bristol Tramways & Carriage Company's Construction Works and the Eastern Coach Works business at Lowestoft which Tilling had hoped to retain.

The Road Transport Executive did not have powers to compulsorily acquire an undertaking, but could place area schemes before the Commission for consideration and action as it thought fit.

The terms achieved by Heaton were generally considered very reasonable, perhaps deliberately so, for we see it was not long after, that the very

large Scottish Motor Traction Group, followed closely by J. H. Watts 'Red & White' Group, had also negotiated terms for the transfer of their undertakings.

The BET Group was profoundly shocked by Heaton's unilaterial action which it truly regarded as a 'stab in the back' of the worst kind. With the backing of its shareholders, the Board considered it could give a better deal than they would receive from the BTC and declared it would use every endeavour to keep its independence to 'the last wheel'.

Eastern National, at this moment, was still a subsidiary of the parent National Omnibus & Transport Co. which held £450,000 of its £1 shares alongside an equal number recently passed to the Railway Executive. The Company also held £10,486 of £1 shares out of £250,000 in 'Westcliff', where there was no railway shareholding, and some shares in 'London Coastal Coaches' which owned the Victoria Coach Station in London, which in turn also owned a coach hiring section.

Thus, by 1949, the BTC had quietly, and without fuss, become possessed of a very substantial amount of the British omnibus and coach industry, with chassis and body building facilities of no mean order laid on. Only the BET Group and the municipal undertakings, and a host of small operators, were still independent.

The post-war Eastern Coach Works design is featured in this view of No. 3922 at Chelmsford bus station. Shelters were later erected on the far perimeter wall after the Hicks business was bought in 1950.

S. N. White

Under George Cardwell, who became the first Chairman of the Executive, a number of Tilling's chief officers now took control of all the English and Welsh businesses (the Scottish operators being placed in a separate management section), by what came to be known as the Tilling Group Management Board. Thus, so long as it pursued a policy compatible with BTC requirements, its existence ensured that it was very much a case of 'business as usual'. The travelling public was almost unaware of any change having taken place. The more observant may perhaps have noted the disappearance of the Tilling Crewe House emblem from the timetables and handbills from about mid-year.

Returning to 1947, the policy of the ENOC of steadily improving facilities was continued by modest additional times or later journeys over the entire operating area.

The large programme of post-war house building now demanded new transport facilities and led to several extensions of services or new routes being started. The more important as detailed below:

In the Midland Area

10 — Baldock—Bygrave; pre-war service restored
36B — Diverson to serve Wavendon
52D — Luton—Harts Lane—Stopsley; extended to Rochester Avenue
55 — New service; Luton—Ramridge End—Stopsley
57 — Luton—Leagrave; extended to Hockwell Ring
63 — Luton—Dallow Road; extended to Warren Road
109 — Aylesbury locals extended to now run
    (a) Southcourt—Hayden Hill
    (b) Southcourt—Bierton
    (c) Southcourt—Broughton Turn

In the Eastern Area

2B — Chelmsford local; extended to Oxney Green)
13B — Bishop's Stortford—Clavering)
20 — Sudbury—Clare)
28 — Colchester—Layer Road) All restored
114 — Clacton-on-Sea local) pre-war
115A — Clacton-on-Sea local) services
116 — Clacton-on-Sea local)

The new rolling stock coming forward into the fleet carried a post-war design of bodywork, which was fitted with the new Tilling pattern enlarged destination equipment comprising two displays at front and rear. At the top was a single line aperture for the ultimate destination, and beneath, a two line unit to show the service number and at least two passing points. The other innovation peculiar to Eastern National was the adoption of suffixes to the route number for any journeys not proceeding the full length of the route, which on longer routes, with a variety of short journeys, took the suffixes as far as 'M', requiring an inordinate amount of

blind linen and, at times, a considerable amount of turning for crews. It hardly needs saying that the system did not remain in use for very long.

On 30th September 1947, King's Cross Coach Station, London, ceased to be available for this purpose any more, so a temporary site was organized on a 'bombed site' at the corner of Judd Street and Cromer Street, close by Euston Road, a short distance westward from the old coach station. Although designated as 'temporary', it remained in use for a further seven years!

Improvement in the supplies of raw materials, and the return of men to civilian life after the war, gradually enabled production of new vehicles to begin in fairly huge quantities. The country was getting back on its feet and demands for public transport were approaching new peaks. During 1947, the Company took delivery of sixty three new vehicles which included seven Bedford OB/Duple 29 seat coaches, the first new coaches delivered during the past decade. Bedford also provided eight further OB chassis on which Beadle 30 seat saloon bodies were fitted. Two of these were not actually licensed until 1949 and the reason for the delay is unknown. The first new Leyland chassis since 1937 arrived in the shape of eighteen PD1 with ECW double-deck bodies, and the remainder were constructed on Bristol chassis; fourteen L5G/ECW 35 seat saloons, nine K5G/ECW double-decks and seven L5G/ECW dual-purpose 31 seat saloons. The latter had semi-coach seating

Eight of these Beadle-bodied Bedford OBs were delivered in 1947. Vehicle No. 3929 is seen at Clacton bus station.

G. R. Mills

and a colour scheme which incorporated a much greater area of cream. There were no vehicles acquired during the year, but Beadle provided a solitary rebuild on vehicle No. 3437, which was to be the final repair task undertaken by them.

The restoration of the remaining pre-war coastal express services followed in 1948 and were soon in great demand. One small operator, Mr Walley of St. Osyth, was taken over. He had provided a summer seasonal service between the village and the beach, which was now joined to the Clacton—St. Osyth short journeys on service 101 to give a desired through facility which became 101B.

Closer liaison with neighbouring 'Westcliff' was noticeable from now on. The Eastern National 70 and 'Westcliff' 2/2B services between Southend and Grays now became a joint working with full inter-availability of tickets at the same time as a new jointly run service 84 was introduced from South Benfleet (Tarpots) to Grays.

In June, there was considerable revision to services in the Braintree and Halstead area, giving greatly improved headways to some villages, which included the formation of a new route from The Maplesteads to Halstead and Greenstead Green, taking portions from service 22 and the former 18A. In July, the last of the pre-war local services at Clacton was resumed. The latest changes were:

In the Eastern Area

2B — Oxney Green section diverted to serve Beeches Road area (Chelmsford)
29 — New: As noted above
8B — Bishop's Stortford—Woodside Green; extended to Great Canfield
84 — New: As noted above, joint with 'Westcliff'
101B— New: Clacton—St. Osyth Beach (ex-Walley)
111 — Walton-on-Naze—Harwich
117 — Magdalen Green—Holland-on-Sea
'K' — (Express service) Enfield—Southend-on-Sea (formerly 'Borough')

In the Midland Area

36F — Bedford—North Crawley; diverts to serve Bourne End
41 — Hitchin—Royston; extended to Cambridge (pre-war facility restored)
81 — Bedford—Kempston; alternate buses to run to Gibraltar Corner

Express Services (pre-war now restored)

'E' — Bedford—Great Yarmouth
'F' — Luton—Bournemouth
'G' — Luton—Margate
'H' — Luton—Portsmouth/Southsea
'J' — Luton—Great Yarmouth
'P' — Bedford—Dovercourt Bay
'Q' — Luton—Dovercourt Bay

It was gradually becoming more difficult to organize suitable extensions or alterations to existing services, in order to provide the best facilities to new housing developments in and around Luton and Dunstable. Because of competing applications being submitted to the Licensing Authority by both the Company and Luton Corporation, it was suggested the two should consult more closely with a view to securing some mutually amicable arrangement which would save much time in the traffic court, and at the same time would be beneficial to both operators and public alike. Acting upon this suggestion, the two parties got together and duly negotiated an agreement for full coordination of all services within a defined area which would be operated as a single enterprise to be known as Luton & District Transport. This was ratified by both sides and sealed on 11th October 1948. The burden of working out this comprehensive union of the two systems in detail was borne almost entirely by John Kershaw, the Company Area Traffic Superintendent with Mr Ronald Rogers, the Corporation Deputy Manager. Mr Kershaw joined the former 'National' Company when they took over his business at North Petherton, Somerset in 1927. Full details of this are given in *Volume One*.

The new vehicle deliveries for 1948 eased somewhat with just thirty seven being taken into stock. Bristol was the sole provider of chassis in which the

A 1947 Bristol K5G, originally No. 3942, stands at Billericay railway station before departing to Outwood Common on one of the former 'City' routes. The photograph was taken in August 1965, shortly before the vehicle was sold.

G. R. Mills

popular K5G totalled twenty seven units, all fitted with ECW double-deck bodies. Eastern Coach Works were called to supply the bodywork on the remainder; four double-decks on K6B chassis (six cylinder Bristol AVW engine) and six L5Gs, three as 31 seat dual-purpose saloons and three as 35 seat single-decks. No acquired stock was absorbed.

An acute shortage of buses within London Transport caused the Government to consider the allocation, on a temporary basis, of approximately two hundred new buses to them which would have otherwise been supplied to the provinces. Eight of the K5Gs, new in 1947, soon made their way to London for a period of several months working from Camberwell, Nunhead and Norwood depots. All were returned by March 1950.

The new Luton & District Transport commenced operation on 1st January 1949 and became a very successful undertaking. It was reported that for the Corporation it represented a saving of £35,000 in a year but the Company's savings were never disclosed. Its greatest benefit to the public was the linking of separate services to provide cross-town facilities, and a reduction in the number of town centre terminal points.

The Corporation's contribution in the formation of Luton & District Transport was represented by the following services:

1 — Seymour Avenue—Pembroke Avenue
1A — Seymour Avenue—Leagrave, Hockwell Ring
2 — Waller Avenue—Vauxhall Works
3 — Seymour Avenue—Electrolux Works
4 — Park Square—Dunstable Road
5 — Luton—Dunstable direct—Studham
6 — Luton—Dunstable, via Houghton Regis
7 — Fountains Road—Cutenhoe Road
8 — Biscot Mill—Farley Hill
9 — Russell Rise—Hart Lane (circular)
10/11 — Library—Round Green (10)—Stopsley (11)
12 — Library—Richmond Hill—Round Green
13 — Library—Biscot Road—Leagrave
14 — Bridge Street—Biscot Road—Biscot Mill
15 — Bridge Street—Old Bedford Road—Biscot Mill (SU)
16 — Bridge Street—Bramingham Lane *
17 — Richmond Hill—Vauxhall Works *
18 — Farley Hill—Vauxhall Works *
19 — Library—Dunstable, via Leagrave (SU)
20 — Biscot Mill—Vauxhall Works *
21 — Stopsley—Vauxhall Works—Airport *
22 — Park Square—Dunstable Road, via Selborne Road
23 — Park Square—Airport
24 — Cutenhoe Road—Vauxhall Works *

They were all day services except those marked * which catered for works traffic only, and 'SU' which ran only on Sundays.

The Eastern National services fell into two groups:

(a) those fully integrated with Corporation routes
52D — Park Square—Hart Lane—Stopsley
55 — Park Square—Crawley Road—Stopsley
56/A — Cutenhoe Road/Vauxhall—Limbury
57 — LMR Station—Leagrave
63 — Alma Street—Warren Road

(b) Services which continued unchanged or continued beyond the agreement area, but still came within the co-ordination arrangements.
3 — Whipsnade—Dunstable—Toddington—BEDFORD
3B — Dunstable—Tebworth—Toddington
12 — Luton—Streatley—SHEFFORD
12A — Luton—Streatley—PEGSDON
16 — Luton—Dunstable—AYLESBURY

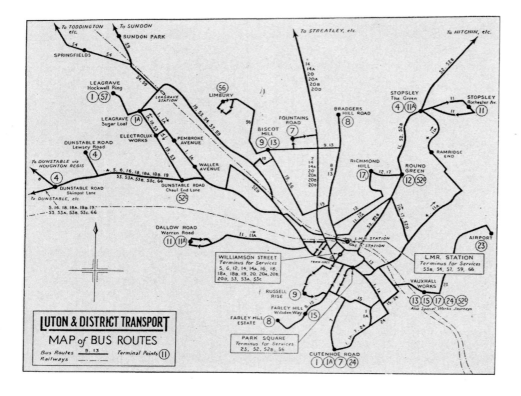

18 — (group) Luton—Dunstable—Leighton Buzzard
20/A — Luton—Streatley—BEDFORD
52/B — Luton—Great Offley—BALDOCK/STOTFOLD
53 — Luton—Dunstable, via Leagrave
53A — Luton—Dunstable (direct)
53B — Luton—Dunstable—Whipsnade Zoo
53C — Luton—Dunstable—(Hambling Place)
66 — Luton—Dunstable—BLETCHLEY

All Eastern National services entering Luton were included in the scheme up to the boundary point, continuing to the destination shown in capital letters.

The co-ordination arrangements were effected as follows:

LCT services 1, 1A, 2, 3 and 7, were combined to run Fountains Road/Cutenhoe Road—Hockwell Ring as 1, 1A and 7

LCT service 4 and EN 55 linked to run Dunstable Road—Park Square—Stopsley as service 4

LCT services 5 and 6 continued unchanged

LCT service 8 to run Bradgers Hill Road—Farley Hill, extended to Farley Hill Estate

LCT service 9 to run Russell Rise—Biscot Mill (vice service 8)

LCT services 10/11 and EN63 linked to run Warren Road—Bridge Street—Stopsley as services 11/11A

LCT service 12 continued unchanged

LCT service 13 and EN57 combined to run the LMR Station—Leagrave as service 57

LCT service 14 and EN56/56A combined to run Park Square—Limbury as service 56

LCT service 15 ceased: now Farley Hill—Vauxhall Works, ex-LCT service 18

LCT service 16 part transferred to Eastern National to run as service 14A

LCT service 17 continued unchanged

LCT service 18 renumbered 15 q.v.

LCT service 19 continued unchanged

LCT service 20 renumbered 13 q.v.

LCT services 21, 22 and EN52D combined to run Dunstable Road—Hart Lane—Round Green or the Airport as service 52D

LCT service 23 continued unchanged

LCT service 24 continued unchanged

The new arrangements reduced the number of separate services from thirty two to twenty two, ignoring those running to points over the boundary, and yet still provided a better service for the travelling public. A new timetable booklet, of Tilling shape and layout, replaced the former small size Corporation timetable, although both were produced by Index Publishers, Dunstable.

One of the dual-purpose versions of the L5G saloon, showing the high-backed seats and reverse colour schemes to standard. Vehicle No. 296 (formerly No. 3969) is seen leaving Maldon bus station in April 1962.

G. R. Mills

It was customary for Bedford depot to place its newest double-decks on the long distance route 7 to Oxford. Here, No. 3992, the last of the Leyland PD1s, awaits its return journey from Gloucester Green bus station, Oxford.

R. H. G. Simpson

The co-ordination had no effect on the two fleets as each party was pledged to provide sufficient and suitable vehicles to maintain its agreed proportion of mileage, which also formed the basis for division of receipts.

Looking now at Company matters in the Midland Area this year, there were a few other developments in services to be noted.

4C — Included into the New service 83 q.v.
7D — Bedford—Oxford; frequency doubled, City of Oxford now sharing the times
35B — Biggleswade—Royston; diverted to serve Abingdon Pigotts
38A — New: St. Ives—Wyton—Broughton
43A — New: Huntingdon—Wyton—St. Ives
48 — Elstow—Bedford—Clapham; extended to Air Ministry Road
75A — New: Huntingdon—Kimbolton—Catworth—Huntingdon (circular)
76 — Huntingdon—Thrapston—Kettering; diverted to serve Leighton Bromswold
82 — Bedford local—Midland Station—Eastcotts—Fenlake (circular)
82A — As 82 in reverse direction
83 — New: Bedford local—Putnoe Lane—Cosmic Avenue, incorporating service 4C
109 — Aylesbury locals, Quarrendon Estate—Southcourt; extended to Stoke Mandeville incorporating service 109A

In the Eastern Section the only changes were:
13A — Extended to Pledgdon, but soon diverted to Henham
4A — Chelmsford local; further extended to Melbourne Avenue
75A — Colchester—Great Wigborough; pre-war service restored
109 — New: Clacton—Great Clacton, via Valley Road
47 — New: Bishop's Stortford—Harlow—Ongar

The last-named new service is of more than passing interest, not only for the Company, which was breaking entirely new ground, but also for the villages between Harlow and Ongar which, despite lying not more than twenty three miles from London, now enjoyed their first regular public transport! Also of importance is the fact that it brought Eastern National into Harlow, where a new town was in the course of development just within the LTE boundary to which the villages over the border would now require transport for reasons of shopping or employment.

Thirty eight new vehicles joined the fleet in 1949, swelling the ranks of standard post-war deliveries. Bristol provided twenty three chassis and ECW bodied them as ten 35 seat saloons on L5G frames and thirteen double-decks on K5G frames. Nine Beadle chassisless saloons also arrived with Bedford units and petrol engines, but two years later these were changed to Gardner 4LK oil units. Lastly, late in the year, six Bedford OB/Duple 29 seat coaches arrived and were stored in readiness for the 1950 summer season. During the year a programme to update twenty three double-decks to the latest pattern was undertaken by Eastern Coach Works, Lowestoft. This involved Bristol G, Leyland TD4 and TD5 chassis, dating from between 1935 and 1937 which were all rebodied following chassis overhaul. Two Dennis Lancets, Nos. 3479 and 3584, were rebodied using the 1939 Beadle saloon bodies latterly carried on Leylands, Nos. 2813 and 2815.

Hicks Bros. of Braintree, the largest independent operating in North-Central Essex, disposed of its business to the BTC with effect from 1st January 1950. Its Clacton-based excursion and tours section was, however, retained with six coaches for continuance by the family under the style of 'Cansdall Coaches', running in the well-known Royal Blue and Daffodil Yellow livery with the fleetname in a similar style to the parent. Hicks had started in 1913 with a single motorized passenger-cum-goods service from Felstead to Braintree and elsewhere. They moved to Braintree in the mid-1920s and established themselves in Fairfield Road where a good garage was built, which is the present Braintree depot of the Company. There was also a sub-depot at Silver End which is still used by Eastern National today. The business was continued under its own name for the time being with Eastern National maintaining overall supervision, until the time was ready for it and other Company structural changes to be implemented.

None of Hicks Bros. services appeared in the Company timetable until early 1952 using Hicks route numbers (which were never carried on its buses) pre-fixed by 'H'. Its own bus station at Park Road, Chelmsford, just south of the Duke Street railway arch, was soon closed and all services operated from the Eastern National bus station just north of the railway arch. Having acquired Hicks, the Company was now free to introduce a new cross-town facility at Chelmsford from Broomfield to Oxney Green as service 3. The Broomfield—Great Waltham part of the former 3 route was now combined with service 52 to Pleshey, with Hicks' service from Dunmow covering the remainder. The Oxney Green section was from part of service 2, Chelmsford—Ongar. Other changes in 1950 are summarised below:

2B — Further extended into Chignal Estate to Queensland Avenue
21A — Braintree—Felstead Factory; withdrawn (covered by Hicks service 10)
23A — Braintree—Halstead; part diverted via Penny Pots
50A — Chelmsford—Flacks Green; extended to Fairstead
63 — New: Maldon—Burnham-on-Crouch, via North Fambridge
75 — Colchester—Mersea Island; summer extension to Sea View Avenue
78 — Colchester—Brightlingsea; extended to Bellfield Avenue
123A — New: Clacton—Weeley—Bradfield—Manningtree

The only alteration to report in the Midland Section was the diversion of service 8, Bedford—Biggleswade, to call at Girtford.

Beadle's own design of lightweight, chassisless vehicle was a popular and economical choice in the 1940s. Here is No. 4014 en route to Clacton with a full complement of 33 passengers.

W. J. Haynes

Vehicle deliveries in 1950 observed a change in the construction and use regulations whereby the overall dimensions of two axle PSVs was slightly increased. Manufacturers quickly took advantage of the new scope being offered by introducing 'blown-up' versions of current models. The Company first took delivery of ten Bristol L5G/ECW saloons measuring in at the old dimension of 7ft. 4in. x 27ft. 6in., followed by ten coaches by ECW on the L6B chassis of similar size. Seventeen old dimension Bristol K5G/ECW double-decks, each measuring 7ft. 4in. x 26ft., was followed by seven slightly larger KS5G models of 7ft. 6in. x 27ft. The new version of the L, officially designated LL, provided the base for ten 39 seat saloons with Gardner 5LW engines and these measured 7ft. 6in. x 30ft., enabling an extra four seats to be included. Bedford OB/Duple coaches completed the deliveres of new rolling stock.

The fairly large intake of forty eight vehicles from Messrs Hicks brought in a varied selection of buses and coaches, predominantly of double-deck type, in which the latter was represented by twenty one Leylands and eight Guys. Fourteen coaches were included on a motley selection of chassis comprising Leyland, Dennis, Albion, Bedford, Guy and Austin manufacture. One Dennis and four Leyland saloons concluded the Hicks fleet. A further Maudslay Marathon coach and two Guy Arab double-decks were later delivered in Eastern National livery which had been on order by Hicks when taken over.

The Hicks vehicles were repainted into the Company's green and cream livery, but retained their familiar 'Hicks' emblem and fleet number until the 1954 reorganization when the Company's name and new numbering system was universally adopted. During the period 1950—54, twenty six of the original Hicks vehicles were disposed of and most were replaced by standard rolling stock drawn from the Company's ranks carrying 'On Hire' labels. Among the Leyland double-decks acquired from Hicks was one based on a Tiger coach chassis. This particular vehicle had been rebodied from coach to double-deck in 1939, the Tiger chassis being almost identical to a Titan but, at 17ft. 6in., having a wheelbase 1ft. longer.

Arriving in time for the summer season were four AEC Regent open-top double-decks, acquired especially from Brighton, Hove & District. They were given a separate sequence of fleet numbers commencing at 101, to which was added more over the next few years as further open-tops were acquired, reaching No. 108 in 1954. They operated at Clacton and Southend, the latter contingent being a familiar sight along the five miles of esplanade from Shoeburyness to Leigh-on-Sea, via Thorpe Bay, Southend and Westcliff.

The Company took delivery of eighteen Bedford OB coaches with the well-proportioned 29 seat Duple bodies. Here, No. 4068 is seen standing at Pier Avenue, Clacton in readiness for one of the many day excursions in the area.

R. A. Jenkinson

The British Transport Commission/Road Passenger Executive had about this time reached certain decisions regarding its large portfolio of operating units, with a view to eliminating certain anomolous situations which could now be remedied, as former competing services were now in common ownership.

In June 1951, the first big reshuffle by the RPE, between Western National, Red & White and Bristol Tramways, took place in the Gloucestershire area. Another scheme soon followed which was to bring to an end the artificial division of Grays, in which London Transport ruled over the western half whilst Eastern National and one or two others covered the eastern portion. The RPE negotiated an agreement with the LTE to operate all services in the Grays and Tilbury area except those running out into Eastern National territory. This permitted the reintroduction of cross-town facilities after a lapse of seventeen years (see *Chapter One* for earlier details).

As a preliminary to the change, Eastern National acquired two local routes still being run by the Benjamin family trading as 'Our Bus', who were the last private operator to work stage services in the Grays district out of the host that once infested that area. This was effected on 15th September 1951 when their times, which had been fully co-ordinated with those of Eastern

Chelmsford bus station is the scene of this photograph taken in the late 1950s. The vehicle is 1359 (formerly No. 4146), one of the standard KSW5Gs, new in 1951. The shelters added, when the Hicks business was acquired, can be seen on the left, and a Bristol LD waits in the background.

R. F. Mack

National, were taken over without any change, and incorporated into services 32A and 32B . . . but not for long. Two weeks later, on 30th September, the following services were passed over to the LTE together with the garage in Argent Street and twenty eight buses.

31 — Grays—Little Thurrock—Tilbury, which became part of LT service 371/A
32 — Grays—Orsett (Stanford-le-Hope section retained), to LT service 323 (part)
32A — Grays—Nutberry, to LT service 323A
32B — Grays—Fairway, to LT service 323B
35 — Grays—Shell Haven/Coryton, to LT service 349
37A — Grays—Chadwell St. Mary—Tilbury Ferry to part of LT service 370A
37B — Tilbury Docks—Chadwell St. Mary—to LT service 379
44 — Grays—Orsett—Bulphan, to part of LT service 323
45 — Grays—East Tilbury—Linford—(Stanford-le-Hope section retained), to LT service 380
57 — Tilbury Docks—Nutberry, to LT service 357
81 — Tilbury Docks—East Tilbury (Bata Works) to LT service 367
82 — Grays—East Tilbury (Bata Works), to LT service 368
85 — Grays—Woodside Estate, to part of LT service 328/A

The above LT route numbers were not put into use immediately, as all the above services were continued until 2nd January 1952 using their old crews, buses and route numbers during a period of familiarization under the Executive when all transferred to the LTE garage, where a batch of LTE vehicles had been drafted in, and the new pattern of omnibus services was introduced. The Eastern National buses were now returned and Argent Street ceased to be operational. It was retained for storage purposes for a time and then sold to the Grays Co-operative Society as a transport depot but later demolished entirely to make way for a car-park which now covers the site.

Following the closure of Grays depot, the Company began preparations for the provision of passenger facilities for Basildon New Town, just getting under way. There was no garage nearer than Chelmsford, so as an interim move, a small temporary garage was established in Bull Road, Vange, starting with the three vehicles required for the early departures on the 51/53 routes to Chelmsford and Harwich/Clacton. The two small retained portions of the services 32 and 45 were soon taken off.

In the Aylesbury area, two private operators sold their businesses to the Company about the end of 1951. They were R. R. Coaches Ltd., trading as 'Red Rose', which ran on an equal footing with the Company on service 106 to Halton Camp, via Wendover, and 'Queens Park Coaches', which had its own separate route to Halton Camp, via Weston Turville, which now became a new 107 service. The former had been operated by several owners since about 1925 until coming into the possession of Robert McGill and his wife in 1929, from whom it was bought. The latter route was acquired from the executors of W. M. Oborne, who had established the service prior to 1931. Nine vehicles of mixed manufacture were taken over. The only other change of note in the Midland Section was the introduction, on 1st January, of a new 104A service between Aylesbury and Tring, via Marsworth.

The following are the more important service developments in the Eastern Area during 1951:

9 — Diverted to serve Cock Clarks

12 — New: Chelmsford—Rettendon—West and South Hanningfield

16 — Extended from Sudbury to Clare, ex-part of service 20

18B — Colchester—Halstead; to run via Aldham Village ex-service 26

20 — See services 16 and 30

20 — New: Colchester—Tenaring Hospital

26 — Colchester—Great Tey; to run via Wakes Colne (part to service 18B)

27 — New: Colchester—Wormingford Aerodrome

30 — Halstead—Pebmarsh; extended to Long Melford ex-service 20

33 — Renumbered 29

49 — New: Bishop's Stortford—Harlow (as service 47 but on different days)

80 & 84 — Services to Bata Works, East Tilbury; transferred to 'Westcliff' following closure of Grays garage

110 — New: Clacton local to Sacketts Grove

124 — New: Clacton—Colchester—Black Notley Hospital

Fifty one new vehicles were delivered in 1951 comprising eight Bristol LL5G/ECW saloons, fourteen LWL5G/ECW saloons, twenty eight Bristol KSW5G/ECW double-decks and one Bristol K5G/ECW double-deck, the chassis of which was assembled from parts salvaged from No. 4005, an earlier K5G of 1948, which had been seriously involved in an accident.

The change in vehicle dimensions was now fully implemented by the supply of chassis constructed to full legal width, hence the 'W' appearing in the KS and LL type designations. These vehicles were 8ft. wide, although not any longer and, apart from looking distinctly broad externally, they also provided the passenger with a noticeably wider seat without reducing the width of the gangway. As an interim measure, single-deck bodies of full 8ft. width were permitted on the 7ft. 6in. wide LL chassis and the eight vehicles delivered in 1951 were to this pattern. All 8ft. wide vehicles were supplied with white steering wheels instead of the usual black, as an instant reminder to drivers not accustomed to the larger vehicle.

The nine vehicles acquired from 'Queen's Park Coaches', Aylesbury consisted of two Bedford and two Dennis saloons, and one Dennis, one Bedford and three Leyland coaches. They were allocated an unusual series of fleet numbers prefixed by 'L', which were not actually carried on the vehicles. All had been disposed of by the end of 1952.

During the year, four Gardner oil engine conversions were completed when 4LK units replaced the Bedford petrol engines in Beadle/Bedfords Nos. 4011—4014.

With the Grays services passing to the London Transport Executive on 30th September, the destiny of the thirty four vehicles based there was placed in the balance. The executive was not too interested in the vehicle type allocated but, at the same time, could not spare enough of their own to convert to their liking. Six of the vehicles were new Bristol double-decks and the Company seized these back on the day before new operations commenced. The remaining twenty eight vehicles were temporarily loaned and carried London Transport side titles and holders for their usual running numbers, which were specially painted red. These were:

No. 3420 Dennis single-deck	No. 3877 Guy Arab double-deck
No. 3479 Dennis single-deck	No. 3878 Guy Arab double-deck
No. 3481 Dennis single-deck	No. 3879 Guy Arab double-deck
No. 3482 Dennis single-deck	No. 3880 Guy Arab double-deck
No. 3485 Dennis single-deck	No. 3881 Guy Arab double-deck
No. 3628 Bristol J single-deck	No. 3882 Guy Arab double-deck
No. 3631 Bristol J single-deck	No. 3883 Guy Arab double-deck
No. 3632 Bristol J single-deck	No. 3884 Guy Arab double-deck
No. 3679 Bristol J single-deck	No. 3897 Bristol L single-deck
No. 3721 Bristol J single-deck	No. 3898 Bristol L single-deck
No. 3722 Bristol J single-deck	No. 3905 Bristol L single-deck
No. 3874 Bristol L single-deck	No. 3906 Bristol L single-deck
No. 3875 Guy Arab double-deck	No. 3927 Bedford OB single-deck
No. 3876 Guy Arab double-deck	No. 3929 Bedford OB single-deck

The wide-bodied LWL saloons seated 39 passengers and were the last type of saloon bought for crew operation.

G. R. Mills

The executive managed to do without the use of the Dennis and Bedford saloons, and to make up the deficit of these and six double-decks, previously mentioned, fourteen standard STL double-decks were drafted in. By 2nd February, a full complement of vehicles was made up by LT and all the Company's stock was duly returned.

In common with many businesses, the passenger transport industry was seriously affected by a large rise in operating costs, chiefly in wages and the price of fuel, but also because of the imposition of purchase tax and the rapid rise of rates. Hitherto, it had been possible to contain rising expenditure by reason of the much heavier passenger loadings, although fares were still the same as pre-war. Applications for a fares increase was granted; a very modest increase amounting to only one halfpenny on those up to 6d., one penny on fares to 1/-, and 2d up to 1/9d, and so on pro rata. The reader must remember these are pre-decimalization figures.

Another important stage in the BTC's strategy of regrouping its businesses was reached this year, when the whole of Eastern National's Midland Section was transferred to the United Counties Omnibus Company based at Northampton. It was deemed to be more conveniently administered from Northampton than from the comparatively remote Chelmsford end, and

Three of these L6B coaches were acquired with the Westcliff business in 1952. Westcliff had built up tremendous goodwill in their coaching activities, and their name was allowed to continue for some considerable time with the new owners, as can be seen in this view of No. 324 standing at Southend (Victoria) railway station yard in September 1961.

G. R. Mills

would also increase the scope of United Counties to approximate more closely with the Commission's preferred size of operating unit. At the same time the 'Westcliff' business was to be fully integrated into Eastern National, leaving it in much the same size as before. However, a little more time was to elapse before this could be implemented, although the last timetable to be issued by 'Westcliff' appeared in June 1952, control having passed officially during the preceding month.

Meanwhile, Hicks Bros. had continued trading as such. Its express route from Bishop's Stortford to Clacton was now lettered 'P', a new route from Dunmow to Broxted started (H18) and a new Witham local, to Ebenezer Close, began as part of service H52, with some extra timings in other services here and there. The H22 London service, which had terminated for many years at Chenies Mews, off Tottenham Road, was now transferred to the Euston Square terminal.

The last but one independent stage operator working into Chelmsford was taken over this year when H. L. Stracey's service to Little Baddow by the back lanes became EN 7. In the Midland Section, there were a few alterations to note before all passed to United Counties on 1st May; viz:

18 — (group) Part diverts to serve Eggington
48 — Elstow—Clapham; diverted to serve Mile Road (Broad Avenue)
51 — Letchworth circulars; New loop route to serve Elderfield
75 — Huntingdon—Kimbolton circular diverts, via Tilbrook

This last diversion, on 16th March 1952, was the last piece of new ground to be covered by Eastern National before the transfer to United Counties, after just six weeks of operation.

In the Eastern Area (now the only operating area) several new services were started in 1952 among other changes, viz:

5 — New: Chelmsford local Woodhall Estate—Galleywood
14A — Chelmsford local; extended to Wood Street
38 — New: Bishop's Stortford—Thaxted (rail replacement service)
121 — New: Clacton local to Meadowview Camping Ground
— New: West Mersea—Wethersfield Air Base (Express for USAF)

During the year, the former Hicks services were renumbered into a new series using their former numbers with 300 added.

The transfer of the Company's Midland Area to United Counties, and the acquisition of 'Westcliff' created a major change in the fleet profile at 1952. Among the losses were eighty nine Bristol K and twelve Leyland PD1 double-decks, forty one Bristol L/LL and twenty J saloons, and six Bristol L coaches. These, together with smaller quantities of other types, amounted to 246 vehicles. On the plus side came seventy four Bristol K/KSW double-decks, seventeen Bristol J saloons, with fourteen Bedford and eleven Bristol LS coaches. Other models made the intake up to 268 units among which was

Above: The 'Benfleet' and 'Canvey' constituents in the Westcliff fleet included several Daimler double-decks, of which No. 1218, with a Roberts body, is an interesting example photographed in June 1962.

G. R. Mills

Above left: Solid construction in the Eastern Coach Works body can be clearly seen in this view of one of the many Bristol LS6G 39 seat coaches. Vehicle No. 364, originally in the Westcliff fleet, had adopted the Eastern National name by 1964, when this picture was taken.

G. R. Mills

Left: Six Seddon single-decks with Perkins engines and Plaxton 31 seat bodies came to the Company from Westcliff. All had originally been in the 'City' fleet.

notably twelve Leyland PD1A and twenty eight Daimler double-decks. The Company's fleet had drawn a net increase of twenty two units which was a close and satisfactory compromise. In addition to these vehicles, there was a small quantity of lorries, vans, cars, etc.

New vehicles continued to arrive, although the 1952 total was down somewhat on previous years. Fourteen Bristol KSW double-decks, eight LWL saloons and one Bristol LS5G dual-purpose saloon, with 41 seats and dual entrance/exit, made up the year's quota.

The latter vehicle requires special attention in that it was the fourth production model of Bristol's new underfloor-engined chassis. The LS was designed for lightweight single-decks and was of fully forward control layout, in which the driving position was placed ahead of the front axle. The design and general arrangement was conceived by Bristol as far back as 1920 but, at that time, there seemed to be little demand for such a vehicle. The framework was of light alloy construction, sufficient enough to contain the working components and be driven to Lowestoft for bodying. The bodywork was, however, a strengthening feature for this semi-integral design

This vehicle was new to Westcliff as an open-top in 1937 but became enclosed in 1942. In 1949, the roof was again removed so that the Bristol G could be used on popular sea front services. Westcliff did not use fleet numbers, and this picture was taken from Southend Pier prior to 1954 when the vehicle became No. 1246 in the Company fleet.
R. F. Mack

and contributed largely to its ultimate rigidity. This vehicle was rebuilt in 1958 to a 38 seat coach with just one door for use in connection with the Coach Air Service at Southend.

Other matters concerning vehicles in 1952 included the acquisition of three Bristol G/Tilling-bodied open-top double-decks (ex-Brighton & Hove), the fitment of a further five Gardner 4LK engines to Beadle/Bedford chassisless saloons, and the rebodying of twelve Bristol K double-decks by ECW. Ten of these dated from 1937, and one each of 1940 and 1942 vintage. This concluded the heavy programme of vehicle rebodying which hitherto constituted a prominent feature of Company policy.

Until 1952, vehicles carried their stock numbers on cast metal plates, with a coloured background particular to the depot to which it had been allocated. The depot colourings were arranged thus:

Eastern Section

Chelmsford (including Bishop's Stortford) — Light Green
Grays and Southend — Dark Green
Maldon — White
Colchester, West Mersea, Brightlingsea, Dedham and Sudbury — Yellow
Clacton (including Walton and Dovercourt) — Dark Blue
Vehicles withdrawn for disposal — Red

Midland Section

Bedford (including Cambridge, Stony Stratford, St. Neots, Yardley Hastings, Biggleswade and Huntingdon) — Black
Luton (including Leighton Buzzard, Clophill and Toddington) — Brown
Aylesbury — Light Blue
Hitchin — Grey
Vehicles withdrawn for disposal — Red

After the Midland Section had been transferred to United Counties, the Eastern Section continued the depot plates without change until 1954 when a new system was introduced to coincide with the fleet renumbering as detailed later in this book.

On 4th January 1953, a new edition of the Company timetable appeared, in which the whole of the 'Westcliff' services, using their own service numbers, prefixed 'W', together with the timetables of the former 'City Coach' services acquired on behalf of the BTC, were numbered in a new series commencing at 251.

A short account of 'Westcliff' and its principal acquisitions appears in the Acquired Operators Appendix. This year (1953) the 'Westcliff' group of express coach services was brought into the Company lettered series, mostly using up the vacancies created by the transfer to United Counties the previous year.

These were:

D — Southend-on-Sea—London ('Westcliff')
E — Southend-on-Sea—Brighton/Worthing
F — Southend-on-Sea—Eastbourne
G — Southend-on-Sea—Folkestone } all ex-'Multiways' 1946
H — Southend-on-Sea—Hastings
J — Southend-on-Sea—Margate
M — Southend-on-Sea—Great Yarmouth (New this year by 'Westcliff')

The 'Westcliff' express and touring services enjoyed an enormous goodwill with London booking agencies, as well as within its own operating area, which the Company recognized fully by continuing to promote these activities in its own publicity as 'Westcliff Coach Service' right up until 1961!

Now that all stage carriage services within the Southend area were in the hands of Eastern National, 'Westcliff' or Southend Corporation, the way was at last clear to initiate the desideratum, so long cherished by both parties, for an integrated transport system within the heavily populated, and still growing conurbation, which now extended well beyond the boundaries of the County Borough.

There had been a limited degree of co-ordination as outlined earlier, but now preparations for a fully co-ordinated system over a wider area was envisaged, extending westward to a line from the west end of Canvey Island to Battlesbridge, from which points the River Thames formed a southern boundary, as the River Crouch similarly did to the north with the North Sea on the east.

On 4th December the small service hitherto provided by Mr. T. W. Rolf from Woodham Walter, through Colicky Green to Maldon, was taken over by the Company and allotted service 67. Three other new services were introduced this year, with a few other changes as detailed below:

1B — Chelmsford—Little Baddow; extended to Boreham Turn
2B — Chelmsford (local); further extended in Chignal Estate to Welland Avenue
8B — Bishop's Stortford—Great Canfield; further extended to High Roding
11A — Combined with service 12, Chelmsford—Hanningfields
14A — Chelmsford local; New section to Finchley Avenue, via Lady Lane
24 — New: Halstead—Wethersfield Air Base
46 — Chelmsford—Matching Green; extended to Harlow
54 — New: Chelmsford—Boreham Race Track (only operated this year — track closed)
77 — New: Colchester—Great Bentley
109 — Clacton—Valley Farm Camp; extended to Holland-on-Sea
122 — New: Harwich—Dovercourt Holiday Camp

Hicks Bros. introduced the following this year:

331 — New: Braintree—Wethersfield Air Base
312 — New: Braintree—Leighs—Boreham Race Track } (only operated this year — track closed)
320 — New: Dunmow—Walthams—Boreham Race Track

H19B — Combined with service 319
317 — New: The section to Coopers End

The joint service 84 of Eastern National/'Westcliff', which had been combined with 'Westcliff' 2B service in 1951, was now revived to run from South Benfleet through Basildon to Homesteads and Grays by 'Westcliff' only, which itself also commenced a new service, Basildon—Pitsea Station W44, to meet the needs of the growing number of housing completions in the new town. A fair number of years would elapse before a railway station was built there, although the line passed right through the town centre.

Following the enormous change in fleet profile during 1952, the vehicular events of 1953 and 1954 are somewhat insignificant with the return to delivery of standard buses and coaches. Thirty four new vehicles came in 1953 comprising eighteen Bristol KSW double-decks, seven LS5G coaches with ECW bodies seating 39, six LS5G saloons with 43 seats and dual entrance/exit arrangement, and three LS5G with similar bodies but with entrance/exit arrangement,

One of the former Westcliff dual-purpose LS5G saloons is seen here at Victoria Coach Station, London awaiting passengers for the Southend Airport service.

coach type seats classified as dual-purpose. In the late 1950s, the dual door vehicles were converted to one door with revised seating.

Some of the KSWs had an improved seating arrangement on the upper deck. Instead of the usual straight row of four seats, they were now slightly staggered so that each passenger had his own 'piece' to sit on. Under the old arrangement the fourth passenger, sitting nearest the gangway, usually found him/herself left with only a portion of their entitlement and when the bus took a sharp turn to the left, the unfortunate traveller was unable to prevent a somewhat undignified slide into the gangway! The new seating found favour with all but a few courting couples, who considered it a disadvantage after a late night outing to the cinema.

The temporary coach station at Judd Street, near King's Cross, had to be vacated by 17th January 1954 so the Company's express services, and those of the other BTC operators which used or called at it, were now extended to the Victoria Coach Station, thereby adding thirty minutes running time to all journeys. Another temporary coach stop/pick-up point was arranged in Euston Square, about a quarter of a mile further westward of Judd Street, where a booking/enquiry office was set up using a converted single-deck bus, normally employed for a similar purpose at shows and for promotional purposes. This sufficed for several years pending the opening of a permanent station in the area.

Bristol KSW double-deck No. 1408 (formerly No. 4190) stands at the 'temporary' Euston Coach Station, London which, in fact, lasted for several years!

C. F. Klapper

In 1954, the plans for the new arrangements in the South Essex area were completed, as well as those for the final welding together of a single system of services absorbed from 'Westcliff', Hicks Bros. and 'City Coach' Company. Southend Corporation had finally closed down its trolley bus routes, and the Eastern and Kursaal Circular routes were taken over by motor buses on 10th February and the Western Circle on 28th October, in readiness for the grand changeover at the year end after not quite thirty years of silent service. 'Westcliff' also introduced further service developments during this interim period, viz:

W13 — New: Southend—Hullbridge, via Lower Hockley
W14 — Southend—Basildon Industrial Sites—Romford, via Arterial Road
252 — Part to run from Brentwood to Shenfield, via Priests Lane
253 — Brentwood—Shotgate; extended to Rawreth
257 — Laindon—Wickford; extended to Rettendon, incorporating EN 12B
258 — Laindon—Pipps Hill; extended to Vange
262 — New: Brentwood local. Bishops Hall Estate—Three Arch Estate
W26A — Benfleet—Canvey Casino; extended to Seaview Road South

and Eastern National, the following:

7 — Chelmsford—Little Baddow; extended to Maldon to include service 67
8 — Chelmsford—Berners Roding, experimental — ran three months only
12B — Combined with 'Westcliff' service 257 (see above)
13 — Part now diverts to serve Littlebury
14B — Chelmsford—Springfield Park; extended to Brook End
16 — Colchester—Sudbury; now diverts to serve Cornard Estate
50 — Chelmsford—Fairstead; extended to Braintree
63 — Maldon—Fambridge; extended to Steeple Stone
67 — Became part of service 7 (see above)
75 — Colchester—West Mersea; extended to East Mersea ex-service 76
75D — Combined with service 76 to run Colchester—Fingringhoe—West/East Mersea
125 — New: Clacton—Castle Hill (local)

The tours and excursions department was now being expanded quite rapidly as vehicles for this work became available. A considerable number of additional places from which tours could be operated had been acquired with the various businesses taken over since 1939, but little use could be made of them hitherto. The Company was also seeking further points which could be conveniently added to the network. A further accession this year was the Laindon-based tours and excursions (but no stage route) of Gidea Park Coaches Ltd. which also had a picking up point in Brentwood. 'Westcliff' now instituted a full programme of tours and excursions from Brentwood where a new office/enquiry bureau had opened at 3 High Street.

By 1954, matters had been allowed to settle and consideration was turned towards the replacement of some of the former 'Westcliff' fleet. The first eight vehicles to be withdrawn were Bristol J05Gs, Nos. 224, 242, 243, 244 and 246, AEC Regents Nos. 1167 and 1168 and Daimler No. 1201.

Twenty five new vehicles were delivered consisting of thirteen Bristol LD/ECW double-decks, five LS5G/ECW 43 seat dual door saloons, four LS5G/ECW 45 seat saloons, two Bristol SC lightweight saloons and one LS5G 39 seat coach. The dual door vehicles were converted to one door with increased seating in 1960. The double-decks deserve special mention in that the LD was a new generation chassis incorporating all the latest ideas and, when bodied, managed to achieve an overall low height of 13ft. 4in., just ¼in. more than the K series which it superseded. The outstanding feature was the stepped down rear axle which enabled a sunken gangway on the lower deck to extend throughout the entire length of the vehicle, thus doing away with any step up from the rear platform. With the possibility of having a reduced height lower deck floor, the need for a sunken gangway upstairs was also eliminated, so a flat floor, with conventional two-by-two seats each side of a centre gangway, was produced on both decks. The cautionary notice for lower deck passengers on the offside to 'lower head when leaving seat' was no longer required and altogether a much more popular vehicle had now arrived for the travelling public, thanks largely to the drop centre rear axle. The Bristol LD also heralded the arrival of the cowled radiator and, for the first time, the familiar shape exposed unit was hidden and became synonymous with an older breed of vehicle.

A few second-hand vehicles joined the ranks in 1954. Two Dennis Lancets came from the Romford-based 'Gidea Park Coaches', three AEC Regents and one Bristol G, all in open top form, arrived from Brighton, six Bristol K double-decks were taken over from the Thames Valley Company at Reading, and one Bristol G double-deck arrived from Eastern Counties, Norwich.

The fleet numbering system had by now reached a most unsatisfactory situation. Hitherto, all new vehicles had been numbered in an on-going common sequence which had started at 2001 with the former 'National' Company in 1919 and by now had reached 4233! Added to this were large batches of vehicles taken over from Hicks and 'Westcliff', plus a few other oddities which possessed much lower numbers or, as in the case of 'Westcliff', many without any fleet number at all. Clearly something had to be done to create a sensible identification system and, on 18th July 1954, the entire fleet was renumbered into the following groups:

1 — 100 acquired single-decks (after renumbering)
100 — 1000 single decks
1001 — 1100 acquired double-decks (after renumbering)
1101 — 2000 double-decks

One of the 1954 Bristol LD6Gs photographed near Newbury Park Station on the 'famous' service 251. This is an Eastern National vehicle using the Westcliff side titles.

P. J. Marshall

The first Bristol LS saloons were dual-entrance and here No. 394 (formerly No. 4225) is seen outside Castle Road garage, Clacton.

At the same time, single-decks and double-decks were arranged in chassis types, with Bristol vehicles placed last. In most cases types were placed in order of chassis number. Ten years later the fleet numbering was further refined, details of which are given later. For ease of reference *Appendix A* has been arranged to show the successive fleet numbers which each vehicle carried during its time connected with the Eastern National fleet.

The engineering administration was now established in two centres, one called Eastern, and based at New Writtle Street, Chelmsford, and the other called Southern, based at Fairfax Drive, Prittlewell, Southend-on-Sea. All vehicles now carried small identification symbols above the stock number, Eastern Area using triangles and Southern Area using circles, coloured as follows:

Eastern Area		*Southern Area*	
Chelmsford	red	Southend (London Road)	red
Bishop's Stortford	red	Hadleigh	white
Maldon	white	Canvey	white
Halstead	black	Basildon	yellow
Colchester	yellow	Southend (Tylers Avenue)	light blue
Braintree	dark blue	*Wood Green	brown
Clacton	light blue		
Brentwood	brown		

*Wood Green was transferred to the Eastern Area in 1956, and the brown circle became an orange triangle with a white dot at its centre.

By 1954, many of the former 'Westcliff' vehicles, which had formerly sported the standard Tilling red and cream livery, were appearing in the Company's green and cream colours, but with 'Westcliff' side titles. Similarly most of the former 'City' vehicles lost their brown and cream colour scheme to become green and cream, but carried 'Westcliff' names except for those vehicles used especially on the famous service 251 which 'City' pioneered between Southend and Wood Green. Here the vehicles became green and cream, retaining the 'City' name as a gesture to the goodwill this service enjoyed.

The same applied to the former Hicks vehicles which, despite going green, retained their Hicks name. When replacements were needed in the Hicks, 'City' or 'Westcliff' fleets, some existing Eastern National vehicles would join their ranks and have the appropriate fleetnames applied. This arrangement continued until after the 1955 reorganization, when all vehicles adopted the Company's name except some coaches which continued until the early 1960s using the 'Westcliff' title.

Traffic administration was of a slightly different nature, dividing the Company into three centres rather than two. A Northern Area was based at the omnibus station, Jackson Road, Clacton-on-Sea, later moving to Queen Street, Colchester. The Duke Street omnibus station at Chelmsford formed the Central area headquarters and, at Southend-on-Sea, the Southern Area was commanded from 17/21 London Road.

EASTERN NATIONAL
WESTCLIFF-ON-SEA

TIME TABLES
OF
ALL SERVICES
1/-

14th NOVEMBER, 1954
AND UNTIL FURTHER NOTICE

Chapter Six

Virtual Monopoly   1955-1961

The BTC's strategy for its omnibus and coach subsidiaries in the area which closely approximated to the administrative county of Essex, excluding the LTE special area, attained its logical conclusion in 1955 when all the licences and rolling stock of the enlarged 'Westcliff' and of 'Hicks Bros.' undertakings were transferred to Eastern National, which now assumed full control for all of the BTC's business interests in that area. At about the same time, the new partnership with Southend-on-Sea Corporation Transport was established as Southend & District Joint Services which now became the sole provider of passenger transport within the co-ordinated area. This removed all problems of competing applications for licences at the Traffic Commissioners, and also ensured that each partner would receive its agreed proportion of the total revenue earned, no matter from which route or on whose vehicle it had been received.

A short biographical note regarding the 'Westcliff Motor Services' appears in *Appendix B* where all the acquired businesses are listed.

Some account of the rather chequered experience of the Corporation undertaking in the earlier years, and its relations with 'Westcliff' which led up to the formation of the Joint Services, will not be out of place here.

About the time of Queen Victoria's Diamond Jubilee in 1898, which was marked by the erection of a large figure of the Queen on a pedestal at the top of Pier Hill, with her outstretched arm pointing in the direction of the public conveniences, the Local Board was considering the question of providing improved transport facilities for its rapidly growing population and visitors. At that time, the only conveyances were a few ancient double-deck horse-drawn omnibuses provided by two local jobmasters, Peter Trigg and Sydney Smith.

The Local Board resolved to install a system of tramways throughout the area under its control and also over the boundary to Leigh-on-Sea which was then a separate UDC, but also happy with the proposals. The Council took advantage of the recently-enacted Light Railway legislation which simplified procedures, and reduced the expense before any railway or tramway could be built under the old arrangements which required the promotion of a Bill in Parliament. Southend was, in fact, the first local authority to obtain a Light Railway Order from the Board of Trade to construct its tramways.

The system opened on 19th July 1901 with lines to Leigh-on-Sea, Prittlewell, Southchurch and the beach near Luna Park, later known as The Kursaal. The only extension (opened in sections) was along the Eastern Esplanade to Thorpe Bay and north through The Boulevards to join the Southchurch terminus, which permitted circular running. On 1st April 1914, Southend achieved the status of a County Borough having a little earlier absorbed Leigh-on-Sea and Southchurch.

The Corporation had been anxious to extend the tramways into other parts of the Borough, but was continually frustrated in its efforts to provide the facilities desired by the residents so long as no trams passed along their particular street! Other obstacles were the low railway bridge by the LT&S station in High Street which was very narrow at its lower end, and the steepness of Pier Hill. Such were the contentious matters over which the Corporation kept deferring a decision and eventually avoided by securing powers to operate motor buses in 1912. It then ordered seven motor omnibuses but, here again, unable to decide the most suitable pattern, bought three Straker-Squire and three Tilling-Stevens single decks with various types of body, and a small Edison battery-powered saloon bus. They arrived in 1914 and were put to work on two routes, one of which was a total failure and quickly withdrawn but, before they could be tried elsewhere, half the fleet (the three Straker-Squires) had been commandeered by the War Office which did not favour Tilling-Stevens in their ranks. The latter continued in service, but proved unprofitable, so the Corporation withdrew

Typical of the standard Bristol LS saloon is No. 1205 (formerly No. 379), and one that had been in the Westcliff fleet. It is seen on the short working of service 34, Chelmsford–Pitsea.

T. M. Smith

them in 1916 and sold them, but nobody has yet discovered where they went.

When the Armistice came in 1918, the question to provide transport facilities once again arose, but the Corporation was still thoroughly frightened by its previous experience and ducked the issue by granting licences to the Westcliff & Southend-on-Sea Charabanc Co. Ltd., predecessor of 'Westcliff Motor Services', to provide a service from the top of Pier Hill to Westcliff (Plough Hotel), via Clifftown which became a popular and profitable service. The 'Westcliff' Company had been formed by the fusion of the charabanc department of two jobmasters' businesses; Holmes Bros. and Sydney Smith (aforesaid), with the Southend-on-Sea Charabanc Co. Ltd., in 1913.

By 1925, the tramway track to Prittlewell had deteriorated so drastically that it required relaying but, being the least profitable line in the system, the Corporation was reluctant to embark on the heavy expenditure and opted to experiment with a pair of rail-less trolleybuses which were eventually purchased. Others were bought later and the route extended at each end so that it ran from Eastwood Boulevard to The Kursaal. Further trolleybus sections followed but the trams continued to operate on the remaining routes.

By 1929, 'Westcliff' and other private operators were providing several more omnibus services within the Borough. The Corporation summoned enough courage to determine it should also be operating its own buses and, accordingly, ordered seven AEC Regal saloons for use on two routes for which it had refused to grant licences to others. This brought it into conflict with the other applicants with whom there had been earlier difficulties and who now appealed to the Minister of Transport. During the course of resulting delays, the new Traffic Act had become law and the Corporation now found itself in the invidious and somewhat ridiculous position of being unable to issue to itself the licences it had refused others! The Corporation had now to apply to the Traffic Commissioners for licences, just as any other newcomer would have to, but because of the objections lodged by the established operators, they too were refused. Meanwhile, the seven new buses languished in the depot patiently awaiting their maiden trip. After prolonged and unsuccessful hearings at the Traffic Court, the Corporation was forced to the conclusion that it would have to buy out some existing services if it was ever to find work for its buses. This was done during 1932 by negotiation and, at the same time, agreement was reached for the Corporation to operate the local services in the eastern half of the Borough, the company operators to work within the western half. The Corporation buses finally commenced work on 5th July 1932 and five company routes, one ex-'Westcliff', three ex-'Blue Buses' and one ex-Borough were transferred on 1st January 1933, some being worked by motor buses and part by trolley buses, becoming one of the few undertakings to use trams, trolley buses and motor buses simultaneously!

The Corporation trams continued without change until 16th July 1938 when the Boulevards section was closed, followed a little later by the

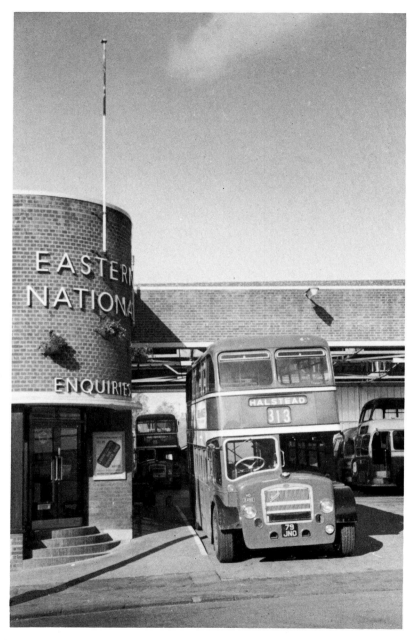

An early morning scene at Halstead depot (now closed) showing one of the 1957 Bristol LDs which has been put out ready for the first service.

Esplanade section, and finally the last were withdrawn on 8th April 1942, since when the motor bus operations have been expanded. Tillings had sought to establish a joint system as far back as 1935, but no agreement for a fully co-ordinated service was possible as the 'Benfleet' and 'City' companies were determined to keep their independence. A small step forward was made on 1st October 1947 when the Corporation's Leigh — Thorpe Bay circular was linked with the 'Westcliff' Leigh — Highlands as a joint service.

The Southend Joint Services commenced working on 2nd January 1955 with no alteration to the services whatsoever, but a number of routes exchanged operator during a period of familiarization until the summer timetables came into force, and then some new cross-town facilities appeared as follows:

'Westcliff' 6/6A joined SCT 64 to run Newington Crescent — Eastwood as 6/6A

'Westcliff' 9/9A joined SCT 5A to run Shoeburyness — Eastwoodbury as 9/9A

'Westcliff' 19/19A joined SCT 68 to run Shoebury Common — Leigh-on-Sea as 68/68A; a new marine drive of nearly six miles

To avoid unnecessary repetition of route lists for the contributing undertakings, readers should consult part three of *Appendix B* where all services are listed in the new numerical sequence and where it shows their origins with the previous number suitably prefixed 'E' for former Eastern National route, 'H' for former Hicks Bros., 'S' for former Southend Corporation and 'W' for the ex-'Westcliff' services, of which those from 251 upwards are of the late 'City' coach company.

The question of renumbering of services was worked out early in 1955 because, if left, there would have been duplication of numbers in several areas. The Corporation had only adopted numbers during the last five years but it was very haphazard and can only be described as chaotic as it was using 5A/B; 25/A/B/C/D; 28/A/B/C; 51/A; 52/A; 61/A/B/C; 62; 63/A/B; 64; 68; 69 and Z.

The route renumbering arrangement was well thought out. Southend Corporation numbers already cleared those in use by 'Westcliff' but the numbers in the sixties duplicated some used by Eastern National, and two 'Westcliff' numbers duplicated the Eastern National routes entering Southend. As the greatest concentration of services and buses lay in this area it was left virtually unaltered except for 'Westcliff' service 19/19A which was eliminated by linking it with Corporation routes, and the infrequent service 11A which was allotted the vacant number 13. The Corporation service 51 was changed to 66, and service 52 disappeared in the route changes so that only those routes numbered in the sixties duplicated Eastern National elsewhere. The former 'City' routes had been numbered from 251 upwards and Hicks Bros. from 300 upwards, while the

A facsimile of a Company leaflet, dated October 1957, giving details of winter coach services to and from London.

Index Publishers

Clacton/Harwich services in the 100 and upwards series were all well clear. The renumbering was therefore worked out as follows:

14th August	Maldon area services using 60 upwards now had 30 added
21st August	Basildon area to take numbers preceding the 251 batch
28th August	Bishop's Stortford completely renumbered in the 300 series, using any not allocated to ex-Hicks Bros. services
11th September	Halstead/Braintree routes to also occupy vacant 300 numbers
18th September	Chelmsford services, except those in the forties and fifties — (e.g. 1—14) now received numbers starting at 30; others left unchanged
2nd October	Colchester had 70 added to those services in the 15—29 group and would now follow those in the 75 upwards series which were left unchanged

The final result came out thus:

1—29	Southend/Canvey area	
30—59	Chelmsford services	
60—69	Southend/Canvey area	
70—89	Colchester area	
90—99	Maldon area	
100 upwards	Clacton/Harwich area	
231 upwards	Campbell's routes to be acquired	
241—250	Basildon area	
251 upwards	Brentwood/Billericay services	
300 upwards	Bishop's Stortford/Braintree/Halstead area	

As time passed, exceptions to these groupings began to creep in. For instance some services which became joint with Eastern Counties received numbers used by that concern in the 200 series and certain variations of a main route were given numbers 100 above or below, such as service 251, which had variants 151 and 351. Both were well out of sequence, although it is unlikely that the travelling public would have felt any great concern in the matter.

A few service changes deserve mention. Continuing its policy of developing town services, the Company arranged for Braintree to be so served this year for the first time when service 312 appeared. Efforts to provide better facilities at Harlow New Town were now projected to The Stow, which was the New Town Shopping Centre, with some journeys diverting to serve the industrial area, but no local travel was permitted over the extension. Another improvement was the linking of services 335, Braintree—Witham with service 60, Witham—Maldon, to give through facilities. Also newly started were services 242 Basildon—Coryton and 263 from Brentwood—St. Vincent's Hamlet, which actually lay within LTE territory.

The express services of 1955 saw little change but one significant alteration was the provision on service D (Southend—London) of a picking-up point at the Jolly Cricketers, near Basildon, providing its first direct link to the metropolis. The number of daily departures was also increased.

Standardization on the Bristol chassis and Eastern Coach Works body was now very typical of any Tilling group company, and practically all deliveries of new vehicles consisted of models produced at the Bristol and Lowestoft factories. The replacement programme for 1955 witnessed the arrival of fifty one new vehicles, comprising twenty LS5G 45 seat saloons and thirty one LD double-decks, of which eighteen were fitted with Gardner 5LW engines and the remainder with Bristol AVW six cylinder units. Seven of the saloons returned to ECW during 1956 for seat reduction to 41 and to be suitably adapted for one man operation. In February 1960, the same vehicles reverted to 45 seaters but still retained the one man features. A further eight second-hand K5G double-decks were acquired from United Counties, five of which had originally been in the Eastern National fleet before the separation of the Midland Area.

The main event of 1956 was the purchase of J. W. Campbell & Sons of Pitsea, from whom ten vehicles and six routes were obtained on 19th February. These received route numbers from 231 upwards and were continued with little change for some time. Campbell was the last private stage operator in South Essex, so Eastern National was now in complete possession of all road services in Basildon New Town and much of the surrounding area.

The express coach network was further enlarged this year with two fresh services. To provide separate facilities from the Tilbury/Grays area to

One of the 1957 Bristol SC lightweight saloons. Bus services were expected to continue in all weathers, including the snows of January 1963.

G. R. Mills

Holland-on-Sea and Walton-on-Naze, the new service R was interworked with service N, and service S from Harlow and Bishop's Stortford was introduced to Felixstowe.

Southend & District Joint Services commenced three express services:

X24 Canvey—Benfleet—Hadleigh to Westcliff and Rochford Hospitals, reviving, to some extent, a facility provided by Pearce's Motor Services in the 1930s.

X90 Leigh-on-Sea—Roots Hall (Southend United Football Ground) originally Corporation route Z.

X92 Basildon—Westcliff and Rochford Hospitals — a new service.

A new facility into Harlow New Town was a stage working of part of service 322 from Dunmow and, at Clacton, two extensions were made for the convenience of holiday-makers; the local 110 service now ran to Chester Camp and service 125 to Highlands Camp.

An interesting selection of vehicles came with the purchase of J. W. Campbell at Pitsea in February. Of the ten vehicles acquired, eight were on various models of Albion chassis, including one CX37 Weymann-bodied double-deck and three CX13 all-weather bodied 33 seat coaches. An AEC Regent with Northern Coachbuilders double-deck body and a Bedford OWB saloon made up the fleet, but the Bedford and three of the oldest Albions were not used by Eastern National. None of the vehicles remained with the Company for more than twelve months.

Thirty seven new vehicles formed the 1956 intake, comprising thirty four LD double-decks, nineteen with Gardner 5LW engines and the rest with Bristol AVW units. Vehicle No. 1515 was the 1,000th LD built and was actually delivered to the Company in January 1957. It carried a commemorative plaque on the front bulkhead of the lower saloon. Three LS5G 45 seat saloons also arrived, two of which returned to ECW in June to have their seating reduced to 41 with the introduction of one man operation. Both were returned to 45 seaters early in 1960 but still retained the one man features.

Two Bristol K5G double-decks, which had originally been Eastern National Nos. 3807 and 3750, were acquired from United Counties. Both had passed to the latter company at the separation of the Midland Area.

Further improvement to the express services came in 1957 when service P from Harlow New Town to Clacton, etc. was divided to give separate facilities for Holland-on-Sea and Walton-on-Naze, which was designated Q, and the original service A, from London to Clacton, now obtained additional picking-up points at Great Clacton and Weeley. Service C was extended at weekends from Maldon to Bradwell Power-Station, and service D, from Southend to London, was now rerouted right through the town centre at Basildon, via Pitsea and Vange, instead of using the Arterial Road, and further strengthened to six, the number of daily return runs, with two extras between London and Basildon.

Stage routes saw few changes in 1957, but Chelmsford received better connections to Southend by a new route 11A which ran direct instead of detouring via East Hanningfield. New services were 243 Pitsea—Basildon local and 313/314 from Bishop's Stortford to Stansted Airport, via either Stansted Village or Plaw Hatch. Another town service was also started from Bishop's Stortford (South Street) via the town centre to Heath Row. At Clacton, a new section to route 77 arrived to cater for visitors at Shang-ri-la Camp at Aingers Green.

An important development was the further electrification of the East Coast railway line from Liverpool Street, London, beyond Shenfield to Chelmsford, which now enjoyed a fast fixed interval service with modern open-plan rolling stock such as it had never known before, some effects of which will be noted later in this book. At the end of 1957, electrification was also carried down from Shenfield to Southend (Victoria) Station, with equally improved facilities.

In 1957, new vehicles totalled thirty eight and also saw the arrival of fourteen more lightweight 35 seat saloons on the Bristol SC chassis with Gardner 4LK engines. Thirteen LD double-decks, eight with AVW engines and five with Gardner engines, and four LS5G saloons entered the stage fleet while

The original Bristol LDL 70 seat rear entrance double-deck, and forerunner of the FLF range. Here, No. 2510 (formerly No. 1541) has been used on the short-lived service 253 extension to Upminster.

G. R. Mills

the coach fleet took delivery of five LS6Gs with 34 seat bodies. Towards the end of the year, the LS chassis was superseded by the MW (Medium Weight) frame which, unlike its predecessor, was a true chassis without any dependence on a body for rigidity. The main frame of the MW featured an amidships section that cranked upwards over the area occupied by the engine, thereby giving improved ground clearance. Two of these chassis were supplied with 6HLW engines, one bodied as a 34 seat coach and the other as a 45 seat saloon. In 1963, the five LS coaches were upseated to 39 in order to provide further accommodation for the growing express market.

Eastern National was now firmly committed to exploit each and every opportunity to expand the express network, which it clearly identified as its best area of growth, and fresh ideas appeared in 1958. An important liaison was established with Air Charter Ltd. which had already developed a range of air routes to Continental destinations via Southend Airport. Eastern National provided the coach link with the London terminal at Euston Square being used for this purpose, with an additional pick-up arranged at Ilford, near Gants Hill Underground Station. At first, up to five daily departures were required.

On 13th June, the old established business of Rose Bros. Ltd., at

The chassis has progressed from LS to MW, and Eastern Coach Works have yet to create a new design for the 39 seat coach body but this is, nevertheless, very businesslike in appearance. Vehicle No. 333 (formerly No. 481) is one of the six which were new in 1959.

G. R. Mills

Chelmsford was purchased. Its best known activity had been a coach service to London, dating from 1929, which had practically attained an hourly headway, frequently calling for much duplication at weekends. Rose had a rather mixed fleet in a yellow livery with black lining and used the fleet-name 'Primrose Coaches'. The service had been adversely affected by the new electric train service, as had the Company's own service to London (Bow) which was now reduced from a half-hourly to hourly headway for the same reason. 'Primrose' also had a summer express service to Great Yarmouth which was designated V, and there was a summer service to Steeple Stone, on the Blackwater Estuary, which was combined with service 93. It had its share of the local private hire work and excursions and tours from both Witham and Chelmsford. The extensive taxi and car hire section was retained by Rose.

There were additional express coach facilities in 1958 from the Tilbury/Grays area to serve Clacton, via Laindon and Chelmsford, designated T, and another from Southend to Bournemouth, via Basildon as U.

Only two small additions to stage services call for comment; service 96 Maldon—Woodham Ferrers Station now continued through to Wickford and Basildon, and a short spur off the 320 route at Great Yeldham was made to serve Toppesfield.

The growing population of Basildon had, by now, reached almost 50,000, and improved travel facilities were introduced, following the completion of the Laindon Link from the town centre to near Laindon railway station, along which service 244 from Pitsea to Basildon via Vange now ran, giving rail commuters an alternative route to London which would save them time and money.

Deliveries of new vehicles in 1958 was highlighted by the appearance of the first 30ft. long double-deck in the shape of the lengthened LD, designated LDLX6G. Taking the fleet number 1541, it carried ten extra seats than the LD, and enjoyed a prototype air suspension on the rear axle, giving an improved ride and a constant step height from the ground, no matter how heavily laden. Other new vehicles comprised nineteen LD double-decks, only two of which had the AVW engine, six SC lightweight saloons and twenty MW chassis, four with 6HLW engines and 39 seat coach bodies and the remainder with 5HLW engines and 41 seat stage bodies.

Seven L6B coaches with 31 seat full-front bodies were acquired from United Counties together with one Leyland PS1 with Duple 35 seat coach body. The latter vehicle, together with three of the L6Bs, had originally been with Eastern National before the separation of the Midland Area. In June, a 41 seat Thurgood-bodied Leyland coach was taken over from the 'Primrose Coaches' of Rose Bros., and this was operated for a short time in the 'Primrose' livery.

The relentless spiral of increasing wages chasing increased prices, coupled with the general extension of private motoring, was becoming a source of anxiety for the management, and as there was always a long delay between submitting an application for increased fares and the time it could become effective, the expected benefits often became nugatory. Each time it became necessary to raise fares, public transport found itself on the slippery slope of diminishing returns. Services in the rural areas were the worst affected, and country folk in areas where public transport has always been minimal have found ways of dealing with this situation which became easier with the increase in private motoring. People who worked at the larger centres of employment still enjoyed suitable bus facilities from many points, but had perforce to embark on car sharing arrangements, which often had the benefit of giving door to door travel at low cost. The bravest turned to the 'moped' for individual transport; it was cheap to buy and cheap to run although perhaps a little uncomfortable in winter. The bus could not satisfactorily compete with these alternatives, hence the attention to develop urban routes and express coastal services to the limit. The latter could still flourish for fares were often considerably lower than the train, and there were now plenty of the older generation with increased spending power who had never possessed a car, or were likely to do so. Tours and excursion facilities and trips to special events likewise received special attention, for there were now twenty one distinct and separate district groupings each with its own tours programme. At Brentwood, the tours also picked up on the

Picking up outside the Prince of Wales, Marks Tey, is one of the initial batch of Bristol FLF double-decks new in 1960. Vehicle No. 2717 (formerly No. 1588) has its radiator in the earlier conventional position.

G. R. Mills

London County Council's Harold Hill Estate. Eastern National literature for the promotion of this aspect of the business was of a very high standard and always freely available at as many points as possible.

A new express service, designated W, made its appearance in 1959 to run direct from Southend to Jaywick, giving a much swifter journey than the 19/19A stage service and permitting a much longer day by the sea. A direct service from Chelmsford to Basildon was arranged this year by splitting service 34, with half the journeys going to Basildon as 34A, the rest continuing to Pitsea as previously. At Clacton the 113 local service to Jaywick was now worked through from Great Clacton to give a further cross-town facility. Service 48 from Chelmsford to Mill Beach ran for the last time in the summer of 1959, reflecting the changing habits of the travelling public who could now afford to take longer trips to more interesting places. The opening of new lengths of motorway and dual carriageways enabled day trippers to reach an increasing variety of places hitherto reserved for their true holiday.

Seventeen LD double-decks joined the fleet in 1959, this time fitted with the Gardner 5LW engine. Twenty seven MW chassis were also supplied, eleven as 41 or 45 seat saloons and ten as 41 seat dual-purpose saloons, all of which had the 5HLW engine. Six coaches completed the order as 39 seaters powered by the 6HLW unit.

On 17th September 1960, the local service run by Mesdames Mawdsley and Brown, from Rowhedge into Colchester, was acquired. It was in continuation of that worked for many years by Mr T. Fale, who is known to have been on that road with his carrier's van as long ago as 1914. This service always put up at the Plough Hotel yard but was transferred some time later to the bus station and numbered 76A. One bus was for a time out-stationed at Rowhedge for this purpose.

In November, another Pitsea—Basildon local service was started as 241, and the Braintree town service was extended to serve the Skitts Hill area. One country extension was that of the 319 service beyond Wethersfield to Cornish Hall End.

The first change to note in the Southend Joint Services was the substitution of the 7/8 group of services to run through to Shoeburyness instead of the 9/9A group, giving through running to the coast from Rayleigh, Hockley and Rochford. There were no changes to the express network this year.

The development of the LDL chassis and its trials with various BTC companies ended with the production of the F series of low slung double-deck chassis. These were available in short and long form (FS and FL), and front or rear entrance, the former being identified by an additional F in the designation (FSF or FLF). The F series enjoyed the provision of air-operated brakes in place of the vacuum-assisted type found on earlier models. Twenty of the new breed double-deck vehicles were supplied in the FLF form, fifteen with Gardner 6LX engines and the remainder with the improved Bristol BVW engines. Two 60 seat double-decks came on the shorter FS chassis, having rear entrances and 5LW engines. New vehicles further included the supply of twenty two MW chassis, five of which had 41 seat coach bodies and 6HLW engines, and the remainder bodied as 45 seat saloons powered by the 5HLW unit. One Bristol K5G open-top double-deck was acquired from Brighton, Hove & District and two Bedford saloons came from Mawdsley and Brown, only one of which was used by Eastern National.

The requirements of the increasing population of the Basildon area was outstripping the facilities available on the coaches starting their journeys at Southend, and a whole range of relief departures were started in 1961 to pick up at Pitsea and Basildon, where there were immediate connecting buses from Laindon, Billericay and Wickford. These carried the same running letter as the Southend services but with the addition of a 1. Thus E/1 went to Worthing; F/1 was to Eastbourne; G/1 for Folkestone; H/1 for Hastings and J/1 for Margate. This was the last year that Eastern National used letter designations for its coach services now that they had more than exhausted the alphabet. During the winter, a new scheme, using numerals prefixed by X, was evolved in time for the printing of the 1962 programmes, details of which will be given in the next chapter.

On 12th November 1961, George Digby's bus service (in succession to Fred Heath) which had run since the early 1920s from Wormingford, via West

This vehicle was one of four Bristol LL6G coaches acquired from Tilling Transport (BTC) Ltd., which had since been placed under Eastern National supervision. Built especially for London sightseeing trips, the Eastern Coach Works body had roof lights added for greater visibility. Vehicle No. 018 is seen at Marks Tey in August 1964.

G. R. Mills

Bergholt to Colchester, was taken over, removing one more of the long-established private operators. This service was combined with the 76 route from Colchester to Fingringhoe and the recently acquired 76A to Rowhedge, to form the first cross-town facility not provided by the Colchester Transport Department. At the same time, the outstation at Rowhedge was closed.

The closure of the Colne Valley branch railway called for Eastern National to provide a replacement bus service at the end of the year which was numbered 89 to run via Halstead and the Hedinghams to Haverhill. Another new town service began this year from Brentwood to Hutton Drive as service 264 and the arrival of more 'Lodekka' double-deck omnibuses enabled the famous ex-City 251 service between Wood Green and Southend to resume its customary routing between Wickford and Rawreth, via Shotgate, as these vehicles could negotiate Blue Brick Bridge. In its wake, a new service 250 from Southend to Wickford, via Rettendon Turnpike, was started and the single-deck 'Shotgate Shuttle' could now be dispensed with, but a new 249 service from Brentwood, to serve the Shotgate Industrial Estate, was started at the same time. Two new services for employees at the new Bradwell Power-Station also started in 1961, service 97 from Maldon, through Steeple, and 98 from Althorne, via Burnham and Southminster. Something completely new was the appearance of Eastern National buses on the Colchester—Ipswich road which had been an Eastern Counties preserve since 1920. Its 207 route now became joint with Eastern National which operated every third journey.

Town services were still very much under review in 1961, as service 265 was rerouted to run from Billericay Station, via Stock Road to Perry Street, and Gooseberry Green to Norsey Road and Sunnymede at a greater frequency. At Basildon the 248 service to Grays, withdrawn in 1958, was revived but still had to take the circuitous route via Vange (Barge) to Corringham owing to the lack of any outlet from Basildon to the A13 road in a south-westerly direction. Development of suitable omnibus services had been hampered by the lack of roads of sufficient width for the larger passenger vehicles.

The diversion, in June, of the 15 group of services (Southend—Romford) to run from Vange through the new Basildon town centre (omitting Nevendon), to regain the former route at Laindon (Fortune of War) gave further facilities for shoppers and commuters to Basildon from a number of other destinations.

Forty new vehicles formed the replacement programme for 1961 comprising fifteen FLF double-decks, nine of which had Gardner 6LX engines and the remainder Bristol BVW units. The twenty five MW chassis were divided between five 34 seat coaches with 6HLW engines, four 45 seat saloons with 5HLW engines and sixteen 41 seat dual-purpose saloons with 5HLW engines. Five Bristol coaches with 35 seat full-front bodies were acquired from the Tillings Transport unit.

Towards the end of 1961, the Company administration was split into three areas, designated Northern, Central and Southern, as follows:

Northern Area based at Jackson Road, Clacton-on-Sea *
   a) Colchester with outstations at Brightlingsea, West Mersea and Stoke-by-
      Nayland
   b) Clacton-on-Sea with outstations at Walton-on-Naze and Dovercourt,
      and summer offices in Pier Avenue, Clacton and at Jaywick Sands
   c) Halstead
   d) Braintree with an outstation at Silver End

Central Area based at the omnibus station, Duke Street, Chelmsford
   a) Chelmsford with an outstation at Dunmow
   b) Maldon
   c) Bishop's Stortford
   d) Brentwood
   e) Wood Green, London N22

Southern Area based at 17/21 London Road, Southend-on-Sea
   a) Southend-on-Sea (with various offices and garages)
   b) Hadleigh
   c) Canvey Island
   d) Basildon

Note: * Early in 1963, this was transferred to a more central location at the
Company premises in Queen Street, Colchester.

The temporary Basildon premises at Bull Road and 125 Timberley Lane,
Vange were vacated in 1961 when a new garage and offices were completed
at Cherrydown, near the new town centre.

Chapter Seven
Uphill Struggle   1962-1969

The policy of expanding the coaching and express services and fostering the within-town facilities, in step with building developments, was pursued with even greater emphasis right through to 1969, at which point this chapter and, indeed, this volume, is brought to a close.

The increased number of express services compelled the adoption of a new system of identification which first appeared in the literature issued in the spring, now using numbers prefixed by X. Detailed diagrams showing the transition of the services from the old to the new systems are shown in *Appendix B*. They can be broadly summarized as follows:

    X10—X15 for London services
    X20—X27 for Southend services
    X40—X43 for Tilbury/Grays services
    X50—X52 for Bishop's Stortford services
    X60—X64 for Basildon services
    X70 upwards for Chelmsford services
    X90 upwards for Southend & District services

The London to Continental Coach/Air services, via Southend Airport, continued without a symbol.

The only changes to the network to record in 1962 are the renumbering of service X24 to X90, and the withdrawal of service X92 in September, which did not attract sufficient traffic.

The provision of through services to Canvey Island from mainland destinations was at long last accomplished in 1962 as a result of the opening of a new approach road, with an underpass at Benfleet Station which cut out the notorious level-crossing. The following services were now linked to the island route 26; service 3 Southend—Benfleet, via Tarpots, and a new 3A service via Essex Way, both going to Leigh Beck on a ten minute headway, the remaining timings of service 26 going to Tarpots and then westward to Pitsea and Basildon, half-hourly. At the same time, the Canvey local 26C service from Winter Gardens became 3C.

Changes to the pattern of operations at Basildon, where the population had reached some 80,000, were to come thick and fast during the next few years in order to keep pace with the completion of housing programmes and the opening of new link roads. Diversions of parts of services 241—244 (local routes to the industrial sites) were now redesignated 141—144. Service 34A to Chelmsford now became 34 and the Wickford—Pitsea section of the former service now became 231.

A new service which commenced in April 1962 was the 22 Southend—Hullbridge direct, via Eastwood and Rayleigh, and during June, the former service 31 journeys to Chelmsford via Hatfield Peverel became 38. The Clacton area also had changes when service 101A, Clacton—Point Clear was changed to 101; service 113, Great Clacton—Town—Jaywick was divided to run in two parts as 121 and 115 respectively, and service 114A, Burrsville Park—Clacton became part of 114 which, presumably, was done as four characters could not be displayed on a triple-roll indicator blind.

Another change was the extension of service 252, Hutton (Bracken Bank)—Brentwood, to Warley (Woodman Road), using a section off the 261 route which now ran from Stondon Massey, via Hook End to Brentwood Station only . On 2nd July, Eastern National took over the business of Wright Bros. of Harlow, without vehicles. This company had for a few months previously been operating a contract on behalf of the official receiver for the benefit of employees of the British Oxygen Company.

The Company's responsibilities were further increased in 1962 when the administration and engineering requirements of Tillings Transport (BTC) Ltd. was transferred from Grays Inn Road, London to Chelmsford. These coaches enjoyed a special pale grey livery with maroon wings which, after takeover, changed to the familiar Tilling cream and green coach style.

The unmistakable Mk. 2 Bristol MW is represented here by vehicle No. 389. New to Tilling in 1962, this 34 seat coach was absorbed in 1968.

Vehicles moved in and out of the two separate fleets in accordance with traffic requirements and, so far as the public were concerned, it was all one unit.

Once again two basic vehicle types formed the replacement rolling stock programme for 1962. Twenty six FLF double-decks, split between twelve with Gardner 6LX engines and fourteen with Bristol BVW units, arrived together with twenty two MW chassis. The latter were again bodied in three different groups, eight coaches with 6HLW engines and seating split between 34 and 39, eight 45 seat saloons with 5HLW engines and six 41 seat dual-purpose saloons also with the 5HLW unit. Acquired from Tillings Transport were two Bristol LL6G coaches with full-front 35 seat bodied and two LS6G coaches of similar seating capacity. In April 1965, all four were raised in seating capacity to 37. Special mention should be made that three of the FLF6Bs were supplied as 55 seat coaches for use on service X10 between Southend and London.

Great activity, both in stage and express routes, was experienced in 1963. Of particular significance was the provision in London of adequate terminal facilities, after so many years of 'making do' with the temporary arrangements at Euston Square and previously at Judd Street.

The news that the long-established business of Moore Bros. at Kelvedon was to be taken over came as something of a shock to many people, not least

This vehicle was one of the first Bristol RELH 47 seat coaches to be placed in service. No. 579, new in 1964, used mainly on the Company's Continental tours.

R. A. Jenkinson

to the residents of that town where they had been in business for a century and a half. Kelvedon without any Moore's buses and coaches seemed unthinkable to many but, after hearing Harold Moore's statement that, 'We have run out of Moores', the reason became clear. The entire business including the premises and the fleet of three saloon buses, twelve coaches and twenty four serviceable double-decks, was acquired with traffic licences for twelve routes, an express service to Yarmouth and excursions and tours from Braintree, Coggeshall and Kelvedon, particulars of which are as follows:

ENOC No.	Moore No.	Serving	Remarks
38	17	Maldon-Chelmsford, via Hatfield Peverel	Daily, hourly
53	2	Colchester—Chelmsford, via Kelvedon and Witham	Daily, hourly
70	1	Colchester—Braintree, via Coggeshall	Daily, ½ hourly maximum
71	31	Colchester—Earls Colne, via Easthorpe, Kelvedon and Coggeshall	Freq. Kelvedon to Coggeshall 3/4 through runs daily
72	32	Colchester—Tolleshunt Knights, via Stanway and Tiptree	Mon.—Fri. School/Workers
73	3	Colchester—Kelvedon, via Birch and and Tiptree (Ship)	Daily, hourly to Tiptree and garage runs Kelvedon
74	16	Colchester—Tolleshunt Knights, via Birch and Tiptree	2/4 trips daily
331	18	Braintree—West Mersea via Kelvedon and Tiptree	summer Sundays
332	26	Braintree—Pattiswick	2 trips Weds.
334	(3)	Tiptree—Silver End, via Kelvedon	Mon.—Fri. workers
X71	—	Silver End—Yarmouth, via Braintree and Coggeshall	summer Sats.

The above continued unchanged until 1964 when they were more fully integrated into the service network. By way of a change, the network at Basildon remained fairly stable this year, but the 236 Pitsea—Bata Works route was combined with the 245 route from Basildon to the same point. The 260 route, Ongar—Brentwood—Laindon was completely reconstructed; the Laindon—Bulphan portion became 257; the Bulphan or West Hordon or Old Dog—Brentwood Station became service 265; the Warley (Headley Arms)—Brentwood—Blackmore, via Kelvedon Common, now incorporated the London Transport 339A route Warley—Coxtie Green and the

Blackmore—Ongar portion was added to the 261, which thus became Little Warley—Brentwood—Hook End—Blackmore—High Ongar—Ongar. The section between Headley Arms and Great Warley (Waterworks) was abandoned with service 40 Brentwood—Grays covering. Service 260 was also fully co-ordinated with the London Transport 339 route, Warley—Brentwood—Ongar, direct to Epping and Harlow.

At Chelmsford, the 44A town service was divided, Vicarage Road runs became 44 and those via Moulsham Drive, 44A, and service 55, Westlands to Springfield Green, via Beeches Road, became 56A. Service numbers were revised for the Colchester—West Mersea and Brightlingsea routes, and Clacton area arranged new numbers for some deviations from the main route to eliminate the use of suffixes, all shown in the route diagrams.

New services in 1963 were the 124 to connect the Tudor Estate, near Jaywick, with Clacton and Holland; and 283 from Halstead to Sudbury and Stowmarket, which was well outside Eastern National territory. This was originally the 'outer half' of the former 'Corona' coach route from London which was dually-licensed, working as a stage service over this section. After the demise of 'Corona', it passed to Mulley's of Ixworth who, in turn, sold it to Eastern Counties on 4th November 1962. It became joint with Eastern National as from 13th May 1963 whereupon the X14 service was combined with it, working next as Eastern Counties route X, which continued through to Bury St. Edmunds.

In May, the Company began to use the new coach station at Northdown Street, King's Cross, London, recently taken over from Tilling Transport which also continued to use it. It was rebuilt from the former premises of Pat Hearn Ltd., one of the oldest proprietors of coaches in London, by now part of Tilling Transport. It was thoroughly modernized with comfortable waiting accommodation and a very attractive pedestrian entrance from Pentonville Road complete with travel bureau. All the London express services were now channelled through it or terminated there.

The express network was further enlarged for the 1963 season by the extensions to existing facilities and opening up new services in quite a new direction. Having exhausted almost all the possibilities to Essex resorts from within its own ground, a new outward look to distant destinations could be seen. The X28 Southend—Cambridge and X29 to Derby (through the Midlands) services appeared, and a direct X44 service from Basildon also started, while the former Moore's Yarmouth express now continued as X71. Extensions were made from Clacton to Walton on service X27 and from Hastings to Eastbourne on the X23; the X24 now diverted to include Ramsgate, and the X26 to accept bookings through to the Isle of Wight in conjunction with Red Funnel Steamers from Southampton.

The acquisition of Moore's business in February brought forty one vehicles into the Eastern National fleet, all but five of which were of Guy manufacture. Two further Guy double-decks, on order for Moores, joined the Company later. The Guys were of the Arab series, ranging from Mk. I to Mk. IV, and one was converted to a towing wagon, another without any

A facsimile of a Company leaflet, giving details of the London—Southend express coach service which used FLF double-deck vehicles in special livery.

Index Printers

body, three as dual-purpose saloons and seven as coaches. The remaining vehicles consisted of three Commer coaches and two Bedford coaches. All were sold by Eastern National by the end of 1965. Thirty nine new vehicles joined the Company in 1963 and followed a similar pattern in recent years. Thirty two FLF double-decks divided between fourteen with Gardner 6LX engines, and eighteen with Bristol BVW units, plus seven MWs supplied as six 45 seat saloons and one 39 seat coach, with five and six cylinder engines respectively. Further intakes of second-hand stock included one Bristol K6B and five K5G double-decks from Wilts & Dorset, and nine coaches from Tillings Transport Ltd. The latter consisted of four MW6G 34 seaters, three LL6G 35 seaters and two LS6B 34 seaters. The provision of double-deck coaches on service X10 was strengthened by three more FLF6Bs being so equipped to carry 55 passengers.

In 1964, there occurred the most extensive reorganization of stage services ever carried out in the Company's history. The opening of Nethermayne, the long awaited link road, going south-west from Basildon to the A13 road, was the signal for a general recasting of numerous services in that area. This included the cross-country 51/53 routes from Tilbury to Clacton and Harwich, which had remained unchanged for over thirty years, with corresponding repercussions throughout the eastern half of the system. The opportunity also enabled the services of Moore, 'City Coach' and parts of 'Westcliff', all of which were still almost intact, to be welded into an integrated network tailored to current requirements, with some valuable economies to help overcome the acute shortage of platform staff which existed in the south-east area of Essex. A similar and to some extent related exercise was simultaneously undertaken with Southend & District Joint Services. The list of alterations is far too long to be dealt with here, but all are recorded on the route diagrams shown in *Appendix B*. The rerouting of the 51/53 services *(see above)* and the division of service 251, Wood Green—Southend, at Billericay, so that alternate trips passed through Basildon, meant that the new town now had direct bus services to almost all parts of the Eastern National network. Also, from Canvey to Basildon the 26 service was now extended westward to Upminster and Romford.

Another event that was to benefit the Company was the opening of the Dartford Tunnel under the River Thames, to link Essex with Kent, and so eliminate long delays during the season at the Tilbury-Gravesend ferry, or the long detour via North Woolwich or the Blackwall Tunnel. Eastern National had long prepared plans for this event, as of course had the operators on the other side of the water. All concerned got together to provide a totally new group of joint services via the tunnel, jointly operated and promoted as Dartford Tunnel Coachways (DTC), for which a very distinctive and rather jolly motif was devised, which could be used by all the partners.

The first DTC services which used common X series numbers were:

X30 Southend—Basildon to Bognor—Southsea	Joint with Southdown
X32 Clacton—Basildon to Dover—Folkestone	Joint with East Kent
X33 Walton—Basildon to Chatham—Hastings	Joint with Maidstone & District
X34 Clacton—Basildon to Margate—Ramsgate	Joint with East Kent

A fine view of Bristol MW6G No. 1432 climbing North Hill, Colchester, on the ex-Sudbury service 86.

The other changes to the express network this year included the extension of service X15 from Maldon to Mill Beach and West Mersea; combining the X51 Harlow—Jaywick with the X50 Bishop's Stortford—Clacton, and the merging of services X60—X64 from Pitsea to the coast, with the similar X20—X24 starting at Southend. There was also a new X43 Southend—Skegness service started this year. The important London to Southend Coach/Air services were now numbered X1 and extended to commence at Victoria Coach Station, London, calling at King's Cross and additional picking up points en route. It was also extended at the other end to run from the airport to the Pier Hill Coach Station, to provide connections with a steamer route to Paris or Ostend in conjunction with Eagle Steamers which called at the pier. A new enquiry and booking office opened this year at 29 High Street, Harlow in the former premises of Wright Bros.

Closure of the Wivenhoe—Brightlingsea branch railway called for replacement buses as from 15th June 1964. These quite inexplicably took passengers to the small country station at Alresford as route 74 with one trip to the Wivenhoe Station. The majority then ran through to Colchester to terminate at the bus station, but without contact at either of the Colchester railway stations. Town services continued to receive attention with ad-

Later Bristol FLFs were fitted with Cave-Browne-Cave heating in which the conventional radiator was removed, and two smaller units, controlled by varivane shutters, were housed at each side of the destination box. Here No. 2872 pulls away from Southend bus station, bound for Grays.

G. R. Mills

ditional facilities being provided at Billericay, Brentwood, Chelmsford and Witham. At Bishop's Stortford, part of the London Transport service 350A from the town to Havers Lane Estate was taken over and combined with the existing 309 town route.

Amidst all this welter of reorganization, it was deemed necessary to completely renumber the whole fleet once again! Ten years had passed since the last renumbering and a new system, breaking each model down into groups, spaced at intervals of 100, enabled greater scope for the future without the fear of clashes. The second scheme was introduced on Sunday, 9th August 1964, and was along the following lines:

Coaches
100 — Commer TS3
200 — Bristol LL
300 — Bristol LS and MW
400 — Bristol RELH
500 — Bedford

Single-Deck
1000 — second-hand Tiger Cub ex Mansfield
            and District
1100 — Bristol L, LL and LWL
1200 — Bristol LS
1300 — Bristol MW
1400 — Bristol MW dual-purpose
1500 — later Bristol RELL
1600 — Bristol RELH dual-purpose

Double-Deck
2000 — Guy
2100 — Leyland PD1 and PD2
2200 — Bristol K
2300 — Bristol KS and KSW
2400 — Bristol LD and FS
2500 — Bristol LD and FS
2600 — Bristol FLF coach
2700 — Bristol FLF
2800 — Bristol FLF

Fifty eight new vehicles arrived in 1964, among them being some interesting departures from Bristol ECW tradition in the form of six Bedford/Duple 41 seat coaches. The most exciting newcomer was the Bristol RE which heralded the new 36ft. length of which all manufacturers were quick to take advantage. The RE was unusual in having an engine at the rear and the ECW 47 seat body, with forced air ventilation, and sealed windows gave little indication of this feature. Powered by the Gardner 6HLX engine, through a five speed syncromesh gearbox, they looked very impressive and formed the basis of the next generation in vehicle design. The RE was suitable for bus and coach bodies in low and high frame heights and both could be made available in long or short versions. Fifteen chassis were supplied to the Company, seven bodied as full coaches and the rest as dual-purpose saloons. Other replacement vehicles comprised three MW6G 39 seat coaches and thirty four FLFs, twenty with Gardner 6LX engines and the rest with the Bristol BVW unit. Two of the latter were supplied as 55 seat coaches for the X services. The intake for 1964 was completed with the purchase of three 34 seat MW6G coaches from United Counties.

There was another long list of service changes in 1965, mainly effected on 11th April. Many resulted from experience gained after the last upheval, but not a few could be attributed to further new road layouts at Basildon, and the need to equate working costs with revenue. Thus the changes included a further weeding out of lightly-used country routes and some axeing of Sunday workings. On the other hand, town services were improved as was the express network. The more important happenings were the entire withdrawal of the Sunday service on routes 19A, 33A, 34, 34A, 72, 231, 232 and 252. Other withdrawals were part of route 79 (covered by Osborne), routes 82 and 83 were combined, Wiston spur on route 85 ceased, the 283 only ran on Saturdays, the deviation to Littlebury service on 301, and parts of service 320 also came off.

The sleek lines of the Bristol RELH coach body is enhanced by the broad centre band. Purchased in 1968, vehicle No. 407 was used primarily on trips to the Continent but, on occasions, would be found on local services as is the case here at Fairfield Road, Chelmsford.

G. R. Mills

A second straight line across Essex was made this year when the separate services between Bishop's Stortford—Braintree, Braintree—Colchester, and Colchester—Harwich were linked to run on an hourly headway and numbered 70. Another linking was the Walton—Colchester 105 service to run on to Maldon as 19, and a joint route with Eastern Counties was started from Harwich to Ipswich, via Manningtree as service 212. Chelmsford received further new town routes, 51, 51A, and 51B, and route 207, Colchester—Ipswich, now diverted via Langham instead of Eastern Counties service 247 doing so.

Little has been said of the Extended Tours Department operated by the Company in succession to 'Westcliff' with whom this was a special activity. They continued to be so promoted under the old name until, at least, 1961, the current programme comprising a choice of five 'Seeing Britain' tours between five and twelve days duration, supplemented by a choice of four shorter spring and autumn tours which had departures from Southend, Brentwood, Romford and London in conjunction with Thomas Cook Ltd. In 1959, a whole new series commenced with departures from Chelmsford, Colchester, Clacton and other points in the northern part of the county, mainly of three days duration with a choice of three destinations. By 1962, these had been expanded to give a choice of eleven and, two years later, the two divisions were combined into a single programme, offering twenty three distinctly different tours from London and all over the Eastern National system.

The express network was again enlarged in 1965 as follows. The X40 now started from Gillingham instead of Tilbury; the X50 was extended to Jaywick Sands; the X10 now had a spur to Canvey Island, its first coach link with London; the X33 now ran on to Eastbourne from Hastings and the X52 was rerouted to give a Felixstowe destination to Halstead and Sudbury for the first time. The spur to Hadleigh on service X14 was now replaced by an Eastern Counties bus connection and service X21 was withdrawn by extending the X23 to cover. Completely new introductions this season were:

X35 Basildon—Tunbridge Wells (DTC)
X45 Sudbury—Basildon (to connect with all the DTC routes)
X46 Southend—Norwich (joint with ECOC route M)
X51 Bishop's Stortford—Southend (joint with Biss Bros.)

The ever increasing quantity of printed marketing material needed to promote the much enlarged express and tours business, led to the decision to set up a printing and graphic design section at New Writtle Street, Chelmsford. One of its first ideas was the creation of a new Company logo to head up its timetables, handbills and general literature, the unique part of the emblem comprising the Colchester Rose with the spire of Chelmsford Cathedral rising from the centre of the bloom. It also appeared with the Company name set round in circular fashion.

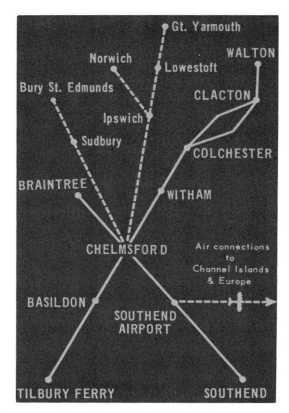

Replacement rolling stock for 1965 comprised thirty four FLF double-decks, sixteen with Gardner 6LX engines and eighteen with the Bristol BVW unit. Two of the latter were finished as 59 seat coaches, and three MW5G 43 seat dual-purpose saloons completed orders for new vehicles. Twelve second-hand coaches were taken over from Tillings Transport Ltd. including seven LS6B, three MW6G and two Bedford SB models, with seating capacities ranging between 39 and 43.

The same policy pattern was continued throughout 1966 by exploiting the coaching side and the town services, but continuing the thinning out of off-peak and rural routes, and also Sunday workings, in an endeavour to maintain financial viability. Mainly implemented in May, some reductions were planned particularly because the continuing staff shortage in South Essex had already led to unannounced service cuts. An interesting innovation this summer was the introduction of a batch of 'Limited Stop' services across the country which gave speedier journeys without the need to pre-book. The Southend trips were arranged to terminate at the Seaway Coach Park, which was within a few steps of the Esplanade, Kursaal and Pier. The map shows the routes taken by these services.

Further services were introduced in the Basildon area, its population now nearly 90,000, with another 7,000 inhabitants at Pitsea, 17,000 at Wickford and 11,000 at Laindon. The existing bus terminal had become stretched to capacity and temporary picking up points had to be organized while work proceeded on a new bus station. The express coaches used the garage at Cherrydown and the 2/2A Southend—Grays buses were also routed through Basildon.

A new feature by the Tours Department, in 1966, was a group of Centred Holidays arranged in Northern Ireland, the Isle of Wight, Bournemouth and Folkestone. Also new was a Chelmsford—Tilbury coach service in connection with the Stena Line of ships to Calais. A range of new express coach routes to the West Country appeared this season, jointly worked with 'Royal Blue' or 'Bristol Greyhound' as follows:

X2 from Sudbury, etc. to West Country resorts
X3 from Southend, etc. to West Country resorts
X4 from Southend to Bristol and Weston-super-Mare
X31 from Clacton/Basildon to Portsmouth/Southsea (DTC)

The X15 London—Maldon did not run in 1966, no doubt as a result of the much-improved train services now in operation, and the X45 Sudbury—Basildon service was extended to Worthing along with a few other small improvements.

The rail replacement service for Brightlingsea, alluded to earlier, was now allowed to run to Colchester North Station to connect with fast trains; a much more useful arrangement. There were a number of minor route changes involving quite a few service number changes, all of which are recorded in *Appendix B*.

The 'Limited Stop' services introduced last year were evidently a success for they were repeated again in 1967, but now running with 400 added to the normal route number instead of using the prefix E. The Southend—Grays route was extended through the tunnel to Dartford, these journeys becoming 402 instead of 2. Three new town services were started at Chelmsford, Bishop's Stortford and Braintree, and one new country service was started from Chelmsford to Fuller Street, via Little Waltham, as service 314. A rather unusual event was the introduction of services from Colchester to Harwich, via Great Oakley, etc. which had been purchased from R. W. Hooks by Ewer's 'Grey Green' coaches. It paralleled its coach route from London to Harwich which now only received a through vehicle when sufficient bookings justified the run, passengers normally travelling by stage bus provided by this company. The service also incorporated the existing service 80 from Colchester to Tendring Hospital, retaining that number, and included a short spur route to Stones Green as 80A. As from 8th October 1967, this service also became part of a new pool known as 'Essex Coach Express' embracing all the services run to Harwich, Clacton-on-Sea and Walton-on-Naze by 'Grey Green', Eastern National and Sutton's Coaches of Clacton.

One more express route to the West Country began between Southend and Ilfracombe in conjunction with 'Royal Blue'. Service X28, Southend—Cambridge, now joint with Eastern Counties, was projected to Northampton and Birmingham, with Midland Red and Premier Travel sharing the timings. The X44 Harwich to Basildon service continued to Horsham (DTC) and Biss Bros. of Bishop's Stortford now shared workings on the X2.

The variety of services now being offered in the Company's travel bureau had become so comprehensive, covering every aspect and type of travel, that it became a full member of the Association of British Travel Agents (ABTA). Two more important new features came into the programme this year with the introduction of 'No Passport' day visits to the Continent via Lympne Airport, and a range of Continental tours took the Company into France, Belgium and Holland for the first time. However, these exciting new ventures were not permitted to distract attention from matters nearer home, for the express route from London to Basildon had been steadily increased until it offered a coach every half-hour to Basildon, whence they divided to run direct by the Arterial Road or by Hadleigh and Leigh to Southend, or to Benfleet and Canvey Island.

A few small extensions to note among the stage services are as follows:

84 from Colchester to Langham Wick arranged jointly with Mrs Bennett
230 extended to Stanford-le-Hope
241 extended to Laindon Station
331 Great Bardfield—Braintree—Witham divided; the section to Witham via the Notleys becoming service 339
338 Heybridge (Brewster House) — Maldon. A new local service

Double-deck replacement was again of paramount importance in 1967 when thirty three FLFs joined the fleet, this time all with Gardner 6LX engines. Three RELH6G 45 seat dual-purpose saloons were transferred from Tillings Transport Ltd. These vehicles had been new to Eastern National in 1964, passing to the Tillings Travel unit in May 1965. The double-decks deserve special mention in that they were the first vehicles in the fleet with semi-automatic transmission.

Another spate of service alterations occurred in 1968, with one of the more significant being the final abandonment of the Romford—Bow section of the former 'Hillman' route from Chelmsford to Bow, the last remnant of that one-time renowned business which despatched a coach every five minutes (three minutes at peak hours) to some point along the line to East Anglia. Some of the former Bow buses now ran to Wood Green instead as service 351, the 30 service, between Chelmsford and Brentwood, being combined with the 40 to Tilbury and, at the same time, the 30B becoming 40A. Also the final stretch of the Wood Green route now worked from Tottenham by way of West Green Road instead of using Bruce Grove and Lordship Lane.

The complex of services between Southend and Basildon were revised with changes of service numbers, and a new service to Rayleigh, the only town for miles around without a direct link, was now started as service 150.

In the coaching field, one more new service appeared from Clacton to Basildon and on to Ashford and Rye (DTC), the X36, and a few extensions to existing routes were effected. Another express pool commenced on 26th May when all services to Suffolk and Norfolk became part of the 'East Anglian Express' operated by Eastern Counties, Eastern National and 'Grey Green', to be later joined by 'Norfolk Coachways'. The X14 service to Bury St. Edmunds now continued through to Norwich, becoming merged into the Eastern Counties route F. Journeys to Canvey on the X10 were now separated as X7, the X1 to Southend became X8 and the X4 to Weston-super-Mare became X9. The X71 became part of the East Anglian pool and the X43 to Skegness did not fulfil expectations and was, therefore, discontinued. At Norwich the X46 now continued on to Cromer and Sheringham, while Frank Harris Coaches of Grays shared in the X3 service to the West Country.

Twenty eight new vehicles joined the fleet in 1968. The REs this year came with semi-automatic transmission and consisted of four long version with 47 seat ECW coach bodies and four short version with 36 seat Duple bodies. Twenty FLFs were also supplied, all with the Gardner 6LX unit, five of which were finished in 55 seat coach layout. Nine MWs formed the annual transfer of vehicles from the Tillings Transport fleet, seven being 34 seaters with the Gardner 6HLW engine. The remaining two were 41 seat dual-purpose saloons with 5HLW engines, which had originally been new to Eastern National in 1961 and transferred to the Tilling unit in May 1965.

A number of changes came into effect in 1969 in time for inclusion in the annual mid-year timetable. These largely simplified service numbering in the Southend Joint or Basildon district. The Southend & District Joint 20/22 group received considerable attention as did services 34 and 34A at Basildon which became 234 and 235, bringing them into the Basildon series from the Chelmsford group, as they no longer went that way. Service 34B was deleted as other services now covered the same ground. For the same reason, service 53A, Grays—Basildon, via Laindon, now became 249 and the 230 Pitsea—Corringham disappeared when the 244/255 and a new 256 were rearranged to run Billericay—Great or Little Burstead—Laindon and Basildon to North Benfleet as 254 or to Fobbing, Corringham and Stanford-le-Hope (255/256).

The express services to the West Country continued to gain in popularity, largely because they cut out the change and wait in London for the connecting coach before continuing, or when transferring from one terminus to another which the railways were/are powerless to do much about. The following additions were made:

X13 Southend—Brentwood ⎫
X14 Sudbury—Bishop's Stortford ⎬ to Torbay resorts
X15 Ipswich—Chelmsford ⎫
X16 Southend—Brentwood ⎬ to Minehead/Ilfracombe

Also new were

X61 Dagenham—Stansted Airport
X62 Southend—Stansted Airport

In 1969, the field of holiday travel and other facilities required the production of a superbly-designed all-colour large quarto booklet to portray all the good things the Company's Excursion and Tours Department had to offer. There were more tours than ever before within the United Kingdom and no fewer than eighteen to Continental destinations covering almost all of Europe, including Austria and Hungary. The number of 'Centred Holidays' was again increased and pick-up points now reached as far as Letchworth, Cambridge and Peterborough, with additional ones within the London area.

The coach/air section was stepped up with facilities being offered in conjunction with Channel Airways through Stansted Airport, and with British Air Ferries via Southend. The 'No Passport' tours had been so well-received that a wider choice was now offered including some which travelled all the way by coach to most of the Normandy coastal resorts, and also to Dunkirk, Bruges and Brussels.

Tillings Travel continued to operate the extensive range of tours in and around London and its surrounding beauty spots for overseas visitors, which for long had been a speciality of P. Hearn Ltd. Later in the year, this section was reconstituted as Tillings Transport (NBC) Ltd. which a few years later, in company with Eastern National's huge Coaching and Travel Department and fleet, formed the basis of National Travel (South-East) Ltd.

The Company was always on the look out for new ideas which might encourage people to make greater use of its services so, in 1969, a free push-chair loan scheme was started, suitably promoted by notices saying 'Don't put off your visit because of baby — Eastern National will loan you a very smart push-chair to make your load lighter and your visit more pleasant'. The 'service' operated at Southend, Chelmsford, Maldon, Colchester, Clacton and Halstead depots/terminals. This innovation must place Eastern National on record as being one of the few omnibus companies to possess pedestrian-operated vehicles for its patrons!

Just before the year ended, a gap in the Company network was filled, between Dunmow and Saffron Walden, hitherto served by F. C. Moore's 'Viceroy' service which, without any prior notice whatever, ceased operation on 11th December. There was no service over the route for the next three days but, on 15th December, Eastern National was able to arrange a tem-

The Bristol RELL formed the basis of replacement single-deck programmes for the late 1960s/early 1970s, and here, No. 1506, new in 1969, stands in Colchester depot yard.

G. R. Mills

porary service which shortly after became an extension of its existing 33 route, Chelmsford—Dunmow, creating a new and useful cross-country link. All journeys now travelled via Little Easton village whereas some of the 'Viceroy' trips stayed on the main road.

Intake of new vehicles in 1969 witnessed the arrival of a third model of the RE for the first time. The long, low stage-bodied version with 53 seats and semi-automatic transmission was powered by the Gardner 6HLX engine, and twenty of these were purchased to replace ageing stock of early 1950 vintage. The rear engined double-deck, already well proven by other manufacturers, was at last produced by Bristol in the shape of the VR. Five of these were delivered to replace KSWs of early 1950 vintage. The VR seating was a modest 70 and therefore was no greater than the FLF at first but, in later years, this figure was increased. The main advantage with the VR, however, was its ability to be one man operated. Four vehicles were purchased second-hand during the year, one Bedford and two FLF coaches coming from Tillings Transport. The latter two had been new to Eastern National in 1963/4 and transferred to Tillings later. The other vehicle came from United Automobile Services, and was a 45 seat LS5G, dating from 1952.

The new generation double-deck arrived just before the end of 1969 in the shape of the Bristol VRT. Vehicle No. 3003 is seen working on one of the busy Clacton town services, soon after delivery.

G. R. Mills

EPILOGUE

This volume closes at 1969, a year in which the omnibus industry started a new epoch, when all major operators were transferred from the Transport Holding Company to a new organization named the National Bus Company, created by the then Minister of Transport, Mrs Barbara Castle. It is doubtful if the travelling public will have been in any way impressed with the alteration, for much that has occurred since then has been associated with higher fares and fewer services, albeit largely the result of circumstances quite beyond the control of the bus operators themselves.

The year 1969 is also noteworthy in that just sixty years earlier, in June 1909, the original fleetname 'National' was born in Chelmsford when the National Steam Car Co. Ltd. was formed by Thomas Clarkson for the construction of omnibuses at Moulsham Works to operate on the streets of London. Eastern National was created out of the parent concern in 1929, registered in 1930 and celebrated its Golden Jubilee in 1980, while 1969 marks the Diamond Jubilee of Clarkson's operations in London. Clarkson could never have imagined, even in his most optimistic moments, when his first four quaint-looking steam-buses started work in London on that November day, what the outcome would eventually be; that his infant company would develop into part of the group of major operating companies to be known as Eastern National, Southern National and Western National. In 1919, the internal combustion engine replaced his steam-engine, in which he had placed so much faith and effort, which events showed to have been misplaced so far as the motor vehicle was concerned. However, there is talk today among the cognoscenti that, in the event of it becoming necessary at some future time to substitute nuclear fuel for fossil fuel as the power source in the automobile, it could then once again be the turn of the steam-engine to return as the prime mover. If this should be the case, then perhaps some of the vast amount of research which Clarkson performed will not have been in vain after all.

Eastern National will undoubtedly have many problems to deal with in the future, for the limit and extent to which private transport may yet reach before saturation point comes cannot now be long delayed. Then perhaps the market for public transport may stabilize so that the Company can devise a suitable strategy, as sure it will, as it has done in the past, to meet that situation and provide the travelling public with the best possible service it can offer.

Appendix A

Rolling Stock

The rolling stock information in this appendix is not fully comprehensive. Consideration of space and the fact that readers seeking detailed information can obtain such material from specialized sources precludes its inclusion. The appendix has been designed to show, at a glance, sufficient basic detail to compare notes and identify illustrations shown throughout the book. Further details can also be found in the captions to the photographs.

The Eastern National fleet was renumbered in 1954 and again in 1964 and, to make identification of stock numbers easy to understand, the appendix has been arranged in one vehicle per line with each successive fleet number starting the entry.

During the period of this volume, much vehicle rebodying and rebuilding was carried out. Some of the Beadle rebuilds were very extensive and a new body was virtually constructed but, during the period when raw materials were scarce, the rebuild often incorporated much that was salvaged from the old. Many were officially classed as rebuilds but could have justifiably been described as rebodies. However, the official description is used throughout and only rebuilds are shown within parenthesis.

In describing the layout of bodywork, the generally accepted coding has been used as it is compact and easily assimilated. It is in three parts; a prefix letter(s) indicating the type of vehicle, followed by numbers denoting the seating capacity, and terminating with letter(s) to show the position and pattern of entrance and exits. The code is:

Prefixes

B   Single-deck saloon
C   Coach (not a charabanc)
Ch Charabanc (forerunner of coach with separate door to each row of seats)
L   Lowbridge height double-deck
H   Highbridge height double-deck
OT Open-top (no roof on double-deck)
F   Preceding B or C denotes that the normally half-cab model has been constructed as 'full front'
DP Dual-purpose (bus body with coach seats)
LC Lowbridge height double-deck coach

Seating

Split numbers show upper deck first

Suffixes

C   Central entrance/exit
D   Dual entrance/exit
F   Front entrance
R   Rear entrance
RO Rear entrance with open stairs
T   Toastrack (bench seating in charabanc fashion, but without doors or sides)

Fleet No.	Regn. No.	Chassis	Make	Layout	Remarks
2002	HK5028	AEC YC		B31	
2003	HK5048	AEC YC		B31	new 1919
2004	HK5114	AEC YC	Hickman	OT28/26RO	
2005	HK5047	AEC YC		B32	
2014	HK6814	AEC YC	Dodson	OT30/26RO	
2016	BM7761	AEC YC		B32	
2021	BM7766	AEC YC	NOTC	OT22/22RO	
2025	BM7812	AEC YC		OT30/26RO	
2028	NO194	AEC YC	Dodson	OT28/26RO	
2029	BM7816	AEC YC	Dodson	OT28/26RO	
2030	BM8018	AEC YC	Hickman	OT28/26RO	
2031	BM8019	AEC YC	Hickman	OT28/26RO	
2033	BM8021	AEC YC	Dodson	OT28/26RO	
2034	BM8022	AEC YC		OT28/26RO	
2042	BM8305	AEC YC	Dodson	OT28/26RO	
2043	BM8320	AEC YC	Dodson	OT28/26RO	
2045	HK7212	AEC YC	Dodson	OT28/26RO	new 1920
2047	BM8365	AEC YC	Hickman	OT28/26RO	
2048	HK7267	AEC YC		B	
2050	HK7288	AEC YC	Dodson	OT28/26RO	
2053	AD6863	AEC YC		B	
2055	HK7545	AEC YC	Dodson	OT28/26RO	
2062	HK7644	AEC YC		OT30/26RO	
2065	AD7310	AEC YC	Dodson	OT30/26RO	
2071	Y8585	AEC YC		B32	
2073	HK8169	AEC YC	Dodson	OT30/26RO	
2074	XA9730	AEC YC	Dodson	OT28/26RO	
2076	XA9894	AEC YC	Hickman	OT28/26RO	
2077	XA9904	AEC YC	Hickman	OT28/26RO	
2079	HK8553	AEC YC	Dodson	OT28/26RO	
2080	XB8077	AEC YC	Dodson	OT28/26RO	
2081	HK8572	AEC YC		B31	
2082	HK8573	AEC YC		OT28/26RO	
2083	HK8635	AEC YC		B31	
2085	Y8983	AEC YC	Dodson	B31 (B32)	
2086	HK8644	AEC YC	Dodson	OT28/26RO	
2088	HK8958	AEC YC	Dodson	OT28/24RO	
2089	HK8957	AEC YC	Dodson	OT28/26RO	
2090	HK9077	AEC YC		OT28/26RO	
2094	Y9287	AEC YC		B31	
2097	HK9406	AEC YC		B32	
2109	YA749	AEC YC	Dodson	OT28/26RO	
2163	NM2010	Burford 30 cwt	Hickman	B14F	new 1922
2168	NO9101	AEC YC	(Hickman)	B30	
2172	NO9560	AEC YC	Hickman	B30	new 1923
2175	NO9940	AEC YC	Dodson	OT28/26RO	
2177	NO9858	AEC YC	Hickman	OT28/26RO	
2179	PU2128	AEC YC	Dodson	OT28/24RO	
2180	NM4458	AEC YC		B30	
2181	PU3052	AEC YC	Dodson	OT28/24RO	
2183	PU2809	AEC YC	Dodson	OT28/24RO	
2184	PU2808	AEC YC	Dodson	OT28/24RO	new 1924
2185	PU3051	AEC YC	Dodson	OT28/24RO	
2188	PU3477	AEC YC	Strachan & Brown	B32	
2191	XF9024	Unic		Ch14	
2201	FX5962	Daimler CK	Strachan & Brown	B22R	
2208	(PU5737)	Chevrolet	London Lorries	B14F	
2214	NM6141	AEC YC	Dodson	OT30/26RO	
2215	PU6992	AEC YC	Dodson	OT30/26RO	
2216	BP9307	AEC YC		OT30/26RO	
2220	PU8663	AEC YC	Dodson	OT30/26RO	new 1925
2221	CC4240	AEC YC	Dodson	OT30/26RO	

Fleet No.	Regn. No.	Chassis	Make	Layout	Remarks
2223	FX7322	Daimler		Ch28	
2224	PU7691	AEC YC	Dodson	OT28/26RO	new 1925
2225	PU7923	AEC YC	Dodson	OT28/26RO	
2226	PU8156	AEC YC		B31	
2228	FX5523	Daimler CK	Strachan & Brown	B22R	
2229	FX6061	Daimler CK	Strachan & Brown	B22R	
2230	FX5042	Daimler CK	Dodson	OT30/26RO	
2232	PU8580	AEC YC	Dodson	OT28/26RO	
2234	PU7841	Lancia Penta	Dodson	B20F	Beadle C20 —/30
2236	NM4481	Dennis 35hp	Dodson	B32R	
2241	BM8249	AEC YC		OT24/24RO	
2245	BM7702	Dennis 40hp		B	
2246	BM8315	Dennis 40hp		B31	C29
2254	NM1020	Dennis	Dodson	B32R	
2255	NM1139	Dennis		B32R	acqd/new 1925
2258	NM1383	Dennis 35hp		B32R	
2270	NM5268	Dennis B	Dodson	B32R	
2271	NM5266	Dennis B	Dodson	B32R	
2273	NM5656	Daimler CK		B24	
2274	NM5657	Daimler CK		B26	
2275	NM5658	Daimler CK	Short	B20	
2276	NM5771	Daimler CK	Short	B20	
2277	NM5948	Daimler CKA	Short	B20	
2278	PU9037	AEC YC	Dodson	OT30/26RO	
2281	LU8940	AEC YC	Dodson	OT30/26RO	
2283	NM7822	Daimler	Dodson	B32	
2287	TW4121	AEC YC	Hickman	OT28/26RO	
2304	TW3699	Guy BB	London Lorries	C25D	
2306	TW4066	Guy BB	London Lorries	C25D	
2307	TW3101	Guy BB	London Lorries	C25D	
2311	TW3614	Guy BB	London Lorries	C25D	new 1926
2312	TW4055	Guy BB	London Lorries	C25D	
2314	TW4095	Guy BB	London Lorries	C25D	
2315	TW3853	Guy BB	London Lorries	C25D	
2318	EW3726	Berliet		B20	
2321	EW4109	Berliet		B20	
2322	EW2576	Daimler CK		B26	
2326	LU8943	AEC YC	Dodson	OT28/26RO	
2328	XM9717	AEC YC	Dodson	OT28/26RO	
2329	XM7092	AEC B	Dodson	OT28/26RO	Possibly YC type, not B
2343	VW196	Leyland PLC1	Strachan & Brown	B26R	
2349	TW8929	Leyland PLC1	London Lorries	C26D	
2350	TW9350	Leyland PLC1	Beadle	C26D	
2354	TW9347	Leyland PLC1	Beadle	C26D	
2375	TW9352	ADC 416A	Strachan & Brown	C28D	
2383	TW8936	ADC 416A	Strachan & Brown	B32D	
2386	TW8930	ADC 416A	Strachan & Brown	B32D	
2393	NM645	Daimler CB		B32	
2394	DD6205	Morris T2		lorry	
2395	DD6204	Morris T2		lorry	
2402	VW198	Leyland PLSC3	Strachan & Brown	B32R	acqd/new 1927
2403	VW199	Leyland PLSC3	Strachan & Brown	B32R	
2409	VW205	Leyland PLSC3	Strachan & Brown	B32R	
2430	TM1932	Leyland PLSC3	Strachan & Brown	B32R	
2431	TM1861	Leyland PLSC3	Strachan & Brown	B32R	
2432	TM1862	Leyland PLSC3	Strachan & Brown	B32R	
2433	VW2133	Leyland PLSC3	Strachan & Brown	B32R	
2434	TM1864	Leyland PLSC3	Strachan & Brown	B32R	
2435	TM1882	Leyland PLSC3	Strachan & Brown	B32R	
2465	UO478	Lancia 6 wheeler		B32	
2490	VW2739	Leyland PLSC3	Strachan	B32R	
2491	VW2506	Leyland PLSC3	Strachan	B32R	
2492	TM2027	Leyland PLSC3	London Lorries	C26F	later downgraded to B26F
2493	TM2048	Leyland PLSC3	London Lorries	C26F	later downgraded to B26F
2494	VW2795	Leyland PLSC3	Strachan	B31R	new 1928
2495	VW2773	Leyland PLSC3	Strachan	B31R	

Fleet No.	Regn. No.	Chassis	Body carried 1929 Make	Layout	Remarks
2496	TM2211	Leyland PLSC3	Strachan	B31R	
2498	TM2264	Leyland PLSC3	Strachan	B31R	Recovery vehicle —/38
2499	VW2903	Leyland PLSC3	Strachan	B31R	
2501	TM2094	Leyland PLSC3	Strachan	B31R	
2502	TM2110	Leyland PLSC3	Strachan	B31R	
2503	TM2126	Leyland PLSC3	Strachan	B31R	
2504	TM2185	Leyland PLSC3	Strachan	B31R	
2505	TM2165	Leyland PLSC3	Strachan	B31R	
2506	VW2990	Leyland PLSC3	Strachan	B31R	
2507	VW3015	Leyland PLSC3	Strachan	B31R	
2516	TM2265	Leyland PLSC3	Strachan	B32R	
2521	VW3512	Leyland PLSC3	Strachan	B32R	
2522	TM2394	Leyland PLSC3	Strachan	B32R	
2523	TM2395	Leyland PLSC3	Strachan	B32R	
2525	TM2439	Leyland PLSC3	Strachan	B32R	
2537	TM2700	Leyland PLSC3	Strachan	C31R	ECOC B30R —/33 (Beadle —/42)
2541	VW4747	Leyland PLSC3	Strachan	C31R	ECOC B30R —/33
2542	VW4744	Leyland PLSC3	Strachan	C31R	ECOC B30R —/33
2543	VW4746	Leyland PLSC3	Strachan	C31R	ECOC B30R —/33
2603	VW4711	Leyland PLSC3	Beadle	B32R	
2609	VW6010	Leyland PLSC3	Beadle	B32R	
2744	NC1843	Daimler		B	
2760	AF2227	AEC YC		Ch30	also described as B30
2783	TM3724	Leyland TD1	Leyland	L24/24RO	
2784	TM3734	Leyland TD1	Leyland	L24/24RO	ECW L27/28R —/42
2785	TM3736	Leyland TD1	Leyland	L24/24RO	
2786	TM3735	Leyland TD1	Leyland	L24/24RO	acqd/new 1928
2787	TM3744	Leyland TD1	Leyland	L24/24RO	
2788	TM3751	Leyland TD1	Leyland	L24/24RO	
2789	TM3824	Leyland TD1	Leyland	L24/24RO	
2790	TM3827	Leyland TD1	Leyland	L24/24RO	
2791	TM3843	Leyland TD1	Leyland	L24/24RO	
2792	TM3846	Leyland TD1	Leyland	L24/24RO	
2796	TM3882	Leyland PLSC3	Strachan	B32R	Beadle B32R —/38
2797	TM3871	Leyland PLSC3	Strachan	B32R	ECW B32R —/39 (Beadle —/41)
2798	TM3872	Leyland PLSC3	Strachan	B32R	ECW B32R —/38
2799	TM3883	Leyland PLSC3	Strachan	B32R	ECW B32R —/38, then Duple B32R —/43
2801	VW7786	Leyland PLSC3	Strachan	B32R	Beadle B32R —/38
2803	VW7347	Leyland PLSC3	Strachan	B32R	Beadle B32R —/38
2804	VW7345	Leyland PLSC3	Strachan	B32R	Beadle B32R —/38
2805	TM3884	Leyland PLSC3	Strachan	B32R	Beadle B32R —/38
2806	TM3885	Leyland PLSC3	Strachan	B32R	ECW B32R —/39
2807	TM3886	Leyland PLSC3	Strachan	B32R	
2808	TM3887	Leyland PLSC3	Strachan	B32R	Beadle B32R —/38
2809	VW7644	Leyland PLSC3	Strachan	B32R	Beadle B32R —/38
2810	VW7645	Leyland PLSC3	Strachan	B32R	Beadle B32R —/38
2811	TM3888	Leyland PLSC3	Strachan	B32R	ECW B32R —/38 Body to 3420
2813	TM3889	Leyland PLSC3	Strachan	B32R	ECW B32R —/39
2814	TM3939	Leyland PLSC3	Strachan	B32R	
2815	TM3940	Leyland PLSC3	Strachan	B32R	Beadle B32R —/39
2817	VW7722	Leyland PLSC3	Strachan	B32R	
2819	VW7787	Leyland PLSC3	Strachan	B32R	Beadle B32R —/38
2820	VW7721	Leyland PLSC3	Strachan	B32R	Beadle B32R —/38
1929					
2822	TM4158	Leyland PLSC3	Strachan	B32R	Beadle B32R —/38
2823	VW8149	Leyland PLSC3	Strachan	B32R	Beadle B32R —/38
2824	TM4159	Leyland PLSC3	Strachan	B32R	ECW B30R —/38
2825	VW8150	Leyland PLSC3	Strachan	B32R	Beadle B32R —/38
2827	TM4245	Leyland PLSC3	Strachan	B32R	Beadle B32R —/38
2828	VW8635	Leyland PLSC3	Strachan	B32R	Beadle B32R —/38 (Beadle —/41)
2830	VW8585	Leyland PLSC3	Strachan	B32R	ECW B30R —/38
2831	VW8633	Leyland PLSC3	Strachan	B32R	Beadle B32R —/38
2832	VW8309	Leyland PLSC3	Strachan	B32R	Beadle B32R —/38
2833	VW8634	Leyland PLSC3	Strachan	B32R	ECW B30R —/38
2834	TM4744	Leyland PLSC3	Strachan	B32R	Beadle B32R —/38

Fleet No.	Regn. No.	Chassis	Body carried 1929 Make	Layout	Remarks
2835	TM4745	Leyland PLSC3	Strachan	B32R	Beadle B32R —/38
2845	TM4593	Leyland PLSC3	Strachan	B32R	ECW B30R —/38
2846	VW8823	Leyland TD1	Leyland	L24/24RO	
2847	VW8822	Leyland TD1	Leyland	L24/24RO	East Lancs L30/26R —/44
2850	TM4710	Leyland TD1	Leyland	L24/24RO	
2875	VX1017	Leyland TS2	Beadle	C26D	ECOC C26F —/35 (B31R —/41)
2886	UU5450	AEC Reliance	Strachan	B32F	
2890	VX647	AEC Reliance	Dodson	B32F	
2893	VX1240	AEC Reliance	Dodson	B32F	
2896	TM5141	AEC Reliance	Strachan	B32F	
2898	TM5200	AEC Reliance	Strachan	B32F	
2901	VX249	Dennis G	Beadle	C14	
2902	VW9565	AEC Regent I	Short	H26/24RO	renumbered 1141 7/54
2903	VX895	AEC Regent I	Short	H26/24RO	
2909	TM4906	Leyland TD1	Leyland	L27/24RO	
2918	TM2209	Karrier WL6/2		H24/24R	
2919	TM2210	Karrier WL6/2		H24/24R	
2920	NM9744	Albion PM28	Strachan & Brown	B32	
2921	TM712	Albion PM28		B32	
2922	NM8857	REO		B26	
2923	HS4493	REO		B25	
2924	TM3082	REO		C20	
2925	VX1560	Gilford CP6	Strachan	B20F	
2926	VX1561	Gilford CP6	Strachan	B20F	
2927	VX1542	Gilford CP6	Strachan	B20F	
2928	VX1541	Gilford CP6	Strachan	B20F	

Section Two — Former National Omnibus & Transport Company vehicles transferred into the Eastern National Omnibus Company by agreement dated October 1930, being those situated at Grays depot, Essex

Fleet No.	Regn. No.	Chassis	Body carried 1929 Make	Layout	Remarks
2001	HK4689	AEC YC	Dodson	OT30/26RO	new 1919
2006	HK5118	AEC YC		OT28/26RO	new 1919
2011	HK6410	AEC YC	NOTC	OT22/22RO	new 1919
2013	HK6418	AEC YC	Hickman	OT28/26RO	new 1919
2015	BM7760	AEC YC	NOTC	OT22/22RO	new 1919
2044	HK8530	AEC YC	(Dodson)	OT28/26RO	new 1920
2046	HK7244	AEC YC		OT28/26RO	new 1920
2051	HK7554	AEC YC		OT28/26RO	new 1920
2058	HK7589	AEC YC	Hickman	OT28/26RO	new 1920
2059	HK7588	AEC YC		B31	new 1920
2069	XA9586	AEC YC	Dodson	OT30/26RO	new 1920
2099	BM9938	AEC YC	Dodson	OT28/26RO	new 1920
2163	NM2010	Burford 30 cwt	Hickman	B14F	new 1922
2178	NO9939	AEC YC	Hickman	OT28/26RO	new 1923
2182	PU2129	AEC YC	Dodson	OT28/24RO	new 1924
2197	PU3464	Chevrolet		B14F	new 1924
2200	FX5836	Daimler CK	Strachan & Brown	B22R	new 1924
2207	NM5678	Chevrolet	London Lorries	B14F	new 1924
2209	PU5738	Chevrolet	London Lorries	B14F	new 1924
2266	NM4052	Dennis	Dodson	B31	acqd 1925
2267	NM4053	Ford T		van	acqd 1925
2268	NM4216	Ford T		van	acqd 1925
2284	XA8519	AEC YC	Dodson	OT28/26RO	new/acqd 1926
2288	EW2475	Thornycroft J		B31	new/acqd 1926
2292	EW2010	Leyland		B26	new/acqd 1926

Fleet No.	Reg. No.	Chassis	Body carried 1929 Make	Layout	Remarks
2301	TW3480	Guy BB	London Lorries	C25D	new/acqd 1926
2325	XB8439	AEC YC	Hickman	OT28/26RO	new/acqd 1926
2351	TW9857	Leyland PLC1	Beadle	C26D	
2360	TW9356	Leyland PLSC3	Strachan & Brown	C32R	ECOC B32R —/33
2363	TW9336	Guy BA	Beadle	C20F	
2367	TW9856	Leyland PLC1	Beadle	C26D	new 1927
2384	TW8937	ADC 416A	Strachan & Brown	B32D	new 1927
2387	TM1401	Guy FCX	Dodson	H34/30R	
2416	TW9338	Guy BB	London Lorries	C26D	
2596	VW4887	Chevrolet LO	Strachan	B13F	
2597	VW4898	Chevrolet LO	Strachan	B13F	new/acqd 1928
2742	VW5681	Leyland PLC1	Beadle	C26D	new/acqd 1928
2745	PR2548	GMC K16RH		B	

Section Three — Former National Omnibus & Transport Company vehicles transferred into Eastern National Omnibus Company by agreement dated 1 Jan 1930, being a proportion of those situated at Shepherd's Bush depot.

Fleet No.	Reg. No.	Chassis	Body carried 1929 Make	Layout	Remarks
2357	TW9353	Leyland PLSC3	Strachan & Brown	C32R	new 1927
2358	TW9354	Leyland PLSC3	Strachan & Brown	C32R	new 1927
2373	VW108	ADC 416A	Strachan & Brown	C28D	
2536	VW4578	Leyland PLSC3	Strachan	C31R	new 1928; ECOC B30R —/33; (Beadle —/42)
2851	TW4093	Saurer 2BH	London Lorries	B12	purchased in 1926

Section Four — Eastern National Omnibus Company vehicle intake from 1/1/30

Fleet Nos. Orig.	1954	1964	Regn. No.	Chassis	Body	Layout	Remarks
1930				Note: Nos. 2929—2979, 2981—2995, and 3000 in WNOC and SNOC fleets			
2980	—	—	TM6315	Leyland LT2	Strachan	B32R	B31R —/40; (? E. Lancs 1944)
2996	—	—	TM6309	Leyland LT2	Strachan	B32R	(? E. Lancs 1944)
2997	—	—	TM6310	Leyland LT2	Strachan	B32R	(? E. Lancs 1944)
2998	—	—	TM6312	Leyland LT2	Strachan	B32R	B31R —/40; (? E. Lancs 1944); B30R
2999	—	—	TM6311	Leyland LT2	Strachan	B32R	B30R —/40; (? E. Lancs 1944); B32R
3001	—	—	TM6313	Leyland LT2	Strachan	B32R	B31R —/40; (? E. Lancs 1944)
3002	—	—	TM6904	Leyland LT2	Strachan	B32R	(? E. Lancs 1944) 5LW later; B29R
3003	—	—	TM6905	Leyland LT2	Strachan	B32R	(? E. Lancs 1944) 5LW later
3004	—	—	TM6906	Leyland LT2	Strachan	B32R	(? E. Lancs 1944)
3005	—	—	TM6907	Leyland LT2	Strachan	B32R	(? E. Lancs 1944)
3006	—	—	TM6908	Leyland TS3	Strachan	B32R	B31R —/41; (? E. Lancs 1944)
3007	—	—	TM6909	Leyland TS3	Strachan	B32R	ECOC DP30R —/33

Fleet No. Orig.	1954	1964	Regn. No.	Chassis	Body	Layout	Remarks
3008	—	—	TM6316	Leyland TS3	Strachan	B32R	(? E. Lancs 1944)
3009	—	—	TM6314	Leyland TS3	Strachan	B32R	B31R —/40; (? E. Lancs 1944)
3010	—	—	TM6405	Leyland TD1	Leyland	L24/24R	Beadle L24/24R —/41
3011	—	—	TM6406	Leyland TD1	Leyland	L24/24R	
3012	—	—	TM6407	Leyland TD1	Leyland	L24/24R	Beadle L24/24R —/41
3013	—	—	TM6408	Leyland TD1	Leyland	L24/24R	Beadle L24/24R —/42
3014	—	—	TM6409	Leyland TD1	Leyland	L24/24R	Beadle L26/26R —/41
3015	—	—	UR6225	Leyland TD1	Leyland	L24/24R	ECW L27/26R —/43
3016	—	—	VX4672	Leyland TD1	Leyland	L24/24R	ECW L27/28R —/41; 5LW later
3017	—	—	VX4673	Leyland TD1	Leyland	L24/24R	Beadle L27/28R —/40; 5LW later
3018	—	—	VX6361	Gilford 1680T		B32	believed delivered early 1931
3019	—	—	VX6362	Gilford 1680T		B32	believed delivered early 1931
3020	—	—	VX4108	AEC Regent I	Short	L26/24R	AEC 8.8 oil ex 3063 4/32
3021	—	—	VX4901	AEC Regent I	Short	L26/24R	(Beadle L26/26R —/43)
3022	—	—	VX4902	AEC Regent I	Short	L26/24R	
3023	—	—	TM6301	AEC Regent I	Short	L26/24R	(Beadle L26/26R —/43)
3024	—	—	TM6302	AEC Regent I	Short	L26/24R	East Lancs L30/26R —/43
3025	1145	—	TM6303	AEC Regent I	Short	L26/24R	East Lancs L30/26R —/43 (Beadle L26/26R —/46)
3026	1144	—	TM6304	AEC Regent I	Short	L26/24R	(Beadle L26/26R —/45)
3027	1142	—	TM6305	AEC Regent I	Short	L26/24R	(Beadle L26/26R —/44)
3028	1143	—	TM6306	AEC Regent I	Short	L26/24R	(Beadle L26/26R —/43)
3029	—	—	TM6307	AEC Regent I	Short	L26/24R	
3030	—	—	TM6308	AEC Regent I	Short	L26/24R	(Beadle L26/26R —/43)
1931			Note: Nos. 3031-3053 in WNOC fleet				
3054	—	—	UR1014	Dennis G		C20	
3055	—	—	UR1870	Dennis G		B20	
3056	—	—	UR5379	Dennis 30 cwt		B14	(ex-Leverett) 'Ashwell & District'
3057	—	—	UR3521	Dennis EV		B32R	
3058	—	—	UR3520	Dennis EV		B32R	
3059	—	—	TM8731	Leyland PLSC3	Strachan	B31R	
3060	—	—	TM8732	Leyland PLSC3	Strachan	B29R	
3061	—	—	EV1751	AEC Regal	Strachan	B28R	
3062	—	—	EV1752	AEC Regal	Strachan	B32R	
3063	—	—	EV1942	AEC Regent	Short	L24/24R	ECW L26/26R by —/45
3064	—	—	EV1946	Thornycroft XC	Strachan	L24/24R	ECW L27/26R —/41
3065	—	—	EV1945	Thornycroft XC	Strachan	L24/24R	ECW L27/26R —/41
3066	—	—	EV1943	Thornycroft XC	Strachan	L24/24R	(6 cyl petrol. Other XCs 4 cyl)
3067	—	—	EV1944	Thornycroft XC	Strachan	L24/24R	ECW L27/26R —/41 (Beadle —/43)
3068	—	—	EV1947	Thornycroft XC	Strachan	L24/24R	ECW L27/26R —/41 (Beadle —/43)
3069	—	—	EV1487	Leyland TD1	Strachan	L27/24R	5LW 11/37; (ECW L27/28R —/41)
3070	—	—	EV1488	Leyland TD1	Strachan	L27/24R	5LW 8/37; (ECW L27/28R —/41)
3071	—	—	EV1486	Leyland TD1	Strachan	L27/24R	5LW 11/36; (ECW L27/28R —/41)
3072	—	—	EV1489	Leyland TD1	Strachan	L27/24R	(ECW L27/28R —/41)
3073	—	—	TM9151	Leyland TD1	Strachan	L27/24R	
3074	—	—	TM9152	Leyland TD1	Strachan	L27/24R	(ECW L27/28R —/41)
3075	—	—	TM8791	AEC Regent	Short	L27/24R	
3076	1153	—	TM8792	AEC Regent	Short	L27/24R	East Lancs L30/26R —/43
3077	1151	—	TM8793	AEC Regent	Short	L27/24R	(Beadle L52R —/44)
3078	1152	—	TM8794	AEC Regent	Short	L27/24R	(Beadle L52R —/45)
3079	—	—	TM8795	AEC Regent	Short	L27/24R	Duple L30/26R —/41; then East Lancs L30/26R —/45
3080	1154	—	TM8796	AEC Regent	Short	L27/24R	Beadle L26/26R —/43
3081	1155	—	TM8797	AEC Regent	Short	L27/24R	Beadle L26/26R —/44
3082	—	—	TM8798	AEC Regent	Short	L27/24R	East Lancs L30/26R —/44
3083	—	—	TM8799	AEC Regent	Short	L27/24R	East Lancs L30/26R —/44
3084	—	—	TM8800	AEC Regent	Short	L27/24R	
3085	—	—	EV1755	AEC Regent	Short	L27/24R	East Lancs L30/26R —/44

Fleet No. Orig.	1954	1964	Regn. No.	Chassis	Body	Layout	Remarks
3086	—	—	EV1754	AEC Regent	Short	L27/24R	East Lancs L30/26R —/44
3087	—	—	EV1753	AEC Regent	Short	L27/24R	East Lancs L30/26R —/44
3088	—	—	EV1224	Leyland TS1	Duple	C26D	ECW B31R of —/38 ex 3756 in 1942
3089	—	—	EV1305	Leyland TS1	Duple	C26D	ECW B31R of —/38 ex 3757 in 1942
3144	—	—	TM8508	Leyland TD1	Strachan	L24/24R	Beadle L27/24R —/40
3145	—	—	TM8509	Leyland TD1	Strachan	L24/24R	Beadle L27/24R —/41
3146	—	—	TM9047	Leyland TD1	Strachan	L24/24R	Beadle L27/24R —/41
3147	—	—	TM9048	Leyland TD1	Strachan	L24/24R	Beadle L27/24R —/41
3148	—	—	TM9049	Leyland TD1	Strachan	L24/24R	Beadle L27/24R —/41
3149	—	—	TM9050	Leyland TD1	Strachan	L24/24R	Beadle L27/24R —/40
3150	—	—	TM9051	Leyland TD1	Strachan	L24/24R	Beadle L27/24R —/40 (Beadle —/43)
3151	—	—	TM9150	Leyland TD1	Strachan	L24/24R	Beadle L27/24R —/40
3152	—	—	TM9184	Leyland TD1	Strachan	L24/24R	Beadle L27/24R —/41
3153	—	—	TM9185	Leyland TD1	Strachan	L24/24R	Beadle L27/24R —/41
3159	—	—	TW9799	Leyland PLC1	Strachan	C32	
3160	—	—	VW6216	Leyland TS2	Strachan	C30	ECOC C26F —/35
3161	—	—	VW8166	Leyland PLSC3	Leyland	B30R	
3162	—	—	VW8256	Leyland PLSC3	Leyland	B30R	
3163	—	—	VX822	Leyland TD1	Leyland	L27/24RO	
3164	—	—	VX823	Leyland TD1	Leyland	L27/24RO	(L24/24RO —/37)
3165	—	—	VX3583	Leyland LT1	Leyland	B30	
3166	—	—	VX3584	Leyland LT1	Leyland	B30	
3167	—	—	VX5121	Leyland TD1	Leyland	L24/24R	(Beadle L26/26R —/41)
3168	—	—	VX5122	Leyland TD1	Leyland	L24/24R	(Beadle L26/26R —/41)
3169	—	—	VX5304	Leyland TD1	Leyland	L27/24R	(Beadle L26/26R —/41)
3170	—	—	VX5305	Leyland TD1	Leyland	L27/24R	(Beadle L26/26R —/41)
3171	—	—	NO3513	Leyland M	LGOC K	OT24/22RO	
3172	—	—	HK8121	Leyland X4	LGOC K	OT24/22RO	
3173	—	—	NO6402	Leyland G	LGOC K	OT24/22RO	
3174	—	—	CT5736	Thornycroft J	LGOC	OT48RO	
3175	—	—	NN3135	Thornycroft J	LGOC	OT48RO	
3176	—	—	FE4974	Thornycroft J	LGOC	OT48RO	
3177	—	—	CT5909	Thornycroft J	LGOC K	OT24/22RO	
3178	—	—	CT6389	Thornycroft J	LGOC K	OT48RO	
3179	—	—	NN4045	Thornycroft J	LGOC	OT48RO	
3180	—	—	CT6002	Thornycroft J	LGOC	B32	
3181	—	—	CT6084	Thornycroft J	LGOC	OT38RO	
3182	—	—	PU9404	Thornycroft J	LGOC K	OT24/22RO	(ex-Silver Queen)
3183	—	—	CT5630	Thornycroft J	LGOC	OT48RO	
3184	—	—	CT5760	Thornycroft J	LGOC K	OT24/22RO	
3185	—	—	FU59	Thornycroft J	LGOC	OT48RO	
3186	—	—	CT6139	Thornycroft J	LGOC	OT48RO	
3187	—	—	CT6138	Thornycroft J	LGOC K	B26R	
3188	—	—	KN9793	Thornycroft J	LGOC K	OT24/22RO	
3189	—	—	AA5700	Thornycroft J	LGOC K	OT24/22RO	
3190	—	—	OH1399	Thornycroft J	LGOC K	OT24/22RO	
3191	—	—	TW4448	Chevrolet T		Ch14	
3192	—	—	TW5060	Chevrolet T		Ch14	
3193	—	—	KM8484	Chevrolet T		B14	
3194	—	—	CT8956	Chevrolet LM		B14	
3195	—	—	TW9800	Chevrolet LM		C14	
3196	—	—	TW9801	Chevrolet LM		B14	
3197	—	—	VW1608	Chevrolet LM		B14	
3198	—	—	VW961	Chevrolet LM		C14	
3199	—	—	CT9313	Chevrolet LM	Applewhite	B20F	
3200	—	—	CT9370	Chevrolet LM	Applewhite	B20F	
3201	—	—	VW5252	Chevrolet LO	Applewhite	B20F	
3202	—	—	VW6214	Chevrolet LO	Applewhite	B20F	
3203	—	—	VW6215	Chevrolet LO	Applewhite	C20F	
3204	—	—	VW8483	Chevrolet LP	Applewhite	C20F	
3205	—	—	VW9083	Chevrolet LP		C20F	
3206	—	—	FW224	Chevrolet LQ		B20	

Note: Nos. 3154-3158 in WNOC fleet

Fleet No. Orig.	1954	1964	Regn. No.	Chassis	Body	Layout	Remarks
3207	—	—	VX1605	Chevrolet		B20	(ex-Silver Queen)
3208	—	—	VX2843	Chevrolet LQ		B20	
3209	—	—	VX2842	Chevrolet LQ		B20	
3210	—	—	VX6948	Chevrolet U		C20	
3211	—	—	PU712	Guy BA		B20	
3212	—	—	PU1274	Guy BA		B20	
3213	—	—	MY2126	AEC Regent	Short	L24/24RO	
3214	—	—	VX3378	AEC Regal	Metcalfe	B32	
3215	—	—	XN6774	Leyland LB5		OT48RO	
3216	—	—	XL7513	Leyland LB5		OT48RO	
3217	101	—	VX1592	Leyland TS2	Metcalfe	B32	East Lancs B31F by —/45
3218	—	—	TW1544	Lancia Tetra		B	
3219	—	—	VW3421	Lancia Penta		B26	(ex-Enterprise)
3220	—	—	YH7108	Lancia Z	Alldays	B	
3221	—	—	VW5015	Lancia Penta		C20	
3222	—	—	VW4585	Lancia		C26	
3223	—	—	VW4684	Gotfredson		B32	
3224	—	—	TW2931	Gotfredson		B20	
3225	—	—	TW8488	Berliet CT6		B20	
3226	—	—	TW8487	Berliet CT6		B20	
3281	—	—	EW3306	Thornycroft J		OT36RO	
3282	—	—	RP761	Morris		B	
3283	—	—	EW590	Leyland S4		OT36RO	(ex-Hinsby)
3284	—	—	EW3244	Ford		B20	
3285	—	—	EW3022	Daimler CB		B20	
1932							
3295	—	—	MJ438	Leyland TD2	Strachan	L30/26R	5LW 5/36
3296	—	—	MJ439	Leyland TD2	Strachan	L30/26R	5LW 3/36; (Beadle —/43)
3297	—	—	EV6056	Leyland TD2	Strachan	L30/26R	5LW 3/36; (ECW —/41)
3298	—	—	EV6057	Leyland TD2	Strachan	L30/26R	5LW 4/36
3299	—	—	EV6058	Leyland TD2	Strachan	L30/26R	5LW 4/36; (ECW —/41)
3300	—	—	EV6059	Leyland TD2	Strachan	L30/26R	5LW 2/36
3301	—	—	EV6060	Leyland TD2	Strachan	L30/26R	5LW 5/36
3302	—	—	EV6052	Leyland TD2	Strachan	L30/26R	5LW 5/36
3303	—	—	EV6053	Leyland TD2	Strachan	L30/26R	5LW 5/36
3304	—	—	MJ401	Leyland TS4	Beadle	C26R	B32R
3305	—	—	MJ402	Leyland TS4	Beadle	C26R	B32R
3306	—	—	MJ403	Leyland TS4	Beadle	C26R	B32R 5LW 2/38
3307	—	—	MJ404	Leyland TS4	Beadle	C26R	B32R 5LW 1/38
3308	—	—	MJ405	Leyland TS4	Beadle	C26R	B32R 5LW 4/38
3309	—	—	EV5676	TSM B39A7	Beadle	B32R	
3310	—	—	EV5677	TSM B39A7	Beadle	B32R	
3311	—	—	EV5678	TSM B39A7	Beadle	B32	
3312	—	—	MJ284	TSM B39A7	Beadle	B32	
3313	—	—	MJ282	TSM B39A7	Beadle	B32	
3314	—	—	MJ281	TSM B39A7	Beadle	B32	
3315	—	—	MJ283	TSM B39A7	Beadle	B32	
3316	—	—	EV5679	TSM B39A7	Beadle	B32	
3317	—	—	MJ440	Dennis Lancet	Beadle	B32R	(Beadle —/42)(Beadle —/43)
3318	—	—	MJ441	Dennis Lancet	Beadle	B32R	(Beadle —/42)
3319	—	—	EV6054	Dennis Lancet	Beadle	B32R	(Beadle —/41)
3320	—	—	EV6055	Dennis Lancet	Beadle	B32R	(Beadle —/42)
3321	—	—	EV6061	Dennis Lancet	Beadle	B32R	(Beadle —/42)
3322	—	—	MJ285	AEC Regent	Strachan	L30/26R	
3323	—	—	MJ286	AEC Regent	Strachan	L30/26R	5LW 11/37
3324	—	—	MJ287	AEC Regent	Strachan	L30/26R	
3325	—	—	MJ288	AEC Regent	Strachan	L30/26R	
3326	—	—	MJ289	AEC Regent	Strachan	L30/26R	5LW 12/37; (ECW —/41)
3327	—	—	EV6333	AEC Regent	Strachan	L30/26R	5LW 2/38; (ECW —/41)
3328	—	—	EV5783	AEC Regent	Strachan	L30/26R	(ECW —/41)
3329	—	—	EV5784	AEC Regent	Strachan	L30/26R	5LW 2/38; (ECW —/41)
3330	—	—	EV5785	AEC Regent	Strachan	L30/26R	(ECW —/41)
3331	—	—	EV6062	AEC Regal	Duple	C26	5LW 7/36
3332	—	—	MJ406	AEC Renown	Short	L66R	(Beadle —/43)
3333	—	—	MJ407	AEC Renown	Short	L66R	5LW 10/36; (Beadle —/44)

Note: Nos. 3227-3280 in WNOC fleet   Note: Nos. 3286-3294 in WNOC fleet

Fleet No. Orig.	1954	1964	Regn. No.	Chassis	Body	Layout	Remarks
3334	—	—	MJ290	AEC Renown	Short	L66R	5LW 10/36
3335	—	—	MJ291	AEC Renown	Short	L66R	5LW 9/36

Note: Western National and Southern National continued the common fleet numbering sequence up to and including 3393 after which Eastern National continued from 3394 with the other two companies adopting their own system. Fleet numbers from 3394 onwards were, however, used by Western National and Southern National but only for stock acquired from other operators.

1933

Fleet No. Orig.	1954	1964	Regn. No.	Chassis	Body	Layout	Remarks
3394	—	—	AEV764	Dennis Lancet	ECOC	B36R	(Beadle —/42)
3395	—	—	AEV765	Dennis Lancet	ECOC	B36R	(Beadle —/42)
3396	—	—	AEV766	Dennis Lancet	ECOC	B36R	(Beadle —/42)
3397	—	—	AEV767	Dennis Lancet	ECOC	B36R	(Beadle —/42) (Beadle —/43)
3398	—	—	AEV768	Dennis Lancet	ECOC	B36R	
3399	—	—	AEV769	Dennis Lancet	ECOC	B36R	
3400	—	—	AEV770	Dennis Lancet	ECOC	B36R	(Beadle —/44)
3401	—	—	AEV771	Dennis Lancet	ECOC	B36R	
3402	—	—	AEV772	Dennis Lancet	ECOC	B36R	(Beadle —/42)
3403	—	—	AEV773	Dennis Lancet	ECOC	B36R	(Beadle —/42)
3404	—	—	AEV774	Dennis Lancet	ECOC	B36R	(Beadle —/42)
3405	—	—	AEV775	Dennis Lancet	ECOC	B36R	(Beadle —/42)
3406	—	—	AEV776	Dennis Lancet	ECOC	B36R	(Beadle —/42)
3407	—	—	AEV777	Dennis Lancet	ECOC	B36R	(Beadle —/42)
3408	—	—	AEV778	Dennis Lancet	ECOC	B36R	(Beadle —/42)(Beadle —/43)
3409	—	—	AEV779	Dennis Lancet	ECOC	B36R	(Beadle —/41)
3410	—	—	AEV780	Dennis Lancet	ECOC	B36R	(Beadle —/42)
3411	—	—	AEV781	Dennis Lancet	ECOC	B36R	(Beadle —/42)
3412	—	—	AEV782	Dennis Lancet	ECOC	B36R	(Beadle —/42)
3413	—	—	AEV783	Dennis Lancet	ECOC	B36R	(Beadle —/42)
3414	—	—	AEV784	Dennis Lancet	ECOC	B36R	(Beadle —/42)
3415	—	—	AEV785	Dennis Lancet	ECOC	B36R	(Beadle —/42)
3416	—	—	AEV786	Dennis Lancet	ECOC	B36R	(Beadle —/42)
3417	—	—	AEV787	Dennis Lancet	ECOC	B36R	(Beadle —/42)
3418	—	—	AEV788	Dennis Lancet	ECOC	B36R	(Beadle —/42)(Beadle —/43)
3419	—	—	AEV789	Dennis Lancet	ECOC	DP32R	(Beadle —/42)(Beadle —/43 twice)(Beadle —/44)
3420	—	—	AEV790	Dennis Lancet	ECOC	DP32R	(Beadle —/42)(Beadle —/44) ECW B32R ex-2811 —/49
3421	—	—	AEV791	Dennis Lancet	ECOC	DP32R	(Beadle —/42)
3422	—	—	AEV792	Dennis Lancet	ECOC	DP32R	
3423	—	—	AEV793	Dennis Lancet	ECOC	DP32R	(Beadle —/42)(Beadle —/44)
3424	—	—	AEV794	Leyland TS4	ECOC	C26F	
3425	—	—	AEV795	Leyland TD2	ECOC	L28/28R	
3426	—	—	AEV796	Leyland TD2	ECOC	L28/28R	
3427	—	—	AEV797	Leyland TD2	ECOC	L28/28R	Duple L30/26R —/41
3428	—	—	AEV798	Leyland TD2	ECOC	L28/28R	(Beadle —/46)
3429	—	—	AEV799	Leyland TD2	ECOC	L28/28R	
3430	—	—	AEV800	Leyland TD2	ECOC	L28/28R	
3431	—	—	AHK649	Leyland TD2	Park Royal	L28/28R	
3432	—	—	TX5630	TSM B10A2	Vickers	32	
3433	—	—	HJ7639	TSM B10A2	Vickers	31	
3434	—	—	HJ9952	Gilford 166SD		28	
3435	—	—	JN1224	Gilford 1680T		31	
3436	—	—	HJ9955	Morris Viceroy		B20R	originally Rayleigh MS
3437	1149	—	KR4997	AEC Regent	Short	L24/24R	(Beadle L26/26R —/47) two gangways on upper deck
3438	—	—	JN343	AEC Regent	Park Royal	L50R	
3439	—	—	CN4520	AEC Regent	Short	L50R	
3440	—	—	JN2310	AEC Regent	Park Royal	L27/28R	
3441	—	—	MY2542	AEC Regent	Short	L50R	(ex-Borough)
3442	—	—	JN2767	AEC Regent	Park Royal	L27/28R	
3443	—	—	HJ8954	Gilford 1660T	Wycombe	31	
3444	—	—	TS8211	Gilford 1660T	Wycombe	B32	
3445	—	—	JN213	Gilford 1680T	Beadle	C32	
3446	—	—	HJ8199	Gilford 1660T	Wycombe	B31R	
3447	—	—	JN256	Gilford 168SD	Duple	C26F	originally Rayleigh MS
3448	—	—	JN257	Gilford 168SD	Duple	C26F	
3449	—	—	HJ9956	Morris Viceroy		B20R	

Fleet No. Orig.	1954	1964	Regn. No.	Chassis	Body	Layout	Remarks
3450	—	—	GK428	Leyland TS3		C26R	
3451	—	—	GK439	Leyland TS3		C26R	
3452	—	—	GK441	Leyland TS3		C26R	
3453	—	—	GK443	Leyland TS3		C26R	
3454	—	—	GK444	Leyland TS3		C26R	
3455	102	—	GN5141	Leyland TS3		C26R	Beadle B31R —/43
3456	—	—	GN5142	Leyland TS3		C26R	(ex-AOC Ltd)
3457	—	—	GN5143	Leyland TS3		C26R	
3458	—	—	GN5144	Leyland TS3		C26R	
3459	103	—	GN5146	Leyland TS3		C26R	Beadle B31R —/43
3460	—	—	GN5147	Leyland TS3		C26R	
3461	—	—	GH7089	Leyland TS3		C26R	
3462	—	—	KX5872	Chevrolet U		B14	
3463	—	—	KX6039	Chevrolet U		B14	
3464	—	—	YM5524	Dennis 4 ton		OT48RO	
3465	—	—	YE3930	Dennis 4 ton		OT48RO	
3466	—	—	XP3760	Dennis 4 ton		OT48RO	
—	—	—	GH7084	Leyland TS3		C26R	
—	—	—	GH7090	Leyland TS3		C26R	
—	—	—	GK5717	Leyland TS3		C26R	(un-numbered vehicles ex-AOC Ltd)
—	—	—	GN4867	Leyland TS3		C26R	
—	—	—	GN5145	Leyland TS3		C26R	
—	—	—	GN5149	Leyland TS3		C26R	
3467	—	—	GD8694	Albion PM28	Pickering	B31	(ex-'Chiltern')
3468	—	—	TM7541	Dennis GL	Thurgood	B20	(ex-'Malebird') (Recovery Veh 12/35)
3469	—	—	VX7574	AJS Pilot	Petty	B26	(ex-'Pullman')
3470	—	—	VX702	Gilford 15SD	(Economy)	B28	
3471	—	—	VW2934	REO Sprinter	(Economy)	B26	
3472	—	—	TM8402	REO Gold Crown		B26	(ex-'Milton' Beds)
—	—	—	NH9892	Star Flyer		B	
—	—	—	KX1467	Chevrolet		B14F	un-numbered vehicles ex-Bates
—	—	—	PP7280	REO Pullman		B20	

1934

Fleet No. Orig.	1954	1964	Regn. No.	Chassis	Body	Layout	Remarks
3473	—	—	AVW451	Dennis Lancet	ECOC	DP32R	
3474	—	—	AVW452	Dennis Lancet	ECOC	DP32R	(Beadle —/43)
3475	—	—	AVW453	Dennis Lancet	ECOC	DP32R	
3476	—	—	AVW454	Dennis Lancet	ECOC	DP32R	
3477	—	—	AVW455	Dennis Lancet	ECOC	DP32R	(Beadle —/42)
3478	—	—	AVW456	Dennis Lancet	ECOC	DP32R	(Beadle —/42)
3479	—	—	AVW457	Dennis Lancet	ECOC	DP32R	(Beadle —/42)(Beadle —/44 twice) ECW B30R of 1938 ex-2813 —/49
3480	—	—	AVW458	Dennis Lancet	ECOC	DP32R	(Beadle —/42)(Beadle —/44)
3481	—	—	AVW459	Dennis Lancet	ECOC	DP32R	(Beadle —/42)
3482	—	—	AVW460	Dennis Lancet	ECOC	DP32R	(Beadle —/42)(Beadle —/43)
3483	—	—	AVW461	Dennis Lancet	ECOC	DP32R	
3484	—	—	AVW462	Dennis Lancet	ECOC	DP32R	(Beadle —/42)(Beadle —/43)
3485	—	—	AVW463	Dennis Lancet	ECOC	DP32R	(Beadle —/42)
3486	—	—	AVW464	Dennis Lancet	ECOC	DP32R	(Beadle —/42)(Beadle —/44)
3487	—	—	AVW465	Dennis Lancet	ECOC	DP32R	(Beadle —/42)(Beadle —/44)
3488	—	—	AVW466	Dennis Lancet	ECOC	DP32R	(Beadle —/42)(Beadle —/44 twice)
3489	—	—	AVW467	Dennis Lancet	ECOC	DP32R	(Beadle —/42)(Beadle —/44)
3490	—	—	AVW468	Dennis Lancet	ECOC	DP32R	(Beadle —/42)
3491	—	—	AVW469	Dennis Lancet	ECOC	DP32R	(Beadle —/42)(Beadle —/43 twice)
3492	—	—	AVW470	Dennis Lancet	ECOC	DP32R	(Beadle —/43)
3493	—	—	GK3409	Gilford 1660T	Wycombe	C31F	
3494	—	—	GK3410	Gilford 1660T	Wycombe	C31F	
3495	—	—	GK3411	Gilford 1660T	Wycombe	C31F	(ex-ECOC)
3496	—	—	UL7692	Dennis F	Dennis	C20	(Nos. 3496-3499 reused)
3497	—	—	UU5144	Dennis F	Dennis	C20	
3498	—	—	UU5147	Dennis F	Dennis	C20	
3499	—	—	GF9510	Dennis F	Dennis	C20	

Orig.	1954	1964	Regn. No.	Chassis	Body	Layout	Remarks
3496	—	—	TM6724	Gilford 1680T	Strachan	C30F	
3497	—	—	TM6725	Gilford 1680T	Strachan	C30F	(ex-'Strawhatter')
3498	—	—	TM7005	Gilford 1680T	Strachan	C30F	
3499	—	—	TM8375	Gilford 1680T	Strachan	C30F	
3500	—	—	VW7551	Gilford 15SD	Metcalfe	B26F	
3501	—	—	VW9568	Gilford 166SD		C26F	
3502	—	—	VX7851	Gilford 168SD	Duple	C26F	
3503	—	—	VX9493	Gilford 168SD	Duple	C26F	
3504	—	—	EV828	Gilford 1680T		B32	(ex-'Bird')
3505	—	—	VX4166	Gilford 1660T		C31	
3506	—	—	VW9850	GMC T42		B26	
3507	—	—	VX1072	REO Gold Crown	Bush & Twiddy	B20	
3508	—	—	VX2418	REO Pullman		B26	
3509	—	—	VX6549	REO Pullman		B26	
3510	144	—	AEV88	AEC Regal	Duple	C32R	Rebodied during war
3511	—	—	BHK741	Leyland TD2	ECOC	L30/26R	
3512	—	—	BHK742	Leyland TD2	ECOC	L30/26R	
3513	—	—	EW7802	Dennis Lancet		B32	(ex-'Golden Arrow')
3514	—	—	TM8465	Gilford 1680T	Strachan	C30F	
3515	—	—	TM8735	Gilford 1680T	Strachan	C30F	(ex-'Strawhatter')
3516	—	—	TM8805	Gilford 1680T	Strachan	C30F	
3517	—	—	TM8815	Gilford 1680T	Strachan	C30F	
3518	—	—	EV5742	Chevrolet		B14	(ex-Johnson)
3519	—	—	VX9906	Commer Invader		B20F	(ex-'East Bergholt & District')
3520	143	—	AHK792	AEC Regal	Waveney	C32	(Beadle —/45)
3521	—	—	EV7338	Gilford 1680T	(Wycombe)	C30F	
3522	—	—	EV7579	Gilford 1680T	(Wycombe)	C30F	
3523	—	—	EV7339	Gilford 1680T	(Wycombe)	C30F	(ex-Hillman)
3524	—	—	EV7580	Gilford 1680T	(Wycombe)	C30F	
3525	—	—	EV7581	Gilford 1680T	(Wycombe)	C30F	
3526	—	—	VX5364	Dennis GL		B20	
3527	—	—	PL4925	Dennis Dart		B20	
3528	—	—	VX9516	Dennis GL	Duple	B20F	(ex-Patten)
3529	—	—	EV2531	Dennis EV		B32	
3530	—	—	EV6784	Dennis Lancet		B32	
3531	—	—	VX6863	Dennis GL		B20	
1935							
3532	—	—	BTW471	Dennis Lancet	ECOC	DP32R	B32R
3533	—	—	BTW472	Dennis Lancet	ECOC	DP32R	B32R
3534	—	—	BTW473	Dennis Lancet	ECOC	DP32R	B32R (Beadle —/42)
3535	—	—	BTW474	Dennis Lancet	ECOC	DP32R	B32R (Beadle B35R —/42)
3536	—	—	BTW475	Dennis Lancet	ECOC	DP32R	B32R (Beadle B31R —/42)
3537	—	—	BTW476	Dennis Lancet	ECOC	DP32R	B32R B31R during war
3538	—	—	BTW477	Dennis Lancet	ECOC	DP32R	B32R B31R during war
3539	—	—	BTW478	Dennis Lancet	ECOC	DP32R	B32R
3540	—	—	BTW479	Dennis Lancet	ECOC	DP32R	B32R
3541	—	—	BTW480	Dennis Lancet	ECOC	DP32R	B32R (Beadle B35R —/43)
3542	—	—	BTW481	Dennis Lancet	ECOC	DP32R	B32R
3543	—	—	BTW482	Dennis Lancet	ECOC	DP32R	B32R (Beadle B35R —/43)
3544	—	—	BTW483	Dennis Lancet	ECOC	DP32R	B32R (Beadle —/43)
3545	—	—	BTW484	Dennis Lancet	ECOC	DP32R	B32R (Beadle B31R —/43) (Beadle —/44)
3546	—	—	BTW485	Dennis Lancet	ECOC	DP32R	B32R (Beadle —/43)
3547	—	—	BTW486	Dennis Lancet	ECOC	DP32R	B32R (Beadle B35R —/43)
3548	—	—	BTW487	Dennis Lancet	ECOC	DP32R	B32R (Beadle B32R —/43) (Beadle —/43)
3549	—	—	BTW488	Dennis Lancet	ECOC	DP32R	B32R (Beadle —/42) (Beadle —/43)
3550	—	—	BTW489	Dennis Lancet	ECOC	DP32R	B32R (Beadle —/43) (Beadle —/44)
3551	—	—	BTW490	Dennis Lancet	ECOC	DP32R	B32R
3552	—	—	BTW491	Dennis Lancet	ECOC	DP32R	B32R (Beadle —/42)
3553	—	—	BTW492	Dennis Lancet	ECOC	DP32R	B32R (Beadle B35R —/43)
3554	—	—	BTW493	Dennis Lancet	ECOC	DP32R	B32R (Beadle —/43)
3555	—	—	BTW494	Dennis Lancet	ECOC	DP32R	B32R (Beadle B36R —/42) B32R

Orig.	1954	1964	Regn. No.	Chassis	Body	Layout	Remarks
3556	—	—	BTW495	Leyland TD3	ECOC	L28/28R	
3557	—	—	BTW496	Leyland TD3	ECOC	L28/28R	
3558	—	—	BTW497	Leyland TD3	ECOC	L28/28R	
3559	—	—	BTW498	Leyland TD3	ECOC	L28/28R	(Beadle —/45) ECW L27/26R —/49
3560	—	—	BTW499	Leyland TD3	ECOC	L28/28R	
3561	—	—	BTW500	Leyland TD3	ECOC	L28/28R	
3562	142	—	EV6296	AEC Regal	Metal Bodies	B32	Willowbrook B36F —/43
3563	—	—	VX3262	GMC T42		B26	
3564	—	—	VX7062	Gilford 168SD		C26	
3565	—	—	VX7063	Gilford 168SD		C26	
3566	—	—	VX9495	Gilford 1680T		C32	
3567	—	—	VW9851	GMC T30		B20	
3568	—	—	VX5715	Gilford 1660T		C32	(ex-'Quest')
3569	—	—	VX9494	Gilford 1680T		C32	
3570	—	—	VX1070	REO Pullman		B26	
3571	—	—	AHK611	Bedford WLB	Economy	20	
3572	—	—	VX5346	Gilford 1660T		C32	
3573	—	—	VX7853	Gilford AS6	Duple	C20	
3574	—	—	VX2289	Gilford 1660T		C32	
3575	—	—	VX7846	Chevrolet U		B14	
3576	—	—	GV899	Bedford WLB	Duple	C20F	(ex-Underwood)
3577	141	—	MV2272	AEC Regal		C32	Beadle B32R —/42
3578	—	—	EV6338	Bedford WLB		B20	
3579	—	—	VX6515	Gilford 1680T		C32	
3580	—	—	VX5043	Dennis GL		C20	(ex-Davies)
3581	—	—	VW4951	Dennis 30cwt		C20	
3582	—	—	MS9336	Gilford 1660T		C32	(ex-Stanford Motors)
3583	—	—	VW5044	Gilford 1660T		C26	
3584	—	—	CPU196	Dennis Lancet	Dennis	C32C	Beadle B30R of /39 ex 2815 —/49
3585	—	—	CPU197	Dennis Lancet	Dennis	C32C	(Beadle —/43) Beadle B35F —/43
3586	—	—	MY8142	Guy FBB	Duple	B32	
3587	—	—	MP5344	Guy FBB		29	(ex-'Primrose' (Mersea))
3588	—	—	MK6400	Guy BB		B32	
3589	—	—	WG325	Gilford 1680T		C32F	
3590	—	—	WG324	Gilford 1680T	Wycombe	C32F	(ex-'Horn')
3591	—	—	EV6953	Gilford AS6		B20	
3592	—	—	EV695	Gilford AS6		B20	
3593	—	—	VX5600	AEC Regal	Metcalfe	C32	
3594	—	—	VX4640	AEC Regal	Metcalfe	C32	
3595	—	—	CTW191	Dennis Ace	Dennis	B20F	
3596	—	—	CTW192	Dennis Ace	Dennis	B20F	
3597	—	—	CTW193	Dennis Ace	Dennis	B20F	(Beadle —/43)
3598	—	—	CTW194	Dennis Ace	Dennis	B20F	
3599	—	—	CTW195	Dennis Ace	Dennis	B20F	(Beadle —/43)
3600	—	—	CTW196	Dennis Ace	Dennis	B20F	
3601	—	—	CTW197	Dennis Ace	Dennis	B20F	
3602	—	—	CTW198	Dennis Ace	Dennis	B20F	
3603	—	—	CTW199	Dennis Ace	Dennis	B20F	
3604	—	—	CTW200	Dennis Ace	Dennis	B20F	
3605	—	—	CTW201	Dennis Ace	Dennis	B20F	(Beadle —/43)
3606	—	—	CTW202	Dennis Ace	Dennis	B20F	
3607	—	—	CTW203	Dennis Ace	Dennis	B20F	(Beadle —/44)
3608	—	—	CTW204	Dennis Ace	Dennis	B20F	(Beadle —/43)
1936							
3609	—	—	CTW205	Dennis Ace f/c	Dennis	C20C	
3610	—	—	CTW206	Dennis Ace f/c	Dennis	C20C	
3611	—	—	CTW207	Dennis Ace f/c	Dennis	C20C	(Beadle —/44)
3612	—	—	CTW208	Dennis Ace f/c	Dennis	C20C	
3613	—	—	CTW209	Dennis Ace f/c	Dennis	C20C	
3614	—	—	CTW210	Dennis Ace f/c	Dennis	C20C	
3615	233	—	DEV451	Bristol JO5G	ECOC	DP31F	
3616	234	—	DEV452	Bristol JO5G	ECOC	DP31F	
3617	235	—	DEV453	Bristol JO5G	ECOC	DP31F	(Beadle —/46)
3618	236	—	DEV454	Bristol JO5G	ECOC	DP31F	
3619	237	—	DEV455	Bristol JO5G	ECOC	DP31F	

Fleet Nos. Orig.	1954	1964	Regn. No.	Chassis	Body	Layout	Remarks
3620	—	—	DEV456	Bristol JO5G	ECOC	DP31F	
3621	238	—	DEV457	Bristol JO5G	ECOC	DP31F	
3622	—	—	DEV458	Bristol JO5G	ECOC	DP31F	(Beadle —/46)
3623	239	—	DEV459	Bristol JO5G	ECOC	DP31F	
3624	240	—	DEV460	Bristol JO5G	ECOC	DP31F	ECW B32R —/43
3625	—	—	DEV461	Bristol JO5G	ECOC	DP31F	
3626	—	—	DEV462	Bristol JO5G	ECOC	DP31F	
3627	—	—	DEV463	Bristol JO5G	ECOC	DP31F	
3628	—	—	DEV464	Bristol JO5G	ECOC	DP31F	
3629	—	—	DEV465	Bristol JO5G	ECOC	DP31F	
3630	241	—	DEV466	Bristol JO5G	ECOC	DP31F	(Beadle —/40)
3631	—	—	DEV467	Bristol JO5G	ECOC	DP31F	(Beadle —/41)(Beadle —/46)
3632	—	—	DEV468	Bristol JO5G	ECOC	DP31F	(Beadle —/41)
3633	—	—	DEV469	Bristol JO5G	ECOC	DP31F	
3634	1233	—	DEV470	Bristol GO5G	Brush	L27/26R	(Beadle —/43) ECW L27/28R —/49
3635	1234	—	DEV471	Bristol GO5G	Brush	L27/26R	ECW L27/28R —/44
3636	—	—	DEV472	Bristol GO5G	Brush	L27/26R	
3637	—	—	DEV473	Bristol GO5G	Brush	L27/26R	
3638	—	—	DEV474	Bristol GO5G	Brush	L27/26R	
3639	1235	—	DEV475	Bristol GO5G	Brush	L27/26R	
3640	1236	—	DEV476	Bristol GO5G	Brush	L27/26R	ECW L27/28R —/49
3641	1237	—	DEV477	Bristol GO5G	Brush	L27/26R	ECW L27/28R —/49
3642	1238	—	DEV478	Bristol GO5G	Brush	L27/26R	ECW L27/28R —/49
3643	1239	—	DEV479	Bristol GO5G	Brush	L27/26R	ECW L27/28R —/49
3644	1240	—	DEV480	Bristol GO5G	Brush	L27/26R	ECW L27/28R —/49
3645	1241	—	DEV481	Bristol GO5G	Brush	L27/26R	ECW L27/28R —/44
3646	1242	—	DEV482	Bristol GO5G	Brush	L27/26R	ECW L27/28R —/44
3647	—	—	DEV483	Leyland TD4	Brush	L28/28R	
3648	—	—	DEV484	Leyland TD4	Brush	L28/28R	
3649	—	—	DEV485	Leyland TD4	Brush	L28/28R	ECW L24/24R —/49 (Second-hand)
3650	—	—	DEV486	Leyland TD4	Brush	L28/28R	
3651	—	—	DEV487	Leyland TD4	Brush	L28/28R	
3652	—	—	DEV488	Leyland TD4	Brush	L28/28R	

1937

Fleet Nos. Orig.	1954	1964	Regn. No.	Chassis	Body	Layout	Remarks
3653	1249	—	ENO931	Bristol GO5G	ECW	L24/24R	(Beadle —/44) ECW L27/28R —/49
3654	1250	—	ENO932	Bristol GO5G	ECW	L24/24R	ECW L27/28R —/49
3655	1251	—	ENO933	Bristol GO5G	ECW	L24/24R	ECW L27/28R —/49
3656	—	—	ENO934	Leyland TD4	ECW	L24/24R	
3657	—	—	ENO935	Leyland TD4	ECW	L24/24R	ECW L27/26R —/49
3658	1107	—	ENO936	Leyland TD4	ECW	L24/24R	(Beadle —/44) ECW L27/26R —/49
3659	1108	—	ENO937	Leyland TD4	ECW	L24/24R	(Beadle —/44) ECW L27/26R —/49
3660	—	—	ENO938	Leyland TD4	ECW	L24/24R	
3661	—	—	ENO939	Leyland TD4	ECW	L24/24R	ECW L27/26R —/49
3662	—	—	ENO940	Leyland TD4	ECW	L24/24R	
3663	—	—	ENO941	Leyland TS7	ECW	C31F	
3664	—	—	ENO942	Leyland TS7	ECW	C31F	
3665	—	—	ENO943	Leyland TS7	ECW	C31F	
3666	—	—	ENO944	Bristol JO5G	ECW	B31R	
3667	250	—	ENO945	Bristol JO5G	ECW	B31R	
3668	251	—	ENO946	Bristol JO5G	ECW	B31R	
3669	—	—	ENO947	Bristol JO5G	ECW	B31R	
3670	—	—	ENO948	Bristol JO5G	ECW	B31R	
3671	—	—	ENO949	Bristol JO5G	ECW	B31R	
3672	249	—	ENO950	Bristol JO5G	ECW	B31R	
3673	—	—	ENO951	Bristol JO5G	ECW	B31R	
3674	252	—	ENO952	Bristol JO5G	ECW	B31R	
3675	—	—	ENO953	Bristol JO5G	ECW	B31R	
3676	253	—	ENO954	Bristol JO5G	ECW	B31R	
3677	—	—	ENO955	Bristol JO5G	ECW	B31R	
3678	254	—	ENO956	Bristol JO5G	ECW	B31R	
3679	255	—	ENO957	Bristol JO5G	ECW	B31R	
3680	256	—	ENO958	Bristol JO5G	ECW	B31R	
3681	257	—	ENO959	Bristol JO5G	ECW	B31R	
3682	—	—	ENO960	Bristol JO5G	ECW	DP31F	
3683	—	—	ENO961	Bristol JO5G	ECW	DP31F	
3684	258	—	ENO962	Bristol JO5G	ECW	DP31F	
3685	259	—	ENO963	Bristol JO5G	ECW	DP31F	
3686	—	—	ENO964	Dennis Lancet	ECOC	B31R	(Beadle —/43 twice)
3687	—	—	ENO965	Dennis Lancet	ECOC	B31R	
3688	—	—	MJ7021	Bedford WLB	Strachan	B20	Lorry by —/45
3689	—	—	ANM532	Albion PK115	Strachan	C32F	(ex-Union Jack)
3690	—	—	GG5821	Albion PV70	Cowieson	B32	
3691	—	—	MJ4350	Albion PV70		B32	
3692	—	—	CG1126	Thornycroft FWD	Strachan	L50R	
3693	—	—	GG9600	Albion Venturer	Brush	H51R	
3694	—	—	AN0132	Dennis Lancet	Duple	B36	(ex-Berry)
3695	—	—	APP272	Dennis Lancet	Dennis	B32	
3696	—	—	HX4358	AEC Regal	Park Royal	32	
3697	—	—	DPU73	Bedford WTB	Duple	C26R	
3698	—	—	CEV394	Bedford WTL	Motts	C25F	
3699	—	—	CNO740	TSM B39A7	Duple	C36F	
—	—	—	KV54	Maudslay ML7		H	not operated, ENOC waiting room —/36
3700	—	—	ALW678	Commer Centaur		20	(ex-Union Jack)
3701	—	—	VX7875	Gilford 1680T		C31	
3702	—	—	VX4333	Gilford 1660T	Duple	B32	
3703	—	—	VW7087	Dennis G		B18	(ex-Berry)
3704	—	—	UF3067	TSM B10A2	Short	B32R	
3705	—	—	EV8316	Morris RP		C20	
3706	—	—	FEV175	Leyland TD5	Brush	L28/28R	ECW L27/26R —/49
3707	—	—	FEV176	Leyland TD5	Brush	L28/28R	ECW L27/26R —/49
3708	—	—	FEV177	Leyland TD5	Brush	L28/28R	ECW L27/26R —/49
3709	—	—	FEV178	Leyland TD5	Brush	L28/28R	ECW L27/26R —/49
3710	—	—	FEV179	Leyland TD5	Brush	L28/28R	ECW L27/26R —/49
3711	—	—	FEV180	Leyland TD5	Brush	L28/28R	ECW L27/26R —/49
3712	—	—	FEV181	Leyland TD5	Brush	L28/28R	ECW L27/26R —/49
3713	—	—	FEV182	Leyland TD5	Brush	L28/28R	ECW L27/26R —/49
3714	—	—	FHK751	Bristol JO5G	ECW	B31R	
3715	260	—	FNO788	Bristol JO5G	ECW	B31R	
3716	261	—	FNO789	Bristol JO5G	ECW	B31R	
3717	262	—	FNO790	Bristol JO5G	ECW	B31R	
3718	—	—	FNO791	Bristol JO5G	ECW	B31R	
3719	—	—	FNO792	Bristol JO5G	ECW	B31R	
3720	—	—	FNO793	Bristol JO5G	ECW	B31R	
3721	263	—	FNO794	Bristol JO5G	ECW	B31R	
3722	—	—	FNO795	Bristol JO5G	ECW	B31R	
3723	—	—	FNO796	Bristol JO5G	ECW	B31R	
3724	264	—	FNO797	Bristol JO5G	ECW	B31R	
3725	—	—	FNO798	Bristol JO5G	ECW	B31R	
3726	265	—	FNO799	Bristol JO5G	ECW	B31R	
3727	—	—	FNO800	Bristol JO5G	ECW	B31R	
3728	—	—	FPU508	Bristol K5G	ECW	L24/24R	
3729	—	—	FPU509	Bristol K5G	ECW	L24/24R	ECW L27/28R —/52
3730	—	—	FPU510	Bristol K5G	ECW	L24/24R	ECW L27/28R —/52
3731	—	—	FPU511	Bristol K5G	ECW	L24/24R	ECW L27/28R —/52
3732	1257	2200	FPU512	Bristol K5G	ECW	L24/24R	ECW L27/28R —/52
3733	—	—	FPU513	Bristol K5G	ECW	L24/24R	ECW L27/28R ex-UCOC 1/60
3734	1258	—	FPU514	Bristol K5G	ECW	L24/24R	ECW L27/28R —/52
3735	—	—	FPU515	Bristol K5G	ECW	L24/24R	ECW L27/28R —/52
3736	—	—	FPU516	Bristol K5G	ECW	L24/24R	L27/28R
3737	—	—	FPU517	Bristol K5G	ECW	L24/24R	ECW L27/28R —/52
3738	—	—	FPU518	Bristol K5G	ECW	L24/24R	L27/28R

Fleet Nos. Orig.	1954	1964	Regn. No.	Chassis	Body	Layout	Remarks
3739	1259	—	FPU519	Bristol K5G	ECW	L24/24R	(Beadle —/44)
3740	1260	—	FPU520	Bristol K5G	ECW	L24/24R	(Beadle —/44)
3741	1261	—	FPU521	Bristol K5G	ECW	L24/24R	(Beadle —/44)
3742	1262	—	FPU522	Bristol K5G	ECW	L24/24R	(Beadle —/44)
3743	—	—	FPU523	Bristol K5G	ECW	L27/28R	
1938							
3744	—	—	GNO688	Bristol K5G	ECW	L26/24R	L24/24R; ECW L27/28R —/52
3745	—	—	GNO689	Bristol K5G	ECW	L26/24R	L24/24R
3746	—	—	GNO690	Bristol K5G	ECW	L26/24R	L24/24R
3747	1270	—	GNO691	Bristol K5G	ECW	L26/24R	L24/24R
3748	—	—	GNO692	Bristol K5G	ECW	L26/24R	L24/24R
3749	—	—	GNO693	Bristol K5G	ECW	L26/24R	L24/24R
3750	—	—	GNO694	Bristol K5G	ECW	L26/24R	L24/24R
3751	1271	—	GNO695	Bristol K5G	ECW	L26/24R	L24/24R
3752	—	—	GNO696	Bristol K5G	ECW	L26/24R	L24/24R
3753	—	—	GNO697	Bristol K5G	ECW	L26/24R	L24/24R
3754	—	—	GNO698	Bristol K5G	ECW	L26/24R	L24/24R; ECW L27/28R —/52
3755	—	—	GNO699	Bristol K5G	ECW	L26/24R	L24/24R
3756	—	—	GNO700	Dennis Lancet	ECW	B31R	Body to 3088 and body from 3758 —/42 (? later a coach)
3757	—	—	GNO701	Dennis Lancet	ECW	B31R	Body to 3089 —/42 (later coach)
3758	—	—	GNO702	Dennis Lancet	ECW	B31R	Body to 3756 —/42 (later coach)
3759	—	—	GPU411	Bristol L5G	ECW	B31R	
3760	266	—	GPU412	Bristol L5G	ECW	B31R	
3761	—	—	GPU413	Bristol L5G	ECW	B31R	
3762	267	—	GPU414	Bristol L5G	ECW	B31R	
3763	268	—	GPU415	Bristol L5G	ECW	B31R	
3764	—	—	GPU416	Bristol L5G	ECW	B31R	
3765	—	—	GPU417	Bristol L5G	ECW	B31R	
3766	—	—	GPU418	Bristol L5G	ECW	B31R	
3767	269	—	GPU419	Bristol L5G	ECW	B31R	
3768	—	—	GPU420	Bristol L5G	ECW	B31R	
3769	270	—	GPU421	Bristol L5G	ECW	B31R	
3770	—	—	GPU422	Bristol L5G	ECW	B31R	
3771	—	—	GPU423	Bristol L5G	ECW	B31R	
3772	—	—	GPU424	Bristol L5G	ECW	B31R	
3773	—	—	GPU425	Bristol L5G	ECW	B31R	
3774	271	—	GPU426	Bristol L5G	ECW	B31R	
3775	272	—	GPU427	Bristol L5G	ECW	B31R	
3776	—	—	GPU428	Bristol L5G	ECW	B31R	
3777	273	—	GPU429	Bristol L5G	ECW	B31R	
3778	—	—	GPU430	Bristol L5G	ECW	B31R	
3779	274	—	GPU431	Bristol L5G	ECW	B31R	
3780	275	—	GPU432	Bristol L5G	ECW	B31R	
3781	—	—	GPU433	Bristol L5G	ECW	B31R	
3782	276	—	GPU434	Bristol L5G	ECW	B31R	
3783	—	—	GPU435	Bristol L5G	ECW	B31R	
3784	—	—	GPU436	Bristol L5G	ECW	B31R	
3785	—	—	GPU437	Bristol L5G	ECW	B31R	
3786	—	—	GPU438	Bristol L5G	ECW	B31R	
3787	—	—	VT297	TSM B10A		B32	(ex-Huntingdon Coaches)
3788	—	—	UR4047	Chevrolet LQ		20	(ex-'Offordian')
3789	—	—	EW6556	Dennis GL	Thurgood	B20	
3790	—	—	GH9947	Gilford 168SD	Duple	C26F	
3791	—	—	DB9318	TSM B10A2	Tilling	B31R	
3792	—	—	DB9324	TSM B10A2	Tilling	B31R	
3793	—	—	DB9328	TSM B10A2	Tilling	B31R	(ex-'North Western')
3794	—	—	DB9336	TSM B10A2	Tilling	B31R	
3795	—	—	DB9339	TSM B10A2	Tilling	B31R	
3796	—	—	DB9341	TSM B10A2	Tilling	B31R	
3797	—	—	EV7290	Bedford WLB	Thurgood	B20	(ex-'Clavering & District')
3798	—	—	DB5294	Leyland TS1	Leyland	C32R	(Beadle —/44)
3799	—	—	MJ449	Dennis Lancet	Duple	B32R	(ex-'Westorning & District')
3800	—	—	MJ7180	Bedford WLB		B20	
3801	—	—	DB5228	TSM B10A	Tilling	B36R	
3802	—	—	DB9342	TSM B10A2	Brush	B31R	(ex-'North-Western')
3803	—	—	DB9351	TSM B10A2	Brush	B31R	
3804	—	—	DB9355	TSM B10A2	Brush	B31R	
3805	—	—	TR5295	Leyland TD1	Short	OT27/24RO	(ex-Hants & Dorset) (Beadle L26/26R —/46)
3806	—	—	TR5326	Leyland TD1	Short	OT27/24RO	(ex-Hants & Dorset)
3807	—	—	GTW888	Bristol K5G	ECW	L24/24R	
3808	—	—	GTW889	Bristol K5G	ECW	L24/24R	L26/24R
3809	—	—	GTW890	Bristol K5G	ECW	L24/24R	
3810	—	—	GTW891	Bristol K5G	ECW	L24/24R	L27/24R
3811	—	—	GTW892	Bristol K5G	ECW	L24/24R	L26/24R
3812	1266	—	GTW893	Bristol K5G	ECW	L24/24R	L27/24R
3813	—	—	GTW894	Bristol K5G	ECW	L24/24R	
3814	—	—	GTW895	Bristol K5G	ECW	L24/24R	
3815	—	—	DTW271	Bedford WTB		C26F	(ex-Starling)(Beadle —/46)
1939							
3816	—	—	GV2366	Dennis Lancet	Duple	C26	normal control
3817	—	—	GV5940	Bedford WTB	Duple	C20F	
3818	—	—	GV5941	Bedford WTB	Duple	C26F	C25F (ex-'Transit Bus')
3819	—	—	BU7186	Dennis Lancet	Duple	C32R	(Beadle —/42)
3820	—	—	NV5508	Bedford WLB		B20F	
3821	—	—	NV6225	Bedford WTL		B20F	(ex-Meadows via UCOC)
3822	—	—	RA5365	Leyland PLSC3	Leyland	B32F	
3823	—	—	RA6602	Leyland PLSC3	Leyland	B32F	
1940							
3820	—	—	JEV411	Bristol K5G	ECW	L27/28R	
3821	—	—	JEV412	Bristol K5G	ECW	L27/28R	
3822	—	—	JEV413	Bristol K5G	ECW	L27/28R	
3823	—	—	JEV414	Bristol K5G	ECW	L27/28R	
3824	—	—	JEV415	Bristol K5G	ECW	L27/28R	
3825	—	—	JEV416	Bristol K5G	ECW	L27/28R	
3826	—	—	JEV417	Bristol K5G	ECW	L27/28R	
3827	—	—	JEV418	Bristol K5G	ECW	L27/28R	
3828	—	—	JEV419	Bristol K5G	ECW	L27/28R	
3829	—	—	JEV420	Bristol K5G	ECW	L27/28R	ECW L27/28R —/52
3830	—	—	JEV421	Bristol K5G	ECW	L27/28R	
3831	—	—	JEV422	Bristol K5G	ECW	L27/28R	
3832	—	—	JEV423	Bristol K5G	ECW	L27/28R	
3833	—	—	JEV424	Bristol K5G	ECW	L27/28R	
3834	—	—	JEV425	Bristol K5G	ECW	L27/28R	
3835	—	—	JEV426	Bristol K5G	ECW	L27/28R	
3836	—	—	JEV427	Bristol K5G	ECW	L27/28R	
3837	—	—	JEV428	Bristol K5G	ECW	L27/28R	
3838	—	—	JEV429	Bristol K5G	ECW	L27/28R	
3839	—	—	JEV430	Bristol K5G	ECW	L27/28R	
1941							
3840	—	—	JEV431	Bristol K5G	ECW	L27/28R	
3841	—	—	JEV432	Bristol K5G	ECW	L27/28R	
3842	—	—	JEV433	Bristol K5G	ECW	L27/28R	
3843	—	—	JEV434	Bristol K5G	ECW	L27/28R	
3844	—	—	JEV435	Bristol K5G	ECW	L27/28R	
3845 — 3869				Not used due to cancellation of order for Bristol L5G/ECW saloons			
3870	—	—	CHK801	Bedford WTL	Duple	C26	(ex-Simpson)
3871	—	—	DNO42	Albion Victor		B26	
1942							
3872	—	—	JPU460	Bristol K5G	Duple	L27/28R	ECW L27/28R —/52
3873	—	—	JPU461	Bristol K5G	Duple	L27/28R	
3874	278	—	HHT459	Bristol L6GG	ECW	B31F	(ex-Bristol T & CC) later L5G and B33F (New with gas producer unit)

Orig.	Fleet Nos. 1954	1964	Regn. No.	Chassis	Body	Layout	Remarks
3875	1175	—	JTW146	Guy Arab I 5LW	Brush	L27/28R	
3876	1176	—	JTW147	Guy Arab I 5LW	Brush	L27/28R	
3877	1177	—	JTW148	Guy Arab I 5LW	Brush	L27/28R	
1943							
3878	1178	—	JTW233	Guy Arab I 5LW	Brush	L27/28R	
3879	1179	—	JTW234	Guy Arab I 5LW	Brush	L27/28R	
3880	1180	—	JTW235	Guy Arab I 5LW	Brush	L27/28R	
3881	1181	—	JTW236	Guy Arab I 5LW	Brush	L27/28R	
3882	1182	—	JTW237	Guy Arab I 5LW	Brush	L27/28R	
3883	1183	—	JTW238	Guy Arab I 5LW	Brush	L27/28R	
3884	1184	—	JTW239	Guy Arab I 5LW	Brush	L27/28R	
1944							
3885	1274	2201	JVW430	Bristol K5G	ECW	L27/28R	prototype low-bridge body
1945							
3886	—	—	DR9838	Leyland TD2	Weymann	L24/24R	(ex-Plymouth Corpn. rebuilt L27/26R and 5LW fitted on acqn)
3887	1105	—	DR9839	Leyland TD2	Weymann	L24/24R	
3888	—	—	DR9864	Leyland TD2	Leyland	L24/24R	
3889	—	—	KHK513	Bristol K5G	ECW	L27/28R	
3890	—	—	KHK514	Bristol K5G	ECW	L27/28R	
1946							
3891	1278	2203	KNO442	Bristol K5G	ECW	L27/28R	
3892	—	—	KNO443	Bristol K5G	ECW	L27/28R	
3893	1279	—	KNO596	Bristol K5G	ECW	L27/28R	
3894	—	—	KNO597	Bristol K5G	ECW	L27/28R	
3895	—	—	KNO598	Bristol K5G	ECW	L27/28R	
3896	—	—	KNO599	Bristol L5G	ECW	B35R	
3897	279	—	KNO600	Bristol L5G	ECW	B35R	
3898	280	—	KNO601	Bristol L5G	ECW	B35R	
3899	—	—	KNO602	Bristol L5G	ECW	B35R	
3900	—	—	KNO603	Bristol L5G	ECW	B35R	
3901	—	—	KNO604	Bristol L5G	ECW	B35R	
3902	—	—	KNO605	Bristol L5G	ECW	B35R	
3903	—	—	KNO606	Bristol L5G	ECW	B35R	
3904	—	—	KNO607	Bristol L5G	ECW	B35R	
3905	281	—	KNO608	Bristol L5G	ECW	B35R	
3906	282	—	KNO609	Bristol L5G	ECW	B35R	
3907	284	—	KNO610	Bristol L5G	ECW	B35R	
3908	283	—	KNO611	Bristol L5G	ECW	B35R	
1947							
3909	—	—	KNO612	Bristol L5G	ECW	B35R	
3910	—	—	KNO613	Bristol L5G	ECW	B35R	
3911	285	—	KNO614	Bristol L5G	ECW	B35R	
3912	286	—	KNO615	Bristol L5G	ECW	B35R	
3913	287	—	KNO616	Bristol L5G	ECW	B35R	
3914	288	—	KNO617	Bristol L5G	ECW	B35R	
3915	289	—	KNO618	Bristol L5G	ECW	B35R	
3916	290	—	KNO619	Bristol L5G	ECW	B35R	
3917	291	—	KNO620	Bristol L5G	ECW	B35R	
3918	—	—	KNO621	Bristol L5G	ECW	B35R	
3919	292	—	KNO622	Bristol L5G	ECW	B35R	
3920	—	—	KNO623	Bristol L5G	ECW	B35R	
3921	—	—	KNO624	Bristol L5G	ECW	B35R	
3922	293	—	KNO625	Bristol L5G	ECW	B35R	
3923	154	—	HKK26	Beadle Commer	Beadle	B35R	delivered —/45; later 4LK
3924	162	—	LNO150	Beadle Bedford	Beadle	B33R	delivered —/46; later 4LK
3925	186	—	LPU615	Bedford OB	Beadle	B30F	Perkins P6 oil engine by —/52
3926	187	—	LPU616	Bedford OB	Beadle	B30F	
3927	188	—	LPU617	Bedford OB	Beadle	B30F	
3928	189	—	LPU618	Bedford OB	Beadle	B30F	Perkins P6 oil engine by —/52
3929	190	—	LPU619	Bedford OB	Beadle	B30F	
3930	—	—	LPU620	Bedford OB	Beadle	B30F	
3931	191	—	LPU621	Bedford OB	Beadle	B30F	first licensed 1949
3932	—	—	LPU622	Bedford OB	Beadle	B30F	first licensed 1949

Orig.	Fleet Nos. 1954	1964	Regn. No.	Chassis	Body	Layout	Remarks
3933	183	—	LPU623	Bedford OB	Duple	C29F	
3934	182	—	LPU624	Bedford OB	Duple	C29F	
3935	—	—	LPU625	Bedford OB	Duple	C29F	
3936	—	—	LPU626	Bedford OB	Duple	C29F	
3937	—	—	LPU627	Bedford OB	Duple	C29F	
3938	184	—	LPU628	Bedford OB	Duple	C29F	
3839	185	—	LPU629	Bedford OB	Duple	C29F	
3940	—	—	MPU1	Bristol K5G	ECW	L27/28R	
3941	—	—	MPU2	Bristol K5G	ECW	L27/28R	
3942	1281	2209	MPU3	Bristol K5G	ECW	L27/28R	
3943	1283	2211	MPU4	Bristol K5G	ECW	L27/28R	
3944	1282	2210	MPU5	Bristol K5G	ECW	L27/28R	
3945	1284	2212	MPU6	Bristol K5G	ECW	L27/28R	
3946	1285	2213	MPU7	Bristol K5G	ECW	L27/28R	
3947	1288	2216	MPU8	Bristol K5G	ECW	L27/28R	
3948	—	—	MPU9	Bristol K5G	ECW	L27/28R	
3949	—	—	MPU10	Bristol K5G	ECW	L27/28R	
3950	—	—	MPU11	Bristol K5G	ECW	L27/28R	
3951	—	—	MPU12	Bristol K5G	ECW	L27/28R	
3952	—	—	MPU13	Bristol K5G	ECW	L27/28R	
3953	1291	2219	MPU14	Bristol K5G	ECW	L27/28R	
3954	1293	2221	MPU15	Bristol K5G	ECW	L27/28R	
3955	—	—	MPU16	Bristol K5G	ECW	L27/28R	
3956	1294	2222	MPU17	Bristol K5G	ECW	L27/28R	
3957	—	—	MPU18	Bristol K5G	ECW	L27/28R	delivered 1948
3958	—	—	MPU19	Bristol K5G	ECW	L27/28R	
3959	1295	2223	MPU20	Bristol K6B	ECW	L27/28R	
3960	1296	2224	MPU21	Bristol K6B	ECW	L27/28R	
3961	1297	2225	MPU22	Bristol K6B	ECW	L27/28R	
3962	—	—	MPU23	Bristol K5G	ECW	L27/28R	
3963	1300	2228	MPU24	Bristol K6B	ECW	L27/28R	
3964	1301	2229	MPU25	Bristol K5G	ECW	L27/28R	
3965	294	—	MPU26	Bristol L5G	ECW	DP31R	
3966	295	—	MPU27	Bristol L5G	ECW	DP31R	
3967	—	—	MPU28	Bristol L5G	ECW	DP31R	
3968	—	—	MPU29	Bristol L5G	ECW	DP31R	
3969	296	—	MPU30	Bristol L5G	ECW	DP31R	
3970	297	—	MPU31	Bristol L5G	ECW	DP31R	
3971	298	—	MPU32	Bristol L5G	ECW	DP31R	
3972	299	—	MPU33	Bristol L5G	ECW	DP31R	
3973	300	—	MPU34	Bristol L5G	ECW	DP31R	delivered 1948
3974	—	—	MPU35	Bristol L5G	ECW	DP31R	
3975	—	—	MPU36	Leyland PD1	ECW	L27/26R	
3976	—	—	MPU37	Leyland PD1	ECW	L27/26R	
3977	—	—	MPU38	Leyland PD1	ECW	L27/26R	
3978	—	—	MPU39	Leyland PD1	ECW	L27/26R	
3979	—	—	MPU40	Leyland PD1	ECW	L27/26R	
3980	—	—	MPU41	Leyland PD1	ECW	L27/26R	
3981	—	—	MPU42	Leyland PD1	ECW	L27/26R	
3982	—	—	MPU43	Leyland PD1	ECW	L27/26R	
3983	1114	—	MPU44	Leyland PD1	ECW	L27/26R	
3984	—	—	MPU45	Leyland PD1	ECW	L27/26R	
3985	—	—	MPU46	Leyland PD1	ECW	L27/26R	
3986	—	—	MPU47	Leyland PD1	ECW	L27/26R	
3987	1115	—	MPU48	Leyland PD1	ECW	L27/26R	
3988	1118	—	MPU49	Leyland PD1	ECW	L27/26R	
3989	1119	—	MPU50	Leyland PD1	ECW	L27/26R	
3990	1120	—	MPU51	Leyland PD1	ECW	L27/26R	
3991	1121	2106	MPU52	Leyland PD1	ECW	L27/26R	
3992	—	—	MPU53	Leyland PD1	ECW	L27/26R	
1948							
3993	1302	2230	NNO93	Bristol K5G	ECW	L27/28R	
3994	1303	2231	NNO94	Bristol K5G	ECW	L27/28R	
3995	1304	2232	NNO95	Bristol K5G	ECW	L27/28R	
3996	—	—	NNO96	Bristol K5G	ECW	L27/28R	

Orig.	Fleet Nos. 1954	1964	Regn. No.	Chassis	Body	Layout	Remarks
3997	—	—	NNO97	Bristol K5G	ECW	L27/28R	
3998	—	—	NNO98	Bristol K5G	ECW	L27/28R	
3999	—	—	NNO99	Bristol K5G	ECW	L27/28R	
4000	—	—	NNO100	Bristol K5G	ECW	L27/28R	London Transport, Camberwell
4001	—		NNO101	Bristol K5G	ECW	L27/28R	London Transport, Camberwell
4002	—	—	NNO102	Bristol K5G	ECW	L27/28R	London Transport, Camberwell
4003	—	—	NNO103	Bristol K5G	ECW	L27/28R	London Transport, Nunhead
4004	1314	2242	NNO104	Bristol K5G	ECW	L27/28R	London Transport, Nunhead
4005	1317	2245	NNO105	Bristol K5G	ECW	L27/28R	London Transport, Norwood (Chassis to 3850 —/51)
4006	1315	2243	NNO106	Bristol K5G	ECW	L27/28R	London Transport, Norwood
4007	1316	2244	NNO107	Bristol K5G	ECW	L27/28R	London Transport, Nunhead
4008	301	—	NNO108	Bristol L5G	ECW	B35R	
4009	—	—	NNO109	Bristol L5G	ECW	B35R	
4010	—	—	NNO110	Bristol L5G	ECW	B35R	
1949							
4011	163	—	NVX525	Beadle Bedford	Beadle	B33R	later B35R 4LK 51/52
4012	164	—	NVX526	Beadle Bedford	Beadle	B33R	later B35R 4LK 51/52
4013	165	—	NVX527	Beadle Bedford	Beadle	B33R	later B35R 4LK 51/52
4014	166	—	NVX528	Beadle Bedford	Beadle	B33R	later B35R 4LK 51/52
4015	167	—	NVX529	Beadle Bedford	Beadle	B33R	later B35R 4LK 51/52
4016	168	—	NVX530	Beadle Bedford	Beadle	B33R	later B35R 4LK 51/52
4017	169	—	NVX531	Beadle Bedford	Beadle	B33R	later B35R 4LK 51/52
4018	170	—	NVX532	Beadle Bedford	Beadle	B33R	later B35R 4LK 51/52
4019	171	—	NVX533	Beadle Bedford	Beadle	B35R	later B35R 4LK 51/52
4020	302	—	ONO41	Bristol L5G	ECW	B35R	
4021	303	—	ONO42	Bristol L5G	ECW	B35R	
4022	304	—	ONO43	Bristol L5G	ECW	B35R	
4023	305	—	ONO44	Bristol L5G	ECW	B35R	
4024	—	—	ONO45	Bristol L5G	ECW	B35R	
4025	306	—	ONO46	Bristol L5G	ECW	B35R	
4026	307	—	ONO47	Bristol L5G	ECW	B35R	
4027	308	—	ONO48	Bristol L5G	ECW	B35R	
4028	309	1107	ONO49	Bristol L5G	ECW	B35R	
4029	310	1108	ONO50	Bristol L5G	ECW	B35R	
4030	1318	2246	ONO51	Bristol K5G	ECW	L27/28R	London Transport, Catford
4031	1319	2247	ONO52	Bristol K5G	ECW	L27/28R	London Transport, Catford
4032	1320	2248	ONO53	Bristol K5G	ECW	L27/28R	London Transport, Catford
4033	1321	2249	ONO54	Bristol K5G	ECW	L27/28R	London Transport, Norwood
4034	—	—	ONO55	Bristol K5G	ECW	L27/28R	London Transport, Norwood
4035	—	—	ONO56	Bristol K5G	ECW	L27/28R	
4036	—	—	ONO57	Bristol K5G	ECW	L27/28R	
4037	1328	2256	ONO58	Bristol K5G	ECW	L27/28R	
4038	1327	2255	ONO59	Bristol K5G	ECW	L27/28R	
4039	1329	2257	ONO60	Bristol K5G	ECW	L27/28R	
4040	—	—	ONO61	Bristol K5G	ECW	L27/28R	
4041	—	—	ONO62	Bristol K5G	ECW	L27/28R	
4042	1322	2250	ONO63	Bristol K5G	ECW	L27/28R	
1950							
4043	1331	2259	ONO64	Bristol K5G	ECW	L27/28R	
4044	1332	2260	ONO65	Bristol K5G	ECW	L27/28R	
4045	1334	2262	ONO66	Bristol K5G	ECW	L27/28R	
4046	1335	2263	ONO67	Bristol K5G	ECW	L27/28R	
4047	1336	2264	ONO68	Bristol K5G	ECW	L27/28R	
4048	1337	2265	ONO69	Bristol K5G	ECW	L27/28R	
4049	—	—	ONO70	Bristol K5G	ECW	L27/28R	
4050	1338	2266	ONO71	Bristol K5G	ECW	L27/28R	
4051	1339	2267	ONO72	Bristol K5G	ECW	L27/28R	
4052	—	—	ONO73	Bristol K5G	ECW	L27/28R	
4053	—	—	ONO74	Bristol K5G	ECW	L27/28R	
4054	—	—	ONO75	Bristol K5G	ECW	L27/28R	
4055	1340	2268	ONO76	Bristol K5G	ECW	L27/28R	
4056	—	—	ONO77	Bristol K5G	ECW	L27/28R	
4057	1341	2269	ONO78	Bristol K5G	ECW	L27/28R	
4058	—	—	ONO79	Bristol K5G	ECW	L27/28R	
4059	1342	2270	ONO80	Bristol K5G	ECW	L27/28R	
4060	311	—	ONO81	Bristol L5G	ECW	B35R	
4061	312	—	ONO82	Bristol L5G	ECW	B35R	
4062	313	—	ONO83	Bristol L5G	ECW	B35R	
4063	—	—	ONO84	Bedford OB	Duple	C29F	⎫
4064	—	—	ONO85	Bedford OB	Duple	C29F	⎪
4065	192	—	ONO86	Bedford OB	Duple	C29F	⎬ delivered late 1949
4066	195	—	ONO87	Bedford OB	Duple	C29F	⎪
4067	194	—	ONO88	Bedford OB	Duple	C29F	⎪
4068	193	—	ONO89	Bedford OB	Duple	C29F	⎭
4069	196	—	ONO90	Bedford OB	Duple	C29F	
4070	197	—	ONO91	Bedford OB	Duple	C29F	
4071	198	—	ONO92	Bedford OB	Duple	C29F	
4072	199	—	ONO93	Bedford OB	Duple	C29F	
4073	200	—	ONO94	Bedford OB	Duple	C29F	
4074	314	—	ONO988	Bristol L5G	ECW	B35R	
4075	315	1113	ONO989	Bristol L5G	ECW	B35R	
4076	—	—	ONO990	Bristol L5G	ECW	B35R	
4077	316	1114	ONO991	Bristol L5G	ECW	B35R	
4078	317	—	ONO992	Bristol L5G	ECW	B35R	
4079	318	1116	ONO993	Bristol L5G	ECW	B35R	
4080	—	—	ONO994	Bristol L5G	ECW	B35R	
4081	—	—	ONO995	Bristol LL5G	ECW	B39R	
4082	329	1117	ONO996	Bristol LL5G	ECW	B39R	
4083	330	1118	ONO997	Bristol LL5G	ECW	B39R	
4084	—	—	ONO998	Bristol LL5G	ECW	B39R	
4085	—	—	ONO999	Bristol LL5G	ECW	B39R	
4086	331	1119	RHK121	Bristol LL5G	ECW	B39R	
4087	—	—	RHK122	Bristol LL5G	ECW	B39R	
4088	332	1120	RHK123	Bristol LL5G	ECW	B39R	
4089	—	—	RHK124	Bristol LL5G	ECW	B39R	
4090	—	—	RHK125	Bristol LL5G	ECW	B39R	
4091	333	1121	RHK126	Bristol LL5G	ECW	B39R	⎫
4092	334	1122	RHK127	Bristol LL5G	ECW	B39R8	⎪
4093	—	—	RHK128	Bristol LL5G	ECW	B39R8	⎪
4094	335	1123	RHK129	Bristol LL5G	ECW	B39R8	⎬ delivered early 1951
4095	—	—	RHK130	Bristol LL5G	ECW	B39R8	⎪
4096	336	1124	RHK131	Bristol LL5G	ECW	B39R8	⎪
4097	—	—	RHK132	Bristol LL5G	ECW	B39R8	⎭
4098	319	—	PTW101	Bristol L6B	ECW	FC26F	FC30F —/53
4099	320	—	PTW102	Bristol L6B	ECW	FC31F	
4100	321	—	PTW103	Bristol L6B	ECW	FC31F	
4101	325	—	PTW104	Bristol L6B	ECW	FC31F	
4102	326	—	PTW105	Bristol L6B	ECW	FC31F	
4103	327	—	PTW106	Bristol L6B	ECW	FC31F	
4104	—	—	PTW107	Bristol L6B	ECW	FC31F	
4105	—	—	PTW108	Bristol L6B	ECW	FC31F	
4106	—	—	PTW109	Bristol L6B	ECW	FC31F	
4107	328	—	PTW110	Bristol L6B	ECW	FC31F	
1	—	—	VX4732	Leyland TD1	Leyland	L24/24R	⎫
39	—	—	BNO206	Dennis Ace	Duple	C20	⎪
41	—	—	BTW374	Leyland LT5A	Wilkes & Mead	C35F	⎪
43	—	—	CNO579	Leyland LT7	Duple	B39	⎪
44	—	—	VX5662	Leyland TS1	Duple	DP32F	⎪
45	105	—	TF6615	Leyland LT2	Wilkes & Mead	C32F	⎬ (ex-Hicks) legally to ENOC 1955
46	104	—	TF5756	Leyland LT2	Leyland	B36F	⎪
47	—	—	DHK511	Albion PK115	Waveney	32	⎪
49	—	—	DPU747	Leyland TD4	Park Royal	L27/26R	⎪
50	—	—	WH810	Leyland TD1	Leyland	L24/24RO	⎪
51	1101	—	WH1551	Leyland TD1	Leyland	L27/24R	⎪
52	1102	—	WH1552	Leyland TD1	Leyland	L27/24R	⎪
54	—	—	WH1554	Leyland TD1	Leyland	L27/24R	⎭

Fleet Nos. Orig.	1954	1964	Regn. No.	Chassis	Body	Layout	Remarks
55	—	—	EHK733	Albion PK115	Waveney	C32	
58	—	—	CHK788	Dennis Ace f/c	Duple	C20F	
59	1109	—	FHK141	Leyland TD5	Strachan	L27/26R	
60	—	—	FTW391	Dennis Lancet	Park Royal	B39F	
61	—	—	FTW997	Albion PK115	Duple	C26F	
62	—	—	VX8349	Leyland TS1	Park Royal	L27/26R	originally a coach
63	—	—	MW5198	Leyland TD1	Park Royal	L27/26R	
64	—	—	ADK810	Bedford WTB	Duple	C25F	
65	1104	—	HF6705	Leyland TD1	Park Royal	L27/26R	
66	—	—	CK4266	Leyland TD1	Leyland	L27/24R	
67	—	—	CK4219	Leyland TD1	Leyland	L27/24R	
68	1103	—	CK4209	Leyland TD1	Leyland	L24/24R	
69	—	—	CK4270	Leyland TD1	Leyland	L24/24R	
70	—	—	CK4263	Leyland TD1	Leyland	L24/24R	
71	—	—	HF6703	Leyland TD1	Park Royal	L27/24R	
72	—	—	HF5881	Leyland TD1	Leyland	L27/24R	
74	—	—	TF2340	Leyland TD1	Leyland	L28/24R	
75	1185	—	JVX716	Guy Arab II	Weymann	L27/28R	
76	1186	—	KEV217	Guy Arab II	Strachan	L27/26R	(ex-Hicks)
77	1187	—	KEV690	Guy Arab II	Strachan	L27/28R	legally to ENOC 1955
78	1188	—	LPU125	Guy Arab II	Strachan	L27/26R	
79	153	—	MNO330	Guy Arab III	Wilkes & Mead	C35F	
80	125	—	MEV174	Leyland PS1/1	Thurgood	B35F	
81	1117	2105	MNO193	Leyland PD1	Leyland	L27/26R	OT33/26R by 2/61
82	1116	2104	MNO194	Leyland PD1	Leyland	L27/26R	OT33/26R by 4/61
83	152	—	MPU68	Guy Arab III	Wilkes & Mead	C35F	
84	1189	—	NEV609	Guy Arab II	Strachan	L27/26R	
85	1190	—	NEV610	Guy Arab II	Strachan	L27/26R	
86	1106	—	WH4908	Leyland TD3	Strachan	L27/26R	
87	—	—	NEV248	Bedford OB	Duple	C29F	
88	—	—	NEV961	Bedford OB	Wilkes & Mead	C29F	
89	—	—	NEV962	Bedford OB	Wilkes & Mead	C29F	
90	1191	—	OVW756	Guy Arab III	Strachan	L27/28R	
91	1192	—	OVW757	Guy Arab III	Strachan	L27/28R	
92	221	—	OVX854	Austin CXB	Wilkes & Mead	C29F	
4108	222	—	PTW623	Maudslay MIII	Duple	FC33F	Ordered by Hicks
4109	1193	—	PTW624	Guy Arab III	Strachan	L27/28R	Ordered by Hicks
4110	1194	—	PTW625	Guy Arab III	Strachan	L27/28R	Ordered by Hicks
4111	—	—	RPU521	Bristol KS5G	ECW	L27/28R	
4112	—	—	RPU522	Bristol KS5G	ECW	L27/28R	
4113	1348	2305	RPU523	Bristol KS5G	ECW	L27/28R	
4114	1349	2306	RPU524	Bristol KS5G	ECW	L27/28R	
4115	—	—	RPU525	Bristol KS5G	ECW	L27/28R	
4116	—	—	RPU526	Bristol KS5G	ECW	L27/28R	
4117	—	—	RPU527	Bristol KS5G	ECW	L27/28R	
101	1157	—	GW6259	AEC Regent	ECW	OT30/26R	(ex-'Brighton & Hove')
102	1158	—	GW6263	AEC Regent	ECW	OT30/26R	
103	1159	—	GW6296	AEC Regent	ECW	OT30/26R	
104	1160	—	GW6299	AEC Regent	Beadle	OT30/26R	

1951

Fleet Nos. Orig.	1954	1964	Regn. No.	Chassis	Body	Layout	Remarks
3850	—	—	TTW268	Bristol K5G	ECW	L27/28R8	(chassis ex-4005 —/51)
4118	—	—	SHK511	Bristol KSW5G	ECW	L27/28R	
4119	1351	2308	SHK512	Bristol KSW5G	ECW	L27/28R	
4120	1352	2309	SHK513	Bristol KSW5G	ECW	L27/28R	
4121	337	1125	RHK133	Bristol LL5G	ECW	B39R8	
4122	338	1126	RHK134	Bristol LWL5G	ECW	B39R	
4123	339	1127	RHK135	Bristol LWL5G	ECW	B39R	
4124	—	—	RHK136	Bristol LWL5G	ECW	B39R	
4125	—	—	SHK514	Bristol LWL5G	ECW	B39R	
4126	340	1128	SHK515	Bristol LWL5G	ECW	B39R	
4127	341	1129	SHK516	Bristol LWL5G	ECW	B39R	
4128	342	1130	SHK517	Bristol LWL5G	ECW	B39R	
4129	343	1131	TNO666	Bristol LWL5G	ECW	B39R	
4130	—	—	TNO667	Bristol LWL5G	ECW	B39R	
4131	—	—	TNO668	Bristol LWL5G	ECW	B39R	
4132	347	1135	TNO669	Bristol LWL5G	ECW	B39R	
4133	348	1136	TNO670	Bristol LWL5G	ECW	B39R	
4134	349	1137	TNO671	Bristol LWL5G	ECW	B39R	
4135	350	1138	TNO672	Bristol LWL5G	ECW	B39R	
4136	1353	2310	SHK518	Bristol KSW5G	ECW	L27/28R	
4137	—	—	SHK519	Bristol KSW5G	ECW	L27/28R	
4138	—	—	SHK520	Bristol KSW5G	ECW	L27/28R	
4139	1354	2311	SHK521	Bristol KSW5G	ECW	L27/28R	
4140	1355	2312	SHK522	Bristol KSW5G	ECW	L27/28R	
4141	1356	2313	SHK523	Bristol KSW5G	ECW	L27/28R	
4142	—	—	SHK524	Bristol KSW5G	ECW	L27/28R	
4143	1357	2314	SHK525	Bristol KSW5G	ECW	L27/28R	
4144	1358	2315	SHK526	Bristol KSW5G	ECW	L27/28R	
4145	—	—	SHK527	Bristol KSW5G	ECW	L27/28R	
4146	1359	2316	SHK528	Bristol KSW5G	ECW	L27/28R	
4147	1360	2317	SHK529	Bristol KSW5G	ECW	L27/28R	
4148	—	—	TNO673	Bristol KSW5G	ECW	L27/28R	
4149	—	—	TNO674	Bristol KSW5G	ECW	L27/28R	
4150	1364	2321	TNO675	Bristol KSW5G	ECW	L27/28R	
4151	1365	2322	TNO676	Bristol KSW5G	ECW	L27/28R	
4152	—	—	TNO677	Bristol KSW5G	ECW	L27/28R	
4153	—	—	TNO678	Bristol KSW5G	ECW	L27/28R	
4154	1366	2322	TNO679	Bristol KSW5G	ECW	L27/28R	
4155	1369	2326	TNO680	Bristol KSW5G	ECW	L27/28R	
4156	1370	2327	TNO681	Bristol KSW5G	ECW	L27/28R	
4157	1371	2328	TNO682	Bristol KSW5G	ECW	L27/28R	
4158	1372	2329	TNO683	Bristol KSW5G	ECW	L27/28R	
4159	1373	2330	TNO684	Bristol KSW5G	ECW	L27/28R	
4160	1374	2331	TNO685	Bristol KSW5G	ECW	L27/28R	
L121	—	—	ABH358	Leyland KP3	Duple	C20	
L122	—	—	APP528	Leyland SKP3	Duple	C26	
L123	—	—	CPP236	Bedford WTB	Duple	B20F	
L124	—	—	EKX691	Dennis Lancet	Perris	B39R	(ex Queens Park Coaches)
L125	—	—	FPP545	Bedford WTB	Duple	C20F	
L126	—	—	GPP473	Dennis Lancet	Willowbrook	B35F	
L127	—	—	GPP497	Bedford OWB	Duple	B30F	
L128	—	—	KKX408	Leyland PS1	Duple	C35F	
L129	—	—	MPP450	Dennis Lancet	Yeates	C35F	

1952

Fleet Nos. Orig.	1954	1964	Regn. No.	Chassis	Body	Layout	Remarks
4161	1375	2332	TNO686	Bristol KSW5G	ECW	L27/28R	
4162	1376	2333	TNO687	Bristol KSW5G	ECW	L27/28R	
4163	1377	2334	TNO688	Bristol KSW5G	ECW	L27/28R	
4164	1378	2335	TNO689	Bristol KSW5G	ECW	L27/28R	
4165	1379	2336	TNO690	Bristol KSW5G	ECW	L27/28R	
4166	351	1139	TTW570	Bristol LWL5G	ECW	B39R	
4167	352	1140	TTW571	Bristol LWL5G	ECW	B39R	
4168	353	1141	TTW572	Bristol LWL5G	ECW	B39R	
4169	354	1142	TTW573	Bristol LWL5G	ECW	B39R	
4170	355	1143	TTW574	Bristol LWL5G	ECW	B39R	
4171	356	1144	TTW575	Bristol LWL5G	ECW	B39R	
4172	357	1145	TTW576	Bristol LWL5G	ECW	B39R	
4173	358	1146	TTW577	Bristol LWL5G	ECW	B39R	
4174	359	1200	UEV829	Bristol LS5G	ECW	DP41D	
4175	—	—	No record of this number being used				
4176	1381	2338	UEV831	Bristol KSW5G	ECW	L27/28R	C38F —/58; DP38F —/62; B43F 11/62
4177	1382	2339	UEV832	Bristol KSW5G	ECW	L27/28R	
4178	1383	2340	UEV833	Bristol KSW5G	ECW	L27/28R	
4179	1384	2341	UEV834	Bristol KSW5G	ECW	L27/28R	
4180	1385	2342	UEV835	Bristol KSW5G	ECW	L27/28R	
4181	1388	2345	UEV836	Bristol KSW5G	ECW	L27/28R	
4182	1389	2346	UEV837	Bristol KSW5G	ECW	L27/28R	
4183	1390	2347	UEV838	Bristol KSW5G	ECW	L27/28R	
4184	1391	2348	UEV839	Bristol KSW5G	ECW	L27/28R	
105	1231	—	NJ8721	Bristol GO5G	Tilling	OT30/26R	(ex-'Brighton & Hove')
106	1232	—	NJ8722	Bristol GO5G	Tilling	OT30/26R	
107	1243	—	NJ9057	Bristol GO5G	Tilling	OT30/26R	

Left table:

Orig.	Fleet Nos. 1954	1964	Regn. No.	Chassis	Body	Layout	Remarks
LT2	106	—	BYM919	Leyland TS7T	Heaver	B39C	
LT8	107	—	CUL802	Leyland TS7T	Heaver	B41C	B39C 9/52
LT10	108	—	CUL804	Leyland TS7T	Heaver	B39C	
LT11	109	—	CUL805	Leyland TS7T	Heaver	B39C	
LT14	110	—	CXL827	Leyland TS7T	Heaver	FB39C	
LT16	111	—	CXW441	Leyland TS7T	Heaver	B43C	
LT18	112	—	CYO190	Leyland TS7T	Heaver	FB43C	FB39C 9/52
LT20	113	—	CYO192	Leyland TS7D	Heaver	B39C	
LT25	114	—	DUC901	Leyland TS7D	Heaver	B39C	
LT26	115	—	DUC902	Leyland TS7D	Heaver	B39C	
LT27	116	—	DUC903	Leyland TS7D	Heaver	B39C	
LT32	117	—	DUC908	Leyland TS7D	Heaver	B39C	LT2-LT32 G2-G6 LS2-LS9 and G7 originally City
G2	118	—	HVW213	Leyland TEC2	Duple	FDP39C	
G3	119	—	HVW214	Leyland TEC2	Duple	FDP39C	
G4	120	—	HVW215	Leyland TEC2	Duple	FDP39C	
G5	121	—	HVW216	Leyland TEC2	Duple	FDP39C	
G6	122	—	HVW217	Leyland TEC2	Duple	FDP39C	
LS2	123	—	LHK413	Leyland PS1/1	Duple	C35F	
LS3	124	—	LHK414	Leyland PS1/1	Duple	C35F	
LS4	126	—	LHK415	Leyland PS1/1	Duple	C35F	
LS5	127	—	LPU684	Leyland PS1/1	Duple	C35F	
LS6	128	—	LPU685	Leyland PS1/1	Duple	C35F	
LS7	129	—	LPU686	Leyland PS1/1	Duple	C35F	
LS8	130	—	LPU687	Leyland PS1/1	Duple	C35F	
LS9	131	—	LPU688	Leyland PS1/1	Duple	C35F	
G7	132	—	NVX170	Leyland PS2/11	Heaver	B39C	originally had two front axles
	133	—	FJN212	Leyland PSU1/15	Burlingham	C39C	
	134	—	FJN210	Leyland PSU1/15	Burlingham	C39C	
	135	—	FJN211	Leyland PSU1/15	Burlingham	C39C	133-138 ordered by City but new to Westcliff
	136	—	FJN218	Leyland PSU1/15	Burlingham	C39C	
	137	—	FJN208	Leyland PSU1/15	Burlingham	C39C	
	138	—	FJN209	Leyland PSU1/15	Burlingham	C39C	
	145	—	AHJ404	AEC Regal	Duple	C32F	
	146	—	AHJ405	AEC Regal	Duple	C32F	
	147	—	BHJ132	AEC Regal	Duple	C30F	bus livery 3/59
	148	—	BJN116	AEC Regal	Duple	C30F	bus livery 4/59
	149	—	BJN117	AEC Regal	Duple	C30F	bus livery 4/59
	150	—	BJN118	AEC Regal	Duple	C30F	
	151	—	BJN119	AEC Regal	Duple	C30F	
C5	155	—	KTW247	Commer Q4	Mulliner	B32F	
C6	156	—	LPU689	Commer Q4	Heaver	B33F	
C7	157	—	LPU690	Commer Q4	Heaver	B33F	
C8	158	—	LPU691	Commer Q4	Heaver	B33F	
C9	159	—	LPU692	Commer Q4	Heaver	B33F	
C10	160	—	LPU693	Commer Q4	Heaver	B33F	
C11	161	—	LPU694	Commer Q4	Heaver	B33F	Perkins P6 engines — C5-C11 B21-B52 originally City
B21	172	—	KPU859	Bedford OB	Mulliner	B30F	
B22	173	—	KPU871	Bedford OB	Mulliner	B30F	
B24	174	—	KTW237	Bedford OB	Mulliner	B30F	
B31	175	—	KTW244	Bedford OB	Mulliner	B30F	
B30	176	—	KTW243	Bedford OB	Mulliner	B30F	
B27	177	—	KTW240	Bedford OB	Mulliner	B30F	
B26	178	—	KTW239	Bedford OB	Mulliner	B30F	
B29	179	—	KTW242	Bedford OB	Mulliner	B30F	
B36	180	—	KVW952	Bedford OB	Mulliner	B30F	
B32	181	—	KVW948	Bedford OB	Mulliner	B30F	
B51	201	—	MVW285	Bedford OB	Duple	C29F	
B52	202	—	MVW286	Bedford OB	Duple	C29F	
	203	—	CJN299	Bedford OB	Duple	C29F	
	204	—	DHJ22	Bedford OB	Duple	C29F	
	205	—	DHJ23	Bedford OB	Duple	C29F	
	206	—	DHJ24	Bedford OB	Duple	C29F	
B53	207	—	MVW287	Bedford OB	Duple	C29F	originally City
	208	—	DHJ623	Bedford OB	Duple	C29F	
	209	—	DHJ624	Bedford OB	Duple	C29F	
	210	—	DHJ625	Bedford OB	Duple	C29F	

All vehicles in this column ex-Westcliff, legally to ENOC 1955

Right table:

Orig.	Fleet Nos. 1954	1964	Regn. No.	Chassis	Body	Layout	Remarks
	211	—	DJN548	Bedford OB	Duple	C29F	
	212	—	DJN551	Bedford OB	Duple	C29F	
	213	—	DJN552	Bedford OB	Duple	C29F	
	214	—	DJN553	Bedford OB	Duple	C29F	
S3	215	—	OEV410	Seddon Mk IV	Plaxton	B31F	
S2	216	—	OEV409	Seddon Mk IV	Plaxton	B31F	S1-S6 originally City —
S4	217	—	OEV411	Seddon Mk IV	Plaxton	B31F	all fitted
S5	218	—	OEV412	Seddon Mk IV	Plaxton	B31F	with Perkins
S6	219	—	OEV413	Seddon Mk IV	Plaxton	B31F	P6 engines
S1	220	—	OEV408	Seddon Mk IV	Plaxton	B31F	
	223	—	JN6880	Bristol JO5G	ECOC	B36R	
	224	—	JN6881	Bristol JO5G	ECOC	B36R	
	225	—	JN6882	Bristol JO5G	ECOC	B36R	
	226	—	JN6883	Bristol JO5G	ECOC	B36R	
	227	—	JN6885	Bristol JO5G	ECOC	B36R	
	228	—	JN6886	Bristol JO5G	ECOC	DP32R	
	229	—	JN6888	Bristol JO5G	ECOC	DP32R	
	230	—	JN6889	Bristol JO5G	ECOC	DP32R	
	231	—	JN7499	Bristol JO5G	ECOC	B36R	
	232	—	JN7501	Bristol JO5G	ECOC	DP32R	
	242	—	JN8560	Bristol JO5G	ECOC	B35R	
	243	—	JN8561	Bristol JO5G	ECOC	B35R	
	244	—	JN8563	Bristol JO5G	ECOC	B35R	
	245	—	JN8564	Bristol JO5G	ECOC	B35R	
	246	—	JN8565	Bristol JO5G	ECOC	B35R	
	247	—	JN8566	Bristol JO5G	ECOC	B35R	
	248	—	JN8567	Bristol JO5G	ECOC	B35R	
	277	—	AJN826	Bristol L5G	ECW	B35R	
	322	—	EHJ27	Bristol L6B	ECW	FC31F	
	323	—	EHJ28	Bristol L6B	ECW	FC31F	
	324	—	EHJ29	Bristol L6B	ECW	FC31F	
	344	1132	EJN633	Bristol LWL5G	ECW	B39R	
	345	1133	EJN634	Bristol LWL5G	ECW	B39R	
	346	1134	EJN635	Bristol LWL5G	ECW	B39R	
	360	300	EJN636	Bristol LS6G	ECW	C39F	
	361	301	EJN637	Bristol LS6G	ECW	C39F	
	362	302	EJN638	Bristol LS6G	ECW	C39F	
	363	303	EJN639	Bristol LS6G	ECW	C39F	ECW C39F 9/57
	364	304	EJN640	Bristol LS6G	ECW	C39F	
	369	309	FJN164	Bristol LS6G	ECW	C39F	
	370	310	FJN165	Bristol LS6G	ECW	C39F	
	371	311	FJN166	Bristol LS6G	ECW	C39F	
	374	312	FJN167	Bristol LS6G	ECW	C39F	
LD3	1110	2100	LEV919	Leyland PD1/1	Beadle	L26/26R	OT33/26R 4/59
LD4	1111	2101	LEV920	Leyland PD1/1	Beadle	L26/26R	OT33/26R 12/58
LD1	1112	2102	LEV917	Leyland PD1/1	Alexander	H30/26R	OT33/26R —/58
LD2	1113	2103	LEV918	Leyland PD1/1	Alexander	H30/26R	OT33/26R —/58
LD5	1122	—	NVX302	Leyland PD1A	Roberts	L27/26R	
LD6	1123	—	NVX303	Leyland PD1A	Roberts	L27/26R	
LD7	1124	—	NVX304	Leyland PD1A	Roberts	L27/26R	
LD8	1125	—	NVX305	Leyland PD1A	Roberts	L27/26R	LD1-LD15 originally City
LD9	1126	—	NVX306	Leyland PD1A	Roberts	L27/26R	
LD10	1127	—	NVX307	Leyland PD1A	Roberts	L27/26R	
LD11	1128	2108	NVX308	Leyland PD1A	Beadle	L27/26R	OT33/26R —/58
LD12	1129	2109	NVX309	Leyland PD1A	Beadle	L27/26R	OT33/26R 12/56
LD13	1130	2110	NVX310	Leyland PD1A	Beadle	L27/26R	OT33/26R 12/58
LD14	1131	2111	NVX311	Leyland PD1A	Beadle	L27/26R	OT33/26R —/58
LD16	1132	2112	NVX313	Leyland PD1A	Beadle	L27/26R	OT33/26R 2/60
LD15	1133	2113	NVX312	Leyland PD1A	Beadle	L27/26R	OT33/26R 2/60
LD22	1134	2114	FJN203	Leyland PD2/12	Leyland	L27/26R	
LD20	1135	2115	FJN201	Leyland PD2/12	Leyland	L27/26R	
LD23	1136	2116	FJN204	Leyland PD2/12	Leyland	L27/26R	
LD21	1137	2117	FJN202	Leyland PD2/12	Leyland	L27/26R	
LD25	1138	2118	FJN206	Leyland PD2/12	Leyland	L27/26R	
LD24	1139	2119	FJN205	Leyland PD2/12	Leyland	L27/26R	
	1140	—	GW6273	AEC Regent	ECW	OT30/26R	originally Brighton & Hove

All vehicles in this column ex-Westcliff, legally to ENOC 1955

Orig.	1954	1964	Regn. No.	Chassis	Body	Layout	Remarks
	1147	—	GJ2005	AEC Regent	ECW	OT30/26R	originally Brighton & Hove
	1148	—	GJ2004	AEC Regent	ECW	OT33/26R	
	1150	—	HX2980	AEC Regent	ECW	OT30/26R	ex-demonstrator
	1156	—	HF7435	AEC Regent	NCB	H30/26R	1156 originally Benfleet and Canvey
	1161	—	JN3716	AEC Regent	Weymann	L27/26R	
	1162	—	JN3228	AEC Regent	Weymann	L27/26R	
	1163	—	JN3229	AEC Regent	Weymann	L27/26R	
	1164	—	JN3718	AEC Regent	Weymann	L27/26R	
	1165	—	JN3717	AEC Regent	Weymann	L26/26R	
	1166	—	JN4294	AEC Regent	ECW	L27/28R	
	1167	—	JN4295	AEC Regent	Weymann	L26/26R	
	1168	—	JN4744	AEC Regent	Weymann	L24/24R	
	1169	—	JN4745	AEC Regent	ECW	L27/28R	
	1170	—	JN4746	AEC Regent	Weymann	L24/24R	
	1171	—	JN4747	AEC Regent	Weymann	L24/24R	
	1172	—	MVW971	AEC Regent	Weymann	H29/28R	re-registered just before acquisition
	1173	—	MVW970	AEC Regent	Weymann	H29/24R	
	1174	—	NPU170	AEC Regent	Weymann	H28/28R	
	1195	—	FOP340	Daimler CWG5	Duple	H30/26R	CWA6 after —/52
	1196	—	FOP360	Daimler CWA6	Duple	H30/26R	
	1197	—	FOP364	Daimler CWA6	Duple	H30/26R	
	1198	—	JVW561	Daimler CWA6	Duple	H30/26R	
	1199	—	FOP429	Daimler CWA6	Duple	H30/26R	
	1200	—	FOP431	Daimler CWA6	Duple	H30/26R	
	1201	—	FOP385	Daimler CWA6	Park Royal	H30/26R	
	1202	—	FOP416	Daimler CWA6	Park Royal	H30/26R	
	1203	—	FOP417	Daimler CWA6	Park Royal	H30/26R	
	1204	—	FOP452	Daimler CWA6	Duple	H30/26R	
	1205	—	FOP459	Daimler CWA6	Park Royal	H30/26R	1172-1215 originally Benfleet and Canvey
	1206	—	FOP461	Daimler CWA6	Park Royal	H30/26R	
	1207	—	FOP462	Daimler CWA6	Park Royal	H30/26R	
	1208	—	FOP465	Daimler CWA6	Park Royal	H30/26R	
	1209	—	KEV534	Daimler CWA6	Brush	H30/26R	
	1210	—	KEV535	Daimler CWA6	Brush	H30/26R	
	1211	—	KEV536	Daimler CWA6	Brush	H30/26R	
	1212	—	KHK863	Daimler CWA6D	Brush	H30/26R	
	1213	—	KNO71	Daimler CWA6D	Brush	H30/26R	
	1214	—	KHK864	Daimler CWA6	Brush	H30/26R	
	1215	—	KNO72	Daimler CWA6	Brush	H30/26R	
D1	1216	—	NVX171	Daimler CVD6	Roberts	L27/26R	
D2	1217	—	NVX172	Daimler CVD6	Roberts	L27/26R	
D3	1218	—	NVX173	Daimler CVD6	Roberts	L27/26R	
D4	1219	—	NVX174	Daimler CVD6	Roberts	L27/26R	1216-1222 originally City
D5	1220	—	NVX175	Daimler CVD6	Roberts	L27/26R	
D6	1221	—	NVX176	Daimler CVD6	Roberts	L27/26R	
D7	1222	—	ONO289	Daimler CVD6	Strachan	L27/28R	
	1223	—	JN6890	Bristol GO5G	Brush	L27/26R	
	1224	—	JN6891	Bristol GO5G	Brush	L27/26R	
	1225	—	JN6892	Bristol GO5G	ECW	L27/28R	
	1226	—	JN6893	Bristol GO5G	ECW	L27/28R	
	1227	—	JN6894	Bristol GO5G	ECW	L27/28R	
	1228	—	JN6895	Bristol GO5G	Brush	L27/26R	
	1229	—	JN6896	Bristol GO5G	Brush	L27/26R	
	1230	—	JN6897	Bristol GO5G	Brush	L27/26R	
	1244	—	JN8570	Bristol GO5G	ECOC	OT30/26R	
	1245	—	JN8571	Bristol GO5G	ECOC	OT30/26R	
	1246	—	JN8572	Bristol GO5G	ECOC	OT30/26R	
	1247	—	AAP829	Bristol GO5G	Tilling	H30/26R	originally Brighton & Hove
	1252	—	JN9540	Bristol K5G	ECW	L27/28R	
	1253	—	JN9541	Bristol K5G	ECW	L27/28R	
	1254	—	JN9542	Bristol K5G	ECW	L27/28R	
	1255	—	JN9543	Bristol K5G	ECW	L27/28R	
	1256	—	JN9544	Bristol K5G	ECW	L27/28R	
	1263	—	AHJ401	Bristol K5G	ECW	L27/28R	
	1264	—	AHJ402	Bristol K5G	ECW	L27/28R	
	1265	—	AHJ403	Bristol K5G	ECW	L27/28R	

All vehicles in this column ex-Westcliff, legally to ENOC 1955

Orig.	1954	1964	Regn. No.	Chassis	Body	Layout	Remarks
	1267	—	AJN823	Bristol K5G	ECW	L27/26R	
	1268	—	AJN824	Bristol K5G	ECW	L27/26R	
	1269	—	AJN825	Bristol K5G	ECW	L27/26R	
	1272	—	BHJ532	Bristol K5G	ECW	L27/28R	
	1273	—	BHJ533	Bristol K5G	ECW	L27/28R	
	1275	—	BJN111	Bristol K5G	ECW	L27/28R	
	1276	—	BJN112	Bristol K5G	ECW	L27/28R	
	1277	—	BJN113	Bristol K5G	ECW	L27/28R	
	1280	—	BJN114	Bristol K5G	ECW	L27/28R	
	1286	2214	CHJ250	Bristol K5G	ECW	L27/28R	
	1287	2215	CHJ251	Bristol K5G	ECW	L27/28R	
	1289	2217	CHJ252	Bristol K5G	ECW	L27/28R	
	1290	2218	CHJ253	Bristol K5G	ECW	L27/28R	
	1292	2220	CHJ254	Bristol K5G	ECW	L27/28R	
	1298	2226	CHJ255	Bristol K6B	ECW	L27/28R	
	1299	2227	CHJ256	Bristol K6B	ECW	L27/28R	
	1305	2233	CJN321	Bristol K5G	ECW	L27/28R	
	1306	2234	CJN322	Bristol K5G	ECW	L27/28R	
	1307	2235	DHJ21	Bristol K5G	ECW	L27/28R	
	1308	2236	CJN323	Bristol K6B	ECW	L27/28R	
	1309	2237	CJN324	Bristol K5G	ECW	L27/28R	London Transport, Leyton
	1310	2238	CJN325	Bristol K5G	ECW	L27/28R	LT Holloway, Riverside
	1311	2239	CJN326	Bristol K5G	ECW	L27/28R	LT Holloway, Riverside
	1312	2240	CJN327	Bristol K6B	ECW	L27/28R	
	1313	2241	CJN328	Bristol K5G	ECW	L27/28R	
	1323	2251	DHJ607	Bristol K5G	ECW	L27/28R	
	1324	2252	DHJ608	Bristol K5G	ECW	L27/28R	
	1325	2253	DHJ610	Bristol K6B	ECW	L27/28R	
	1326	2254	DHJ612	Bristol K6B	ECW	L27/28R	
	1330	2258	DHJ611	Bristol K6B	ECW	L27/28R	
	1333	2261	DHJ609	Bristol K5G	ECW	L27/28R	
	1343	2300	DJN554	Bristol KS5G	ECW	L27/28R	
	1344	2301	DJN556	Bristol KS5G	ECW	L27/28R	
	1345	2302	DJN557	Bristol KS5G	ECW	L27/28R	
	1346	2303	DJN558	Bristol KS6B	ECW	L27/28R	
	1347	2304	DJN559	Bristol KS6B	ECW	L27/28R	
	1350	2307	DJN560	Bristol KSW6B	ECW	L27/28R	
	1361	2318	EJN627	Bristol KSW5G	ECW	L27/28R	
	1362	2319	EJN628	Bristol KSW5G	ECW	L27/28R	
	1363	2320	EJN629	Bristol KSW5G	ECW	L27/28R	
	1367	2324	EJN630	Bristol KSW5G	ECW	L27/28R	
	1368	2325	EJN631	Bristol KSW5G	ECW	L27/28R	
	1380	2337	EJN632	Bristol KSW5G	ECW	L27/28R	
	1386	2343	FJN156	Bristol KSW5G	ECW	L27/28R	
	1387	2344	FJN157	Bristol KSW5G	ECW	L27/28R	
	1392	2349	FJN158	Bristol KSW5G	ECW	L27/28R	
	1393	2350	FJN159	Bristol KSW5G	ECW	L27/28R	
	1394	2351	UEV830	Bristol KSW5G	ECW	L27/28R	
	1395	2352	UEV840	Bristol KSW5G	ECW	L27/28R	
	1396	2353	UEV841	Bristol KSW5G	ECW	L27/28R	
	1397	2354	UEV842	Bristol KSW5G	ECW	L27/28R	
	1398	2355	UVX664	Bristol KSW5G	ECW	L27/28R	
	1399	2356	UVX665	Bristol KSW5G	ECW	L27/28R	
	1400	2357	UVX666	Bristol KSW5G	ECW	L27/28R	
	375	313	FJN168	Bristol LS6G	ECW	C39F	
	376	314	FJN169	Bristol LS6G	ECW	C39F	
	378	1204	FJN162	Bristol LS5G	ECW	DP41D	C38F 4/59: DP38F —/62: B43F
	379	1205	FJN163	Bristol LS5G	ECW	DP41D	C38F 4/59: DP38F —/62: B43F
	1404	2361	FJN160	Bristol KSW5G	ECW	L27/28R	
	1405	2362	FJN161	Bristol KSW5G	ECW	L27/28R	
	1415	2372	VNO867	Bristol KSW5G	ECW	L27/28R	
	1416	2373	VNO868	Bristol KSW5G	ECW	L27/28R	
	1417	2374	WNO472	Bristol KSW5G	ECW	L27/28R	staggered seats upstairs

All vehicles in this column ex-Westcliff, legally to ENOC 1955

Left table

Fleet Nos. Orig.	1954	1964	Regn. No.	Chassis	Body	Layout	Remarks
	1418	2375	WNO473	Bristol KSW5G	ECW	L27/28R	staggered seats on upper deck
	1419	2376	WNO476	Bristol KSW5G	ECW	L27/28R	
	1420	2377	WNO477	Bristol KSW5G	ECW	L27/28R	(ex-Westcliff) legally to ENOC 1955
	1421	2378	WNO474	Bristol KSW5G	ECW	L27/28R	OT33/28R 1/66
	1422	2379	WNO475	Bristol KSW5G	ECW	L27/28R	OT33/28R 2/66
	1423	2380	WNO478	Bristol KSW5G	ECW	L27/28R	OT33/28R 3/66
	1426	2383	WNO479	Bristol KSW5G	ECW	L27/28R	OT33/28R 5/66
1953							
4185	1401	2358	VNO855	Bristol KSW5G	ECW	L27/28R	
4186	1403	2360	VNO856	Bristol KSW5G	ECW	L27/28R	special cooling system
4187	1402	2359	VNO857	Bristol KSW5G	ECW	L27/28R	
4188	1406	2363	VNO858	Bristol KSW5G	ECW	L27/28RD	
4189	1407	2364	VNO859	Bristol KSW5G	ECW	L27/28RD	staggered seats upper deck
4190	1408	2365	VNO860	Bristol KSW5G	ECW	L27/28RD	
4191	1409	2366	VNO861	Bristol KSW5G	ECW	L27/28RD	
4192	1410	2367	VNO862	Bristol KSW5G	ECW	L27/28RD	
4193	1411	2368	VNO863	Bristol KSW5G	ECW	L27/28RD	
4194	1412	2369	VNO864	Bristol KSW5G	ECW	L27/28RD	
4195	1413	2370	VNO865	Bristol KSW5G	ECW	L27/28RD	
4196	365	305	UEV843	Bristol LS5G	ECW	C39F	
4197	366	306	UEV844	Bristol LS5G	ECW	C39F	later LS6G
4198	367	307	UEV845	Bristol LS5G	ECW	C39F	
4199	368	308	UEV846	Bristol LS5G	ECW	C39F	later LS6G
4200	372	1201	VNO869	Bristol LS5G	ECW	DP41D	DP38F —/58 DP43F 12/62
4201	373	1202	VNO870	Bristol LS5G	ECW	DP41D	DP38F —/58 DP43F 12/62
4202	377	1203	VNO871	Bristol LS5G	ECW	DP41D	DP38F 3/59 DP43F 11/62
4203	1414	2371	VNO866	Bristol KSW5G	ECW	L27/28R	
4204	1424	2381	WNO482	Bristol KSW5G	ECW	L27/28R	OT33/28R 1/66
4205	1425	2382	WNO483	Bristol KSW5G	ECW	L27/28R	OT33/28R 10/65 — staggered seats on upper deck
4206	1429	2386	WNO484	Bristol KSW5G	ECW	L27/28R	OT33/28R 11/65
4207	1430	2387	WNO485	Bristol KSW5G	ECW	L27/28R	OT33/28R 3/66
4208	1431	2400	XVX19	Bristol LD5G	ECW	L33/25R	special cooling system 8/59
4209	1434	2403	XVX20	Bristol LD5G	ECW	L33/25R	
4210	1435	2404	XVX21	Bristol LD5G	ECW	L33/25R	delivered 1954
4211	1438	2407	XVX22	Bristol LD5G	ECW	L33/25R	
4212	1439	2408	XVX23	Bristol LD6B	ECW	L33/25R	
4213	1440	2409	XVX24	Bristol LD6B	ECW	L33/25R	
4214	1441	2410	XVX25	Bristol LD6B	ECW	L33/25R	
4215	1427	2384	WNO480	Bristol KSW5G	ECW	L27/28R	OT33/28R 10/65 — staggered seats on upper deck
4216	1428	2385	WNO481	Bristol KSW5G	ECW	L27/28R	OT33/28R 5/66
4217	388	1211	WVX444	Bristol LS5G	ECW	B43D	B45F 7/60
4218	386	1209	WVX446	Bristol LS5G	ECW	B43D	B45F 7/60
4219	387	1210	WVX447	Bristol LS5G	ECW	B43D	B45F 7/60
4220	383	1206	WVX441	Bristol LS5G	ECW	B43D	B45F 12/59
4221	384	1207	WVX442	Bristol LS5G	ECW	B43D	B45F 9/59
4222	385	1208	WVX443	Bristol LS5G	ECW	B43D	B45F 7/59
1954							
4223	390	1212	WVX445	Bristol LS5G	ECW	B43D	B45F 6/60
4224	393	1215	YVW121	Bristol LS5G	ECW	B43D	B45F 8/60
4225	394	1216	YVW122	Bristol LS5G	ECW	B43D	B45F 9/60
4226	—	—	No record of this number being used				
4227	1432	2401	XVX26	Bristol LD5G	ECW	L33/25R	
4228	1433	2402	XVX27	Bristol LD5G	ECW	L33/25R	
4229	—	—	No record of this number being used				
4230	380	315	VVX367	Bristol LS5G	ECW	C39F	delivered 1953
4231	381	316	VVX368	Bristol LS5G	ECW	C39F	
4232	382	317	VVX369	Bristol LS5G	ECW	C39F	
4233	389	318	XTW152	Bristol LS5G	ECW	C39F	later LS6G
	391	1213	YPU138	Bristol LS5G	ECW	B43D	B45F 9/58
	392	1214	YPU139	Bristol LS5G	ECW	B43D	B45F 10/58
	139	—	OEV817	Dennis Lancet	Duple	C33F	(ex-Gidea Park Coaches)
	140	—	PTW641	Dennis Lancet	Gurney Nutting	C34F	
108	1248	—	ANJ831	Bristol GO5G	ECW	OT33/26R	(ex-Brighton & Hove)
—	395	—	724APU	Bristol SC4LK	ECW	B35F	(ECW B35F 6/56)

Right table

Fleet Nos. Orig.	1964	Regn. No.	Chassis	Body	Layout	Remarks
396	—	725APU	Bristol SC6P	ECW	B35F	4LK —/58; B35F by 3/62
397	1217	473BEV	Bristol LS5G	ECW	B45F	
398	1218	474BEV	Bristol LS5G	ECW	B45F	
399	1219	475BEV	Bristol LS5G	ECW	B45F	(ECW B41F 11/56) B45F 2/60
400	1220	476BEV	Bristol LS5G	ECW	B45F	Commer TS3 —/54; 5HLW 4/60
1436	2405	XVX28	Bristol LD5G	ECW	L33/25R	
1437	2406	XVX29	Bristol LD5G	ECW	L33/25R	
1442	2411	XVX30	Bristol LD6B	ECW	L33/25R	(ECW L33/27R —/56 after accident)
1443	2412	XVX31	Bristol LD6B	ECW	L33/25R	
1001	—	AVF354	Bristol GO5G	ECOC	H30/26R	(ex-Eastern Counties)
1002	—	BRX911	Bristol K5G	ECW	L24/24R	
1003	—	BRX912	Bristol K5G	ECW	L24/24R	
1004	—	BRX914	Bristol K5G	ECW	L24/24R	(ex-Thames Valley)
1005	—	BRX915	Bristol K5G	ECW	L24/24R	
1006	—	BRX919	Bristol K5G	ECW	L24/24R	
1007	—	BRX924	Bristol K5G	ECW	L24/24R	
1008	—	GJ2011	AEC Regent	Tilling	OT33/26R	treelopper —/58 (ex-Brighton & Hove)
1009	—	GJ2012	AEC Regent	Tilling	OT33/26R	
1010	—	GN6200	AEC Regent	Tilling	OT33/26R	
1955						
401	1221	567CTW	Bristol LS5G	ECW	B45F	
402	1222	568CTW	Bristol LS5G	ECW	B45F	
403	1223	569CTW	Bristol LS5G	ECW	B45F	(ECW B41F 11/56) (ECW B45F 2/60)
404	1224	570CTW	Bristol LS5G	ECW	B45F	
405	1225	832CVX	Bristol LS5G	ECW	B45F	
406	1226	833CVX	Bristol LS5G	ECW	B45F	
407	1227	966DHK	Bristol LS5G	ECW	B45F	
408	1228	967DHK	Bristol LS5G	ECW	B45F	
409	1229	29ENO	Bristol LS5G	ECW	B45F	
410	1230	30ENO	Bristol LS5G	ECW	B45F	
411	1231	31ENO	Bristol LS5G	ECW	B45F	(ECW B41F 11/56) (ECW B45F 2/60)
412	1232	854ETW	Bristol LS5G	ECW	B45F	(ECW B41F 11/56) (ECW B45F 2/60)
413	1233	855ETW	Bristol LS5G	ECW	B45F	(ECW B41F 6/56) B45F 2/60
414	1234	856ETW	Bristol LS5G	ECW	B45F	(ECW B41F 6/56) B45F 2/60
415	1235	857ETW	Bristol LS5G	ECW	B45F	
416	1236	858ETW	Bristol LS5G	ECW	B45F	
417	1237	859ETW	Bristol LS5G	ECW	B45F	(ECW B41F 10/56) (ECW B45F 2/60)
418	1238	860ETW	Bristol LS5G	ECW	B45F	
419	1239	861ETW	Bristol LS5G	ECW	B45F	(ECW B41F 10/56) (ECW B45F 2/60)
420	1240	862ETW	Bristol LS5G	ECW	B45F	
1444	2413	205BPU	Bristol LD6B	ECW	L33/25R	
1445	2414	206BPU	Bristol LD6B	ECW	L33/25R	
1446	2415	207BPU	Bristol LD6B	ECW	L33/25R	
1447	2416	208BPU	Bristol LD6B	ECW	L33/25R	
1448	2417	209BPU	Bristol LD6B	ECW	L33/25R	
1449	2418	210BPU	Bristol LD5G	ECW	L33/25R	
1450	2419	211BPU	Bristol LD5G	ECW	L33/25R	
1451	2420	212BPU	Bristol LD5G	ECW	L33/25R	
1452	2421	213BPU	Bristol LD5G	ECW	L33/25R	
1453	2422	214BPU	Bristol LD5G	ECW	L33/25R	
1454	2423	882CEV	Bristol LD5G	ECW	L33/25R	
1455	2424	883CEV	Bristol LD5G	ECW	L33/25R	
1456	2425	884CEV	Bristol LD5G	ECW	L33/25R	
1457	2426	885CEV	Bristol LD5G	ECW	L33/25R	
1458	2427	561CTW	Bristol LD5G	ECW	L33/27R	

Orig.	Fleet Nos. 1964	Regn. No.	Chassis	Body	Layout	Remarks
1459	2428	562CTW	Bristol LD6B	ECW	L33/27R	
1460	2429	563CTW	Bristol LD6B	ECW	L33/27R	LD6G —/69
1461	2430	564CTW	Bristol LD6B	ECW	L33/27R	
1462	2431	565CTW	Bristol LD6B	ECW	L33/27R	
1463	2432	566CTW	Bristol LD6B	ECW	L33/27R	
1464	2433	968DHK	Bristol LD5G	ECW	L33/27R	
1465	2434	969DHK	Bristol LD5G	ECW	L33/27R	
1466	2435	970DHK	Bristol LD5G	ECW	L33/27R	
1467	2436	971DHK	Bristol LD5G	ECW	L33/27R	
1468	2437	972DHK	Bristol LD5G	ECW	L33/27R	
1469	2438	973DHK	Bristol LD5G	ECW	L33/27R	
1470	2439	974DHK	Bristol LD5G	ECW	L33/27R	
1471	2440	975DHK	Bristol LD5G	ECW	L33/27R	
1472	2441	976DHK	Bristol LD5G	ECW	L33/27R	
1473	2442	977DHK	Bristol LD5G	ECW	L33/27R	
1474	2443	978DHK	Bristol LD5G	ECW	L33/27R	
1475	2444	501EEV	Bristol LD5G	ECW	L33/27R	
1476	2445	502EEV	Bristol LD5G	ECW	L33/27R	
1477	2446	503EEV	Bristol LD5G	ECW	L33/27R	
1478	2447	504EEV	Bristol LD5G	ECW	L33/27R	
1479	2448	505EEV	Bristol LD5G	ECW	L33/27R	
1480	2449	32ENO	Bristol LD5G	ECW	L33/27R	
1481	2450	33ENO	Bristol LD5G	ECW	L33/27R	
1482	2451	34ENO	Bristol LD6B	ECW	L33/27R	
1483	2452	35ENO	Bristol LD6B	ECW	L33/27R	
1484	2453	36ENO	Bristol LD6B	ECW	L33/27R	LD6G 6/69
1011	—	FPU523	Bristol K5G	ECW	L27/28R	originally ENOC 3743)
1012	—	NV9817	Bristol K5G	ECW	L27/28R	
1013	—	NV9818	Bristol K5G	ECW	L27/28R	(ex-United Counties)
1014	—	VV6351	Bristol K5G	ECW	L27/28R	originally — ENOC 3745
1015	—	GNO689	Bristol K5G	ECW	L27/28R	
1016	—	GNO693	Bristol K5G	ECW	L27/28R	ENOC 3749
1017	—	JEV421	Bristol K5G	ECW	L27/28R	ENOC 3830
1018	—	JEV425	Bristol K5G	ECW	L27/28R	ENOC 3834
1956						
421	1241	437FEV	Bristol LS5G	ECW	B45F	
422	1242	438FEV	Bristol LS5G	ECW	B45F	(ECW B41F 6/56) B45F 2/60
423	1243	439FEV	Bristol LS5G	ECW	B45F	(ECW B41F 6/56) B45F 1/60
1485	2454	433FEV	Bristol LD5G	ECW	L33/27R	
1486	2455	434FEV	Bristol LD5G	ECW	L33/27R	
1487	2456	435FEV	Bristol LD5G	ECW	L33/27R	
1488	2457	436FEV	Bristol LD5G	ECW	L33/27R	
1489	2458	320GPU	Bristol LD6B	ECW	L33/27R	
1490	2459	321GPU	Bristol LD6B	ECW	L33/27R	
1491	2460	322GPU	Bristol LD5G	ECW	L33/27R	
1492	2461	323GPU	Bristol LD5G	ECW	L33/27R	
1493	2462	324GPU	Bristol LD5G	ECW	L33/27R	
1494	2463	325GPU	Bristol LD5G	ECW	L33/27R	
1495	2464	882GVX	Bristol LD5G	ECW	L33/27R	
1496	2465	267GVW	Bristol LD6B	ECW	L33/27R	
1497	2466	268GVW	Bristol LD6B	ECW	L33/27R	
1498	2467	883GVX	Bristol LD6B	ECW	L33/27R	
1499	2468	884GVX	Bristol LD6B	ECW	L33/27R	
1500	2469	885GVX	Bristol LD6B	ECW	L33/27R	
1501	2470	817HNO	Bristol LD6B	ECW	L33/27R	
1502	2471	818HNO	Bristol LD6B	ECW	L33/27R	
1503	2472	819HNO	Bristol LD6B	ECW	L33/27R	
1504	2473	820HNO	Bristol LD6B	ECW	L33/27R	
1505	2474	506HTW	Bristol LD6B	ECW	L33/27R	
1506	2475	507HTW	Bristol LD6B	ECW	L33/27R	
1507	2476	508HTW	Bristol LD6B	ECW	L33/27R	
1508	2477	509HTW	Bristol LD6B	ECW	L33/27R	
1509	2478	538HVX	Bristol LD5G	ECW	L33/27R	
1510	2479	539HVX	Bristol LD5G	ECW	L33/27R	

Orig.	Fleet Nos. 1964	Regn. No.	Chassis	Body	Layout	Remarks
1511	2480	540HVX	Bristol LD5G	ECW	L33/27R	
1512	2481	541HVX	Bristol LD5G	ECW	L33/27R	
1513	2482	295JHK	Bristol LD5G	ECW	L33/27R	
1514	2483	296JHK	Bristol LD5G	ECW	L33/27R	
1515	2484	297JHK	Bristol LD5G	ECW	L33/27R	(carried plaque '1000th LD built')
1516	2485	298JHK	Bristol LD5G	ECW	L33/27R	
1517	2486	75JNO	Bristol LD5G	ECW	L33/27R	
1518	2487	76JNO	Bristol LD5G	ECW	L33/27R	
001	—	KNO53	Albion CX13	Pickering	B34F	
002	—	MTW844	Albion CX13	Allweather	C33F	(ex-Campell)
003	—	MTW843	Albion CX13	Allweather	C33F	
004	—	MTW842	Albion CX13	Allweather	C33F	
005	—	LTW470	Albion CX13	Strachan	B32F	
006	—	JPK847	Bedford OWB	Duple	B28F	not operated by ENOC
1019	—	FVO322	AEC Regent	NCB	L27/28R	to ENOC livery
1020	—	PPU187	Albion CX37	Weymann	L27/26R	
—	—	EVX346	Albion PW141	Metcalfe	C32F	
—	—	GEV694	Albion PH114		C20F	
1021	—	GTW888	Bristol K5G	ECW	L27/28R	(ex-United Counties)
1022	—	GNO694	Bristol K5G	ECW	L27/28R	
1957						
424	—	601JPU	Bristol SC4LK	ECW	B35F	
425	—	602JPU	Bristol SC4LK	ECW	B35F	
426	—	603JPU	Bristol SC4LK	ECW	B35F	
427	—	604JPU	Bristol SC4LK	ECW	B35F	
428	320	613JPU	Bristol LS6G	ECW	C34F	C39F —/63 C34F 12/65
429	321	614JPU	Bristol LS6G	ECW	C34F	C39F —/63 C34F 12/65
430	322	615JPU	Bristol LS6G	ECW	C34F	C39F —/63
431	323	616JPU	Bristol LS6G	ECW	C34F	C39F —/63
432	324	617JPU	Bristol LS6G	ECW	C34F	C39F —/63
433	328	618JPU	Bristol MW6G	ECW	C34F	
434	1300	1858F	Bristol MW6G	ECW	B45F	
435	—	605JPU	Bristol SC4LK	ECW	B35F	
436	—	606JPU	Bristol SC4LK	ECW	B35F	
437	—	607JPU	Bristol SC4LK	ECW	B35F	
438	—	608JPU	Bristol SC4LK	ECW	B35F	
439	—	609JPU	Bristol SC4LK	ECW	B35F	
440	—	610JPU	Bristol SC4LK	ECW	B35F	
441	1244	1859F	Bristol LS5G	ECW	B45F	
442	1245	1860F	Bristol LS5G	ECW	B45F	
443	1246	1861F	Bristol LS5G	ECW	B45F	
444	1247	1862F	Bristol LS5G	ECW	B45F	
445	—	611JPU	Bristol SC4LK	ECW	B35F	
446	—	612JPU	Bristol SC4LK	ECW	B35F	
447	—	9572F	Bristol SC4LK	ECW	B35F	
448	—	9573F	Bristol SC4LK	ECW	B35F	B33F —/63
1519	2488	77JNO	Bristol LD5G	ECW	L33/27R	
1520	2489	78JNO	Bristol LD5G	ECW	L33/27R	
1521	2490	79JNO	Bristol LD5G	ECW	L33/27R	
1522	2491	80JNO	Bristol LD5G	ECW	L33/27R	
1523	2492	81JNO	Bristol LD5G	ECW	L33/27R	
1524	2493	1838F	Bristol LD6B	ECW	L33/27R	
1525	2494	1839F	Bristol LD6B	ECW	L33/27R	
1526	2495	1840F	Bristol LD6B	ECW	L33/27R	
1527	2496	1841F	Bristol LD6B	ECW	L33/27R	
1528	2497	1842F	Bristol LD6B	ECW	L33/27R	
1529	2498	1843F	Bristol LD6B	ECW	L33/27R	
1530	2499	1844F	Bristol LD6B	ECW	L33/27R	
1531	2500	1845F	Bristol LD6B	ECW	L33/27R	
1958						
449	1301	1863F	Bristol MW5G	ECW	B45F	OMB modification 9/59
450	—	9574F	Bristol SC4LK	ECW	B35F	
451	—	9575F	Bristol SC4LK	ECW	B35F	
452	—	9576F	Bristol SC4LK	ECW	B35F	
453	—	9577F	Bristol SC4LK	ECW	B35F	

Fleet Nos. Orig.	Fleet Nos. 1964	Regn. No.	Chassis	Body	Layout	Remarks
454	—	9578F	Bristol SC4LK	ECW	B35F	
455	—	9579F	Bristol SC4LK	ECW	B35F	
456	329	7015HK	Bristol MW6G	ECW	C39F	
457	330	7016HK	Bristol MW6G	ECW	C39F	
458	331	7017HK	Bristol MW6G	ECW	C39F	
459	332	7018HK	Bristol MW6G	ECW	C39F	
460	1302	1864F	Bristol MW5G	ECW	B41F	
461	1303	1865F	Bristol MW5G	ECW	B41F	
462	1304	1866F	Bristol MW5G	ECW	B41F	
463	1305	1867F	Bristol MW5G	ECW	B41F	
464	1306	201MHK	Bristol MW5G	ECW	B41F	
465	1307	202MHK	Bristol MW5G	ECW	B41F	
466	1308	203MHK	Bristol MW5G	ECW	B41F	(ECW B45F 1/60)
467	1309	204MHK	Bristol MW5G	ECW	B41F	
468	1310	205MHK	Bristol MW5G	ECW	B41F	
469	1311	206MHK	Bristol MW5G	ECW	B41F	
470	1312	207MHK	Bristol MW5G	ECW	B41F	
471	1313	208MHK	Bristol MW5G	ECW	B41F	
472	1314	209MHK	Bristol MW5G	ECW	B41F	
473	1315	210MHK	Bristol MW5G	ECW	B41F	
474	1316	211MHK	Bristol MW5G	ECW	B41F	
1532	2501	1846F	Bristol LD6B	ECW	L33/27R	LD6G —/69
1533	2502	1847F	Bristol LD6B	ECW	L33/27R	LD6G --/69
1534	2503	1848F	Bristol LD5G	ECW	L33/27R	
1535	2504	1849F	Bristol LD5G	ECW	L33/27R	
1536	2505	1850F	Bristol LD5G	ECW	L33/27R	
1537	2506	1851F	Bristol LD5G	ECW	L33/27R	
1538	2507	1852F	Bristol LD5G	ECW	L33/27R	
1539	2508	1853F	Bristol LD5G	ECW	L33/27R	
1540	2509	1854F	Bristol LD5G	ECW	L33/27R	
1541	2510	236LNO	Bristol LDLX6G	ECW	L37/33R	prototype air suspension
1542	2511	1855F	Bristol LD5G	ECW	L33/27R	
1543	2512	1856F	Bristol LD5G	ECW	L33/27R	
1544	2513	1857F	Bristol LD5G	ECW	L33/27R	
1545	2514	351LPU	Bristol LD5G	ECW	L33/27R	
1546	2515	352LPU	Bristol LD5G	ECW	L33/27R	
1547	2516	353LPU	Bristol LD5G	ECW	L33/27R	
1548	2517	354LPU	Bristol LD5G	ECW	L33/27R	
1549	2518	355LPU	Bristol LD5G	ECW	L33/27R	
1550	2519	356LPU	Bristol LD5G	ECW	L33/27R	
1551	2520	357LPU	Bristol LD5G	ECW	L33/27R	
007	—	EBD238	Bristol L6B	ECW	FC31F	
008	—	EBD239	Bristol L6B	ECW	FC31F	
009	—	EBD240	Bristol L6B	ECW	FC31F	
010	—	EBD241	Bristol L6B	ECW	FC31F	originally ENOC
011	—	PTW107	Bristol L6B	ECW	FC31F	(ex-United Counties) 4102
012	—	PTW108	Bristol L6B	ECW	FC31F	4103
013	—	PTW109	Bristol L6B	ECW	FC31F	4104
014	—	KKX408	Leyland PS1	Duple	C35F	L128
015	—	SEV814	Leyland PSU1/15	Thurgood	C41F	(ex-Primrose (Chelmsford))
1959						
475	1317	212MHK	Bristol MW5G	ECW	B41F	(ECW B45F 1/60)
476	1318	213MHK	Bristol MW5G	ECW	B41F	(ECW B45F 1/60)
477	1319	214MHK	Bristol MW5G	ECW	B41F	(ECW B45F 1/60)
478	1400	215MHK	Bristol MW5G	ECW	DP41F	
479	1401	216MHK	Bristol MW5G	ECW	DP41F	
480	1402	217MHK	Bristol MW5G	ECW	DP41F	
481	333	280NHK	Bristol MW6G	ECW	C39F	
482	334	281NHK	Bristol MW6G	ECW	C39F	
483	335	282NHK	Bristol MW6G	ECW	C39F	
484	336	283NHK	Bristol MW6G	ECW	C39F	
485	337	284NHK	Bristol MW6G	ECW	C39F	
486	338	285NHK	Bristol MW6G	ECW	C39F	
487	1403	1251EV	Bristol MW5G	ECW	DP41F	
488	1404	1252EV	Bristol MW5G	ECW	DP41F	
489	1405	1253EV	Bristol MW5G	ECW	DP41F	
490	1406	1254EV	Bristol MW5G	ECW	DP41F	fitted with roof luggage rack 11/60
491	1407	1255EV	Bristol MW5G	ECW	DP41F	
492	1408	1256EV	Bristol MW5G	ECW	DP41F	
493	1409	1257EV	Bristol MW5G	ECW	DP41F	
494	1320	1258EV	Bristol MW5G	ECW	B45F	OMB modification 11/59
495	1321	1259EV	Bristol MW5G	ECW	B45F	
496	1322	1260EV	Bristol MW5G	ECW	B45F	
497	1323	1261EV	Bristol MW5G	ECW	B45F	
498	1324	1262EV	Bristol MW5G	ECW	B45F	
499	1325	1263EV	Bristol MW5G	ECW	B45F	
500	1326	1264EV	Bristol MW5G	ECW	B45F	
501	1327	1265EV	Bristol MW5G	ECW	B45F	
1552	2521	358LPU	Bristol LD5G	ECW	L33/27R	
1553	2522	359LPU	Bristol LD5G	ECW	L33/27R	
1554	2523	360LPU	Bristol LD5G	ECW	L33/27R	
1555	2524	47PPU	Bristol LD5G	ECW	L33/27R	
1556	2525	48PPU	Bristol LD5G	ECW	L33/27R	
1557	2526	49PPU	Bristol LD5G	ECW	L33/27R	
1558	2527	50PPU	Bristol LD5G	ECW	L33/27R	
1559	2528	51PPU	Bristol LD5G	ECW	L33/27R	
1560	2529	52PPU	Bristol LD5G	ECW	L33/27R	
1561	2530	53PPU	Bristol LD5G	ECW	L33/27R	
1562	2531	54PPU	Bristol LD5G	ECW	L33/27R	
1563	2532	55PPU	Bristol LD5G	ECW	L33/27R	
1564	2533	56PPU	Bristol LD5G	ECW	L33/27R	
1565	2534	57PPU	Bristol LD5G	ECW	L33/27R	
1566	2535	58PPU	Bristol LD5G	ECW	L33/27R	
1567	2536	59PPU	Bristol LD5G	ECW	L33/27R	
1568	2537	60PPU	Bristol LD5G	ECW	L33/27R	
1960						
502	1328	1266EV	Bristol MW5G	ECW	B45F	
503	1329	1267EV	Bristol MW5G	ECW	B45F	
504	1330	1268EV	Bristol MW5G	ECW	B45F	
505	1331	1269EV	Bristol MW5G	ECW	B45F	
506	1332	1270EV	Bristol MW5G	ECW	B45F	
507	339	3384VW	Bristol MW6G	ECW	C41F	
508	340	3385VW	Bristol MW6G	ECW	C41F	
509	341	3386VW	Bristol MW6G	ECW	C41F	
510	342	3387VW	Bristol MW6G	ECW	C41F	
511	343	3388VW	Bristol MW6G	ECW	C41F	
512	1333	2723VX	Bristol MW5G	ECW	B45F	
513	1334	2724VX	Bristol MW5G	ECW	B45F	
514	1335	2725VX	Bristol MW5G	ECW	B45F	
515	1336	2726VX	Bristol MW5G	ECW	B45F	
516	1337	2727VX	Bristol MW5G	ECW	B45F	
517	1338	2728VX	Bristol MW5G	ECW	B45F	
518	1339	2729VX	Bristol MW5G	ECW	B45F	
519	1340	2730VX	Bristol MW5G	ECW	B45F	
520	1341	2731VX	Bristol MW5G	ECW	B45F	
521	1342	2732VX	Bristol MW5G	ECW	B45F	
522	1343	2733VX	Bristol MW5G	ECW	B45F	
523	1344	2734VX	Bristol MW5G	ECW	B45F	
1569	2538	61PPU	Bristol FS5G	ECW	L33/27R	
1570	2539	62PPU	Bristol FS5G	ECW	L33/27R	
1571	2700	80TVX	Bristol FLF6G	ECW	L38/32F	
1572	2701	81TVX	Bristol FLF6G	ECW	L38/32F	
1573	2702	82TVX	Bristol FLF6G	ECW	L38/32F	
1574	2703	83TVX	Bristol FLF6G	ECW	L38/32F	
1575	2704	84TVX	Bristol FLF6G	ECW	L38/32F	
1576	2705	85TVX	Bristol FLF6G	ECW	L38/32F	
1577	2706	86TVX	Bristol FLF6G	ECW	L38/32F	
1578	2707	87TVX	Bristol FLF6G	ECW	L38/32F	
1579	2708	88TVX	Bristol FLF6G	ECW	L38/32F	
1580	2709	89TVX	Bristol FLF6B	ECW	L38/32F	
1581	2710	90TVX	Bristol FLF6B	ECW	L38/32F	
1582	2711	91TVX	Bristol FLF6B	ECW	L38/32F	

Orig.	Fleet Nos. 1964	Regn. No.	Chassis	Body	Layout	Remarks
1583	2712	92TVX	Bristol FLF6B	ECW	L38/32F	FLF6G —/67
1584	2713	93TVX	Bristol FLF6B	ECW	L38/32F	
1585	2714	94TVX	Bristol FLF6G	ECW	L38/32F	
1586	2715	95TVX	Bristol FLF6G	ECW	L38/32F	
1587	2716	96TVX	Bristol FLF6G	ECW	L38/32F	
1588	2717	97TVX	Bristol FLF6G	ECW	L38/22F	
1589	2718	98TVX	Bristol FLF6G	ECW	L38/32F	
1590	2719	99TVX	Bristol FLF6G	ECW	L38/32F	
1023	—	CAP131	Bristol K5G	ECW	OT32/26R	(ex-Brighton & Hove)
	—	KEV423	Bedford OWB	Duple	B31F	} (ex-Mawdsley and Brown)
	—	MVX596	Bedford OB	Mulliner	B31F	
1961						
524	1410	2735VX	Bristol MW5G	ECW	DP41F	
525	1411	2736VX	Bristol MW5G	ECW	DP41F	
526	1412	2737VX	Bristol MW5G	ECW	DP41F	
527	1413	2738VX	Bristol MW5G	ECW	DP41F	
528	1414	2739VX	Bristol MW5G	ECW	DP41F	
529	1415	2740VX	Bristol MW5G	ECW	DP41F	to Tilling 5/65; ENOC —/68
530	1416	2741VX	Bristol MW5G	ECW	DP41F	
531	1417	2742VX	Bristol MW5G	ECW	DP41F	
532	344	569UVX	Bristol MW6G	ECW	C34F	C39F 2/66
533	345	570UVX	Bristol MW6G	ECW	C34F	C39F 2/66
534	346	571UVX	Bristol MW6G	ECW	C34F	C39F 2/66
535	349	572UVX	Bristol MW6G	ECW	C34F	
536	350	573UVX	Bristol MW6G	ECW	C34F	C39F 3/66
537	1418	804WVW	Bristol MW5G	ECW	DP41F	to Tilling 5/65; ENOC —/68
538	1419	805WVW	Bristol MW5G	ECW	DP41F	
539	1420	806WVW	Bristol MW5G	ECW	DP41F	
540	1421	807WVW	Bristol MW5G	ECW	DP41F	
541	1422	201YVX	Bristol MW5G	ECW	DP41F	
542	1423	202YVX	Bristol MW5G	ECW	DP41F	
543	1424	203YVX	Bristol MW5G	ECW	DP41F	C39F 12/65
544	1425	204YVX	Bristol MW5G	ECW	DP41F	
545	1345	205YVX	Bristol MW5G	ECW	B45F	
546	1346	206YVX	Bristol MW5G	ECW	B45F	
547	1347	207YVX	Bristol MW5G	ECW	B45F	
548	1348	208YVX	Bristol MW5G	ECW	B45F	
1591	2720	801WVW	Bristol FLF6B	ECW	L38/32F	
1592	2721	802WVW	Bristol FLF6B	ECW	L38/32F	
1593	2722	803WVW	Bristol FLF6B	ECW	L38/32F	
1594	2723	171XNO	Bristol FLF6B	ECW	L38/32F	
1595	2724	172XNO	Bristol FLF6B	ECW	L38/32F	
1596	2725	170XNO	Bristol FLF6B	ECW	L38/32F	
1597	2726	173XNO	Bristol FLF6G	ECW	L38/32F	
1598	2727	174XNO	Bristol FLF6G	ECW	L38/32F	
1599	2728	175XNO	Bristol FLF6G	ECW	L38/32F	
1600	2729	176XNO	Bristol FLF6G	ECW	L38/32F	
1601	2730	177XNO	Bristol FLF6G	ECW	L38/32F	
1602	2731	178XNO	Bristol FLF6G	ECW	L38/32F	
1603	2732	179XNO	Bristol FLF6G	ECW	L38/32F	
1604	2733	180XNO	Bristol FLF6G	ECW	L38/32F	
1605	2734	181XNO	Bristol FLF6G	ECW	L38/32F	
016	205	MXB744	Bristol LL6G	ECW	FC35F	
017	206	MXB745	Bristol LL6G	ECW	FC35F	
018	207	MXB746	Bristol LL6G	ECW	FC35F	} ex-Tilling
019	208	MXB747	Bristol LL6G	ECW	FC35F	
020	209	MXB748	Bristol LL6G	ECW	FC35F	
1962						
549	1349	209YVX	Bristol MW5G	ECW	B45F	
550	1350	210YVX	Bristol MW5G	ECW	B45F	
551	1351	211YVX	Bristol MW5G	ECW	B45F	
552	1352	212YVX	Bristol MW5G	ECW	B45F	
553	1353	MOO174	Bristol MW5G	ECW	B45F	
554	1354	MOO175	Bristol MW5G	ECW	B45F	
555	1355	MOO176	Bristol MW5G	ECW	B45F	
556	1356	MOO177	Bristol MW5G	ECW	B45F	
557	352	OO9543	Bristol MW6G	ECW	C39F	C32F —/63: DP41F as 1435 1/69
558	353	OO9544	Bristol MW6G	ECW	C39F	C32F —/63: DP41F as 1436 1/69
559	354	OO9545	Bristol MW6G	ECW	C39F	C32F —/63: DP41F as 1437 1/69
560	355	OO9546	Bristol MW6G	ECW	C39F	C32F —/63: DP41F as 1438 1/69
561	359	OO9547	Bristol MW6G	ECW	C39F	C32F —/63: DP41F as 1439 4/69
562	360	OO9548	Bristol MW6G	ECW	C34F	
563	361	OO9549	Bristol MW6G	ECW	C34F	
564	362	OO9550	Bristol MW6G	ECW	C34F	
565	1426	MOO178	Bristol MW5G	ECW	DP41F	
566	1427	MOO179	Bristol MW5G	ECW	DP41F	
567	1428	MOO973	Bristol MW5G	ECW	DP41F	
568	1429	MOO974	Bristol MW5G	ECW	DP41F	
569	1430	MOO975	Bristol MW5G	ECW	DP41F	
570	1431	MOO976	Bristol MW5G	ECW	DP41F	
1606	2735	182XNO	Bristol FLF6B	ECW	L38/32F	
1607	2736	183XNO	Bristol FLF6B	ECW	L38/32F	
1608	2600	184XNO	Bristol FLF6B	ECW	LC37/18F	} purchased for service X10
1609	2602	185XNO	Bristol FLF6B	ECW	LC37/18F	
1610	2601	186XNO	Bristol FLF6B	ECW	LC37/18F	
1611	2737	EOO579	Bristol FLF6G	ECW	L38/32F	
1612	2738	EOO580	Bristol FLF6G	ECW	L38/32F	
1613	2739	EOO581	Bristol FLF6G	ECW	L38/32F	
1614	2740	EOO582	Bristol FLF6G	ECW	L38/32F	
1615	2741	EOO583	Bristol FLF6G	ECW	L38/32F	
1616	2742	EOO584	Bristol FLF6B	ECW	L38/32F	
1617	2743	EOO585	Bristol FLF6B	ECW	L38/32F	
1618	2744	EOO586	Bristol FLF6B	ECW	L38/32F	
1619	2745	EOO587	Bristol FLF6B	ECW	L38/32F	
1620	2746	EOO588	Bristol FLF6B	ECW	L38/32F	
1621	2747	EOO589	Bristol FLF6B	ECW	L38/32F	
1622	2748	EOO590	Bristol FLF6B	ECW	L38/32F	
1623	2749	EOO591	Bristol FLF6B	ECW	L38/32F	Gardner 6LW 6/67
1624	2750	JWC710	Bristol FLF6G	ECW	L38/32F	
1625	2751	JWC711	Bristol FLF6G	ECW	L38/32F	
1626	2752	JWC712	Bristol FLF6G	ECW	L38/32F	
1627	2753	JWC713	Bristol FLF6G	ECW	L38/32F	
1628	2754	JWC714	Bristol FLF6G	ECW	L38/32F	
1629	2755	JWC715	Bristol FLF6G	ECW	L38/32F	
1630	2756	JWC716	Bristol FLF6G	ECW	L38/32F	
1631	2757	JWC717	Bristol FLF6G	ECW	L38/32F	
1632	2758	JWC718	Bristol FLF6B	ECW	L38/32F	
021	200	MXB739	Bristol LL6G	ECW	FC35F	
022	204	MXB743	Bristol LL6G	ECW	FC35F	(ex-Tilling)
023	319	OBD901	Bristol LS6G	ECW	C35F	C37F 4/65
024	325	OBD902	Bristol LS6G	ECW	C35F	C37F 4/65
1963						
571	1357	OWC606	Bristol MW5G	ECW	B45F	
572	1358	OWC607	Bristol MW5G	ECW	B45F	
573	1359	OWC608	Bristol MW5G	ECW	B45F	
574	1360	OWC609	Bristol MW5G	ECW	B45F	
575	1361	OWC610	Bristol MW5G	ECW	B45F	
576	1362	OWC611	Bristol MW5G	ECW	B45F	
577	364	LWC869	Bristol MW6G	ECW	C39F	
1633	2759	RWC600	Bristol FLF6G	ECW	L38/32F	
1634	2760	RWC601	Bristol FLF6G	ECW	L38/32F	
1635	2761	RWC602	Bristol FLF6G	ECW	L38/32F	
1636	2762	RWC603	Bristol FLF6G	ECW	L38/32F	
1637	2603	RWC604	Bristol FLF6B	ECW	L37/18F	

Fleet Nos. Orig.	1964	Regn. No.	Chassis	Body	Layout	Remarks
1638	2763	RWC605	Bristol FLF6B	ECW	L38/32F	
1639	2764	RWC606	Bristol FLF6B	ECW	L38/32F	
1640	2604	RWC607	Bristol FLF6B	ECW	LC37/18F	
1641	2605	RWC608	Bristol FLF6B	ECW	LC37/18F	to Tilling —/?; ENOC —/69
1642	2765	VWC45	Bristol FLF6B	ECW	L38/32F	
1643	2766	VWC46	Bristol FLF6B	ECW	L38/32F	
1644	2767	VWC47	Bristol FLF6B	ECW	L38/32F	
1645	2768	VWC48	Bristol FLF6B	ECW	L38/32F	
1646	2769	VWC49	Bristol FLF6B	ECW	L38/32F	
1647	2770	VWC50	Bristol FLF6G	ECW	L38/32F	
1648	2771	VWC51	Bristol FLF6G	ECW	L38/32F	
1649	2772	VWC52	Bristol FLF6G	ECW	L38/32F	
1650	2773	VWC53	Bristol FLF6G	ECW	L38/32F	
1651	2774	987KOO	Bristol FLF6G	ECW	L38/32F	
1652	2775	988KOO	Bristol FLF6G	ECW	L38/32F	
1653	2776	989KOO	Bristol FLF6G	ECW	L38/32F	
1654	2777	990KOO	Bristol FLF6G	ECW	L38/32F	
1655	2778	991KOO	Bristol FLF6B	ECW	L38/32F	
1656	2779	992KOO	Bristol FLF6B	ECW	L38/32F	
1657	2780	993KOO	Bristol FLF6B	ECW	L38/32F	
1658	2781	994KOO	Bristol FLF6B	ECW	L38/32F	
1659	2782	995KOO	Bristol FLF6B	ECW	L38/32F	
1660	2783	934LWC	Bristol FLF6G	ECW	L38/32F	
1661	2784	935LWC	Bristol FLF6G	ECW	L38/32F	
1662	2785	936LWC	Bristol FLF6B	ECW	L38/32F	
1663	2786	937LWC	Bristol FLF6B	ECW	L38/32F	
1664	2787	938LWC	Bristol FLF6B	ECW	L38/32F	
1049	2018	581AOO	Guy Arab IV	Massey	L34/33R	ordered by Moore, new to ENOC
1050	2019	582AOO	Guy Arab IV	Massey	L34/33R	
025	—	HYM685	Bedford OB	Duple	C29F	
026	—	RTW222	Bedford OB	Duple	C29F	
027	—	LPU940	Guy Arab III	Duple	DP35F	
028	—	LVW124	Guy Arab III	Duple	DP35F	
029	—	LVW125	Guy Arab III	Duple	DP35F	
030	—	KGT378	Guy Arab III	Strachan	C35F	
031	—	KGT381	Guy Arab III	Strachan	C35F	
032	—	KGT379	Guy Arab III	Strachan	C35F	
033	—	KGT380	Guy Arab III	Strachan	C35F	
034	—	PHK531	Guy Arab III	Strachan	C35F	
035	—	PHK532	Guy Arab III	Strachan	C35F	
036	—	PHK534	Guy Arab III	Strachan	C35F	
037	100	576FVW	Commer Avenger	Duple	C41F	
038	101	577FVW	Commer Avenger	Duple	C41F	
039	102	7652VW	Commer Avenger	Yeates	C41F	C37F —/63 C41F —/64
040	—	LTW62	Guy Arab III	Duple	Towing Wagon	
1024	2000	JTW447	Guy Arab I	Massey	L29/28R	
1025	2001	JVW999	Guy Arab II	Massey	L29/28R	
1026	—	JVX555	Guy Arab II	Strachan	L27/28R	
1027	2002	GYL982	Guy Arab II	Strachan	L28/28R8	
1028	2003	GYL981	Guy Arab II	Strachan	L28/28R8	
1029	2004	GYL983	Guy Arab II	Strachan	L28/28R8	semi-derelict condition
1030	2005	GYL984	Guy Arab II	Strachan	L28/28R8	(ex-Moore)
1031	—	JVX556	Guy Arab II	Strachan	L27/28R	
1032	—	JVX557	Guy Arab II	Strachan	L27/28R	
1033	—	JVX558	Guy Arab II	Strachan	L27/28R	
1034	2006	LPU611	Guy Arab III	Massey	L29/28R	
1035	—	LPU612	Guy Arab III	Strachan	L27/28R	
1036	—	ONO537	Guy Arab III	Strachan	L27/28R	
1037	—	ONO538	Guy Arab III	Strachan	L27/28R	
1038	2007	YEV263	Guy Arab IV	Strachan	L28/28R	
1039	2008	52DHK	Guy Arab IV	Strachan	L28/28R	
1040	2009	53DHK	Guy Arab IV	Strachan	L28/28R	
1041	2010	2834F	Guy Arab IV	NCME	L31/32R	
1042	2011	2835F	Guy Arab IV	NCME	L31/32R	
1043	2012	8935NO	Guy Arab IV	Massey	L34/33R	

Fleet Nos. Orig.	1964	Regn. No.	Chassis	Body	Layout	Remarks
1044	2013	8936NO	Guy Arab IV	Massey	L34/33R	
1045	2014	19PVX	Guy Arab IV	Massey	L34/33R	(ex-Moore)
1046	2015	20PVX	Guy Arab IV	Massey	L34/33R	
1047	2016	372WPU	Guy Arab IV	Massey	L34/33R	
1048	2017	373WPU	Guy Arab IV	Massey	L34/33R	
—	—	PHK533	Guy Arab III	(without body)		
041	201	MXB740	Bristol LL6G	ECW	FC35F	
042	202	MXB741	Bristol LL6G	ECW	FC35F	
043	203	MXB742	Bristol LL6G	ECW	FC35F	
044	326	SLA760	Bristol LS6B	ECW	C34F	C37F 5/65
045	327	SLA761	Bristol LS6B	ECW	C34F	C37F 5/65 (ex-Tilling)
046	356	10DLY	Bristol MW6G	ECW	C34F	
047	357	12DLY	Bristol MW6G	ECW	C34F	
048	358	13DLY	Bristol MW6G	ECW	C34F	
049	363	NWC14	Bristol MW6G	ECW	C34F	
1051	2202	DMR836	Bristol K5G	ECW	L27/28R	
1052	2204	DMR838	Bristol K5G	ECW	L27/28R	
1053	2205	DMR839	Bristol K5G	ECW	L27/28R	(ex-Wilts & Dorset)
1054	2206	DMR840	Bristol K5G	ECW	L27/28R	
1055	2207	EAM612	Bristol K6B	ECW	L27/28R	
1056	2208	EAM613	Bristol K5G	ECW	L27/28R	
1964						
578	400	AVX961B	Bristol RELH6G	ECW	C47F	
579	401	AVX962B	Bristol RELH6G	ECW	C47F	
580	402	AVX963B	Bristol RELH6G	ECW	C47F	C42F 8/69
581	403	AVX964B	Bristol RELH6G	ECW	C47F	C42F 12/65
582	404	AVX965B	Bristol RELH6G	ECW	C47F	C42F 12/65
583	405	AVX966B	Bristol RELH6G	ECW	C47F	C42F 12/65
584	406	AVX967B	Bristol RELH6G	ECW	C47F	C42F 12/65
585	500	BNO109B	Bedford SB13	Duple	C41F	
586	501	BNO110B	Bedford SB13	Duple	C41F	
587	502	BNO111B	Bedford SB13	Duple	C41F	
588	503	BNO112B	Bedford SB13	Duple	C41F	
589	504	BNO113B	Bedford SB13	Duple	C41F	
590	505	BNO114B	Bedford SB13	Duple	C41F	
591	1600	BNO101B	Bristol RELH6G	ECW	DP47F	
592	1601	BNO102B	Bristol RELH6G	ECW	DP47F	
593	1602	BNO103B	Bristol RELH6G	ECW	DP47F	to Tilling 5/65; ENOC —/67
594	1603	BNO104B	Bristol RELH6G	ECW	DP47F	to Tilling 5/65; ENOC —/67
595	1604	BNO105B	Bristol RELH6G	ECW	DP47F	
596	1605	BNO106B	Bristol RELH6G	ECW	DP47F	
597	1606	BNO107B	Bristol RELH6G	ECW	DP47F	
598	1607	BNO108B	Bristol RELH6G	ECW	DP47F	to Tilling 5/65; ENOC —/67
599	365	BNO115B	Bristol MW6G	ECW	C39F	
600	366	BNO116B	Bristol MW6G	ECW	C39F	
601	367	BNO117B	Bristol MW6G	ECW	C39F	
1665	2788	AVX956B	Bristol FLF6B	ECW	L38/32F	
1666	2789	AVX957B	Bristol FLF6G	ECW	L38/32F	
1667	2790	AVX958B	Bristol FLF6G	ECW	L38/32F	
1668	2791	AVX959B	Bristol FLF6G	ECW	L38/32F	
1669	2792	AVX960B	Bristol FLF6G	ECW	L38/32F	
1670	2793	BVX667B	Bristol FLF6B	ECW	L38/32F	
1671	2606	BVX668B	Bristol FLF6B	ECW	LC37/18F	
1672	2607	BVX669B	Bristol FLF6B	ECW	LC37/18F	
1673	2794	BVX670B	Bristol FLF6B	ECW	L38/32F	
1674	2795	BVX671B	Bristol FLF6G	ECW	L38/32F	
1675	2796	BVX672B	Bristol FLF6G	ECW	L38/32F	
1676	2797	BVX673B	Bristol FLF6B	ECW	L38/32F	
1677	2798	BVX674B	Bristol FLF6B	ECW	L38/32F	
1678	2799	BVX675B	Bristol FLF6B	ECW	L38/32F	
1679	2800	BVX676B	Bristol FLF6B	ECW	L38/32F	
1680	2801	BVX677B	Bristol FLF6B	ECW	L38/32F	
1681	2802	BVX678B	Bristol FLF6G	ECW	L38/32F	
1682	2803	BVX679B	Bristol FLF6B	ECW	L38/32F	
1683	2804	BVX680B	Bristol FLF6B	ECW	L38/32F	
050	347	YBD200	Bristol MW6G	ECW	C34F	
051	348	YBD201	Bristol MW6G	ECW	C34F	(ex-United Counties)
052	351	YBD202	Bristol MW6G	ECW	C34F	

Fleet Nos.	Regn. No.	Chassis	Body	Layout	Remarks
1964					
2805-2806	BVX681-682B	Bristol FLF6G	ECW	L38/32F	
2807	BVX683B	Bristol FLF6B	ECW	L38/32F	
2808-2811	FWC426-429B	Bristol FLF6B	ECW	L38/32F	
2812-2815	GNO788-791B	Bristol FLF6G	ECW	L38/32F	
2816-2819	HEV994-997B	Bristol FLF6G	ECW	L38/32F	
1965					
2820	JHK452C	Bristol FLF6B	ECW	L38/32F	
2821	JHK453C	Bristol FLF6G	ECW	L38/32F	
2822-2823	JHK454-455C	Bristol FLF6B	ECW	L38/32F	
2824-2826	JHK459-461C	Bristol FLF6G	ECW	L38/32F	
2827	JHK462C	Bristol FLF6B	ECW	L38/32F	
2828-2829	KNO951-952C	Bristol FLF6B	ECW	L38/32F	2828 Gardner 6LW 3/65
2830-2832	KNO953-955C	Bristol FLF6G	ECW	L38/32F	
2833-2835	LWC659-661C	Bristol FLF6B	ECW	L38/32F	
2836-2840	LWC662-666C	Bristol FLF6G	ECW	L38/32F	
2841-2845	MVX878-882C	Bristol FLF6B	ECW	L38/32F	
2846-2848	MVX883-885C	Bristol FLF6G	ECW	L38/32F	
2849-2851	NTW942-944C	Bristol FLF6G	ECW	L38/32F	
2608-2609	KNO949-950C	Bristol FLF6B	ECW	LC37/22F	
1432-1434	JHK456-458C	Bristol MW5G	ECW	DP43F	OMB 4/65
368-369	OJJ749-750	Bristol LS6B	ECW	C39F	
370	OJJ751	Bristol LS6B	ECW	C41F	
371-375	OLU752-756	Bristol LS6B	ECW	C39F	
376-377	PYO757-758	Bristol LS6B	ECW	C39F	
378	SLA759	Bristol LS6B	ECW	C34F	(ex-Tilling)
379	SLA762	Bristol LS6B	ECW	C34F	
380-382	VYO767-769	Bristol MW6G	ECW	C41F	C39F 12/65
383	1BXB	Bristol MW6G	ECW	C39F	
384	NWC15	Bristol MW6G	ECW	C39F	
506	6BXB	Bedford SB8	Duple	C41F	
507	8BXB	Bedford SB8	Duple	C41F	
380	SLA763	Bristol LS6B	ECW	C43F	
1966					
2852-2854	OVX296-298D	Bristol FLF6G	ECW	L38/32F	
2855-2856	OPU824-825D	Bristol FLF6B	ECW	L38/32F	
2857-2858	OPU822-823D	Bristol FLF6B	ECW	L38/32F	
2859-2863	RHK344-348D	Bristol FLF6B	ECW	L38/32F	
2864-2868	RVW390-394D	Bristol FLF6B	ECW	L38/32F	
2869-2873	RWC941-945D	Bristol FLF6G	ECW	L38/32F	
2874-2877	STW762-765D	Bristol FLF6B	ECW	L38/32F	
2878-2880	SVX277-279D	Bristol FLF6B	ECW	L38/32F	
2881-2883	UEV219-221E	Bristol FLF6G	ECW	L38/32F	
318	SLA763	Bristol LS6B	ECW	C34F	(ex-Tilling)
385-386	2-3BXB	Bristol MW6G	ECW	C34F	

Fleet Nos.	Regn. No.	Chassis	Body	Layout	Remarks
1967					
2884-2889	WNO972-977F	Bristol FLF6G	ECW	L40/30F	
2890-2896	WNO978-984F	Bristol FLF6G	ECW	L40/30F	
2897-2906	WVX524-533F	Bristol FLF6G	ECW	L40/30F	
2907-2913	WWC737-743F	Bristol FLF6G	ECW	L40/30F	
2914-2916	WWC744-746F	Bristol FLF6G	ECW	L40/30F	
1602-1603	BNO103-104B	Bristol RELH6G	ECW	DP45F	(ex-Tilling: see 1964)
1607	BNO108B	Bristol RELH6G	ECW	DP45F	
1968					
407-410	YHK724-727F	Bristol RELH6G	ECW	C47F	
413-416	YTW537-540F	Bristol RESH6G	Duple (N)	C36F	
2610-2612	AVW401-403F	Bristol FLF6G	ECW	LC37/18F	
2613-2614	AVX974-975G	Bristol FLF6G	ECW	LC37/18F	
2917-2926	AEV811-820F	Bristol FLF6G	ECW	L40/30F	
2927-2930	AVW396-399F	Bristol FLF6G	ECW	L40/30F	
2931	AVX973G	Bristol FLF6G	ECW	L40/30F	
387-388	4-5BXB	Bristol MW6G	ECW	C34F	
389	9DLY	Bristol MW6G	ECW	C34F	
390	11DLY	Bristol MW6G	ECW	C34F	
391-392	OWC181-182D	Bristol MW6G	ECW	C34F	(ex-Tilling)
393	OWC183D	Bristol MW6G	ECW	C34F	
1415	2740VX	Bristol MW5G	ECW	DP41F	see 1961
1418	804WVW	Bristol MW5G	ECW	DP41F	see 1961
1969					
1500-1504	CVW854-858G	Bristol RELL6G	ECW	B53F	
1505-1509	EPU186-190G	Bristol RELL6G	ECW	B53F	
1510-1514	FVX612-616H	Bristol RELL6G	ECW	B53F	
1515-1519	FWC438-442H	Bristol RELL6G	ECW	B53F	
3000-3004	CPU979-983G	Bristol VRTSL6G	ECW	L39/31F	
508	BPU21B	Bedford SB13	Duple (N)	C41F	
2605	RWC608	Bristol FLF6B	ECW	LC37/18F	see 1963 (ex-Tilling)
2607	BVX669B	Bristol FLF6B	ECW	LC37/18F	see 1964
1248	PHN858	Bristol LS5G	ECW	B45F	(ex-United Auto)

Appendix B
Route Diagrams

Diagrams showing the development and duration of every stage and express service worked by Eastern National.

PART ONE: Eastern Area Stage Routes 1929—1955 (pages 117—122)
Eastern National Route Numbers 1, 1A, 1B, 2, 2A, 2B, 3, 3A, 4, 4A, 4B, 5, 6, 7, 8, 8A, 8B, 8C, 9, 10, 10A, 10B, 11, 11A, 12, 12A, 12B, 13, 13A, 13B, 13C, 13D, 13E, 14, 14A, 14B, 14C, 15, 16, 17, 17A, 18, 18A, 18B, 19, 19A, 20, 21, 21A, 21B, 22, 23, 23A, 24, 25, 26, 27, 28, 29, 30, 31, 31A, 32, 32A, 32B, 33, 35, 36, 37, 37A, 37B, 38, 39, 39A, 39B, 39C, 40, 40A, 41, 42, 43, 44, 45, 46, 47, 48, 49, 50, 50A, 51, 52, 53, 54, 55, 56, 57, 58, 59, 60, 61, 62, 63, 64, 65, 66, 67, 68, 70, 71, 72, 75, 75A, 75B, 75C, 75D, 75E, 76, 77, 77A, 77B, 78, 80, 81, 82, 83, 84, 85, 101, 101A, 101B, 102, 103, 103A, 104, 104A, 104B, 105, 106, 107, 107A, 108, 109, 110, 111, 112, 113, 114, 114A, 115, 115A, 116, 117, 118, 118A, 119, 119A, 119B, 120, 121, 122, 123, 123A, 124, 125, 164.

PART TWO: Midland Area Stage Routes 1929—1955 (pages 123—128)
Eastern National Route Numbers 1, 2, 2A, 3, 3A, 3B, 3C, 4, 4A, 4B, 4C, 4D, 5, 5A, 6, 7, 7A, 7B, 7C, 7D, 7E, 8, 8A, 8B, 8C, 8D, 8E, 8F, 8G, 9, 9A, 9B, 9C, 9D, 10, 11, 12, 12A, 13, 14, 14A, 15, 15A, 16, 16A, 16B, 17, 18, 18A, 18B, 18C, 19, 20, 20A, 20B, 20C, 20D, 21, 22, 23, 24, 24A, 25, 25A, 26, 27, 27A, 27B, 28, 28A, 28B, 29, 29A, 30, 30A, 30B, 30C, 31, 32, 33, 33A, 33B, 33C, 34, 34A, 34B, 34C, 35, 35A, 35B, 35C, 35D, 35E, 36, 36A, 36B, 36C, 36D, 36E, 36F, 36G, 37, 38, 38A, 38B, 39, 40, 41, 41A, 42, 42A, 43, 43A, 44, 45, 46, 47, 48, 48A, 49, 50, 50A, 51, 51A, 51B, 51C, 52, 52B, 52C, 52D, 53, 53A, 53B, 53C, 54, 55, 56, 56A, 57, 58, 59, 63, 64, 65, 66, 67, 68, 69, 70, 71, 72, 73, 74, 75, 76, 77, 78, 80, 80A, 81, 82, 82A, 83, 101, 102, 103, 104, 104A, 105, 106, 107, 108, 109, 109A, 110, 359.

PART THREE: All Eastern National and Southend District Joint Services 1955—1969 (pages 129—148)
1955 Route Numbers 1, 2, 2A, 2B, 2C, 2D, 3, 3A, 3B, 3C, 4, 4A, 4B, 5, 5A, 6, 6A, 6B, 6C, 7, 7A, 7B, 8, 8A, 9, 9A, 9B, 10, 11, 11A, 11E, 12, 13, 13A, 14, 14A, 14B, 14D, 14E, 15, 15A, 15B, 15C, 16, 16A, 17, 17A, 18, 19, 19A, 19E, 20, 20A, 21, 22, 22A, 22B, 22C, 23, 23A, 24, 24A, 25, 25A, 25B, 25C, 26, 26A, 26B, 26C, 26F, 27, 28, 28A, 28B, 28C, 29, 29A, 29B, 30, 30A, 30B, 31, 31A, 31B, 31C, 31E, 32, 32A, 33, 33A, 34, 34A, 34B, 34C, 35, 36, 37, 38, 39, 40, 40A, 41, 42, 42A, 43, 43A, 44, 44A, 44B, 44C, 45, 46, 47, 47A, 48, 49, 49A, 50, 50A, 50B, 51, 51A, 51B, 52, 53, 53A, 53C, 53E, 54, 55, 55A, 56, 57, 58, 58C, 61, 61A, 61B, 61C, 62, 63, 63A, 63B, 64, 65, 66, 67, 67A, 68, 68A, 69, 70, 70A, 70B, 71, 72, 73, 73A, 74, 74A, 75, 75A, 75B, 75C, 76, 76A, 77, 77A, 78, 78A, 79, 80, 80A, 80B, 81, 82, 83, 84, 85, 86, 87, 87A, 88, 88A, 88B, 89, 89A, 90, 91, 92, 93, 94, 94A, 95, 96, 97, 98, 99, 100, 101, 101A, 101B, 102, 103, 104, 105, 106, 107, 108, 109, 110, 111, 112, 113, 113A, 114, 114A, 115, 115A, 116, 117, 118, 119, 119A, 120, 120A, 121, 122, 123, 124, 125, 126, 126A, 128, 129, 130, 131, 141, 142, 143, 144, 145, 147, 148, 150, 151, 153, 158, 159, 207, 212, 224, 230, 231, 232, 233, 234, 235, 236, 241, 242, 243, 244, 245, 246, 247, 248, 249, 250, 251, 252, 253, 254, 255, 256, 257, 258, 259, 260, 261, 262, 263, 264, 265, 266, 283, 299, 300, 301, 302, 303, 304, 305, 306, 307, 308, 309, 310, 311, 312, 313, 314, 315, 316, 317, 319, 320, 321, 322, 323, 324, 325, 329, 330, 331, 332, 333, 334, 335, 336, 337, 338, 339, 347, 348, 349, 351, 352, 353, 402, 411, 419, 446, 453.

PART FOUR: Express Routes 1929—1961 (page 149)
Eastern Area Symbols A, B, C, D, E, F, G, H, J, K, L, M, N, P, Q, R, S, T, U, V, W.
Midland Area Symbols D, E, F, G, H, J, M, P, Q.

PART FIVE: Express Routes 1962—1969 (pages 150—151)
Eastern Area Routes X1, X2, X3, X4, X5, X7, X8, X9, X10, X11, X12, X13, X14, X15, X16, X20, X21, X22, X23, X24, X25, X26, X27, X28, X29, X30, X31, X32, X33, X34, X35, X36, X40, X41, X42, X43, X44, X45, X46, X50, X51, X52, X60, X61, X62, X63, X64, X70, X71.
East Anglian Routes EAX1, EAX2, EAX3, EAX12, EAX35, EAX52.
Essex Coast Routes ECX4, ECX33, ECX80.

Compiled by F. D. Simpson
Drawn by R. J. Crawley

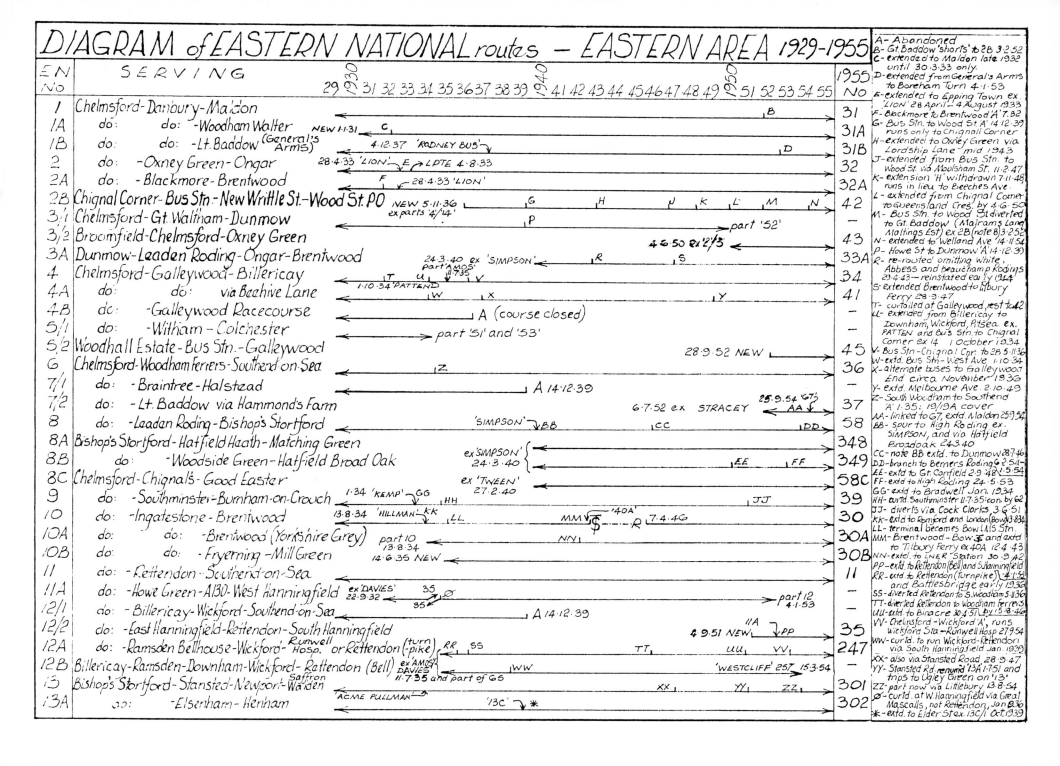

DIAGRAM of EASTERN NATIONAL routes – EASTERN AREA 1929-1955

Timeline columns: 29 1930 31 32 33 34 35 36 37 38 39 1940 41 42 43 44 45 46 47 48 49 1950 51 52 53 54 55

EN No	SERVING	Notes	1955 No
1	Chelmsford-Danbury-Maldon	B	31
1A	do: do: -Woodham Walter	NEW 1.1.31 C	31A
1B	do: do: -Lt. Baddow (General's Arms)	4.12.37 'RODNEY BUS' D	31B
2	do: -Oxney Green-Ongar	28.4.33 'LION' E LPTE 4.8.33	32
2A	do: -Blackmore-Brentwood	F 28.4.33 'LION'	32A
2B	Chignal Corner-Bus Stn.-New Writtle St.-Wood St. PO	NEW 5.11.36 ex parts '4/14' G H J K L M N	42
3/1	Chelmsford-Gt. Waltham-Dunmow	P part '52'	—
3/2	Broomfield-Chelmsford-Oxney Green	4.6.50 ex '2/3'	43
3A	Dunmow-Leaden Roding-Ongar-Brentwood	24.3.40 ex 'SIMPSON' part 'AMOS' 11.7.35 R S	33A
4	Chelmsford-Galleywood-Billericay	T U V	34
4A	do: do: via Beehive Lane	1.10.34 'PATTEN' W X Y	41
4B	do: -Galleywood Racecourse	A (course closed)	—
5/1	do: -Witham-Colchester	part '51' and '53'	—
5/2	Woodhall Estate-Bus Stn.-Galleywood	28.9.52 NEW	45
6	Chelmsford-Woodham Ferrers-Southend-on-Sea	Z	36
7/1	do: -Braintree-Halstead	A 14.12.39	—
7/2	do: -Lt. Baddow via Hammond's Farm	6.7.52 ex STRACEY 25.9.54 '67' AA	37
8	do: -Leaden Roding-Bishop's Stortford	'SIMPSON' BB CC DD	58
8A	Bishop's Stortford-Hatfield Heath-Matching Green	ex 'SIMPSON' 24.3.40	348
8B	do: -Woodside Green-Hatfield Broad Oak	EE FF	349
8C	Chelmsford-Chignals-Good Easter	ex 'TWEEN' 27.2.40	58C
9	do: -Southminster-Burnham-on-Crouch	1.34 'KEMP' GG HH JJ	39
10	do: -Ingatestone-Brentwood	13.8.34 'HILLMAN' KK LL MM S R 7.4.46	30
10A	do: do: -Brentwood (Yorkshire Grey)	part 10 13.8.34 NN	30A
10B	do: do: -Fryerning-Mill Green	14.6.35 NEW	30B
11	do: -Rettendon-Southend-on-Sea		11
11A	do: -Howe Green-A130-West Hanningfield	ex 'DAVIES' 22.9.32 35 Ø 35	—
12/1	do: -Billericay-Wickford-Southend-on-Sea	A 14.12.39 part 12 4.1.53	—
12/2	do: -East Hanningfield-Rettendon-South Hanningfield	4.9.51 NEW 11A PP	35
12A	do: -Ramsden Bellhouse-Wickford-Runwell Hosp. or Rettendon (-pike) (turn)	RR SS TT UU VV	247
12B	Billericay-Ramsden-Downham-Wickford-Rettendon (Bell)	ex 'AMOS' 'DAVIES' 11.7.35 and part of 65 WW 'WESTCLIFF' 257 15.3.54	—
13	Bishop's Stortford-Stansted-Newport-Saffron Walden	XX YY ZZ	301
13A	do: -Elsenham-Henham	'ACME PULLMAN' '13C' *	302

Legend:

A- Abandoned
B- Gt. Baddow 'shorts' to 2B 3.2.52
C- extended to Maldon late 1932 until 30.3.33 only.
D- extended from General's Arms to Boreham Turn 4.1.53
E- extended to Epping Town ex. 'LION' 28 April – 4 August 1933
F- Blackmore to Brentwood 'A' 7.32
G- Bus Stn. to Wood St. 'A' 14.12.39 runs only to Chignall Corner
H- extended to Oxney Green via Lordship Lane mid 1943
J- extended from Bus Stn. to Wood St. via Moulsham St. 11.2.47
K- extension 'H' withdrawn 7.11.48 runs in lieu to Beeches Ave.
L- extended from Chignal Corner to Queensland Cres. by 4.6.50
M- Bus Stn. to Wood St diverted to Gt. Baddow (Malrams Lane Maltings Est) ex 2B (note B) 3.2.52
N- extended to Welland Ave 14.11.54
P- Howe St. to Dunmow 'A' 14.12.39
R- re-routed omitting White, Abbess and Beauchamp Rodings 29.4.43 — reinstated early 1944
S- extended Brentwood to Tilbury Ferry 28.9.47
T- curtailed at Galleywood, rest to 42
U- extended from Billericay to Downham, Wickford, Pitsea ex. PATTEN and Bus Stn. to Chignal Corner ex 14 1 October 1934
V- Bus Stn.-Chignal Corr. to 2B 5.11.36
W- extd. Bus Stn.-West Ave 1.10.34
X- alternate buses to Galleywood End circa November 1936
Y- extd. Melbourne Ave. 2.10.49
Z- South Woodham to Southend 'A' 1.35: 19/19A cover
AA- linked to 67, extd. Maldon 25.9.54
BB- spur to High Roding ex. SIMPSON, and via Hatfield Broadoak 24.3.40
CC- note BB extd. to Dunmow 28.7.46
DD- branch to Berners Roding 6.2.54
EE- extd to Gt. Canfield 2.9.48
FF- extd to High Roding 24.5.53
GG- extd to Bradwell Jan. 1934
HH- curtld. Southminster 11.7.35: con. by 62
JJ- diverts via Cock Clarks. 3.6.51
KK- extd to Romford and London (Bow) 13.8.34
LL- terminal becomes Bow LAIS Stn.
MM- Brentwood-Bow 'S' and extd. to Tilbury Ferry ex 40A 12.4.43
NN- extd. to LNER Station 30.9.42
PP- extd. to Rettendon (Bell) and S. Hanningfield
RR- extd. to Rettendon (Turnpike) 4.1.53 and Battlesbridge early 1930
SS- diverted Rettendon to S. Woodham 5.11.36
TT- diverted Rettendon to Woodham Ferrers
UU- extd. to Bicacre 30.4.51 by 15.8.46
VV- Chelmsford-Wickford 'A', runs Wickford Sta.-Runwell Hosp 27.9.54
WW- curtld. to run Wickford-Rettendon via South Hanningfield Jan. 1939
XX- also via Stansted Road. 28.9.47
YY- Stansted Rd. renumd '13A' 1.7.51 and trips to Ugley Green on '13'
ZZ- part now via Littlebury 13.8.54
Ø- curtld. at W. Hanningfield via Great Mascalls, not Rettendon, Jan 1936
*- extd. to Elder St ex. 13C/1 Oct. 1939

Bus route history chart — "EN No. / SERVING / 1929–1955 timeline / 1955 No. / NOTES"

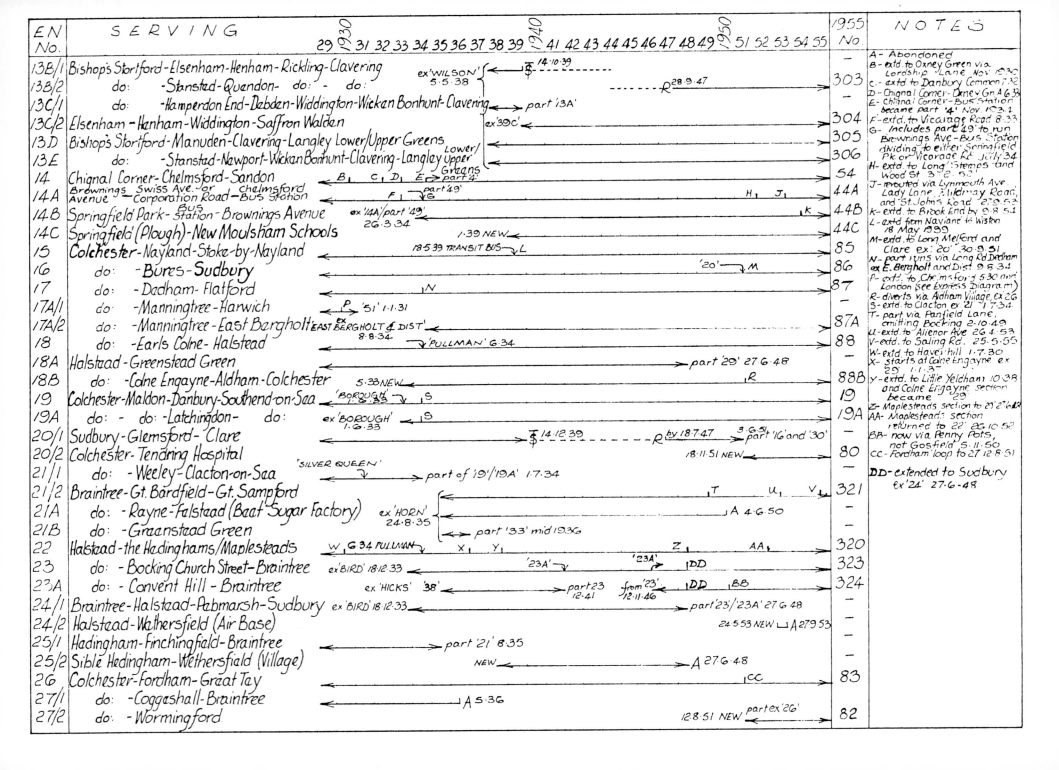

EN No.	SERVING	1955 No.
13B/1	Bishop's Stortford–Elsenham–Henham–Rickling–Clavering (ex 'WILSON' 5.5.38)	—
13B/2	do: –Stansted–Quendon– do: – do:	303
13C/1	do: –Hamperdon End–Debden–Widdington–Wicken Bonhunt–Clavering (part '13A')	—
13C/2	Elsenham–Henham–Widdington–Saffron Walden (ex '39C')	304
13D	Bishop's Stortford–Manuden–Clavering–Langley Lower/Upper Greens	305
13E	do: –Stansted–Newport–Wicken Bonhunt–Clavering–Langley Upper Greens (part '4')	306
14	Chignal Corner–Chelmsford–Sandon	54
14A	Brownings Ave. or Swiss Ave. Chelmsford–Corporation Road–Bus Station	44A
14B	Springfield Park–Bus Station–Brownings Avenue (ex '14A'/part '49' 26.3.34)	44B
14C	Springfield (Plough)–New Moulsham Schools (1.39 NEW)	44C
15	Colchester–Nayland–Stoke-by-Nayland (18.5.39 TRANSIT BUS)	85
16	do: –Bures–Sudbury	86
17	do: –Dedham–Flatford	87
17A/1	do: –Manningtree–Harwich ('51' 1.1.31)	—
17A/2	do: –Manningtree–East Bergholt (ex 'EAST BERGHOLT & DIST' 8.8.34)	87A
18	do: –Earls Colne–Halstead ('PULLMAN' 6.34)	88
18A	Halstead–Greenstead Green (part '29' 27.6.48)	—
18B	do: –Colne Engayne–Aldham–Colchester (5.33 NEW)	88B
19	Colchester–Maldon–Danbury–Southend-on-Sea ('BOROUGH' 1.8.33)	19
19A	do: – do: –Latchingdon– do: (ex 'BOROUGH' 1.6.33)	19A
20/1	Sudbury–Glemsford–Clare (part '16' and '30')	—
20/2	Colchester–Tendring Hospital (18.11.51 NEW)	80
21/1	do: –Weeley–Clacton-on-Sea ('SILVER QUEEN') (part of '19'/'19A' 1.7.34)	—
21/2	Braintree–Gt. Bardfield–Gt. Sampford	321
21A	do: –Rayne–Falstead (Beet Sugar Factory) (ex 'HORN' 24.8.35) (A 4.6.50)	—
21B	do: –Greenstead Green (part '33' mid 1936)	—
22	Halstead–the Hedinghams/Maplesteads (6.34 PULLMAN)	320
23	do: –Bocking Church Street–Braintree (ex 'BIRD' 18.12.33)	323
23A	do: –Convent Hill–Braintree (ex 'HICKS' '38')	324
24/1	Braintree–Halstead–Pebmarsh–Sudbury (ex 'BIRD' 18.12.33) (part '23'/'23A' 27.6.48)	—
24/2	Halstead–Wethersfield (Air Base) (24.5.53 NEW) (A 27.9.53)	—
25/1	Hedingham–Finchingfield–Braintree (part '21' 8.35)	—
25/2	Sible Hedingham–Wethersfield (Village) (NEW) (A 27.6.48)	—
26	Colchester–Fordham–Great Tay	83
27/1	do: –Coggeshall–Braintree (A 5.36)	—
27/2	do: –Wormingford (12.8.51 NEW, part ex '26')	82

NOTES

A – Abandoned
B – extd. to Oxney Green via Lordship Lane Nov 1930
C – extd. to Danbury Common 7.32
D – Chignal Corner–Oxney Gn. A 6.38
E – Chignal Corner–Bus Station became part '4' Nov 1931
F – extd. to Vicarage Road 8.33
G – Includes part '49' to run Brownings Ave–Bus Station dividing to either Springfield Pk or Vicarage Rd July 34
H – extd. to Long Stomps and Wood St 3.2.52
J – rerouted via Lynmouth Ave, Lady Lane, Bildray Road, and St. John's Road 27.9.52
K – extd. to Brook End by 9.8.51
L – extd. from Nayland to Wiston 18 May 1939
M – extd. to Long Melford and Clare ex '20' 30.9.51
N – part runs via Long Rd Dedham
P – extd. to Chelmsford 5.30 and London (see Express Diagram)
R – diverts via Aldham Village, ex 26
S – extd. to Clacton ex '21' 1.7.34
T – part via Panfield Lane, omitting Bocking 2.10.49
U – extd. to Alienor Ave 26.4.53
V – extd. to Saling Rd. 25.5.55
W – extd. to Haverhill 1.7.30
X – starts at Colne Engayne ex '29' 1.1.3?
Y – extd. to Little Yeldham 10.38 and Colne Engayne section became '29'
Z – Maplesteads section to '29' 27.6.4?
AA – Maplesteads section returned to '22' 26.10.52
BB – now via Penny Pots, not Gosfield 5.11.50
CC – Fordham loop to 27 12.8.51
DD – extended to Sudbury ex '24' 27.6.48

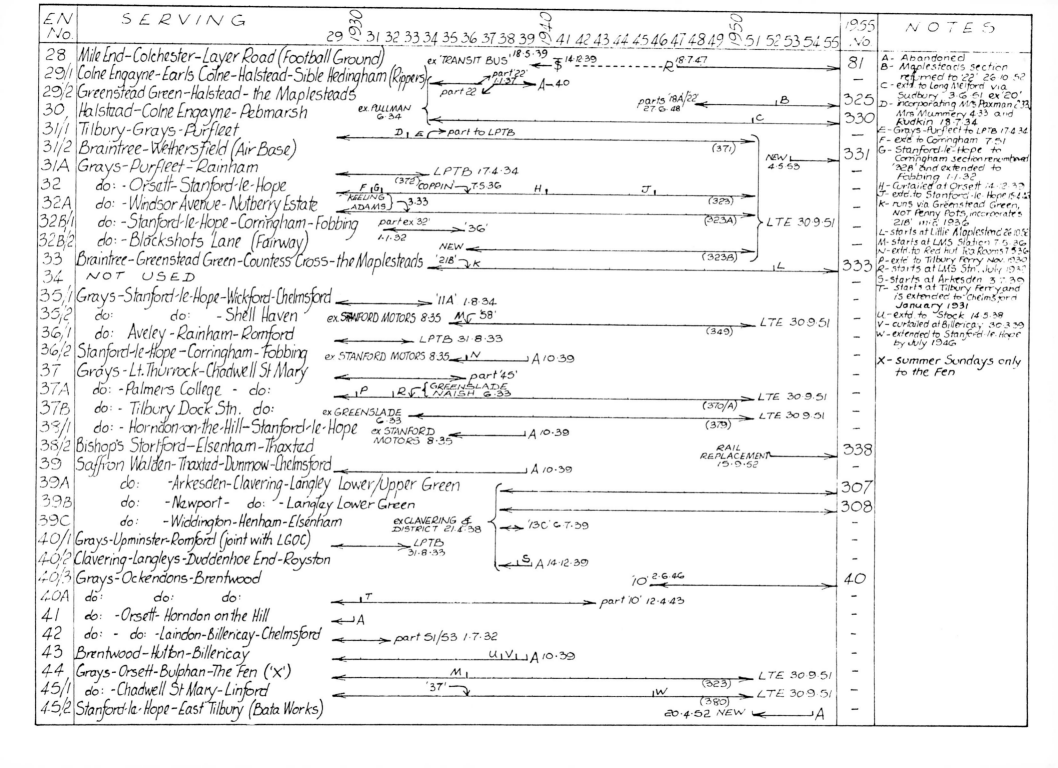

Chart header (columns): EN No. | SERVING | 1930 29 31 32 33 34 35 36 37 38 39 1940 41 42 43 44 45 46 47 48 49 1950 51 52 53 54 55 | 1955 No. | NOTES

EN No.	SERVING	1955 No.
28	Mile End–Colchester–Layer Road (Football Ground) — ex 'TRANSIT BUS' 18.5.39 $ 14.12.39 R 18.7.47	81
29/1	Colne Engayne–Earls Colne–Halstead–Sible Hedingham (Rippers) — part '22' 1.37 A–40 part 22	—
29/2	Greenstead Green–Halstead–the Maplesteads — parts 18A/22 27.6.48 B	325
30	Halstead–Colne Engayne–Pebmarsh — ex. PULLMAN 6.34 C	330
31/1	Tilbury–Grays–Purfleet — D E part to LPTB	—
31/2	Braintree–Wethersfield (Air Base) — (371) NEW 4.5.53	331
31A	Grays–Purfleet–Rainham — LPTB 17.4.34	—
32	do: –Orsett–Stanford-le-Hope — F G (372) COPPIN 7.5.36 H J	—
32A	do: –Windsor Avenue–Nutberry Estate — KEELING ADAMS 3.33 (323)	—
32B/1	do: –Stanford-le-Hope–Corringham–Fobbing — part ex 32' 1.1.32 '36' (323A) LTE 30.9.51	—
32B/2	do: –Blackshots Lane (Fairway) — NEW	—
33	Braintree–Greenstead Green–Countess Cross–the Maplesteads — '218' K (323B) L	333
34	NOT USED	—
35/1	Grays–Stanford-le-Hope–Wickford–Chelmsford — '11A' 1.8.34	—
35/2	do: do: – Shell Haven — ex. STANFORD MOTORS 8.35 M '58' LTE 30.9.51	—
36/1	do: Aveley–Rainham–Romford — LPTB 31.8.33 (349)	—
36/2	Stanford-le-Hope–Corringham–Fobbing — ex STANFORD MOTORS 8.35 N A 10.39	—
37	Grays–Lt. Thurrock–Chadwell St Mary — part '45'	—
37A	do: –Palmers College– do: — P R GREENSLADE NAISH 6.33 LTE 30.9.51	—
37B	do: – Tilbury Dock Stn. do: — ex GREENSLADE 6.33 (370/A) LTE 30.9.51	—
38/1	do: – Horndon-on-the-Hill–Stanford-le-Hope — ex STANFORD MOTORS 8.35 A 10.39 (379)	—
38/2	Bishop's Stortford–Elsenham–Thaxted — RAIL REPLACEMENT	338
39	Saffron Walden–Thaxted–Dunmow–Chelmsford — A 10.39 RAIL REPLACEMENT 15.9.52	—
39A	do: –Arkesden–Clavering–Langley Lower/Upper Green	307
39B	do: –Newport– do: –Langley Lower Green	308
39C	do: –Widdington–Henham–Elsenham — ex CLAVERING & DISTRICT 21.4.38 '13C' 6.7.39	—
40/1	Grays–Upminster–Romford (joint with LGOC) — LPTB 31.8.33	—
40/2	Clavering–Langleys–Duddenhoe End–Royston — S A 14.12.39	—
40/3	Grays–Ockendons–Brentwood — '10' 2.6.46	40
40A	do: do: do: — T part '10' 12.4.43	—
41	do: –Orsett–Horndon on the Hill — A	—
42	do: – do: –Laindon–Billericay–Chelmsford — part 51/53 1.7.32	—
43	Brentwood–Hutton–Billericay — U V A 10.39	—
44	Grays–Orsett–Bulphan–The Fen ('X') — M LTE 30.9.51	—
45/1	do: –Chadwell St Mary–Linford — '37' W (323) LTE 30.9.51	—
45/2	Stanford-le-Hope–East Tilbury (Bata Works) — (380) 20.4.52 NEW A	—

NOTES

A – Abandoned
B – Maplesteads section reformed to '22' 26.10.52
C – extd. to Long Melford via Sudbury 3.6.51 ex '20'
D – incorporating M/S Paxman 6.33 Mrs Mummery 4.33 and Rudkin 18.7.34
E – Grays–Purfleet to LPTB 17.4.34
F – extd. to Corringham 7.51
G – Stanford-le-Hope to Corringham section renumbered '32B' and extended to Fobbing 1.1.32
H – Curtailed at Orsett 14.12.39
J – extd. to Stanford-le-Hope 15.4.??
K – runs via Greenstead Green, NOT Penny Pots, incorporates '218' m.d. 1936
L – starts at Little Maplestead 26.10.52
M – starts at LMS Station 7.5.36
N – extd. to Red Hut Tea Rooms 7.5.36
P – extd. to Tilbury Ferry Nov. 1930
R – starts at LMS Stn. July 193?
S – starts at Arkesden 3.7.39
T – Starts at Tilbury Ferry and is extended to Chelmsford January 1931
U – extd. to Stock 14.5.38
V – curtailed at Billericay 30.3.39
W – extended to Stanford-le-Hope by July 1946

X – summer Sundays only to the Fen

EN No.	SERVING	(timeline 29 1930 31 32 33 34 35 36 37 38 39 1940 41 42 43 44 45 46 47 48 49 1950 51 52 53 54 55)	1955 No.
46	Chelmsford-Roxwell-Willingale	'SIMPSON' →B ←————————— C	4-6
47	Bishop's Stortford-Hatfield Heath-Harlow-Matching Green-Moreton-Ongar	4·6·49 NEW ├───────── G/D	47
48	Chelmsford-Hatfield Peverel-Mill Beach	←—————————————————————	48
49/1	Chelmsford-Springfield Park	1·3·30 NEW ├——→ part '14A/14B' 26·3·34	—
49/2	Bishop's Stortford-Harlow (Old Town)	1·5·51 NEW ├── G/D	49
50	Chelmsford-Hatfield Peverel-Terling	1·7·30 NEW ├———————— E ├— F ├——→	50
50A	do: -Russell Green-Flacks Green	ex WILKINSON 1942 ←———————————	50A
51	do: -Colchester-Harwich	ex '5/17A' 7·30 ├— H	51
52	do: -Great Waltham-Pleshey	ex PLESHEY BELLE mid 1931 ←———— J	52
53	do: -Colchester-Weeley-Clacton-on-Sea	121 ├ K ├ L ←——————————	53
54/1	Clacton-Weeley-Manningtree-Holbrook-Ipswich	NEW M 11·31 ├◄ '123' 1·32	—
54/2	Tilbury Town-Orsett Infirmary	├————— A 10·39	—
54/3	Chelmsford-Little Waltham-Boreham Race Track	31·8·52 NEW ├— A 1953 (Track closed)	—
55	Tilbury Town-Stifford Hospital	ex RUDKIN'S TILBURY SAFETY COACHES 18·7·34 ├————— A 10·39	—
56	do: -West Tilbury (Wilson's farm) *	├————— A 10·39	—
57	do: -Nutberry Corner	├————————————→ (357) LTE 30·9·51	—
58	Grays-Stanford-le-Hope-Shell Haven	ex DAY AND BEDINGFIELD 1·8·34 ←→ part 35/59 7·5·36	—
59	Red Hut- do: - do:	part ex 58 ├————— A 16·1·41	—
60	Maldon-Wickham Bishops-Witham	N ├◄ '67' ←————————————— P	90
61	do: -Althorne-Southminster-Burnham-on-Crouch	←— R ←—————————————	91
62	do: -Steeple- do: -Bradwell-on-Sea	←— S ←—————————————	92
63/1	do: -Purleigh-South Woodham-Wickford	←→ part '12A'/'66' 11·7·35	—
63/2	do: -North Fambridge-Burnham-on-Crouch	5·11·50 NEW ├——— T ├——→	93
64	do: -Heybridge Basin-Mill Beach-Goldhanger	ex 'QUEST' 1·1·35 '65' ↓ →part 65 ←—————	94
65	do: ---direct--to--- do:	part '64' ├ ex. U ├◄'64' 1·7·37 ←—————	95
66	do: -Cock Clarks-Cold Norton-North Fambridge	├ V ├ W ├ X ├ Y ├ Z ←———	96
67/1	do: -Local: Mundon Road-Centre-Heybridge	←→ part 60 1·8·35	—
67/2	do: -Colickey Green-Woodham Walter	ex ROLF 4·2·53 ← part 7 26·9·54	—
68	do: -Braintree (Crittall's Works)	←——→ incl. in '60', A by 1·41	—
69	N O T U S E D		—
70	Southend-Pitsea-Corringham-Stanford-le-Hope-Grays	←————————— AA ————————→	2/2B
71	Leigh-on-Sea-Eastwood (Jones Corner)	Operated by 'BOROUGH SERVICES' 1·6·33 ←— 'WESTCLIFF' route 'G' 30·10·40	—
72	do: -Westcliff (Somerset Crescent)	←— 'WESTCLIFF' route 'G' 30·10·40	—
73	} N O T U S E D		—
74	}		—
75	Colchester-Abberton-West Mersea	ex 'UNDERWOOD' 1·1·35 ←— BB '75B' ↓ ←————— CC ——→	75

NOTES

A- Abandoned
B- extd. to Matching Green 24·3·40
C- extd. to Harlow ex part 8A 4·1·53
D- extd. to Harlow New Town Centre 28·8·55 (see also note G)
E- extd. to Fairstead 10·11·52
F- extd. to Braintree 29·9·54
G- Bishop's Stortford to Harlow section to '49' 28·8·55
H- through from Tilbury Ferry ex. '42 July 1952
J- incorporating part 3' 4·6·50
K- (as note H)
L- including '121' and runs via Wivenhoe and St. Osyth but NOT Weeley, July 1933
M- joint with E.C.O.C.
N- starts at Mundon Road ex '67' 1·8·35
P- extd. to South House Estate 15·15?
R- garage journey run via Ostend
S- garage journey run via St. Lawrence 1·1·38
T- diverted to run from Althorne via Mayland to Steeple Stone 1·6·54
U- runs direct to Goldhanger
V- rerouted to run Purleigh to North Fambridge 11·7·35. The section to Cock Clarks 'A'
W- curtailed at Cold Norton 1·7·37
X- extd. to Stow Maries by 8·43
Y- extd. to Maldon East Station and Woodham Ferrers Stn 28·4·46
Z- starts from Maldon Bus Stn 3·2·52
AA- ENOC take over operating 30·10·40
BB- see also services 75A and 75C which used separate times over the same route until 1·10·37
CC- through to East Mersea 1·8·54
*- service for pea pickers

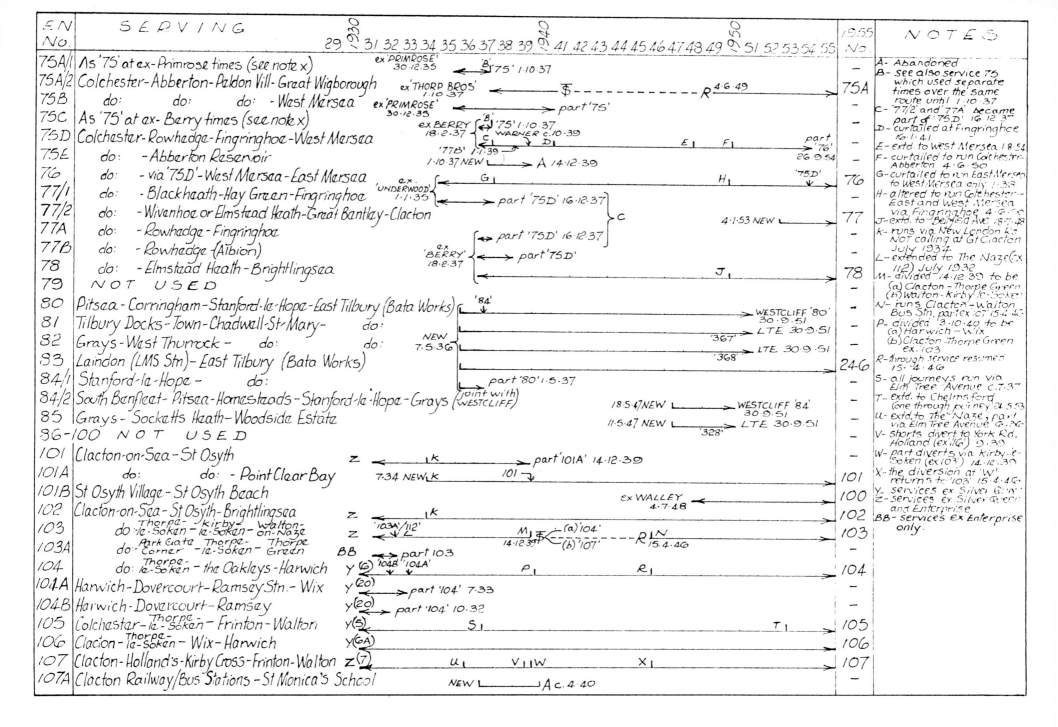

EN No.	SERVING	1930 ... 1940 ... 1950 ... 1955 diagram	1955 No.	NOTES
75A/1	As '75' at ex-Primrose times (see note x)	ex 'PRIMROSE' 30.12.35 — 'B' '75' 1.10.37	—	A - Abandoned
75A/2	Colchester-Abberton-Peldon Vill-Great Wigborough	ex 'THORP BROS' 1.10.37 — $ ---- R 4.6.49	75A	B - see also service 75 which used separate times over the same route until 1.10.37
75B	do: do: do: - West Mersea	ex 'PRIMROSE' 30.12.35 — part '75'	—	C - '77/2' and '77A' became part of '75D' 16.12.37
75C	As '75' at ex-Berry times (see note x)	ex BERRY 18.2.37 'B' '75' 1.10.37 WARNER c.10.39	—	D - curtailed at Fingringhoe 16.1.41
75D	Colchester-Rowhedge-Fingringhoe-West Mersea	C / D E F part '76' 26.9.54	—	E - extd. to West Mersea 18.54
75E	do: - Abberton Reservoir	'77B' 1.1.39 → 1.10.37 NEW ⊢→ A 14.12.39	—	F - curtailed to run Colchester-Abberton 4.6.50
76	do: - via '75D'-West Mersea-East Mersea	ex 'UNDERWOOD' 1.1.35 G H '75D'	76	G - curtailed to run East Mersea to West Mersea only 1.38
77/1	do: - Blackheath-Hay Green-Fingringhoe	part '75D' 16.12.37	—	H - altered to run Colchester-East and West Mersea via Fingringhoe 4.6.50
77/2	do: - Wivenhoe or Elmstead Heath-Great Bentley-Clacton	C 4.1.53 NEW	77	J - extd. to Belfield Ave. 18.7.48
77A	do: - Rowhedge - Fingringhoe	part '75D' 16.12.37	—	K - runs via New London Rd. Not calling at Gt Clacton July 1934
77B	do: - Rowhedge (Albion)	ex 'BERRY' 18.2.37 part '75D'	—	L - extended to The Naze (ex 112) July 1932
78	do: - Elmstead Heath - Brightlingsea	J	78	M - divided 14.12.39 to be (a) Clacton - Thorpe Green (b) Walton - Kirby-le-Soken
79	NOT USED		—	N - runs Clacton-Walton Bus Stn. part ex 107 15.4.46
80	Pitsea - Corringham - Stanford-le-Hope - East Tilbury (Bata Works)	'84' WESTCLIFF '80' 30.9.51	—	P - divided 13.10.40 to be (a) Harwich - Wix (b) Clacton-Thorpe Green ex.103
81	Tilbury Docks - Town - Chadwell-St-Mary - do:	LTE 30.9.51	—	R - through service resumed 15.4.46
82	Grays - West Thurrock - do: do:	NEW 7.5.36 '367' LTE 30.9.51	—	S - all journeys run via Elm Tree Avenue c.7.37
83	Laindon (LMS Stn) - East Tilbury (Bata Works)	'368'	24-6	T - extd. to Chelmsford (one through journey 21.5.53
84/1	Stanford-le-Hope - do:	part '80' 1.5.37	—	U - extd. to The Naze, part via Elm Tree Avenue c.36
84/2	South Benfleet - Pitsea - Homesteads - Stanford-le-Hope - Grays	(joint with WESTCLIFF) 18.5.47 NEW WESTCLIFF '84' 30.9.51	—	V - Shorts divert to York Rd, Holland (ex 11G) 9.39
85	Grays - Socketts Heath - Woodside Estate	11.5.47 NEW '328' LTE 30.9.51	—	W - part diverts via Kirby-le-Soken (ex 103) 14.12.39
86-100	NOT USED			X - the diversion at 'W' returns to '103' 15.4.46
101	Clacton-on-Sea - St Osyth	Z K part '101A' 14.12.39	—	Y - services ex Silver Gem
101A	do: do: - Point Clear Bay	7.34 NEW K 101	101	Z - services ex Silver Queen and Enterprise
101B	St Osyth Village - St Osyth Beach		100	BB - services ex Enterprise only.
102	Clacton-on-Sea - St Osyth - Brightlingsea	Z K ex WALLEY 4.7.48	102	
103	do: Thorpe-le-Soken - Kirby-le-Soken - Walton-on-Naze	Z '103A/112' M $ (a)'104' R N 15.4.46 (b)'107'	103	
103A	do: Park Gate Corner - Thorpe-le-Soken - Thorpe Green	BB part 103	—	
104	do: Thorpe-le-Soken - the Oakleys - Harwich	Y(6) '104B' '104A' P R	104	
104A	Harwich-Dovercourt-Ramsey Stn. - Wix	Y(20) part '104' 7.33	—	
104B	Harwich-Dovercourt-Ramsey	Y(20) part '104' 10.32	—	
105	Colchester-Thorpe-le-Soken - Frinton - Walton	Y(5) S T	105	
106	Clacton - Thorpe-le-Soken - Wix - Harwich	Y(6A)	106	
107	Clacton-Holland's-Kirby Cross-Frinton-Walton	Z(7) U V W X	107	
107A	Clacton Railway/Bus Stations - St Monica's School	NEW ⊢→ A c.4.40	—	

EN No.	SERVING	Timeline (1929–1955)	1955 No.
108	Clacton-Tendring-Manningtree-East Bergholt	Y (8) ... ₤10.39 ... R →	108
109/1	Walton-on-Naze – Brightlingsea	Y (9) A 10.31	–
109/2	Clacton Bus/Railway Stations – Gt. Clacton (Ship)	4.6.49 NEW ⌐ B →	109
110/1	Harwich-Manningtree-East Bergholt	Y (10) A 10.32	110
110/2	Clacton Bus Station-Sackett's Grove	3.6.51 NEW →	110
111	Harwich-Oakleys-Thorpe-le-Soken-Walton-on-Naze	Y (11) ₤10.39 — R 11.7.48 →	111
112/1	The Naze-Walton Station-Lower Kirby	Y (16) C → part '103' 7.33	112
112/2	Jaywick-Town (Sea front)-Holland (King's Ave)	R 3.6.51 ex '115A' →	112
113/1	Jetty-Town-Great Clacton-Holland	Y (13) A	–
113/2	Railway Station-Town-Wash Lane-Jaywick	NEW 26.3.34 ... D →	113
114	Clacton Jetty-Town-Magdalen Green	Y (14) E F G H ₤10.39 R 27.7.47 →	114
114A	Town Circular: Bus Stn.-Gt. Clacton-Gorse Lane-Holland Rd-Bus Stn.	NEW 7.35 →	114A
115	Jaywick-Town-Magdalen Green *	ZZ (15) ₤3.10.40 - R J 23.10.44 K →	115
115A/1	do: -Marine Parade-Holland-on-Sea (Kings Cliff)	NEW 7.32 ₤10.39 (see '112/2')	–
115A/2	do: -Town-Railway Stn.-Holland (Kings Cliff)	1.6.47 NEW →	115A
116/1	Clacton Jetty-Rush Green-Cemetery	Z (12) → part '114'	–
116/2	Jaywick-Town-Railway Stn.-Holland (Kings Cliff)	NEW 7.33 ₤10.39 — R L 15.4.46 →	116
117/1	Clacton-Rly. Stn.-Valley Rd. Corner-Holland ⊠	Z (17) A 10.32	–
117/2	Magdalen Green-Town-Railway Stn.-Holland Sand Pits	NEW 5.34 M ₤10.39 R N 7.4.7.48 P R →	117
118	Harwich-Marine Parade-Parkeston Quay	Y (19)	118
118A	do: - Main Road - do:	Y (19) A 10.33	–
119	do: -Dovercourt (White Horse) via Marine Parade	Y (19A) S	119
119A	do: - do: do: via Main Road	Y (19A) S	119A
119B	do: - Royal Oak Football Ground	Y (?) A	–
120/1	do: - Upper Dovercourt Tollgate	Y (18)	–
120/2	do: - Upper Dovercourt Holiday Camp via Main Road	T NEW ⌐ ₤10.39 (see '122/2')	–
120A	do: -Upper Dovercourt via Marine Parade	26.7.32 NEW	–
121/1	Clacton -St Osyth-Wivenhoe-Colchester	Y (4/21A) → part '53' 1.7.33	–
121/2	do: - Meadowview Holiday Camp	1.6.52 NEW →	121
122/1	Parkeston Quay - Upper Dovercourt	Y (22) A 31.12.50	–
122/2	Harwich-Dovercourt Holiday Camp via Main Road	1.8.53 ex '120/2' R →	122
123	Clacton-Weeley-Tendring-Mistley-Ipswich (joint ECOC) ex 1.1.32	ex '54' U V W →	123
123A	do: do: do: -Bradfield-Manningtree	4.6.50 NEW ⌐ A 4.6.51	–
124	do: - Colchester- Black Notley Hospital	3.6.51 NEW →	124
125	do: - Great Clacton (Castle Hill)	4.7.54 NEW →	125
164	Royston-Buntingford-Great Hormead-Standon	ex '64'/'65' ENOC Midland Area 14.8.38 ← X AA BB UCOC C '188' CC 6.5.53	–

Column year headers: 29 30 31 32 33 34 35 36 37 38 39 40 41 42 43 44 45 46 47 48 49 50 51 52 53 54 55 | 1955 No.

NOTES

A - Abandoned
B - extended to Valley Farm 7.50
C - extd. to Kirby Cross Stn 6.32
D - susp. from 3.10.40 to 16.1.41
E - diverted to run Magdalen Green-Gorse Lane via Town, Railway Stn and Valley Rd including part '116' 3.32
F - starts from Jaywick 6.33
G - extended to Marine Hotel, Rush Green, Magdalen Green, Great Clacton, Cemetery to Gorse Lane 26.3.34
H - runs Jaywick-Town-Burrsville Park PO 1.7.37
J - curtailed to run Bus Stn-Coppins Green 23.10.44
K - full service restored 28.7.45
L - Holland terminal extended to York Road 15.4.46
M - Holland terminal now to Kings Cliff 7.38
N - Holland terminal extended to Brighton Road 14.7.48
P - Town-Magdalen Green section withdrawn 2.10.49
R - Holland terminal extended to Fernwood Ave 24.5.53
S - extended to Upper Dovercourt (Tollgate) ex '120'/'120A' 18.52
T - to services 119/119A (see note S)
U - no longer joint with ECOC from 1.1.34
V - diverts to call at Thorpe Green mid 1935
W - now direct to Thorpe Green omitting Weeley
X - withdrawn from 10.39 until 14.12.39
Y - Services ex Silver Queen
Z - services ex Silver Queen and Enterprise
AA - extended from Standon to Bishops Stortford c. June 1950
BB - Working shared with UCOC 1.1.52
CC - transferred entirely to UCOC 6.5.53 and thereafter worked Royston-Buntingford only. Remainder A

* In winter only runs Town-Magdalen Green
⊠ School service
ZZ - ex Enterprise only

DIAGRAM of all EASTERN NATIONAL omnibus routes in the MIDLAND AREA 1929–1952

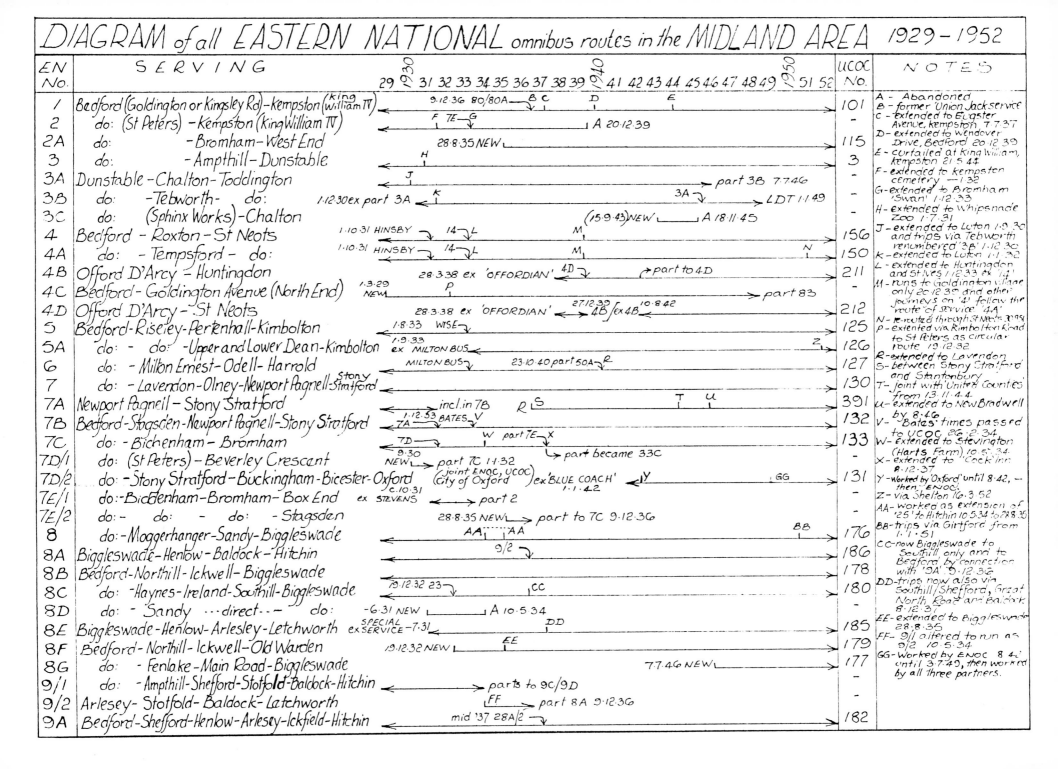

EN No.	SERVING	Timeline annotations (29 '30 31–39 '40 41–49 '50 51 52)	UCOC No.
1	Bedford (Goldington or Kingsley Rd)–Kempston (King William IV)	9.12.36 80/80A — B C — D — E	101
2	do: (St Peters) – Kempston (King William IV)	F 7E G — A 20.12.39	-
2A	do: – Bromham–West End	28.8.35 NEW	115
3	do: – Ampthill–Dunstable	H	3
3A	Dunstable–Chalton–Toddington	J — part 3B 7.7.46	-
3B	do: –Tebworth– do:	1.12.30 ex part 3A — K — 3A — LDT 1.1.49	-
3C	do: (Sphinx Works)–Chalton	(15.9.43) NEW — A 18.11.45	-
4	Bedford – Roxton – St Neots	1.10.31 HINSBY — 14 L — M	156
4A	do: – Tempsford – do:	1.10.31 HINSBY — 14 L — M — N	150
4B	Offord D'Arcy – Huntingdon	28.3.38 ex 'OFFORDIAN' — 4D — part to 4.D	211
4C	Bedford – Goldington Avenue (North End)	1.3.29 NEW — P — part 8B	-
4D	Offord D'Arcy – St Neots	28.3.38 ex 'OFFORDIAN' — 27.12.39 4B/ex4B 10.8.42	212
5	Bedford–Riseley–Pertenhall–Kimbolton	1.8.33 WISE	125
5A	do: – do: –Upper and Lower Dean–Kimbolton	1.9.33 ex MILTON BUS — Z	126
6	do: – Milton Ernest–Odell– Harrold	MILTON BUS — 23.10.40 part 50A R	127
7	do: – Lavendon–Olney–Newport Pagnell–Stony Stratford		130
7A	Newport Pagnell – Stony Stratford	incl. in 7B — R S — T U	391
7B	Bedford–Stagsden–Newport Pagnell–Stony Stratford	1.12.33 BATES — 7A V	132
7C	do: – Bichenham – Bromham	7D — W part 7E X	133
7D/1	do: (St Peters) – Beverley Crescent	9.30 NEW — part 7C 1.1.32	-
7D/2	do: – Stony Stratford–Buckingham–Bicester–Oxford	c.10.31 (Joint ENOC, UCOC) (City of Oxford) ex 'BLUE COACH' 1.1.42 — Y — GG	131
7E/1	do: –Bichenham–Bromham– Box End	ex STEVENS — part 2	-
7E/2	do: – do: – do: – Stagsden	28.8.35 NEW — part to 7C 9.12.36	-
8	do:–Moggerhanger–Sandy–Biggleswade	AA AA — BB	176
8A	Biggleswade–Henlow–Baldock–Hitchin	9/2	186
8B	Bedford–Northill–Ickwell–Biggleswade		178
8C	do: –Haynes–Ireland–Southill–Biggleswade	19.12.32 23 — CC	180
8D	do: – Sandy …direct… do:	-6.31 NEW — A 10.5.34	-
8E	Biggleswade–Henlow–Arlesley–Letchworth	SPECIAL ex SERVICE -7.31 — DD	185
8F	Bedford– Northill– Ickwell–Old Warden	19.12.32 NEW — EE	179
8G	do: – Fenlake–Main Road–Biggleswade	7.7.46 NEW	177
9/1	do: – Ampthill–Shefford–Stotfold–Baldock–Hitchin	parts to 9C/9D	-
9/2	Arlesey– Stotfold– Baldock– Letchworth	FF — part 8A 9.12.36	-
9A	Bedford–Shefford–Henlow–Arlesey–Ickfield–Hitchin	mid '37 28A/2	182

NOTES

A – Abandoned
B – former 'Union Jack' service
C – extended to Elgster Avenue, Kempston 7.7.37
D – extended to Wendover Drive, Bedford 20.12.39
E – curtailed at King William, Kempston 21.5.44
F – extended to Kempston cemetery –1.32
G – extended to Bromham 'Swan' 1.12.33
H – extended to Whipsnade Zoo 1.7.31
J – extended to Luton 1.9.30 and trips via Tebworth renumbered '3B' 1.12.30
K – extended to Luton 1.1.32
L – extended to Huntingdon and St Ives 1.12.33 ex '14'
M – runs to Goldington village only 20.12.39 and other journeys on '4' follow the route of service '4A'
N – re-routed through St Neots 2.9.51
P – extended via Kimbolton Road to St Peters as circular route 19.12.32
R – extended to Lavendon
S – between Stony Stratford and Stantonbury
T – joint with 'United Counties' from 13.11.44
U – extended to New Bradwell by 8.46
V – 'Bates' times passed to UCOC 26.12.34
W – extended to Stevington (Harts Farm) 5.34
X – extended to 'Cock' Inn 8.12.37
Y – Worked by 'Oxford' until 8.42, – then 'ENOC'
Z – via Shelton 16.3.52
AA – Worked as extension of '25' to Hitchin 10.5.34 to 28.8.35
BB – trips via Girtford from 1.7.51
CC – now Biggleswade to Southill only and to Bedford by connection with '9A' 9.12.36
DD – trips now also via Southill/Shefford, Great North Road and Baldock 8.12.37
EE – extended to Biggleswade 28.8.35
FF – 9/1 altered to run as 9/2 10.5.34
GG – Worked by ENOC 8.42 until 3.7.49, then worked by all three partners.

EN No.	SERVING	29 1930 31 32 33 34 35 36 37 38 39 1940 41 42 43 44 45 46 47 48 49 1950 51 52	UCOC No.	NOTES
9B	Bedford - Shefford - Meppershall - Shillington - Hitchin	mid '37 27B-28/2 → B →	42	A - Abandoned
9C	do: - do: - Henlow - Baldock - Hitchin	part 9/1 ← A c.10.5.34	-	B - Meppershall - Hitchin only from 20.12.39
9D	do: - do: - do: - direct - do:	part 9/1 ← A c.8.35	-	C - extended to New Inn 7.5.36
10/1	do: - Salph End - Renhold	→ part of '34C' 10.5.34	-	D - via Manor Road, Barton from - 8.33
10/2	Baldock - Bygrave	28.8.35 NEW ← $4.39 --- 25.8.46 R →	43	E - extended to Waresley by 1.30
11	Bedford - Milton Ernest - Sharnbrook - Rushden	← →	124	F - extended to Tring 23.3.33 incorporating former Aylesbury Omnibus Co., Bright Bros. and 'X' Services
12	Luton - Pegsdon - Shillington - Shefford (White Hart)	C renumbered '14' 18.9.49	-	
12A	do: - Streatley - Pegsdon/Hexton Village 23.3.33 ex 'BLUE BIRD'	D renumbered '14A' 18.9.49	-	G - extended to Aylesbury ex '101' 18.11.35
13	Stony Stratford - Whaddon - Horwoods - Winslow	→ to 'UNITED COUNTIES' 1.12.33	-	H - diverted via Marsworth Church 4.5.47 to 1.1.51
14/1	St. Neots - Buckden - Huntingdon - St Ives	→ part '4/4A' 1.12.33	-	J - passed to LGCS 1.1.32
14/2	SEE '12'	18.9.49 ex '12' ←	14	k - extended to Ivinghoe Aston 26.3.49
14A	SEE '12A'	18.9.49 ex '12A' ←	14A	L - extended to LMSR Stn - 9.30
15	Biggleswade - Potton - Gamlingay	← E → part '35C' 1.1.32	-	M - extended to Aylesbury incorporating '105' 1.11.34
15A	do: - Langford - Henlow	← → part '25' 1.1.32	-	N - Aylesbury - to Bierton locals to '109' 6.7.47
16	Luton - Dunstable - Totternhoe - Eddlesborough	F '101' G →	16	P - extended to LMSR Stn - 9.30
16A	Tring - Long Marston - Leighton Buzzard	8.33 ex 'CHILTERN' H --- H →	16A	R - extended to Wing and Burcott ex 'XL' and Aylesbury Omnibus Co and at the other end extended to Vauxhall Works, Luton ex 'XL' and incorporating the Dunstable - Leighton Buzzard section of 'SAFEWAY'.
16B/1	Luton - Dunstable - Studham	← J →	-	
16B/2	Leighton Buzzard - Billington - Horton - Ivinghoe	10.5.34 JELLEY ← k →	16B	
17	Bedford - Ampthill - Aspley Guise - Woburn - L. Buzzard	L 10.5.34 '105' M N part to '109' →	141	
18	Luton - Dunstable - Hockliffe - Leighton Buzzard	P R S →	18	
18A	do: - do: - Eddlesborough - do:	by 7.30 NEW JELLEY → 10.5.34	18A	S - trips via Eggington 16.3.52
18B	do: - do: - Tilsworth - do:	← T →	18B	T - ran as '18' until - 10.32
18C	Eddlesborough - Totternhoe - do:	1.8.33 BRIGHT BROS ← A 20.12.39	-	U - through from Bedford via Stagsden 10.5.34
19	Luton - Dunstable - Houghton Regis	→ LUTON CORPORATION 23.3.33	-	V - curtailed to run Ampthill - Eversholt 23.10.40
20	Bedford - Ampthill - Clophill - Silsoe - Luton	← →	142	
20A	do: - Elstow - do: - do: - do:	← →	143	
20B/1	Clophill - Ampthill - Flitwick - do: - do:	← '20D' →	-	
20B/2	do: - Greenfield - Pulloxhill - do: - do:	NEW →	144	
20C	do: - Maulden - Ampthill Town/Station	NEW ← →	146	
20D	AS '20B/1'	by 18.11.35 ex '20B' ← →	145	
21/1	Biggleswade - Dunton - Wrestlingworth	← → included in '29A'	-	
21/2	Toddington - Westoning - Ampthill - Clophill (with variations)	2.6.38 ex WESTONING & DIST → part '54'	-	
22	Newport Pagnell - Fenny Stratford - Bletchley	← U → $ --- 21.5.44 R →	166	
23/1	Bedford - Cotton End - Haynes	→ part '8C' 19.12.32	-	
23/2	Clophill - Woburn Sands or Flitwick - Woburn	2.6.38 ex WESTONING & DIST ← V →	33	

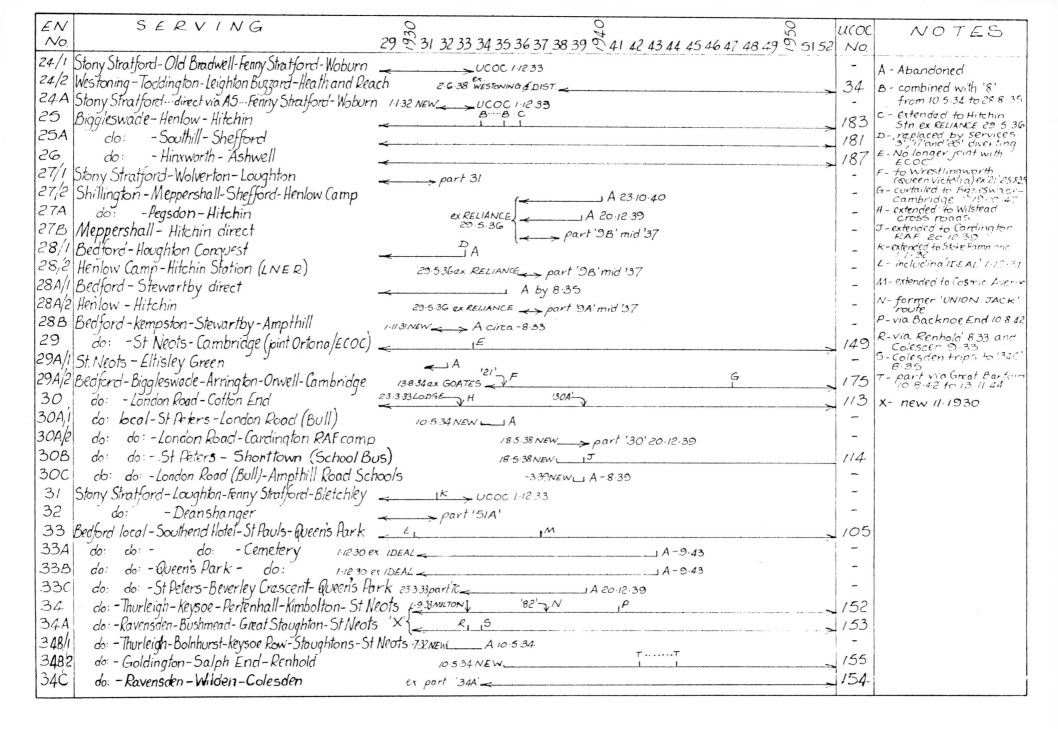

EN No.	SERVING	29 '30 31 32 33 34 35 36 37 38 39 '40 41 42 43 44 45 46 47 48 49 '50 51 52	UCOC No.	NOTES
24/1	Stony Stratford - Old Bradwell - Fenny Stratford - Woburn	← UCOC 1·12·33	–	A - Abandoned
24/2	Westoning - Toddington - Leighton Buzzard - Heath and Reach	2·6·38 ex WESTONING & DIST. →	34	B - combined with '8' from 10·5·34 to 28·8·35
24A	Stony Stratford ... direct via A5 ... Fenny Stratford - Woburn	1·1·32 NEW → UCOC 1·12·33	–	C - extended to Hitchin Stn. ex RELIANCE 29·5·36
25	Biggleswade - Henlow - Hitchin	B ... B ... C ← →	183	D - replaced by services '3','17'and '26' diverting
25A	do: - Southill - Shefford	← →	181	E - No longer joint with ECOC
26	do: - Hinxworth - Ashwell	← →	187	F - to Wrestlingworth (Queen Victoria) ex '21' 25·8·34
27/1	Stony Stratford - Wolverton - Loughton	← → part 31	–	G - curtailed to Biggleswade - Cambridge 9·7·39 to 13·11·47
27/2	Shillington - Meppershall - Shefford - Henlow Camp	ex RELIANCE 29·5·36 { A 23·10·40	–	H - extended to Wilstead cross roads
27A	do: - Pegsdon - Hitchin	{ A 20·12·39	–	J - extended to Cardington RAF 20·12·39
27B	Meppershall - Hitchin direct	{ → part '9B' mid '37	–	K - extended to Stoke Hammond 1·7·36
28/1	Bedford - Houghton Conquest	D A ←	–	L - including 'IDEAL' 1·12·31
28/2	Henlow Camp - Hitchin Station (LNER)	29·5·36 ex RELIANCE ← → part '9B' mid '37	–	M - extended to Cosmic Avenue
28A/1	Bedford - Stewartby direct	← A by 8·35	–	N - former 'UNION JACK' route
28A/2	Henlow - Hitchin	29·5·36 ex RELIANCE ← → part '9A' mid '37	–	P - via Backnoe End 10·8·42
28B	Bedford - Kempston - Stewartby - Ampthill	1·11·31 NEW ← → A circa 8·33	–	R - via Renhold 8·33 and Colesden 9·33
29	do: - St Neots - Cambridge (joint Ortona/ECOC)	E ← →	149	S - Colesden trips to 1·34 8·35
29A/1	St. Neots - Eltisley Green	← A	–	T - part via Great Barford 10·8·42 to 13·11·44
29A/2	Bedford - Biggleswade - Arrington - Orwell - Cambridge	13·8·34 ex GOATES → '21' F G ← →	175	X - new 11·1930
30	do: - London Road - Cotton End	23·3·33 LODGE → H '30A' ← →	113	
30A/1	do: local - St Peters - London Road (Bull)	10·5·34 NEW ← → A	–	
30A/2	do: do: - London Road - Cardington RAF camp	18·5·38 NEW → part '30' 20·12·39	–	
30B	do: do: - St Peters - Shorttown (School Bus)	18·5·38 NEW ← J	114	
30C	do: do: - London Road (Bull) - Ampthill Road Schools	3·39 NEW ← A - 8·39	–	
31	Stony Stratford - Loughton - Fenny Stratford - Bletchley	← K → UCOC 1·12·33	–	
32	do: - Deanshanger	← → part '51A'	–	
33	Bedford local - Southend Hotel - St Pauls - Queen's Park	L M ← →	105	
33A	do: do: - do: - Cemetery	1·12·30 ex IDEAL ← → A - 9·43	–	
33B	do: do: - Queen's Park - do: -	1·12·30 ex IDEAL ← → A - 9·43	–	
33C	do: do: - St Peters - Beverley Crescent - Queen's Park	23·3·33 part 7C ← → A 20·12·39	–	
34	do: - Thurleigh - Keysoe - Pertenhall - Kimbolton - St Neots	9·33 MILTON { '82' N P ← →	152	
34A	do: - Ravensden - Bushmead - Great Staughton - St Neots 'X' {	R S ← →	153	
34B/1	do: - Thurleigh - Bolnhurst - Keysoe Row - Staughtons - St Neots	7·32 NEW ← A 10·5·34	–	
34B/2	do: - Goldington - Salph End - Renhold	10·5·34 NEW ← T ...... T →	155	
34C	do: - Ravensden - Wilden - Colesden	ex part '34A' ← →	154	

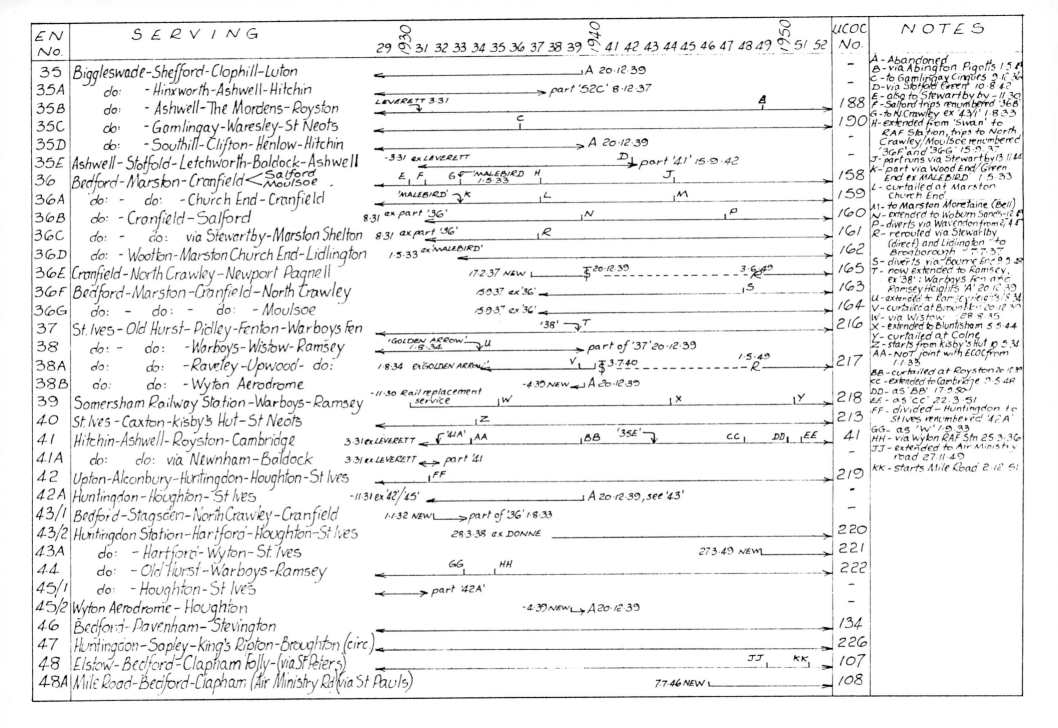

EN No.	SERVING	(1929–1952 timeline)	UCOC No.	NOTES
35	Biggleswade-Shefford-Clophill-Luton	A 20.12.39	–	A – Abandoned
35A	do: – Hinxworth-Ashwell-Hitchin	part '52C' 8.12.37	–	B – via Abington Pigotts 1.5.?
35B	do: – Ashwell-The Mordens-Royston	LEVERETT 3.31 .... A	188	C – to Gamlingay Cinques 9.12.3?
35C	do: – Gamlingay-Waresley-St Neots	C	190	D – via Stotford Green 10.8.4?
35D	do: – Southill-Clifton-Henlow-Hitchin	A 20.12.39	–	E – also to Stewartby by – 11.30
35E	Ashwell-Stotfold-Letchworth-Baldock-Ashwell	-3.31 ex LEVERETT D part '41' 15.9.42	–	F – Salford trips renumbered '36B'
36	Bedford-Marston-Cranfield < Salford / Moulsoe	E F G 'MALEBIRD' 1.5.33 H J	158	G – to N.Crawley ex '43/1' 1.8.33
36A	do: – do: – Church End-Cranfield	'MALEBIRD' K L M	159	H – extended from 'Swan' to RAF Station, trips to North Crawley/Moulsoe renumbered '36F' and '36G' 15.9.37
36B	do: – Cranfield-Salford	8.31 ex part '36' N P	160	J – part runs via Stewartby 13.11.44
36C	do: – do: via Stewartby-Marston Shelton	8.31 ex part '36' R	161	K – part via Wood End/Green End ex MALEBIRD 1.5.33
36D	do: – Wootton-Marston Church End-Lidlington	1.5.33 ex 'MALEBIRD'	162	L – curtailed at Marston Church End
36E	Cranfield-North Crawley-Newport Pagnell	17.2.37 NEW S 20.12.39 R 3.6.49	165	M – to Marston Moretaine (Bell)
36F	Bedford-Marston-Cranfield-North Crawley	15.9.37 ex '36' S	163	N – extended to Wobum Sands 12.6.?
36G	do: – do: – do: – Moulsoe	15.9.37 ex '36'	164	P – diverts via Wavendon from 2/4 5?
37	St Ives-Old Hurst-Pidley-Fenton-Warboys Fen	'38' T	216	R – rerouted via Stewartby (direct) and Lidlington to Brogborough – 7.7.37
38	do: – do: – Warboys-Wistow-Ramsey	'GOLDEN ARROW' 1.8.34 U part of '37' 20.12.39	–	S – diverts via Bourne End 9.9.3?
38A	do: – do: – Raveley-Upwood- do:	1.8.34 Ex 'GOLDEN ARROW' V S 3.7.40 R 1.5.49	217	T – now extended to Ramsey, ex '38': Warboys Fen and Ramsey Heights 'A' 20.12.39
38B	do: – do: – Wyton Aerodrome	-4.39 NEW A 20.12.39	–	U – extended to Ramsey Heights 1.8.34
39	Somersham Railway Station-Warboys-Ramsey	-11.30 Rail replacement service W X Y	218	V – curtailed at Broughton 20.12.39
40	St Ives-Caxton-kisby's Hut-St Neots	Z	213	W – via Wistow – 28.8.35
41	Hitchin-Ashwell-Royston-Cambridge	3.31 ex LEVERETT '41A' AA BB '35E' CC DD EE	41	X – extended to Bluntisham 5.5.44
41A	do: do: via Newnham-Baldock	3.31 ex LEVERETT part '41'	–	Y – curtailed at Colne
42	Upton-Alconbury-Huntingdon-Houghton-St Ives	FF	219	Z – starts from kisby's Hut 10.5.31
42A	Huntingdon-Houghton-St Ives	-11.31 ex '42'/'45' A 20.12.39, see '43'	–	AA – Not joint with ECOC from 1.1.33
43/1	Bedford-Stagsden-North Crawley-Cranfield	1.1.32 NEW part of '36' 1.8.33	–	BB – curtailed at Royston 20.12.39
43/2	Huntingdon Station-Hartford-Houghton-St Ives	28.3.38 ex DONNE	220	CC – extended to Cambridge 9.5.48
43A	do: – Hartford-Wyton-St Ives	27.3.49 NEW	221	DD – as 'BB' 17.9.50
44	do: – Old Hurst-Warboys-Ramsey	GG HH	222	EE – as 'CC' 22.3.51
45/1	do: – Houghton-St Ives	part '42A'	–	FF – divided – Huntingdon to St Ives renumbered '42A' 17.9.33
45/2	Wyton Aerodrome – Houghton	-4.39 NEW A 20.12.39	–	GG – as 'W' 1.9.33
46	Bedford-Pavenham-Stevington		134	HH – via Wyton RAF Stn 25.3.36
47	Huntingdon-Sapley-King's Ripton-Broughton (circ.)		226	JJ – extended to Air Ministry road 27.11.49
48	Elstow-Bedford-Clapham Folly-(via St Peters)	JJ KK	107	KK – starts Mile Road 2.12.51
48A	Mile Road-Bedford-Clapham (Air Ministry Rd via St Pauls)	7.7.46 NEW	108	

(Timeline header: 29 1930 31 32 33 34 35 36 37 38 39 1940 41 42 43 44 45 46 47 48 49 1950 51 52)

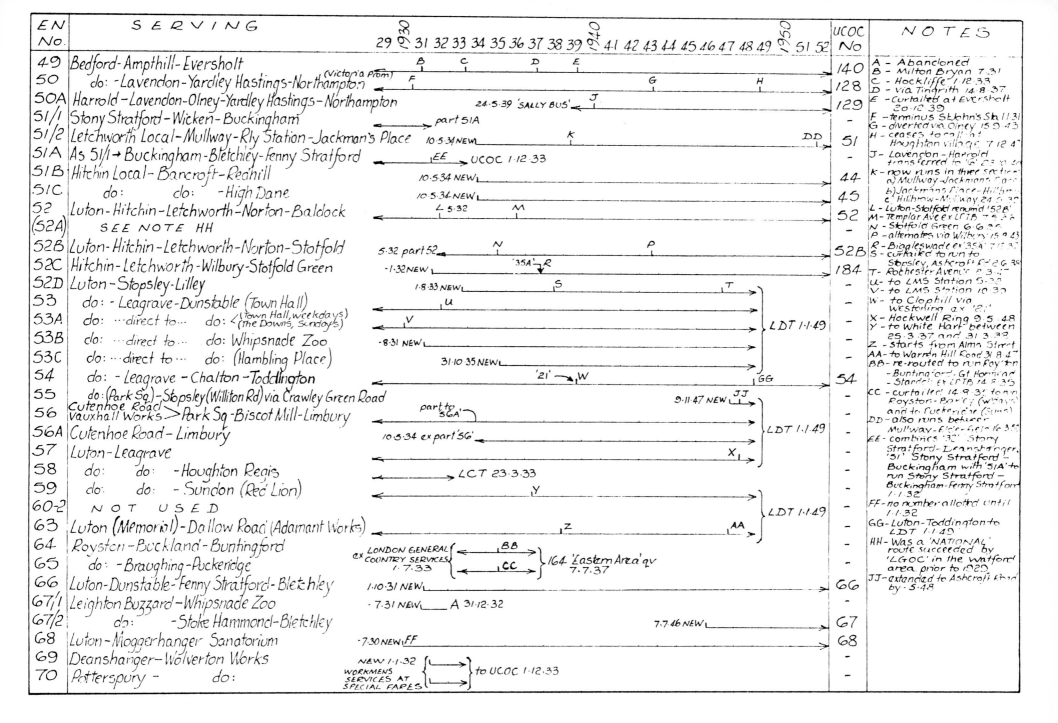

EN No.	SERVING	(timeline 1929–1952)	UCOC No.	NOTES
49	Bedford–Ampthill–Eversholt	B C D E	140	A – Abandoned
50	do: –Lavendon–Yardley Hastings–Northampton (Victoria Prom)	F G H	128	B – Milton Bryan 7.31
50A	Harrold–Lavendon–Olney–Yardley Hastings–Northampton	24.5.39 'Sally Bus' J	129	C – Hockliffe 1.12.33
51/1	Stony Stratford–Wicken–Buckingham	part 51A	–	D – via Tingrith 14.8.37
51/2	Letchworth Local–Mullway–Rly Station–Jackman's Place	10.5.34 NEW K DD	51	E – Curtailed at Eversholt 20.12.39
51A	As 51/1 → Buckingham–Bletchley–Fenny Stratford	EE UCOC 1.12.33	–	F – terminus St John's Str 11.31
51B	Hitchin Local–Barcroft–Redhill	10.5.34 NEW	44	G – diverted via Olney 15.9.43
51C	do: do: –High Dane	10.5.34 NEW	45	H – ceases to call at Houghton village 7.12.47
52	Luton–Hitchin–Letchworth–Norton–Baldock	L 5.32 M	52	J – Lavendon–Harrold transferred to '6' 23.10.44
(52A)	SEE NOTE HH		–	K – now runs in three sections a) Mullway–Jackman's Pce
52B	Luton–Hitchin–Letchworth–Norton–Stotfold	5.32 part 52 N P	52B	b) Jackman's Place–Hitchin
52C	Hitchin–Letchworth–Wilbury–Stotfold Green	–1.32 NEW '35A' R	184	c) Hillbrow–Mullway 24.6.39
52D	Luton–Stopsley–Lilley	1.8.33 NEW S T	–	L – Luton–Stotfold renumd '52B'
53	do: –Leagrave–Dunstable (Town Hall)	1.8.33 NEW U	–	M – Templar Ave ex LGTB 7.5.38
53A	do: ···direct to··· do: (Town Hall, weekdays)(The Downs, Sundays)	V	–	N – Stotfold Green 6.6.38
53B	do: ···direct to··· do: Whipsnade Zoo	–8.31 NEW	–	P – alternates via Wilbury 15.9.43
53C	do: ···direct to··· do: (Hambling Place)	31.10.35 NEW	–	R – Biggleswade ex '35A' 7.8.38
54	do: –Leagrave–Chalton–Toddington	'21' → W GG	54	S – curtailed to run to Stopsley, Ashcroft Rd 26.6.38
55	do:(Park Sq.)–Stopsley (Williton Rd) via Crawley Green Road	9.11.47 NEW JJ	–	T – Rochester Avenue 6.3.49
56	Cutenhoe Road, Vauxhall Works → Park Sq–Biscot Mill–Limbury	part to '56A'	–	U – to LMS Station 5.32
56A	Cutenhoe Road–Limbury	10.5.34 ex part '56' LDT 1.1.49	–	V – to LMS Station 10.32
57	Luton–Leagrave	X	–	W – to Clophill via Westoning ex '21'
58	do: do: –Houghton Regis	→ LCT 23.3.33	–	X – Hockwell Ring 9.5.48
59	do: do: –Sundon (Red Lion)	Y	–	Y – to White Hart between 25.3.37 and 31.3.38
60-2	NOT USED		–	Z – starts from Alma Street
63	Luton (Memorial)–Dallow Road (Adamant Works)	Z AA LDT 1.1.49	–	AA – to Warren Hill Road 31.8.47
64	Royston–Buckland–Buntingford	ex LONDON GENERAL COUNTRY SERVICES 1.7.33 ← BB → 164 'Eastern Area' qv 7.7.37	–	BB – re-routed to run Royston– Buntingford–Gt Hormead– Standon ex LGTB 14.8.35
65	do: –Braughing–Puckeridge	← CC →	–	CC – curtailed 14.8.35 to run Royston–Barley (wdays) and to Puckeridge (Suns)
66	Luton–Dunstable–Fenny Stratford–Bletchley	1.10.31 NEW	66	DD – also runs between Mullway–Elder Field 16.3.50
67/1	Leighton Buzzard–Whipsnade Zoo	–7.31 NEW A 31.12.32	–	EE – combines '32' Stony Stratford–Deanshanger '51' Stony Stratford–Buckingham with '51A' to run Stony Stratford– Buckingham–Fenny Stratford 1.1.32
67/2	do: –Stoke Hammond–Bletchley	7.7.46 NEW	67	FF – no number allotted until 1.1.32
68	Luton–Moggerhanger Sanatorium	–7.30 NEW FF	68	GG – Luton–Toddington to LDT 1.1.49
69	Deanshanger–Wolverton Works	NEW 1.1.32 WORKMENS SERVICES AT SPECIAL FARES → to UCOC 1.12.33	–	HH – Was a 'NATIONAL' route succeeded by 'LGOC' in the Watford area prior to 1929
70	Potterspury– do:		–	JJ – extended to Ashcroft Road by 5.4.8

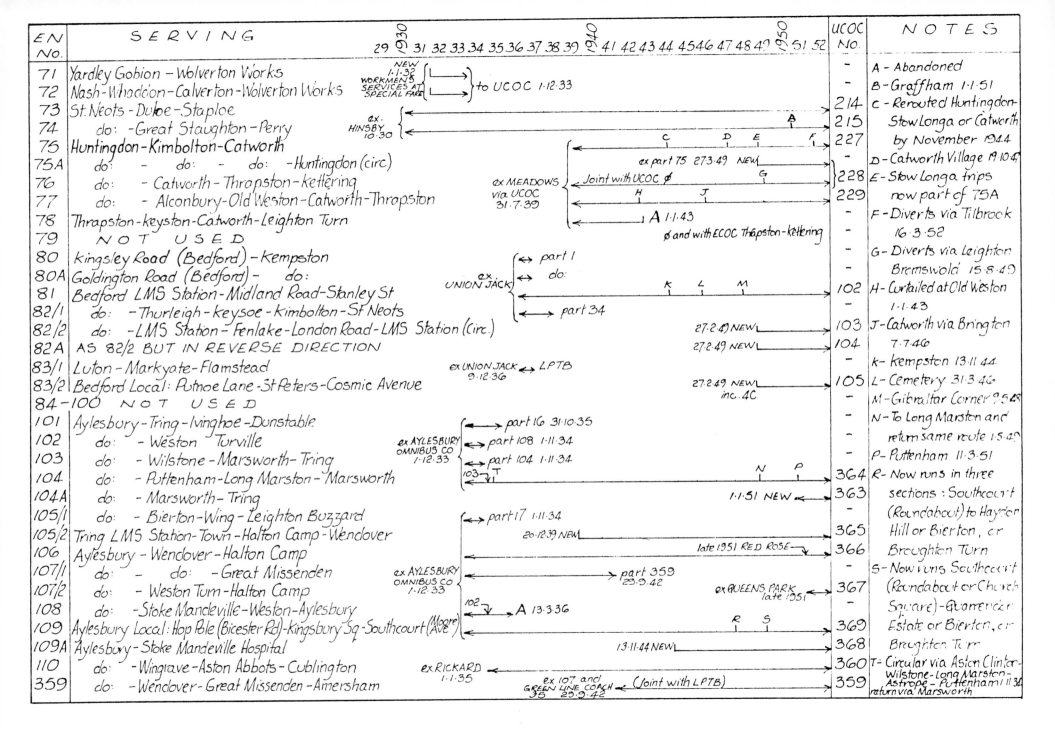

EN No.	SERVING	29 1930 31 32 33 34 35 36 37 38 39 1940 41 42 43 44 4546 47 48 49 1950 51 52	UCOC No.	NOTES
71	Yardley Gobion – Wolverton Works	NEW 1.1.32 WORKMENS SERVICES AT SPECIAL FARE } to UCOC 1.12.33	–	A – Abandoned
72	Nash–Whaddon–Calverton–Wolverton Works		–	B – Graffham 1.1.51
73	St. Neots – Duloe – Staploe	ex. HINSBY 10.30	214	C – Rerouted Huntingdon–
74	do: –Great Staughton–Perry	A	215	Stow Longa or Catworth
75	Huntingdon–Kimbolton–Catworth	C D E F	227	by November 1944
75A	do: – do: – do: –Huntingdon (circ)	ex part 75 27.3.49 NEW	–	D – Catworth Village 19.10.47
76	do: – Catworth–Thrapston–Kettering	ex MEADOWS via UCOC 31.7.39 Joint with UCOC ∅ G	} 228	E – Stow Longa trips
77	do: – Alconbury–Old Weston–Catworth–Thrapston	H J	229	now part of 75A
78	Thrapston–Keyston–Catworth–Leighton Turn	A 1.1.43	–	F – Diverts via Tilbrook
79	NOT USED	∅ and with ECOC Thrapston–Kettering	–	16.3.52
80	Kingsley Road (Bedford) – Kempston	↔ part 1	–	G – Diverts via Leighton
80A	Goldington Road (Bedford) – do:	ex UNION JACK ↔ do:	–	Bromswold 15.8.49
81	Bedford LMS Station–Midland Road–Stanley St	K L M	102	H – Curtailed at Old Weston
82/1	do: –Thurleigh–Keysoe–Kimbolton–St Neots	↔ part 34	–	1.1.43
82/2	do: –LMS Station–Fenlake–London Road–LMS Station (circ.)	27.2.49 NEW	103	J – Catworth via Brington
82A	AS 82/2 BUT IN REVERSE DIRECTION	27.2.49 NEW	104	7.7.46
83/1	Luton – Markyate – Flamstead	ex UNION JACK 9.12.36 ↔ LPTB	–	K – Kempston 13.11.44
83/2	Bedford Local: Putnoe Lane –St Peters –Cosmic Avenue	27.2.49 NEW inc. 4C	105	L – Cemetery 31.3.46
84–100	NOT USED		–	M – Gibraltar Corner 9.5.48
101	Aylesbury–Tring–Ivinghoe–Dunstable	↔ part 16 31.10.35	–	N – To Long Marston and
102	do: – Weston Turville	ex AYLESBURY OMNIBUS CO 1.12.33 ↔ part 108 1.11.34	–	return same route 1.5.49
103	do: – Wilstone–Marsworth–Tring	↔ part 104 1.11.34	–	P – Puttenham 11.3.51
104	do: –Puttenham–Long Marston–Marsworth	103→T N P	364	R – Now runs in three
104A	do: – Marsworth–Tring	1.1.51 NEW	363	sections : Southcourt
105/1	do: – Bierton–Wing–Leighton Buzzard	↔ part 17 1.11.34	–	(Roundabout) to Hayden
105/2	Tring LMS Station–Town–Halton Camp–Wendover	20.12.39 NEW	365	Hill or Bierton, or
106	Aylesbury – Wendover – Halton Camp	late 1951 RED ROSE	366	Broughton Turn
107/1	do: – do: –Great Missenden	ex AYLESBURY OMNIBUS CO 1.12.33 part 359 29.9.42	–	S – Now runs Southcourt
107/2	do: – Weston Turn–Halton Camp	ex QUEENS PARK late 1951	367	(Roundabout or Church
108	do: –Stoke Mandeville–Weston–Aylesbury	102↓ A 13.3.36	–	Square)–Quarrendon
109	Aylesbury Local: Hop Pole (Bicester Rd)–Kingsbury Sq–Southcourt (Moore) (Ave)	R S	369	Estate or Bierton, or
109A	Aylesbury–Stoke Mandeville Hospital	13.11.44 NEW	368	Broughton Turn
110	do: –Wingrave–Aston Abbots–Cublington	ex RICKARD 1.1.35	360	T – Circular via Aston Clinton–
359	do: –Wendover–Great Missenden–Amersham	ex 107 and GREEN LINE COACH 35 29.9.42 (Joint with LPTB)	359	Wilstone–Long Marston–Astrope–Puttenham 11.34 return via Marsworth

DIAGRAM of all EASTERN NATIONAL omnibus routes 1955-1969

PRE 1955 NO.	1955 NO.	SERVING	1955–1969 notes
w1 / w2	1	Southend-Thundersley-Rayleigh	
ENTO	2/1	do: -Corringham-Grays	70 →25.9.55 ... 25.5.66 B C Wdn 26.5.68
—	2/2	do: - do: - Orsett-Grays	26.5.68 2A/2
w2A	2A/1	do: - <West Horndon / Little Warley> Romford	15/15A 13.9.59
—	2A/2	do: - Corringham-Orsett-Grays	27.4.64 256.66 D 2/2 25.6.6
w2B	2B	do: - Homesteads - Grays	part 53 25.6.66
w2C	2C	do: - Shellhaven/Coryton	235 30.5.67
—	2D	do: - Homesteads - Orsett - Grays	11.4.65 NEW 248 25.5.66
w3	3	do: - Tarpots - South Benfleet	E 5.2.62 F 19.4.64
—	3A	do: - Essex Way - South Benfleet - Canvey	5.2.62 NEW F 19.4.64
—	3B	was not used	
—	3C	Leigh Beck (Canvey) - Winter Gardens	18.6.62 26C
w4	4	Southend - Landwick	
w4A	4A	do: - Wakering - Shoeburyness	G 15.6.58
w4B	4B	do: - Little Wakering	
w5	5/1	do: - North Shoebury - Shoeburyness	part 5A/25 3.6.56
—	5/2	do: - do: - do:	15.6.58 part 25 ... A 11.4.65
S5A	5A/1	do: - Thorpe Bay - Shoeburyness (Ness Rd.)	part 9/9A 28.5.55
—	5A/2	do: -Thorpe Bay Stn.-Shoeburyness (Railway Stn)	NEW 25.9.55 part 3/3A 19.4.64
w6	6	do: - Prittlewell Chase - Rayleigh (High St)	H 28.5.55 J 17.6.62 K 19.4.64
part w6A	6A	do: - Carlton Avenue - do: do:	H 28.5.55 J 17.6.62 K 19.4.64
—	6B/1	Westcliff ('Plough') - Prittlewell Chase - Rayleigh (High St)	20.4.64 NEW 6C 27.5.68
—	6B/2	Newington Avenue - Chalkwell Park - Eastwood (Kent Elm)	27.5.68 part ex16/NEW
—	6C	as 6B/1	27.5.68 6B/1

NOTES:

B Diverted via Basildon Town Centre 25.5.68

C Extended to Dartford 23.7.67: Dartford journeys became '402' 2.10.67

D Diverted via Basildon Town Centre 25.6.66

E Extended to Canvey (Leigh Beck) 5.2.62

F Through from Shoeburyness (ex 5A/2) 19.4.64

G To run via North Shoebury Corner instead of via Rose Inn

H From 28.5.55 to 19.6.55 only ran through from Newington Ave. (Archer Ave) ex '64' and curtailed at Rayleigh (Weir): Applied again from 3.6.56

J Extended to Archer Avenue (Roedean Avenue) 17.6.62

K Curtailed at Eastwood (Kent Elm Corner) 19.4.64

PRE 1955 No.	1955 No.	SERVING	1955	1956	1957	1958	1959	1960	1961	1962	1963	1964	1965	1966	1967	1968	1969
w 7	7	Southend - Ashingdon - Rayleigh				B 15.6.58											→
—	7A	do: (Pier Hill) - Ashingdon - Lower Hockley												5.12.66 ex 13 C			→
—	7B	do: do: - do: - South Fambridge												5.12.66 ex 13A C			→
w 8	8	do: - Hawkwell - Rayleigh												4.12.66 D			→
w 8A	8A	do: - Stroud Green - Rayleigh				16.6.58 E								4.12.66 F			→
w 9	9	do: - Eastwoodbury via Rochford Road				15.6.58 G						K					→
w 9A	9A	do: - do: via Warners Way #		13.1.57 H	15.6.58 G			26.6.61 J					5.12.66 L			→
w 9B	9B	do: - Sutton Schools do:															→
w 10	10	do: - Rochford - Paglesham															→
E 11	11	Chelmsford - Southend via East Hanningfield	M 4.7.55														→
—	11A	do: - do: via Main Road	9.6.57 ex 11														→
—	11E	do: - do: (Limited Stop)											22.5.66 NEW →	311/411 28.5.67		
w 12	12	Southend - Wallasea Bay															→
w 13	13	do: - Hullbridge via Ashingdon											26.5.66 N P 5.12.66			→
w 11	13A	do: - South Fambridge - via Ashingdon	3.6.55 11										7B 3.12.66 →			
w 14	14/1	do: - Romford via Arterial Road ✱					14.9.59 S								Wdn 8.1.68		
—	14/2	do: - Basildon Bus Stn. via Arterial Road												ex part of 14D 8.1.68		
—	14A/1	do: - Romford via Arterial Road and Alma Works					ex part 14 14.9.59								Wdn 8.1.68		
—	14A/2	do: - Basildon Bus Stn. via Arterial Road and Industrial Sites												ex part of 14D 8.1.68		
—	14B	do: - Rayleigh Stn. via Arterial Road											14.5.66 NEW			
—	14D	do: - Laindon via Arterial Road										12.4.65 ex part 14 T 7.6.65 →	14/14A 8.1.68		
—	14E	Eastwood (Kent Elm) - Basildon (Carreras Works)											NEW		

NOTES:
B Extended to Shoeburyness (Cambridge) incorporating parts of '9' and '9A' qv
C ex Minibus service (unlicensed) 5.12.66
D Extended to Shoeburyness (Cambridge) interworks with '7' 4.12.66
E Extended to Rayleigh Station 16.6.58
F Extended to Pier Hill 4.12.66
G Shoeburyness section became '7' (qv) 15.6.58
H Cockethurst section withdrawn 13.1.57
J ECKO Works - Eastwoodbury withdrawn 26.6.61
K Extended to Southend Airport between 20.4.64 and 14.9.64
L Shoeburyness - Southend (Central Station) withdrawn 5.12.66
M Part to run via main road, not calling at East Hanningfield, which was renumbered to '11A' 9.6.57

N Curtailed at Lower Hockley 26.5.66
P Curtailed at Ashingdon 5.12.66
S via West Horndon only 14.9.59
T Curtailed at Basildon 7.6.65
✱ via West Horndon or via Alma Works
Extended to Cockethurst Corner on Sundays

PRE 1955 NO.	1955 NO.	SERVING	1955	1956	1957	1958	1959	1960	1961	1962	1963	1964	1965	1966	1967	1968	1969
—	15/1	Southend – Romford via West Horndon					13.9.59 ex 2A		B 25.6.61			26/151 19.4.64					
—	15/2	do: - Upminster - do:											13.12.65 ex 15B			C 8.1.68	
—	15A/1	do: - Romford via Alma Works					13.9.59 ex 2A		B 25.6.61			14A/15B/151 19.4.64					
—	15A/2	as 15A/1											13.12.65 ex 15B			D 8.1.68	
—	15B	as 15/1							26.6.61 old 15			20.4.64 E	15/15A 13.12.65				
—	15C	Romford (Roneo Corner) – Basildon (Carreras Works)										NEW					
—	16/1	Chalkwell Stn. – Westborough Drive – Rayleigh (High St)	8.6.57 65		F	G				H 18.6.62		16A 20.4.64					
—	16/2	Temple Sutton – Westcliff-on-Sea – Eastwood (Kent Elm Corner)										20.4.64 NEW				27.5.68 J K 24.9.68	
—	16A	as 16/1										20.4.64 16					
w17	17	Southend (Pier Hill) – Woodcutters Arms – Eastwood via Mountdale										L 19.4.64					
—	17A	do: do: do: via Blenheim Chase Gardens		NEW 3.6.56								part 17 19.4.64					
w18	18	Southend – Foulness															
E19	19/1	do: – Danbury – Colchester – Clacton											M N	part to 19E 25.9.66			
E19A	19A/1	do: – Latchingdon – do: - do:											M N				
w19	19/2	do: – (Kursaal) – Chalkwell Stn. – Leigh-on-Sea (Elm)	67/67A														
w19A	19A/2	do: do: – Chalkwell Park – do:	68/68A														
—	19E	Colchester – Clacton (Limited Stop)											25.5.66 NEW P 419 28.5.67				
—	20/1	Southend – Wickford via Rayleigh (Weir) – Battlesbridge										19.4.64 250	14/14A and 22 group 22.5.66				
—	20/2	do: - Runwell Hospital												20.5.69 20C			
—	20A	do: - Wickford via Grove Road and Battlesbridge												20.5.69 22B			
w21	21	Leigh-on-Sea Stn. – Church – Prittlewell (Hobleythick Lane)	S				T 15.6.59										
w22	22/1	do: Church – Stn. – Thames Drive – Dawes Heath – Hullbridge					part 25A 14.6.59										
—	22/2	Southend – Eastwood – Hullbridge							18.4.62 NEW			U 19.4.64					

NOTES:
B Diverted via Basildon 25.6.61
C Extended to Romford 8.1.68
D Southend-Pitsea section withdrawn 8.1.68
E Also via Alma Works 20.4.64
F Extended to Rayleigh Station 16.6.58
G Diverted via Progress Road / Rayleigh Road 31.3.59
H Curtailed at Kent Elm Corner
J Curtailed to run Southend – Temple Sutton only 27.5.58
K Diverted to Hamstel Road/Eastern Avenue vice Temple Sutton 24.9.68
L Diverted to start Temple Sutton vice '61B', incorporating '16' to cover ex '17A' and run via Blenheim Chase 19.4.64

M Via Progress Road 19.4.64 to 22.5.66
N Via London Road, Rayleigh and Carpenter's Arms vice Rawreth Lane; and Colchester – Maldon section doubled (vice Moore's).
P Extended to Holland-on-Sea 31.10.66
S To run via Station, Thames Drive vice 'Elm' and London Road 26.9.55
T Extended to Rochford 15.6.59
U Extended to Southend (Central Station) incorporating part '25A' 19.4.64

PRE 1955 No.	1955 No.	SERVING	1955–1969 timeline annotations
—	22A	Southend (Central Station) – West Hockley via Grove Road	ex 20 / 22.5.66 NEW → 20A
—	22B	do: do: – Wickford via Grove Road and Battlesbridge	22.5.66 NEW → 20/1
—	22C	do: do: – Runwell Hospital	23.5.66 / 22.5.66 NEW → 20/2 20.5.69
w23	23	Leigh-on-Sea Stn. – Church – Eastwood Rd – Jones Corner	B 25.9.55 C D E 14.6.59 F 22.5.66
w23A	23A	do: – do: – Elmsleigh Drive – Kent Elm Corner	G 25.9.55 H 17.6.62 J 19.4.64 K 22.5.66
w24	24/1	do: – Rayleigh via Victoria House	L 25.9.55 M 14.6.59 N 17.6.62 P 19.4.64 R 22.5.66 → 24A 26.5.68
—	24/2	Thorpe Bay – Southend – Dawes Heath – Rayleigh Station (ex 25A diverted via Westcliff Station and Leigh Cliffs)	26.5.68 { 25A 24
—	24A	as 24/1	
s/w25	25	Highlands – Leigh-on-Sea – Southend (Victoria Circus)	3.6.56 S 15.6.58 T U 14.6.59
s/w25A	25A	do: – Southchurch – Thorpe Bay	15.6.58 V W 14.6.59 X 19.4.64 → 24 26.5.68 (part to 22)
s/w25B	25B	do: – Woodgrange Drive – Thorpe Bay	part to '25' 15.6.58
s—	25C	Southend Pier/Kursaal – Leigh-on-Sea (Elm) DANCES	} A by 1964
s—	—	do: – Southchurch (White Horse) DANCES	
w26	26	South Benfleet – Canvey (Leigh Beck)	Y 5.2.62 Z 19.4.64
w26A	26A/1	do: – do: (Sea View Road South)	part 26
—	26A/2	Canvey (ENOC depot) – Basildon (Carreras Works)	NEW
w26B	26B	South Benfleet – Canvey (Thorney Bay Camp)	
—	26C	Canvey (Leigh Beck) – Winter Gardens	NEW 5.2.62 AA 3C 18.6.62
—	26F	Basildon (Town Centre) – Ford Works, Dunton	NEW
w27	27	South Benfleet – Wickford	BB 6.6.67

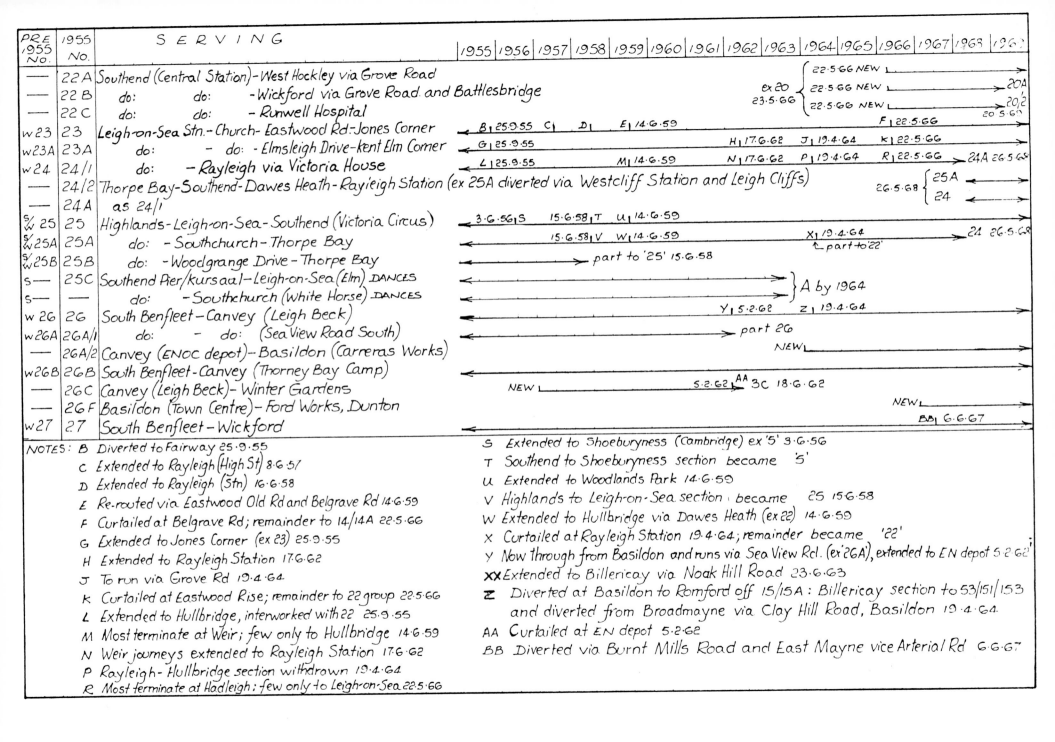

NOTES:
B Diverted to Fairway 25.9.55
C Extended to Rayleigh (High St) 8.6.57
D Extended to Rayleigh (Stn) 16.6.58
E Re-routed via Eastwood Old Rd and Belgrave Rd 14.6.59
F Curtailed at Belgrave Rd; remainder to 14/14A 22.5.66
G Extended to Jones Corner (ex 23) 25.9.55
H Extended to Rayleigh Station 17.6.62
J To run via Grove Rd 19.4.64
K Curtailed at Eastwood Rise; remainder to 22 group 22.5.66
L Extended to Hullbridge, interworked with 22 25.9.55
M Most terminate at Weir; few only to Hullbridge 14.6.59
N Weir journeys extended to Rayleigh Station 17.6.62
P Rayleigh – Hullbridge section withdrawn 19.4.64
R Most terminate at Hadleigh; few only to Leigh-on-Sea 22.5.66

S Extended to Shoeburyness (Cambridge) ex '5' 3.6.56
T Southend to Shoeburyness section became '5'
U Extended to Woodlands Park 14.6.59
V Highlands to Leigh-on-Sea section became 25 15.6.58
W Extended to Hullbridge via Dawes Heath (ex 22) 14.6.59
X Curtailed at Rayleigh Station 19.4.64; remainder became '22'
Y Now through from Basildon and runs via Sea View Rd (ex 26A), extended to EN depot 5.2.62
XX Extended to Billericay via Noak Hill Road 23.6.63
Z Diverted at Basildon to Romford off 15/15A: Billericay section to 53/151/153 and diverted from Broadmayne via Clay Hill Road, Basildon 19.4.64
AA Curtailed at EN depot 5.2.62
BB Diverted via Burnt Mills Road and East Mayne vice Arterial Rd 6.6.67

PRE 1955 NO.	1955 NO.	SERVING	1955	1956	1957	1958	1959	1960	1961	1962	1963	1964	1965	1966	1967	1968	1969
—	28	Hamstel Rd.- North Ave.- Victoria Circus- London Rd.- Chalkwell Schools * 28/29 group and 63A										B					
s28A	28A	Western circular (clockwise) via Fairfax Drive		←—	C 3.6.56 →remainder to 29/2 3.6.56												
s28B	28B	Western circular (anticlockwise) via Fairfax Drive		←—	D →remainder to 28 3.6.56												
s28C	28C	Kursaal — Priory Park		←——→ A 28.1.57													
—	29/1	Western circular (anticlockwise) via Prittlewell Chase	part 28B ←——→ 28, 29/2, 29A 3.6.56														
—	29/2	Hamstel Rd.- Southchurch Rd.- Victoria Circus- Fairfax Drive- Chalkwell Sch. * ex 28A, 28B, 63A, 63B 3.6.56										E					
—	29A/1	Western circular (clockwise) via Prittlewell Chase	part 28A ←——→ 28, 29/2, 29A 3.6.56														

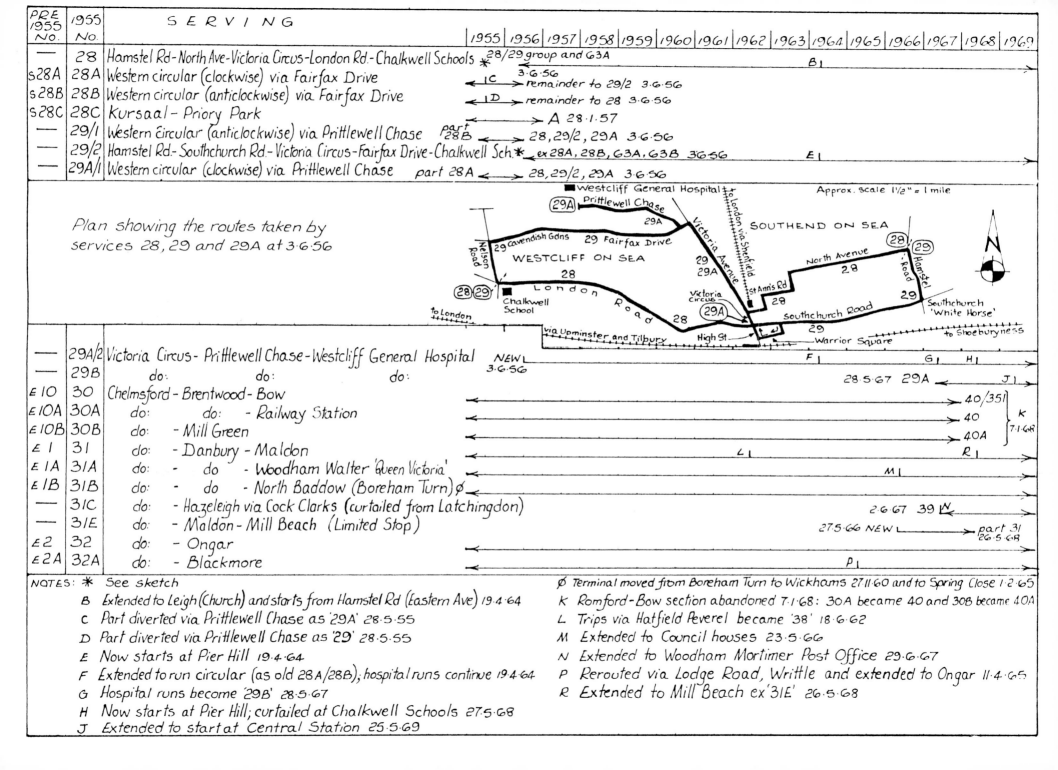

Plan showing the routes taken by services 28, 29 and 29A at 3.6.56

			1955	1956	1957	1958	1959	1960	1961	1962	1963	1964	1965	1966	1967	1968	1969
—	29A/2	Victoria Circus- Prittlewell Chase- Westcliff General Hospital	NEW 3.6.56									F			G	H	
—	29B	do: do: do:												28.5.67 29A →		J
E10	30	Chelmsford - Brentwood - Bow	←——————————————————→ 40/351														
E10A	30A	do: do: - Railway Station	←——————————————————→ 40 }k													7.1.68
E10B	30B	do: - Mill Green	←——————————————————→ 40A }													
E1	31	do: - Danbury - Maldon	←—————————————————— L —————— R													
E1A	31A	do: - do - Woodham Walter 'Queen Victoria'	←——————————————————— M													
E1B	31B	do: - do - North Baddow (Boreham Turn) ø	←———————————————————													
—	31C	do: - Hazeleigh via Cock Clarks (curtailed from Latchingdon)												2.6.67 39 N →		
—	31E	do: - Maldon - Mill Beach (Limited Stop)											27.5.66 NEW →part 31 26.5.68				
E2	32	do: - Ongar	←———————————————————													
E2A	32A	do: - Blackmore	←——————————————————— P													

NOTES: * See sketch

B Extended to Leigh (Church) and starts from Hamstel Rd (Eastern Ave) 19.4.64
C Part diverted via Prittlewell Chase as '29A' 28.5.55
D Part diverted via Prittlewell Chase as '29' 28.5.55
E Now starts at Pier Hill 19.4.64
F Extended to run circular (as old 28A/28B); hospital runs continue 19.4.64
G Hospital runs become '29B' 28.5.67
H Now starts at Pier Hill; curtailed at Chalkwell Schools 27.5.68
J Extended to start at Central Station 25.5.69

ø Terminal moved from Boreham Turn to Wickhams 27.11.60 and to Spring Close 1.2.65
K Romford - Bow section abandoned 7.1.68: 30A became 40 and 30B became 40A
L Trips via Hatfield Peverel became '38' 18.6.62
M Extended to Council houses 23.5.66
N Extended to Woodham Mortimer Post Office 29.6.67
P Rerouted via Lodge Road, Writtle and extended to Ongar 11.4.65
R Extended to Mill Beach ex '31E' 26.5.68

PRE 1955 No.	1955 No.	SERVING	1955	1956	1957	1958	1959	1960	1961	1962	1963	1964	1965	1966	1967	1968	1969

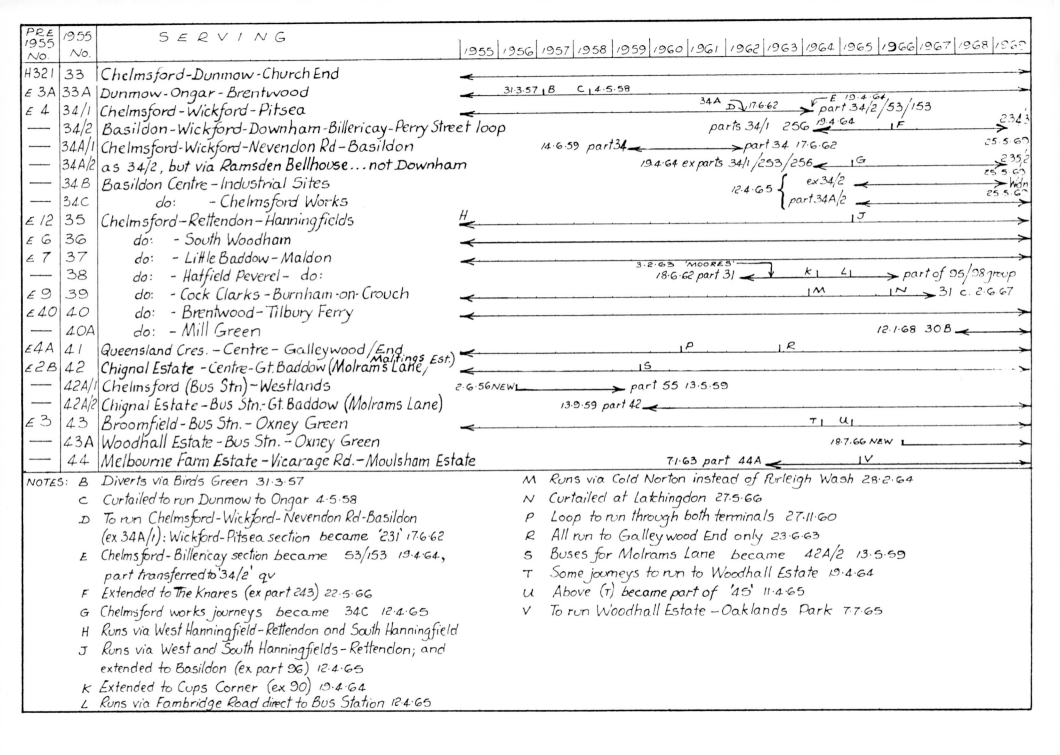

PRE 1955 No.	1955 No.	SERVING	1955–1969 entries
H321	33	Chelmsford – Dunmow – Church End	◄──────────────────►
E 3A	33A	Dunmow – Ongar – Brentwood	◄── 31.3.57 │B C │4.5.58
E 4	34/1	Chelmsford – Wickford – Pitsea	◄──── 34A D↓17.6.62 ►E 19.4.64 part 34/2/53/153
—	34/2	Basildon – Wickford – Downham – Billericay – Perry Street loop	parts 34/1 256 19.4.64 F 234/3
—	34A/1	Chelmsford – Wickford – Nevendon Rd – Basildon	14.6.59 part 34 ◄──────► part 34 17.6.62 25.5.69
—	34A/2	as 34/2, but via Ramsden Bellhouse ... not Downham	19.4.64 ex parts 34/1/253/256 ◄── G 235/2 25.5.69
—	34B	Basildon Centre – Industrial Sites	12.4.65 { ex 34/2 ◄──► Wdn 25.5.69
—	34C	do: – Chelmsford Works	{ part 34A/2 ◄──────►
E 12	35	Chelmsford – Rettendon – Hanningfields	H ◄──────────────── J ──────►
E 6	36	do: – South Woodham	◄──────────────────►
E 7	37	do: – Little Baddow – Maldon	◄──────────────────►
—	38	do: – Hatfield Peverel – do:	3.2.63 'MOORES' 18.6.62 part 31 ◄── K │ L │ ► part of 95/98 group
E 9	39	do: – Cock Clarks – Burnham-on-Crouch	◄──────── M ──── N ──► 31 c. 2.6.67
E 40	40	do: – Brentwood – Tilbury Ferry	◄──────────────────►
—	40A	do: – Mill Green	12.1.68 30B ◄──
E 4A	41	Queensland Cres. – Centre – Galleywood/End	◄── P │ R │ ►
E 2B	42	Chignal Estate – Centre – Gt. Baddow (Molrams Lane / Maltings Est.)	◄── S │ ►
—	42A/1	Chelmsford (Bus Stn) – Westlands	2.6.56 NEW ──► part 55 13.5.59
—	42A/2	Chignal Estate – Bus Stn. – Gt. Baddow (Molrams Lane)	13.9.59 part 42 ◄──
E 3	43	Broomfield – Bus Stn. – Oxney Green	◄──────── T │ U │ ►
—	43A	Woodhall Estate – Bus Stn. – Oxney Green	18.7.66 NEW │ ──►
—	44	Melbourne Farm Estate – Vicarage Rd. – Moulsham Estate	7.1.63 part 44A ◄──── V ──►

NOTES:
B Diverts via Birds Green 31.3.57
C Curtailed to run Dunmow to Ongar 4.5.58
D To run Chelmsford – Wickford – Nevendon Rd – Basildon (ex 34A/1): Wickford – Pitsea section became '231' 17.6.62
E Chelmsford – Billericay section became 53/153 19.4.64, part transferred to '34/2' qv
F Extended to The Knares (ex part 243) 22.5.66
G Chelmsford works journeys became 34C 12.4.65
H Runs via West Hanningfield – Rettendon and South Hanningfield
J Runs via West and South Hanningfields – Rettendon; and extended to Basildon (ex part 96) 12.4.65
K Extended to Cups Corner (ex 90) 19.4.64
L Runs via Fambridge Road direct to Bus Station 12.4.65

M Runs via Cold Norton instead of Purleigh Wash 28.2.64
N Curtailed at Latchingdon 27.5.66
P Loop to run through both terminals 27.11.60
R All run to Galleywood End only 23.6.63
S Buses for Molrams Lane became 42A/2 13.5.59
T Some journeys to run to Woodhall Estate 19.4.64
U Above (T) became part of '45' 11.4.65
V To run Woodhall Estate – Oaklands Park 7.7.65

PRE 1955 No.	1955 No.	SERVING	1955	1956	1957	1958	1959	1960	1961	1962	1963	1964	1965	1966	1967	1968	
E14A	44A	West Ave/Brownings Ave – Moulsham Drive – Moulsham St.	←			B		C		D			E		F	G	
E14B	44B	West Ave/Brownings Ave – Bus Stn – Springfield Park – Brook End	←			H			J				K		L	G	
E14C	44C	Springfield – Moulsham Schools	←										→		part 53 30·10·67		
E5	45	Woodhall Estate – Bus Stn – Wood St – Galleywood	←						M		N P part 43 ↓11·4·65						
E46	46	Chelmsford – Harlow	←	R													
E47	47	Ongar – Harlow via First Avenue	←	R										S	47A ↓ by 8·68		
—	47A	do: – do: via Edinburgh Way												5·9·66 part 47 → → 47 by 12·68			
E48	48/1	Chelmsford – Mill Beach	←					⌋ A 31·8·60									
—	48/2	do: – Springfield Park/Brook End					25·6·61 part 45 ←			T	U						
E49	49	Bishop's Stortford – Harlow via First Avenue	←	R													
—	49A	do: – do via Edinburgh Way											23·5·66 part 49 ←				
E50	50	Chelmsford – Terling – Braintree	←										V				
E50A	50A	do: – Flacks Green	←					W			X						
—	50B	do: – to/via Boreham Village									19·4·64 part 50A ←						
E51	51/1	Tilbury – Chelmsford – Colchester – Harwich	←									Y → part 70 11·4·65					
S51	51	Southend (Victoria Circus) – Kursaal via Southchurch Ave	← 66 28·5·55														
—	51/2	Chelmsford – Great Baddow via London Road/Moulsham Estate											7·6·65 NEW L				
—	51A	do: – do: via Waterhouse Lane/Moulsham Estate											7·6·65 NEW L				
—	51B	do: – do: via Westway/Moulsham Estate											7·6·65 NEW L				
E52	52	do: – Pleshey	←														

NOTES:
B Starts Melbourne Farm Estate and runs via Langton Ave 27.10.57
C Part via Vicarage Road to Moulsham Drive 14.9.58
D Extended to Moulsham Lodge Estate, Lewis Drive (Gloucester Ave) 5.6.60
E Vicarage Road section became '44' 7.1.63
F Starts Wicklow Avenue and extended to Shopping Centre 6.6.65
G Extended to Heath Drive 25.9.66
H Some start from West Avenue via North Avenue 27.10.57
J Diverted to Moulsham Lodge Estate; Springfield Park section became '45'.
K Part starts Pennine Road/Wicklow Avenue 19.4.64
L All do as (k) above and extend to Moulsham Lodge Estate shops 6.6.65
M Diverted from Galleywood End to Springfield Park ex '44B' 25.6.61
N Curtailed at 'Eagle' 23.6.63 and extended to Galleywood End (Skinner's Lane) 15.9.63
P Starts Chignal Estate (Sundays) 19.4.64 and daily 27.9.64.
R Extended to Harlow Town Centre 26.11.56

S Journeys via Industrial Estate became '47A' 5.9.66
T Terminal extended to St Margarets Rd instead of Sandford Rd 23.9.62
U Starts from Chignal Estate 19.4.64
V Does not call at Rectory Green between Terling and Fairsted 13.12.65
W Trips through or to Boreham Village
X Above (w) became 50B 19.4.64 qv
Y Curtailed to run Colchester – Harwich only 19.4.64

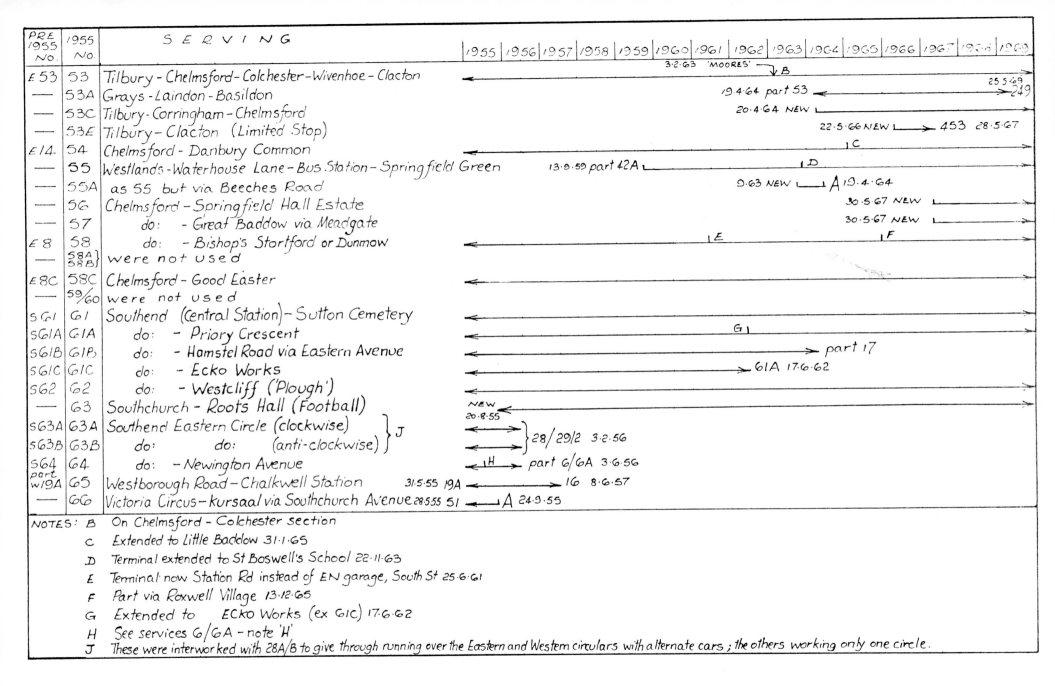

PRE 1955 No.	1955 No.	SERVING	1955	1956	1957	1958	1959	1960	1961	1962	1963	1964	1965	1966	1967	1968	1969
E53	53	Tilbury - Chelmsford - Colchester - Wivenhoe - Clacton									3.2.63 'MOORES' ↓B						25.5.69
—	53A	Grays - Laindon - Basildon										19.4.64 part 53					→ 249
—	53C	Tilbury - Corringham - Chelmsford										20.4.64 NEW					
—	53E	Tilbury - Clacton (Limited Stop)												22.5.66 NEW	→ 453 28.5.67	
E14	54	Chelmsford - Danbury Common										⌐C					
—	55	Westlands - Waterhouse Lane - Bus Station - Springfield Green	13.9.59 part 42A									⌐D					
—	55A	as 55 but via Beeches Road								9.63 NEW ⌐A 19.4.64							
—	56	Chelmsford - Springfield Hall Estate												30.5.67 NEW			
—	57	do: - Great Baddow via Meadgate												30.5.67 NEW			
E8	58	do: - Bishop's Stortford or Dunmow					⌐E							⌐F			
—	58A} 58B}	were not used															
E8C	58C	Chelmsford - Good Easter															
—	59/60	were not used															
S61	61	Southend (Central Station) - Sutton Cemetery															
S61A	61A	do: - Priory Crescent								G1							
S61B	61B	do: - Hamstel Road via Eastern Avenue											→ part 17				
S61C	61C	do: - Ecko Works								→ 61A 17.6.62							
S62	62	do: - Westcliff ('Plough')															
—	63	Southchurch - Roots Hall (Football)	NEW 20.8.55														
S63A	63A	Southend Eastern Circle (clockwise) } J		28/29/2 3.2.56													
S63B	63B	do: do: (anti-clockwise) }															
S64	64	do: - Newington Avenue	⌐H part 6/6A 3.6.56														
part w19A	65	Westborough Road - Chalkwell Station	31.5.55 19A → 16 8.6.57														
—	66	Victoria Circus - Kursaal via Southchurch Avenue	28.5.55 51 ⌐A 24.9.55														

NOTES:
B   On Chelmsford - Colchester section
C   Extended to Little Baddow 31.1.65
D   Terminal extended to St Boswell's School 22.11.63
E   Terminal now Station Rd instead of EN garage, South St 25.6.61
F   Part via Roxwell Village 13.12.65
G   Extended to   ECKO Works (ex 61C) 17.6.62
H   See services 6/6A - note 'H'
J   These were interworked with 28A/B to give through running over the Eastern and Western circulars with alternate cars; the others working only one circle.

PRE 1955 No.	1955 No.	SERVING	1955–1969 changes
67	67	Leigh-on-Sea (Elm)-Ridgeway-Kursaal-Shoebury Common	19 (1955) · B (1956) · C (1957) · D (1958) · E (1965)
W19 / W19A	67A	Leigh-on-Sea (Elm)-Chalkwell Park-Kursaal-Shoebury Common	19A (1955) → part 67 19.5.56
S68	68	as 67A but diverting at Lifstan Way to Hamstel Road	19 1W 1X · G
	68A	Leigh-on-Sea(Elm)-Chalkwell Pk-Kursaal-Hamstel Road- (Eastern Avenue)	19A/68 ← part 68 19.5.56
S69	69	Chalkwell Schools-ECKO Works	← · H
E70	70/1	Southend-Pitsea-Stanford-le-Hope-Grays	← 2/1 25.9.55
—	70/2	Colchester-Coggeshall-Braintree	ex 'MOORES' 3.2.63 · J · S
—	70A/1	Bishop's Stortford-Harwich (direct between Bradfield and Mistley)	12.4.65 part 70 ← · A 4.12.67
—	70A/2	Kelvedon-Coggeshall < Braintree / Colchester	27.5.68 ex part 71 ←
—	70B	Bishop's Stortford-Harwich via Pyes Bridge	13.4.65 part 70 ←
—	71	Colchester-Copford-Kelvedon-Coggeshall-Earls Colne	ex 'MOORES' 3.2.63 ← · K
—	72/1	do: -Black Pits-Haynes Green-Tolleshunt Knights	do: 4.2.63 ← 73/73A 17.5.64
—	72/2	do: -Copford-Easthorpe	19.4.64 ex part 71
—	73/1	do: -Birch-Tiptree-Kelvedon	ex 'MOORES' 3.2.63 ← L 19.2.64
—	73/2	do: -Black Pits-Messing-Tiptree-Tolleshunt Knights	20.4.64 { parts 71-74 ←
—	73A	do: - do: -Haynes Green-Tiptree-Tolleshunt Knights	{ parts 71-74 ←
—	74/1	do: -Birch-Tiptree-Tolleshunt Knights	part 19/19A ex'MOORES' 3.2.63 ↓ → 73/73A 19.2.64
—	74/2	do: -Brightlingsea via Alresford Station	Limited Stop Rail Replacement 15.6.64 { · M
—	74A	Wivenhoe Station-Brightlingsea	{ · N
E75	75	Colchester-West Mersea-East Mersea	← · P
E75A	75A/1	do: -Peldon Village-Great Wigborough	← → 79 18.9.63
—	75A/2	do: do: -West Mersea-East Mersea	29.9.63 part 75 ←

NOTES:
B   Extended to Leigh-on-Sea (Thames Drive) via London Road 19.5.56
C   Extended to Shoeburyness (Cambridge) 24.5.58
D   Extended to Shoeburyness (East Beach) 16.5.59
*E Diverted to Hamstel Road (Eastern Avenue) 5.6.65
F   Extended to Leigh-on-Sea (Thames Drive) via Marine Parade, Leigh Church and Ridgeway 19.5.56
*G Diverted to Shoeburyness (East Beach) 5.6.65
H   Also runs Leigh Church to Roots Hall for football match (ex X91) 21.8.65
J   Combined with '51' and '310' to form through route Bishop's Stortford- Braintree - Colchester - Harwich 11.4.65
K   To run Kelvedon - Earls Colne only 19.4.64: Colchester - Easthorpe transferred to new '72': Messing served by '73'.
L   Covered by '19/19A' and other services

M   Extended to North Street and part runs direct 23.5.66
N   Extended to Colchester Bus Station 23.5.66
P   Extended to East Mersea (ex 76) 1.6.63
S   Split at Colchester 26.5.68; passengers must change buses
*   Notes E and G - These two routes exchanged terminals
W   Extended to Leigh (Elm) via Kursaal and Chalkwell Station 28.5.55

X   Diverted at Leigh Broadway to Thames Drive via Marine Parade 19.5.56

PRE 1955 No.	1955 No.	S E R V I N G	1955	1956	1957	1958	1959	1960	1961	1962	1963	1964	1965	1966	1967	1968	1969
—	75B	Colchester – Peldon Turn – West and East Mersea via Blue Row									29·9·63 part 75 ←						
—	75C	do: – Peldon Village – do: via do:											8·1·66 part 75 etc. ←			
E76	76	do: – Fingringhoe – do:	←							76A/1 ↓	B (ex DIGBY)					→
—	76A/1	do: (Plough) – Rowhedge (Regent St)						17·9·60 ex 'MAWDSLEY & BROWN' ← → part 76 3·6·61								
—	76A/2	Wormingford – Colchester – Fingringhoe via High Park Corner									15·9·63 part 76 ←						
E77	77	Colchester – Alresford – Great Bentley – Clacton	←								part 77 ↓ C → } part 102 11·4·65 qv					
—	77A	do: – Wivenhoe – Alresford Heath – Great Bentley								29·9·62 NEW →							
E78	78	do: – Brightlingsea	←									D		→
—	78A	do: – Brightlingsea via Wivenhoe									29·9·63 NEW ←	D		→
—	79/1	do: (Bus Park/North Station) – Roman Way Camp (Joint OSBORNE'S) 13·11·58 NEW					→					99 16·9·63				
—	79/2	do: – Great Wigborough									18·9·63 ex 75A ← → to OSBORNE'S after 11·12·65				
E20	80	do: – Tendring Hospital ('EXPRESS')	←											E ∗	→
—	80A	do: – Stones Green via Horsley Cross and Beaumont											8·10·67 ex HOOKS ← ∗	→
—	80B	do: – do: – Honey Pot Lane – Harwich												25·5·68 NEW ← ∗ →
E28	81	do: (Mile End) – Layer Road (Football service)	←												→
E27	82	do: – Fordham – Wormingford Aerodrome	←							83 ↓ F				→
E26	83	do: – Aldham – Great Tey	←						G		82 14·4·65 →
—	84/1	do: – Langham (Fruit picking)	←											Wdn by 1969
—	84/2	do: – Langham Wick (co-ordinated with Mrs Bennett)											31·5·67 part ex BENNETT H ← →
E15	85	do: – Nayland – ⟨ Wiston / Stoke-by-Nayland (co-ordinated with Norfolks)	←								J		K	→
E16	86	do: – Sudbury – Clare	←					L		M	N →
E17	87	do: – Dedham – East Bergholt	←									P	→
E17A	87A	do: – Manningtree – East Bergholt	←									R	→

NOTES:
B Extended to Wormingford 12·11·61
C Part via Wivenhoe became '77A' 29·9·63
D Extended to Regent Road, Brightlingsea 11·4·65
E Now stage, extended to Harwich via Little Bentley, Frith's Farm and Wix: ex HOOKS/GREY GREEN 2·10·67
∗ 80/80A/80B: These three work as part of ECX80 (qv). All licensed to ENOC/GREY GREEN/SUTTONS
F Part extended to Great Tey (ex 83) 14·4·65
G To run via Aldham Village 4·10·61
H Co-ordinated with Mrs Bennett
J Extended to Blunden's Stoke 9·6·63
K Wiston section abandoned 11·4·65

L Part via Great Cornard 29·8·60
M All via Great Cornard 21·11·64
N Glemsford – Clare section abandoned 17·10·65
P Re-routed via Manningtree 11·4·65 but curtailed 12·12·65 to run via Heath to Dedham
R Curtailed 12·12·65 to run either to Dedham or Dedham Heath with one trip on Thursdays to East Bergholt only. Remainder now with ECOC as 221 through from Colchester – Ipswich. ENOC's '70' covers Mistley section.

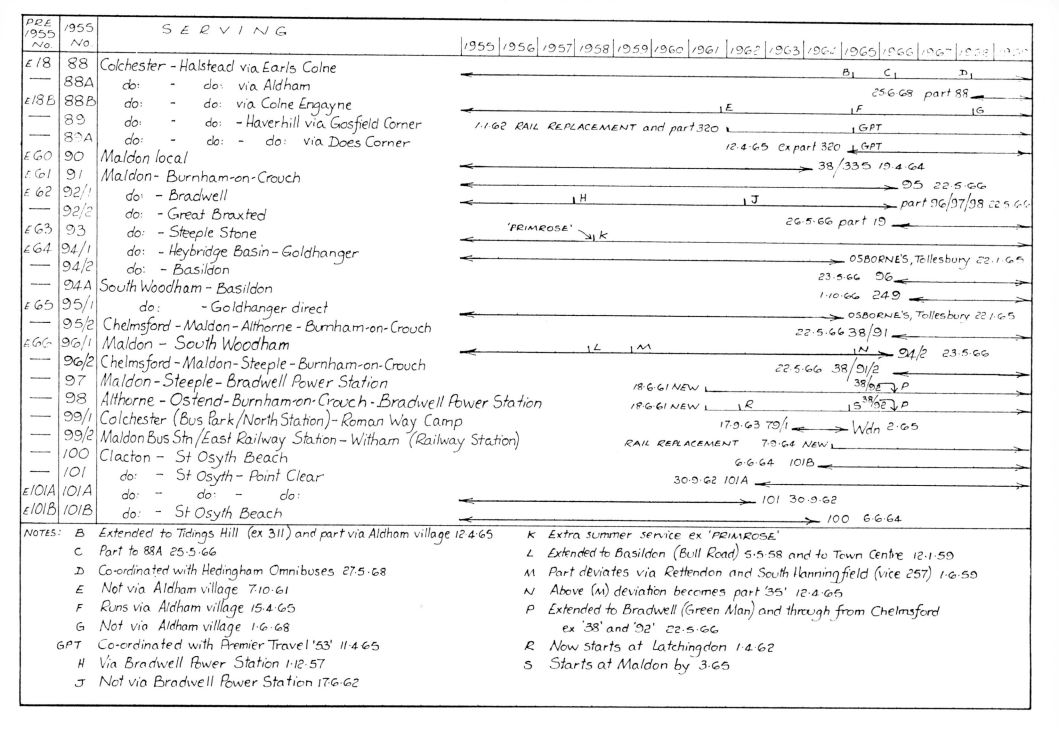

PRE 1955 No.	1955 No.	SERVING	1955	1956	1957	1958	1959	1960	1961	1962	1963	1964	1965	1966	1967	1968	1969
E18	88	Colchester – Halstead via Earls Colne											B C	D		
—	88A	do: – do: via Aldham											25.6.68 part 88			
E18B	88B	do: – do: via Colne Engayne						E				F		G	
—	89	do: – do: – Haverhill via Gosfield Corner	1.1.62 RAIL REPLACEMENT and part 320									GPT			
—	89A	do: – do: – do: via Does Corner									12.4.65 ex part 320	GPT			
E60	90	Maldon local											38/335 19.4.64		
E61	91	Maldon – Burnham-on-Crouch											95 22.5.66		
E62	92/1	do: – Bradwell					H			J			part 96/97/98 22.5.66		
	92/2	do: – Great Braxted										26.5.66 part 19			
E63	93	do: – Steeple Stone	'PRIMROSE' K												
E64	94/1	do: – Heybridge Basin – Goldhanger											OSBORNE'S, Tollesbury 22.1.65		
—	94/2	do: – Basildon										23.5.66 96			
—	94A	South Woodham – Basildon										1.10.66 249			
E65	95/1	do: – Goldhanger direct										OSBORNE'S, Tollesbury 22.1.65			
—	95/2	Chelmsford – Maldon – Althorne – Burnham-on-Crouch										22.5.66 38/91			
E66	96/1	Maldon – South Woodham					L M					N 94/2 23.5.66			
—	96/2	Chelmsford – Maldon – Steeple – Burnham-on-Crouch										22.5.66 38/91/2			
—	97	Maldon – Steeple – Bradwell Power Station						18.6.61 NEW				38/92 P			
—	98	Althorne – Ostend – Burnham-on-Crouch – Bradwell Power Station						18.6.61 NEW	R			S 38/92 P			
—	99/1	Colchester (Bus Park/North Station) – Roman Way Camp								17.9.63 79/1	Wdn 2.65				
—	99/2	Maldon Bus Stn/East Railway Station – Witham (Railway Station)	RAIL REPLACEMENT 7.9.64 NEW												
—	100	Clacton – St Osyth Beach									6.6.64 101B				
—	101	do: – St Osyth – Point Clear								30.9.62 101A					
E101A	101A	do: – do: – do:								101 30.9.62					
E101B	101B	do: – St Osyth Beach									100 6.6.64				

NOTES:

B   Extended to Tidings Hill (ex 311) and part via Aldham village 12.4.65
C   Part to 88A 25.5.66
D   Co-ordinated with Hedingham Omnibuses 27.5.68
E   Not via Aldham village 7.10.61
F   Runs via Aldham village 15.4.65
G   Not via Aldham village 1.6.68
GPT   Co-ordinated with Premier Travel '53' 11.4.65
H   Via Bradwell Power Station 1.12.57
J   Not via Bradwell Power Station 17.6.62

K   Extra summer service ex 'PRIMROSE'
L   Extended to Basildon (Bull Road) 5.5.58 and to Town Centre 12.1.59
M   Part deviates via Rettendon and South Hanningfield (vice 257) 1.6.59
N   Above (M) deviation becomes part '35' 12.4.65
P   Extended to Bradwell (Green Man) and through from Chelmsford ex '38' and '92' 22.5.66
R   Now starts at Latchingdon 1.4.62
S   Starts at Maldon by 3.65

PRE 1955 No.	1955 No.	SERVING	1955	1956	1957	1958	1959	1960	1961	1962	1963	1964	1965	1966	1967	1968	1969
E102	102	Clacton - St Osyth - Brightlingsea										77/77A ↓B					→
E103	103	do: - Thorpe-le-Soken - Walton-on-Naze											→ A part to 128 11.4.65				
E104	104	do: - Wix - Harwich											↓C		↓D		→
E105	105	Colchester - Thorpe-le-Soken - Walton-on-Naze							E‖	F‖	G‖				H‖	→
E106	106	Clacton - Oakleys - Harwich												J‖	k‖		→
E107	107	do: - Kirby-le-Soken - Walton-on-Naze							L‖						M‖	→
E108	108/1	do: - Tendring - East Bergholt		←‖N							ø 128 6.6.64					
—	108/2	do: - Kirby-le-Soken - Ashes Corner - Walton-on-Naze						ex '107'			←				P‖	→
E109	109/1	do: - Valley Farm Camp					↑R				ø 129 6.6.64					
—	109/2	do: - direct to Ashes Corner - Walton-on-Naze						ex '107'			←				P‖	→
E110	110/1	do: - Sacketts Grove		←‖S							ø 130 6.6.64					
—	110/2	Holland (Fernwood) - Clacton - Jaywick													‖T	→
E111	111/1	Walton-on-Naze - Harwich							U‖		ø 131 6.6.64					
—	111/2	Wargrave Rd. - Coppins Green - Clacton - Holland - Fernwood Avenue												←‖	‖V	→
E112	112	Holland (kings Ave) - Clacton - Jaywick (Sea front Route)				W‖		X‖		Y‖	Z‖					→
—	113/1	Clacton Station - Bus Station - Wash Lane - Jaywick				AA‖			BB‖	CC 115/121 2.6.62						
—	113/2	Clacton - Burrsville Park - (circular going out via Thorpe Road)								29.9.63 part 114 ←						
—	113A	Valley Rd (Yeoman's Works) - Clacton - Jaywick (Tudor Estate)												9.9.68 ex 126A ‖	‖A	

NOTES:

B Runs via Great Bentley 11.4.65 ex 77/77A : Extended to Regent Road 11.4.65; curtailed at Old Railway Station 28.5.66; restored to Regent Road 31.10.66

C Runs (a) Harwich-Stones Green/Bradfield and (b) Clacton - Dovercourt 28.5.66

D Part extended to Manningtree 27.5.68

E Summer only Chelmsford-Walton through trip abandoned 9.63

F Via Walton Road instead of Elm Tree Avenue 27.9.64

G Extended to Maldon ex 19/19A 11.4.65

H Via Elm Tree Avenue instead of Walton Road 3.11.68

J Part via Back Road, Oakleys ex HOOKS 2.10.67

k Part extended to Stones Green 8.9.68

L Trips via Kirby-le-Soken and Ashes Farm become 108/2, and trips via Ashes Farm Corner become 109/2 — both on 29.9.63

M Extended to Jaywick Sands ex 110/115 8.9.68

N To run via Mistley Heath 7.7.57

P Extended to Jaywick Sands ex 110/115 8.9.68

R Valley Farm - Holland section withdrawn after 9.9.59

S Extended to Chester Camp 2.6.56

T Jaywick Sands section becomes part of 107/108/109 9.9.68

U Extended to The Naze 14.7.63

V Rerouted from 'Roaring Donkey' to Fleetwood Avenue loop 9.9.68 incorporating part of '115'.

W Part diverted to Holland (Cliff Road) 1.6.59

X Diverted to Holland (Fernwood Avenue) 3.6.61

Y Diverted to Holland (Brighton Road) 1.10.62 - 30.5.63

Z All to Fernwood Avenue 1.6.63

AA Extended to Great Clacton, Highfield or Bockings Elm 1.6.59, but Highfield only 1.6.60

BB Winter service becomes 115A 1.10.61

CC Route divided 2.6.62

ø Summer services only which did not operate from 9.63 to 6.64

PRE 1955 No.	1955 No.	SERVING	Timeline (1955–196–)
E114	114	Burrsville Park - Clacton - Jaywick Sands	B … C … D E F
E114A	114A/1	do: circle in both directions	part 114 30.9.62
—	114A/2	Jaywick Sands - Yeoman's Factory, Clacton	27.5.68 NEW
E115	115	Magdalen Green - Town - Jaywick	G H … 17.2.6?/11
E115	115A	Holland (King's Cliff) - Railway Stn - Bus Stn - Jaywick	$ … 6.7.58 R J K L 110/2 29.9.63 … 8.9.68
E116	116/1	Holland (York Road) - do: do: do:	M N P 126 30.9.63
—	116/2	Harwich - Parkeston Quay via Fronks Rd and Hall Lane	6.6.64 part 118 R S
E117	117/1	Clacton - Railway Stn - Valley Farm - Holland (Fernwood Ave)	T U 111 1.10.63
—	117/2	Harwich - Parkeston Quay via Main Road	29.9.63 part 118 V
E118	118	Harwich - Parkeston Quay (either route 116/2 or 117/2)	W X
E119	119	do: - Dovercourt Tollgate via Marine Parade and Fronks Rd	Y Z
E119A	119A	do: - do: Tollgate and Transit Camp via Main Rd.	120/2 29.9.63
—	120/1	Dovercourt Railway Station - Holiday Camp	120A 29.9.63
—	120/2	Harwich Quay - Main Rd - Dovercourt (Transit Camp)	29.9.63 ex 119A AA BB
—	120A	Dovercourt Railway Station - Holiday Camp	29.9.63 ex 120/1 … Wdn by 1969
E121	121	Clacton - Little Clacton (Meadow View Camp)	CC DD
E122	122	Harwich - Dovercourt (Caravan Camp) via Main Road	EE FF
E123	123	Clacton - Tendring - Manningtree - Ipswich	GG HH

NOTES:

B — Jaywick-Clacton withdrawn; runs via Valley Road 2.6.56
C — Runs via Thorpe Road and Highlands Camp or via Valley Rd 16.7.61
D — As 'c' but not calling at Highlands Camp 30.9.62
E — To run circular via Thorpe Road and Valley Road or vice versa 1.4.63
F — Outward journey run via Thorpe Road, becoming 113/2 29.9.63
G — Starts from Croft Road 1.10.61
H — Now from Wargrave Road incorporating part of 113/1 and runs via Wash Lane 2.6.62
J — Extended to Kings Parade, Queensway 5.7.59
K — To Fernwood Avenue (ex part 117) and via Wash Lane (ex 113) 1.10.61
L — Wash Lane route became 115 2.6.62
M — To Cliff Rd in half-season, extended to Kings Parade in full season 1959; and throughout from 3.6.61
N — To Fernwood Avenue 2.6.62
P — Ran Brighton Road through to Jaywick (Tudor Estate) 1.6.63
R — Some via boating lake from 1964
S — Extended to Harwich Quay and via Highfield Avenue 6.6.65
T — Starts from Croft Road 2.10.61
U — From Wargrave Road and via Turpins Avenue 2.6.62
V — From Harwich Railway Stn. by 6.6.64 and extended to Quay 27.9.64
W — Runs via boating lake becoming 116/2, and via Main Rd becoming 117/2 29.9.63
X — From Harwich Railway Station by 6.6.64
Y — From Harwich Rly. Stn. by 6.6.64; trips via boating lake became 124 6.6.64
Z — Part via boating lake (ex 124) 8.9.68
AA — From Railway Station by 6.6.64
BB — Now from Quay 28.5.66
CC — Extended to Jaywick Sands 2.6.56
DD — Incorporated in part of 113/1 (Jaywick section) 2.6.62 and runs via Rly. Stn.
EE — From Railway Station and via boating lake 6.6.64
FF — Extended to Harwich Quay 5.6.65
GG — Became joint with ECOC 29.1.61
HH — Spur to Rigby Avenue, Mistley 3.1.66 and via Bradfield Heath also, incorporating part of 128 28.5.66

PRE 1955 No.	1955 No.	SERVING	1955	1956	1957	1958	1959	1960	1961	1962	1963	1964	1965	1966	1967	1968	1969
E124	124/1	Clacton - Colchester - Black Notley Hospital									224 - 29.9.63						
—	124/2	Harwich - Dovercourt Transit Camp via Fronks Rd and Hall Lane										6.6.64 part 119				part 119 8.9.68	
—	125	Clacton - Great Clacton (Castle Hill)		B													
—	126	Holland (Brighton Rd) - Clacton - Jaywick (Tudor Estate) *									30.9.63 116		C D			E	
—	126A	Yeoman's Factory - Clacton														26.5.68 NEW 113A 9.9.68	
—	128	Clacton - East Bergholt										6.6.64 108		A part became 123 28.5.66			
—	129	do: - Valley Farm Camp										6.6.64 109					
—	130	do: - Socketts Grove - Chester Camp										6.6.64 110					
—	131	Walton-on-Naze — Harwich										6.6.64 111	F		G	5.8.69 A	
—	141	Great Knightleys - Basildon Industrial Site No.1 via Long Riding								7.8.62 part 241	H		J			
—	142	Laindon (Town Centre) - do: do: do: No.2 via Upper Mayne								30.7.62 NEW	K		L M			
—	143	The Knares — do: do: do: No.1 via Clay Hill Road								19.6.62 part 243	N				148 9.9.68	
—	144	Laindon (Railway Stn) - do: do: do: No.1 via Whitmore Way								18.6.62 part 244						
—	145	Corringham — do: do: do: No.1								6.62 NEW						
—	147	Pitsea - Basildon (Town Centre) - Standard Telephone Works											18.7.66 NEW			
—	148	Laindon - The Knares - Basildon Industrial Site No.1 via Whitmore Way													9.9.68 part 143/1	
—	150	Rayleigh - Wickford - Basildon													8.1.68 NEW	
—	151	Southend (Tylers Ave) - Pitsea - Basildon - Brentwood - London (Wood Green): formed from 15/15A/26/251										14.4.64	P	R			
—	153	Tilbury - Chadwell - Corringham - Basildon - Chelmsford - Colchester - Wivenhoe: parts of 34/51/53/248										19.5.64					
—	158	Basildon Industrial Site No.2 - Langdon Hills											12.4.65 part 258				
—	159	Laindon (Railway Stn) - Basildon Industrial Site No.2 via St Nicholas Lane													by 9.68 NEW	
—	207	Colchester - Stratford St Mary - Ipswich (joint with ECOC)							29.1.61 ECOC 207 solus				S			
—	212	Harwich - Manningtree - Ipswich (joint with ECOC)											12.4.65 NEW		T		
—	224	Clacton - Colchester - Black Notley Hospital										29.9.63 124					

NOTES:
- B Extended to Highlands Camp 2.6.56 and also to Jaywick Sands from 1.7.56 to 8.9.56
- C Via sea front only 5.6.65
- D Via Holland Rd 28.5.66 and extended to Crossways 24.7.66
- E To Fernwood Avenue 9.9.68
- F Extended to Harwich Quay from Walton Bus Stn via Elm Tree Ave 5.5.65
- G Part to now run to Walton and Stones Green 7.10.67
- H Extended to Ballard's Walk 19.6.63
- J Curtailed at Town Centre 12.4.65
- K Extended to Laindon 16.4.63
- L Via Great Knightleys 29.9.64
- M Extended to Industrial Site No.1 12.4.65
- N Extended to The Knares 10.3.63
- P Extended to Southend (Seaway) 31.7.64
- R Journeys via Chesnut Avenue, Tottenham ceased 23.5.66
- S Part via Langham ex ECOC '247' 12.4.65
- T Some via Wix 27.5.68
- * Via sea front summer and via Holland Road winter

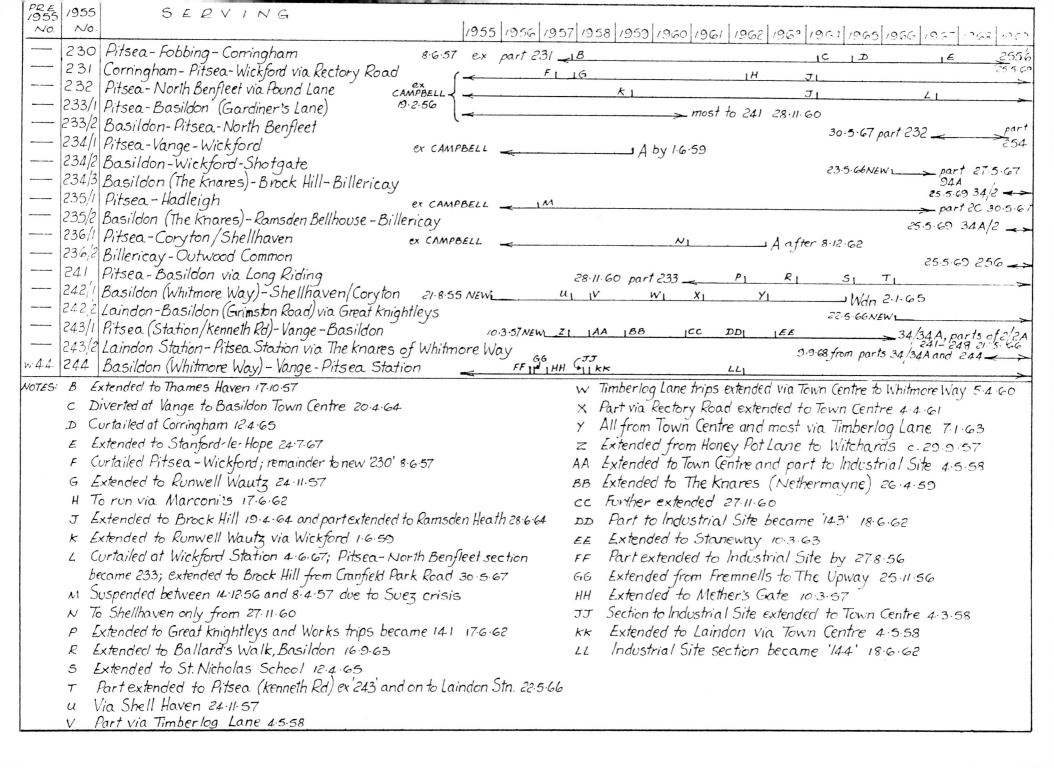

PRE 1955 NO.	1955 NO.	SERVING	1955	1956	1957	1958	1959	1960	1961	1962	1963	1964	1965	1966	1967	1968	1969

- — 230 Pitsea-Fobbing-Corringham 8.6.57 ex part 231 ←B ————————————————————————— C ——— D ——————————— E ——————— 255/6
- — 231 Corringham-Pitsea-Wickford via Rectory Road 255/60
- — 232 Pitsea-North Benfleet via Pound Lane ex CAMPBELL 19.2.56 { ←———————— F | G ——————————————— H ——— J ————————————————→ 30.5.67 part 232 ← part 234
- — 233/1 Pitsea-Basildon (Gardiner's Lane) { ←———————— K ——————————— J ———————————— L ————————————→
- — 233/2 Basildon-Pitsea-North Benfleet { ←——————————————————→ most to 241 28.11.60
- — 234/1 Pitsea-Vange-Wickford ex CAMPBELL ←——————————| A by 1.6.59
- — 234/2 Basildon-Wickford-Shotgate 23.5.66NEW ————————→ part 27.5.67 94A
- — 234/3 Basildon (The knares)-Brock Hill-Billericay 25.5.69 34/2 ←
- — 235/1 Pitsea-Hadleigh ex CAMPBELL ←————| M ————————————————————————————→ part 2C 30.5.67
- — 235/2 Basildon (The knares)-Ramsden Bellhouse-Billericay 25.5.69 34A/2 ←
- — 236/1 Pitsea-Coryton/Shellhaven ex CAMPBELL ←——————————————————| N ———————| A after 8.12.62
- — 236/2 Billericay-Outwood Common 25.5.69 256 ←
- — 241 Pitsea-Basildon via Long Riding 28.11.60 part 233 ← P | R | S | T |
- — 242/1 Basildon (Whitmore Way)-Shellhaven/Coryton 21.8.55 NEW ————— U | V ——— W | X | Y |————→ Wdn 2.1.65
- — 242/2 Laindon-Basildon (Grimston Road) via Great knightleys 22.5.66 NEW
- — 243/1 Pitsea (Station/kenneth Rd)-Vange-Basildon 10.3.57 NEW — Z | AA | BB | CC | DD | EE |————→ 34/34A, parts of 2/2A 241-248 21.5.66
- — 243/2 Laindon Station-Pitsea Station via The knares of Whitmore Way 9.9.68 from parts 34/34A and 244 ←
- w.44 244 Basildon (Whitmore Way)-Vange-Pitsea Station ←————— FF | GG | HH | JJ | KK ————————— LL |

NOTES:
B Extended to Thames Haven 17.10.57
C Diverted at Vange to Basildon Town Centre 20.4.64
D Curtailed at Corringham 12.4.65
E Extended to Stanford-le-Hope 24.7.67
F Curtailed Pitsea-Wickford; remainder to new '230' 8.6.57
G Extended to Runwell Wautz 24.11.57
H To run via Marconi's 17.6.62
J Extended to Brock Hill 19.4.64 and part extended to Ramsden Heath 28.6.64
K Extended to Runwell Wautz via Wickford 1.6.59
L Curtailed at Wickford Station 4.6.67; Pitsea-North Benfleet section became 233; extended to Brock Hill from Cranfield Park Road 30.5.67
M Suspended between 14.12.56 and 8.4.57 due to Suez crisis
N To Shellhaven only from 27.11.60
P Extended to Great knightleys and Works trips became 14.1 17.6.62
R Extended to Ballard's Walk, Basildon 16.9.63
S Extended to St. Nicholas School 12.4.65
T Part extended to Pitsea (kenneth Rd) ex '243' and on to Laindon Stn. 22.5.66
U Via Shell Haven 24.11.57
V Part via Timberlog Lane 4.5.58

W Timberlog Lane trips extended via Town Centre to Whitmore Way 5.4.60
X Part via Rectory Road extended to Town Centre 4.4.61
Y All from Town Centre and most via Timberlog Lane 7.1.63
Z Extended from Honey Pot Lane to Witchards c.29.9.57
AA Extended to Town Centre and part to Industrial Site 4.5.58
BB Extended to The Knares (Nethermayne) 26.4.59
CC Further extended 27.11.60
DD Part to Industrial Site became '143' 18.6.62
EE Extended to Stoneway 10.3.63
FF Part extended to Industrial Site by 27.8.56
GG Extended from Fremnells to The Upway 25.11.56
HH Extended to Mether's Gate 10.3.57
JJ Section to Industrial Site extended to Town Centre 4.3.58
KK Extended to Laindon via Town Centre 4.5.58
LL Industrial Site section became '144' 18.6.62

PRE 1955 No.	1955 No.	SERVING	1955	1956	1957	1958	1959	1960	1961	1962	1963	1964	1965	1966	1967	1968	1969
W 80	245	Pitsea – Bata Works	←					B						C			→
E 83	246	Laindon – Bata Works	←													→┤ A 24.5.68
E12A	247	Wickford – Runwell Hospital	←									D					→
W 84	248/1	Basildon – Pitsea – Grays via Homesteads	←			┘ Wdn 3.5.58											
—	248/2	do: – Corringham – Orsett – Grays					25.6.61 NEW ┘					19.4.64 →┘ part 153	R 22.5.66 *			→
—	249/1	Billericay – Crays Hill – Wickford – South Woodham											23.5.66 ←E┘ part 94A 30.5.67			
—	249/2	Basildon – Laindon – Horndon-on-the-Hill – Orsett – Grays													25.5.69 53A ←
—	250/1	Southend (Tylers Ave) – Turnpike Corner – Wickford						17.9.61 part 251 ←			→ 20 19.4.64				
—	250/2	Basildon – Wickford – Shotgate										7.6.65 NEW ┘	F			
W251	251	Southend (Tylers Ave) – Wood Green via Battlesbridge	←					G			H				J	→
W252	252	Brentwood (High St) – Hutton (Bracken Bank)	←			K				L						→
W253	253	do: – Rawreth (Carpenters Arms)	←						M	N	P	R┘ S				
W254	254	do: – Great Burstead – Laindon	←			T				U	V	W				X	
W255	255	do: – Little Burstead – Laindon	←			Y				Z						AA	
W256	256/1	Billericay – Sunnymede Estate	←				BB		CC			DD			25.5.69 236 ┘	
—	256/2	Billericay – Little Burstead – Basildon – Fobbing – Corringham – Stanford-le-Hope													ex 230/255 ←

NOTES:
B Part from Basildon via Homesteads 27.1.59
C Basildon section via Town Centre, and Pitsea section via Corringham 13.12.65
D Extended to Basildon Town Centre 19.4.64
E Basildon section became 94A 1.10.66
F Extended to Brentwood 23.5.66, and Wickford to Basildon section became '234' 23.5.66
G Via Shotgate 25.6.61; Battlesbridge shuttle to '250' 17.9.61
H Half service became '151' and extended to Southend (Seaway) 31.7.64
J To run via West Green Road via Bruce Grove and Lordship Lane (Tottenham) 7.1.68
K Starts at Railway Stn. and runs via Three Arch Estate and Bracken Bank to Shenfield Stn. 4.5.58
L Extended from Station to Woodman Road ex '261' 17.6.62
M Wickford to Rawreth section withdrawn 25.5.61
N Extended to Shotgate 17.6.62
P Curtailed at Wickford Station and extended to Upminster Station 22.5.63
R Curtailed to run Upminster – Hutton Industrial Site (part to 34A) 19.4.64
S Via Warley (Ford's) 19.7.64
T Extended to Basildon Town Centre 4.5.58

U Spur to Laindon Station withdrawn 17.6.62
V Billericay – Brentwood section withdrawn 10.3.63 and extended to Billericay Railway Station
W Part extended to Laindon 20.4.64
X Brentwood – Billericay section withdrawn, and remainder extended from Laindon to North Benfleet via Basildon Town Centre and Pitsea
Y Extended to Basildon Town Centre 4.5.58
Z Spur to Laindon Station and Billericay – Brentwood section withdrawn 17.6.62 and remainder extended to Billericay Railway Station.
AA Brentwood – Billericay section withdrawn and remainder extended from Laindon to Stanford-le-Hope via Basildon and Fobbing 25.5.69
BB To run Perry Street – Billericay – Sunnymede – Outwood Common 6.12.59
CC Reverted back from Perry Street to Billericay Station 4.6.61
DD Perry Street section became 34/34A 19.4.64 and rerouted via Hillside Road instead of Norsey Road.
* Resumed to run via Homesteads (part starts at Pitsea)

PRE 1955 No.	1955 No.	SERVING	1955	1956	1957	1958	1959	1960	1961	1962	1963	1964	1965	1966	1967	1968	1969
w257	257/1	Laindon-Wickford-Rettendon			←————— B ————————→ A (Diversion of 94 covers)												
	257/2	do: - Bulphan									23.5.63 part 260 ←—C			D		
w258	258	do: - Pipps Hill circular/Vange			←				E F		G	H J					
w259	259	do: - Langdon Hills			←								K				
w260	260	do: - Brentwood-Warley/Ongar			←						L M						
w261	261	Brentwood (Woodman Rd)-Hook End-Stondon Massey			←					N P							
w262	262	Brentwood local: Bishop's Hall Estate-Town-Hornbeam Close			←							R					
w263	263	Brentwood-St Vincent's Hamlet	22.7.55 NEW L														
—	264	do: – Hulton Drive							4.4.61 NEW S								
—	265	do: – Herongate/Old Dog/West Horndon Station/Bulphan									22.5.63 part 260 ←— T						
—	266	Little Warley-Brentwood-Hook End-Stondon Massey-Ongar-Fyfield										part 33A 11.4.65 NEW L U		V		
—	283	Halstead (ENOC office)-Sudbury-Bildeston-Stowmarket							4.11.62 ex CORONA/MULLEY (by ECOC)		←— W			→ECOC 7.1.68 only	
—	299	Bishop's Stortford local: Station Rd-Haymead's Hospital-Beldams Lane-London Rd-Station Rd											30.5.67 NEW L			
—	300	do: : as 299 but in reverse direction												30.5.67 NEW L			
E13	301	Bishop's Stortford (South St)-Ugley Green-Saffron Walden		←					X	Y	Z					
E13A	302	Bishop's Stortford-Stansted Airport/Debden/Birchanger		←		AA			X					BB		

NOTES:
B Rerouted via Church Road, and Whitmore Way via Gardiners Lane South 29.4.57
C Extended to Basildon Town Centre 29.9.63, and Saturday service became '265' 9.11.63
D Laindon Station spur withdrawn 27.5.68
E To run Laindon Stn. via Wash Rd. to Church Rd. (Basildon Rd) 28.11.60. Vange section withdrawn
F Part extended to Basildon (Marconi's) ex 15/15A 25.6.61
G To run via Arterial Rd. vice Wash Rd. to Industrial Site No 2/Church Rd. (Basildon Rd) 25.5.63
H Part extended to Basildon Town Centre 28.9.64
J Section to Industrial Site No 2 became '158', part via Pipps Hill or to Church Road became '259' 12.4.65, section to Town Centre diverted via Great Knightleys
K Runs Church Rd./Basildon Rd. or Town Centre via Pipps Hill (ex part 258) 12.4.65
L On 22.5.63 (a) Laindon-Bulphan became '257'; (b) Bulphan-Brentwood Stn. became '265'; (c) section Warley (Headley Arms)-Waterworks withdrawn; (d) Brentwood-Ongar section curtailed at Blackmore (Ongar section to 261); (e) Includes Warley-Coxtie Green ex London Transport 339A, and co-ordinated with London Transport 339 Warley-Brentwood-Ongar-Harlow
M Diverted at Headley Arms to Ford's 19.7.64
N Station to Woodman Road section to 252 17.6.62
P Rerouted Little Warley-Brentwood-Hook End-Stondon Massey (Tipps Cross)-Blackmore-Ongar, incorporating part of '260' 22.5.63

R Extended to Shenfield Stn. via Hulton (Sundays) vice '252' 11.4.65
S Terminus at Wainright Ave. until road adopted by 26.11.61
T Extended to Basildon Town Centre (ex '257') 9.11.63
U Curtailed at Ongar 7.11.65
V Starts at Brentwood Station. Section to Little Warley became part of '261' 8.1.68
W ENOC participation from 13.5.63
X Services 301, 302, 303/1, 305, 306, 310/1, 313/1, 314/1 and 317 :- Bishop's Stortford terminal moved from ENOC depot, South Street to Station Road 25.6.61
Y Part via Audley End Station 7.9.64 and via Widdington (ex 304) 20.4.64
Z No deviation via Littlebury from 13.12.65
AA Airport section to '313' 7.4.57 and curtailed at Debden Green 29.5.57
BB Extended to Thaxted incorporating '338' 26.5.68

PRE 1955 NO.	1955 NO.	SERVING	1955	1956	1957	1958	1959	1960	1961	1962	1963	1964	1965	1966	1967	1968	1969
E13B	303/1	Bishop's Stortford - Rickling - Clavering - Lower Langley							X₁			→ part 305/306 27.1.64					
—	303/2	do: - Stansted - (Skyways) via Rye Street												22.5.66 ex 313	B₁		
E13C	304/1	Elsenham - Saffron Walden											→ part 301 12.12.65				
—	304/2	as 303/2 via Plaw Hatch / Passenger Terminal												22.5.66 ex 314	C₁		
E13D	305	Bishop's Stortford (South Street) - Manuden - Clavering - Upper Langley							X₁ D₁		E₁ F₁						
E13E	306	do: - Newport - Wicken Bonhunt - Lower Langley							X₁		G₁						
E39A	307	Saffron Walden - Arkesden - Clavering															
E39B	308	do: - Newport - do: - Lower Langley															
—	309	Bishop's Stortford local: South St - Town - Heath Row	4.3.57 NEW₁						H₁				J₁				
H10	310/1	do: (FALCON) - Dunmow - Braintree						K₁	L₁ X₁				→ part 70 11.4.65				
—	310/2	Chelmsford - Braintree - Convent Hill - Gosfield - Halstead											13.12.65 ex 311				
H11	311	do: do:						M₁					N₁ P₁ R				
—	312/1	Braintree local: Cressing Road - Bailey Bridge Road	NEW₁						S₁				→ 321 12.12.65				
—	312/2	Chelmsford - Braintree - Bocking - Penny Pot - Halstead											13.12.65 ex 311				
—	313/1	Bishop's Stortford - Stansted - Takeley - Coopers End - Stansted (Skyways) 7.4.57 NEW₁							X₁				→ 303 13.12.65				
—	313/2	Chelmsford - Braintree - Halstead via Convent Hill and Penny Pot										12.12.65 ex 311					
—	314/1	Bishop's Stortford # - Plaw Hatch - extended as 313/1 7.4.57 NEW₁							X₁				→ 304 13.12.65				
—	314/2	Chelmsford - Little Waltham - Fuller Street													11.8.67 NEW₁		
H15	315	Braintree - Gt. Saling < Bardfield Saling - New Green / Turn Lindsell / Dunmow - Bishop's Stortford											T₁				
H16	316	Bran End - Felsted - Howe Street - Chelmsford															
H17	317	Bishop's Stortford (FALCON) - Broxted or Coopers End ✱			V₁				X₁							U₁	

NOTES:
B Terminal redesignated The Hall, Caravan Site 27.5.68
C Hall Caravan Site section became part of '317' 30.9.68
D Wicken Bonhunt section withdrawn 7.4.62
E Deviated to Wicken Bonhunt (ex 303) 2.2.64 but withdrawn 28.10.64
F Curtailed at Lower Langley 12.4.65
G Part via Stansted village (ex 303) 27.1.64
H Extended to Manston Drive 5.5.60
J Extended to Havers Lane Estate (ex London Transport 350/350A) 4.11.64
K Terminal to South Street 1.4.57 instead of 'Falcon'
L To Railway Station 10.9.59
M Extended to Halstead (ex 323/4), and part to Tidings Hill or Notleys 11.5.58
N Tidings Hill section to '88' 12.4.65
P Variations on Braintree - Halstead section became '310', '312' and '313'. Notleys section withdrawn 12.12.65
R 'Limited Stop' journeys to Southend 22.5.66
S Extended to Skitts Hill 29.1.61

T Rerouted to run Braintree - Rayne - Stebbing Green or Bardfield Saling to Stebbing village - Bran End / Lindsell or Dunmow - Bishop's Stortford 14.4.65
U Part runs to The Hall Caravan Site (ex 304) 30.9.68
V Rerouted (from South St) to run via (a) Takeley - Coopers End - Molehill Green (part via Bambers End) - Broxted or (b) via Burton End - Tye Green to Molehill Green 24.11.57
✱ Routing — (a) Circular via Takeley (or some call Bambers Green) - Broxted - Tye Green - Burton End or (b) via Takeley to Coopers End
AA Box Stansted Road and via ENOC depot, South Street
X Services 301, 302, 303/1, 305, 306, 310/1, 313/1, 314/1 and 317:- Bishop's Stortford terminal moved from ENOC depot, South Street to Station Road 25.6.61

PRE 1955 No.	1955 No.	SERVING	1955	1956	1957	1958	1959	1960	1961	1962	1963	1964	1965	1966	1967	1968	1969
H19	319	Braintree - Beazley End - Wethersfield Air Base and village							B							C	
E22	320/1	Halstead - Maplesteads - Hedinghams - Little Yeldham - Haverhill					D			E			F 89/89A 11.4.65				
—	320/2	Braintree Bus Park - Vauxhall Drive											20.3.67 NEW				
E21	321/1	do: - Wethersfield Air Base - Great Bardfield - Gt Sampford											352 19.4.64 *				
—	321/2	do: - Bailey Bridge Road - Skitts Hill											12.12.65 312				
H22	322	do: - Dunmow - Harlow - London		G							H J				K L		
E23	323/1	do: - Halstead - Sudbury				M							part 380 28.5.64				
—	323/2	Halstead - Pebmarsh - Sudbury											30.5.68 330				
E24A	324/1	Braintree - Halstead via Convent Hill and Penny Pots				311 11.5.58											
—	324/2	Halstead - Great Maplestead											19.10.65 325				
E29	325/1	do - Greenstead Green - Braintree												P R		S	
H29	329	Felsted - Willows Green - Rayne (Pods Lane)														T	
E30	330	Halstead - Sudbury - Long Melford									323		u				
E31	331/1	Braintree - Wethersfield Air Base (via Gosfield)			A from 15.6.57											323/2 30.5.68	
—	331/2	do: - Kelvedon - West Mersea (summer only)									⊗ 3.2.63 ex MOORE'S		V A after 25.9.65				
—	331/3	Great Bardfield - Panfield Lane - Braintree - Notleys - Witham											ex 351,352 30.5.67 W				
—	332/1	Braintree - Pattiswick via Bradwell									3.2.63 ex MOORE'S		325 12.4.65				
—	332/2	Great Bardfield - Braintree - Witham via Bocking - Notleys											ex 352 28.5.67 W				
E33	333	Braintree - Little Maplestead											X Y Z				
—	334	Tiptree - Silver End									4.2.63 ex MOORE'S		AA				

NOTES:
B Extended to Cornish Hall End 27.8.60
C Curtailed at Wethersfield 'Dog' 29.5.68
D Spur from Great Yeldham - Toppesfield 7.6.58
E Ridgewell - Haverhill section became '89' 1.1.62
F Maplesteads section to '325' 11.4.65, rest to '89'/'89A'
* Only Braintree - Bardfield to '352'; Great Sampford section abandoned
G Part to Harlow New Town from Dunmow 27.11.56
H To new Kings Cross Coach Station 13.5.63
J Extended to Sudbury 11.4.65
K Extended to Great Cornard 28.5.67
L Incorporating part of '336' 26.5.68
M Became '311' 11.5.58 on Braintree to Halstead section; Sudbury bus continues as 323/1
N Became circular from Halstead via Great and Little Maplesteads 2.4.67
P Part to Great Maplestead ex '320/1' or to Pattiswick ex '322/1' 12.4.65

R Great Maplestead section to 324 19.10.65
S Curtailed to become Halstead - Greenstead Green 27.5.68; Pattiswick section became '333'
T Via Pods Lane 29.5.68 (instead of TO Pods Lane)
u Incorporating part of 323 and curtailed at Sudbury 28.5.64
⊗ First day of operation by ENOC 2.6.63
V Starts from Halstead 6.6.65
W Divided 26.5.68; Braintree - Notleys - Witham section became '339'
X Extended to Purls Hill Corner (Great Maplestead) 14.4.65
Y Curtailed at Countess Cross 28.9.66
Z Incorporating Braintree - Pattiswick section of 325 27.5.68
AA Extended to Tolleshunt Knights by 6.2.65 and Kelvedon to Silver End section abandoned 5.7.65

PRE 1955 NO.	1955 NO.	SERVING	Timeline (1955–1969) notes
E60 H35 }	335	Braintree-Silver End (direct)-Witham-Hawbridge Estate-Maldon	B	C	D	E	
—	336/1	Halstead-Little Maplestead-Sudbury	25.5.64 NEW ... F ... part 322 26.5.68
—	336/2	as 335 but via Avenue, Witham	27.5.68 part 335
—	337	Ebenezer Close-Witham-Maldon	27.5.68 parts 335/353
E38	338/1	Bishop's Stortford (EN depot, South St)-Thaxted	X ... 302 27.3.69
—	338/2	Heybridge-Maldon	27.5.68 part 335
—	339	Braintree-Notleys-Witham	26.5.68 parts 331/332
E8B	347	Bishop's Stortford (South St)-High Roding	G	X	H
E8A	348	do: do: do: -Matching Green	X	A after 11.12.65
H49	349	do: do: -Great Hallingbury	part 347 15.6.58
—	351/1	Great Bardfield-Panfield Lane-Braintree-Witham	13.12.65 ex part 321 ... 331 30.12.67
—	351/2	Chelmsford-Brentwood-Wood Green	7.1.68 ex 30/30A
H52	352	Braintree-Notleys-Witham	J ... part 332/2 28.5.67
—	353	Witham local-Maltings Road-Ebenezer Close	20.4.64 ex parts 335/352 ... 337
—	402	Southend-Grays-Dartford	2.10.67 part 2
—	411	do: -Chelmsford-St Osyth-Clacton-Walton-on-Naze	28.5.67 ex 53E/11E
—	419	do: -Maldon-Weeley-Clacton-Walton-on-Naze	28.5.67 ex parts 11E/19E/53E
—	446	Harlow-Chelmsford	26.5.68 NEW
—	453	Tilbury-Grays-Chelmsford-Clacton-Walton-on-Naze	28.5.67 53E

(Services 402, 411, 419, 446, 453 bracketed: } LIMITED STOP)

NOTES:
B Buses via Polish Camp cease 20.10.59
C Extended to South House Estate and via Oak Rd, Heybridge (ex part 90) and spur to Great Totham (Braxted Turn) withdrawn 19.4.64
D Diverted via Cups Corner to Bus Station (ex 38) 12.12.65
E Garage runs to Kelvedon became 336/2, 337 or 338/2 26.5.68
F Extended to Great Cornard 28.5.67
G Diverted via Great Hallingbury ex 349 15.6.58

H Curtailed at Woodside Green (The Gate) 15.12.65, but extended to Forest Hall Farm 10.1.66
J Extended to Great Bardfield (ex 321) 13.4.64 and Ebenezer Close section became '353'
X Services 338/1, 347 and 348:- Bishop's Stortford terminal moved from ENOC depot, South Street to Station Road 25.6.61

DIAGRAM of EXPRESS SERVICES (Eastern Area) 1929–1961

Symbol	TERMINAL POINTS	(timeline 29 1930 31 32 33 34 35 36 37 38 39 1940 41 42 43 44 45 46 47 48 49 1950 51 52 53 54 55 56 57 58 59 1960 61)	
A	London-Colchester-Clacton	ex'NATIONAL' — C — $ — R —	12
—	do:- do:- do: (via North London) ex'NATIONAL'	A	
—	do:- do: - Harwich	NEW A } Licences refused	
B	do:- Braintree-Halstead-Hedinghams/Great Bardfield (HORN) ex'BIRD' (ex 'HORN')	'HORN' — D — $ — R — E —	14
C	do: - Maldon	ex'QUEST' — $ — R —	15
D	do: - Southend	— $ — R —	10
E	Southend-Brighton-Worthing	F — G	20
F	do: - Eastbourne		21
G	do: - Folkestone	ex'WESTCLIFF' }	22
H	do: - Hastings		23
J	do: - Margate		24
K	do: - Enfield	'BOROUGH' — 'B' — $ — R — H —	11
L	Tilbury - Great Yarmouth	'TILBURY COACHING' — $ — R — J —	40
M	Southend - Great Yarmouth	'WESTCLIFF' —	25
N	Tilbury - Clacton - Jaywick Sands (via Laindon)	NEW — $ — R — J — K —	41
P	Bishops Stortford - Clacton	ex HICKS BROS — M — N — C — P —	50
Q	Harlow - Clacton - Jaywick Sands	part 'P' —	51
R	Tilbury - Clacton - Walton on Naze (via Laindon)	NEW J — S	42
S	Harlow - Felixstowe (via B183 to Dunmow)	NEW — L —	52
T	Tilbury - Clacton - Jaywick Sands	ex 'N' —	43
U	Southend - Bournemouth	NEW —	26
V	Chelmsford - Great Yarmouth	ex 'PRIMROSE' —	70
W	Southend - Clacton - Jaywick Sands	NEW —	27

MIDLAND AREA EXPRESS SERVICES

D	Bedford-Clacton *	NEW 1933 ∅	
E	do: - Great Yarmouth	NEW 1932 #	
F	Luton - Bournemouth		
G	do: - Margate	ex Hill 1934	
H	do: - Southsea	t/as STRAWHATTER	
J	do: - Great Yarmouth		
M	do: - Southend *	NEW 1936	
P	Bedford - Dovercourt	NEW 1937	
Q	Luton - Dovercourt	NEW 1937	

NOTES (Midland)

∅ Extended to Jaywick Sands 1949
Feeder from Ramsey, Warboys and Huntingdon 1949
* 'D' and 'M' interworked. Passengers for the other destination exchanged at Baldock.
'D' and 'M' were suspended 1940-1945
Remainder suspended 1940-1947

All passed to 'UNITED COUNTIES' after the 1951 season

NOTES

A - service abandoned
B - operated by 'BOROUGH'
C - extended to Jaywick Sands
D - Braintree-Great Bardfield / Halstead-Hedinghams section now by bus connection
E - extended to Hedinghams (Weds and Sats)
F - now calls at Basildon 'Jolly Cricketers'
G - re-routed via New Town and Pitsea
H - now operated by Eastern National
J - feeder services from Aveley and Ockendon
K - re-routed via Basildon
L - re-routed via Bishop's Stortford
M - ran as H12 until 1952
N - now starts at Harlow New Town
P - extended to Walton-on-Naze
R - service resumed
S - re-routed via Basildon
$ - temporarily suspended
NB: Letter symbols did not come into use until 1936

The Company's Official Booking Agents Display this sign:-

COACH BOOKING AGENCY EASTERN NATIONAL

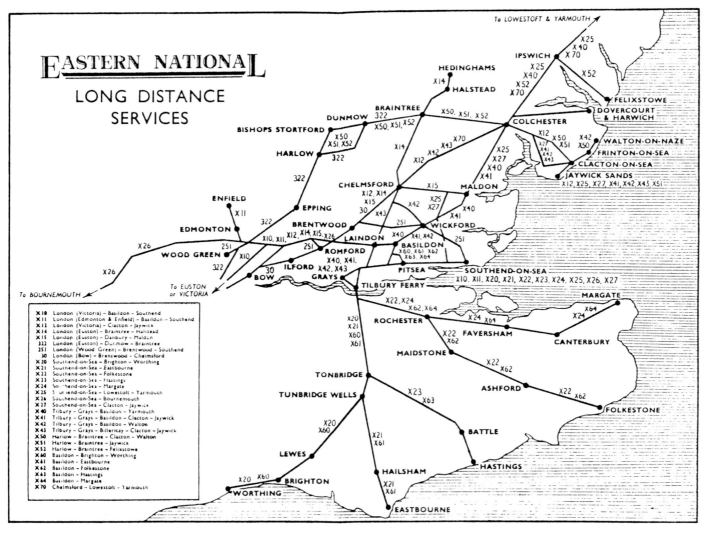

EASTERN NATIONAL

LONG DISTANCE SERVICES

Company map issued 1962 showing Express service network after adoption

of new identification symbols

To LOWESTOFT & YARMOUTH

IPSWICH
X25
X40
X70
X25
X40
X52
X70

HEDINGHAMS
X14

HALSTEAD

FELIXSTOWE

DOVERCOURT & HARWICH

BRAINTREE
322

DUNMOW

BISHOPS STORTFORD
X50
X51, X52

HARLOW

322

X50, X51, X52

X50, X51, X52

322

COLCHESTER

X50, X51, X52

X14

X70

X12

X43

X12

X25
X27
X40
X41

WALTON-ON-NAZE
X42
X50
X51

FRINTON-ON-SEA
X27
X41
X42
X43

CLACTON-ON-SEA

JAYWICK SANDS
X12, X25, X27, X41, X42, X43, X51

ENFIELD
X11

EPPING

CHELMSFORD
X12, X14
X15
30
X43

X15

X25
X27

MALDON

X40

X42

X41

WICKFORD

X40
251

322

EDMONTON

BRENTWOOD
X10, X11, X12, X14, X15, X26

LAINDON

X40
X41, X42

BASILDON
X60, X61, X62
X63, X64

X26

WOOD GREEN
251
X10

322

ROMFORD
X40, X41,
X42, X43

ILFORD
30

251

PITSEA

SOUTHEND-ON-SEA
X10, X11, X20, X21, X22, X23, X24, X25, X26, X27

To BOURNEMOUTH

X26

To EUSTON or VICTORIA

BOW

GRAYS

TILBURY FERRY

MARGATE
X24

X22, X24
X62, X64

ROCHESTER
X20
X21
X60
X61

X24 X64

FAVERSHAM
X22
X62

CANTERBURY

MAIDSTONE

X22
X62

ASHFORD

X22 X62

FOLKESTONE

TONBRIDGE

TUNBRIDGE WELLS

X23
X63

BATTLE

X20
X60

X21
X61

LEWES

HAILSHAM

HASTINGS

X20 X60
BRIGHTON

X21
X61

WORTHING

EASTBOURNE

X10 London (Victoria) - Basildon - Southend
X11 London (Edmonton & Enfield) - Basildon - Southend
X12 London (Victoria) - Clacton - Jaywick
X14 London (Euston) - Braintree - Halstead
X15 London (Euston) - Danbury - Maldon
322 London (Euston) - Dunmow - Braintree
251 London (Wood Green) - Brentwood - Southend
30 London (Bow) - Brentwood - Chelmsford
X20 Southend-on-Sea - Brighton - Worthing
X21 Southend-on-Sea - Eastbourne
X22 Southend-on-Sea - Folkestone
X23 Southend-on-Sea - Hastings
X24 Southend-on-Sea - Margate
X25 Southend-on-Sea - Lowestoft - Yarmouth
X26 Southend-on-Sea - Bournemouth
X27 Southend-on-Sea - Clacton - Jaywick
X40 Tilbury - Grays - Basildon - Yarmouth
X41 Tilbury - Grays - Basildon - Clacton - Jaywick
X42 Tilbury - Grays - Basildon - Walton
X43 Tilbury - Grays - Billericay - Clacton - Jaywick
X50 Harlow - Braintree - Clacton - Walton
X51 Harlow - Braintree - Jaywick
X52 Harlow - Braintree - Felixstowe
X60 Basildon - Brighton - Worthing
X61 Basildon - Eastbourne
X62 Basildon - Folkestone
X63 Basildon - Hastings
X64 Basildon - Margate
X70 Chelmsford - Lowestoft - Yarmouth

Notes to Diagram opposite ⟹

A - service abandoned, in most cases replaced by other facilities

B - now joint with Biss Bros

C - worked in conjunction with Harris's Coaches, Grays

D - branch to Canvey Island

E - above extended to X7

F - extended to Bury St Edmunds / Hadleigh, merged with EC 'X'.

H - Hadleigh section abandoned

J - extended to Mill Beach and West Mersea

K - extended to Eastbourne

L - diverts to run via Ramsgate to Margate

M - diverts to run via Margate to Ramsgate

N - extended to Walton-on-Naze

O - extended to Northampton and Birmingham (Joint with Midland Red and Premier Travel)

P - now starts at Southend

Q - now starts at Gillingham

R - not beyond Clacton this year

S - extended to Horsham

T - extended to Worthing

U - extended to Sheringham

V - curtailed to start at Braintree

※ - commenced 1958 as Coach/Air service. No symbol until 1964.

- Joint with Eastern Counties, Royal Blue and Grey Green. Listed and advertised by ENOC but not licensed to ENOC.

(T) part of Dartford Tunnel Coachways. Joint with East Kent, Maidstone & Dist. or Southdown

EN = Eastern National
EC = Eastern Counties
G-G = Grey-Green of George Ewer & Co.

DIAGRAM of EXPRESS SERVICES ('Eastern Area') 1962 - 1969

Left table

X..	TERMINAL POINTS	1962 → 63 64 65 66 67 68 69
1	London – Southend via Airport (direct)	* →X8
2	Sudbury – Brixham (Joint 'Royal Blue')	NEW ⌐B →X14
3	Southend – do: do:	NEW ⌐C →X13
4	do: – Weston-super-Mare (Joint Bristol Greyhound)	NEW ⌐ →X9
5	do: – Ilfracombe (Joint 'Royal Blue')	NEW ⌐ →X16
7	London – Canvey Island	part X10 ← →
8	do: – Southend via Airport	X1 ← →
9	Southend – Weston-super-Mare (Joint Bristol Greyhound)	X4 ← →
10	London – Southend via Basildon	D ← D →E
11	Enfield – Southend	K ← →
12	London – Clacton – Jaywick Sands	A ← → EC X4
13	Southend – West Country	NEW →
14/1	London – Halstead	B ← F →H → EC 'F'
14/2	Sudbury – West Country	NEW ⌐
15/1	London – Maldon	C ← J →A
15/2	Ipswich – Ilfracombe	# NEW ⌐ →
16	Southend – Ilfracombe	NEW ⌐ →
20	do: – Worthing	E ← →
21	do: – Eastbourne	F ← →A
22	do: – Folkestone	G ← →
23	do: – Hastings	H ← K →
24	do: – Margate	J ← L →M
25	do: – Great Yarmouth	M ← →
26	do: – Bournemouth	U ← →
27	do: – Clacton – Jaywick Sands	W ← N →
28	do: – Cambridge (Joint E.C.O.C)	NEW ⌐ →O
29	do: – Derby (Joint Barton Transport, Skills, Trent)	NEW ⌐ →
30	do: – Southsea	(T) NEW ⌐
31	Basildon – Southsea	(T) NEW ⌐
32	Clacton – Folkestone	(T) NEW ⌐
33	Walton-on-Naze – Hastings	(T) NEW ⌐K
34	Clacton – Thanet Resorts	(T) NEW ⌐
35	Basildon – Tunbridge Wells	(T) NEW ⌐ →P
36	Clacton – Rye	(T) NEW ⌐ →

Right table

X..	TERMINAL POINTS	1962 → 63 64 65 66 67 68 69
40	Tilbury – Great Yarmouth	(T) L ← →Q
41	do: – Clacton – Jaywick Sands	N ← N →A
42	do: – Walton-on-Naze	R ← R →N
43/1	do: – Clacton – Jaywick Sands	T ← →A
43/2	Southend – Skegness	NEW ⌐ →A
44	Basildon – Harwich	(T) NEW ⌐ →S
45	Sudbury – Basildon	(T) NEW ⌐ →T
46	Southend – Norwich	NEW ⌐ →U X51
50	Harlow – Walton-on-Naze	P ← →
51/1	do: – Clacton – Jaywick Sands	Q ← → part X50
51/2	Bishop's Stortford – Southend	NEW ⌐
52	Harlow – Felixstowe	S ← → EAX52
60/1	Pitsea – Worthing	E/1 ← → part X20
60/2	London – Stansted Airport	NEW ⌐
61/1	Pitsea – Eastbourne	F/1 ← → part X21
61/2	Dagenham – Stansted Airport	NEW ⌐
62/1	Pitsea – Folkestone	G/1 ← → part X22
62/2	Southend Airport – Stansted Airport	NEW ⌐
63	Pitsea – Hastings	H/1 ← → part X23
64	do: – Thanet Resorts	J/1 ← → part X24
70	Chelmsford – Great Yarmouth	V ← → EAX3
71	Silver End – Great Yarmouth	ex MOORE'S ⌐ V → EAX2

EAX.. EAST ANGLIAN EXPRESS – commenced 25.5.68

1	London – Felixstowe (via East London)	ex EC'A'/G-G1 ←
2	do: – Great Yarmouth (via Bury St Edmunds)	ex EC'P'/EN'X71' ←
3	do: – Great Yarmouth (via Ipswich)	ex EN'X70'/EC'F'.8/G-G3 ←
12	Harwich – Sheringham	ex EC'Q8/G-G12 ←
35	London – Felixstowe/Great Yarmouth (via North London)	ex GG 35 ←
52	London – Felixstowe via Harlow	ex EN'X52' ←

ECX ESSEX COAST EXPRESS – commenced 2.10.67

4	London – Walton-on-Naze (via East London)	ex EN'X12'/G-G4/SUTTON ←
33	London – Walton-on-Naze (via North London)	ex G-G 33 ←
80	London – Harwich	ex G-G2/HOOK8 ←

Appendix C
Acquired Operators

Biographical notices of all the acquired operators and their predecessors arranged alphabetically. All of them, whether large or small, have made their contribution to the life of the community they served, but as few are likely to be remembered, or will have had their story recorded, they are placed in this appendix before all trace has been lost in the mists of time.

Acme Pullman Services Ltd.
Adams, Ben (Finchingfield)
Adams, E. (Grays)
Akers, A. (see Bird Motor Service)
Allen, Thomas F. (Kempston)
Allen, Wm. A. (Canvey)
Amersham & District
Amos, S. A. (see under S.A.A. Motors)
Argent, Thos. & Wm.
Ashdown, F. H. (see Rodney Bus)
Ashwell & District
Associated Coaches (Ongar) Ltd.
Aylesbury Line
Aylesbury Motor Bus Co.
Aylesbury Omnibus Co. Ltd.

Balfour Beatty & Co. Ltd
Barling & Wakering Motor Service
Barrett, B. E. Ltd. (Luton)
Barrett, F. (Thaxted)
Bates, John H.
Beaumont & Priest Ltd./Beaumont—
  Safeway
Beeston, B. & Sons Ltd.
Benfleet & District Motor Services Ltd.
Benjamin, E. & E. (see under 'Our Bus')
Berry, A. W. & Sons
Bird Motor Service
Bluebird Motor Coaches, The (Tiptree)
Bluebird Service (Luton)
Blue Buses (Eastwood)
Blue Coach Service (Bedford)
Bonham, A. M. (see Milton Bus, Bedford)
Borough Services Ltd., The
Brentwood & District Motor Services Ltd.
Bright Bros.

Brown, A. V. (see Bluebird, Tiptree)
Brown, W. & Sons (Warboys)
Browne Bros. (Chelmsford)
Burnham & District

Cambridge Blues (Arrington)
Campbell, J. W. & Sons Ltd.
Canvey & District Motor Transport
  Co. Ltd.
Canvey Auxiliary Motors
Carding, R. A. (see Wonder Bus)
Charles & George Holmes & Sydney
  Smith Ltd.
Charter, Leslie
Chiltern Bus Service
Christmas, P. W. (see XMAS Bus Service)
City Coach Company Ltd.
Clacton & District Motor Services Ltd.
Clark, A. E. Sen/Jun.
Clark & Mathews (see Mayblossom
  Service)
Clavering & District Bus Services
Clench, H. H. (see Dreadnought Bus
  Service)
Collingridge, — —
Comfy Coaches (Yardley Hastings)
Commercial Car Hirers Ltd.
Cooper, C. and E. J. (see Ideal Bus)
Coppin, H. & Son
Corona Coaches (see Eastern Counties
  Omnibus Co. Ltd.)
Cracknell, S. G.
Crow, W. G.
Cummings, C. S. (see Royal Blue,
  Braintree)
Curtis, E. (see Ongar & District)

Davies, E.
Dawson, J. (see Malebird Bus)
Day, — — (West Mersea)
Day & Bedingfield
Death, George
Digby, George
Don Motor Hire Service/Donne, H.
  (see Huntingdon Coaches Ltd.)
Dreadnought Bus Service

East Bergholt & District Services
Eastern Counties Omnibus Co. Ltd.
Eastward Coaches
Edmunds & Hart (see Shoeburyness
  Motor Services)
Edward Hillman's Saloon Coaches Ltd.
  (see Hillman's Coaches)
Edwards Hall Motors Ltd. (see Blue Buses)
England, A. F.
Enterprise Bus Co. (Clacton) Ltd.
Essex Public Services Ltd.
Evans Coaches
Ewer, George & Co. Ltd. (see Grey-Green
  Coaches)

Fale, T. W.
Fitch & Son/Fitch & Son (Clacton) Ltd.
Forbes, A. J.
Ford, A. A.
Fraser Smith, A.
French, E. D. (see Wakering Motor Brake)
Fuller, F. H. (see Regent Motor Service)
Furber, Mrs E. S. (see East Bergholt &
  District Services)

Gammond, G. O. (see Blue Coach Service,
  Bedford)
Gant, Allen
Gaylard, Henry
Gidea Park Coaches Ltd.
Gilbert, R. H. (see Milton Bus, Stanford)
Goates, J. (see Cambridge Blues)
Goggins family (see Transit Bus)
Golden Arrow Service
Gozzett, J. H. (see Quest Motor Services)
Great Eastern Railway Co.
Greenleaf, James
Greenslade, A. R. (see Tilbury & District
  Motor Services)
Grey-Green Coaches
Griffin Bus Service

Griffiths, T. W. H. (see Pullman Service)
Groom, H.

Hadleigh Garage & Transport Co. Ltd.
Hadleigh Motor Bus Co. Ltd.
Harding, Major (see Griffin Bus)
Harding, — — (Orsett)
Harding, A. M. (Southend) (see next
  entry)
Harding's Coaches Ltd.
Harrington A. and S.
Hart, Eric E. (see Shoeburyness Motor
  Services)
Hatton, G.
Hearn, Pat Ltd.
Heath, F. C.
Helliker, W. C.
Henderson, John
Henman, Herbert
Hicks Bros.
Hill, H. E. (see Strawhatter Coaches)
Hilliar, A. C.
Hillman, Edward (see next entry)
Hillman's Saloon Coaches Ltd.
Hinds, H. J. & Co./Hinds & Savage
Hinsby, J. and S.
Hinton, F. J. (see Laindon & District)
Hiscock, V. D.
Hitchins, — — (Dunmow)
Holmes, Charles and George
Holmes & Smith Ltd.
Hooks Bros., R. W.
Horn Motor Coach Co.
Huggins, — — (Stanford-le-Hope)
Huntingdon Coaches Ltd.
Hunwick, Arthur
Hutley's Motor Bus Service

Ideal Bus Service
Intermediate Bus Service

Jelley, M. E.
Johnson, R. H. K.
Jones & Harris

Keeling, F. W. (see also Adams, E.)
Kemp, John & Son
Kershaw, A. J.
Knight, Len (see Intermediate Bus)
Knight, Mrs S. J. (see Sally Omnibus
  Service)

Laindon & District Motor Service
Lake, G. W.
Lamb Bros. (see Renown Bus Service)
Leggett Dyer & Co. Ltd.
Leigh, Hadleigh and Rayleigh Omnibus
  Co. Ltd.
Leverett, H. (see Ashwell & District)
Lion Coaches Ltd.
Local Bus, The (see Adams, E. and
  Keeling, F. W.)
Lodge, D.
London Country Buses (see London
  Passenger Transport Board/London
  Transport Executive)
London General Country Services Ltd.
London & North Eastern Rly. Co.
Luton Corporation

MacDermott Roe, E. J. R.
Malebird Bus Co.
Martin and Inman
Matravers, Fred (see Victory Bus)
Mawdsley & Brown
May Blossom Service
Meadows, J. & Son
Mersea, Colchester & District Transport
  & Bus Co. Ltd.
Mersea Engineering & Transport Co.
Milton Bus Service (Bedford)
Milton Bus Service (Stanford)
Minney, Alfred (see Comfy Coaches)
Mitchell, Wm. O. (see Barling and
  Wakering Motor Service)
Moore Bros. Ltd. (Kelvedon)
Moore, F. C. Ltd. (see Viceroy Coaches)
Morley, L. R. (see Rochford & District)
Motor Belle, The (see Harding's Coaches
  Ltd.)
Mulley's Motorways (see Eastern Counties
  Omnibus Co. Ltd.)
Multiways Ltd.
Mummery, Mrs F.

Naish, J. J.
New Empress Saloons Ltd.
New Imperial Motors
Nickolds, P. F.
Nugus, F. H./Saloon Coaches

Oborne, W. M. (Exors. of (see Queens
  Park Coaches)

Offordian Coaches
'Old Tom' Motor Service
Ongar & District Motor Services
Orange Luxury Coaches (Portsmouth)
  Ltd.
'Our Bus'

Patten's Coaches Ltd.
Paxman, Mrs M. A. (Grays)
Pearse's Garage & Motor Works/Pearse's
  Motor Services Ltd.
Peck Bros.
People's Motor Services Ltd.
'Pleshey Belle', The
Pope, J. H. (see 'Reliance', Hockliffe)
Premier Line Ltd.
Prentice, E. & Son Ltd. (see Chiltern
  Bus Service)
Pride Associated Coaches
'Pride of the Marshes'
Primrose Bus Service (West Mersea)
Primrose Coaches (Chelmsford)
Public (see Essex Public Services)
Pudney, M. (see 'Reliance', The)
Pullman Service

Queens Park Coaches
Quest Motor Services

R. R. Coaches Ltd.
Rayleigh Motor Services Ltd.
Red Rose Garage Ltd. (see R. R. Coaches)
Regent Motor Service
Reliance Bus (Hockliffe)
Reliance Coaches (Meppershall)
Reliance Coaches (West Mersea)
'Reliance', The (Halstead)
Renown Bus Service
Rickard, A. T.
Rochford & District Motor Services Ltd.
Rodney Bus Service
Rolfe, T. W.
Rose Bros. (Chelmsford) Ltd. (see Prim-
  rose Coaches)
Rowlatt and Miles
'Royal Blue' (Braintree)
Royal Blue Cars (Southend) 1913
Royal Blue Cars (Southend) 1921
Royal Blue Coaches (Dovercourt)
Royal Red Charabancs/Coaches (see
  Westcliff and Southend-on-Sea Motor
  Charabanc Co. Ltd.)

Rudkins, C. W. (see Tilbury Safety
  Coaches Ltd.)
Ryall, Percy

S. A. A. Motors
'Safeway'
Sally Omnibus Service
Saywood, J./Saywood & Coleman
Scott, E. & Sons (see Golden Arrow)
Seamarks Bros. (see Westoning & Dist.)
Sefton, Henry (Hadleigh)
Sefton, H. E. (Althorne) (see Burnham
  and District)
Service Saloons Ltd.
Seymour, G. B. (see New Imperial Motors
  or Rayleigh Motor Services Ltd.)
Shoeburyness Motor Services Ltd.
Silver End Development Co. Ltd.
Silver Queen Motor Omnibus Co. Ltd.
  (see Clacton & District)
Simpson, C. & Sons
Skinner, Mr C. J. and Mrs I. M. (see
  Tilbury Coaching Services Ltd.)
Slade, F. Lewis (see Offordian Coaches)
Smith, G. I. (see Westoning & District)
Smith, Sydney (Southend)
Smith, Wm. (Canvey)
Southend-on-Sea Motor Charabanc Co.
  Ltd.
Southend Charabanc Co.
Springett, H. & Son
Stanford Motors Ltd.
Starling, G. E. & Sons
Stevens, J.
Stracey, H. L.
Straps & Barber (see 'Union Jack')
Strawhatter Coaches
Suckling, G./Suckling & Haxell's Motor
  Services
Sullens, T. and Son
Swallow Coaches (Tilbury) (see Tilbury
  Safety Coaches)

Tabersham Bros. (see Pride Associated
  Coaches Ltd.)
Taylor, C. M. (see Horn Motor Coach Co.)
Taylor, Chas. (see Reliance Coaches,
  Meppershall)
The Local Bus (see Adams, E. and
  Keeling, F. W.
The Transit Bus

Thorpe Bros. (see Reliance, W. Mersea)
Thundersley, Hadleigh & District Motors
  Ltd.
Tilbury Coaching Services Ltd.
Tilbury & District Motor Services
Tilbury Safety Coaches Ltd.
Tilling Transport/(NBC) Ltd.
Timberlake, H. W.
Tween, H.

Underwood, P. H.
'Union Jack' (Luton) Omnibus Co. Ltd.
United Counties Omnibus Co. Ltd.

Venture Bus
Viceroy Coaches
Victory Bus (Stanford-le-Hope)
Victory Service (Coggeshall)
Viking Motor Coaches

Waite, W. A. (see Wilkinson, J. A.)
Wakering Motor Brake
Walley, S.
Warner, C. N.
Webster, Tom (see 'Old Tom' Motor
  Service)
Wells and Son (see Royal Blue,
  Dovercourt)
Wendrome Coaches (see Viking)
Westcliff & Southend-on-Sea Motor
  Charabanc Co. Ltd.
Westcliff-on-Sea Motor Services Ltd.
Weston, G. (Eastwood)
Weston, G. A. (Westcliff) (see Southend-
  on-Sea Motor Charabanc Co. Ltd.)
Westoning & District Bus Service
Wickford Carriage Co. Ltd.
Wickford Omnibus Services Ltd.
Wilkinson, J. A.
Williams, D. E. Sen./Jun.
Wilson, H.
Wise, A. and F.
Witherington, A. J.
Wonder Bus Service
Wright Bros. Ltd.

XL Motor Service
XMAS Bus Service

Young, E. W.
Young, A. H. (see New Empress Saloons)

153

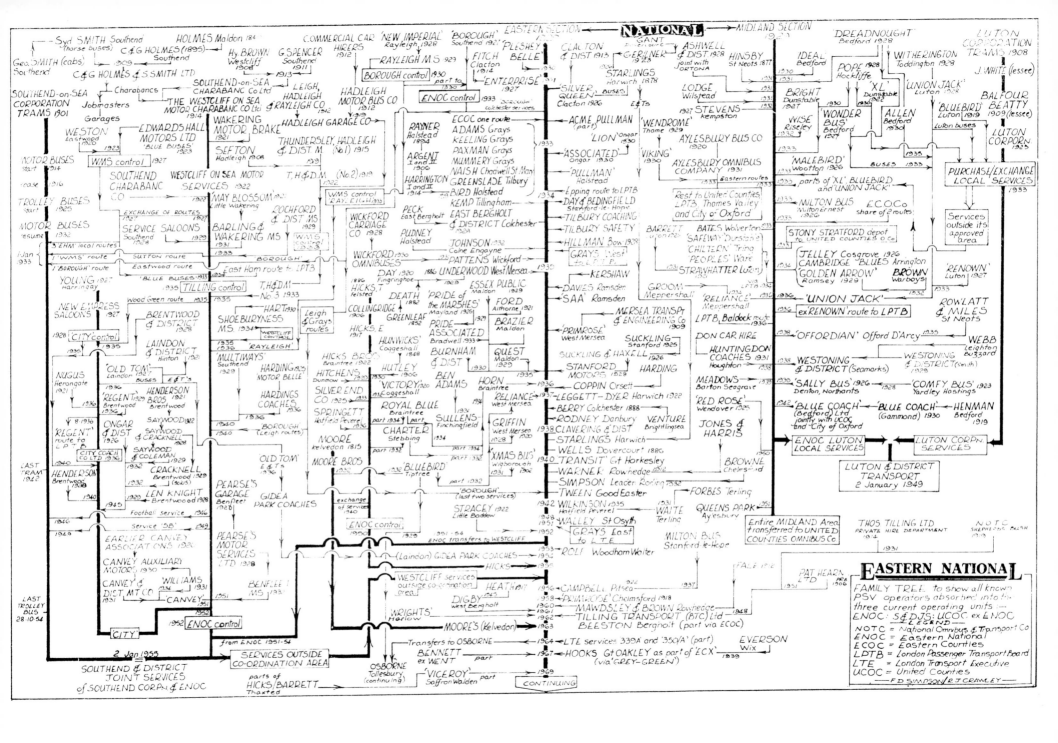

EASTERN NATIONAL

FAMILY TREE to show all known PSV operators absorbed into the three current operating units :— ENOC; S&DJS; UCOC ex ENOC

LEGEND

NOTC = National Omnibus & Transport Co
ENOC = Eastern National
ECOC = Eastern Counties
LPTB = London Passenger Transport Board
LTE = London Transport Executive
UCOC = United Counties

—F.D. SIMPSON/R.J. CRAWLEY—

ACME PULLMAN SERVICES LTD.   205 Bishopsgate, London EC2

'Acme' pioneered a frequent coach service from London, via Loughton, to Epping and Bishop's Stortford with a fleet of extremely comfortable and speedy coaches. It successfully captured all the 'long riders' from 'General' buses south of Epping and emptied the 'National'/LGCS buses thence to Bishop's Stortford. A few journeys continued north to Saffron Walden and Newmarket which had an adverse effect on service EN13 covering that road. The only measure that LGCS could take to protect itself was to buy off 'Acme' which it did on 22nd September 1932. Service EN13 acquired additional timings as from 17th March 1933 and extra fare protection a little later. Subsequent developments are detailed in *Chapter Two*.

ADAMS, Ben   Finchingfield, Essex

Ben Adams operated a motor-carrier service from Bardfield to Braintree Railway Station which put up at the 'Horse and Groom' on weekdays taking the direct route, but deviating on Wednesdays to take in Jaspers Green and Panfield. It passed to Sullens of Finchingfield about 1930.

ADAMS, E.   52 Clarence Road, Grays, Essex

This operator worked jointly, but traded separately with Keeling (q.v.) who both used the fleetname 'The Local Bus' which ran from Grays centre to the Nutberry Estate, via Windsor Avenue. He was authorized to be on the route from 7a.m. to 9.30a.m., 12 noon to 2.30p.m. and from 3.30p.m. to 8.45p.m. He sold the service to the Leighton Coach Company (which ran a service to London that was acquired by the LPTB) which in turn sold it to Eastern National in February 1933; no vehicles changing hands.

ALLEN, Thomas F.   13 Cleveland Street, Kempston, Bedfordshire

His career in transport began as a driver for Clench's 'Dreadnought' Bus Service (q.v.) at Bedford, becoming a proprietor when he took over the Bedford—St. Neots route, via Kimbolton, when that business collapsed. Another driver, L. M. Jarvis, took on the route via Staughton. Allen's basic service was two to four round trips daily beginning with an old Ford Model T 14 seater, progressing to a 20 seat Bedford which he bought new. At busy times Mrs Allen helped by conducting. When Eastern National introduced its own service, revenue was affected and a working agreement between the two was arranged. By 1935, Allen realized his Bedford would soon be due for replacement and was happy to accept the £1,700 offered by England of 'Union Jack' to the chagrin of Eastern National, which enabled Allen to move into a taxi business in Bedford. On Saturdays, when traffic was heavy, Allen would hire Franklin's bus from Carlton, while on lay-over in Bedford, to run relief for him at 15/- a trip as far as Thurleigh. Allen's bus wore blue and yellow/cream livery. His service went to 'Union Jack' on 22nd July 1935.

ALLEN, Wm. A.   Leigh Beck, Canvey Island, Essex

Of the seventeen Canvey busmen, he was one of the more important as he was elected to the office of 'Controller' by members of the Canvey Auxiliary Motors, the local operators' association. He had responsibility for arranging rotas, timetables, fixing substitutes when required, and general liaison with the Council who referred all complaints (of which there were plenty) to him for remedy and report, for which he was remunerated at 4/- per vehicle per week in summer and 2/6d. in winter (20p and 12½p respectively). He had considerable difficulty in collecting subscriptions from certain members whom he eventually had to sue for payment. For a time, he was Secretary and General Manager of the successor, Canvey & District Motor Transport Company Ltd.

AMERSHAM & DISTRICT MOTOR BUS AND HAULAGE CO. Ltd.   Amersham, Bucks.

This company commenced operations 1920/21 with a motor charabanc named *The Somme* and one or two lorries. Buses followed a little later and services developed slowly. When the business began to expand in the later 1920s, the LGOC acquired it and enlarged its operations. It was transferred to the LPTB in 1933 except for part of the Aylesbury—Amersham—Chesham service which was joint with the Aylesbury Omnibus Co. On 21st July 1933, it was divided at Great Missenden, the Aylesbury end reaching the ENOC on 1st December with the rest of the AOC on the date, so that each operator acquired the other's half interest in the retained portion.

ARGENT, Thomas and William   Halstead, Essex

By 1906, Thomas had succeeded to the business of Samuel Rayner of Trinity Street who worked a horse-bus service to Braintree on three days each week. In January 1914, Mr A. Harrington bought Thomas's large omnibus with which he continued the service. At about the same time, William advertised that he was carrying on the service in succession to his father, presumably using Thomas's smaller omnibus, and he would be charging lower fares! It would seem that William did not operate for very long as a Mr Reynolds was on the route soon after, his service ceasing about 1917, but Harrington continued for a few more years, the business being ultimately embodied into Akers 'Bird Service'.

ASHWELL & DISTRICT   Ashwell, Hertfordshire

This was the fleetname of H. Leverett, who commenced in 1927 with a small bus, having built the body himself. It was known locally as Leverett's tin pot! It was the ENOC's first acquisition giving it a second service into Cambridge. Ashwell was a populous village over two miles from its railway station and Leverett had chosen his route well, operating to Hitchin and Letchworth over routes hitherto neglected by 'National'. It must have been a quick success, as during the following year, 1928, he was able to buy two Dennis Gs and extended the route to Royston. In 1929, he bought three more Dennis vehicles and extended the service through to Cambridge in competition with 'Ortona'. As his services passed through the villages which the railway avoided, he soon took away most of the local traffic, so it is unlikely the LNER would have hesitated at buying him off. In October 1930, the ENOC informed Hitchin UDC of the impending purchase which they later made jointly with 'Ortona', but no timetable appeared in the monthly issues until March 1931.

ASSOCIATED COACHES (ONGAR) LTD.   Chingford, Essex

This company operated a coach service between Ongar, Epping, Chingford and London with 'Forest King' as a fleetname. Business passed to 'Green Line' on 31st March 1932 after some difficulties with the Licensing Authority. One of its Directors at this time was H. H. Clench, former owner of the Dreadnought Omnibus Company, Bedford (q.v.). There were also two stage services trading as 'Lion Associated'. These were Epping—Ongar—Chelmsford and Ongar—Blackmore—Chelmsford which the ENOC took on 28th April 1933 following revocation of licences. The company was first registered in June 1930 to take over an existing coach service run by E. Curtis (of Ongar & District Motor Service) and a Mr Thompson. It had also absorbed the 'Lion Motor Service' (q.v.) on 12th January 1931. Attempts to secure licences for several other services were made, but without success.

AYLESBURY LINE   Aylesbury, Buckinghamshire

When 'Premier Line' took over the Aylesbury Motor Bus Company's services, it adopted the fleetname 'Aylesbury Line' which continued to be carried on the buses after acquisition by the ENOC until transferred to their final owners. (See also Aylesbury Omnibus Co. Ltd.).

AYLESBURY MOTOR BUS COMPANY   County Motor Garage, Buckingham Street, Aylesbury, Buckinghamshire

This company was started in 1920 by Mr E. W. Young, who soon after took over the garage business which included the Ford car agency, a make of vehicle which figured in the bus fleet. In 1924, rolling stock comprised eight Daimlers, of which four were double-decks, and four saloons; one AEC saloon, six Ford saloons and two Ford charabancs. On 17th August 1931 his operations passed to 'Premier Line' as detailed in *Chapter Two*, the business now trading as 'Aylesbury Line Services'. Timetables were published regularly in conjunction with a local printer's guide to rail and bus services which was accompanied by a map (q.v.) clearly showing the extent of the undertaking.

In the early days, there had been competition between Young and 'National' which withdrew from the Leighton Buzzard road by agreement. In 1924, there was an arrangement with the LGOC/'National' which regularized the position vis-a-vis the LGOC 'Country Area'. The main stipulations provided (a) that NOTC could extend from Berkhamsted to Aylesbury at times to be agreed, which was in fact exercised from January 1929 and, (b) the AMBC may continue to run to Berkhamsted (but no further) and also to Amersham and Chesham, limited over the last named portion to four journeys on

weekdays and two only on Sundays, otherwise it may not operate within thirty miles of Charing Cross or anywhere within the 'National' Company's area. The boundary between the latter two concerns was, starting at Ivinghoe, it followed the B488 road to Linslade and then kept to the north side of the B4032 as far as Winslow and then followed the A413 to Buckingham where it met City of Oxford and Midland Red territory. Patrons of the 'Aylesbury' company were aided in identifying their buses after dark by the green light carried at the front of the vehicle.

AYLESBURY OMNIBUS COMPANY LTD.   Aylesbury, Buckinghamshire

This company was formed by 'Premier Line' Ltd. to take over the unincorporated Aylesbury Motor Bus Company. It was acquired by Eastern National on 11th May 1933 in the interests of Tilling and other undertakings, and continued to manage it during its dismemberment. Nine days later, the 'Viking' coach service from Thame was also placed under its control. The division of the Aylesbury Omnibus Company was effected in several stages which are clearly shown on the map in *Chapter Two*. The last component passed to the London Passenger Transport Board on 12th December 1933. The services to be retained by Eastern National were embodied on the first day of that month when the routes were allotted numbers commencing at 101, and at about the same time the former 'Viking' route was abandoned.

Aylesbury Omnibus Company
3d. single 'Setright' ticket. Details completed by insertion into the conductor's machine.

BALFOUR BEATTY & CO. LTD. 66 Queen Street, London
This company owned electric light and power undertakings and also owned or leased several tramway systems, one of which was the small network at Luton. This tramway was owned by the Corporation which, when it opened in 1908, leased it to the construction firm J. G. White and Co. About a year later they transferred it to Balfour Beatty. On 21st February 1923, the Corporation repossessed the tramway which it continued to operate and manage. For later events see under Luton Corporation and *Chapter Two*.

BARLING & WAKERING MOTOR SERVICE 4 Tylers Avenue, Southend-on-Sea, Essex
The above service was operated by W. O. Mitchell, a motor engineer at the above address,

AYLESBURY MOTOR 'BUS ROUTES.

ROUTES served by AYLESBURY Motor-'bus Co......

Connections.............

'Look for the GREEN LIGHT at night'

Official map as published in the company timetables.

using a small omnibus in navy blue livery until his application for a licence from the traffic commissioners was refused in 1931. He appears to have operated it in succession to an earlier operator known as 'The May Blossom Service' owned by Clarke and Matthews. 'Westcliff' took up the service which was embodied into its existing service 4A which soon after became 4B.

BARRETT, B. E. LTD. Langley Garage, Luton, Bedfordshire
This operator had one of the more important garage and motor agency businesses in the borough. It also had a road haulage department and owned charabancs for private hires and excursions. It started a regular service to Margate in the 1920s which passed to H. E. Hill (Strawhatter Coaches) in 1931 when licensing was introduced, and then to the ENOC in July 1934.

BARRETT, F. Town Street, Thaxted, Essex
This was a one man operator who held licences as follows: to Elsenham Station (Suns.), to Braintree (Weds.), to Saffron Walden (Tues.) and the local station bus at train times. About 1934, the Saffron Walden route and his Elsenham and Thaxted services passed to 'Viceroy' (q.v.) and his other services were given up on 28th November 1938.

BATES, John H. 32 Jersey Road, Wolverton, Buckinghamshire
This was one of 'The Five' local operators on the Stony Stratford—Stantonbury route who were troublesome both to 'National' and the ENOC until the advent of the rota working arrangement evolved in 1932. His buses were in a blue livery and had names such as *Blue Belle*, *Blue Bird* and *Blue Pullman* but, by the time the ENOC applied for its licences in August 1933, his fleet was described as being 'in very poor condition'. The ENOC took over one of the five set rotas which was added to its own times, and these first appeared in the timetable of 1st December 1933 but only remained there until the following February. The service with his vehicles was transferred to United Counties on 24th February 1934 as part of the general tidying up of routes in that area.

BEAUMONT—SAFEWAY (BEAUMONT & PRIEST LTD) Cambridge Road Garage, Enfield, Middlesex
This company was formed from two separate businesses; Beaumont's Coach Service of W. D. Beaumont and the Safeway Saloon Coaches of Arthur Wellington Priest, which joined forces in March 1931. W. D. Beaumont had earlier run a London—Bedford service which was sold to Birch Bros., and Priest had earlier traded with his brother as 'Imperial'. After various attempts to establish a coach service, they started a London—Dunstable and Leighton Buzzard route as 'Safeway', soon becoming 'Beaumont—Safeway', which was worked from a garage in North Street, Leighton Buzzard, although one or two coaches were still stationed at the London end. At busy times, when relief vehicles were required, hiring was resorted to, usually from A. F. England at Dunstable who would pay his driver 2s. 6d. for the return run! The London—Dunstable section was acquired by the LPTB on 27th April 1934, the ENOC taking the remaining piece to Leighton Buzzard and the use of the North Street garage which has continued with the ENOC and UCOC ever since.

BEESTON, B. & SONS LTD. East Begholt, Essex
In 1951, this old established family business was acquired by Eastern Counties which, in 1962, in conjunction with Eastern National, rationalized the group of overlapping services on the Ipswich—Manningtree—Colchester corridor. This resulted in Eastern National working all the times between Mistley/Manningtree and Colchester, including Beeston's fomer interests over that road. (See also Peck Bros.)

BENFLEET & DISTRICT MOTOR SERVICES LTD. London Road, Hadleigh, Essex
After his departure from 'Westcliff' on 29th October 1932, H. R. Bridge promoted the above to take over the near defunct Pearse's Motor Services (q.v.) of High Street, South Benfleet from Major Albert Pearse, in exchange for four hundred acres of Pitsea marshes. The major's fleet of near dilapidated buses were mostly off the road because of stop notices placed upon them, but Bridge soon provided replacements with three new TSM/Park Royal-bodied double-decks which were supplemented with acquired stock from time to time. An utterly reliable and courteous service was established and 'Benfleet' soon drew the public, who loyally supported it, becoming a real money spinner with often three vehicles being required on a single timing out of Southend. A few other minor services that Pearse operated were soon dropped, with the exception of the Wickford market journey which became 'Westcliff' service 27 and the main line was incorporated into route 3. The Bridges sold out to the British Transport Commission on 2nd March 1951.

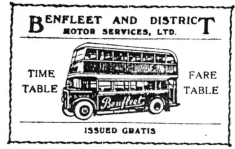

From OCT. 1st, 1934 to MAY 31st, 1935.

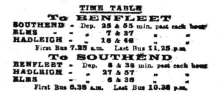

Top left: Half of front cover of 'Benfleet' 8pp timetable book, actual size 5½in. x 4½in.

Left: 9d. single 'Setright' ticket, details completed by conductor inserting ticket in the machine.

Above: 'Benfleet' made good use of the reverse of its tickets to provide every passenger with a timetable.

BERRY, A. W. & SONS Port Lane Motor Works, Colchester, Essex and also at Brightlingsea (Victoria Place) and West Mersea (Kingsland Road) Essex

Excepting 'Silver Queen' this was the Company's most important purchase in the Colchester district. The Berrys had the distinction of working the first timetabled horse-bus service from Colchester to West Mersea (there were earlier carriers) in 1888, and also of owning the very first public motor conveyance in the area by placing a Daimler motor wagonette on this road about 1899. The Berrys carried on an engineering business at Port Lane where they built a complete steam wagon for a local brewery.

In 1905 they faced the first competition from a self-propelled vehicle when the Great Eastern Railway commenced its service between the same points, but withdrew it on 27th February 1909 following an agreement between the parties for the maintenance of the service to connect with the trains. Later that year, however, another newcomer appeared using a Bell omnibus and a Durkopp charabanc. This was Mr W. J. W. Shiers, trading as Mersea Transport and Engineering Company, which was succeeded in 1916 by the Mersea, Colchester and District Transport and Bus Company Ltd. (possibly the longest title in the book) but always known as the 'Primrose' which was the colour of the vehicles. There was intense rivalry between this company and Berrys, especially after it elected to invade Berry's Brightlingsea route as well, which also involved the 'Silver Queen' Company. Following negotiations, 'Primrose' withdrew from the Brightlingsea road which became Berry's prerogative, and the Wivenhoe road was left to 'Silver Queen'. Later, Berrys bought off the 'Venture' bus, operated by a local man between Brightlingsea and Colchester using a small Ford Model T. Berry operated the following routes:

a) Colchester—Abberton—West Mersea	became EN 75C/75D	
b) Colchester—Alresford—Brightlingsea	became EN 78	
c) Colchester—Rowhedge—West Mersea	became EN 75D	
d) Colchester—Rowhedge—Fingringhoe	became EN 77A	
e) Colchester—Rowhedge (Albion)	became EN 77B	
f) Brightlingsea—Thorpe-le-Soken (Market)	was discontinued	
g) Brightlingsea—Tendring (Hospital)	was discontinued	

h) Brightlingsea/West Mersea—Colchester—London Express Coach Service, run on Fridays, Saturdays, Sundays and Mondays, was operated but a licence was refused even after appeal to the Traffic Commissioners.

Excursions and tours were offered from Colchester, Brightlingsea, West Mersea, Thorington Cross, Elmstead and Alresford. An office at Scheregate (opposite the bus station) at Colchester served as a booking/enquiry office, parcels depot and inspectors' room.

The Berry fleet, which was always in brown in latter years, comprised about sixteen vehicles of very mixed types. At take-over there were the following: 1 AEC Regal, 4 Gilford, 2 Tilling-Stevens, 2 International, 4 Dennis (all different), 2 Bedford and an ADC. All were single-decks although some were fitted with opening sunshine tops. In earlier years Daimler, Humber, FIAT, Straker-Squire, ex-LGOC AEC 'B' types, Weigal, Vulcan, REO and a Wells could have been seen at work on their services.

Above right: An excellent timetable and fares folder was regularly issued, and a full programme of excursions and tours were offered. The Company took over the Brightlingsea garage and office, but none of the Colchester or West Mersea premises.

BIRD MOTOR SERVICE Chapel Hill, Halstead, Essex

Mr A. Akers was landlord of the Bird in Hand public house and, in 1919, started conveying workpeople to Braintree, which became a regular daily service after Harrington gave up his horse omnibus over that route. He continued Harrington's Thursday market trip to Sudbury and adopted the name 'Bird Motor Service', probably because of his other occupation. Later he introduced a Friday market bus to Chelmsford which was superseded by his Braintree times being arranged to connect with Hicks Bros. daily Braintree—Chelmsford route. A short-lived service was also run from Braintree to Black and White Notleys until another operator (Springett) appeared with a through service from Witham. He was an 'early bird' too with an express service to London through from Hedingham, as related in *Chapter Two*. His entire operations, garage and fleet of five coaches and six buses, passed to the ENOC on 18th December 1934. The Rosemary Lane garage continued in use until the Company's new premises in High Street were completed in 1938.

BLUEBIRD MOTOR COACHES Bluebird Garage, Tiptree, Essex
A. V. Brown (Victor) was in business as a garage proprietor at Tiptree and, like many others, included car hire and some haulage with a lorry among his activities. In the middle 1920s, he moved into operating buses and coaches which he pursued quite ambitiously so that by 1930 he had put together quite a network of services, but not without giving some concern to other neighbouring bus owners. Brown's fleet consisted of Chevrolet, Bedford, REO and Gilford saloons. In 1931 he was operating the following services:

a) Tolleshunt Knights—Tiptree—Colchester
b) Goldhanger—Tiptree—Colchester
c) Tollesbury—Tolleshunt D'Arcy—Birch—Colchester
d) Tollesbury—Tolleshunt D'Arcy—Mill Beach—Maldon
e) Maldon—Hatfield Peverel—Chelmsford
f) West Mersea—Abberton—Colchester
g) Tollesbury—Tiptree—London (Express Coaches)

All the above services were started by him as new routes except (f) which was taken over from Harding, t/a Griffin (q.v.); (e) began as a Chelmsford—Hatfield Peverel—Witham Station service on which the competition was too hot, so he diverted it at Hatfield Peverel to run to Maldon, which proved to be a good route. All the above routes except (g) received licences from the Traffic Commissioners, also for excursions and tours from Tiptree.

Rather surprisingly in 1932, Brown decided to cease running buses and disposed of his services as follows: (f) went to Thorpe Bros. of West Mersea, (a) and (e) to Moore Bros. Kelvedon and (b) (c) and (d) to Osbornes of Tollesbury (who are still operating them). Eventually (a), (e) and (f) passed to Eastern National.

BLUEBIRD SERVICE Garage: Old Bedford Road, Luton, Bedfordshire
Office: 2 Bridge Street, Luton, Bedfordshire
This was the fleetname of Hinds & Savage Ltd. who started in 1919 at High Town Road with charabancs and road haulage. The latter was disposed of to the Luton Haulage Co. and, early in 1927, local omnibus services commenced running to several parts of the town not served by the Corporation trams or by 'National', except in one case. This was the 'Bluebird' service to Biscot Mill/Leagrave which took a slightly different route from 'National' for part of the way. At the terminus, the 'Bluebird' crew could see when an opposition bus was on its way and so time their own departure so that they reached the point of junction sufficiently ahead of 'National' to effectively clear the road of waiting passengers. Until 1931, the business was conducted by H. J. Hinds solus, when E. Savage joined him as manager and the limited company formed.

In the mid-1920s the business was moved to Wardown garage in New Bedford Road. Early in 1932, A. F. England's 'Union Jack' (Luton) Omnibus Co. took control of the business which had six routes at work. These continued under the 'Bluebird' name until 22nd March 1933 when the services were sold to Luton Corporation as part of his sale of the three subsidiaries. The 'Bluebird' services were as follows:

Manchester Square—Leagrave
Manchester Square—Biscot Mill
Manchester Square—Stockingstone Road } Taken over and operated by
Manchester Square—Colin Road Luton Corporation
Manchester Square—Hexton and Pegsdon

local section to Bramingham Turn to Corporation. Rest to the ENOC as a new 12A service.

Manchester Square—Whipsnade Zoo, via Leagrave and Dunstable

Luton—Dunstable part to Corporation, rest abandoned.

BLUE BUSES Eastwood Rise, Eastwood, Southend-on-Sea, Essex
This was the unofficial fleetname of Edwards Hall Motors Ltd. as it was always so named in the local timetables and guides, or in the press. It was started by H. R. Bridge in 1923 to provide improved bus facilities to Eastwood village where he was developing an estate. 'Westcliff' declined to improve its service to the area but, nevertheless, indulged in every tactic it could to drive him off the road. The business prospered, however, so that by 1927 the following unnumbered services were in operation:

a) Southend—Wickford, via Leigh, Eastwood and Rayleigh
b) Southend—Wickford, via Prittlewell, Eastwood and Rayleigh
c) Southend—Hullbridge, via Prittlewell, Rayleigh and Hambro Hill
d) Leigh—Hockley, via Eastwood and Rayleigh
e) Leigh—Hambro Hill, via Hadleigh, Dawes Heath and Rayleigh
f) Leigh—Rayleigh, via Hadleigh, Thundersley and Rayleigh
g) Leigh—Hadleigh local
h) Leigh—South Benfleet, via Hadleigh and Vicarage Hill
i) Leigh—Southend Pier, via Grand Drive, Ridgeway and Sea Front

By 1927, fresh competition was beginning to assert itself on various routes, so Bridge and 'Westcliff' decided to settle their differences, rationalize their conflicting services and concentrate upon making life as difficult as possible for the opposition instead of themselves. The 'Blue Buses' now continued as a subsidiary of 'Westcliff', mainly engaged on some new local services in Southend while 'Westcliff' dealt with the country routes. There were about fourteen buses in the 'Blue Bus' fleet; five Vulcans of 1923/4, two REOs of 1925 and six Dennis vehicles of 1926. Thereafter, the fleet was augmented as required by transfers of elderly Daimler saloons from the 'Westcliff' fleet. Following the sale of the Southend local routes to the Corporation (see 'Westcliff' notes) at the end of 1932, the business was soon combined with the parent and wound up on 14th March 1933, the remaining routes at Leigh being designated by 'Westcliff' as E, F, G, and H.

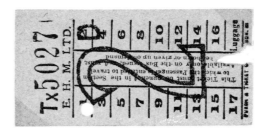

Punch type ticket headed E. H. M. Ltd.
2d. blue with numbered stages.

159

BLUE COACH SERVICE 125 Marlborough Road, Bedford, Bedfordshire

This was the fleetname of George Oliver Gammond who had started 'on the buses' at Chatteris, Cambridgeshire and, having sold his service jointly to the 'Ortona' and Peterborough Electric Traction companies in 1929, next went to Bedford where he purchased Herbert Henman's charabanc business located at the above address. The rolling stock was really out of date so he acquired five second-hand vehicles to get started, most of which are said to have come from Cooper, whose garage was nearby, and who had just sold his 'Ideal' service to the Company.

With considerable vision he quickly spotted the need for improved road facilities southwest of Bedford and, on 5th July 1930, commenced his new long route all the way to Oxford through Olney, Newport Pagnell, Wolverton, Stony Stratford, Buckingham, Finmere, Bicester and Kidlington. Journeys to any of these places or between them were very inconvenient by train, and bus connections were even more sketchy, and no other long distance coach service went that way. The service consisted of two round trips on weekdays with one on a Sunday, and although there were stage fares throughout, he organized booking offices all over Bedford and Oxford and important points in between to facilitate the planning of his loadings over this long route, of all but three hours running time. Very good business was done at weekends and holiday times, frequently calling for his entire fleet of five to be used to run a single timing. One coach was permanently based at Buckingham to operate regular relief trips thence to Stony Stratford but, at busy times, this would need to run all the way and Zachariah Radford's solitary coach at Finmere would be hired to do these short runs.

Gammond also managed to carry out some school contract work in Bedford on Mondays to Fridays which did not interfere with his full commitment at the weekends and holiday times.

Gammond's activities were a matter of considerable concern to Eastern National, United Counties and City of Oxford who eventually were able to acquire his service jointly in 1942, in the circumstances outlined in *Chapter Four*, and in spite of his avowed intention of never selling to Eastern National or any combine company.

BOROUGH SERVICES LTD., THE 49/51 London Road, Southend-on-Sea, Essex

This was probably the most successful of the independent omnibus businesses in the Southend area and had been promoted by Arthur Rogers who had a retail business in Eastwood, and H. H. Smith, a resident of Westcliff. After several abortive attempts to secure licences from Southend Watch Committee, they finally succeeded on 31st October 1927, when four were granted for a new service to Eastwood which was already served by several other routes. They discovered a new direction via Boston Avenue, Shakespeare Avenue and Fairfax Drive and then by an anti-clockwise loop along Picketts Lane, Eastwood Schools, the Woodcutters Arms and back to Fairfax Drive. Two new 26 seat Gilford saloons, registered on 6th December, were used to open the service on a half-hourly frequency, which was doubled in the following March when a Dennis G and a Tilling-Stevens were put on. Rogers and Smith were evidently quite satisfied with their enterprise for they now bombarded the Watch Committee with various applications which met with an equal number of refusals. At this date 'Westcliff Motor Services' had friends in the right places.

On 23rd September 1928, they secured a licence to run a single omnibus between Southend, Grays and Rainham. In the event, the Grays—Rainham portion was never worked and the solitary bus managed to do six round trips per day between Southend and Grays which now enjoyed its first direct service to the sea. 'Westcliff' intended that the new concern should not get away unchallenged and responded in the spring by ex-

Borough

1½d. single 'Setright' ticket. Amount already printed on ticket so no additional information requires to be added. This type of ticket is used because the machine does not print any halfpenny values.

tending its Stanford-le-Hope service to Grays every half hour, a move which virtually killed the ENOC Grays—Stanford-le-Hope route, causing it to be curtailed at Orsett, except on Sundays. There were further refusals to grant licences to 'Borough' until 25th March 1929 when one extra vehicle was allowed for the Grays route and, in May, a licence for one coach was forthcoming, presumably for summer excursion traffic. Later in 1929, following a police order, four extra licences for use on existing services were granted because of overcrowding on its buses, and two more were secured for a Leigh—Eastwood service.

On 26th February 1929, the business was converted into a limited company and Mr George Horlock joined the Board. When the Corporation exercised its powers to operate motor buses and extend its trolley vehicle system, it bought the 'Borough' service between Southend and Eastwood as part of the agreement made in 1932 between the Corporation and the private operators, in which the borough was divided into Company and Corporation zones. (See the entry on 'Westcliff').

Because it was becoming impossible to expand by obtaining licences for new services, 'Borough' instead took control, during 1931, of Rayleigh Motor Services who owned services between Rayleigh—Rochford—Southend, Hullbridge—Rayleigh—Eastwood—Southend, and the Southend—Maldon—Colchester through service. 'Borough' now had a foot in the ENOC operating centres of Grays and Colchester. These moves by 'Borough' provoked the ENOC into action for there were other eligible businesses in the district and the decision was taken to remove this ambitious operator by acquisition. A sufficiently attractive bid was made and the ENOC secured control on 19th May 1933. Because the ENOC was restricted to only work into Southend over the agreed Eastwood Road, only the Colchester services could be transferred to itself, and 'Borough' was kept in being to operate its other services and so too was 'Rayleigh' (q.v.).

A new service was jointly started by 'Borough' and 'Westcliff' in July 1934 from Leigh Railway Station to Somerset Crescent to serve new housing development. It was designated 72 in the ENOC series and B by 'Westcliff'. 'Borough' continued without change until 30th October 1940 when it was placed in a state of suspended animation brought about by war conditions, the two Leigh routes being halved in frequency because of civil evacuation, and consequently each needed only one vehicle supplied by 'Westcliff' and the 'Borough' vehicles used on the 72 Southend—Grays service became 'Eastern National' by agreement. 'Borough' was finally extinguished in 1947 when 'Westcliff' and the ENOC had become nationalized, there being no useful purpose in keeping it alive any longer. The 'Borough' fleet carried the ENOC stock numbers but remained legally owned by 'Borough'. The vehicles in 'Borough' ownership when the business was acquired received numbers 3432—3449. Thereafter, vehicles were transferred to or from as service requirements demanded.

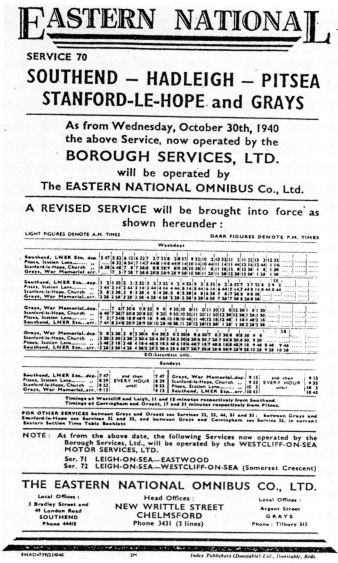

This is the end of 'Borough'!

BRENTWOOD & DISTRICT MOTOR SERVICES LTD. Great Eastern Street, Brentwood, Essex

Operations commenced about 1928/9 by W. H. Malden who had earlier been concerned with buses in the Laindon area using a quaint assortment of second-hand vehicles which, among other interesting stock, included a former Clement-Talbot ambulance of 1922 vintage with a back entrance and a small Guy J of 1923. The first service broke new ground by running from Brentwood to Hutton (Bracken Bank). Soon after, some old Gilford coaches were employed on a route to Laindon and Billericay, going through Little Burstead, which had not previously enjoyed any bus facilities at all. The garage was in the former stables of the Essex Arms Hotel in Great Eastern Street, and the office was at 23 South Drive, Warley. In the spring of 1936, the business was taken over by 'City' (q.v.) becoming their service numbers 2 and 3. Numerous attempts had been made to open up other routes but the necessary licences were not forthcoming.

BRIGHT BROS. 15 Burr Street, Dunstable, Bedfordshire

In 1927, Dan Bright bought a REO coach for private hire and excursion work. It was licensed to his wife Priscilla but his son Len did the driving. His other son, Horace, at this time drove a bus in Salter's 'Ideal' fleet (see Volume One). After Salter had been acquired by 'National', Horace and Len considered there was still room for another to make a living on the Dunstable—Edlesborough section of that route. Further REOs were obtained, and Horace generally worked the service bus while Len attended to any coaching activities.

The market service between Leighton Buzzard and Ivinghoe, formerly run by J. H. Pope ('Reliance') was now operated and, after the opening of Whipsnade Zoo, there was regular Sunday working, though mostly as excursion rather than stage service. The rolling stock was kept at the rear of Scott's garage off The Square in Dunstable, although one is reported to have used the old Salter garage in Luton Road. Operations were taken over by the ENOC on 23rd March 1933, and both brothers became employees of the Company. No vehicles were transferred.

BROWN, W. & SONS Warboys, Huntingdonshire

This operator received a licence for a market service from Warboys to St. Ives in 1931 which was not renewed in 1932. It is thought that it was incorporated into Scott's 'Golden Arrow' service from Ramsey through Warboys to St. Ives which passed to the ENOC during June 1934.

BROWNE BROS. Springfield Road, Chelmsford

A business started in the early 1920s offering excursions and private hire from premises adjacent to the river bridge and the first vehicles were charabancs on ex-RAF Crossley chassis, in dark green. At the licensing of 1931, they were granted licences for two vehicles and in 1932 they acquired two Albion PKA26 vehicles which passed with the business when it was sold to Simpson & Sons of Leaden Roding.

BURNHAM & DISTRICT Oakleigh Garage, Althorne, Essex

Henry Sefton started a service with the above-named, between Burnham-on-Crouch and Maldon in 1928, with one or two journeys working through to Chelmsford. He was in competition with 'Pride of the Marshes' between Latchingdon and Maldon and with 'National' to Chelmsford. Earnings were not sufficient and his two saloons were repossessed. These he replaced with a pair of White buses which had begun life with 'United'. They had sold off a quantity very cheaply after proving to be unreliable which, to his cost, many a small owner like Sefton, tempted by the low price, quickly discovered. 'Quest' took over the Maldon service and 'Pride of the Marshes' carried on the Chelmsford run for a time.

CAMBRIDGE BLUES Arrington Bridge, Cambridgeshire

J. Goates, who traded as above, commenced in the late 1920s to run to Cambridge from Arrington. Subsequently it was extended to start from Biggleswade and developed later into a Bedford—Cambridge daily service, which was acquired by the ENOC on 13th August 1934, so gaining a third service into the university town where it used yet a third terminal point in Gonville Place. For a while the ENOC continued to outstation two buses at Arrington which ceased when the new garage opened at Biggleswade. No vehicles were taken over with the business which became ENOC service 29A.

A Chevrolet 14 seat saloon of J. Goates, Arrington Bridge, which is very typical of the small country proprietor. Eastern National acquired the business on 13th August 1934.

D. S. Deacon

CAMPBELL, J. W. & SONS LTD. Station Garage, Pitsea, Essex

This company was registered on 1st November 1933 to continue an existing business of the same name which is known to have owned an AEC charabanc as early as 1923, but also traded as coal merchants and cartage contractors. Buses were worked in a small way between Pitsea, Vange and Basildon, daily; Pitsea to Nevendon for scholars, to Wickford on Mondays for the market, and a workmen's service to Shell Haven. Later, a peak hour facility was run between Hadleigh and Pitsea Station for commuters via Bowers Gifford and Tarpots Corner. In November 1937, Campbell took over operation of the Milton Bus Service from Corringham to Pitsea and Wickford, and also from Pitsea to North Benfleet, which Milton had ceased operating at an earlier date.

Latterly, Campbell's fleet was in a green livery and almost exclusively of Albion make but, at the time he was taken over by Eastern National on 19th February 1956, there was

also an AEC Regent double-deck and one Bedford OWB saloon, but very little of the acquired stock was retained by the new owners. It is believed that Campbell's early services were originally worked by Vange Motors or Bell Hill Garage, or both.

The Pickering-bodied Albion CX13 acquired from Campbell of Pitsea, in February 1956. Note the Company's fleet number, 001, has been applied, although Campbell's name still prevails.

Campbell
Punch type multi-value exchange ticket, with own advertisement on the reverse side.

CANVEY & DISTRICT MOTOR TRANSPORT CO. LTD. Leigh Beck, Canvey Island, Essex

This company was the successor to Canvey Auxiliary Motors (q.v.), composed of fifteen owner/operator shareholders who elected the two Clarks, G. Lake, G. Hatton, W. A. Allen and V. D. Hiscock as the first Directors. Their first meeting is said to have been held on the upper deck of a bus! The fifteen worked on a rota of duties as drivers, conductors, cleaners, washers, mechanics or in the office as clerks. Seeking to rid itself of the former incompetent image, the new company rather went to the other extreme by investing in a fleet of twenty seven omnibuses, no fewer than twenty being the largest procurable, six-wheeled covered-top double-decks mainly from municipalities, with a few small Dennis saloons from London Transport. Full 'Fare-Board' type tickets now appeared and London pattern running numbers were affixed to the buses, presumably under the direction of Mr Stinson who had been appointed General Manager. A depot was established at Small Gains garage, although most of the fleet would have stood outside. The service ran every twenty minutes in winter, increasing to every fifteen minutes in summer from 5.30a.m. until 1.03 the following morning. It was not long before there was discord among the Directors, and also among those who were not Directors, which caused frequent changes in the composition of the Board. On one occasion they resigned en bloc, Mr Stinson taking his departure and W. A. Allen becoming Secretary and General Manager.

In the meantime, having acquired 'Benfleet & District', H. R. Bridge decided that 'Canvey' could make a useful addition to his business portfolio, and by discreet enquiry was able to buy up shares from those wanting their capital out. By 1934, more than half the shares were in Bridge hands and H. R. and H. A. Bridge were now in control, and before long had also bought out Williams (q.v.).

The service now continued with little change until 1951 when it was sold to the BTC at the same time as 'Benfleet & District'. The excursions and tours section had been hived off a few years earlier to Norman, the son of H. R. Bridge, who continued them as 'Supreme Coaches' which still flourishes on a much enlarged scale with later generations of the family.

Canvey & District
Two 'Setright' tickets — 7d. yellow return and 1d. rose for goods.

CANVEY AUXILIARY MOTORS   Canvey Island, Essex

This association succeeded to one, if not two earlier associations which had been formed about 1920 by the many small owners who worked on the 3½ mile 'road' across to the island from Benfleet Station, using an incredible assortment of conveyances, be they cab, car, truck or van, so long as it had four wheels and could go! Its object was to exclude any newcomers, fix fares and times and arrange a working rota among the seventeen members. The island was joined to the mainland by a stony causeway which could be crossed at certain states of the tide. The rule was that if water appeared through the floor boards, no more buses would cross until the next ebb tide; passengers, in the meantime, rowing over by boat.

In 1926, Canvey Island was constituted into a new Urban District and one of the first Acts of the new council was to introduce Hackney Carriage Regulations and Licensing, the seventeen members of the Association each receiving licences at the start. They were:

Allen, W. A.	Gaylard, H.	Lake, G. W.
Crow, W. G.	Hatton, G. N.	MacDermott Roe, G. R.
Clark, A. E., Junior	Hilliar, A. C.	Nickolds, P. F.
Clark, A. E., Senior	Hiscock, V. D.	Ryall, P.
Fraser-Smith, A.	Helliker, W. C.	Smith, W.
Timberlake, H. W.	Williams, D. E., Senior	

The council was perpetually bombarded with complaints regarding the bus service and found it almost impossible to apportion responsibility for alleged timings not operated, buses leaving at wrong times and out of turn, using unlicensed or inadequate vehicles at busy times, etc. . . . so it ordered the 'Auxiliary' to nominate a 'controller' from amongst its members, the choice falling upon W. A. Allen (q.v.) whose duties are detailed under his name. Proceedings were taken against a number of the owners for using unlicensed motors or drivers, as many as six or seven being found when spot checks were made. The minutes reveal that many vehicles were still unfit for service when the annual parade of inspection came round, so that owners were often granted additional time to 'get his bus back on the road' and so on. In fact, after several periods of grace, Timberlake was still unable to take up his licence which passed instead to Fraser-Smith, reducing the membership to sixteen. As more people took up residence on Canvey Island, and traffic increased, so things slowly improved and by 1929/30 most of the dreadful old vehicles (mainly Ford Ts) had run themselves into the ground to be chiefly replaced by 14 seat Chevrolets, although one or two owners managed to buy a small Dennis or REO with a 20 seat body.

When the new licensing arrangements were introduced in 1931, the Traffic Commissioners would not accept the 'Auxiliary's' application due to it being very difficult to attach responsibility to any particular individual, nor was it prepared to issue licences to sixteen separate owners working on 3½ miles of route. The problem was overcome by converting the 'Auxiliary' into a limited company in which each owner became a shareholder with the exception of D. E. Williams who demurred. He was, however, able to persuade the authorities to issue him with a licence to operate alone. The new company was entitled Canvey & District Motor Transport Co. Ltd. and was registered on 29th October 1931.

CHARLES & GEORGE HOLMES & SYDNEY SMITH LTD.   Southend-on-Sea, Essex
See under Holmes, Charles and George; Holmes & Smith Ltd.; Smith, Sydney; or Westcliff Motor Services.

CHARTER, Leslie   Stebbing, Essex
This was a small one man business that succumbed shortly after the new licensing regu-

lations, which caused his licences to be revoked for non-compliance with the conditions. He had four routes: (a) Lindsell—Dunmow, (b) Stebbing—Haverhill, (c) Stebbing—Saffron Walden, and (d) Thaxted—Braintree, via Lindsell and Stebbing, all of which ran on the appropriate market days. In February 1932, the service ceased and Hicks incorporated most of (d) with its existing route, and 'Viceroy' (q.v.) continued (a) and parts of (c).

CHILTERN BUS SERVICE   Chiltern Garage, Tring, Hertfordshire
This was the fleetname of E. Prentice and Son Ltd. whose business had been bought by LGCS on 10th May 1933. There were two regular services: (a) Aylesbury—Berkhamsted—Watford, which was worked jointly with LGCS (ex-'National'), Aston, 'West Herts' and Aylesbury Bus Co. and (b) Tring—Leighton Buzzard, which route lay within the ENOC area to which it was transferred on the same day with one Albion saloon.

CITY COACH COMPANY LTD.   Ongar Road, Brentwood, Essex
Much has already appeared in print regarding this business, which will be covered fairly briefly here. It was descended from the City Motor Omnibus Company Ltd. which operated buses in London until compulsorily acquired by London Transport. However, in 1928, it broadened its operations by acquiring New Empress Saloons Ltd. which had pioneered the Wood Green to Southend omnibus route and assiduously developed it in every way. First it extended it westward to Kentish Town where it connected with the 'City' 536 omnibus route from Highgate to Elmers End, via the West End.

Soon after, 'Westcliff' put on a competing service and the parties worked a co-ordinated timetable (not joint) on a fifteen minute headway over the forty eight mile route. In 1934 'City' negotiated the purchase of the 'Westcliff' share of the service which was effective from 1st January 1935. In 1936, the purchase of some small operators in the Brentwood area was negotiated. The first, 'Brentwood & District', was followed by Nugus of Herongate, 'Old Tom' of Laindon and the 'Regent' bus of Brentwood. About this time the City Motor Omnibus Company became City Coach Company.

The fleet of Leyland Lions and Dennis saloons on the main service were now replaced by new Leyland six-wheeled saloons, while Commer and Dodge saloons served the country services. Some new Leyland Tiger coaches arrived in 1938 but all were taken over by the War Department, never to return.

In 1937, a local service to Woodman Road, Warley was started and an extension of the Laindon—Nevendon route to Rayleigh was made after the granting of a licence. Following an appeal from 'Westcliff', which did not in fact have a service on that road, it was successfully revoked.

J. Henderson of Brentwood, who operated to Doddinghurst and Hook End, but gave up when the blitz started, was replaced by 'City'. The Wood Green—Southend service in November 1939 was reduced by half east of Brentwood, and in 1942 the route was split into three separate sections and the Kentish Town—Wood Green portion withdrawn, as was the Romford—Brentwood section in the middle, which caused such an outcry that partial restoration came very quickly.

In 1945, Curtis's 'Ongar & District' service was taken over, several small owners having been absorbed into it earlier. The full Kentish Town to Southend operation was resumed in 1946 and a fleet of Daimler and Leyland double-decks were ordered as replacements for the ageing Leyland TS7T six-wheelers. The latter had given sterling service on this heavily-trafficked route which called for excessive duplication. The new buses had to be diverted between Wickford and Rawreth, via Battlesbridge, because of the low Blue Brick Bridge at Shotgate which, to maintain connections, required the provision of a shuttle saloon over the original section between Wickford and the Carpenters Arms at Rawreth. Other post-war developments were the extension of the Hook End route, northward to Stondon Massey and south to Woodman Road, via Brentwood Station and Headley Chase, and a new route ran from Laindon Station to Langdon Hills. Traffic was never fully regained on the section between Kentish Town and Wood Green and was consequently abandoned from 1st October 1947.

The Mallender family sold the business with over one hundred vehicles to the British Transport Commission in February 1952, bringing to an end a great family enterprise

One of the City Coach Company Leyland Tiger six-wheelers, twelve of which eventually passed to the Company, via Westcliff, in 1952. These vehicles carried 39 passengers.
Duple

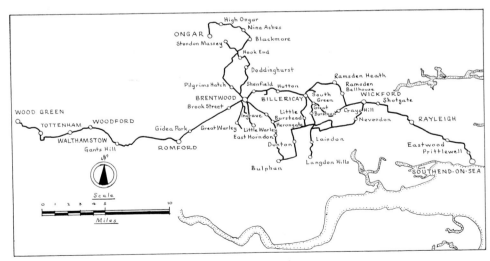

Services operated by the City Coach Co. Ltd., — 1951.

On WEEK-DAYS, between [illegible] a.m. and 9.58 p.m., the vehicles departing from Brentwood to Southend connect with the Services operated by The Brentwood & District Motor Services Ltd. to Laindon, and to Hutton (Bracken Bank).
On Sundays, the Bracken Bank Service does not operate. Tickets are not interchangeable. Please see separate Time Table.

TIME TABLE OF THE

NEW EMPRESS CITY SALOONS

BETWEEN

[illegible] Laindon and [illegible] and Hutton (Bracken Bank) and [illegible]
On Sundays the Laindon [illegible] only operated. Tickets are not interchangeable. Please see separate Time Table.

LONDON (LEIGHTON ROAD by KENTISH TOWN STATION AND WOOD GREEN) & SOUTHEND-ON-SEA (Tylers Avenue, High Street)

Daily Service, commencing 12th January, 1935, and until further notice.

	N.S.	N.S.	N.S.	N.S.	N.S.																														
	a.m.	a.m.	a.m.	a.m.	a.m.	a.m.	a.m.	a.m.	a.m.	a.m.	a.m.	a.m.	a.m.	a.m.	a.m.	a.m.	a.m.	a.m.	a.m.	a.m.	a.m.	a.m.	a.m.	a.m.	a.m.	a.m.	a.m.	a.m.	p.m.	p.m.	p.m.	p.m.	p.m.	p.m.	p.m.
LONDON (Kentish Town)	5.15		5.55	6.05		6.25		6.55		7.25		7.55		8.25		8.55		9.25		9.55		10.25		10.55		11.25		11.55		12.25		12.55		1.25	
LONDON (Wood Green)	5.34	6.00	6.15	6.25	6.30	6.45	7.00	7.15	7.30	7.45	8.00	8.15	8.30	8.45	9.00	9.15	9.30	9.45	10.00	10.15	10.30	10.45	11.00	11.15	11.30	11.45	12.00	12.15	12.30	12.45	1.00	1.15	1.30	1.45	2.00
TOTTENHAM (Bruce Grove)	5.44	6.12	6.27	6.37	6.42	6.57	7.12	7.27	7.42	7.57	8.12	8.27	8.42	8.57	9.12	9.27	9.42	9.57	10.12	10.27	10.42	10.57	11.12	11.27	11.42	11.57	12.12	12.27	12.42	12.57	1.12	1.27	1.42	1.57	2.12
TOTTENHAM (Broad Lane)	5.48	6.16	6.31	6.41	6.46	7.01	7.16	7.31	7.46	8.01	8.16	8.31	8.46	9.01	9.16	9.31	9.46	10.01	10.16	10.31	10.46	11.01	11.16	11.31	11.46	12.01	12.16	12.31	12.46	1.01	1.16	1.31	1.46	2.01	2.16
WALTHAMSTOW	5.56	6.25	6.40	6.50	6.55	7.10	7.25	7.40	7.55	8.10	8.25	8.40	8.55	9.10	9.25	9.40	9.55	10.10	10.25	10.40	10.55	11.10	11.25	11.40	11.55	12.10	12.25	12.40	12.55	1.10	1.25	1.40	1.55	2.10	2.25
WOODFORD (Gates' Corner)	6.01	6.30	6.45	6.55	7.00	7.15	7.30	7.45	8.00	8.15	8.30	8.45	9.00	9.15	9.30	9.45	10.00	10.15	10.30	10.45	11.00	11.15	11.30	11.45	12.00	12.15	12.30	12.45	1.00	1.15	1.30	1.45	2.00	2.15	2.30
ILFORD (East Av, Brands Cr)	6.09	6.40	6.55	7.05	7.10	7.25	7.40	7.55	8.10	8.25	8.40	8.55	9.10	9.25	9.40	9.55	10.10	10.25	10.40	10.55	11.10	11.25	11.40	11.55	12.10	12.25	12.40	12.55	1.10	1.25	1.40	1.55	2.10	2.25	2.40
ROMFORD	6.22	6.55	7.10	7.18	7.25	7.40	7.55	8.10	8.25	8.40	8.55	9.10	9.25	9.40	9.55	10.10	10.25	10.40	10.55	11.10	11.25	11.40	11.55	12.10	12.25	12.40	12.55	1.10	1.25	1.40	1.55	2.10	2.25	2.40	2.55
(A) BRENTWOOD	6.38	7.13	7.28		7.43	7.58	8.13	8.28	8.43	8.58	9.13	9.28	9.43	9.58	10.13	10.28	10.43	10.58	11.13	11.28	11.43	11.58	12.13	12.28	12.43	12.58	1.13	1.28	1.43	1.58	2.13	2.28	2.43	2.58	3.13
BILLERICAY		7.30	7.45		8.00	8.15	8.30	8.45	9.00	9.15	9.30	9.45	10.00	10.15	10.30	10.45	11.00	11.15	11.30	11.45	12.00	12.15	12.30	12.45	1.00	1.15	1.30	1.45	2.00	2.15	2.30	2.45	3.00	3.15	3.30
RAMSDEN BELLHOUSE						8.24				9.24				10.24				11.24				12.24				1.24				2.24				3.24	
WICKFORD		7.48	8.03		8.18	8.33	8.48	9.03	9.18	9.33	9.48	10.03	10.18	10.33	10.48	11.03	11.18	11.33	11.48	12.03	12.18	12.33	12.48	1.03	1.18	1.33	1.48	2.03	2.18	2.33	2.48	3.03	3.18	3.33	3.48
RAYLEIGH		8.03	8.18		8.33	8.48	9.03	9.18	9.33	9.48	10.03	10.18	10.33	10.48	11.03	11.18	11.33	11.48	12.03	12.18	12.33	12.48	1.03	1.18	1.33	1.48	2.03	2.18	2.33	2.48	3.03	3.18	3.33	3.48	4.03
EASTWOOD		8.13	8.28		8.43	8.58	9.13	9.28	9.43	9.58	10.13	10.28	10.43	10.58	11.13	11.28	11.43	11.58	12.13	12.28	12.43	12.58	1.13	1.28	1.43	1.58	2.13	2.28	2.43	2.58	3.13	3.28	3.43	3.58	4.13
SOUTHEND (Victoria Circus)		8.23	8.38		8.53	9.08	9.23	9.38	9.53	10.08	10.23	10.38	10.53	11.08	11.23	11.38	11.53	12.08	12.23	12.38	12.53	1.08	1.23	1.38	1.53	2.08	2.23	2.38	2.53	3.08	3.23	3.38	3.53	4.08	4.23
SOUTHEND (Tylers Avenue)		8.25	8.40		8.55	9.10	9.25	9.40	9.55	10.10	10.25	10.40	10.55	11.10	11.25	11.40	11.55	12.10	12.25	12.40	12.55	1.10	1.25	1.40	1.55	2.10	2.25	2.40	2.55	3.10	3.25	3.40	3.55	4.10	4.25

																												Monday to Friday, from Rayleigh only			S.O.	Monday to Friday, from Rayleigh only	
	p.m.	p.m.	p.m.	p.m.	p.m.	p.m.	p.m.	p.m.	p.m.	p.m.	p.m.	p.m.	p.m.	p.m.	p.m.	p.m.	p.m.	p.m.	p.m.	p.m.	p.m.	p.m.	p.m.	p.m.	p.m.	p.m.	p.m.	p.m.	p.m.	p.m.	p.m.	p.m.	p.m.
LONDON (Kentish Town)	1.55		2.25		2.55		3.25		3.55		4.25		4.55		5.25		5.55		6.25		6.55		7.25		7.55		8.25			8.55			9.10
LONDON (Wood Green)	2.15	2.30	2.45	3.00	3.15	3.30	3.45	4.00	4.15	4.30	4.45	5.00	5.15	5.30	5.45	6.00	6.15	6.30	6.45	7.00	7.15	7.30	7.45	8.00	8.15	8.30	8.45		9.00	9.15			9.30
TOTTENHAM (Bruce Grove)	2.27	2.42	2.57	3.12	3.27	3.42	3.57	4.12	4.27	4.42	4.57	5.12	5.27	5.42	5.57	6.12	6.27	6.42	6.57	7.12	7.27	7.42	7.57	8.12	8.27	8.42	8.57		9.12	9.27			9.42
TOTTENHAM (Broad Lane)	2.31	2.46	3.01	3.16	3.31	3.46	4.01	4.16	4.31	4.46	5.01	5.16	5.31	5.46	6.01	6.16	6.31	6.46	7.01	7.16	7.31	7.46	8.01	8.16	8.31	8.46	9.01		9.16	9.31			9.46
WALTHAMSTOW	2.40	2.55	3.10	3.25	3.40	3.55	4.10	4.25	4.40	4.55	5.10	5.25	5.40	5.55	6.10	6.25	6.40	6.55	7.10	7.25	7.40	7.55	8.10	8.25	8.40	8.55	9.10		9.25	9.40			9.55
WOODFORD (Gates Corner)	2.45	3.00	3.15	3.30	3.45	4.00	4.15	4.30	4.45	5.00	5.15	5.30	5.45	6.00	6.15	6.30	6.45	7.00	7.15	7.30	7.45	8.00	8.15	8.30	8.45	9.00	9.15		9.30	9.45			10.00
ILFORD (Eastern Ave, Brands Corner)	2.55	3.10	3.25	3.40	3.55	4.10	4.25	4.40	4.55	5.10	5.25	5.40	5.55	6.10	6.25	6.40	6.55	7.10	7.25	7.40	7.55	8.10	8.25	8.40	8.55	9.10	9.25		9.40	9.55			10.10
ROMFORD	3.10	3.25	3.40	3.55	4.10	4.25	4.40	4.55	5.10	5.25	5.40	5.55	6.10	6.25	6.40	6.55	7.10	7.25	7.40	7.55	8.10	8.25	8.40	8.55	9.10	9.25	9.40		9.55	10.10			10.25
(A) BRENTWOOD	3.28	3.43	3.58	4.13	4.28	4.43	4.58	5.13	5.28	5.43	5.58	6.13	6.28	6.43	6.58	7.13	7.28	7.43	7.58	8.13	8.28	8.43	8.58	9.13	9.28	9.43	9.58		10.13	10.28			10.43
BILLERICAY	3.45	4.00	4.15	4.30	4.45	5.00	5.15	5.30	5.45	6.00	6.15	6.30	6.45	7.00	7.15	7.30	7.45	8.00	8.15	8.30	8.45	9.00	9.15	9.30	9.45	10.00	10.15		10.30	10.45			11.00
RAMSDEN BELLHOUSE			4.24				5.24				6.24				7.24				8.24				9.24				10.24						
WICKFORD	4.03	4.18	4.33	4.48	5.03	5.18	5.33	5.48	6.03	6.18	6.33	6.48	7.03	7.18	7.33	7.48	8.03	8.18	8.33	8.48	9.03	9.18	9.33	9.48	10.03	10.18	10.33	10.40	10.48	11.03		11.10	11.18
RAYLEIGH	4.18	4.33	4.48	5.03	5.18	5.33	5.48	6.03	6.18	6.33	6.48	7.03	7.18	7.33	7.48	8.03	8.18	8.33	8.48	9.03	9.18	9.33	9.48	10.03	10.18	10.33	10.48	10.55	11.03	11.18	11.23	11.25	11.33
EASTWOOD	4.28	4.43	4.58	5.13	5.28	5.43	5.58	6.13	6.28	6.43	6.58	7.13	7.28	7.43	7.58	8.13	8.28	8.43	8.58	9.13	9.28	9.43	9.58	10.13	10.28	10.43	10.58	11.05	11.13	11.28	11.33	11.35	11.43
SOUTHEND (Victoria Circus)	4.38	4.53	5.08	5.23	5.38	5.53	6.08	6.23	6.38	6.53	7.08	7.23	7.38	7.53	8.08	8.23	8.38	8.53	9.08	9.23	9.38	9.53	10.08	10.23	10.38	10.53	11.08	11.15	11.23	11.38	11.43	11.45	11.53
SOUTHEND (Tylers Avenue)	4.40	4.55	5.10	5.25	5.40	5.55	6.10	6.25	6.40	6.55	7.10	7.25	7.40	7.55	8.10	8.25	8.40	8.55	9.10	9.25	9.40	9.55	10.10	10.25	10.40	10.55	11.10	11.17	11.25	11.40	11.45	11.47	11.55

	N.S.	N.S.	N.S.	N.S.	N.S.																														
	a.m.	a.m.	a.m.	a.m.	a.m.	a.m.	a.m.	a.m.	a.m.	a.m.	a.m.	a.m.	a.m.	a.m.	a.m.	a.m.	a.m.	a.m.	a.m.	a.m.	a.m.	a.m.	a.m.	a.m.	a.m.	a.m.	a.m.	p.m.	p.m.	p.m.	p.m.	p.m.	p.m.	p.m.	p.m.
SOUTHEND (Tylers Avenue)			5.55	6.10	6.25	6.40	6.55	7.10	7.25	7.40	7.55	8.10	8.25	8.40	8.55	9.10	9.25	9.40	9.55	10.10	10.25	10.40	10.55	11.10	11.25	11.40	11.55	12.10	12.25	12.40	12.55	1.10	1.25	1.40	1.55
SOUTHEND (Victoria Circus)			6.00	6.15	6.30	6.45	7.00	7.15	7.30	7.45	8.00	8.15	8.30	8.45	9.00	9.15	9.30	9.45	10.00	10.15	10.30	10.45	11.00	11.15	11.30	11.45	12.00	12.15	12.30	12.45	1.00	1.15	1.30	1.45	2.00
EASTWOOD			6.10	6.25	6.40	6.55	7.10	7.25	7.40	7.55	8.10	8.25	8.40	8.55	9.10	9.25	9.40	9.55	10.10	10.25	10.40	10.55	11.10	11.25	11.40	11.55	12.10	12.25	12.40	12.55	1.10	1.25	1.40	1.55	2.10
RAYLEIGH			6.20	6.35	6.50	7.05	7.20	7.35	7.50	8.05	8.20	8.35	8.50	9.05	9.20	9.35	9.50	10.05	10.20	10.35	10.50	11.05	11.20	11.35	11.50	12.05	12.20	12.35	12.50	1.05	1.20	1.35	1.50	2.05	2.20
WICKFORD			6.37	6.52	7.07	7.22	7.37	7.52	8.07	8.22	8.37	8.52	9.07	9.22	9.37	9.52	10.07	10.22	10.37	10.52	11.07	11.22	11.37	11.52	12.07	12.22	12.37	12.52	1.07	1.22	1.37	1.52	2.07	2.22	2.37
RAMSDEN BELLHOUSE					7.16				8.16				9.16				10.16				11.16				12.16				1.16				2.16		
BILLERICAY			6.55	7.10	7.25	7.40	7.55	8.10	8.25	8.40	8.55	9.10	9.25	9.40	9.55	10.10	10.25	10.40	10.55	11.10	11.25	11.40	11.55	12.10	12.25	12.40	12.55	1.10	1.25	1.40	1.55	2.10	2.25	2.40	2.55
(B) BRENTWOOD	6.45		7.15	7.30	7.45	8.00	8.15	8.30	8.45	9.00	9.15	9.30	9.45	10.00	10.15	10.30	10.45	11.00	11.15	11.30	11.45	12.00	12.15	12.30	12.45	1.00	1.15	1.30	1.45	2.00	2.15	2.30	2.45	3.00	3.15
ROMFORD	7.05	7.20	7.35	7.50	8.05	8.20	8.35	8.50	9.05	9.20	9.35	9.50	10.05	10.20	10.35	10.50	11.05	11.20	11.35	11.50	12.05	12.20	12.35	12.50	1.05	1.20	1.35	1.50	2.05	2.20	2.35	2.50	3.05	3.20	3.35
ILFORD (East Av, Brands Cr)	7.23	7.38	7.53	8.08	8.23	8.38	8.53	9.08	9.23	9.38	9.53	10.08	10.23	10.38	10.53	11.08	11.23	11.38	11.53	12.08	12.23	12.38	12.53	1.08	1.23	1.38	1.53	2.08	2.23	2.38	2.53	3.08	3.23	3.38	3.53
WOODFORD (Gates Corner)	7.30	7.45	8.00	8.15	8.30	8.45	9.00	9.15	9.30	9.45	10.00	10.15	10.30	10.45	11.00	11.15	11.30	11.45	12.00	12.15	12.30	12.45	1.00	1.15	1.30	1.45	2.00	2.15	2.30	2.45	3.00	3.15	3.30	3.45	4.00
WALTHAMSTOW	7.35	7.50	8.05	8.20	8.35	8.50	9.05	9.20	9.35	9.50	10.05	10.20	10.35	10.50	11.05	11.20	11.35	11.50	12.05	12.20	12.35	12.50	1.05	1.20	1.35	1.50	2.05	2.20	2.35	2.50	3.05	3.20	3.35	3.50	4.05
TOTTENHAM (Broad Lane)	7.40	7.55	8.10	8.25	8.40	8.55	9.10	9.25	9.40	9.55	10.10	10.25	10.40	10.55	11.10	11.25	11.40	11.55	12.10	12.25	12.40	12.55	1.10	1.25	1.40	1.55	2.10	2.25	2.40	2.55	3.10	3.25	3.40	3.55	4.10
TOTTENHAM (Bruce Grove)	7.50	8.05	8.20	8.35	8.50	9.05	9.20	9.35	9.50	10.05	10.20	10.35	10.50	11.05	11.20	11.35	11.50	12.05	12.20	12.35	12.50	1.05	1.20	1.35	1.50	2.05	2.20	2.35	2.50	3.05	3.20	3.35	3.50	4.05	4.20
LONDON (Wood Green)	7.56	8.11	8.26	8.41	8.56	9.11	9.26	9.41	9.56	10.11	10.26	10.41	10.56	11.11	11.26	11.41	11.56	12.11	12.26	12.41	12.56	1.11	1.26	1.41	1.56	2.11	2.26	2.41	2.56	3.11	3.26	3.41	3.56	4.11	4.26
LONDON (Kentish Town)	8.10	8.25		8.55		9.25		9.55		10.25		10.55		11.25		11.55		12.25		12.55		1.25		1.55		2.25		2.55		3.25		3.55		4.25	

																														Monday to Friday to Rayleigh only	Monday to Friday to Rayleigh only	S.O.
	p.m.	p.m.	p.m.	p.m.	p.m.	p.m.	p.m.	p.m.	p.m.	p.m.	p.m.	p.m.	p.m.	p.m.	p.m.	p.m.	p.m.	p.m.	p.m.	p.m.	p.m.	p.m.	p.m.	p.m.	p.m.	p.m.	p.m.	p.m.	p.m.	p.m.	p.m.	p.m.	p.m.
SOUTHEND (Tylers Avenue)	2.10	2.25	2.40	2.55	3.10	3.25	3.40	3.55	4.10	4.25	4.40	4.55	5.10	5.25	5.40	5.55	6.10	6.25	6.40	6.55	7.10	7.25	7.40	7.55	8.10	8.25	8.40	8.55	9.10	9.25	9.55	10.25	10.55
SOUTHEND (Victoria Circus)	2.15	2.30	2.45	3.00	3.15	3.30	3.45	4.00	4.15	4.30	4.45	5.00	5.15	5.30	5.45	6.00	6.15	6.30	6.45	7.00	7.15	7.30	7.45	8.00	8.15	8.30	8.45	9.00	9.15	9.30	10.00	10.30	11.00
EASTWOOD	2.25	2.40	2.55	3.10	3.25	3.40	3.55	4.10	4.25	4.40	4.55	5.10	5.25	5.40	5.55	6.10	6.25	6.40	6.55	7.10	7.25	7.40	7.55	8.10	8.25	8.40	8.55	9.10	9.25	9.40	10.12	10.42	11.12
RAYLEIGH	2.35	2.50	3.05	3.20	3.35	3.50	4.05	4.20	4.35	4.50	5.05	5.20	5.35	5.50	6.05	6.20	6.35	6.50	7.05	7.20	7.35	7.50	8.05	8.20	8.35	8.50	9.05	9.20	9.35	9.50	10.20	10.50	11.20
WICKFORD	2.52	3.07	3.22	3.37	3.52	4.07	4.22	4.37	4.52	5.07	5.22	5.37	5.52	6.07	6.22	6.37	6.52	7.07	7.22	7.37	7.52	8.07	8.22	8.37	8.52	9.07	9.22	9.37	9.52	10.07	10.37	11.07	
RAMSDEN BELLHOUSE		3.16				4.16				5.16				6.16				7.16				8.16				9.16				10.16			
BILLERICAY	3.10	3.25	3.40	3.55	4.10	4.25	4.40	4.55	5.10	5.25	5.40	5.55	6.10	6.25	6.40	6.55	7.10	7.25	7.40	7.55	8.10	8.25	8.40	8.55	9.10	9.25	9.40	9.55	10.10	10.25			
(B) BRENTWOOD	3.30	3.45	4.00	4.15	4.30	4.45	5.00	5.15	5.30	5.45	6.00	6.15	6.30	6.45	7.00	7.15	7.30	7.45	8.00	8.15	8.30	8.45	9.00	9.15	9.30	9.45	10.00	10.15	10.30	10.45			
ROMFORD	3.50	4.05	4.20	4.35	4.50	5.05	5.20	5.35	5.50	6.05	6.20	6.35	6.50	7.05	7.20	7.35	7.50	8.05	8.20	8.35	8.50	9.05	9.20	9.35	9.50	10.05	10.20	10.35	10.50	11.05			
ILFORD (Eastern Ave, Brands Corner)	4.08	4.23	4.38	4.53	5.08	5.23	5.38	5.53	6.08	6.23	6.38	6.53	7.08	7.23	7.38	7.53	8.08	8.23	8.38	8.53	9.08	9.23	9.38	9.53	10.08	10.23	10.38	10.53	11.08	11.23			
WOODFORD (Gates Corner)	4.15	4.30	4.45	5.00	5.15	5.30	5.45	6.00	6.15	6.30	6.45	7.00	7.15	7.30	7.45	8.00	8.15	8.30	8.45	9.00	9.15	9.30	9.45	10.00	10.15	10.30	10.45	11.00	11.15	11.30			
WALTHAMSTOW	4.20	4.35	4.50	5.05	5.20	5.35	5.50	6.05	6.20	6.35	6.50	7.05	7.20	7.35	7.50	8.05	8.20	8.35	8.50	9.05	9.20	9.35	9.50	10.05	10.20	10.35	10.50	11.05	11.20	11.35			
TOTTENHAM (Broad Lane)	4.25	4.40	4.55	5.10	5.25	5.40	5.55	6.10	6.25	6.40	6.55	7.10	7.25	7.40	7.55	8.10	8.25	8.40	8.55	9.10	9.25	9.40	9.55	10.10	10.25	10.40	10.55	11.10	11.25	11.40			
TOTTENHAM (Bruce Grove)	4.35	4.50	5.05	5.20	5.35	5.50	6.05	6.20	6.35	6.50	7.05	7.20	7.35	7.50	8.05	8.20	8.35	8.50	9.05	9.20	9.35	9.50	10.05	10.20	10.35	10.50	11.05	11.20	11.35	11.50			
LONDON (Wood Green)	4.41	4.56	5.11	5.26	5.41	5.56	6.11	6.26	6.41	6.56	7.11	7.26	7.41	7.56	8.11	8.26	8.41	8.56	9.11	9.26	9.41	9.56	10.11	10.26	10.41	10.56	11.11	11.26	11.41	11.56			
LONDON (Kentish Town)	4.55		5.25		5.55		6.25		6.55		7.25		7.55		8.25		8.55		9.25		9.55		10.25		10.55		11.25		11.55				

N.S.—Not Sundays and Public Holidays. S.O.—Saturdays only. Buses leaving Kentish Town and Tylers Avenue at 25 minutes past the hour, proceed via Ramsden Bellhouse, commencing at 6.25 a.m.
Market Days: Wickford—Monday; Romford—Wednesday; Billericay—Thursday.

A reduced facsimile of the London—Southend timetable after 'City' had acquired the 'Westcliff' interest on that route, which included the hourly diversion via Ramsden Bellhouse which was soon after transferred to a shuttle service so that all through journeys travelled by the main road through South Green and Crays Hill.

which had earned untold goodwill. 'Westcliff' took over operation and for a time the 'City' fleetname was continued on the London service. Moreover, 'City' transfers were applied to some Eastern National vehicles brought in, and for many a day this service was still, to thousands of passengers, the 'City' route, and never service 251, its new designation. When 'City' moved its headquarters to Brentwood in 1938, it built a fine new administrative and engineering block in Ongar Road, the latter portion of which is still used by Eastern National, the other part now being used by British Thermos.

Table of 'City' coach services acquired by Westcliff Motor Services

City No.	Serving	WMS No.
1	London—Romford—Brentwood—Billericay—Wickford—Southend	251
1A	Brentwood—Billericay—Ramsden—Wickford—Shotgate	253
2	Brentwood—Shenfield—Hutton (Bracken Bank)	252
3	Brentwood—Billericay—Little Burstead—Laindon Station	255
4	Ongar—Blackmore or Great Warley—Brentwood—Herongate— Old Dog or West Horndon or Bulphan—Dunton—Laindon	260
4A	Little Warley—Brentwood	part 260
5	Brentwood—Billericay—Great Burstead—Laindon Station	254
6 group	Laindon Station—Wash Road—Pipps Hill—Basildon Road (circle)	258
7	Billericay—Jacksons Lane—Sunnymede Estate	256
9	Laindon (Hotel)—Basildon Road—Nevendon—Wickford	257
11	Woodman Road—Brentwood—Doddinghurst—Hook End—Stondon	261
15	Laindon Station—Langdon Hills (Crown)	259

City Coach Company

Three 'Setright' tickets — 9d. day return (for use on ex-'Ongar & District' route only) pale buff; 2d. excess fare — stone; 1/- single for London—Southend route — yellow.

TIME TABLES OF SERVICES

SERVICE NO. 1.

SOUTHEND (High Street, Tylers Avenue) and LONDON (Wood Green, Lordship Lane).

Via Eastwood, Rayleigh, Wickford, Billericay, Brentwood, Romford, Ilford, Woodford, Walthamstow, Tottenham.

LAINDON STATION CIRCULAR.

Above and facing page: Facsimile reduction of the last City Coach Co. timetables before absorption by Westcliff, dated winter 1951/52.

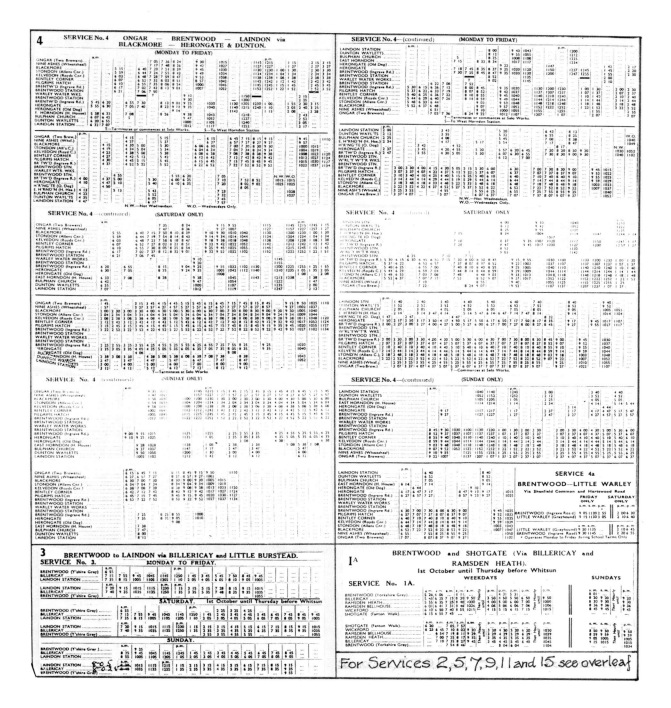

4 SERVICE No. 4 ONGAR — BRENTWOOD — LAINDON via BLACKMORE — HERONGATE & DUNTON.
(MONDAY TO FRIDAY)

SERVICE No. 4—(continued) (MONDAY TO FRIDAY)

SERVICE No. 4—(continued) (SATURDAY ONLY)

SERVICE No. 4 (SATURDAY ONLY)

SERVICE No. 4—(continued) (SUNDAY ONLY)

SERVICE No. 4—(continued) (SUNDAY ONLY)

SERVICE No. 4a
BRENTWOOD—LITTLE WARLEY
Via Shenfield Common and Hartswood Road

N.W.—Not Wednesdays. W.O.—Wednesdays Only.
T—Terminates at Selo Works.
S—To West Horndon Station.

3 BRENTWOOD to LAINDON via BILLERICAY and LITTLE BURSTEAD.
SERVICE No. 3. MONDAY TO FRIDAY.
SATURDAY. 1st October until Thursday before Whitsun.
SUNDAY.

1A BRENTWOOD and SHOTGATE (Via BILLERICAY and RAMSDEN HEATH).
1st October until Thursday before Whitsun
SERVICE No. 1A. WEEKDAYS   SUNDAYS

For Services 2, 5, 7, 9, 11 and 15 see overleaf

continued—
CITY COACH CO:

2 SERVICE No. 2. BRENTWOOD—HUTTON (Bracken Bank).
MONDAY TO SATURDAY.   SUNDAY
Will operate during school terms only. Both Monday—Friday only.

5 BRENTWOOD to LAINDON via BILLERICAY and GREAT BURSTEAD.
SERVICE No. 5. MONDAY TO FRIDAY.
SATURDAY.   SUNDAY.

7 SERVICE No. 7—BILLERICAY (Sunnymede Estate) to BILLERICAY (Sun Corner)
OCTOBER to THURSDAY BEFORE WHITSUN
NS—Not Sundays. SO—Sundays Only.

9 SERVICE No. 9. LAINDON to WICKFORD (Monday Only).

BRENTWOOD (Woodman Road) and STONDON CHURCH.
SERVICE No. 11. VIA DODDINGHURST and HOOK END
WEEK-DAYS
SUNDAYS
SO—Operates on Saturdays only.
MF—MONDAY TO FRIDAY SO SATURDAY ONLY

15 LAINDON STATION to "THE CROWN HOTEL," LANGDON HILLS.
SERVICE No. 15. MONDAY—FRIDAY.
SATURDAYS.
SUNDAYS.
2½d. FARE ONLY

167

CLACTON & DISTRICT MOTOR SERVICES LTD. Clacton-on-Sea, Essex

This company had been one of W. P. Allen's promotions and was registered on 4th December 1913 to operate omnibuses and charabancs in the East Essex area using the fleetname 'Silver Queen'. W. P. Allen had also promoted motor bus undertakings at Dartford, Folkestone and Ramsgate in Kent, at Grantham and Louth in Lincolnshire, and in Worcester and elsewhere. Some of his businesses became associated with British Electric Traction, resulting in him holding directorships in the East Kent Road Car Co., Aldershot & District Traction and Lincolnshire Road Car Co., all of which had absorbed his companies over the years.

At Clacton, the other Directors were F. H. Tozer and A. P. Allt, the Secretary was F. Ives, and the registered office was at College Hill Chambers, London EC4. When Allen selected Clacton as an operating centre, he had the field virtually to himself. At this time there was only one motor charabanc working in the town, a Leyland with tiered seating named *Swiftsure*, which is believed to have begun working in 1911. There were also several local proprietors who ran cabs and horse-brakes, most of which sought passengers during the season by standing along the seaward end of Pier Avenue.

The motor bus/charabanc was late arriving at Clacton, although it must be mentioned that the Great Eastern Railway had, between 1906—8, operated a seasonal motor route to St. Osyth. It is believed this was started when the appearance of an electric tramway threatened. In 1904, the Clacton and St. Osyth Light Railway Company was authorized to construct a line from the Pier, via the Railway Station and Great Clacton. This, of course, was the section the promoters really wanted and hoped to build first as far as Great Clacton village, and then quietly forget about the country portion! Negotiations with the Clacton UD dragged on for some considerable time because they would not consent unless the entire line was constructed. Eventually the powers lapsed and were not renewed, whereupon the GER, finding the buses rather unprofitable, except at high season, decided to abandon its service.

During this time, the original horse-bus owners maintained their long established service. The oldest service, started by a local jobmaster named Reed, when Clacton was first being developed, ran between the town and Weeley Railway Station until the GER opened the branch from Thorpe-le-Soken Station, on the Walton-on-Naze line, on 1st May 1882. He then maintained a daily service of about eight trips to Great Clacton, with one extended to St. Osyth (increased to two in summer) for the benefit of visitors. Soon after the turn of the century, Horace Scragg of Meredith Road was in possession of the business, which was always located in Orwell Road and, by 1914, had passed to Arthur Rampling when the omnibus section ceased. The usual jobmasters' activities were continued, together with a fleet of cabs, etc., and by the 1920s, it was in the hands of E. M. Appleby who replaced the horses with motors and added household removals.

The other horse-bus owner was Mr William Rampling who also ran a daily omnibus from St. Osyth. This appears to have ceased at about the same time as 'Silver Queen' started its first route from Clacton to St. Osyth, together with their motor tours. However, before its first operating season was over, war was declared on Germany, with the result that the business was almost closed down with the exception of some rudimentary service to St. Osyth, and the fleet reduced to just three vehicles, two of which were cars.

At the end of 1918, the fleet strength was four omnibuses and two cars, and a year later sufficient omnibuses had been obtained to enable services, usually consisting of two or three trips daily, to be started between Clacton and Colchester, via Weeley or St. Osyth and Wivenhoe; to Brightlingsea; to Walton, via Thorpe; to Harwich; and between Walton and Colchester where a branch depot was established in the yard of the Angel Hotel in High Street. Other services were started from Clacton in 1920, and also from Colchester where there was sharp competition with 'National' which was busy opening

up services, as well as other operators, notably Berry & Sons on the Colchester—Brightlingsea route. It was not long before an agreement had very sensibly been reached between these two, following a ruinous fare war. (Details in Volume One). It was also agreed that 'Silver Queen' would leave the Colchester—Brightlingsea service to Berry for operation, providing they kept off the Wivenhoe road which now became a 'Silver Queen' preserve. An amicable atmosphere henceforth prevailed between the three operators. By the summer of 1922, the 'Silver Queen' network was virtually complete, except for the addition of further infilling, and the development of town services. During 1922, the first competition from within appeared in the shape of the 'Enterprise' bus service, started by Fitch & Sons (q.v.) who had been jobmasters in Clacton for many years. There was now to be great rivalry between the two concerns with both bus services and charabanc trips. However, in the later 1920s, some rapport was established between them when several services became a joint operation or, by co-ordination of timetables, several services were arranged to leave at standard departure times.

As Clacton continued to grow, both as a popular resort and residential town, the omnibus and charabanc services prospered to the extent that, by June 1926, when the company changed its name to 'Silver Queen Motor Omnibus Co. Ltd.', there were forty five Leyland buses and twenty five Leyland charabancs in the fleet. A number of these vehicles dated from well before 1914 and carried some distinctly quaint bodywork. It would not be untrue to describe the 'Silver Queen' fleet at this time as a veritable travelling museum!

An interesting feature of these buses was the arrangement for the 'Silver Queen' name to be painted in large shaded characters on a separate board which was screwed to the waist panel. This could be removed when buses came in for repaint, refitted afterwards, thus saving the cost of fresh signwriting whenever painting was required.

The Directors were now W. P. Allen, A. W. Shrimpton (local manager) and Harry Hyams, with Thomas L. Summers fulfilling the duties of Secretary from 64 Victoria Street, London SW1. The local office and depot was at Jackson Road and there was a branch depot at Walton-on-Naze where the office was at the end of the High Street near the bus terminal known as the 'Kino Stand'. The garage was in the foundry at The Naze, formerly the works of Warner & Company which had manufactured a variety of pumps for manual or power operation.

At Clacton bus terminus, which was common with 'Enterprise' and 'National', there was always a line of buses to be seen and, at one time, a good deal of jockeying or obstruction by drivers of the rival concerns was frequently made in an effort to get a leading position on the rank. A considerable amount of touting went on at the charabanc stand in an endeavour to capture passengers before they reached either the 'Enterprise' stand a little farther along Rosemary Road, or Suttons' Crossley coaches a few doors away in Pier Avenue, and 'National' whose office and stand was a little lower down nearer the Pier.

In 1926, the company expanded into a full branch at Dovercourt by taking over a group of local services from Starling & Son who had acquired them from the LNER in September 1923. These had previously been operated by the Great Eastern Railway and earlier by Mr A. Gant, as noted in the text. Harwich Corporation granted 'Silver Queen' licences for six buses to which the following special conditions were imposed: All passengers were to be insured against personal injury to the extent of £1,000 each; local labour, paid at district rates, must be employed in the running and repair of the cars, and a substantial garage (which later passed to the ENOC) is to be built forthwith in Kingsway, Dovercourt. In 1929, a number of Thornycroft J type buses came into the fleet, displacing many of the more ancient Leylands. The new arrivals came from the associated 'Silver Queen' business in Lincolnshire which had recently been reorganized with some other bus businesses into the Lincolnshire Road Car Company which, it would seem, did not require them. Nearly all carried bodies from former London General K type double-decks. From 1927, some Chevrolets and Lancias with fourteen and twenty seat body-work began to enter the fleet to help counter the activities of 'Enterprise' which generally used smaller, but faster, vehicles than 'Silver Queen'. Latterly, a few Leyland Lions and Tigers came into the fleet and, shortly before the sale to Eastern National, six Leyland Titan covered-top double-decks were purchased. The last major transaction by 'Silver Queen' was to acquire the competing 'Enterprise' company. This it completed in 1930 although both continued to work separately until after acquisition by the ENOC.

As the business expanded over the years, additional garage space in Clacton became necessary, and accommodation was obtained in Castle Road. Buses were outstationed at St. Osyth, at Brightlingsea, at Great Oakley and, for three to four months each summer, two vehicles were sent to East Bergholt to work services to Clacton and Dovercourt for the season, one of which was outstationed during the rest of the year at Tendring.

'Silver Queen' had an arrangement with the New Medway Steam Packet Co. whereby circular tickets were issued permitting combined omnibus/boat tours between Clacton, Walton and Felixstowe on its paddle steamer *Queen of the South*.

The timetable booklets, which included faretables and map, were somewhat sketchy affairs, issued from time to time, and seldom contained details of the rather short high season timings. They were supplied by Magnet Advertising of London. 'Silver Queen' has been credited with the running of a coach service to London, but so far nothing has been discovered to confirm this. The acquisition of 'Silver Queen' and 'Enterprise' by the ENOC removed much of the colour from the transport scene in the Tendring Hundred but there was, however, still a wide choice of operators and vehicles to be seen in the area, particularly on the long distance express services, excursions and tours, a large proportion of which used the large Eastern National coach park in Wash Lane.

A map and timetable of the 'Silver Queen' omnibus routes will be found under the title Silver Queen Omnibuses Ltd.

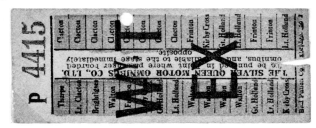

Punch type tickets. 2/- return with stages numbered for 'up' or 'down' journeys — yellow. Weekly Ticket Exchange (seldom used) with stages named, punched at boarding point and available to the place named opposite — white with pink stripes. The reverse of a 1d. single to show company's advertisement.

CLARK, A. E., (Senior) and CLARK, A. E. (Junior) Albert Garage, Leigh Beck, Canvey Island, Essex

Both were members of the Canvey Association and also served on the board of the Canvey & District Motor Transport Co. Ltd. under which further information can be obtained.

CLAVERING & DISTRICT BUS SERVICES Wicken Road, Clavering, Essex

Rather remarkable to relate H. Wilson, proprietor of the above services, succeeded in developing a fair proportion of his network of services after the introduction of licensing in 1931, none of which was achieved by the purchase of other operators' services. He was located in an area which had been neglected by 'National' and the succeeding Eastern National and, although there were some facilities from other small operators passing through from more distant places, no one had made any effort to exploit the potential business available until Wilson saw the opportunities. At 1931, Wilson was operating the following services:

a) The Langleys—Arkesden—Wicken Bonhunt—Clavering—Manuden—Bishop's Stortford (Thursdays, Saturdays and Sundays)
b) Clavering—Wicken Bonhunt—Newport—Quendon—Stansted—Bishop's Stortford (weekdays)
c) Clavering—Wicken Bonhunt—Newport—Saffron Walden (Tuesdays)
d) Clavering—Wicken Bonhunt—Arkesden—Clavering—Langleys—Duddenhoe End—Royston (Wednesdays)

On 23rd September 1933, he was granted licences for two new services, viz:

e) Sheepcote Green—Clavering—Wicken Bonhunt—Rickling—Ugley—Henham—Stansted—Bishop's Stortford (one run weekdays, two on Sundays)
f) The Langleys—Clavering—Wicken Bonhunt—Newport—Quendon—Stansted—Bishop's Stortford, which ran Monday to Friday in lieu of (b), and a group of excursions and tours starting from Clavering and six other villages.

On 24th December 1934, two further licences were forthcoming for:

g) Clavering—Arkesden—Wendens Ambo—Audley End Station—Saffron Walden (Saturdays only)
h) Dunmow—Bambers Green—Molehill Green—Elsenham—Henham—Widdington—Newport—Saffron Walden (Tuesdays and Saturdays)

This last venture was not quite so successful as his other services, and the section between Dunmow and Henham was discontinued from 14th October 1935. In February 1936, he applied successfully for a second group of excursions and tours providing another four picking up points. On 28th June 1937, he was granted another stage service to run:

j) Widdington—Debden Aerodrome—Debden Green—Hamperden End—Henham—Elsenham—Stansted—Bishop's Stortford (Thursdays, Saturdays and Sundays)

In the following December, this was extended to start from Clavering to call also at Wicken Bonhunt and Newport, but also to give a Friday service. Early in 1938, Wilson sought a licence to provide an express service on Wednesdays, Saturdays and Sundays from eleven of 'his' villages, including Clavering to Clacton-on-Sea, but was refused. This was his final act in developing a fine network of routes to serve a scattered collection of small villages, for four months later Eastern National had come to terms with him to take over operation of his services with effect from 21st April 1938, including one Bedford bus. For a time, the Company had two buses out-stationed at Clavering, reduced later to one only with the wartime reductions in service levels.

COLLINGRIDGE, — Felstead, Essex
This carrier took over the service, worked by Thomas Hicks, about the turn of the century which continued until about 1914 when it returned to the Hicks family to be motorized by Ernest.

COMFY COACHES 69 Little Street, Yardley Hastings, Northamptonshire
Alfred Minney, who traded as above, started in 1923 using a 14 seat Chevrolet which had longitudinal seating entered from a rear door. He ran to Northampton (Black Boy Yard) and the service steadily developed in response to public demand and was extended to start from Lavendon and later from Harrold. He offered a more frequent service than that provided by the Northampton Motor Bus Company's route which was later taken over by 'National', and probably accounts for his success as he later needed another Chevrolet which was followed by a Star Flyer. Unfortunately this was bought just as the Knight's 'Sally Bus Service' was getting into its stride, which proved too much for him to compete against, so he sold the service to them as detailed under that notice. Alfred joined 'National' as a driver, but his brother Douglas went to 'The Sally'. At busy times, especially at weekends, Alfred's other brother, Reginald, was pressed into service, and Agnes, his wife, would assist with conducting.

COMMERCIAL CAR HIRERS LTD. Luton, Bedfordshire
This was a company promoted for the purpose of opening up omnibus services using Commer vehicles, which would be supplied on favourable terms to purchasers of the service once it had been established. This occured at Leigh-on-Sea where a service was developed to become the basis of the Hadleigh Motor Bus Company (q.v.).

COPPIN, H. & SON Springfield Garage, Orsett Grays, Essex
These were successors to Harding of the same village (q.v.), who provided a frequent service to Grays (Kings Arms) which the Company acquired on 7th May 1936. This was then diverted to the LMS station yard which avoided the use of the level crossing in the town centre. The times became part of existing service 32. No rolling stock was acquired.

CRACKNELL, S. G. Ongar Road, Brentwood, Essex
S. G. Cracknell was a driver for Saywood (q.v.), who later elected to work his own bus for which he bought a Ford A round about 1928. It was in a greenish-brown livery with his name along the full length in large 'palace script' writing. He worked on his former employer's route and extended it from Blackmore to Ongar. The Ford was replaced by a REO which came from Moore Bros. (q.v.), and was still being used when he sold the service to Curtis of the 'Ongar & Distrct' service in 1932.

CROW, W. G. Canvey Island, Essex
One of the seventeen Canvey busmen (see 'Canvey Auxiliary Motors).

DAVIES, E. Tresco, Ramsden Bellhouse, Essex
Little information has come to light concerning this operator prior to licensing, although

he seems to have worked in harmony with his close neighbour Amos, and Kershaw of Wickford whose services passed to him. In 1931, he obtained licences for the following:

1 Ramsden to Chelmsford, via the Hanningfields S and W (Fridays)
2 Ramsden to Chelmsford direct, via Stock 'Ship' (Saturdays)
3 Wickford to Rettendon, via Turnpike Corner (Mondays)
4 Ramsden to Wickford Railway Station, via Jacksons Corner (Weekdays)

A little later the following were added, ex-Kershaw

5 Basildon to Wickford and Rettendon, via Chalk Street (Mondays)
6 Wickford to Shotgate local service

Of the above, the licence for 1 was revoked in 1932 and the ENOC put on service 11A as a replacement. Services 2, 3, 4 and part of 5, together with part of the Amos business were now all combined into a new ENOC service 12 and 12B. The Basildon part of 5 and the whole of 6 were abandoned as both were well covered by other services.

DAY, — West Mersea, Essex
In the early 1920s, a Mr Day joined the several others all seeking to make a business on the West Mersea to Colchester run. He also pioneered a new service between Colchester and Fingringhoe, via Blackheath while others ran via Rowhedge. He sold both services to P. H. Underwood (circa 1929) from whom they ultimately came to the ENOC to join the 75 etc. group of services.

DAY, P. W. & BEDINGFIELD, C. R. Stanford-le-Hope, Essex
One of the many small bus owners at Grays, they were granted licences to run (a) Homesteads (Balmoral Avenue)—Stanford-le-Hope—Grays—Purfleet; and (b) Homesteads—Stanford-le-Hope—Shell Haven (shift times). As (a) entered the LPTB area, the whole was acquired by the Board on 1st August 1934 which passed the parts east of Grays to the ENOC on the same day, whereupon they became new services 58 and 59. No vehicles were involved. Day & Bedingfield claim to have been operating a West Thurrock—Grays—Orsett service, but were unsuccessful in getting a licence for it.

DEATH, George West Mersea, Essex
This operator succeeded to James Greenleaf's carrier service between West Mersea and Colchester, which he sold to the first of three generations of Underwoods (circa 1885), eventually passing to Eastern National in 1935.

DIGBY, George West Bergholt, Essex
After World War II, this operator succeeded to the service of Fred Heath to Colchester. He gave about six daily journeys and extended the route a short distance to serve Westwood Park until Eastern National took over operation on 12th November 1961 to become part of service 76A.

DREADNOUGHT BUS SERVICE 13 Cutliffe Grove, Bedford, Bedfordshire
After a rather unsettled career, between 1924 and 1927, involving several partnerships operating 'pirate' omnibuses in London, Henry Herbert Clench went to Bedford where he set up the above-named business in March 1928. The office was at the above address where his manager resided, the buses working from St. Peter's garage in Balsall Street. At

least eight buses of assorted manufacture were employed but, by 1930, the service and the vehicles had become so run down that the Corporation refused to renew his licences, whereupon he installed 'gift boxes' in the buses for passengers' contributions, as he was not charging fares. No doubt he got plenty of passengers many of whom were free riders! He soon found himself in arrears with his hire purchase payments and the buses were re-possessed one by one and the business finally collapsed later that year.

Clench had latterly been operating the following services, although he had operated on a number of other routes licenced and unlicenced:

a) Midland Station—Stanley Street (taken over by 'Wonder Bus')
b) Southend Hotel—Queens Park (times incorporated into ENOC service 33)
c) Bedford—Kimbolton—St. Neots (taken over by T. F. Allen, (q.v.))
d) Bedford—Staughton—St. Neots (most taken over by L. M. Jarvis)
e) Bedford—Pavenham—Harrold (taken over by Franklin of Carlton)
f) Biggleswade—Sandy—St. Neots (lapsed, no takers)

Allen's route came to the Company later as did the 'Wonder Bus'. Franklin sold out to Birch Bros. and Jarvis is believed to have eventually become part of the Woolston's service. At this time, there were no fewer than seven proprietors all criss-crossing each other between Bedford and St. Neots.

In October/November 1930, Eastern National started services 34/34A over much the same ground, but did not find the going easy and were able to come to some operating agreement with T. F. Allen who, none the less, disposed of his service to 'Union Jack' before it finally passed to the Company.

EAST BERGHOLT & DISTRICT SERVICES St. Johns, Ipswich Road, Colchester, Essex
The ENOC acquired the above service from Mrs E. S. Furber on 8th August 1934. She had continued operation from her husband who had earlier taken it over from the Peck Bros. (q.v.). It offered 7/8 daily journeys between East Bergholt and Colchester, via Manningtree and Ardleigh, in direct competition with Messrs Beeston. There were also excursions and tours from East Bergholt, Manningtree, Colchester and some of the intermediate villages. A Commer 'Invader' and an AEC 'Regal' were included in the deal, the latter bus lasting until 1957!

There were a great many vehicles passing in and out of this business which is due to Mr Furber having garage connections (Grosvenor Motors) which dealt in commercial vehicles and PSVs. It is possible that Peck Bros. had been supplied with buses by Grosvenor Motors which repossessed them with the service.

EASTERN COUNTIES OMNIBUS COMPANY LTD. Thorpe Road, Norwich, Norfolk
On 1st January 1934, Eastern National acquired the above company's half interest in three stage services which had for several years been jointly operated by the two concerns. In the Midland Area, there were two; service 29, Bedford—St. Neots—Cambridge and service 41, Hitchin—Royston—Cambridge. The third lay in the Eastern Area, being the 123 service, Clacton-on-Sea—Manningtree—Ipswich. There was no further joint working with Eastern Counties until 25th June 1961 when that company's 207 Ipswich—Colchester service became jointly worked, Eastern National performing one trip in three. On 11th April 1965, a new jointly-operated route 212 was started between Ipswich—Manningtree and Harwich.

Three years earlier, on 11th April 1962, Eastern Counties acquired Mulley's Motorways' express coach route from Bury St. Edmunds/Stowmarket/Hadleigh to Sudbury, Halstead and London, which had formerly been run by 'Corona Coaches'. The Stowmarket—Halstead section was licensed as a stage route which Eastern Counties numbered 283 and this became joint with Eastern National on 13th May 1963. At the same time, the latter's X14 London—Halstead coach service was integrated with the Eastern Counties express route X between London and Bury St. Edmunds, the Hadleigh portion of which was now only served by a bus connection.

About the same time, Eastern National and Eastern Counties rationalized their overlapping services between Ipswich, Manningtree and Colchester, whereby the former now worked all the timings south of Manningtree and the latter, those to the north. In so doing, Eastern National succeeded to the former interests on this road of B. Beeston & Sons of East Bergholt who had been acquired by Eastern Counties in 1951.

EASTWARD COACHES London
Eastward took over the operations of Evans' Coaches in January 1930, only three months after they started the first coach service from East London to Chelmsford with eleven trips daily. In the following October, it acquired additional timings from Benjamin Davis between London and Brentwood, but was itself in financial difficulty soon after, probably because of the very intense competition then building up on this route which was shared with Green Line, Hillman, Sunset and Victory, as well as the ordinary buses. The fleet of Gilford coaches was repossessed by the makers, and Hillman's Coaches incorporated the Eastward timings into its own very frequent schedule.

ENGLAND, A. F. Lovers Walk and Britain Street, Dunstable, Beds.
A. F. England was an astute businessman as well as an omnibus proprietor who became a 'bit of a nuisance' to the ENOC for several years. His main involvement in the bus field may be summarized thus: he started his XL service in April 1927, its main activity being a Luton—Dunstable—Leighton Buzzard route which poached traffic from the 'National'/ENOC identical service. In 1931 he acquired control of the 'Union Jack' (Luton) Omnibus Co. Ltd. (q.v.) and, in the following year, the 'Bluebird Services' of Hinds and Savage Ltd. (q.v.), including some involvement in the Toddington and Westoning district. The 'Union Jack' business was now moved over to Dunstable where could be seen the remarkable phenomenon of the 'Union Jack' of England in Britain Street, which also changed its name to Englands Lane, just round the corner from his premises.

England's next move was to negotiate a deal with Luton Corporation which, as mentioned in *Chapter One*, had just turned down an offer from the ENOC to operate the town transport. It is not known if he did this for fear of the Corporation interfering with his services, or whether it was done to thwart the ENOC. It was probably the latter because only three days after this deal he purchaed the Lamb Bros. 'Renown' service and then moved to Bedford where he bought R. A. Carding's 'Wonder Bus' services and later T. F. Allen's business. By this time the ENOC and LPTB agreed it was time England was 'got out of the way' for they were concerned he may next make a deal with Birch Bros. Accordingly, the ENOC made a successful bid for these services in December 1936, selling the former 'Renown' route to LPTB in January 1937, so ending A. F. England's activities in the motor bus world. However, he retained his interests in the haulage sphere and next moved into hire purchase facilities for private car buyers.

ENTERPRISE BUS CO. (CLACTON) LTD. Rosemary Road, Clacton-on-Sea, Essex
This interesting concern originated as a jobmaster's run by Messrs Fitch & Son at 6—10 Rosemary Road, and was well-established prior to World War I. Here was a considerable range of stabling and other buildings where they kept cabs, carriages, brakes and so on. It is not known when the business became motorized but, by the summer of 1922, they

were operating a fleet of Ford T one ton vehicles with either 14 seat saloon or open charabanc bodywork. They were supplied and bodied by Harold J. Willett of Colchester, and were on pneumatic tyres with a high speed rear axle. The saloons must have been rather draughty at times, having only half doors at the front and no rear doors or emergency exit. They were provided with electric interior lighting, carried a luggage rail around the roof, and cost no more than £297. 10s. 0d. each complete. A yellow livery with black beading was adopted and the fleetname appeared in large black 'palace script' writing along the full length of its side panels.

The buses were put to work on the more heavily trafficked 'Silver Queen' routes where, in the main, they were generally very successful because of their higher turn of speed and handiness. Enterprise pioneered a few services such as those to Thorpe Green, Holland Cliffs and Clacton cemetery.

The business was converted into a limited company on 22nd March 1923 as A. Fitch & Sons (Clacton) Ltd. the Board consisting of F. A. Fitch, Mrs C. S. Hilton and E. S. Lilley. By 1926/7, the two last named had been replaced by Mr Wilson Blyth, who became Managing Director, and Mr W. L. Blyth. The registered offices next moved to 36 Rosemary Road, which was also the booking office and point from where the excursions and tours started. Towards the end of the year, the business underwent a further reorganization and, on 23rd November, it became the Enterprise Bus Company (Clacton) Ltd. Mrs K. Blyth, Mr M. O. Langridge and Mr W. H. Vincent joined the other Directors on the Board. The capital was set down at £5,000.

Expansion continued and as larger vehicles became necessary for certain duties, particularly in summer season, some very interesting buses joined the fleet. These included two Leyland open-toppers from Arthur Partridge of London 'Chocolate Express' fame, one of which was the almost immortal first independent omnibus to take to the London streets in 1923. A number of Lancias, again fast and comfortable, were put into service together with a pair of Berlinet 20 seaters and, very unusually, a brace of 2 ton Gotfred-sons, an American product, in spite of the name. A big step forward was made in 1929 when a Leyland Tiger and an AEC Regal, with Metcalfe bodies, arrived in company with a Short-bodied 48 seat covered top AEC Regent which, together, caused quite a stir in the opposing 'Silver Queen' camp. They probably contributed to the 'modus vivendi' which was shortly afterwards concluded between the two parties, so eliminating most of the fierce competition engaged in over the years.

Within another eighteen months, 'Silver Queen' purchased the business outright, shortly before it was itself acquired by the ENOC, whereupon the registered office once again travelled a little further along Rosemary Road to number 71.

Sixteen vehicles passed to the ENOC of which one, Leyland Tiger No. 3217, proved to be remarkably reliable, surviving to be renumberd 101 in 1954 after twenty five years of operation! This vehicle has the distinction of being the longest serving PSV in the ENOC fleet.

The entire Enterprise bus routes are indicated in the schedule of services acquired from 'Silver Queen' to which readers should refer. Enterprise issued its own quite presentable timetable booklet which was prepared by a London firm of advertising contractors.

ESSEX PUBLIC SERVICES LTD. 46 Bishopsgate, London EC2
Little is known of this ephemeral business which was registered on 21st May 1929 by H. J. Falkus and A. W. Falkus for the purpose (inter alia) of operating omnibus services. There was an unsuccessful attempt to acquire a licence for a Southend-on-Sea to London service and, for a short period, one of the Falkus family was a Director of Pearse's Motor Service at Benfleet. It is also known that some ex-London 'pirate' Straker-Squire open-top double-decks were bought and sent to Maldon to inaugurate omnibus services in that district. The buses were based on a piece of ground near the East Railway Station, but it has not been possible to discover the services that were worked, or for how long. It has been suggested that when the buses departed after their short sojourn at Maldon, J. W. Gozzett, whose property almost overlooked the Station Road, felt that there was business to be done if suitable vehicles were employed, and so started his 'Quest Coach' services in earnest.

EVANS COACHES London
Evans opened the first London—Chelmsford coach service and was taken over by Eastward Coaches (q.v.) after a very short life.

FALE, Thomas William Rowhedge, Essex
In 1912, the above is listed as a fishmonger in Rowhedge but, by 1914, as a carrier which, presumably, he had taken over from an earlier owner running daily to Colchester where he set up at The Plough. In the early 1920s he acquired a motor bus but eschewed the new corporation bus park that everyone else used and continued at The Plough. In 1937, the service was in the hands of Mrs Fale who carried on the service until after the war when it continued with Mrs Mawdsley and Mrs Brown who still kept the same terminus. This was a famous carrier house which was only demolished a few years ago, and the site is now covered by a large traffic circle.

FITCH & SON/FITCH & SON (CLACTON) LTD. Rosemary Road, Clacton-on-Sea, Essex
See under 'Enterprise Motors'.

FORBES, A. J. The Street, Terling, Essex
This operator provided a bus service in the 1920s between Terling, Chelmsford, Witham and Braintree on various days until 12th October 1931 when Mr W. A. Waite of the Old

Punch type tickets with numbered stages. 1d. single — white with advert on reverse side; 3d. single — rose.

Post Office, Terling, received licences to run to Chelmsford and Braintree, the Witham service being abandoned, since when, no bus has run between those places. At the end of 1935, Waite also gave up the service, part of which was added to J. A. Wilkinson's times which were taken over by the ENOC to become part of its 50 and new 50A services in 1942.

FORD, A. A.   Three Ways Garage, Althorne, Essex
This operator was in the garage business from the early 1920s which included a car hire and taxi service and, later, a small 14 seat saloon bus which he ran in between his other activities according to demand or his availability. In 1931, he made various applications for licences without great success. One was from North Fambridge through Althorne, via Cock Clarks to Maldon which he abandoned in 1934, and another from Burnham-on-Crouch to Southend on one day a week was also short-lived. Gozzett's 'Quest Service' took up the North Fambridge to Maldon route, and Ford continued as a private hire operator and garage proprietor.

FRASER SMITH, A.   Canvey Island, Essex
This operator was one of the seventeen owners and a member of the Association with whom there was a long running dispute, and with the Council, as he refused to operate to the times on his licence, claiming that he only picked up ticket holders. His licence was then suspended and he appealed to the Commissioner who upheld the Council, so he eventually undertook to come into line. He acquired Timberlake's interest when the latter could not make his vehicle roadworthy.

GAYLARD, Henry   High Street, Canvey Island, Essex
See under 'Canvey Auxiliary Motors'.

GANT, Allen   Pound Farm, Upper Dovercourt, Essex
The above farmer was the first to provide a regular service of omnibuses to Harwich, for which purpose he acquired a pair of old London horse-buses which, by all accounts, had seen better days well before starting a new life beside the sea about the turn of the century. The service ceased in 1914 and was continued by the Great Eastern Railway (q.v.).

GIDEA PARK COACHES LTD.   Romford, Essex
A. E. Blane had operated buses in the Romford area from about 1925 until his services were compulsorily taken over by the London Passenger Transport Board. He next turned his attention to coaching operations by acquiring an interest in the Victory Omnibus Company (q.v.), with a coaching subsidiary, Gidea Park Coaches Ltd. which kept its fleet in the yard behind the White Hart Hotel, Romford. This location had incidentally been the former home for 'National' buses when they operated services in the Romford area. In 1936, Gidea Park Coaches acquired the excursions and tours previously worked by Webster at Laindon as part of his 'Old Tom' motor service. Later, a picking up point was secured at Brentwood which formed the nucleus of a large expansion in that area. Eastern National bought the service in 1954 with two Dennis Lancet coaches and the Laindon portion became the basis for further development at that point with Basildon.

GOLDEN ARROW SERVICE   55 Great Whyte, Ramsey, Huntingdonshire
E. Scott and Son selected the above fleetname when they set up their own services after driving for the Peterborough Electric Traction Company which operated around Ramsey. The Scotts filled in some gaps in existing services there, and also went on to working mar-

ket services to Peterborough (2) and to St. Ives when traffic was plentiful. In 1934, the ENOC and ECOC jointly acquired the services which were divided as follows in June of that year:

To ENOC 1 Ramsey—St. Ives via two routes added to existing service 38 with a new 38A. Also believed to include some times from Brown, Warboys (q.v.).
2 Ramsey—Bury—Wistow which was absorbed by suitable diversions of the existing 39 and 44 routes.
3 One Dennis Lancet saloon which was a little over one year old.

To ECOC 1 Two services to Peterborough.
2 Ramsey—Wennington—Raveley.
3 Ramsey—Whittlesey.

GREAT EASTERN RAILWAY COMPANY   Liverpool Street Station, London EC
This company started running motor buses in East Anglia as early as 1904 but gradually disposed of the service when satisfactory arrangements could be made with a local operator. Its Chelmsford area routes, taken over by the National Steam Car Co. in 1913 was, in fact, the germ forming the nucleus of the network still continuing under the Eastern National banner today.

In 1914, the GER decided that a motor bus service between Harwich and Dovercourt was needed in place of an old horse-bus hitherto run by a Mr Alan Gant. It was felt that an up-to-date service, in addition to catering for local traffic would, during the season, be an inducement to visitors to use the company's motor boat service to Shotley or Felixstowe Dock, and for its paddle steamer service up and down the River Orwell to and from Ipswich. Although the GER was still operating buses, it made no attempt to run the new service itself nor, surprisingly, did it arrange for the National Steam Car Company to do so. Instead, it was put out to contract with Thomas Tilling & Sons of London who opened the service on 1st April with some TTA1 petrol-electric double-decks bearing the

Great Eastern Railway Timetable of Harwich—Dovercourt Motor Omnibus Service running at March 1920 (from company timetable)

name 'Great Eastern Railway' along the side panels, but with advertisements for their own activities on the upper deck screening. The crews wore Tilling uniforms and badges and the vehicles were housed in the former GER Clacton bus garage, now moved to West Street, Harwich. Later that year, the TTA1 buses were replaced by Tilling TS3 saloons seating twenty six passengers. The service ran alternatively via Main Road or Fronks Road, both diverting to call at Dovercourt Station en route to and from Upper Dovercourt.

At the end of 1922, the GER became part of the new London & North Eastern Railway which took over the bus service, the last survivor of the former GER's motor bus department.

GREENLEAF, James   West Mersea, Essex
James Greenleaf was working his carrier's cart to Colchester by 1848 which then passed to George Death and then through three generations of Underwoods to reach Eastern National in 1935.

GREY—GREEN COACHES   Stamford Hill, London N16
In October 1967, George Ewer bought the Great Oakley—Colchester stage routes of R. W. Hooks (q.v.), so as to provide a bus connection from its East Coast—London express route for Dovercourt and Harwich at times when there was insufficient through bookings to justify running a branch coach. It was operated by Eastern National as part of the 'Essex Coast Express' pool with George Ewer's 'Grey-Green' and Sutton's Coaches of Clacton-on-Sea as service 80/80A.

GRIFFIN BUS SERVICE   West Mersea, Essex
Mr Harding ran a bus using this title in competition with the four or five established operators on the Colchester road. He sold to Victor Brown who ran the 'Bluebird' service from Tiptree in 1929 and who, in turn, sold to Thorpe Bros. (q.v.) in 1932.

GROOM, H.   Hoo Road, Meppershall, Bedfordshire
This was a small business running to Hitchin two or three times a week for shopping and the cinema, and also had excursions and tours from Henlow, all of which was acquired by C. Taylor's 'Reliance Coaches' (q.v.) in July 1934.

HADLEIGH GARAGE & TRANSPORT CO. LTD. 1A Broadway Market, Hadleigh, Essex
This company was formed by members of the Webb family to continue the business of the Leigh, Hadleigh and Rayleigh Omnibus Co. Ltd., on 18th June 1919. The service is reported to have ceased by 1922 and was taken up by the 'Thundersley, Hadleigh & District Motors'.

HADLEIGH MOTOR BUS COMPANY LTD.   Hadleigh, Essex
This company was registered on 21st October 1912 at Gloucester Mansions, Cambridge Circus, London to take over the service promoted by Commercial Car Hirers in the Leigh-on-Sea area which held 650 shares in the new company. The original Directors were H. J. Mitchell of Hadleigh (manufacturer's agent), J. Webster of Leigh (butcher) and E. P. Williams of Shenfield (solicitor). It also ran the garage attached to the Palace Hotel at Southend where a Maudslay saloon bus was kept for station work. The service passed to the Hadleigh Garage & Transport Company (q.v.). Southend Watch Committee approved transfer of the licences on 30th July 1919 with three buses comprising a Commer, a Tilling-Stevens and a Unic.

HARDING, Mr —   Orsett Grays, Essex
Mr Harding was operating a three times daily horse omnibus from the village by way of Baker Street and Socketts Heath to Grays, in connection with the train service, in the early years of the century which eventually passed to Coppin & Son (q.v.).

HARDING'S COACHES LTD.   Quebec Road, Southend-on-Sea, Essex
This company was formed by Mr A. M. Harding, prior to the sale of his charabanc business to Multiways Ltd. of Southend (q.v.). Harding started in the mid-1920s trading as 'The Motor Belle' and had licences for excursions and tours from Borough Garage in Old Southend Road and (separately) from Marine Parade. He also held an express service from Leigh/Chalkwell Schools/Westcliff (Plough) to Southend football ground, all of which passed to 'Multiways' in July 1936 with whom he continued as Traffic Manager.

HARRINGTON, A. AND S.   North Street, Halstead, Essex
On 23rd February 1914, Mr A. Harrington announced that he had purchased the late Thomas Argent's (q.v.) large omnibus 'which he will continue to operate to Braintree on Mondays, Wednesdays and Saturdays.' During 1915, the business passed into the ownership of S. Harrington who added a Sunday evening service and, in 1919, commenced to run to Sudbury for the market on Thursdays. The business continued until 1924 at which date it was still horse-drawn, and is believed to have been the last regular horse-bus service in the county. The service was continued by A. Akers' 'Bird Coaches' together with driver Eli Bacon who continued in due course with the ENOC, still driving on his old routes.

HATTON, G.   Canvey Island, Essex
One of the seventeen Canvey busmen. See under 'Canvey Auxiliary Motors'.

HEARN LTD., Pat   234 Grays Inn Road, London WC1
Pat Hearn was an early horse omnibus proprietor who belonged to the Atlas and Waterloo, the Camden Town and the King's Cross and Barnsbury Associations, and he commenced working with motor omnibuses in 1906. He found that maintenance costs were so excessive (as did many others) that the motors were withdrawn in August 1907 and he reverted to horse-buses until 1911. Later, motor charabancs and coaches were operated on an increasing scale catering especially for overseas visitors to London requiring sightseeing tours, using up to forty vehicles operating from a garage at Northdown Street, King's Cross until 1948, when the business was taken over by Tilling Transport (q.v.).

HEATH, F.C.   The Garage, West Bergholt, Essex
Fred Heath was the local garage proprietor who also had taxis and cars for hire to which, in the early 1920s, a bus was added. He advertised as 'Heath's Saloon Service' and offered eight to ten daily trips to Colchester, except on Thursdays when there was only six. After the war the service passed to George Digby (q.v.).

HELLIKER, W. C.   Motor Garage, High Street, Canvey Island, Essex
This was one of the seventeen Canvey busmen. See under 'Canvey Auxiliary Motors'.

HENDERSON, John   Ongar Road, Brentwood, Essex
John Henderson started as a taxi proprietor with his brother Alec who became a cycle dealer and John, a garage owner, later moving into bus operation with a service between Kelvedon Common—Brentwood and Warley, which passed through various hands to end

up with 'Ongar & District') (q.v.). About 1929, this operator resumed running with a short-lived service to Navestock, and another to Doddinghurst and Hook End, which flourished. This he continued until 1940 when the blitz began and, without warning, took himself and family in the bus to the fastnesses of West Wales . . . never to return. 'City' took up the service at short notice.

HENMAN, Herbert   125 Marlborough Road, Bedford, Bedfordshire
Herbert Henman was the son of James Alexander Henman, a jobmaster and horse omnibus owner at Melbourne Street, who operated a local service during the first decade of the century, ceasing when H. J. Burridge put on his motor service. Herbert seems to have started about 1919 with a converted Albion lorry, followed by an ex-Army Thornycroft and a pair of small REO charabancs. The first two were green and the latter was in blue, which perhaps accounts for Gammon (q.v.) choosing 'Blue Coach' for his fleetname when he bought the business in 1929.

HICKS BROS.   Fairfield Road, Braintree, Essex
The business can at least be traced back to Felstead in 1878 where it was originally based, and where, at that date, Charles Hicks was a farmer and Thomas Hicks was a baker and confectioner. By 1886 the latter had taken The Swan public house from whence he operated a carrier service which he probably acquired with the inn. The cart went to Chelmsford on Mondays and Fridays, to Braintree on Wednesdays and to Dunmow on Tuesdays. A second vehicle ran from the village to and from the railway station to connect with the trains about six times on weekdays. From 1890, Thomas was also listed as 'Coal Merchant and Carriage Proprietor', then, in 1902, we find Ernest Hicks running a cycle and sports shop in Felstead and the carrier service is in the hands of Mr Collingridge, who was also additionally working to Braintree on Saturdays. By 1912, Ernest had progressed to a motor cycle engineer and, by 1914, had assumed operation of the carrier service from Collingridge using a motorized vehicle. PSV records show that Belhaven and Thornycroft charabancs were purchased that year which would indicate that horses had ceased to be used. The first omnibus appears to have been a 14 seat Ford of 1918 after which many and various cars, charabancs or buses passed through their hands. By 1923, the centre of operations had moved to Fairfield Road, Braintree, the site of the present garage, erected a few years later, and which is now the present Eastern National property. Their first 'big' bus was a Dennis E bought in 1926 followed by a Leyland Lion, but many Fords, Chevrolets and 30 cwt. Dennis models had been used to develop business during the early 1920s, which included mail contracts, taxi service and private car hire work plus charabanc trips to Clacton 'as arranged'.
   The early bus services were, in the main, based on the old carrier routes, although some works services to Halstead and Witham had been introduced with a daily service between

Braintree and Bocking and a route to Bishop's Stortford on three days a week. The first big step forward came in 1928 when a frequent daily route to Chelmsford began in competition with 'National', which only ran on Wednesdays, Fridays, Saturdays and Sundays, and the route to Felstead and Dunmow now became a daily operation. Late in that year, or early in 1929, they purchased Arthur Hutley's service to Coggeshall and Colchester on which road there were two other operators, Fred Matravers red 'Victory' omnibus and the Moore Bros. green saloons. About the same time, a service to Dunmow, via Rayne or Panfield to Stebbing and Bran End was started. At Chelmsford, Hicks secured their own off-street terminal using a site in Park Road on the opposite side of the railway viaduct to the Eastern National bus station. Further progress was made in 1930 with the introduction of the express coach service to London taking a new route via Dunmow and Harlow, which avoided the road via Chelmsford, on which six or seven operators were competing for traffic, and the infrequent Felstead—Dunmow—Chelmsford service also became daily. The services worked by Mr Hitchins from Dunmow were next acquired, enabling them to give a daily service to Bishop's Stortford which was linked to provide a through route across the county to Dunmow, Braintree, Coggeshall and Colchester. On the latter section, the service became joint with 'Victory' bus which was acquired a year or two later.
   The Witham route became a frequent daily service with the take-over of the Silver End Development Company, to be followed shortly after by another operator on the same route, the 'Royal Blue' of C. S. Cummings, part of whose operations were acquired by Horn Coaches (q.v.). About this time, a portion of the small business of Leslie Charter of Stebbing and Barrett of Thaxted was included when both ceased running buses to

A fine view of Hicks garage and booking office at Braintree, control of which passed to the Company in 1950. On the forecourt stands an all-Leyland Lion LT2, which later became No. 104 in the Company fleet.

Stebbing, Lindsell, etc., the remaining parts passing to other operators. The final acquisition was the daily service of Springett and Son of Hatfield Peverel who ran thence to Witham, the Notleys and Braintree, and whose bus and garage were, one night, destroyed by fire.

Hicks Bros. was involved in a long drawn out dispute with Braintree Council which had built a new bus station in Manor Street to which they refused to transfer the buses. They failed to see why they should have to pay the Council for the use of its new facility when they themselves had gone some way to solve the Council's traffic problem by providing off-street loading/standing on its premises and at its own expense. Hicks had built a fine waiting-room, enquiry office and shop to supply passengers with their usual requirements.

In 1940, Hicks and Moore negotiated certain adjustments to their services and tour arrangements in which Hicks withdrew from the Braintree—Colchester road, and the Pattiswick service was now continued by Moore who ceased running to Bocking.

As the years went by, Hicks placed increased faith upon Leyland vehicles for their main routes, although towards the end, a number of Guy Arab models had joined the fleet. During the war period, some experiments were made with HML producer gas trailers. In 1950 Hicks Bros. sold the business to the British Transport Commission which placed it under Eastern National for management supervision until it was fully integrated in 1955. During this time, Hicks still held the licences and additional vehicles were supplied 'on hire' from the parent company in accordance with operating requirements.

Hicks had a branch establishment at Clacton-on-Sea, where the usual tours and excursions were offered during the season from a stand near the junction of Pier Avenue and Rosemary Road. Some Bedford/Duple coaches were used in the familiar blue and yellow livery. This department was not sold with the omnibus business but was retained by the family who continued operation as 'Cansdall Coaches'.

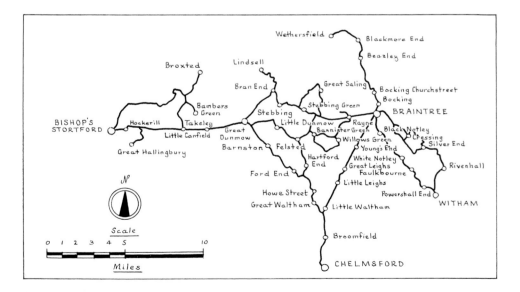

Routes worked by Hicks Bros. Ltd. — 1949

At the time of acquisition, Hicks Bros. were operating the following services:

Hicks No.	Serving	
10	Braintree—Felstead—Dunmow—Bishop's Stortford (certain trips run via Pyes Bridge)	daily
11	Braintree—Leighs—Little Waltham—Chelmsford	daily
12	Bishop's Stortford—Dunmow—Braintree—Coggeshall—Clacton-on-Sea (summer expresss service)	
14	Braintree—Witham (direct workpeoples' service)	weekdays
15	Braintree—Rayne—Great Saling—Stebbing—Bran End—Lindsell	weekdays
	or Stebbling Village/Green—Dunmow/Bishop's Stortford	Tues/Thurs.
16	Bran End—Stebbing—Felstead—Hartford End—Howe Street—Great Waltham—Chelmsford (Tues. only; starts at Felstead)	Thursdays
17	Bishop's Stortford—Takeley—Broxted—Tye Green—Burton End	Thursdays
	Bishop's Stortford—Takeley—Broxted	Saturdays
19	Braintree—Bocking—Beasley End—Blackmore End—Wethersfield	Weds/Sats.
19B	Braintree—Bocking (Courtaulds Mill)	weekdays
21	Dunmow—Ford End—Howe Street—Great Waltham—Chelmsford	daily
22	Braintree—Felstead—Dunmow—Takeley—Hatfield Broad Oak—Harlow—Epping—London (stage to Harlow, express thereafter)	daily
29	Felstead—Willows Green—Crix Green—Rayne (Swan) or Pods Lane—Braintree	Wednesdays
35	Braintree—Theobalds Corner—Cressing	daily
	Braintree—Silver End—Rivenhall—Witham (some trips to Polish Camp)	daily
49	Bishop's Stortford—Great Hallingbury	Thursdays
52	Braintree—the Notleys—Faulkbourne—Witham	daily

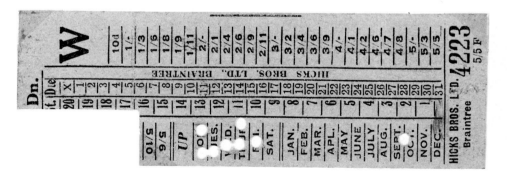

'Willibrew' weekly ticket, cut off by machine at value paid — i.e. 5/10d.; punch hole shows month issued, and daily punch cancellations — buff.

10 BISHOPS STORTFORD—BRAINTREE 10

MONDAY to FRIDAY.

	am	am	am	am	am	am	am	am	Tu P am	PW pm	pm	pm	pm	pm	NW pm	pm	pm	TO pm	pm
Stortford Dep.	......	......	7 45	8 30	8 55	9 20	1030	1130	......	......	1245	2 30	3 45	4 30	5 0	5 35	6 30	6 10	7 0
Takeley Ch.F. ,,	*	......	8 0	8 45		9 35	1045	1145	......	......	1 0	2 45	4 0	4 45	5 15	5 50	6 45	6 25	7 15
Dunmow ,,	6 35	......	8 15	9 0	†	9 50	11 0	12 0	......	......	1 15	3 0	4 15	5 0	5 30	6 5	7 0	6 40	7 30
Lt. Dunmow ,,	6 42	......	8 22	9 7		9 57	11 7	12 7	......	......	1 22	3 7	4 22	5 7	...	6 12	7 7	6 47	7 37
Felstead Ch. ,,	6 50	7 45	8 30	9 15		10 5	1115	1215	12 45	1 33	1 30	3 15	4 30	5 15	......	6 20	7 15	6 55	7 45
Rayne St. Rd. ,,	7 5	8 0	8 45	9 30		1020	1130	1230	1 0	1 45	1 45	3 30	4 45	5 30	......	6 35	7 30	7 10	8 0
Braintree Arr.	7 15	8 10	8 55	9 40		1030	1140	1240	1 10	1 55	1 55	3 40	4 55	5 40	......	6 45	7 40	7 20	8 10

ADDITIONAL JOURNEYS WEDNESDAYS (right-hand columns)

		pm	pm	pm	am	am	P pm	pm	pm	pm	pm	pm
Stortford	Dep.	......	8 20	10 0	......	......	......	......	......	......	5 10	......
Takeley Ch.F	,,	......	8 35	1015	......	......	......	......	......	......	5 25	......
Dunmow	,,	8 0	8 50	1030	......	......	......	2 10	......	......	5 40	......
Lt. Dunmow "Flitch"	,,	8 7	8 57	1037	......	......	......	2 17	......	......	......	......
Felstead Church	,,	8 15	9 5	1045	......	11 0	1 0	2 25	3 30	4 30	......	5 45
Rayne Station Road	,,	8 30	9 20	11 0	......	1115	1 15	2 40	3 45	4 45	......	6 0
Braintree	Arr.	8 40	9 30	1110	......	1125	1 25	2 50	3 55	4 55	......	6 10

	am	am	am	am	am	Tu P am	am	TO am	am	am	pm	pm	pm	pm	pm	pm	P pm	pm	pm	pm
Braintree Dep.	5 50	6 25	7 15	7 45		9 0	9 5	9 30	1015	1115	......	1230	1 30	......	2 30	4 0	4 0	5 0	5 45	6 45
Rayne St. Rd. ,,	6 0	6 35	7 25	7 55		9 10	9 15	9 40	1025	1125	......	1240	1 40	......	2 40	4 10	4 10	5 10	5 55	6 55
Felstead Ch. ,,	6 15	6 50	7 40	8 10		9 25	9 30	9 55	1040	1140	......	1255	1 55	......	2 55	4 25	4 25	5 25	6 10	7 10
Lt. Dunmow ,,	6 23	6 58	7 48	8 18		......	9 38	10 3	1048	1148	......	1 3	2 3	......	3 3	4 33	......	5 33	6 18	7 18
Dunmow ,,	6 30	7 5	7 55	8 25	†	......	9 45	1010	1055	1155	12 5	1 10	2 10	2 30	3 10	4 40	......	5 40	6 25	7 25
Takeley Ch.F ,,	......	7 20	8 10	8 40		......	10 0	1025	1110	......	1220	1 25	2 25	2 45	3 25	4 55	......	5 55	6 40	7 40
Stortford Arr.	......	7 35	8 25	8 55	9 5	......	1015	1040	1125	......	1235	1 40	2 40	3 0	3 40	5 10	......	6 10	6 55	7 55

ADDITIONAL JOURNEYS WEDNESDAYS (right-hand columns)

		pm	pm	pm	am	pm	pm	pm	P pm	pm	
Braintree	Dep.	8 15	......	1025	1030	1230	1 30	3 0	4 0	5 0	......
Rayne Station Road	,,	8 25	......	1035	1040	1240	1 40	3 10	4 10	5 10	......
Felstead Church	,,	8 40	......	1050	1055	1255	1 55	3 25	4 25	5 25	......
Lt. Dunmow "Flitch"	,,	8 48	......	1058	......	......	2 3	......	......	......	......
Du mow	,,	8 55	10 0	......	......	......	2 10	......	......	......	......
Takeley Ch.F	,,	9 10	1015	......	......	......	......	......	......	......	......
Stortford	Arr.	9 25	1030	......	......	......	......	......	......	......	......

P—These Journeys operate via Pyes Bridge

PW—From Watch House via Pyes Bridge. (Not Thursdays). *TO*—Thursdays only. *NW*—Not Wednesday. *P*—Via Pyes Bridge. (Not Thursdays). † To and From Takeley "Green Man"

Tu—Tuesdays Only.

*Connection for this journey departs Dunmow Church, 6.30 a.m. Additional journey—Braintree to Dunmow, Fridays only, depart 4.30 p.m.

ADDITIONAL JOURNEY TO HAYMEADS HOSPITAL (Tuesdays, Wednesdays and Thursdays) } Depart Bishops Stortford, "Falcon" 1.45 p.m., 3.45 p.m. Depart Haymeads Hospital, 1.55 p.m., 3.55 p.m.

SATURDAY ONLY.

		am	am	am	am	am	am	pm	P pm	pm	pm	pm
Stortford, "Falcon"	Dep.	......	......	7 45	8 30	1015	1130	1225	......	1245	......	2 0
Takeley Chaff Factory	,,	......	......	8 0	8 45	1030	1145	1240	......	1 0	......	2 15
Dunmow	,,	6 35	......	8 15	9 0	1045	12 0	1255	......	1 15	......	2 30
Lt. Dunmow "Flitch"	,,	6 42	......	8 22	9 7	1052	12 7	......	......	1 22	......	2 37
Felstead Church	,,	6 50	7 45	8 30	9 15	11 0	1215	......	1 30	1 30	2 30	2 45
Rayne, Station Road	,,	7 5	8 0	8 45	9 30	1115	1230	......	1 45	1 45	2 45	3 0
Braintree	Arr.	7 15	8 10	8 55	9 40	1125	1240	......	1 55	1 55	2 55	3 10

		pm	pm	pm	pm	pm	pm	pm	pm	pm	pm	pm
Stortford "Falcon"	Dep	......	3 15	......	4 30	......	5 45	......	7 0	8 30	......	10 0
Takeley Chaff Factory	,,	......	3 30	......	4 45	......	6 0	......	7 15	8 45	......	1015
Dunmow	,,	......	3 45	......	5 0	......	6 15	......	7 30	9 0	9 0	1030
Lt. Dunmow "Flitch"	,,	......	3 52	......	5 7	......	6 22	......	7 37	9 7	9 7	1037
Felstead Church	,,	3 45	4 0	4 45	5 15	5 45	6 30	6 45	7 45	9 15	9 15	1045
Rayne Station Road	,,	4 0	4 15	5 0	5 30	6 0	6 45	7 0	8 0	9 30	9 30	11 0
Braintree	Arr.	4 10	4 25	5 10	5 40	6 10	6 55	7 10	8 10	9 40	9 40	1110

		am	am	am	am	am	am	pm	pm	pm
Braintree	Dep.	5 50	6 25	7 15	9 0	1015	1130	1245	1 0	2 0
Rayne Station Road	,,	6 0	6 35	7 25	9 10	1025	1140	1255	1 10	2 10
Felstead Church	,,	6 15	6 50	7 40	9 25	1040	1155	1 10	1 25	2 25
Lt. Dunmow "Flitch"	,,	6 23	6 58	7 48	9 33	1048	12 3	1 18	......	2 33
Dunmow	,,	6 30	7 5	7 55	9 40	1055	1210	1 25	......	2 40
Takeley Chaff Factory	,,	......	7 20	8 10	9 55	1110	1225	1 40	......	2 55
Stortford, "Falcon"	Arr.	......	7 35	8 25	1010	1125	1240	1 55	......	3 10

		pm	pm	pm	P pm	pm	pm	pm	pm	pm	pm	pm	pm	pm
Braintree	Dep.	2 0	3 15	3 15	4 15	4 30	5 15	5 45	6 15	7 0	8 15	......	......	1025
Rayne Station Road	,,	2 10	3 25	3 25	4 25	4 40	5 25	5 55	6 25	7 10	8 25	......	......	1035
Felstead Church	,,	2 25	3 40	3 40	4 40	4 55	5 40	6 10	6 40	7 25	8 40	......	......	1050
Lt. Dunmow "Flitch"	,,	......	3 48	......	......	5 3	......	6 18	......	7 33	8 48	......	......	1058
Dunmow	,,	......	3 55	......	......	5 10	......	6 25	......	7 40	8 55	9 0	10 0	......
Takeley Chaff Factory	,,	......	4 10	......	......	5 25	......	6 40	......	7 55	......	9 15	1015	......
Stortford "Falcon"	Arr.	......	4 25	......	......	5 40	......	6 55	......	8 10	......	9 30	1030	......

P—These Journeys operate via Pyes Bridge

SUNDAY ONLY

		am	am	pm	pm	pm	pm	pm	pm	pm	pm	pm
Stortford "Falcon"	Dep.	......	1130	1245	2 15	3 15	4 30	5 45	6 25	7 10	8 30	10 0
Takeley Chaff Factory	,,	......	1145	1 0	2 30	3 30	4 45	6 0	6 40	7 25	8 45	1015
Dunmow	,,	1030	12 0	1 15	2 45	3 45	5 0	6 15	6 55	7 40	9 0	1030
Lt. Dunmow "Flitch"	,,	1037	12 7	1 22	2 52	3 52	5 7	6 22	......	7 47	9 7	1037
Felstead Church	,,	1045	1215	1 30	3 0	4 0	5 15	6 30	......	7 55	9 15	1045
Rayne Station Road	,,	11 0	1230	1 45	3 15	4 15	5 30	6 45	......	8 10	9 30	11 0
Braintree	Arr.	1110	1240	1 55	3 25	4 25	5 40	6 55	......	8 20	9 40	1110

			am	am	pm	pm	pm	pm	pm	pm	pm	pm
Braintree	Dep.	......	1015	1130	1 0	2 0	3 15	4 30	5 45	7 5	8 25	1025
Rayne Station Road	,,	......	1025	1140	1 10	2 10	3 25	4 40	5 55	7 15	8 35	1035
Felstead Church	,,	......	1040	1155	1 25	2 25	3 40	4 55	6 10	7 30	8 50	1050
Lt. Dunmow "Flitch"	,,	......	1048	12 3	1 33	2 33	3 48	5 3	6 18	7 38	8 58	1058
Dunmow	,,	......	1055	1210	1 40	2 40	3 55	5 10	6 25	7 45	9 5	..
Takeley Chaff Factory	,,	......	1110	1225	1 55	2 55	4 10	5 25	6 40	8 0	9 20	......
Stortford "Falcon"	Arr.	......	1125	1240	2 10	3 10	4 25	5 40	6 55	8 15	9 35	......

HICKS BROS., LTD

11 BRAINTREE—CHELMSFORD Via LEIGHS, WALTHAM and BROOMFIELD 11

MONDAY TO FRIDAY INCLUSIVE.

		am	P	am	am	am	am	am	am	am	am	pm	pm	pm	pm
Braintree	Dep.	6 35	6 55	7 15	8 0	8 15	9 0	9 45	1030	11 0	1130	1230	1 30	2 0	2 30
Green Dragon	,,	6 42	7 2	7 22	8 7	8 22	9 7	9 52	1037	11 7	1137	1237	1 37	2 7	2 37
St. Anne's Castle	,,	6 48	7 8	7 28	8 13	8 28	9 13	9 58	1043	1113	1143	1243	1 43	2 13	2 43
Chatham Green	,,	6 54	7 14	7 34	8 19	8 34	9 19	10 4	1049	1119	1149	1249	1 49	2 19	2 49
Ash Tree Corner	,,	7 0	7 20	7 40	8 25	8 40	9 25	1010	1055	1125	1155	1255	1 55	2 25	2 55
Angel, Broomfield	,,	7 7	7 27	7 47	8 32	8 47	9 32	1017	11 2	1132	12 2	1 2	2 2	2 32	3 2
Broomfield Lodge	,,	7 10	7 30	7 50	8 35	8 50	9 35	1020	11 5	1135	12 5	1 5	2 5	2 35	3 5
Chelmsford, E.N. O'bus Stn.	Arr.	7 15	7 35	7 55	8 40	8 55	9 40	1025	1110	1140	1210	1 10	2 10	2 40	3 10

		pm	pm	pm	pm	pm	pm	pm	pm	pm	pm	pm
Braintree	Dep.	3 0	3 30	4 0	4 30	5 0	5 50	6 30	6 45	7 30	8 15	9 30
Green Dragon	,,	3 7	3 37	4 7	4 37	5 7	5 57	6 37	6 52	7 37	8 22	9 37
St. Annes Castle	,,	3 13	3 43	4 13	4 43	5 13	6 3	6 43	6 58	7 43	8 28	9 43
Chatham Green	,,	3 19	3 49	4 19	4 49	5 19	6 9	6 49	7 4	7 49	8 34	9 49
Ash Tree Corner	,,	3 25	3 55	4 25	4 55	5 25	6 15	6 55	7 10	7 55	8 40	9 55
Angel, Broomfield	,,	3 32	4 2	4 32	5 2	5 32	6 22	7 2	7 17	8 2	8 47	10 2
Broomfield Lodge	,,	3 35	4 5	4 35	5 5	5 35	6 25	7 5	7 20	8 5	8 50	10 5
Chelmsford, E.N. O'bus Stn.	Arr.	[illegible]	[illegible]	[illegible]	[illegible]	[illegible]	[illegible]	[illegible]	[illegible]	[illegible]	[illegible]	[illegible]

Chelmsford, E.N. O'bus Stn.	Dep.	[illegible]
Broomfield Lodge	,,	[illegible]
Angel, Broomfield	,,	[illegible]
Ash Tree Corner	,,	[illegible]
Chatham Green	,,	[illegible]
St. Anne's Castle	,,	[illegible]
Green Dragon	,,	[illegible]
Braintree	Arr.	[illegible]

Chelmsford, E.N. O'bus Stn.	Dep.	[illegible]
Broomfield Lodge	,,	[illegible]
Angel, Broomfield	,,	[illegible]
Ash Tree Corner	,,	[illegible]
Chatham Green	,,	[illegible]
St. Annes Castle	,,	[illegible]
Green Dragon	,,	[illegible]
Braintree	Arr.	[illegible]

SATURDAY

Braintree	Dep.	[illegible]
Green Dragon	,,	[illegible]
St. Annes Castle	,,	[illegible]
Chatham Green	,,	[illegible]
Ash Tree Corner	,,	[illegible]
Angel, Broomfield	,,	[illegible]
Broomfield Lodge	,,	[illegible]
Chelmsford, E.N. O'bus Stn.	Arr.	[illegible]

Braintree	Dep.	[illegible]
Green Dragon	,,	[illegible]
St. Anne's Castle	,,	[illegible]
Chatham Green	,,	[illegible]
Ash Tree Corner	,,	[illegible]
Angel, Broomfield	,,	[illegible]
Broomfield Lodge	,,	[illegible]
Chelmsford E.N. O'bus Stn.	Arr.	[illegible]

Chelmsford, E.N. O'bus Stn.	Dep.	[illegible]
Broomfield Lodge	,,	[illegible]
Angel, Broomfield	,,	[illegible]
Ash Tree Corner	,,	[illegible]
Chatham Green	,,	[illegible]
St. Anne's Castle	,,	[illegible]
Green Dragon	,,	[illegible]
Braintree	Arr.	[illegible]

		pm	pm	pm	pm	pm	pm	pm	pm	pm	pm	pm	pm	pm
Chelmsford, E.N. O'bus Stn.	Dep.	[illegible]	[illegible]	[illegible]	[illegible]	[illegible]	[illegible]	[illegible]	[illegible]	[illegible]	[illegible]	[illegible]	[illegible]	[illegible]
Broomfield Lodge	,,	3 50	4 20	4 50	5 20	5 50	6 20	6 50	7 20	7 50	8 20	9 5	9 55	1030
Angel, Broomfield	,,	3 53	4 23	4 53	5 23	5 53	6 23	6 53	7 23	7 53	8 23	9 8	9 58	1033
Ash Tree Corner	,,	4 0	4 30	5 0	5 30	6 0	6 30	7 0	7 30	8 0	8 30	9 15	10 5	1040
Chatham Green	,,	4 6	4 36	5 6	5 36	6 6	6 36	7 6	7 36	8 6	8 36	9 21	1011	1046
St. Annes Castle	,,	4 12	4 42	5 12	5 42	6 12	6 42	7 12	7 42	8 12	8 42	9 27	1017	1052
Green Dragon	,,	4 18	4 48	5 18	5 48	6 18	6 48	7 18	7 48	8 18	8 48	9 33	1023	1058
Braintree	Arr.	4 25	4 55	5 25	5 55	6 25	6 55	7 25	7 55	8 25	8 55	9 40	1030	11 5

P—Priority Journeys—Priority given to Weekly Ticket holders.

PF—Priority given as above, on Fridays only.

During School Terms only the following additional journeys will operate. Monday to Friday—Depart, Chelmsford for Braintree 4.5 p.m. Depart, Broomfield Hospital for Chelmsford 8.40 a.m.

Works Service—Depart, Hoffmanns for Braintree, Monday to Thursday, 5.20 p.m.; Friday, 5.35 p.m. Depart, Marconis for Braintree, Monday to Friday, 5.35 p.m.

SUNDAY

		am	am	am	pm	pm	pm	pm	pm	pm	pm	pm	pm	pm
Braintree	Dep.	6 40	9 0	10 0	12 0	1 0	2 0	3 0	4 0	5 0	6 0	6 30	7 30	8 15
Green Dragon	,,	6 47	9 7	10 7	12 7	1 7	2 7	3 7	4 7	5 7	6 7	6 37	7 37	8 22
St. Anne's Castle	,,	6 53	9 13	1013	1213	1 13	2 13	3 13	4 13	5 13	6 13	6 43	7 43	8 28
Chatham Green	,,	6 59	9 19	1019	1219	1 19	2 19	3 19	4 19	5 19	6 19	6 49	7 49	8 34
Ash Tree Corner	,,	7 5	9 25	1025	1225	1 25	2 25	3 25	4 25	5 25	6 25	6 55	7 55	8 40
Angel, Broomfield	,,	7 12	9 32	1032	1232	1 32	2 32	3 32	4 32	5 32	6 32	7 2	8 2	8 47
Broomfield Lodge	,,	7 15	9 35	1035	1235	1 35	2 35	3 35	4 35	5 35	6 35	7 5	8 5	8 50
Chelmsford, E.N. O'bus Stn.	Arr.	[illegible]	[illegible]	[illegible]	[illegible]	[illegible]	[illegible]	[illegible]	[illegible]	[illegible]	[illegible]	[illegible]	[illegible]	[illegible]

Chelmsford, E.N. O'bus Stn.	Dep.	[illegible]
Broomfield Lodge	,,	[illegible]
Angel, Broomfield	,,	[illegible]
Ash Tree Corner	,,	[illegible]
Chatham Green	,,	[illegible]
St. Anne's Castle	,,	[illegible]
Green Dragon	,,	[illegible]
Braintree	Arr.	[illegible]

SERVICES INDEX.

Service No.	Places Served.
10.	Braintree, Rayne, Felstead, Dunmow, Takeley, Stortford.
11.	Braintree, Leighs, Little Waltham, Broomfield, Chelmsford.
14.	Braintree, Witham Direct. (Works Service only.)
15.	Braintree, Stebbing, Lindsell, Dunmow, Stortford.
16.	Stebbing, Felstead, Chelmsford.
17.	Broxted, Tye Green, Stortford.
19.	Braintree, Bocking, Wethersfield.
21.	Dunmow, Ford End, Howe Street, Great Waltham, Broomfield, Chelmsford
22.	Braintree, Felstead, Dunmow, Takeley, Sheering, London.
29.	Felstead, Willows Green, Braintree.
35.	Braintree, Silver End, Witham.
52.	Braintree, Notleys, Witham.

15 BRAINTREE—STEBBING—DUNMOW. BISHOP'S STORTFORD 15

WEEK-DAYS ONLY

			WS am	NT pm	TO pm	T pm	NT pm	SO pm	NS pm	SO pm
Braintree Bus Park	Dep	......	10 0	1245	1230	......	3 45	5 30	5 45	10 0
Rayne Station Road	,,	......	1010	1255	1240	......	3 55	5 40	5 55	1010
Saling "Oak"	,,	......	1015	1 0	1245	......	4 0	5 45	6 0	1015
Great Saling Church	,,	......	1020	1 5	1250	......	4 5	5 50	6 5	1020
Andrews' Field	,,	......	1025	1 10	1255	......	4 10	5 55	6 10	1025
Stebbing Green	,,	......	......	......	......	1 50	......	......	......	......
Stebbing "White Hart"	,,	......	1035	1 20	1 5	1 55	4 20	6 5	6 20	1035
Stebbing Bran End	,,	......	1040	1 25	1 10	2 0	4 25	6 10	6 25	1040
Linsell, Priors Hall	,,	......	1047	1 32	......	......	4 32	......	......	......
Dunmow	,,	......	......	......	1 25	2 15	......	......	......	......
Takeley Chaff Factory	,,	......	......	......	1 40	......	......	......	......	......
Bishop's Stortford	Arr	......	......	......	1 55	......	......	......	......	......

		am	WS am	NT pm	T pm	NT pm	TO pm	SO pm	WO pm	
Bishop's Stortford	Dep	......	......	......	......	......	4 0	......	......	......
Takeley Chaff Factory	,,	......	......	......	......	......	4 15	......	......	......
Dunmow	,,	......	......	......	3 45	......	4 30	......	......	......
Linsell, Priors Hall	,,	......	1050	1 33	......	4 33	......	......	......	......
Stebbing Bran End	,,	6 35	1057	1 40	4 0	4 40	4 45	6 15	6 25	......
Stebbing "White Hart"	,,	6 40	11 2	1 45	4 5	4 45	4 50	6 20	6 30	......
Stebbing Green	,,	......	......	......	4 10	......	......	......	......	......
Andrews' Field	,,	6 50	1112	1 55	......	4 55	5 0	6 30	6 40	......
Great Saling Church	,,	6 55	1117	2 0	......	5 0	5 5	6 35	6 45	......
Saling "Oak"	,,	7 0	1122	2 5	......	5 5	5 10	6 40	6 50	......
Rayne Station Road	,,	7 5	1127	2 10	......	5 10	5 15	6 45	6 55	......
Braintree Bus Park	Arr	7 15	1137	2 20	......	5 20	5 25	6 55	7 5	......

WS—Wednesday and Saturday. *T*—Tuesday only. *WO*—Wednesday only. *TO*—Thursday only. *SO*—Saturday only. *NT*—Not Thursday. *NS*—Not Saturday.

16 STEBBING and CHELMSFORD Via FELSTEAD 16

		FO am	TO am	FO pm
Stebbing Bran End	Dep.	9 15	......	1250
Stebbing "White Hart"	,,	9 20	......	1255
Stebbing Green	,,	9 25	......	1 0
Felstead Church	,,	9 35	9 25	1 10
"Apple Trees"	,,	9 39	9 29	1 14
Howe Street	,,	9 43	9 33	1 18
"Six Bells"	,,	9 46	9 36	1 21
Ash Tree Corner	,,	9 50	9 40	1 25
"Angel," Broomfield	,,	9 57	9 47	1 32
Broomfield Lodge	,,	10 0	9 50	1 35
Chelmsford, E.N. Bus Stn.	Arr.	10 5	9 55	1 40

		FO Noon	TO pm	FO pm
Chelmsford, E.N. Bus Stn.	Dep.	12 0	1215	3 45
Broomfield Lodge	,,	12 5	1220	3 50
"Angel," Broomfield	,,	12 8	1223	3 53
Ash Tree Corner	,,	12 15	1230	4 0
"Six Bells"	,,	12 19	1234	4 4
Howe Street	,,	12 22	1237	4 7
"Apple Trees"	,,	12 26	1241	4 11
Felstead Church	,,	12 30	1245	4 15
Stebbing Green	,,	12 40	......	4 25
Stebbing "White Hart"	,,	12 45	......	4 30
Stebbing Bran End	Arr.	12 50	......	4 35

FO—Fridays Only. *TO*—Tuesdays Only.

17 BROXTED—TYE GREEN—STORTFORD. 17

THURSDAY ONLY

		am	pm	pm		pm
Stortford	Dep	1045	1230	1 30	......	4 0
Takeley "Four Ashes"	,,	11 0	1245	1 45	......	4 15
Broxted Church	,,	1115	1 0	2 0	......	4 30
Tye Green	,,	1125	......	......	......	......
Burton End	,,	1135	......	......	......	......
Stortford	Arr	1145	......	......	......	......

			pm	pm	pm	pm
Stortford	Dep	......	......	......	3 0	......
Burton End	,,	......	......	......	3 10	......
Tye Green	,,	......	......	......	3 20	......
Broxted Church	,,	......	1 0	2 0	3 30	4 30
Takeley "Four Ashes"	,,	......	1 15	2 15	3 45	4 45
Stortford	Arr	......	1 30	2 30	4 0	5 0

SATURDAY ONLY

		pm	pm	pm	pm
Stortford	Dep	2 55	4 45	8 15	10 0
Takeley	,,	3 10	5 0	8 30	10 5
Broxted	Arr	3 25	5 15	8 45	1030

		pm	pm	pm	pm
Broxted	Dep	2 5	3 30	5 15	8 50
Takeley	,,	2 20	3 45	5 30	9 5
Stortford	Arr	2 35	4 0	5 45	9 20

19 W BRAINTREE—WETHERSFIELD 19 W

WEDNESDAYS AND SATURDAYS

		am	Noon	pm	pm	* pm	pm	pm
Braintree, Bus Park	Dep.	10 0	12 0	2 0	4 0	5 22	6 0	8 45
Gauden Road	,,	10 5	12 5	2 5	4 5	5 27	6 5	8 50
Bocking (Courtaulds	,,	10 8	12 8	2 8	4 8	5 30	6 8	8 53
Bovington Hall	,,	10 12	12 12	2 12	4 12	5 34	6 12	8 57
Beasley End	,,	10 16	12 16	2 16	4 16	5 38	6 16	9 1
Blackmore End	,,	10 20	12 20	2 20	4 20	5 42	6 20	9 5
Wethersfield ("The Dog")	Arr.	10 28	12 28	2 28	4 28	5 50	6 28	9 13

		* am	am	pm	pm	pm	pm	pm
Wethersfield ("The Dog")	Dep.	7 0	10 30	12 30	2 30	4 30	6 30	9 15
Blackmore End	,,	7 8	10 38	12 38	2 38	4 38	6 38	9 23
Beasley End	,,	7 12	10 42	12 42	2 42	4 42	6 42	9 27
Bovington Hall	,,	7 16	10 46	12 46	2 46	4 46	6 46	9 31
Bocking (Courtaulds)	,,	7 20	10 50	12 50	2 50	4 50	6 50	9 35
Gauden Road	,,	7 23	10 53	12 53	2 53	4 53	6 53	9 38
Braintree (Bus Park)	Arr.	7 28	10 58	12 58	2 58	4 58	6 58	9 43

* Operates on Mondays to Fridays inclusive.

Above and overleaf: Reduced facsimile of Hicks Bros. roadside poster timetables. One of the last issued.

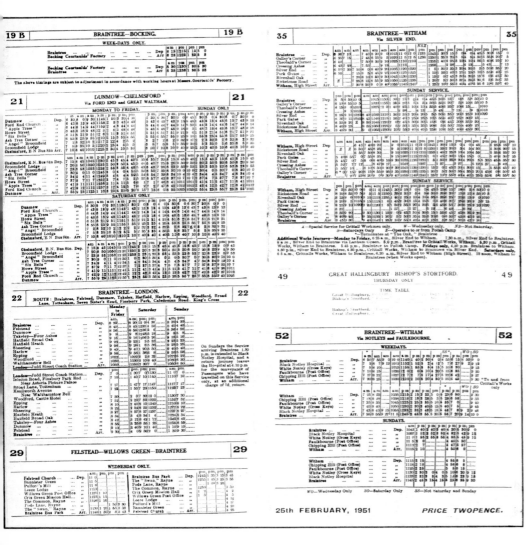

Left: 'Speed Setright' printed for single fare of 1/2d. — red print on yellow paper roll.

HILLIAR, A. C.   Canvey Island, Essex

A member of the seventeen Canvey Island Bus Owners' Association (q.v.) and for a short time was the Chairman of the later 'Canvey & District Motor Transport Company'.

HILLMAN'S SALOON COACHES LTD./EDWARD HILLMAN   52b/c Romford Road London E15

EDWARD HILLMAN'S SALOON COACHES LTD.   London Road, Romford, Essex

The meteoric rise and even more rapid demise of Edward Hillman's coaching activities is one of the more colourful stories to emerge from the 'golden age' of the motor bus/ coach, much of which, however, falls outside the scope of this volume as only a small part of his enterprise was acquired by the ENOC. Suffice it to say here, that Hillman began operations in 1928 with a single coach and had, by 1933, about 120 vehicles in service. In little over twelve months there was nothing left. The key to his success was the provision of a quality through service from East London to Chelmsford which the ENOC could not provide because of its agreement with the LGOC. By May 1929, he was giving sixteen daily journeys with new Gilford coaches carrying truly luxurious body-work, such as the public had not before seen on a local bus service.

The LGOC were, at this time, still using open-top S types and the ENOC's Leyland Lions, although speedy and reliable, were definitely very spartan by comparison. The high floor line and old-fashioned rear entrance with a hinged door did not have the same appeal as the latest low loading front entrance coaches, with sliding door, thick floor covering, parcel shelves, attractive light fittings, curtains, clock, etc., so it is therefore not surprising that the public was completely captivated by them. They flocked to ride upon a Hillman coach and it was not long before the old established operators and, finally, the railway found they had lost a very large part of their traffic to the new mode of travel. This, of course, went on in many other places too, and Hillman had his imitators. Some survived and others he acquired, including Evans Coaches and Eastward Coaches (q.v.). He soon extended beyond Chelmsford to Colchester and Clacton and beyond, which the ENOC sought to acquire, as related in *Chapter Two*.

When the service reached its zenith in 1933, there were fifty one daily departures from Bow to Chelmsford, of which fifteen continued on to Colchester and three to Clacton-on-Sea, disregarding those going still further into East Anglia.

The beginning of the end came on 10th January 1934 when his Upminster section was compulsorily acquired by the LPTB together with thirty one coaches, and the Bow to Brentwood section with twenty eight coaches, and his Romford garage and offices. Hillman was now left with the Bow—Chelmsford timings (and those going beyond) but could no longer carry any local traffic west of Brentwood. Hillman's success had naturally not endeared him to the other operators or the railway which now mounted heavy opposition in the traffic courts, leading to further restrictions on the long distance coaches when licences came up for renewal.

Determined to stay in public transport, Hillman turned to air travel and opened his own aerodrome at Maylands between Romford and Brentwood. This he found much more to his liking than operating coaches under the new conditions, so he sold off the remainder by agreement, to concentrate fully on Hillman's Airways which flourished for a few years to become the nucleus, with others, of British Airways. Today Maylands Aerodrome is a golf course and nothing is now left to serve as a reminder of Hillman's enterprise.

HINDS, H. J. & CO./HINDS & SAVAGE   Wardown Garage, Old Bedford Road, Luton, Bedfordshire

See under 'Bluebird'.

HINSBY, J. and S. St. Neots, Huntingdonshire

This business, acquired by the ENOC in 1931, has been traced back to 1877 when James and Samuel Hinsby, trading from Huntingdon Street, St. Neots as corn dealers, also provided a carrier service for goods and passengers to Bedford on Mondays, Wednesdays and Saturdays, the cart returning the same day. By 1885, the same partners had added a steam flour mill to their activities, and ten years later were manufacturing chemical manure and were proprietors of threshing machines. By 1914 they, or presumably their successors trading under the same name, were also engaged in farming but had now replaced the carriers cart with a Leyland double-deck bus. This they worked in competition with London General which had not long taken over the 'Central' company's Bedford depot, later to become part of the ENOC. By 1924, an agreement had been signed between 'National' and Messrs Hinsby, and the Bedford—St. Neots services became jointly operated. Hinsbys also ran a few market services by agreement, which are detailed in the main text. In 1931, Hinsbys gave up their bus interests and sold the services and five vehicles to the ENOC.

Truly a vintage Leyland S4 circa 1912/13 which Eastern National acquired from Hinsby in October 1931, allocating the fleet number 3283!

HISCOCK, V. D. Small Gains, Canvey Island, Essex

This operator was in business as early as 1922 serving as a motor and marine engineer and a bus proprietor, probably using the garage work hack for the purpose when it was necessary to go to Benfleet. In 1926 he bought a new Chevrolet which the Council refused to licence until he agreed to conform to the timetable having hitherto steadfastly refused. Later, he was a Director of the Canvey & District Motor Transport Company until displaced by MacDermott Roe.

HITCHINS, — Dunmow, Essex

One of the many small owners running bus/carrier services in North Essex. His operations were taken over by Hicks just prior to the 1931 licensing and consisted of Dunmow—Bishop's Stortford, via two or three different routes, Dunmow—Chelmsford, Dunmow—Braintree and Dunmow—Eastons—Duton Hill (circular). Hitchins joined Hicks who employed him as inspector.

HOLMES, Charles and George Royal Mews and Alexandra Mews, Southend, Essex

These brothers, whose family were carriers at Maldon as far back as the 1840s, came to Southend in the 1890s to take over the business of jobmasters, carriage hirers and coach brake proprietors at the above address. Their horses and equipages were of the highest standard for private driving, hiring for weddings or to the local undertakers for funerals, complete with hearse. About 1908, they combined with Sydney Smith who owned a similar business which included operating a horse-bus service. They formed a new company entitled Charles and George Holmes and Sydney Smith Ltd., and part of Peter Trigg's charabanc business was also included. When, in 1911, others were beginning to get motorized, they maintained their position by introducing some Thornycroft torpedo charabancs. About 1914, there were proposals for a large London-financed consortium to commence services in the Southend district, so they joined with the rival 'Royal Blue Cars' of the Southend-on-Sea Charabanc Co. Ltd. which changed its name in 1921 to the more familiar Westcliff Motor Services Ltd. The hiring and carriage side of the business was separated to come under another company trading as Holmes and Smith Ltd. (q.v.).

HOLMES & SMITH LTD. Pier Hill, Southend-on-Sea, Essex

This company continued the carriage and car hire section of Charles and George Holmes and Sydney Smith Ltd., later developing into motor garaging and coachwork. For a short time they also held the Westcliff excursions and tours section based at Walthamstow. It was also owner of the Pier Hill Coach Station of which 'Westcliff' was a tenant. The business is still trading today as part of the Curry Motor Group.

HOOKS BROS., R. W. The Garage, Great Oakley, Essex

This business was in being in 1919 as Hooks Brothers and, by 1923, a bus was serving Colchester via Wix and Elmstead on certain days only, and to Manningtree and Ipswich twice weekly. By 1931, it was owned by R. W. Hooks solus, who obtained the following numbered licences, that for service 3 being refused.

1	Great Oakley—Bradfield—Mistley—Ipswich	Tue/Fri.
2	Great Oakley—Wix—Tendring—Mistley—Ipswich (express)	Tue/Fri.
3	The Oakleys—Clacton-on-Sea	Thursdays
4	Great Oakley—Wrabness—Clacton-on-Sea	Thursdays
5	Great Oakley—Harwich	Mon/Fri.
6	Great Oakley—Wix—Beaumont—Tendring—Elmstead—Colchester	Weds/Sats.
7	Great Oakley—Horsley Cross—Little Bentley—Elmstead—Colchester	Mons/Weds/Sats.
8	Excursions and tours from Great Oakley	
9	(later) Dovercourt—Oakleys—Wix—Tendring or Goose Green—Horsley Cross—Little Bentley—Colchester	Mon—Fri.
	and the Severalls Hospital	Sundays

At 1951 Hooks was working services 1 and 2 as above, but services 5 and 6 now started from Stone's Green, service 7 started at Little Oakley (and Wix on Wednesdays and Saturdays only) and service 9 omitted Goose Green but called at Great Bromley on Mondays to Fridays. The Stone's Green working had been acquired from Everson of Wix in 1939.

In December 1946, a serious fire destroyed most of the Hooks fleet which he was able to replace quickly by securing five buses from the 'City Coach Company', Brentwood, comprising two Albions (formerly Ongar & District), one Commer and a Dodge ex-'City', plus an old Leyland Lion (formerly Yorkshire Traction) from which he managed to extract a further eight years service!

In 1961 he took over Everson's school contracts but before selling the Colchester services to 'Grey-Green', in 1967, had discontinued the Ipswich routes. A glance at Hooks' note heading will at once reveal his versatility and flexibility, which enabled so many village bus owners to reduce overheads and permit continuation of bus services long after they would have ordinarily been uneconomic for a larger operator.

R. W. HOOKS

A.M.Inst.B.E.

Bus Services:
Colchester, Twice Daily except Sundays, from Mayes Lane, Little Oakley.
Ipswich, Tuesdays and Fridays, from Mayes Lane, Little Oakley.
Harwich and Dovercourt, Mondays and Fridays.

THE GARAGE, GREAT OAKLEY, ESSEX.

32, 29, 26 and 20-Seater Buses for Hire, also 7-Seater Taxi.

Motor & Cycle Agent. Agent for Royal Enfield, New Hudson, Rudge-Whitworth, Elswick, Raleigh, B.S.A., Triumph, Humber, & James Cycles & Motor Cycles. Any make supplied. Hire-Purchase Terms on all Makes. Good Price allowed on old Cycle. Gramophone Repairs. Wireless Stockists. Agent for Cossor. Prams Re-tyred

'Phone: RAMSEY 49.   October 15th, 194 7

Facsimile reprint of the Hooks letter heading mentioned in the text above.

HORN MOTOR COACH CO.   Horn Hotel Garage, Braintree, Essex

C. M. Taylor, who founded this business in the late 1920s, observed the need for improved travel facilities to the villages in the Upper Blackwater Valley, which were still only served by Ben Adams' carrier service and the ENOC's Wednesday market bus. He put on a successful daily service between Braintree and Great Bardfield and was quick to observe the business which Akers was doing with his 'Bird Coaches' from local villages to London, so he followed suit by giving six daily through services, later settling to four or five. He started a few other routes and, when licensing was introduced, made application for the following:

1 Great Bardfield—Braintree—London, express from Braintree
2 Excursions and tours from Braintree
3 Great Bardfield—Saffron Walden
4 Braintree—Felstead (Beet Sugar Factory)
5 Braintree—Greenstead Green
6 Braintree—Pattiswick
   and later
7 to extend service 1 from Great Bardfield to Great Sampford which resulted as follows:

Emblem carried on the Horn Coaches and used in its timetables.

Services 1, 3, 4, 5 and 7 were granted (1, it is believed, included Ben Adams' service); 2 and 6 were refused; 3 was soon withdrawn, probably unremunerative; 5 had been taken over from 'Royal Blue' (q.v.) and 7 had been acquired from T. Sullens & Son.

The Horn business passed to the ENOC on 24th August 1935 with six coaches, four Gilfords and two AEC Regals. They sported a golden-buff livery with a golden post horn adorning the side and rear panels. The Horn garage in Rayne Road was also taken over and used as a body/paint shop, the Braintree services being worked from Halstead garage.

HUGGINS, —   Stanford-le-Hope, Essex

This was one of the smaller proprietors in the Grays area, trading as the 'Victory Bus', working from Grays—Stanford-le-Hope—Fobbing/Thames Haven. He did not try for licences in 1931 but, instead, threw his lot in with Stanford Motors (q.v.), who were operating almost identical services.

HUNTINGDON COACHES LTD.   Houghton, Huntingdonshire

This company was formed by Harold Donne on 9th March 1931 to trade as the 'Don Motor Hire Service' which held licences for stage operation between St. Ives and Huntingdon, via Houghton, daily, from St. Ives to RAF Wyton, and for excursions and tours from Houghton for which Eastern National applied on 7th February 1938. Transfer was effected on 28th March with one TSM BIOA saloon included in the deal.

HUNWICK, Arthur   Coggeshall, Essex

There were members of the Hunwick family working on the Colchester—Coggeshall road as far back as 1848 using horse-drawn conveyances. They continued through to about 1919 when the trade was taken over by Arthur Hutley (q.v.). For some years, they also operated a horse-drawn bus to Kelvedon Station to meet the trains and this later passed to Moore Bros. of that town.

HUTLEY'S MOTOR BUS SERVICE   Church Street, Coggeshall, Essex

This was a pioneer operator of motor buses who bought one of the very first B type double-decks to be released by the LGOC to private owners in 1913. His main route was always Braintree—Coggeshall—Colchester, except on Fridays when he ran via Earls Colne to Colchester, and via Halstead to Braintree on Wednesdays. On Tuesdays, during the summer, the bus went through to Clacton. In 1928, by which time his vehicle would be fourteen years old, he decided to sell the route to Hicks, so enabling him to concentrate on his other activity of cartage and removals for which he owned a pair of lorries. The bus was in a bright blue livery and nicely lined out.

IDEAL BUS COMPANY Elstow Road, Bedford, Bedfordshire

The above fleetname was adopted by E. J. Cooper whose main activity was a local route in Bedford from the Southend Hotel to High Street and Queens Park, following the same route as the ENOC service 33. It is not known when his service commenced but his timetable first appeared in Timaeus' Bedford Almanac of 1928, which shows he was providing a service every forty minutes. On Sunday afternoons, his bus ran from each outer terminal to the Bedford cemetery. Later, H. H. Clench's 'Dreadnought' buses appeared on this route amongst his various operations, whereupon 'National' and 'Ideal' closed ranks and worked to a co-ordinated timetable in order to meet this competition. As a result of numerous complaints, Bedford Corporation refused to licence Clench after 1929. It is thought the 'Dreadnought' timings were shared 'pro-rata' between the ENOC and 'Ideal'. In 1931, the 'Ideal' service was in the hands of Cecil Cooper who obtained a licence for it and for excursions and tours but, by about the year end, the entire business had passed to the ENOC who provided a ten minute service from January 1932. Three extra trips per hour were introduced on Fridays and Saturdays, the whole being incorporated into services 33, 33A and 33B. No vehicles were acquired, and it is thought they went to Mr G. O. Gammond, proprietor of 'Blue Coach Service', Bedford (q.v.).

INTERMEDIATE BUS SERVICE Brentwood, Essex

This was started by Len Knight (circa 1926/7) using a 14 seat Ford T bus in blue livery on various local routes in between other operators' timings — hence the title. He gradually settled on to the Brentwood—Kelvedon Common route until 1929 when the Council refused to licence his bus any longer due to its poor condition. 'Ongar & District' took up his times and Knight became a driver for 'Green Line Coaches' which was just getting under way at that time.

JELLEY, Malcolm E. Cosgrove, Northants.

Malcolm Jelley operated services around Stony Stratford and Leighton Buzzard. In 1933, the ENOC commenced negotiations to purchase him along with others, in conjunction with the UCOC as detailed in *Chapter Two*. His services all passed to the UCOC on 26th February 1934, but two market services in the Leighton Buzzard area were transferred to the ENOC on 6th March 1934, after operation by the UCOC for one week, which became new service 16B and part of existing 18A.

JOHNSON, R. H. K. Woodlands, Colne Engaine, Essex

Johnson was a late starter when he secured a licence in March 1932 to continue 'The Reliance' service from Halstead to Hedinghams of Mr M. Pudney, who had earlier been refused. In the following August, he was able to obtain licences for a service from Colne Engaine to Halstead and for a market bus from the Maplesteads to Braintree, via Pebmarsh, Greenstead Green and Penny Pot. After two years of working, he sold the service to the ENOC in June 1934 together with one 14 seat Chevrolet saloon.

JONES & HARRIS Rowhedge, Essex

Edgar Jones and Benjamin Harris were carriers on the Rowhedge—Colchester road before World War I, and set up at the Prince of Wales with their cart. The service passed later to Mr C. N. Warner who continued the operation with a small omnibus. In 1939, his times were incorporated into the Eastern National timetable. No vehicles were acquired.

KEELING, F. W. Queens Hotel, Grays, Essex

F. W. Keeling was the partner with E. Adams operating 'The Local Bus' between Grays and Nutberry Estate, which Eastern National acquired in March 1933 for incorporation into its own similar service 32A.

KEMP, John & Son Tillingham, Essex

The only regular service operated by the above operator was a market run on Fridays from Bradwell-on-Sea to Chelmsford, which was acquired by the ENOC in early 1934. The Kemps were mainly engaged in agricultural haulage work and also a little private hire.

KERSHAW, A. J. Wickford, Essex

Beyond knowing that he secured licences for two services which were acquired by Davies of Ramsden Bellhouse (circa 1932), nothing else has been traced of this operator's business.

LAINDON & DISTRICT MOTOR SERVICE Laindon, Essex

J. F. Hinton/Hinton Bros. started running with two or three B type ex-LGOC open-top double-decks about 1921. The main route was a daily circular run from Laindon Station to the Pipps Hill area, supplemented by running buses to Chelmsford, Wickford or Romford on market days and to Brentwood on Saturdays. His business was acquired by Tom Webster of Laindon who traded as 'Old Tom Motor Service'.

LAKE, G. W. Canvey Island, Essex

This operator was a member of the 'Canvey Auxiliary Motors' (q.v.).

LEGGETT DYER & CO. LTD. Kingsway Garage, Dovercourt Bay, Essex

Samuel Legget was working as a cartage contractor soon after World War I, and his business appears to have been the precursor of that formed in 1924 as per title above, trading as motor engineers in Kingsway to which, by 1929, a haulage and charabanc department had been added. They also provided a scheduled goods and passenger service from Harwich Fountain to Thorpe-le-Soken on Mondays, to Ipswich on Tuesdays, Thursdays and Fridays, and to Colchester on Saturdays. When the new licensing came into force, they opted to continue as goods hauliers only, but obtained two licences for excursions and tours for Dovercourt Bay and for Parkeston Quay, which were taken over in June 1937 without the coaches.

LEIGH, HADLEIGH and RAYLEIGH OMNIBUS CO. LTD.

Little is known about this concern which was formed circa 1912 to run as per its title. Towards the end of 1918, the service passed to Hadleigh Garage and Transport Co. Ltd. (q.v.). Service was maintained during the war period using a bus fitted with a coal gas container.

LION COACHES LTD. High Street, Ongar, Essex

This operator commenced daily services between Epping Town, Ongar and Chelmsford, and also between Blackmore and Chelmsford in competition with the ENOC which only operated these routes on Fridays, Saturdays and Sundays. It also ventured a coach service from Ongar through Epping to London, where it had to face severe competition from the 'Associated Coaches' which eventually proved the victor taking over 'Lion' on 12th January 1931. It is thought 'Lion' used that fleetname as their vehicles were garaged at the rear of the Golden Lion public house.

LODGE, D. Wayside, Wilstead, Bedfordshire

This was a small operator who secured a licence to run into Bedford from Wilstead, via London Road or via Elstow Road on two or three days a week. He probably found he did not care for working under the new conditions, and the ENOC took over his licence on 13th May 1932, incorporating his times into its existing 30 service which was extended to Wilstead crossroads. The parish has recently adopted its original, though rather lengthier, name of Willshamstead.

LONDON GENERAL COUNTRY SERVICES LTD. Bell Street, Reigate, Surrey

As noted in the text, the following portions of services owned or operated by the above were transferred to the ENOC.

1 Additional timings ex-'Acme Pullman' between Bishop's Stortford—Saffron Walden to ENOC service 13 from 17th March 1933 (Eastern Area).
2 Tring—Leighton Buzzard section ex-'Chiltern Bus' to ENOC service 16A from 10th May 1933 (Midland Area).
3 Buntingford—Royston and Puckeridge—Royston, which respectively became ENOC services 64 and 65 from 1st July 1933 (Midland Area).

LONDON & NORTH EASTERN RAILWAY COMPANY Marylebone Station, London

The above took over the eastern group of railways at the end of 1922 which included the GER, who owned a motor bus service between Harwich and Upper Dovercourt. This the LNER deemed would be better left to private hands and arrangements were made with H. E. Starling & Sons, a local motor coach operator, to continue the service, under which name later particulars will be found.

LONDON PASSENGER TRANSPORT BOARD/LONDON TRANSPORT EXECUTIVE
55 Broadway, London SW1

A summary of exchanges between ENOC and the above at various dates:

A — To Eastern National
1 Those sections of businesses acquired by the LPTB in Grays which lay outside its 'special area' in 1933/4, which entered ENOC ground.
2 A small section of the 'People's Motor Service' route between Buntingford—Great Hormead and Standon in December 1933 becoming part of ENOC service 64.
3 The Baldock Market Place to Templar Avenue local section which was added to ENOC route 52 when the LPTB curtailed its services to Baldock at Letchworth Station.
4 Coxtie Green—Brentwood—Warley section of service 339 incorporated into ENOC route 260 on 19th July 1964.
5 The Bishop's Stortford South Street to Havers Lane local section of service 350/350A added to the ENOC 309 town service on 4th November 1964.

B — From Eastern National
1 The ENOC services at Grays which lay in the LPTB special area in 1933/4.
2 Chipping Ongar—Epping Town section of ENOC route 2 on 4th August 1933.
3 Aylesbury—Berkhamsted of former Aylesbury Omnibus Company in December 1933.
4 Remaining local services in the Grays area on 30th September 1951.

NB: There have been further transfers either way, since 1969, which fall outside the period covered by this volume

LUTON CORPORATION Park Street, Luton, Bedfordshire

The exchanges of routes as between the Corporation and the Company in 1933 have already been dealt with, so need not be repeated here. After 1933, there were, at times, problems between the Company and the Corporation with regard to the securing of licences for new services in step with urban development. This led the licensing authority to suggest that the parties should endeavour to work more closely with a view to obviate competing applications and some duplication of facilities. The advice was taken and, following negotiations, a completely integrated system of transport for the Luton/Dunstable conurbation was evolved and came into operation on 2nd January 1949 under the title 'Luton and District Transport'. This is chronologically detailed in the text.

MacDERMOTT ROE, E. J. R. Canvey Island, Essex

This member of the Canvey Association started with a six seat Ford wagonette and was later a director of the Canvey & District Motor Transport Co. Ltd.

MALEBIRD BUS COMPANY The Cock Inn, Wootton, Bedfordshire

This was the fleetname adopted by Mr Jack Dawson, which is a little puzzling until one discovers that its owner was also landlord of the Cock Inn and obviously possessed a dry sense of humour. He commenced running a small omnibus between Marston Moretaine and Bedford in 1926, his bus deviating to pick up the villages among the brickyards. It ran to Ampthill and to Lidlington on Sundays. When acquired, on 1st May 1933, he was using a blue-liveried Chevrolet and his operations were fitted into the existing 36 group of services to the Cranfield district, but the Lidlington route was given a new symbol 36D.

MARTIN and INMAN Bramble Farm, Steeple, Essex

These were the founders of the 'Pride of the Marshes' bus service, circa 1926, under which title details will be found.

MAWDSLEY & BROWN Rowhedge, Essex

These two ladies continued the bus service of T. W. Fale's widow from Rowhedge to Colchester until 17th September 1960 using a Commer saloon. The garage was used for a time by Eastern National as an outstation and the service became its 77A.

MAY BLOSSOM SERVICE Little Wakering, Essex

This was the fleetname of Clarke and Matthews, who worked a service to Southend via Barling which passed at an unknown date to W. O. Mitchell of Southend (q.v.).

MEADOWS, J. & SON South View, Polwell Lane, Barton Seagrave, Kettering, Northamptonshire

The above operated some local services in Kettering but also owned a long route working daily through Thrapston to Huntingdon with variations on certain days. A public enquiry had been held on 26th July 1938 to determine whether their licences should be revoked, as a result of warnings and prosecutions for breaches of the operating conditions attached thereto. The outcome was the sale of the entire business to United Counties on 4th December 1938, but difficulty arose with regard to the Huntingdon service, the majority of which crossed over the boundary into Eastern National territory near Thrapston. The service, meanwhile, was operated by the former, pending a decision on its destiny which was not settled until the following April but not implemented until 31st July 1939. Finally, the route was handed to the Company, with United Counties having joint interest which was exercised by operating a couple of journeys on Saturdays and

Sundays, and Eastern National outstationing one bus at Thrapston until the war economy measures caused its recall to Huntingdon garage with a consequential reduction in service. The five buses which were taken by United Counties now found their way into this fleet, occupying numbers 3819 and 3823. The ex-Meadows services, when taken over, were as follows:

75 Huntingdon—Spaldwick—Kimbolton—Catworth (Saturdays)
76 Huntingdon—Spaldwick—Catworth—Bythorn—Thrapston—Cranford—Kettering (daily)
77 Huntingdon—Alconbury—Buckworth—Barham—Old Weston—Brington—Catworth—Bythorn—Thrapston (Saturdays)
78 Thrapston—Bythorn—Catworth—Old Weston—Brington—Catworth—Keyston—Thrapston (Circular, Tuesdays)

The acquisition of these routes made a noticeable extension of territory clearly depicted in the Company's Midland Area route map.

MERSEA, COLCHESTER & DISTRICT TRANSPORT and BUS CO. LTD.   West Mersea, Essex

This company was the successor to the Mersea Engineering & Transport Co. It adopted the title 'Primrose Bus Service' which was a little less ponderous than its registered name. Full details will be found under the shorter title.

MERSEA ENGINEERING & TRANSPORT CO.   The Fires, West Mersea, Essex

This was one of the earliest operators of mechanical transport for passengers in the Colchester area, being second only to the Berry family (q.v.) with whom they joined on the West Mersea—Colchester route in 1909, using a Durkopp charabanc and a Bell omnibus under the direction of Mr W. J. W. Shiers. A little prior to World War I, some ex-London Straker-Squire double-decks came on to the service until peace returned, by which time the business was in the hands of the Mersea, Colchester & District Transport and Bus Company Ltd. which had been formed in 1918 by London interests using the fleetname 'Primrose Bus Service'. Further information can be found under this title.

MILTON BUS SERVICE   Radwell Road, Milton Ernest, Bedfordshire

This was a one man business run by Arthur Marsh Bonham which started in 1926 with a blue and yellow 14 seat Chevrolet kept in a garage behind his house. He ran to Bedford via the main road through Clapham, or via the more circuitous route through Thurleigh and Ravensden, the bus having first started from Sharnbrook and Odell. On Sundays, he ran from Bedford to Riseley, the Deans and Kimbolton. As business improved, he bought a 20 seat Dennis which was in turn replaced by a 26 seat REO. This was too big for his garage and had to be housed elsewhere in the village. At busy times, especially at weekends, his brother would assist by following with his 7 seat taxi, picking up the overflow passengers. He somewhat reluctantly sold his service to the ENOC on 1st September 1933, who were very anxious to ensure it did not reach Birch Bros.

MILTON BUS SERVICE   Stanford-le-Hope, Essex

R. H. Gilbert traded with this name and his original licence was for a service from Stanford to North Benfleet via Corringham, Fobbing, Vange and Pitsea, which was later altered to run from Fobbing to Pitsea, and Vange to Wickford, daily. Campbell of Pitsea took up working the North Benfleet section and later took over the other portion of the service in November 1937, including his Commer Centaur saloon.

MOORE BROS. LTD.   Roslyn Garage, Kelvedon, Essex

This is reputed to be the longest-established business run by the same family providing public conveyance for passengers and goods. It began in 1815 and terminated in 1963 simply because there were no more Moore's left to continue, and it just failed to reach its 150th anniversary. For almost a century, Moore's horse-vans faithfully served Kelvedon, by going to Colchester and Chelmsford twice weekly. Later, the service of Hunwick, to and from Coggeshall, was taken over and the business also owned a temperance hotel and some horse and carriage letting. In 1912, Moores made their first venture with motor vehicles when a 14 seat Daimler brake was purchased, and three Ford cars entered the business twelve months later. Next it was decided to acquire a real motor bus, probably as a result of seeing Hutley's AEC or the 'National' steamers working around Chelmsford. The latter was chosen, and arrived in August 1914. It is not known for how long the steamer was used but, in 1919, three ex-War Department Thornycrofts were purchased, one of which was fitted with the Hurst Nelson body from the steam car chassis. More Ford vehicles were brought into the business, one of which was the van that worked the carrier services, but Chevrolets, REOs and GMCs fulfilled their requirements until 1931 when Gilfords replaced the old Thornycrofts for the main bus work. These were in turn followed by a mixture of Albions and two AEC Regals, and various cars were used to continue the taxi/car hire section. Double-decks reappeared in 1937 when three AEC Regents arrived from City of Oxford with another from South Wales Transport. Early in the war,

Moore's fleet consisted almost entirely of vehicles built by Guy, and here is one of the Arab Mk. 3 dual-purpose saloons carrying the Company's fleet number, 028. Moore was acquired in February 1963, and this view was taken at Colchester just one month later.

G. R. Mills

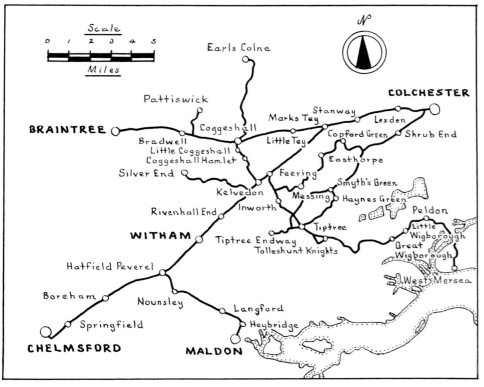

Routes worked by Moore Bros. (Kelvedon) Ltd. — 1962.

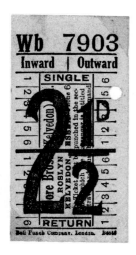

Punch type ticket 2½d. buff, punch in top half for a single fare and below for a return journey. 'Setright' ticket 3d. single — pale green.

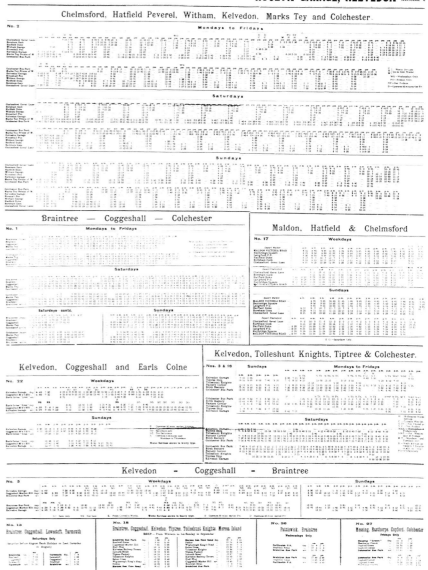

Reduced facsimile of Moore Bros. double-crown poster timetable of 1948; some of the services were combined at a later date.

two Leyland Titans came in, to be soon followed by a Guy Arab, the precursor of many more which became the standard chassis for all bus work, while two Bedfords and three Commer Avengers handled the coaching activities.

The bus services comprised four good daily routes (a) Colchester—Braintree with a maximum half-hourly frequency (b) Colchester—Kelvedon—Chelmsford (c) Maldon—Chelmsford and (d) Colchester—Tiptree, all on hourly headways. Lesser important services ran (e) Colchester—Easthorpe—Kelvedon—Coggeshall—Earls Colne (f) Colchester—Tiptree—Tolleshunt Knights/Kelvedon and (g) Tiptree—Silver End for workers. There was also a summer express route to Lowestoft and Yarmouth, excursions and tours from several centres, plus a summer service from Braintree to West Mersea which enjoyed great popularity before the large increase in private motoring.

MULTIWAYS LTD.   18 Station Road, Westcliff, Southend-on-Sea, Essex

This company was registered in 1929 by Henry Brown (see 'Westcliff') and Mr Twist, with a registered office at 40 Russel Square, London to reputedly operate tours and excursions as a separate entity in the event of the 'Westcliff' stage services being sold or taken over . . . of which there were some rumours at that time.

An interesting pair of vehicles — the Gilford Hera and Dennis Lancet of 'Multiways' whose coastal express services became the nucleus of Dartford Tunnel Coachways. Westcliff acquired the business in 1940 and this view is believed to be of the pre-war road house at Battlesbridge.

However, as nothing occurred along those lines it seems that the business was allowed to go its own way although, on occasions, 'Westcliff' did oppose a 'Multiways' application. It successfully evolved a group of coastal express services and operated the usual excursions and tours with some private hire work. Its coaches were in a brown livery, mostly of Gilford make. On several occasions it moved its base, for a time being located at Brown's Garage, 35 London Road and later at Nelson Street, Southend. It also had a booking office at 429—431 London Road, Westcliff-on-Sea. In 1940, all had come to a stop because of the war conditions, and the licences were sold to 'Westcliff' and the fleet disposed of elsewhere. 'Westcliff' resumed the coastal express routes in 1946 which became services E, F, G, H and L in the Eastern National series, all except for one which formed the nucleus of the 'Dartford Tunnel Coachways'.

MUMMERY, Mrs F.   17 Crescent Avenue, Little Thurrock, Essex
This was one of the better small operators at Grays working the Tilbury—Purfleet route with many others, her licence permitting her to run every eighty minutes, with two extra journeys for workers during the morning and evening peak hours. The business was acquired by the ENOC in April 1933, without vehicles.

NAISH, J. J.   75 Lytton Road, Chadwell St. Mary, Essex
J. J. Naish worked a regular service from Grays to Chadwell St. Mary, via The College, in competition with the ENOC's route 37A. The ENOC applied for his licence on 20th March 1933, taking it over in June without vehicles, the Naish times being incorporated into service 37A.

NEW EMPRESS SALOONS LTD.   Harringay, London N4
This was the brainchild of A. H. Young, who had earlier worked the 'Empress Bus' in inner London. This forty eight mile pioneer service to Southend developed into one of the most remarkable stage services in the country under the control of the City Motor Omnibus Company, which took over his interest in 1928 with seven Dennis and two Maudslay saloons in a purple/maroon livery.

A punch type 2/- return ticket, numerical stages — pale blue.

NEW IMPERIAL MOTORS   Imperial Garage, Crown Hill, Rayleigh, Essex
This company was formed, in 1928, by G. B. Seymour, who owned the garage but licensed the buses in his wife's name from their home at Dawes Heath. The first service worked from Hullbridge, via Rayleigh, Hockley and Rochford to Southend, using Morris saloons. On 15th August 1929, the bus section was converted into a company entitled Rayleigh Motor Services Ltd., under which title subsequent developments will be found.

There was considerable bad feeling between 'Westcliff' and 'New Imperial' crews and Seymour was summoned for assault when there was a display of fisticuffs after a small 'accident' at Hambro Hill. A 'Westcliff' driver would not pull well over to the left or turn down his lights in a narrow section of road, causing Seymour to lose control of his vehicle. He was fined £1 plus costs!

NICKOLDS, Percy F. South View, London Road, Canvey Island, Essex
Percy Nickolds was originally in business as a jobmaster, but seems to have turned to coal retailing and then became a bus owner, using a 14 seat Buick. He was also a member of the Canvey Association (q.v.).

NUGUS, F. H. Coach Station, Herongate, Brentwood, Essex
F. H. Nugus started with his brother in 1921 using a pair of 14 seat Ford T buses between Herongate and Brentwood and Great Warley, a route which was later extended to Bulphan. W. Nugus left to open a garage at East Horndon and F. H. Nugus continued solus until early 1936 when he sold the service to 'City Coach Company'. Earlier, a service ran from Brentwood to Hutton village until others appeared on that road, and an attempt to establish an extension from Bulphan to Grays did not attract sufficient traffic to justify continuation. 'City' took over one Chevrolet, one Bedford and two REO saloons, the Bedford later becoming a van, and surviving until 1952.

OFFORDIAN COACHES, Offord D'Arcy, Huntingdonshire
F. Lewis Slade traded as above with a group of excursion and tours, with further good picking up points at Graveley, Great Paxton, Buckden, Brampton, Huntingdon and Alconbury to which, in 1935, he added similar licences operated by Rowlatt and Miles from St. Neots. This is probably the reason for Eastern National being interested in his activities for his only stage services were a market route to St. Neots on Thursdays, and a like service to Huntingdon on Saturdays, which included a late theatre bus. These services were numbered 4B and 4D after the take-over. The purchase included three vehicles, two of which were formerly with Rowlatt and Miles. Slade also offered a car hire service with Belsize and Sunbeam motor cars.

'OLD TOM' MOTOR SERVICE Manor Road, Laindon, Essex
This was the fleetname of Mr Tom Webster who was in business as early as 1921 carrying out cartage work with a Ford truck converted to a charabanc at weekends. He later ran some buses in competition with Hinton (q.v.) whom he later appears to have taken over or succeeded, his small vehicles being much more suitable to the roads in the district than Hinton's heavy old B type open-top buses. In 1936, he sold the buses to 'City Coach Company' and his excursions and tours to 'Gidea Park Coaches' (q.v.) from whom they eventually passed to Eastern National. Webster was working the following services at the time of sale:

'Old Tom' No.	Serving	'City' No.
1	Laindon—Pipps Hill (circular daily)	6
2	Laindon—Great Burstead—Billericay—Brentwood (daily)	5
3	Laindon—Dunton Wayletts—Bulphan—Brentwood (daily)	7
4	Laindon—Bulphan—Fen—Romford (Wednesday market bus)	8
5	Laindon—Nevendon—Wickford (Monday market bus)	9
6	Laindon—London (Aldgate) (Sunday mornings for Petticoat Lane market before trains started)	10
7	Laindon—Maldon (Thursday and Sunday). This passed as an excursion to 'Gidea Park Coaches'.	—

The fleet, taken over by 'City' from Webster, comprised three 20 seat REOs, one 32 seat Gilford, one 18 seat Bedford, one 24 seat AJS and one 14 seat Chevrolet.

ONGAR & DISTRICT MOTOR SERVICES Station Garage, Ongar Essex
This company was started by E. Curtis on 1st November 1926 using a 14 seat Ford T, quaintly-bodied with longitudinal seating and a back door for access. Livery was red with a black waistband on which the fleetname appeared. Later vehicles carried the name on a circle and bar device in gold. His route was Ongar—High Ongar—Nine Ashes—Blackmore—Kelvedon Common—Bentley—Brentwood, which quickly established itself as it gave a more frequent and utterly reliable service than the several competitors whose services he acquired in the course of time, except that run by 'National/London Transport' which never had more than a lesser share of the traffic. At one time there was a Wednesday Romford market extension, and a service from Brentwood to Stock was also attempted, but no licence could be obtained. At various dates he took over Len Knight, Saywood & Coleman, and S. G. Cracknell. He finally sold to 'City' in March 1945 which became 'City' route 14, together with two Albions, one Dodge and three Bedfords.
 For a time, Curtis had been involved with the 'Associated Coaches' (q.v.) in partnership with R. G. Thompson.

Punch type 8d. return ticket, no stage numbers, punched for 'in' or 'out' only — buff.

ORANGE LUXURY COACHES (PORTSMOUTH) LTD.
Little is known of this company which was formed jointly by 'Westcliff' and Keith & Boyle Ltd., owners of the 'Orange Luxury Coaches' at Kennington and other coastal resorts. It was first registered on 9th May 1929, each nominating two Directors. The head office was at 'Westcliff's' headquarters at Pier Hill, Southend. When in 1932 'Westcliff' sued H. R. Bridge over an alleged breach of contract (which, in fact, Bridge won) one of the 'Westcliff' witnesses was Miss Cassignol (formerly the Secretary to Pearse's Motor Services) who stated her occupation as cashier for Orange Luxury Coaches (Portsmouth) Ltd. More information would be welcome.

'OUR BUS' Grays, Essex
This was the fleetname of the Benjamin family who worked on the local Grays route to Fairway, being the last private small owner to operate in Grays from the many who were there in the 1930s. Eastern National took over their working on 15th September 1951 but held it for only two weeks before passing it, with the other east Grays services, to the London Transport Executive on the last day of that month. Latterly they used a Guy Wolf single-deck on the service.

Punch type ticket locally printed 1½d. — pink. The stage numbering was superfluous for the fare for the whole distance was only 2d.

PATTEN'S COACHES LTD. Runwell Road, Wickford, Essex

About 1929, John Patten, son of the sub-postmaster and village shop proprietor at Ramsden Heath, started running a small bus in competition with the Wickford Omnibus Services route of C. W. Spurling which he took over on 6th May 1931. The company name was changed to Patten's Coaches, the only Directors and shareholders being the two Pattens, father and son. Spurling's Pitsea—Tilbury section was abandoned, and the service concentrated on the Pitsea—Wickford—Billericay—Chelmsford section, the latter place being entered via Beehive Lane and not via Wood Street as did the ENOC services. The business did well, and when the ENOC took over during September 1934, which included the depot in Runwell Road, Wickford, there were six Dennis omnibuses in the fleet, one Dart, one EV, three GLs and one Lancet which had all been registered with John Patten junior, not the company. The vehicles carried an all over light blue livery.

PAXMAN, Mrs M. A. 91 Clarence Road, Grays, Essex

Mrs Paxman had the honour of being the first of the several small operators at Grays to be selected for acquisition following the new licensing. She was one of the many on the Tilbury—Purfleet run, being taken over in February 1933 without vehicles.

PEARSE'S GARAGE & MOTOR WORKS/PEARSE'S MOTOR SERVICES LTD.

High Street, Benfleet, Essex

Both the above-named were under the direction of Major Albert Pearse who started running buses in 1921 mainly for the benefit of commuters to and from Benfleet Station and, a little later, to Southend. Right from the start, there was antagonism with 'Westcliff' when they followed his example with a competing service from Southend using more buses than he. They also prevented him from acquiring additional licences which, on two occasions, were eventually granted after his appeal to the Minister of Transport. He also worked services to Wickford and Stanford-le-Hope, one through to Brentwood via Billericay, with a third, via Vicarage Hill, to Westcliff, all of which were of minor importance compared with the main line to Southend. In 1929, the business became a limited company and a Mr Falkus tried to unsuccessfully control it from his London office. With some difficulty, Pearse managed to extricate himself from the company but not without impoverishing himself, and was, thereafter, always struggling financially. In 1931, he approached H. R. Bridge for help because most of his fleet was off the road with 'stop notices' and he required a quick loan to meet that week's wages bill. Very soon after, H. R. Bridge took control of Pearse's Service in exchange for four hundred acres of Pitsea marshes. The business was soon reconstructed as 'Benfleet & District Motor Services' (q.v.) under the control of the Bridge family. Later details are given under that title.

PECK BROS. East Bergholt, Suffolk

The Peck family, through successive generations since the 1840s or before, had worked a carrier service from East Bergholt to Colchester. In the early 1920s the brothers Eddie and Oswald, whose father still drove the carrier's cart, had employment with B. Beeston & Sons (q.v.) of the same village, who operated motor buses over five routes to Colchester or Ipswich, which were well-established. By the later 1920s the two Pecks, having learned something of the bus business from the Beestons, decided it was time the carrier's cart was replaced by a motor-bus, and so the 'East Bergholt & District service' was born and operated in competition with the Beestons to Colchester, via Manningtree, from which point they also competed with the ENOC. About 1930, the service was taken over by Mrs E. S. Furber whose husband was the owner of Grosvenor Motors which dealt with buses and the like, from whom it is believed the Pecks acquired their rolling stock. Reference should also be made to the 'East Bergholt & District' text.

PEOPLE'S MOTOR SERVICES LTD. Park Road, Ware, Hertfordshire

This was started by Thurgood of Ware, the well-known body builder, after taking over a Mr Mardell who worked from Puckeridge to Ware. Mardell had always managed to start off with his bus a few minutes ahead of 'National'. With his smaller and faster buses, Thurgood steadily developed several new services in East Herts through the villages neglected by 'National', whose heavy omnibuses were totally unsuited for such work. By 1933, he had eight frequent daily services at work, operated by a fleet of twenty one vehicles in brown livery. It was unfortunate that the whole of his activities fell within the LPTB area except for a short length of route near Buntingford which came to the ENOC and was combined with its Midland Area service 64.

'PLESHEY BELLE', THE Pleshey, Essex

For many years two carriers connected Pleshey with the outside world, providing horse and cart services to Chelmsford via Great Waltham on three or fours days a week. In the early 1920s a Mr Harman and a Mr Dowsett (not partners) were on the road and, about 1925, one or both of them invested in a small 14 seat vehicle, painted light blue, which rejoiced in the name The Pleshey Belle. This maintained the service until the advent of licensing by the Traffic Commissioners in 1931 when the service was replaced by ENOC's service 52. The Pleshey Belle set up in the Plough yard which was almost opposite the ENOC bus station in Duke Street. It is believed that the service ceased due to the vehicle being capable of securing a certificate of fitness.

PREMIER LINE LTD. Leysfield Road, Shepherd's Bush, London W12

This was a private company formed by the Directors of Premier Omnibus Co. Ltd., of the same address, to develop a series of coach services to London, the parent already being engaged there with omnibus routes. In the circumstances outlined in *Chapter Two*, 'Premier Line' acquired the Aylesbury Motor Bus Company which became the Aylesbury Omnibus Co. Ltd., eventually passing to the ENOC and other surrounding operators.

PRIDE ASSOCIATED COACHES Rosary Tea Rooms, Mayland, Essex

Formerly the 'Pride of the Marshes' service (q.v.), it was acquired by the Tabersham Bros. who came from the Walthamstow area. Soon after taking over, Sefton's 'Burnham & District' came to an end and Tabersham continued to work his Chelmsford run. Gozzett of 'Quest Motors' took over Sefton's main line to Maldon where he was developing further services since taking up parts of the late 'Essex Public' (q.v.), and was now determined to see the 'Pride' service off the road, with whom open warfare was now waged. The Tabershams next started a thrice daily service to London from Maldon with immediate connections from the Bradwell bus, but not the Burnham buses which were Gozzett's. At some time prior to licensing (dates for events in this area being notoriously difficult to establish) the London route was in the hands of 'Quest Motors' connecting now for Burnham at the same time as 'Pride Associated' was beginning to show signs of getting into a very run down state. By 1932, it had become reduced to only two or three journeys on Mondays to Fridays with a few more at the weekend. The service had become neglected and unreliable. Its timetable dated 1st May 1932 announced naively that 'the proprietors would endeavour to maintain an efficient service, but cannot be responsible for mechanical breakdowns'. By early 1933, things were in such a bad way that the licensing authority stepped in and revoked the licences as from midnight 30th April, leaving the field clear for Gozzett to build up the services in the territory to their fullest extent. At a date unknown, the Tabershams had moved their base from Mayland to Bradwell.

The reason behind the title 'Pride Associated' has never been satisfactorily explained. It is suspected there may have been some link (perhaps H. H. Clench was involved) with the 'Lion Associated' which also had Walthamstow connections. For a time, until the latter also had its licences revoked, the two businesses did make physical contact at Chelmsford, as well as by the Maldon—London coach service.

'PRIDE OF THE MARSHES'   Bramble Farm, Steeple, Essex

This company was started by Herbert Martin and Bernard Inman, circa 1925/6, using the above title, their service being the first real attempt to provide a regular motor service in the thinly-populated Dengie Hundred. The buses were in medium blue, working from Bradwell-on-Sea, via Dengie, to Southminster to connect with the railhead there, with one or two diverting into Burnham-on-Crouch. Most, however, continued via Latchingdon and Steeple to Maldon which was (and is) the natural distributive centre for the area. From about 1928, there was competition when Henry Sefton (q.v.) appeared on the scene with his 'Burnham & District' service. The next year, Martin and Inman (possibly due to this competition) elected to sell the business to the Tabersham Bros. (q.v.) who came to the Rosary Tea Rooms at Mayland, which now became the operating point, the service changing its name to 'Pride Associated' under which title subsequent events are detailed. Martin and Inman are known to have operated with two small Chevrolet buses with typical country carpenter bodywork, also a small Dennis saloon and a Lancia charabanc.

PRIMROSE BUS SERVICE   High Street, West Mersea, Essex

Primrose Bus Service succeeded the Mersea Engineering & Transport Company which was registered as a public company on 13th March 1918, entitled Mersea, Colchester & District Transport & Bus Company Ltd. It also had an office in Lancell Place, Stoke Newington in connection with its haulage interests. The first Board comprised William H. Bishop, William B. Alexander and James Austin. The latter departed during the 1920s to be replaced by Daniel Cock and Roy Littlehayes. One of the first acts of the new company was to acquire some second-hand Karrier double-decks which replaced the ageing Straker-Squires inherited from its predecessor. With these, they opened new bus routes to Brightlingsea, to Rowhedge and to Great Wigborough from Colchester, but singularly failed to dislodge any of the local proprietors already installed on those routes, so retired to continue with its original West Mersea—Colchester service. Its only other new venture appears to have been a weekend charabanc run between London and Clacton-on-Sea, from 1923 to 1926. In the latter part of 1930, three Guy saloons were purchased from the LGOC to replace the Karriers which were demoted to the haulage department. The Guys had formerly seen service with the 'A & W' business at Harrow. They passed to the ENOC with the bus route on 30th December 1935 which was integrated into the 75 group of services. The garage was also taken over, which continued in use with the Company until recently. The Mersea company was also engaged in coal retailing, would undertake ploughing/cultivating by contract using a Samson tractor, and also had a marine engineering department. At the time the buses were sold, there was £8,306 of issued capital in £1 shares held by 191 shareholders.

PRIMROSE COACHES   Townfield Street and 66A Duke Street, Chelmsford, Essex

This was the fleetname adopted by Rose Brothers when they began to work excursions and tours from about 1926, using small pneumatic-tyred charabancs. The business had descended from Mr R. Rose's taxicab and car hire service conducted from the former Lion and Lamb yard in Duke Street. About 1929, an express coach service was started to London, via Brentwood, Eastern Avenue and Finsbury Park to terminate on The Embankment, and later at King's Cross Coach Station. The service was steadily increased until, in 1939, it ran almost hourly when considerable duplication was needed at weekends. A booking office cum waiting-room was opened at 66A Duke Street on the corner

of Market Road, which served as the town centre pick-up point. In 1949, a Daimler CVD6 Strachan-bodied double-deck was purchased to reduce the amount of duplication, but limitations on its use led to it being exchanged for a Leyland PS1 from 'City Coach Company'. The livery was, as the name implies, primrose with black mudguards and roof. The fleet had been very mixed, beginning with Lancia and Laffley; next came two Stars and a Gilford, followed by five Commers and three AJS coaches, two Leyland Cubs and a pair of Bedfords. The post-war period saw Commer, Bedford, Leyland and TSM vehicles in the fleet.

In addition to the London route, Rose Bros. held a licence for a service to Galleywood Racecourse (until it closed), plus excursions and tours from Chelmsford and Witham. As larger coaches came into the fleet, the Lion and Lamb premises became too small, so a modern garage was built in Townfield Street.

With the increase in private motoring and the electrification of the railway to Chelmsford, the London service gradually lost patronage and was finally withdrawn in 1958 as uneconomic. The remainder of the business (except the taxis) was acquired by Eastern National on 13th June 1958 including one Leyland PSU1/15 Thurgood-bodied coach.

Extract from Rose Bros. 'Primrose' Coach Service timetable.

PULLMAN SERVICE   40 Colchester Road, Halstead, Essex

T. W. H. Griffith was rather late in the field but, nevertheless, qualified for a licence to run from Halstead to Colchester in spite of the fact that there were already two long-established services at work on that road; the ENOC, as successor to the old 'National' and S. Blackwell & Son who had worked it since 1920. On 30th June 1933, his service was bought by the ENOC and operated in circumstances as detailed in *Chapter Two*. Griffith continued with the ENOC until his retirement at which time he had charge of the Company's Halstead branch. His three buses comprised an AJS Pilot, a small Gilford and a REO 'Sprinter' which joined the ENOC fleet.

QUEENS PARK COACHES 146 High Street, Aylesbury, Buckinghamshire
Queens Park Coaches were established prior to 1931 by W. M. Oborne when he obtained a licence to work from Aylesbury to Weston Turville, Halton Village and Halton RAF Camp. This service continued without change until it was acquired in June 1951 together with three Leylands, three Dennis Lancets, three Bedfords, plus four garage buildings situated in Walton Road, Queens Park, Aylesbury — hence the fleetname. Part of the garage accommodation was let to the City of Oxford company as their Aylesbury out-station, which arrangement continued with Eastern National until 1951 when all was transferred to United Counties.

One of the constituents to Gozzett's 'Quest', which the Company acquired in 1935, was 'Pride of the Marshes'. This delightful view shows their little Chevrolet and the proud owners.

A Leyland Cub of Queens Park Coaches, which passed to the Company when the business was acquired in 1951.

QUEST MOTOR SERVICES The Causeway, Heybridge, Maldon, Essex
Development of omnibus services in the Maldon area, apart from the routes established by 'National' to Chelmsford and Colchester, were not very satisfactory and some small operators from the villages between the Blackwater and the Crouch estuaries had come and gone. A company calling itself the 'Essex Public', in 1929, started some services from Maldon, which soon faded out. It parked its former London open-top buses on some

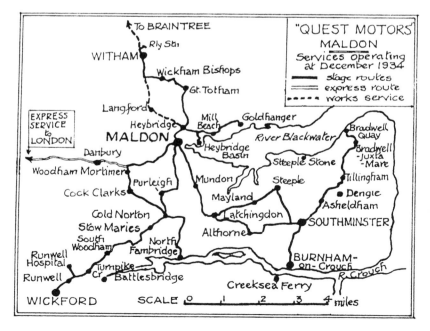

ground near the East Railway Station within view of Gozzett's garage. This is said to have given Gozzett the inspiration to start his own services on a more businesslike basis which he did in 1929, the first service linking Maldon with Witham. Attention was next directed to the Burnham-on-Crouch road following the collapse of Henry Sefton's 'Burnham & District' which brought him in conflict with the Tabersham Bros. service to Bradwell (see 'Pride Associated') with whom open warfare raged. Their business included a coach route to London but had become very run down and came to a sudden end in April 1933 when their licences were revoked due to service irregularities. Gozzett went on to establish other new routes and to continue the former Wickford service of 'Wickford Omnibuses' and another by A. A. Ford of Althorne, plus a new town service, creating quite a respectable network. He also took over Brazier's excursions and tours in Maldon. His activities were giving concern to Eastern National who were determined to buy him out as there was some further potential in the area which it was feared he might add to his growing empire. Negotiations and agreement were reached in 1934 and an application was made for his licences in November which were operated by the new owners from 1st January 1935. Fourteen coaches/buses came with the business and the services were numbered in a new series started at 60 as follows:

60	Maldon—Great Totham—Wickham Bishops—Witham	daily
61	Maldon—Latchingdon—Althorne—Southminster—Burnham-on-Crouch	daily
62	Maldon—Latchingdon—Steeple—Southminster/Burnham—Bradwell	daily
63	Maldon—Purleigh—Stow Maries—Runwell—Wickford	daily
64	Maldon—Heybridge Basin—Mill Beach—Goldhanger	Tues/Fri/Sat/Sun.
65	Maldon—Heybridge—Mill Beach (special summer service)	
66	Maldon—Woodham Mortimer—Cold Norton—North Fambridge	Tues/Thur/Fri/Sat.
67	Mundon Road—Maldon centre—Heybridge (local)	daily
68	Maldon—Braintree (Crittall's Works Service)	
+C	Maldon—Danbury—London (King's Cross) Express	daily
—	Excursions and tours from Maldon and almost every place within the 'Quest' network. (+ was worked through to Burnham by Gozzett).	

Vehicles taken over included one AEC Regal, eight Gilfords, two GMC and one each of REO, Bedford and Chevrolet. Two of these were formerly Brazier.

Gozzett organized a novel scheme in conjunction with the Maldon and Heybridge Chamber of Trade to encourage passengers to use the 'Quest Motors'. All passengers making purchases over a value of 10/- (50p) would have their single fare returned, or a return fare would be returned on spending £1.00 on any day, including Sundays!

R. R. COACHES LTD. Aylesbury Road, Wendover, Buckinghamshire
Better known as 'Red Rose Coaches', this business began in September 1925 by the Lancaster family operating two routes; (a) Halton Camp—Wendover—Aylesbury and (b) Aylesbury—Tring—Berkhamsted, using a fleet comprising four Chevrolets, one Clement-Talbot and a Crossley, which were joined later by another Crossley and an Overland. By 1929, the shares of the company had been purchased by Robert McGill and his wife Rose, who were the sole Directors and shareholders. They gave up the Berkhamsted route at a date unknown, but continued the other route until 1950 when it was taken over by Eastern National, without vehicles.

RAYLEIGH MOTOR SERVICES LTD. Rayleigh and Southend-on-Sea, Essex
This company was formed on 26th August 1929 by G. B. Seymour of Crown Garage, Rayleigh, to continue his 'New Imperial Motors' which ran from Hullbridge through Rayleigh to Rochford and Southend in competition with 'Westcliff' and others. The new company initiated a new through route from Southend to Colchester, via Danbury or Latchingdon and Maldon, which was a success because of poor rail facilities and no through buses. This affected Eastern National services sufficiently to cause the company to put on a similar service. The Hullbridge service was now altered to take a more direct route to Southend, via Eastwood, and a separate route ran via Rochford, both of which competed against 'Westcliff' and others. In June 1930, the expanding 'Borough Services' secured control of 'Rayleigh' and transferred the Colchester services to itself for operation, while 'Rayleigh' continued working the other two. Both Eastern National and 'Westcliff' were much concerned with the activities of 'Borough' and, in 1932, the former gained control of 'Borough' and, of course, 'Rayleigh' also. It now took over the Colchester routes, adding them to its own similar services, and passed control of 'Rayleigh' to 'Westcliff' under which it remained until Tilling took control and wound it up on 19th May 1936. Prior to assuming control, the 'Rayleigh' fleet consisted of five Morris saloons, but 'Borough' soon supplemented these with two new Gilfords and bought four AEC Regent ex-demonstrators for the Colchester routes.

REGENT MOTOR SERVICE Ongar Road, Brentwood, Essex
F. H. Fuller was the owner of the Regent Transport Service which had contracts for the collection and delivery of milk churns from farms to London dairies. One day, in 1929, he returned by train from London to Brentwood Station and boarded Henderson's (q.v.) bus to complete his journey home, but was asked, rather peremptorily, to get off as the bus was full. Henderson was a man of unpredictable temper, whereupon Fuller informed Henderson that if he had no wish to convey him on his bus, there were certain things he could do with it and that he would get his own instead. This is exactly what happened and, in February 1930, the 'Regent' bus service was born. A new 14 seat Chevrolet took to the road starting a new route from Woodman Road or Great Warley—Brentwood Station, and Town to Pilgrims Hatch and Coxtie Green or Canterbury Tye, giving an approximate hourly service. The last-named section was soon dropped, all buses going to Coxtie Green, but soon, another bus was obtained and a half-hourly service was given on Saturdays. In 1931, two medium blue REOs appeared on the service which continued until May 1936, when Fuller sold the vehicles and service to the 'City Coach Company' (q.v.) from which they passed in the following August to the LPTB to become service 339A.

RELIANCE BUS Hockliffe, Bedfordshire
This service was started by J. H. Pope early in 1922 for which he bought three B type ex-LGOC AECs, one a double-deck, another a saloon cut down from a double-deck, the third being a charabanc. He developed several services mainly of the market day or Saturday pattern which reached out to Woburn, Leighton Buzzard, Tring, Luton etc. His operations ceased about 1929 and appear to have been taken up by others, but whether by purchase or default is not known. Part of the business went to A. F. England's 'XL'; one service to Bright Bros., and some to 'Westoning & District'.

RELIANCE COACHES, Crown Garage, Meppershall, Bedfordshire
These were owned by Charles Taylor who catered mainly for private hire work, and also operated a few minor stage services, some of which he had acquired with the business of H. Groom (q.v.) of the same village in August 1934. These consisted of three different services to Hitchin of the shopper, market or cinema pattern, a school service to RAF Henlow, and weekend leave journeys to and from Hitchin Station. All were taken over on 29th May 1936 most being incorporated into the existing service 25, the remaining taking up new services numbered 27, 28 and 28A, but not his excursions and tours which passed a little later to Birch Bros.

RELIANCE COACHES, High Street, West Mersea, Essex
This was the fleetname adopted by the four Thorpe Brothers — Leslie Burton, Kenneth Henry, Donald Jack and Ernest Maurice who, starting in a small way, gradually established themselves in spite of the considerable opposition on the Colchester road. About 1930/31 they took over the old established 'Xmas Bus Service' of P. W. Christmas from Great Wigborough to Colchester and, in 1932, the timings operated by Victor Brown's 'Bluebird' service. On 30th September 1937, they were the last independent on the Mersea Road to sell to Eastern National, this being the last day of operation. No vehicles were taken over with the business. The Mersea timings were added to the existing 75 group of services which were now rearranged (see main text) and the 'Xmas' service became 75A, formerly allocated to the 'Primrose' timings.

'RELIANCE', THE Halstead, Essex
This was the operating name of Mr M. Pudney who, in the late 1920s, elected to enter the omnibus business for which purpose he bought a second-hand ex-London bus which, upon transfer, happened to be bearing the inscription 'The Reliance' on its sides. So this, there and then, became his operating name on various routes he tried around the Halstead area. He eventually settled down on the ENOC route 22 between Halstead and Castle Hedingham for which he was unable to get a licence, so he sold it to R. H. K. Johnson of Colne Engaine who continued it until he sold out to the ENOC.

RENOWN BUS SERVICE Langley Road, Luton, Bedfordshire
This company was run, from July 1927, by Sydney W. and H. C. Lamb, on an approximately hourly frequency between Luton and Flamstead End, using a small fleet of Lancia saloons in an orange/beige livery. They had earlier sought to work on the Luton—Hitchin—Norton route but failed to secure a licence from Luton Watch Committee. They sold their services to A. F. England or, more correctly, to his Union Jack (Luton) Omnibus Co. Ltd. just four days after he had effected his 'big deal' with Luton Corporation on 27th March 1933. England sold it to the ENOC on 24th October 1936, becoming service 80, but not for long as it was soon transferred to the LPTB which was already working on that route as far as Markyate.

RICKARD, A. T. The Garage, Wingrave, Buckinghamshire
This was a small proprietor who also owned the local garage and whose family had earlier been engaged in a carrier service. One James Rickard was on the Leighton Buzzard to Aylesbury road as far back as 1842, setting up at the Buckinghamshire Arms. When licensing started, A. T. Rickard was authorized to run Cublington—Wingrave—Aylesbury on Wednesdays and Saturdays, and to Leighton Buzzard by Mentmore and Ledburn every Tuesday. The latter ceased, however, before the ENOC acquired the service in December 1934, allocating route 110 in the Midland Area series. No vehicle was acquired.

ROCHFORD & DISTRICT MOTOR SERVICES LTD. 6 Tylers Avenue, Southend, Essex
This business commenced operations on 3rd April 1930, the founder, Leonard Redhouse Morley, and his wife, being the sole Directors. He made many applications to Southend Watch Committee and met with numerous refusals, but eventually secured two licences to run from Hancock's yard in Tylers Avenue to Rochford and Creeksea, and was later able to establish a branch route to Hockley. Late in 1931, 'Westcliff' secured control and immediately transferred to 'Rochford' for operation, its route 11 to Fambridge, which continued as such until May 1933 when it was finally absorbed and wound up. 'Rochford' exhorted passengers to 'Get the brown bus habit', or advised 'Special omnibuses kept at Tylers Avenue for the use of return ticket holders only during congested periods', and declared that 'Incivility is a most unlikely occurrence on our buses'.

RODNEY BUS SERVICE, Danbury, Essex
This was the trading name of F. H. Ashdown, whose only service ran from Chelmsford through Danbury to Little Baddow (The Admiral Rodney Inn). It enjoyed considerable local support, not only as the local operator, but also because he offered a more frequent service than the Company. He was frequently in difficulty with the licensing authority over the misuse of relief buses which he was ultimately prohibited from using entirely. The service was acquired on 4th December 1937 becoming part of the existing 1B service. No vehicles were taken nor were his excursions and tours section which flourished for many years with much private hire and contract work.

A little Chevrolet saloon belonging to F. H. Ashdown's 'Rodney Bus Service, Danbury, which passed to the Company in December 1937.

ROLFE, T. W.   The Nurseries, Woodham Walter, Essex

This small service started in the later 1920s and continued virtually without change until taken over by Eastern National in December 1953 to become route 67. The service consisted of a single trip into Maldon on Monday, Wednesday and Friday mornings and four trips ran on Saturdays. In the summer there was an extra service on Wednesdays and Sunday afternoons for the benefit of those wanting to visit the beauty spots at The Old Rodney and Bracken Hill, near Woodham Walter.

ROWLATT and MILES   7 River Terrace, St. Neots, Huntingdonshire

For some years Rowlatt and Miles had operated a small charabanc/tours/private hire business at St. Neots for which they secured a licence in 1931. They sold the undertaking with one Chevrolet and one Dennis GL to F. L. Slade during 1935, who traded as 'Offordian Coaches' (q.v.).

ROYAL BLUE   11 Bishops Avenue, Braintree, Essex

C. S. Cummings, who used the above fleetname, appears to have entered the bus business in 1929 when he put on a forty five minute service from Braintree to Silver End and Witham in competition with the Silver End Development Co. (q.v.). On 20th June 1932, he acquired the Hicks Bros. service 13 from Braintree to Stisted and Pattiswick, but with what significance is not known, for there was no contrary exchange. In December 1933, the Stisted buses were extended to Greensted Green. Cummings seems to have ceased trading early in 1934 when Hicks Bros. and C. M. Taylor ('Horn Coaches') both applied to take over his services. Hicks had, by now, taken over the Silver End company' service to Witham and was successful in taking in Cummings' times also. The Pattiswick working also returned to them, Horn being granted the Braintree to Greensted Green route only. Hicks also acquired the 'Royal Blue' excursions and tours licence for Silver End. Cummings' licences were surrendered in April 1934.

ROYAL BLUE CARS   Southend-on-Sea, Essex

See Southend-on-Sea Motor Charabanc Company Ltd.

N.B: There was a later operator who also traded as 'Royal Blue Cars' with which there was no connection. This was a business, started by Philip Parsons in 1921, which became part of London and Southend Central Motor Services Ltd. which was formed to operate a service to London using two open-top Dennis buses which 'Westcliff' took over when the service ceased during 1926.

ROYAL BLUE COACHES,   Central Garage, Dovercourt, Essex

This old family business was in the hands of Mr William Allen Wells. In the 1880s it was listed in the linen, drapery and stationery line with a post office attached, which seems an unlikely introduction to the motor trade. Wells seems to have been a man of versatility for in 1912 he was at 73 High Street as Stationer, Bookseller, Bible Seller and Fancy Depot, and also in Station Road as Cycle and Motor Car Agent where the business continued to flourish as the Central Garage of Wells & Son. At 1930, they had two 20 seat coaches known as 'The Royal Blue' and a 30 cwt. lorry which ran a goods service to and from Ipswich. The coaches used to stand in Kingsway and private hire work was a feature of the business. In 1938, the goodwill and licence, but not the vehicles, were acquired by Eastern National.

RYALL, Percy   Motor Engineer, The Webley Motor and Cycle Works, Lakeside Corner, Canvey Island, Essex

This was one of the seventeen busmen making up the Canvey Auxiliary Motors.

S. A. A. MOTORS   Park Lane, Ramsden Heath, Essex

Mr S. A. Amos traded as above with a small omnibus to Billericay on weekdays, and via Downham to Wickford for the market on Mondays. His business was obviously affected when daily through services from Chelmsford, Southend-on-Sea, Romford and London were started at frequent intervals by 'Westcliff' and Pattens. He was probably pleased to receive an offer from the ENOC in August 1935, at the same time as his neighbour, Davies, with whom his services had closely worked. The ENOC combined them into new 12A and 12B services with a part incorporated into service 4.

'SAFEWAY'   Cambridge Road Garage, Enfield, Middlesex

This fleetname was used by A. W. Priest who joined forces with W. D. Beaumont, whose services from London to Leighton Buzzard now adopted 'Beaumont-Safeway' as a fleetname, under which title particulars will be found.

SALLY OMNIBUS SERVICE   Denton, Northamptonshire

Mrs S. J. Knight and family started running buses under the above title in the mid-1920s in competition with Alfred Minney's (q.v.) 'Comfy' service and 'National', which came on a little later after taking over the Northampton Motor Bus Company's interest in the Northampton—Lavendon road. In 1928, Minney found the pace too hot and sold his service to the Knights for £500 and went to Bedford to drive for 'National'. The Knights took over the tenancy of Alfred Minney's garage at Yardley Hastings, where they garaged two buses worked by local crews, an arrangement which was continued by the Company and by United Counties after that concern took over.

Under the Knights the service prospered and was extended to Harrold and to Olney; so they were working in three counties. Later certain trips were diverted to serve Lower Brafield. Her sons, Sydney and Charles, dealt with the operational and engineering side while Miss M. E. and Miss Mary Knight devoted their energy to the clerical and administrative aspect of the business. Although really outside the scope of this history it should perhaps be mentioned that, in 1935, the Knights took over C. Wilford's coach and bus business in Northampton, some of which had earlier been taken over from a Mr Mills of Brixworth. They sold the buses to United Counties in 1952, and the coaching section to York Bros. in 1960.

SAYWOOD, Jim   Ongar Road, Brentwood, Essex

Jim Saywood was a driver of Henderson's taxi service (q.v.) until the bus service was started, which he then drove for a few years before taking it over for himself. He died about 1928 and Mrs Saywood continued the service with Mr Coleman, whereupon it was based at Blackmore and continued until 17th May 1932 when 'Ongar & District' made application for the licence. Saywood garaged the bus at the rear of the Castle Inn, Ongar Road. The service ran from Warley to Brentwood, Kelvedon Common and Blackmore.

SEAMARKS BROS.   High Street, Westoning, Bedfordshire

The above bought G. I. Smith's Westoning & District Bus Services on 1st March 1937. They had previously been engaged with their father, R. L. Seamarks in a successful business based at Higham Ferrers where they traded as R. L. Seamarks & Sons. Here they had developed a group of bus services and a range of excursions and tours. During 1936, they exercised an option that had been secured by United Counties Omnibus Company to take over the stage services for the sum of £15,000, including five buses which took effect on Sunday, 24th January 1937. The excursions and tours section was not sold, but continued from Nene garage until 1951 when it was sold to Leicester interests.

Having taken over Smith's business, the Seamarks were much more interested in the coaching aspect of the business and had concluded an agreement with the Company to take from them the stage services (as detailed under Westoning & District Buses) with effect from 2nd June 1938. They continued the business with their well-known green and cream coaches for many years.

SEFTON, Henry   Hadleigh, Essex
Henry Sefton was one of the earliest to venture into mechanical traction in the Leigh area. Between 1908 and circa 1918, he had a small motor waggonette running between Leigh and Hadleigh and then the service continued under the Thundersley, Hadleigh and District Company (q.v.).

SERVICE SALOONS LTD.   Tylers Avenue, Southend-on-Sea, Essex
This company was registered on 28th February 1928 by James Knight and Victor Holmes who bought three ADC front entrance saloons in a light green livery which they placed in competition with 'New Empress Saloons' on the Southend—Brentwood—London service, and against 'Westcliff' on the through route, plus many others working over other sections of the road. By fast running and tight scheduling, these three coaches were expected to perform eleven return trips between Southend and Brentwood, of which one morning and one afternoon run continued through to King's Cross, plus two additional short trips from Southend to Billericay and return, which together totalled over 1,500 miles per week per vehicle! In March 1929, a Gilford coach, acknowledged for its speed, was added, so that the Brentwood runs could now continue as far as Seven Kings, but by now the strain from this kind of work, with but scant maintenance, was beginning to show and unreliability began to set in. Halfway through its second year, the vehicles were repossessed by the finance house at short notice and 'Westcliff' stepped in to pick up the licences. It now extended the service as far as Stratford Broadway running to an hourly headway. There were a number of prosecutions for speeding and other traffic offences.

SHOEBURYNESS MOTOR SERVICES LTD.   West Road, Shoeburyness, Essex
This company, registered to take over the business using the same name, was operated by Eric E. Hart, who was earlier in partnership with Mr Edmunds, and between them a service from Shoeburyness to Southend was started in March 1930 in opposition to 'Westcliff'. Hart secured licences for three vehicles on appeal, in which the Shoebury Council backed them strongly because they considered the service provided by 'West-cliff' was inadequate. They also ran a summer service from Shoebury town to the East Beach. Hart favoured Dennis single and double-decks painted in a pleasing light blue. 'Westcliff' made a very high offer to Hart for the business when it thought that H. R. Bridge was about to take it over. The main service was incorporated into the 'Westcliff' route 5 on 3rd January 1934, the beach route then becoming 5B.

SILVER END DEVELOPMENT COMPANY LTD.   Silver End, Essex
This company was closely connected with the Crittall Metal Window Company of Braintree, being formed as a private company in 1925 by Sir Valentine Crittall with a capital of £2. Sir Valentine had taken inspiration from Cadbury's Bournville and Lever Bros. Port Sunlight, and envisaged the development of a similar garden village complete with its own industrial unit to eventually become a self-contained self-supporting community based on model factory conditions and improved housing, with its own central emporium, public house (the Silver End Hotel), social centre, and so on, not to mention its own bus service to Braintree and Witham. The service commenced with a fleet of Panhard-Levassor saloons which were replaced in 1932 by three Leyland Tigers and after a year or two these were joined by two 20 seat Ford AAs. All were finished in the then standard Crittall

colours of light blue with bright orange lettering. The business was sold to Hicks Bros. in 1934 and they retained the bus depot, which is still in use today with Eastern National.

SILVER QUEEN MOTOR OMNIBUS CO. LTD.   Jackson Road, Clacton-on-Sea
The Silver Queen Motor Omnibus Co. Ltd. was only a renaming about mid-1926 of the former Clacton & District Motor Service Ltd. It was a logical change for its official title was virtually unknown to the travelling public as the fleet had always borne the name 'Silver Queen', as did the timetables and literature.

To avoid dividing what is, in fact, a continuous story, the whole of the happenings of 'Silver Queen' are detailed under the 'Clacton & District' heading. However, the map and reduced facsimile timetable which are titled 'Silver Queen' are shown here.

The Company acquired 'Silver Queen' in 1931, at which time many vehicles were absorbed. Typical of some, but not actually amongst them, was this early Leyland open-top, based at Clacton.

Eastern National

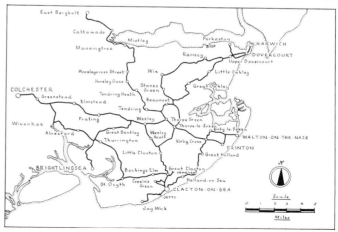

Routes worked by the Silver Queen Motor Omnibus Co. Ltd. — summer 1931.

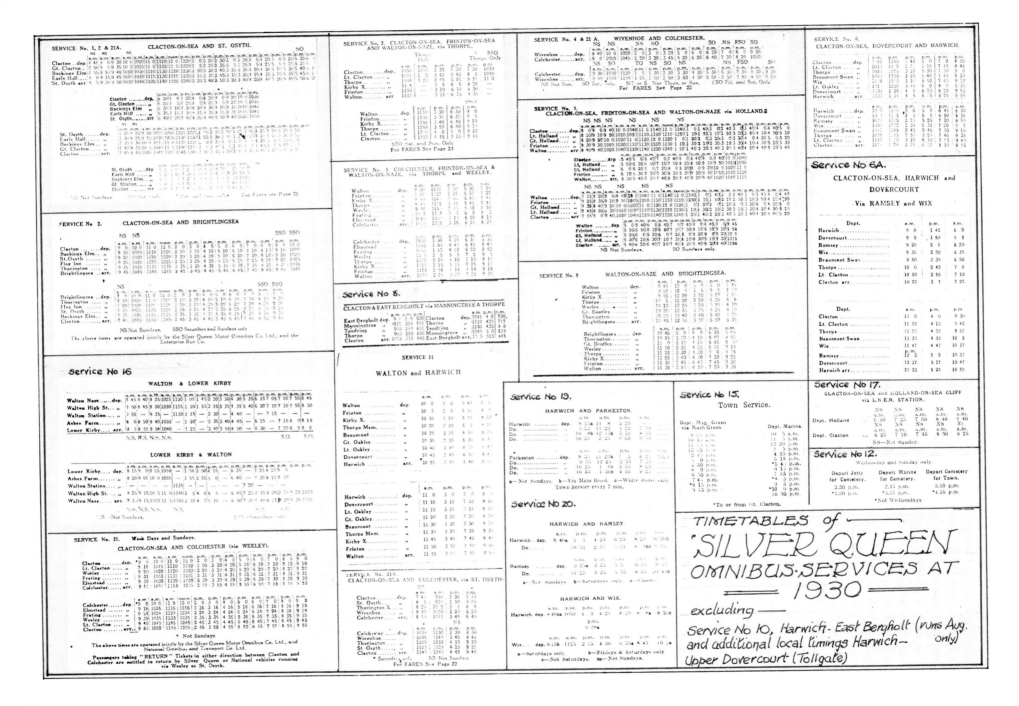

SIMPSON, C. & SONS The Stores, Leaden Roding, Essex

Charles Simpson was on the road with his carrier's cart by 1909, going to Chelmsford on Mondays and Fridays, where he put up at The Fleece, and is believed to also have run to Bishop's Stortford and to Dunmow on certain other days of the week. Leaden Roding lay at the centre of that large area of small scattered villages collectively known as The Rodings or Roothings, some of which were only 25 miles from London yet 8 to 10 miles from a railway station. At this time, there were six carriers providing the sole means of transit for goods and passengers into the area. The first motor bus service came in 1914 when the National Steam Car Company put on a twice weekly bus between Chelmsford and Leaden Roding along what is now the A414 and, by 1920, there were only four carriers at work. Simpson appears to have gradually increased his coverage of the area as the others dropped out. In 1922, he owned a 14 seat Ford but does not seem to have seriously concerned himself with omnibus services until 1928 when he got a Chevrolet bus and a small Vulcan charabanc. By this date, 'National' was still only running on two days a week, although the route had been continued through to Bishop's Stortford.

Simpson now began a daily through service between the two towns with sufficiently encouraging results to justify him acquiring another Chevrolet in March 1929. With this, he started his other main line, crossing the Rodings from Dunmow to Ongar and Brentwood on a daily schedule, both routes making connections at the crossing point at Leaden Roding. This year 'National' increased its service by working four return trips on Saturdays and Sundays, which was of more interest to people at the terminal points than to the villagers.

Simpson next bought a pair of GMC 26 seaters, followed by a Dodge in 1931, and another Chevrolet from Morse of Fyfield who had made some spasmodic attempts at running a bus service from that village. When the time came for applications for licences, Simpson was granted the following:

a) Dunmow—High Roding—Leaden Roding—White Roding—Abbess Roding—Fyfield—Chipping Ongar—Kelvedon Common—Brentwood (working daily)
b) Chelmsford—Good Easter—Leaden/White Rodings to High Roding or to Hatfield Broad Oak—Hatfield Heath—Hallingbury—Bishop's Stortford (running daily)
c) Leaden/White Rodings—Matching Green/Tye—Sheering—Hatfield Heath—Hallingbury—Bishop's Stortford (Thursdays)
d) Leaden/Abbess/Beauchamp Rodings—Fyfield—Willingales Doe/Spain—Roxwell—Chelmsford (Fridays)
e) Leaden/Aythorpe/High Rodings—Great Canfield—Hatfield Broad Oak—Woodside Green—Hallingbury—Bishop's Stortford (Thursdays)

There were some extra short workings on Saturdays on some of the market routes above. They also received licences for up to seven vehicles for excursions and tours from many points, including Dunmow and Bishop's Stortford.

In 1932 Simpson took over the coaching business of Browne Brothers of Chelmsford with their two Albion PKA26 all-weather coaches. Their next effort to improve services in that area was to start a daily route utilizing (c) and (d) with a new link through Ongar—Moreton and the Lavers, Magdalen, High and Little, which had never enjoyed any kind of bus service. It was a brave effort to serve a very thinly-populated district, but traffic did not justify it and the service reverted to the former pattern. One more new service (f) from Leaden Roding to Chelmsford, via Roxwell, for the benefit of work-people, was started and has continued.

Larger vehicles gradually made their appearance in the fleet which included a Dennis Lancet, three more Albions and a 20 seat Vulcan, with the popular Bedford featuring

prominently. Latterly, the fleet was in an all-over reddish maroon. After becoming motorized, the Chelmsford depot moved to the yard behind the Plough, opposite the omnibus station. The family also owned, for many years, the village stores and post office, and a coal merchants business which served a wide area. Simpson's services were taken over on 24th March 1940 with two buses, a Bedford and an Albion Victor. The services were numbered as follows:

(a) became new 3A; (b) and (f) were amalgamated with existing service 8, (c) became new 8A; (e) was the new 8B and (d) was combined with existing service 46.

SMITH, Sydney Marine Avenue, Southend-on-Sea, Essex

The above-named was the son of George Smith, a Southend cab proprietor, who had his own separate business as charabanc and brake owner, also operating a horse-bus service in the town, which ceased when the Corporation trams commenced. In 1908 he joined the Holmes Bros., both businesses combining as Charles and George Holmes and Sydney Smith Ltd., whereunder later information will be found. Reference should also be made to Holmes and Smith Ltd., and Westcliff and Southend Charabanc Company Ltd. Smith remained a Director of Westcliff Motor Services until shortly after Tilling assumed control.

SMITH, William Canvey Island, Essex
See Canvey Auxiliary Motors.

SOUTHEND-ON-SEA MOTOR CHARABANC COMPANY LTD. Southend-on-Sea, Essex

This company was founded on 4th April 1913 by Henry Brown junior and George Spencer, who was the first to open a true automobile works in the Borough. They had some Dennis charabancs trading as the 'Royal Blues' which competed strongly with the 'Westcliff' company's 'Royal Reds' with whom they amalgamated on 23rd April 1914. Both became directors of 'Westcliff', Brown occupying the Chair for some years, and Spencer becoming Managing Director. Later information can be found under 'Westcliff'.

SOUTHEND CHARABANC COMPANY 330 London Road, Southend-on-Sea, Essex

This was run by G. A. Weston after parting company with John Marks in 1920 when their Southend Motor Company ceased trading. He bought a pair of AEC Y type chassis with charabanc bodies known as 'The Cream Cars', which operated on a twice daily run between Southend and London. It ran for about two seasons, and 'Westcliff' added his picking up points in East London to its services from those parts to Southend.

SPRINGETT, H. & SON Hatfield Peverel, Essex

This operator started in the late 1920s with a service to Witham and Braintree, via the Notleys, giving a daily service of between six and ten departures with some extras from Braintree to Black Notley. All appeared to be well-established until disaster struck one night when the garage and bus were completely destroyed by fire. Hicks immediately continued the service by providing a bus which Springett continued to drive for them. The section between Witham and Hatfield Peverel was found to be superfluous and gradually dropped from the timetable, finally being withdrawn as a war economy measure. Springett's ill-fated bus was a Chevrolet, previously in the Bird Motor Service fleet of Akers at Halstead.

STANFORD MOTORS LTD. Corringham Road, Stanford-le-Hope, Essex

This company had been formed on 16th October 1928 to continue Suckling and Haxell's Motor Service, which began operations in February 1926, and was one of the last to continue working independently in this area. Mr David Hamilton was Managing Director and

Secretary, and Albert Haxell was Chairman. Before partnering Haxell, George Suckling had operated a taxi service cum car hire business in Stanford-le-Hope. Their services had been combined with Huggins' 'Victory Bus' just prior to licensing, for which they were granted:

1) Stanford-le-Hope to Grays, via Horndon (became ENOC service 38)
2) Grays to Stanford-le-Hope direct—Thames/Shell Haven (became ENOC service 35)
3) Stanford-le-Hope to Fobbing (The Mill) (became ENOC service 36)

There had earlier been a Laindon to Stanford-le-Hope service which failed to secure a licence. The business was acquired by the ENOC in June 1935 with two Gilford saloons and one Dennis saloon, together with a garage in Corringham Road which the ENOC continued to use until at least 1939. The 'Stanford' fleet also included a Daimler saloon and an ancient Daimler open-top double-deck, which were not taken into stock.

STARLING, G. E. & SONS   Stour Garage, Dovercourt, Essex
Robert Starling was a livery stable keeper and carriage letter at 11 Victoria Place in the 1870s, with a branch establishment at Stour Place. At the turn of the century, the business was in the hands of Edward and Robert Starling who was also a coal merchant at 119 High Street. By 1906, Mrs Mary Ann Starling was running the Victoria Place business and Robert was still at High Street where he was joined in 1914 by Horace Edwin, by which time the Victoria Place establishment ceased to exist. By 1917, Robert and Edwin had opened the Stour Garage with a branch at 39 Cliff Road, trading as coal merchants, funeral furnishers, motor cab proprietors and jobmasters and, by 1922, was trading as per title. The next year they took over operation of the Harwich—Upper Dovercourt service of the LNER which had just taken it over from the Great Eastern Railway, for which they (Starlings) had bought a pair of Guy BB 20 seat saloons. Around 1926, the services were sold to 'Silver Queen' of Clacton-on-Sea who opened a new depot in Kingsway, Dovercourt, but the two Guy buses went to 'Enterprise' at Clacton. The Starlings also had some Guy coaches with which they continued to offer excursions and tours from 39 Cliff Road which the company acquired at the close of the 1938 season with one Bedford coach. At this date the Starlings were undertaking furniture removals and general haulage, and also working in conjunction with the garage business at High Street.

STEVENS, J.   Stevington, Bedfordshire
Very little has been discovered concerning the above who, in 1931/2, received licences to run Bedford—Stevington, via Bromham, or via Kempston and Box End. At the end of the first year, the licences were not renewed, or the service had failed to operate, so the ENOC applied to run instead; the first timetable for service 7E, the replacement service, appearing in the issue dated November 1931. It is believed that the service had earlier been in the hands of a Mr Albert Victor Stevens of 27 Stuart Street, Kempston who, in 1927, owned a 14 seat Chevrolet registered TM1246. The service had been offered to a Mr Osborne of Turvey, Bedfordshire who apparently declined it, whereupon it passed to Mr J. Stevens for operation.

STRACEY, H. L.   Little Baddow, Chelmsford, Essex
About 1922 this operator commenced a bus/carrier service from Little Baddow (Paper Mill Lock) to Chelmsford by the back lanes and Gt. Baddow, which he ran until he retired in 1952, after selling the service to the Company who did not take over his Graham Bros. front entrance saloon bus. His terminus in Chelmsford was Victoria Road.

STRAWHATTER COACHES   45 Park Street West, Luton, Bedfordshire
Henry E. Hill chose this unusual, but not inappropriate, fleetname for a Luton-based business, the main line being a frequent coach service to London which was compulsorily acquired by the LPTB. There was also a group of seasonal coastal express services which were sold back to the ENOC with eight Gilford coaches, details of which are in *Chapter Two*. Hill continued a haulage business with seven lorries.

SUCKLING, George/SUCKLING & HAXELL'S MOTOR SERVICES, Stanford-le-Hope, Essex
George Suckling started with a Ford taxicab in 1925 and was joined, the next year, by Albert Haxell, whereupon the business was enlarged to trade as Suckling & Haxell's Motor Services around Stanford-le-Hope. In 1928, they were joined by David Hamilton and the business was converted into a limited company under the style of Stanford Motors Ltd., under which title further details are given.

SULLENS, T. and SON   3 Bridge Street, Finchingfield, Essex
Sullens continued operation of the carrier service previously worked by Ben Adams through Great Bardfield and Finchingfield to Braintree on Wednesdays. On 7th May 1934, C. M. Taylor, owner of the 'Horn' coaches, applied to take over the service which was combined with his existing Braintree—Great Bardfield service.

THE TRANSIT BUS   The Garage, Mile End, Colchester, Essex
The above business of the Goggin family was first in the hands of Mrs C. E. Goggin but, in 1931, licences were in the name of Mrs J. M. Goggin from whom they were transferred in 1937 to Percy Cecil and Geoffrey Willard Goggin, to be transferred the next year to the former Percy Cecil (solus) with whom they remained only a few months when he sold the service to the Company on 8th August with three vehicles. The regular route was from Wiston through Nayland to Colchester, which was combined with the existing service 15 and a football service from Mile End to Layer Road, Colchester, which received the number 28. Excursions and tours were offered from Mile End and Great Horksley.

THUNDERSLEY, HADLEIGH & DISTRICT MOTORS LTD.   London Road, Hadleigh, . Essex
There were three distinct companies of the above title, the first of which was registered in 1915 as a private company to trade as garage proprietors and to operate buses as indicated in the title. The main route ran Leigh—Hadleigh—Thundersley, taking a circular route. Services later ran from Leigh to Benfleet but these did not remain for long due to competition from Pearse (q.v.), 'Westcliff' and 'Blue Buses'. They ran for a time to Rayleigh, via Dawes Heath, and attempted to thwart 'Blue Buses' on the Leigh—Eastwood route, but without success. In 1919, it took over Henry Sefton's small service, and in the same year it was converted into a new public company of the same name at which date it possessed three motor buses and one motor waggonette (Sefton's), and opened an extensive automobile and general engineering department. In 1922, it took over the Hadleigh Garage & Transport Company (q.v.) and also absorbed the Hadleigh Motor Bus Company, when the fleet consisted of several very old Star single-decks and a very old Maudslay, believed to be one formerly owned by the Palace Hotel. In 1924, when 'Blue Buses' of H. R. Bridge were competing seriously, all the usual tactics of obstruction, racing, and so on were used on the road, but the behaviour of the crews at the Leigh terminus gave rise to numerous complaints of bad language, offensive behaviour and dangerous driving, as rivals crews left the proper stands to be first at the 'church' to capture commuters as

they emerged from the station footpath. It was an old problem; it existed in the days of horse-drawn conveyances when the Leigh drivers would do their utmost to frustrate the Hadleigh drivers who came to be known as the 'Hadleigh Fourpennies'. The situation improved very gradually and ceased when the new Leigh Railway Station opened on a different site. Latterly, the service became just a local run to and from Leigh and Hadleigh, but a new service to the Highlands Estate was started shortly before 'Westcliff' obtained control of the business on 28th December 1932. It registered another company, the third of the same name, but this time private, to administer the property which 'Westcliff' continued to use for vehicle storage until 1951. Henry A. Bridge bought it as part of the transaction when 'Westcliff' purchased the 'Benfleet & District', the 'Supreme' fleet then changing places with the 'Westcliff' vehicles. Three Thornycroft buses came into the 'Westcliff' fleet on 15th June 1935 when Thundersley, Hadleigh & District Motors Ltd. ceased to operate the services, 'Westcliff' having taken the licences.

TILBURY COACHING SERVICES LTD.   31A Dock Road, Tilbury, Essex
Sam and Isobel Skinner formed this company in 1931 at which time their principal activity was a frequent coach service to East Ham, extended into London at weekends, and which passed to the London Passenger Transport Board in March 1934. They also had a summer express coach route to Great Yarmouth and excursions and tours from Tilbury and Grays, the licences for which were applied for by Eastern National on 4th June 1934. No vehicles changed hands.

TILBURY & DISTRICT MOTOR SERVICES   19 Cowper Road, Tilbury, Essex
A. R. Greenslade used the above title for his omnibus business consisting of two services, viz: Tilbury (Dock Station LMS) to Chadwell St. Mary and Tilbury Ferry to Chadwell St. Mary, both via Civic Square and Feenan Highway. The ENOC took over both, the first becoming new 37B and the other being combined into the existing 37A. The precise date of transfer is not known but the licences were granted to the ENOC on 19th June 1933. No vehicles changed hands.

TILBURY SAFETY COACHES LTD.   Dock Road, Tilbury, Essex
Cecil W. Rudkins formed this company to continue his 'Swallow Coaches' which were mainly employed on the popular Tilbury—Grays—Purfleet service, for which he had a six vehicle allowance, the latter going to the LPTB on 18th July 1934, the ENOC taking the Tilbury section on the same day, together with his other services as detailed in *Chapter Two*.

TILLING TRANSPORT   London and Chelmsford
This was originally the private hire arm of Thomas Tilling's London undertaking, subsequently enlarged when it was joined by 'National's' similar London business in 1932. It became nationalized in 1948 and was formed into a separate company known as Tillings Transport (BTC) Ltd. In June 1951, it took over the business of Pat Hearn Ltd. together with a large garage at Northdown Street near King's Cross with a fleet of forty coaches, and the office went to Grays Inn Road. About 1962, control and engineering was transferred to Eastern National at Chelmsford which now developed the garage at Northdown Street into a fine up-to-date terminal for all the London services, the Coach/Air service to Southend Airport and the extensive tours section. Vehicles moved in and out of the two fleets in accordance with operational requirements. In 1969, the title changed to Tillings Transport (NBC) Ltd. continuing until 1974 when this business, and the rest of Eastern National's coaching activities, became the basis for the new National Travel (South East) Ltd.

The final order for Bristol MW coaches in 1966 comprised four 34 seaters for the Tilling fleet. No. T312 is seen outside the University Arms Hotel, Cambridge, while on contract to Thomas Cook & Sons Ltd., — one of Tilling's long standing customers.

G. R. Mills

TIMBERLAKE, H. W.   Canvey Island, Essex
This was one of the Canvey owners whose bus was in too bad a state to operate, so his share passed to A. Fraser Smith (q.v.).

TWEEN, H.   Tye Green, Good Easter, Essex
H. Tween was a one-man bus operator who worked three days a week between Good Easter and Chelmsford, using an old ex-RAF Crossley right up until he surrendered the service to Eastern National on 2nd February 1940. The body had every indication of having been home-made, looking not unlike a flat-topped greenhouse painted green. The service had originally been horse-worked by Mr Tunbridge from Good Easter, passing through Mashbury, from which point it was shared with Mr Sankey whose connection also probably went to Tween.

UNDERWOOD, P. H.   East Mersea, Essex
This is one of the longest-lived services to be acquired by the ENOC, for over fifty years the Underwood family linked East Mersea with the outside world using their carrier's cart and, later, motor bus. The Underwoods first became involved when Philip took over the cart from George Death around 1885, who in turn had succeeded James Greenleaf who is known to have been driving it to Colchester thrice weekly as early as 1848. Philip

was followed by his son Robert, circa 1895, who drove the cart well into the 1920s when grandson Philip Henry continued the service, but now by motor. He traded as Underwood's (Blue and Cream) Saloon Bus Service which ran daily with several additional departures from West Mersea to Colchester. About 1930, he took over the service of a Mr Day who had also worked over this latter section, and also worked from Fingringhoe to Colchester, via Blackheath. Of the five remaining survivors from the very hectic pre-licensing days, Underwood was the first to sell the Mersea service to the ENOC in January 1935. He continued in business at West Mersea as a motor engineer and garage owner in Kingsland Road.

UNION JACK (LUTON) OMNIBUS CO. LTD.   Luton, Bedfordshire

This company was registered on 20th November 1928 to continue a small bus business started by H. J. Witherington of Toddington, Bedfordshire, who had been working a service to Clophill and Ampthill somewhat spasmodically because of vehicle problems. The company was started by C. H. Strapps who was landlord of the Rabbits in Old Bedford Road, and A. E. Barber who kept the Robin Hood in Old Town Street. The Board was made up of P. R. Williams and G. E. Webb, who owned the Excelsior Motor Garage in Albert Road where the registered office was situated. Various bus routes were attempted and they are known to have worked to Aylesbury, Bedford, in and around Luton, and elsewhere, with or without licences, in true pirate fashion. Towards the end of 1929, the last two named Directors separated from the company, by which time it seems to have been working between Leighton Buzzard and the Vauxhall Works. During 1930, however, it was again in trouble and was summoned for more unauthorized operations. In April 1931, control of the business was in the hands of A. F. England who soon added a service to Whipsnade Zoo. When licensing applications were required, he put in for no fewer than six services which were supposed to have been operating. Only the Vauxhall Works and Whipsnade Zoo routes were granted licences, most of the others being awarded to 'Westoning & District' (q.v.) who had operated very similar services considerably longer. The office was next moved to England's headquarters at Britain Street, Dunstable, where he based his XL routes which were also placed with the 'Union Jack' company, soon to be joined by the 'Bluebird' services, the whole being sold to Luton Corporation on 23rd March 1933 as related in the main text. The company did not pass to the Corporation, but was next used by England to buy the 'Renown' service (q.v.) and two other businesses at Bedford (see under A. F. England) which the ENOC finally secured from him in December 1936.

UNITED COUNTIES OMNIBUS COMPANY LTD.   Bedford Road, Northampton, Northamptonshire

Transactions with the above company were mainly for the purpose of passing services to United Counties but, in 1939, there was a deal arranged whereby part of the business of Meadows and Son, Barton Seagrave came to Eastern National. Meadows had a long route from Kettering to Huntingdon which spread, inter alia, into both territories, part of which became jointly worked. Reference should also be made to J. Meadows and Son.

VENTURE BUS   Brightlingsea, Essex

A one bus operator, who traded as above, was acquired by A. W. Berry & Sons in the later 1920s. He worked between Brightlingsea and Colchester with a 14 seat Ford Model T, probably descended from a carrier run.

VICEROY COACHES   Bridge Street Garage, Saffron Walden, Essex

This name was adopted by F. C. Moore for his buses which originated in the Felstead area

Originally in the Meadows fleet, this 1932 Dennis Lancet passed to the Company via United Counties in 1939 as part of the Barton Seagrave business. Vehicle No. 3819 has a Duple body, with seating for 32 passengers.

where, until licensing brought regulation of services, there was considerable competition with Hicks Bros. Moore made seven applications to continue his existing routes but was only granted two licences, viz: Dunmow—Thaxted—Saffron Walden (three or four times daily) and a Friday service to Chelmsford from Gransmore Green, via Cock Green, Leez Priory and Howe Street, which was soon dropped. After a battle in the court, he obtained a licence in the following year for a service to run on Tuesdays from Dunmow to Holders Green, and Hicks received the same, but for a Saturday operation. The arrangement ceased after about twelve months. In 1936, the business moved to Saffron Walden after taking over A. V. Britton of Bridge End Garage who held four licences:

Saffron Walden—Audley End Station	Sundays only when no trains ran
Saffron Walden—Debden—Thaxted	Saturdays
Saffron Walden (and surrounding villages)	
— Clacton-on-Sea	summer express
Excursions and tours from Saffron Walden and eight village picking up points	

In 1937, the business became F. C. Moore Ltd. and, in 1938, he acquired two licences from A. G. Reed of 22 Castle Street for additional excursions and tours plus a Tuesday service from Saffron Walden to Radwinter.

Various services for workpeople, scholars and service personnel were operated, then suddenly, on 11th December 1969, for reasons unknown, operation of the Dunmow service ceased without any prior notice being given. Arrangements were hastily made with Eastern National to take up the service which recommenced on 15th December. It was subsequently joined to the existing 33 Chelmsford—Dunmow service to form a new useful cross-county through service.

VICTORY BUS   Stanford-le-Hope, Essex

This was the title used by Mr Huggins who operated from Grays to Stanford-le-Hope and Thames Haven, which he combined with Stanford Motors (q.v.) instead of making his own separate application for licences.

VICTORY SERVICE   Coggeshall, Essex

This fleetname was adopted by Fred Matravers of Coggeshall, a returned ex-serviceman who, as did many, invested his gratuities in a motor bus, and he chose one of the heavy War Department vehicles which were then very cheaply available. His vehicle carried the usual open-top double-deck body in scarlet, which bore the legend 'Victory' in huge letters on the side panels. To some extent he ran in competition with Hutley (q.v.) but, for some years, operated to Chelmsford, via Braintree on Fridays and also to Clacton on Thursdays and Sundays. After Hicks acquired Hutley's business, the two services were co-ordinated and became joint. Matravers sold the route to Hicks on 29th June 1931 by which time he was using a GMC saloon bus.

VIKING MOTOR COACHES   High Street, Thame, Oxfordshire

The proprietor of this coach line was Mr H. F. King, in continuance of an earlier service known as 'Wendrome' coaches who ran London—Wendover—Princes Risborough—Thame, which King extended to Oxford about 18th December 1930. He used some hire coaches from 'Premier Line' (q.v.) which took over the entire operation during 1932, placing it with its recently-acquired Aylesbury Omnibus Co. Ltd., passing to the ENOC in May 1933. This almost immediately cut off the Thame—Oxford portion and curtailed it at Tring Railway Station. Connections for London passengers were arranged with 'West London Coaches' at Wendover or by train at Tring Station (LMS). For later details see Aylesbury Omnibus Co. H. F. King had formerly been associated with North End Coaches of Portsmouth and Main Lines of London.

WAKERING MOTOR BRAKE   Great Wakering, Essex

This vehicle, of which no particulars are yet known, provided an early public service. It was run by Mr E. D. French from Great Wakering to Shoeburyness Railway Station in connection with the principal trains, but also to Bournes Green where it connected with the Southend Corporation trams. At the end of 1920, Southend Licensing Committee would not confirm the temporary licence he held from the Chief Constable, so 'Westcliff' took up the running which became part of a circular route from Southend, via Bournes Green, to Great Wakering and Shoeburyness, returning via North Shoebury and vice versa.

WALLEY, S.   The Bury, St. Osyth, Essex

For many years Mr Walley provided a summer service between St. Osyth beach and the village, where it connected with the Eastern National services to and from Colchester and Clacton, which was taken over in 1948 to run through to Clacton as service 101B.

WARNER, C. N.   The Limes, Church Hill, Rowhedge, Essex

Charles Newcombe Warner came on to the Rowhedge to Colchester road with his horse-drawn carrier cart before 1914, as successor to Jones & Harris (q.v.), setting up at the Plough Hotel, near St. Botolph Station. In the 1920s, he expanded into a motor bus service, running three times on Mondays, Tuesdays and Wednesdays, four times on Thursdays and Fridays, and every hour on a Saturday; he did not run on a Sunday. Just about the time World War II was declared, his licence was transferred to the Company, which does not appear to have altered its timetable for service 75D! No vehicle was acquired.

WESTON, G.   Eastwood, Southend-on-Sea, Essex

Weston provided the first public conveyance from Eastwood to Leigh by fitting some seating in his motor van which was normally used in connection with his village stores. He also ran unlicensed for a few commuters to Prittlewell Station. When H. R. Bridge started the 'Blue Buses', he was quite willing for his licence to be transferred.

'WESTCLIFF' AND SOUTHEND-ON-SEA MOTOR CHARABANC COMPANY LTD.

Southend-on-Sea, Essex

This was the predecessor of Westcliff-on-Sea Motor Services Ltd. which follows.

WESTCLIFF-ON-SEA MOTOR SERVICES LTD.   Pier Hill, Southend-on-Sea, Essex

Left: Timetable cover in use from 1928 to 1937. *Right:* New timetable cover for 1938, showing one of the rare AEC Ranger touring coaches introduced in 1937. Also shown is the modernized entrance to the Pier (1⅓ miles long).

This concern was, by far, the largest single undertaking to be taken over by Eastern National, having started operations in 1914 when two rival charabanc businesses, operating in the Southend/Westcliff area, came together after rumours reached them that a large London-financed group had intentions to commence a transport system in the area.

The older business was that of Charles and George Holmes and Sydney Smith Ltd., which had descended from a livery stables and carriage hiring operation which had not long introduced motor cars and charabancs, trading as 'The Royal Red Cars'. The other founding partner was the Southend-on-Sea Charabanc Co. Ltd. of Brown and Spencer — the 'Royal Blue Cars'. Brown had been one of the pioneers of motor charabancs in the area, while the latter is credited with having opened the first proper motor garage in the County Borough. Competition between the 'Royal Blues' and the 'Royal Reds' had been very keen.

The combined undertaking was established on 23rd April 1914 as the Westcliff and Southend-on-Sea Charabanc Co. Ltd., and traded as the 'Royal Red Cars' from Pier Hill. Before its first season was completed, war had been declared and most of the fleet was requisitioned by the military. After peace was restored, the company rapidly assembled a new fleet, securing twelve Daimler chassis, mounted with charabanc bodies, to which a further thirteen were added in 1920. These included one Daimler saloon bus and three ex-London B type AEC double-decks.

The only public transport in the Borough at the time was the Corporation trams working on four routes. It had started running some buses in 1914 which ceased in 1916 as they were unremunerative. However, no move was made to resume the service after the war in spite of public demands. Consequently 'Westcliff' decided to fill the gap by starting a service in the spring of 1920 between Pier Hill and Westcliff (Plough Hotel), via Clifftown, using a Daimler saloon carried on pneumatic tyres all round (as, indeed, was its entire fleet, excepting the double-decks). This was an advanced feature at this early date. Later that year, a service was started to Hadleigh and Rayleigh with satisfactory results. In 1921, the title was changed to the handier style of Westcliff Motor Services Ltd. and buses were now running to Rochford and Ashingdon, to Eastwood and Rayleigh, and to Great Wakering and Shoeburyness, which incorporated E. D. French's 'Wakering Motor Brake'.

New services which commenced in 1922 included one reaching to Brentwood via Laindon, and the first taste of competition appeared when Major Pearse of South Benfleet started a service from that point to Southend, with Westcliff replying soon after with a similar facility. The other major event of that year was the inauguration of the famous 'Westcliff' extended tours of between five and twelve days duration. A very high standard was enjoyed and enormous goodwill was earned, not only on their home ground, but with several major travel agencies in London which actively promoted them.

Bus services to several new destinations, including Canvey Island, were introduced in 1922. A new competitor appeared during this year when H. R. Bridge, an estate developer at Eastwood, started his Edwards Hall Motors (better known as the 'Blue Buses') as 'Westcliff' would not improve its service to Eastwood. There next developed a long and bitter battle between the 'Reds' and the 'Blues' in which all the usual tactics were employed, but 'Westcliff' had the benefit of a different weapon — friends in the right places! It had the ability to secure for itself as many licences from the Watch Committee as it could use, and could also obtain the refusal of any licence to which application it objected. This made life very difficult for outsiders, some of whom made successful appeals to the Minister of the grounds of discrimination.

The venture to Canvey Island can only be described as a most unfortunate affair. Not only did buses from Benfleet Station have to splash their way over the stony causeway when the tide was suitable, — at other times passengers were ferried by rowing boat to buses waiting on the island side — but they also had to face no fewer than seventeen island owners working on the 3½ mile route, each of whom took a very poor view at the arrival of an interloper. They made life even more hazardous for the drivers over the only 'road' when the company buses frequently found themselves forced into the deepest ruts or ditches and hemmed in at the terminals by the heterogenous assemblage of vehicles. Buses often became involved in 'accidents' on the causeway, resulting in a wheel being caught in a rut and the vehicle becoming bogged down. One bus was entirely lost in the creek and at least one other became engulfed up to the roof by the rising tide before it could be extricated. After that incident 'Westcliff' decided that Canvey was not the best place to be operating buses, and left the Canvey operators in undisputed possession of the island for another twenty seven years! Things had become more civilized when 'Westcliff' eventually returned.

Competition of a new kind appeared in 1927 when the 'New Empress' Saloons appeared in Southend, having travelled all the way from Harringay, picking up at almost all points and offering several departures daily in smart new Dennis saloons on pneumatic tyres, and without any need to pre-book. The company did the only thing it could to protect its interests by putting on a similar service. Many other operators appeared on various sections or over the whole of the forty eight mile route on which there was a good deal of racing and cutting of fares before regulation put a stop to it. With more competition appearing on their doorstep, 'Westcliff' and 'Blue Buses' decided the time had come to sink their differences and devote their energies to defeating the opposition rather than themselves. The 'Blue Buses' now became a wholly-owned subsidiary of 'Westcliff' and Messrs H. R. and H. A. Bridge occupied places on the Board. An attempt was made by 'Service Saloons' to establish themselves on the London route, but when they came to a sudden stop, in 1929, and their fleet was seized, 'Westcliff' took over their timings and later consolidated them into the Wood Green route, which now ran half-hourly on equal terms with 'City'. The latter had, in the meantime, taken over 'New Empress', so that a fifteen minute frequency over the whole route was attained by working a co-ordinated rather than joint service.

The status quo in Southend was disturbed in 1929 when the Corporation finally made up its mind to play a greater part in the provision of public transport, when it secured powers to operate trolley buses and motor buses. The routes they chose were mainly already covered by 'Westcliff', 'Blue Buses' and 'Borough', or over ground for which others had sought licences but had been refused. The private operators made appeals to the Minister but before any decision could be reached, the new 1930 Traffic Act had become law and the Corporation suddenly found it was unable to issue itself with the licences it had denied to others! It was now in exactly the same position as any other newcomer seeking to start a service, and would have to apply to the Traffic Commissioners for a licence. This was refused to the Corporation because of objections lodged by the affected parties and an appeal still produced the same result. The Corporation was forced to the conclusion that it would have to negotiate with the objectors and eventually agreed to buy five services, three from 'Blue Buses', and one each from 'Westcliff' and 'Borough'. At the same time, the County Borough was divided into two zones, East and West, with the Corporation operating to the east, and the west being left to company operators. The transfer of services was effected on 1st January 1933. Meanwhile, 'Westcliff' had taken over the 'Barling and Wakering' service of W. O. Mitchell in 1931, in which year it also negotiated for control of Morley's Rochford & District Motor Services, who continued to operate its brown buses until fully absorbed in 1933.

Unhappily there had been considerable disunity in the Board room since 1931 when Henry Brown and George Spencer departed for retirement. There had been considerable difficulty in obtaining agreement on policy, and the Bridges were not happy with certain matters regarding the accountancy, or the tenancy arrangements at Pier Hill, which was still owned by Holmes & Smith Ltd. Matters so deteriorated during 1932 that both H. R. and H. A. Bridge resigned. Obtaining release of their capital was the source of some embarrassment to the company, its financial position having suffered as a result of the severe competition and fare cutting. The Bridges were prepared to accept the business of Ardley Bros. at Tottenham in part settlement; in fact it was already held by H. R. Bridge as security for loans advanced to 'Westcliff' to whom it was leased back.

A number of related changes took place about this time. 'Borough' also operated to Grays and had locally secured control of Seymour's 'Rayleigh Motor Services' in June 1930, which gave them two services to Southend and a through route to Colchester via Maldon. Eastern National wanted both 'Rayleigh' and 'Borough' off this route and, equally of course, 'Borough' removed from the Grays route. On 5th January 1933, it secured control of 'Borough' and, as a corollary, 'Rayleigh' also, but could of itself only operate the Colchester service due to a long standing agreement with 'Westcliff'. The difficulty was eventually overcome by transferring control of 'Rayleigh' to 'Westcliff' and making 'Borough' a subsidiary of Eastern National.

The new licensing arrangements soon brought about a more ordered state of affairs in the omnibus world, and the company's fortunes began to improve. Control of the 'Thundersley, Hadleigh & District Motors' was obtained right at the end of 1933 and of 'Shoeburyness Motor Services' from Eric Hart in January 1934. Meanwhile, soon after taking their departure from 'Westcliff', the Bridges had obtained control of 'Pearse's Motor Services' at Benfleet which was reconstructed as Benfleet and District Motor Services Ltd. Two years later, H. R. Bridge obtained control of the Canvey & District Motor Transport Co. Ltd. which, to meet the new licensing requirements, had been created from the former seventeen partner Canvey Association by discreetly buying out the shareholders one by one.

In 1934, the 'Westcliff' interests in North and East London underwent a dramatic change. It is not known whether this was because the Board did not wish to continue operating there or if it was for financial reasons. In July, the Southend to East Ham route was curtailed at Grays when the LPTB took over the section within its special area. About the same time, the 'Westcliff' coaching interests at Walthamstow, together with two of its North London coach routes, were passed to Holmes & Smith Ltd., one of the founding partners which still traded separately as car hirers and motor agents, etc. Henderson Travel, also at Walthamstow and owned jointly with Lambs Ltd., was sold to a Mr Couch and, near the year end, to the surprise of many, it sold the Wood Green to Southend route to its rival 'City Omnibus Company' together with the two other North London express services. This left 'Westcliff' with only the Southend—Victoria Coach Station service, which also picked up at Islington, Dalston and Walthamstow for Leigh, Westcliff and Southend.

At almost the same moment as the above transfer was taking place, Tillings acquired sufficient shares to secure control of the company in December 1934. One of its first actions was to wind up the various subsidiary companies so 'Shoebury Motor Services', 'Rayleigh Motor Services' and 'Thundersley, Hadleigh & District' were all fully integrated during 1935.

Tillings next made overtures to Southend Corporation, with whom it was anxious to reach a much closer working arrangement similar to those it had negotiated with the Brighton, Bristol, Keighley, and York municipal undertakings, but they were declined. One of the stumbling blocks to a fully co-ordinated system was the continued presence of 'Benfleet' and 'City', which had no desire to sell or participate in such an arrangement.

Little of any great importance occurred to 'Westcliff' during the next five years, beyond the steady intake of standard vehicles of Bristol/ECW manufacture until the outbreak of war in 1939, which brought the usual problems common to all bus businesses such as call up of staff, coping with black-out conditions and the requisitioning of vehicles. The latter did not trouble 'Westcliff' as much as it did others as a high proportion of the residents, and most of the schoolchildren, had moved or had been evacuated out of the area, and the relatively large coaching aspect of the business had practically ceased. During this period, 'Westcliff' was able to assist other less fortunate undertakings with the loan of vehicles.

In 1940, 'Westcliff' was able to acquire the licences of Multiways Ltd., a Southend operator with several valuable coastal express services, together with its smaller subsidiary Hardings Coaches Ltd., both of whom had ceased operations for the duration of the hostilities. In October, Tillings decided that there was no need for 'Borough' to continue as a separate operating entity, as no useful purpose was derived from the arrangement, so the two Leigh-on-Sea services were continued by 'Westcliff' and the Grays route became Eastern National.

Some further dialogue with the Southend Corporation, during 1945, proved more fruitful, out of which a co-ordination and pooling scheme was evolved to take effect early in 1946 in which Southend Corporation and 'Westcliff' each had a 45.9 per cent interest, the balance of 8.2 per cent representing Eastern National's share. The Corporation next applied for and obtained consent to operate services outside the boundary of the Borough, and certain changes indicating a closer working relationship could now be seen. Similarly, Eastern National and 'Westcliff' were also working more closely after 1951, when both shared in the provision of new facilities to serve the Basildon New Town, and interavailability of return tickets over common sections of route was at long last introduced.

In 1951, H. R. Bridge felt it was time to take retirement and sold the 'Benfleet' and 'Canvey' business to the BTC who immediately placed them with 'Westcliff' for operation, doubling the frequency on route 3 between Southend and South Benfleet, making the Canvey section a new route 26 and the Wickford route 27. 'Westcliff' now took over the modern 'Benfleet' garage at Hadleigh and the 'Canvey' garage at Leigh Beck but, at the same time, Bridge acquired the former TH&DMS garage at Hadleigh, which 'Westcliff' still used to house the Bridges' coaching interests which were retained and still flourish under the 'Supreme' banner with later generations of the Bridge family in command.

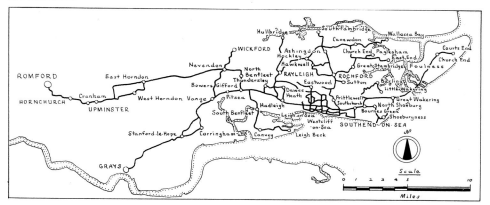

Services operated by Westcliff-on-Sea Motor Services Ltd. — 1951.

The final obstacle to that desideratum of a fully integrated transport system, so long sought for in the area, was removed in February 1952 when the Mallender family sold its City Coach Company of over a hundred units to the BTC. This brought 'Westcliff' three new depots, at Tylers Avenue, Southend, at Lordship Lane, Wood Green, and at North Road, Brentwood, the former 'City' headquarters. A new enquiry office and travel bureau opened almost immediately at 3 High Street, Brentwood, and excursions and tours started.

It was realized that the days of 'Westcliff' were numbered and that another well-known fleetname would soon be passing into oblivion as so recently happened to 'Benfleet', 'Canvey' and 'City', and was also about to happen to 'Hicks'. The long-needed rationalization of services handed down from the above-named operators which were, to all intents and purposes, still working their individual networks, was settled during 1954, and the final day of the old regime was fixed for 2nd January 1955. The following day, there was only Eastern National left and the newly-constituted partnership with Southend Corporation entitled Southend & District Joint Services. However, some indication of the high esteem attached to the old 'Westcliff' tours and coaching section may be gathered by the fact that these continued to be marketed by Eastern National in its literature, by using the 'Westcliff' name for at least another seven years before it became just another memory.

Today, it is almost impossible to find any remains of this once well-known concern. The former 'Westcliff' headquarters at Pier Hill was vacated some years ago. The former 'City' depot at Tylers Avenue, through which millions of Londoners have, over the years, queued after a long day by the sea, with the knowledge that no matter how many were waiting, but providing they were there by the last scheduled departure time, 'City' would keep turning coaches until all had been cleared, has likewise vanished beneath a car-park. The former 'Westcliff' engineering department at Prittlewell has also been vacated and so too have the Canvey and Wood Green depots. Only the former 'Benfleet' garage, since enlarged, and the Brentwood depot, with which 'Westcliff' was associated as an interim measure, now remain.

Further information about the various businesses which 'Westcliff' took over will be found under their own names in this appendix.

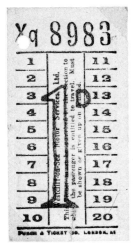

Punch type ticket 1d. single — white. 'Setright' ticket 2½d. single — buff. 'Setright' ticket 4d. single issued from a 'City' machine on a brown paper roll.

NUMERICAL INDEX TO STAGE CARRIAGE SERVICES

Service No.	Route
1	Southend-on-Sea, Leigh-on-Sea, Hadleigh, Thundersley and Rayleigh ...
2	Southend-on-Sea, Leigh-on-Sea, Hadleigh, Pitsea, Vange, Corringham, Stanford-le-Hope and Grays ...
2A	Southend-on-Sea, Leigh-on-Sea, Hadleigh, Pitsea, Vange, Laindon, Upminster, Hornchurch and Romford ...
2B	Southend-on-Sea, Leigh-on-Sea, Hadleigh, Pitsea, Vange, Homesteads, Stanford-le-Hope and Grays ...
2C	Southend-on-Sea, Leigh-on-Sea, Hadleigh, Pitsea, Vange, Corringham, Shellhaven ...
3	Southend-on-Sea, Leigh-on-Sea, Hadleigh, Tarpots and South Benfleet ...
4	Southend-on-Sea, Bournes Green, Wakering and Landwick ...
4A	Southend-on-Sea, Bournes Green, Wakering and Shoeburyness Station ...
4B	Southend-on-Sea, Bournes Green, Barling and Little Wakering ...
5	Southend-on-Sea, Bournes Green and Shoeburyness (Direct) ...
6	Southend-on-Sea (Pier Hill) and Westcliff-on-Sea (Railway Station) ...
6B	Westcliff-on-Sea (Railway Stn.) and Rayleigh (High St.) ...
7	Southend-on-Sea, Rochford, Ashingdon, Hockley and Rayleigh ...
8	Southend-on-Sea, Rochford, Hawkwell, Hockley and Rayleigh ...
8A	Southend-on-Sea, Rochford, Hall Road, Hockley and Rayleigh ...
9 & 9A	Southend-on-Sea and Eastwood (Willson Road) ...
9B	Southend-on-Sea and Sutton (School) ...
10	Southend-on-Sea, Rochford, Stambridge and Paglesham ...
11	Southend-on-Sea, Rochford, Ashingdon, Stambridge, Larks Hill and Fambridge ...
12	Southend-on-Sea, Rochford, Stambridge, Canewdon, Loftmans Corner and Creeksea (Wallasea Bay Yacht Station) ...
17	Southend-on-Sea (Pier Hill), Westcliff-on-Sea, Prittlewell Chase and Eastwood (Woodcutters Arms Hotel) ...
18	Southend-on-Sea, Bournes Green, Wakering and Foulness ...
19	Chalkwell Station and Westborough Road ...
19	Southend-on-Sea (Kursaal), Western Esp., Chalkwell Avenue, Ridgeway, Pall Mall, Elm Hotel, Leigh-on-Sea ...
19A	Southend-on-Sea (Kursaal), Western Esplanade, Chalkwell Avenue, London Road, Elm Hotel, Leigh-on-Sea ...
21	Leigh-on-Sea (Railway Station), Leigh Church and Prittlewell (Hobleythick Lane) ...
22	Leigh-on-Sea (Railway Station), Leigh Church, Hadleigh, Daws Heath, Woodmans Arms, Rayleigh and Hullbridge ...
23	Leigh-on-Sea (Railway Station), Leigh Church, Belfairs Golf Course and Eastwood (Jones' Corner) ...
23A	Leigh-on-Sea (Railway Station), Leigh Church, Elmsleigh Drive and Eastwood (Coombe's Corner) ...
24	Leigh-on-Sea (Church and Station), Thames Drive and Rayleigh (High Street) ...
25A	Highlands Boulevard, Southchurch and Thorpe Bay ...
25B	Highlands Boulevard, Eastern Esplanade and Thorpe Bay ...
26	Leigh Beck Farm (Canvey Island), Haystack and South Benfleet (Canvey Bridge) ...
26A	Casino (Canvey Island), Haystack and South Benfleet (Canvey Bridge) ...
27	South Benfleet, Pound Lane, Nevendon and Wickford ...
80	Pitsea (Station Lane), Vange, Corringham, Stanford and East Tilbury (Bata Shoe Factory) ...
—	Southend-on-Sea (Tylers Avenue), Eastwood, Rayleigh, Wickford, Billericay, Brentwood, Romford, Ilford, Woodford, Walthamstow, Tottenham and London (Wood Green) ...
—	Brentwood, Billericay, Ramsden, Wickford and Shotgate ...
—	Brentwood and Hutton (Bracken Bank) ...
—	Laindon (Railway Station), Billericay, Little Burstead and Brentwood ...
—	Laindon (Railway Station), Dunton, Bulphan, Herongate, Brentwood, Kelvedon, Stondon, Blackmore and Ongar (Two Brewers) ...
—	Brentwood and Little Warley ...
—	Laindon (Railway Station), Billericay, Great Burstead and Brentwood ...
—	Laindon (Railway Station) and Pipps Hill (Circular) ...
—	Billericay (Sun Corner) and Billericay (Sunnymede Estate) ...
—	Laindon Hotel (Rectory Road) and Wickford ...
—	Brentwood (Woodman Road), Doddinghurst, Hook End and Stowdon ...
—	Laindon (Railway Station) and Langdon Hills (Crown Hotel) ...

Complete schedule of stage services as shown in the last 'Westcliff' timetable published 1st June 1952.

WESTONING & DISTRICT BUS SERVICE   High Street, Westoning, Bedfordshire

George Irwin Smith built a small group of bus services under the above fleetname during the later 1920s, utilizing odd parts of Pope's extinct 'Reliance' service at Hockliffe. When applications came before the Traffic Commissioners in 1931, it transpired that A. F. England, of the 'Union Jack' company, had put in almost identical applications to those of Smith which he alleged had been operating for some time. However, these were all disallowed, and Smith received licences for the services for which he applied, which were as follows:

a) Clophill—Ampthill—Greenfield—Westoning—Harlington—Toddington   (daily)
b) Westoning—Eversholt—Toddington—Tebworth—Hockliffe—Leighton Buzzard—
   Heath and Reach   (Tuesdays, Saturdays and Sundays)
c) Westoning—Eversholt—Milton Bryan—Toddington   (Saturdays)
d) Westoning—Ampthill—Woburn—Woburn Sands—Ampthill Circular)
                                       (Thursdays, Saturdays and Sundays)

Smith also had a group of excursions and tours starting from Westoning and, on 27th May 1935, acquired another group operated by F. R. Webb at Leighton Buzzard. For later details see under Seamarks Bros.

WICKFORD CARRIAGE CO. LTD.   Runwell Road, Wickford, Essex

This company was formed by Mr C. W. Spurling, in September 1928, to operate services from Wickford to a number of points poorly-served by existing road and rail services. These ran to Chelmsford, via Downham and Billericay; to Tilbury, via Pitsea and Stanford-le-Hope; and to Maldon, through South Woodham, Stow St. Marys and Purleigh. The first two were linked to make one long route which developed to have some importance, but the latter only came into its own during the summer. Spurling used some small 20 seat buses in brown livery. The company traded only until 27th May 1930 when the business was transferred to Wickford Omnibus Services Ltd.

WICKFORD OMNIBUS SERVICES LTD.   Runwell Road, Wickford, Essex

The above-named continued the services of Wickford Carriage Co. Ltd. and enjoyed an even shorter existence than its parent, for it was taken over and renamed Pattens Coaches Ltd. on 6th May 1931, after less than a year in operation. Pattens only ran the Pitsea to Chelmsford section, the Maldon service being acquired by 'Quest' (q.v.), and the Pitsea to Tilbury section was abandoned as there were more than sufficient buses on that road at the time.

WILKINSON, J. A.   The Homestead, Nounsley, Hatfield Peverel, Essex

This was one of three small operators working out of Terling, as well as Eastern National which, to simplify matters and avoid duplication, will all be dealt with together. The other two were W. A. Waite of the Old Post Office and A. J. Forbes of The Street, whose services had begun as a carrier's cart to Chelmsford run by Mr Wood. Before that, it was with one Thorogood who set up at The Dolphin, Waite moving it latterly to the Rosebery Yard in Springfield Road. It is rather surprising that Eastern National, who had no service to Terling prior to July 1931, were granted a licence when there were already three others all seeking a living off a very thin route. Forbes was licensed to run to Chelmsford on Friday via Russell Green and Boreham, (as was Waite) although Wilkinson also ran on Saturdays and also sent one trip via Crix Corner. Forbes and Waite also had licenses to run to Braintree on Wednesdays, the former going via Fairstead and the latter via Fuller Street, and also gave a Saturday evening cinema run. Forbes was also licensed

to run to Witham on four days. Having obtained his licences Forbes, for reasons unknown, suddenly ceased operating on 12th October 1931 and his Braintree trip on Wednesdays was taken up by Wilkinson. No one took on the Witham service, a road which has not seen a bus for over fifty years, and Waite and Wilkinson covered the Chelmsford route. Eastern National, by the way, ran via Hatfield Peverel. As time went on, Waite got into difficulties, and his service finally came to an end on 6th January 1936 leaving Wilkinson to continue alone until he disposed of his business to the Company in July 1942. The route, via Russell Green, to Chelmsford became the new 50A, but now terminated a little short of Terling at Flacks Green, which avoided the need to send the buses through a deep water splash at the River Ter. The Braintree run was abandoned but restored in slightly different form after hostilities ended, and the service via Crix Corner has never run since.

WILLIAMS, D. E., Senior and WILLIAMS, D. E. Junior   The Den, Foksville Road, Canvey Island, Essex

D. E. Williams, senior, was one of the seventeen Canvey busmen, but he refused to join the Canvey & District Company, preferring to go it alone. The family had been much involved with the development of the island as some were builders, others estate agents and taxi and bus operators. Later, D. E. Williams, senior, became water drainage engineer to the new Council. He secured a licence from the Traffic Commissioners which was suspended in 1932 for the contravention of the conditions, and was restored to D. E. Williams, junior, who continued the service with a pair of ex-London K type double-decks. One curious feature of his licence was the requirement for him to operate the Sunday timetable once in seventeen weeks; clearly a hangover from the days of the seventeen owners on rotation. After H. R. Bridge obtained control of the Canvey & District Motor Transport Company, Williams sold his service to him which also had the benefit of excursions and tours from Leigh Beck. The Williams family also ran the Popular Premier Night Club and the Chris Williams Jazz Band . . . obviously a very versatile lot.

WILSON, H.   The Garage, Clavering, Essex

See under 'Clavering & District'.

WISE A. and F.   Riseley, Bedfordshire

The above were granted a licence in 1931 for a Wednesday and Saturday service to Bedford, over the same route as ENOC service 5 from Kimbolton. Their licence was revoked on 24th June 1932 on the grounds that they had failed to operate the service on a number of occasions (presumably when insufficient passengers appeared), so the ENOC was granted additional timings in replacement. The business had been long-established for we find a Samuel Wise was driving his carrier's cart as far back as 1894 but, by 1906, Frederick was running it; he handed over to the above, circa 1922, when it became motorized. In Samuel's day, there were two other carriers from Riseley, a Thomas Valentine and Mr Wadsworth. By 1914, the latter had given up to Thomas Porter who ceased about 1922, Valentine lasting until 1924, by which time all was in the hands of the Wise family.

WITHERINGTON, A. J.   Toddington Road, Leagrave, Bedfordshire

A. J. Witherington did not operate for long. He started in May 1928 between Luton and Toddington but, when attempting to extend to Ampthill, was refused a licence by Luton Watch Committee who considered his vehicle to be unsuitable. At the end of the year, the Union Jack (Luton) Omnibus Co. Ltd. took over the service.

WONDER BUS SERVICE   29 Park Road, Kempston, Bedfordshire

The above was the fleetname of Albert Charles Carding, trading from about 1927 but later in the hands of his sons R. A. and Percy who seems to have dropped out by the time the business was sold to 'Union Jack' (q.v.) in April 1933. It included one Dennis F saloon which eventually came to the company on acquiring that business.

'Wonder' operated two local services in Bedford (a) George Street to Kempston, which was co-ordinated with the Company's route 1 and (b) from Midland Railway Station to Stanley Street. Carding retained his excursions and tours which were now operated by a new company called Swallow Omnibus and Coach Company. Earlier Carding had also competed with Eastern National on the Bedford—Cranfield route, but his application for a licence was refused by the Licensing Authority.

WRIGHT BROS. LTD.   Harlow, Essex

In the 1930s they described themselves as motor jobmaster's with open and closed cars and coaches for hire day and night. The Directors were George Samuel and Peter W. They had a licence for excursion and tours from Harlow and Sawbridgeworth and, post-war, had been engaged with contract work. Financial difficulties arose, and a receiver was appointed who arranged for Eastern National to continue handling the contracts until arrangements could be completed for the transfer of the business during 1962. A travel bureau was later opened at their former premises in High Street, Old Harlow.

XL MOTOR SERVICE   30 Lovers Walk, Dunstable, Bedfordshire

This was the first of A. F. England's several ambitious ventures into the world of motor bus operation which worked the following services:

1)   Luton—Dunstable—Leighton Buzzard—Wing (became part ENOC 18)
2)   Luton—Houghton Regis—Dunstable (taken over by Luton Corporation)
3)   Leighton Buzzard—Tring (became ENOC 16) — formerly Pope's 'Reliance'
4)   Dunstable—Studham (claimed by England but failed to secure licence)

XL ceased operations on 23rd March 1933 when England's businesses all passed to Luton Corporation.

XMAS BUS SERVICE   Great Wigborough, Essex

In addition to being landlord of the Kings Head Inn at Great Wigborough, Mr P. W. Christmas also ran the village carrier cart which he had taken over from Mr Marlborough back in the 1890s. This went to Colchester, twice weekly, through Peldon and Abberton. He replaced this with a small motor bus in the early 1920s and offered an improved service which ran twice on Mondays and Tuesdays, thrice on Wednesdays, Fridays and Saturdays and, on Thursdays and Sundays it was used for special trips.

About 1930, when he was well past the age when most had retired, Mr Christmas felt it would be wise, in view of the new licensing system about to come into being, to give up, so he sold the route to the Thorpe Bros. of West Mersea (q.v.).

YOUNG, E. W.   County Garages, Buckingham Street, Aylesbury, Buckinghamshire

E. W. Young was proprietor of the Aylesbury Motor Bus Company, which started about 1920, under which title details will be found.

Addendum to Appendix C

Blue Coach (Bedford) and Ideal Bus (Bedford)

Since this appendix was closed for typesetting, the results of some further research recently to hand suggests, but cannot be positively affirmed, that the notices relating to the above named operators require some amendment.

It now appears that the Blue Coach route from Bedford to Oxford, attributed to G. O. Gammond, originated with E. J. Cooper, proprietor of the 'Ideal Bus' circa 1929, which was sold in 1930 to Gammond with some of his coaches soon after the latter had acquired H. Henman's business in Marlborough Road, where the Blue Coaches continued to be based.

Gammond routed his coaches via Bromham, Turvey and Olney to Newport Pagnell, whereas Cooper's travelled direct via Astwood and Stagsden; both continued via Wolverton, Stony Stratford, Buckingham and Bicester to Oxford.

Appendix D
Senior Officers

EASTERN NATIONAL OMNIBUS COMPANY LIMITED (1929—1969)

Periods covered by the senior officers

General Manager
Smith, Bert — Start of period—30.11.37
Pickett, Claude H. S. — 1.12.37—22.7.45
Gavin, James S. — 23.7.45—31.12.54
Richards, Leslie E. — 1.1.55—20.5.60
Bushrod, Robert F. — 1.8.60—End of period

Secretary
Hunt, Richard — Start of period—30.4.32
Pickett, Claude H. S. 1.5.32—31.12.33
Ellis, Henry L. — 1.1.34—28.2.42
Pratt, Bernard J. — 1.6.42—31.3.48
Elsley, Roland — 1.4.48—31.1.67
Wass, Norman — 1.2.67—End of period

Chief Engineer
Morison, William — Start of period—31.7.49
Skinner, William T. — 1.8.49—31.12.62
Kydd, Ian R. — 1.1.63—End of period

Traffic Manager
Bryan, Frank — Start of period—31.5.58
Quilter, L. John — 1.6.58—31.12.62
Hanley, Robert — 1.1.63—End of period

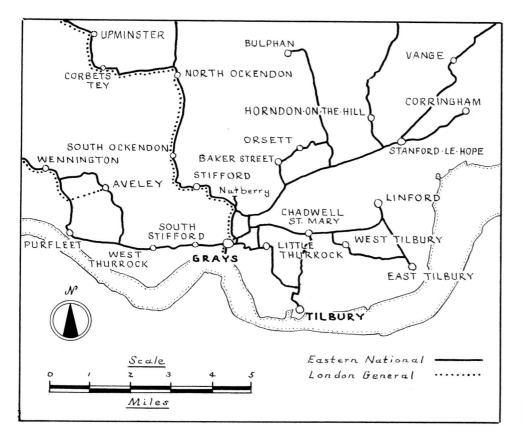

Eastern National and London General routes — 1931.

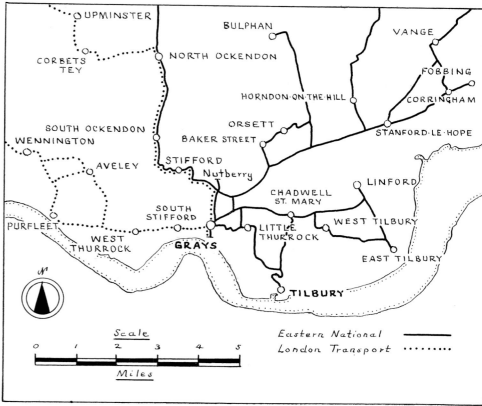

Eastern National and London Transport routes — 1934.

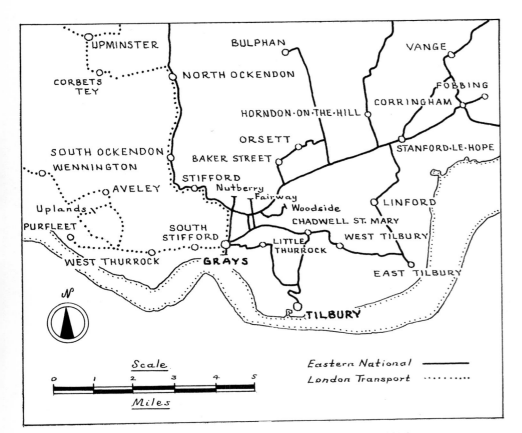

Eastern National and London Transport Routes — 1950.

Eastern National and London Transport Routes — 1952.

EASTERN NATIONAL

No.1 LONDON – EAST COAST, Express Service Car.

TYPES

No.2 PRIVATE PARTY
and EXCURSION Coach

OF

No.3 TILBURY – CLACTON/HARWICH
Through Service Vehicle

No.4 LOCAL SERVICE Vehicle

LUXURY COACHES

No.5 Saloon for
LONDON – HALSTEAD Express Service

EASTERN NATIONAL ADVERTISING

Ad. 952/734

EASTERN NATIONAL

Between **LONDON** and
BRAINTREE, HALSTEAD,
HEDINGHAMS, WETHERSFIELD, FINCHINGFIELD,
GT. BARDFIELD, DANBURY, MALDON

BOOK YOUR SEATS HERE